The Structure of Canadian Government

REVISED EDITION

J.R. MALLORY

Department of Political Science
McGill University

gage PUBLISHING LIMITED
TORONTO ONTARIO CANADA

Canadian Cataloguing in Publication Data

Mallory, J.R., 1916–
The structure of Canadian government

Includes bibliographical references and index.
ISBN 0-7715-5600-4

1. Canada—Politics and government. 2. Canada—Constitutional history. I. Title.

JL64 1971 M34 1984 320.971 C83-099216-2

Originally published in 1971 by The Macmillan Company of Canada under ISBN 0-7705-1152-X

Reprinted 1975, 1977, 1978, 1980, 1981

Co-ordinating Editor: Kathy Austin
Editor: Terry-Lee Wheelband
Cover Design: Brant Cowie/Artplus

1 2 3 4 5 6 7 8 9 WC 88 87 86 85 84
Written, Printed and Bound in Canada

Contents

Preface

The first edition of this book was completed nearly fifteen years ago. Since that time Canadians have had to face and consider a number of profound questions about our political institutions and the values that they embody. We have debated, but not resolved, the place of French-speaking Canadians in a society in which they remain an embattled minority. We have made important changes in the constitution, which may well increase the role of the courts in defining community values. We are just now beginning to face the problem of assigning a suitable place to our native peoples, who were here first, but whose claims to fair treatment have been ignored for centuries. The task of coming to terms with this problem has also reminded us that it is much easier to grant effective political participation to a group which can be clearly identified with a territorial unit where they exercise an amount of power appropriate to defend their rights.

The long debate over the patriation of the constitution was finally resolved with the passage of the 1982 Constitution Act. As a result we have a constitution which is more "written" than it was in the past, we have a number of previously ambiguous matters enshrined in the constitution, and we now have a number of rights set down—in a somewhat limited way—in the Charter of Rights and Freedoms. However, constitutional renewal is an unending process. We may still, in the near future, have to deal with the question of the partition of legislative powers between the two levels of government in a way which is consonant with both modern conditions and the basic character of the original federal bargain. With an amending formula more certain and flexible than in the past such changes not only become feasible, but open the possibility of a less symmetrical federal system in which no province will be quite like the others.

The debate over the 1982 constitution reminded us of the importance of constitutional conventions as a part of our constitutional order. Vague and uncertain as such conventions sometimes are, they are an important part of the internalized rules which underlie the political system. Furthermore, they are an element of flexibility which enables us to adjust to changes in conditions in a way that the often rigid and unimaginative judicial interpretation of positive constitutional law would not.

As one of the consequences of the Charter we are probably now entering an era which will be characterized by a much more positive policy-making and value-setting role for the courts—a role which will strain their credibility and legitimacy much more than in the past. While hitherto the constitutional role of the courts has been characterized by judicial self-restraint, it has also been leavened by dissenting judgments from great jurists like the late Chief Justice Laskin, who did not hesitate to point out where the law was contrary to our contemporary social values, and in the process shamed legislators into changing it.

One of the most agonizing and persistent problems which remains is to come to terms with a necessary special relationship between the two language groups in Canada, which means in part, but not completely, with the role of Quebec in the federation. This attracted a great deal of attention in the sixties and seventies, and recent events in Manitoba have shown that it is unlikely to go away. If the proportions between the two language groups alters significantly the minority will become more apprehensive, while the need for restraint and a sense of historical obligation will be all the more necessary for the majority.

The alienation of Quebecers of the French language is not the only problem which remains at the top of the agenda. The inexorable arithmetic of the electoral process has enhanced the sense of alienation of many western Canadians, and as a consequence the demand for reform of the electoral system is likely to remain with us. This may well lead to a questioning of the appropriateness of the Westminster parliamentary and cabinet system, which inevitably concentrates so much power in the executive that the plurality of a federal system is too frequently put at risk.

Political institutions change because of changes in our perceptions of one another and of changes in the external world around us. As Leonard Woolf said in *After the Deluge*, "political action and the ebb and flow in the political life of a community are determined by the relation between the political matrix and the ideas, beliefs, and desires of individuals."[1] And John Maynard Keynes, in a well-remembered sentence, said "But soon or late, it is ideas, not vested interests, which are dangerous for good or evil."[2] Political institutions change in response to changes in ideas.

In the middle of the last century Walter Bagehot made a useful distinction between the "dignified" and the "efficient" organs of government. The latter represent the working institutions where the real process of government actually goes on, while the former appear to be nothing but surviving archaelogical evidence of the way that government was carried on in the past. Nevertheless, these surviving formal structures, such as the Privy Council or, many would say, the Senate, which today seem to have little meaning, often represent an important landmark in our history and embrace the achievement of some important political or constitutional principle. Government is essentially the institutional embodiment of a

1. Leonard Woolf, *After the Deluge*. (London, 1937). p. 90.
2. J. M. Keynes, *The General Theory of Employment, Interest and Money*. (London, 1936) p. 384.

system of values, and it is important to understand why a particular institution evolved the way it did, because that evolution was important to the development and preservation of the system.

It is necessary to understand the past in order to explain the present. Many of our institutions contain some necessary compromise in the past which settled a dispute serious enough to threaten the survival of the system. Political institutions are more than accepted ways of carrying on the process of government. They also embody the values of the community. Even in the best of societies the crust of civility is thin. Laws alone are insufficient to ensure that power, whether public or private, will not be abused to the point that injustices are created which threaten the stability of the community. What makes constitutional government work is not so much the bundle of laws which order its operation, as the internalized values of fairness which restrain those armed with the authority of the state from the selfish abuse of power.

Politics is more than a spectator sport which can be better appreciated if the audience as well as the players understand the rules. It also happens to be an activity on which our happiness, freedom, and possibly survival depend. While all of us will enhance the quality of our lives by a clearer understanding of the political world in which we live, those of us whose vocation is law or politics are in particular need of such understanding. We should all ponder the words of one of the greatest of our constitutional lawyers,

> . . . every legal change involves a choice of values. . . . Changing a constitution confronts a society with the most important choices, for in the constitution will be found the philosophical principles and rules which largely determine the relations of the individual and of cultural groups to one another and to the state. If human rights and harmonious relations between cultures are forms of the beautiful, then the state is a work of art that is never finished. Law thus takes its place, in its theory and practice, among man's highest and most creative activities.[3]

This book owes much to the unfailing kindness of a large number of politicians and public servants who have tried to improve my understanding of the machinery of government. It owes no less to countless colleagues whose researches eagerly pursued the reality of a rapidly changing process. And it owes much to the generations of students who have endured my efforts to think through the problems of Canadian government. If one of the best ways to understand something is to do it, surely another is to try to teach it. Whatever clarity I have achieved in the end owes more than I can say to my ever-present editor, companion, and dearly-beloved wife. This book is for them all.

J. R. Mallory
Montreal
March 1984

3. F. R. Scott, *Essays on the Constitution*. (Toronto, 1977) p. ix.

1

The Pattern of the Constitution

Most countries of the world today claim to be democracies. Canada is one of the much smaller number that can be called constitutional democracies. The difference is important. From at least the time of the ancient Romans the question has been asked *quis custodiet ipsos custodies*? Or, who controls the controllers? There is a constitutional order if the polity has effective means of preventing the abuse of power, and ensures that those in authority cannot take away the ultimate right of the governed to remove them or reject their policies. How is this to be done? The usual method is to enshrine basic values in the fundamental law of the constitution, which governments and legislatures cannot readily change, but which may be modified by a special and difficult procedure. This was the method pursued by the founders of the American republic, who lavished their considerable learning and experience in producing the constitution of the United States, which defines the powers of government and subjects them to the restraints of fundamental law. They could justly describe the system which they had created as "a government of laws and not of men."

Initially the Canadian solution was different. It derived from the "unwritten" British constitution, where there is no single document which sets down the overriding principles of constitutional government, and where the basic rights of the citizen are protected by the benevolent interpretation of the law by the courts. Through more than a century after Confederation the basic document of the Canadian constitution was the British North America Act, the most important provisions of which confined the two levels of government—federal and provincial—to their own proper spheres. But the Act did little to protect the rights of the citizen. Nevertheless the courts have managed to recognize and protect a number of the basic rights of the citizen even though these rights were not spelled out in the British North America Act.[1] Since the introduction into the Canadian constitution of the Charter of Rights and Freedoms in 1982, this constitutional gap has largely been filled and the constitution of Canada is now much more a "written" one like that of the United States.

Canada has been nourished by the same stream of constitutional ideas, and in many respects the same constitutional atmosphere, as the United States. Both countries have a common tradition of liberty, equality and respect for law. Both have grown out of heterogeneous communities with differences among them so great that a federal form of government was necessary to bring them together.

The similarities end on a point of emphasis. The American constitution was born of war, revolution and the fear of counter-revolution. It has about it the air of leaving nothing to chance. The Canadian constitution was a product of bargaining, of a feeling that the practical operation is more important than the letter of the law, and that the spirit supersedes the letter of the agreement. This has made our constitutional law harder to discover and apply than the American, for it shares the ambiguities of the British constitution. The difference between American and British constitutionalism is essentially this: for the Americans, anything unconstitutional is illegal, however right and necessary it may seem; for the British, anything unconstitutional is wrong, however legal it may be.

To the extent that a constitution is a "written" one, the courts must play an important role as the final guardians and interpreters of the constitution. In the United States, this role of the courts is an omnipresent one since the courts must not only interpret the boundaries between the powers of the national and state governments, but also enforce the restraints which the Bill of Rights imposes on all governments. In Canada, the role of the courts has been more limited. Whereas in the United States the powers of government derive from the people and are expressed and limited in the constitution, Canada inherited the British constitutional idea

1. For example, while the law was never completely clear on the extent that the constitution protected the free discussion and debate which must underlie the process of free government, the Supreme Court nevertheless found a legal basis for protecting them as part of an "unwritten constitution." It is doubtful, however, if the courts would have gone as far as Mr. Justice Abbott, in an *obiter dictum* in the *Padlock* case, and hold that "as our constitutional Act stands, Parliament itself could not abrogate this right of discussion and debate." *Switzman v. Elbling and A.G. for Quebec* [1957] S.C.R. 285. However, these rights are now protected in the Charter of Rights and Freedoms.

of the unlimited sovereignty of the legislature, so that the only role of the courts was to define the boundary between federal and provincial powers. Thus the Canadian courts inherited a more deferential attitude towards legislatures and have been more reluctant to substitute their own judgment of what is constitutionally proper for that of Parliament or a provincial legislature unless there is a clear conflict between them which must be resolved. This judicial attitude is deeply embedded and the inclusion of a Charter of Rights and Freedoms in the constitution may constitute a difficult challenge to the courts when they are confronted with a larger and different role in interpreting the constitution.

The purpose of a constitution is simply to lay down the rules for the operation of the organs of government in relation to one another and in relation to the citizen. The constitution of Canada is not easy either to describe or to discover, for it does not exist in any single document. It is customary to speak of the British North America Act, 1867, together with its various amendments, as "the Canadian constitution," but in fact only a part of the important provisions of the constitution are contained therein.

Our system of government took for granted, and continued in force, an elaborate system of government which had grown up for over a century in the provinces of British North America before Confederation. The B.N.A. Act hardly concerns itself at all, for example, with the organization and powers of the courts of law, or with the structure of the executive or its relationship to Parliament. It does not mention either the Prime Minister or the Cabinet.

Some of these matters are not regulated by law but by "conventions of the constitution." These are rules which are well known and clearly stated, but are not legally enforceable. A breach of these rules is not a breach of the law, though it may be contrary to the spirit of the constitution. A breach of these conventions is unconstitutional but not illegal. The most important areas of the Canadian constitution established by convention rather than by law have been Canada's changing relationship to the United Kingdom—from colony to member of the Commonwealth—and the operation of Cabinet government.

These two areas are closely interrelated and it is the gradual change in them which comprehends the evolution from a number of dependent colonies to an independent and sovereign state. Unlike most other modern states, Canada has never experienced a revolutionary break with the past or an abrupt transfer of sovereignty which laid the foundation for a completely new constitution.

THE BASIC ELEMENTS OF CONSTITUTIONALISM

The three basic elements of the Canadian constitution were all found in the British North American colonies in the eighteenth century. These elements were (1) a system of law, (2) the right to representative institutions and (3) the principle of religious toleration. With them, the firm basis of a constitutional order was laid nearly a century before the frontiers of local self-government began to expand in the nineteenth century.

Under the common law of England, the rights of Englishmen accompanied them overseas. The consequence was that in "settled territories"[2] the common law itself and such of the statute law of England, in general character, accompanied the settlers. Thus, they brought with them their traditional rights, including the legal rights of action which safeguarded English liberty, such as habeas corpus. The case was different for "conquered territories," that is, territories acquired by cession from another European power, for they already had an established system of European law. The abrogation of a system of civilized law by mere conquest could only result in complete confusion and serious damage to the property rights of the inhabitants. It was customary, therefore, to leave the existing system of law undisturbed. This was done when Canada passed from French to British control in 1763. Subsequently, by the Quebec Act, 1774, the colony was made subject to English criminal law, but the civil law was left unchanged. Consequently, although nine Canadian provinces have legal systems based on English common law, the province of Quebec has a system based, in common with the countries of continental Europe, on the Roman civil law.

The right to representative institutions, regarded as inherent in the settled territories, was also necessarily accorded to ceded territory where there were sufficient inhabitants to justify it. Otherwise such territories would naturally be unattractive to English settlers. In practice, the machinery by which local bodies were given legislative powers was the same in both cases.[3] Territories in aboriginal

2. Of the British North American colonies, only Nova Scotia and Newfoundland were regarded as "settled" territories. Nova Scotia was originally claimed by the British Crown in the seventeenth century, and although it changed hands more than once, the courts regarded it as "settled." All of the western provinces of Canada are regarded as acquired by settlement. Cf. Arthur Berriedale Keith, *The Dominions as Sovereign States* (London, 1938), pp. 154-5.

3. In English constitutional law there are two sources of legislative power, *statute* and *prerogative*. Statute law is made by the Sovereign in Parliament in the form

hands which were acquired by settlement were initially governed under the provisions of a charter or letters patent issued under the prerogative. They had no inherent right to elect representatives, to make local laws, or to approve taxes for the cost of local government. What political institutions they might have were those which the Crown, under the prerogative, chose to give them. Since it was impossible to govern territories inhabited by Europeans without some form of local government, the difference in practice between settled and conquered territories became slight. But the constitutional position was not the same. However, once the Crown had granted some form of local representative institutions, this could not be taken away, and the Crown could not revive its right to raise taxes and legislate.[4] This limitation applied, of course, only to the prerogative. When constitutional provisions were made by the Parliament of the United Kingdom, as in the Quebec Act, the right to make new arrangements by a further act of Parliament was not affected.

By the end of the eighteenth century the overseas colonies of the "old British Empire" where there were European settlers, conformed, with minor exceptions, to a standard pattern. The executive power was vested in a Governor. In the exercise of his function he was aided and advised by a Council, whose members he nominated. Legislation was enacted by the passage of bills through an elected Assembly, as well as through the Council (acting as a second legislative chamber), and with the assent of the Governor.[5] Thus the colonial constitutions were similar in outline to the British constitution as it existed in the early years of the eighteenth century. The Council performed the dual function of the House of Lords and the Privy Council.

---

of an act of Parliament. The Sovereign may also legislate without the participation of Parliament by proclamation, letters patent, or some other prerogative instrument. Since the time of the Stuarts the prerogative power to legislate has been steadily shrinking, and the general rule is that once Parliament has dealt with a legislative field the prerogative power to legislate has gone. Nevertheless, there are a few areas in which it is still possible to legislate under the prerogative. Thus, while the British North America Act provides that there shall be a Governor General, the constitution of his office and powers are provided for in a prerogative instrument, the royal letters patent.

4. This was settled in a famous judgment of Lord Mansfield in the case of *Campbell* v. *Hall* in 1774. The case dealt with a dispute which had arisen in Grenada, but the rule laid down has been universally applied ever since.

5. Martin Wight, *The Development of the Legislative Council, 1606-1945* (London, 1946), pp. 29-33.

The English constitution under the early Stuarts was inherently unstable. A clash of interest between King and Parliament grew into a conflict of constitutional principle which led to civil war. Similarly, in North America, a cleavage in interest and outlook between the Governor and the Assembly was bound to emerge when the Governor lay under the control of a distant British government and local interests were focussed in the Assembly. A British constitution of similar design worked only because the Whig magnates, who supported the Crown and dominated the House of Lords after 1688, were also able to control the House of Commons.

The British constitution, which was taken as a model in the government of British colonies overseas, was, except when some powerful interest could hold King, Lords, and Commons together, essentially unstable. Its dangers were revealed when George III, in the early years of his reign, was able to assert considerable dominance over the executive, and the threat appeared of the emergence of a party of "King's friends" who might control the House of Commons and thus undo the established balance of the constitution. The Americans, in their struggle for self-government, perceived the analogy between their own constitutional difficulties and those brought about in Britain by George III. Thus, in drafting the constitutions of the states and in constructing the government of the Union, they sought by a rigid separation of powers to curb the influence of the executive over the legislature.

Perhaps unfortunately, the Americans did not see that an alternative solution to the problem was already being worked out in Britain with the emergence of a Cabinet of Ministers, responsible to the House of Commons. When the time came, at a later date, for the other British North American colonies to gain greater control over their own affairs, it was possible to weigh the merits of the two very different products of the seventeenth-century English constitution.

The third basic constitutional decision which was reached in British North America in the eighteenth century was the principle of religious toleration. In England, Protestantism had been part of the constitution since the sixteenth century. After the expulsion of James II, a Protestant monarchy reinforced a system in which political office was in effect restricted to adherents of the Church of England. This, when applied in Canada and Nova Scotia, imposed a serious obstacle to the participation by French Canadians and Acadians in their own government. The Treaty of Paris contained guarantees of freedom of worship in Canada, and this right was confirmed and amplified in the Quebec Act of 1774.[6] In the same act a special form of oath was provided so that Catholics could hold office in Canada.

REPRESENTATIVE GOVERNMENT

The Quebec Act had asserted that a legislative assembly was unsuited to the circumstances of the colony, and had provided that such legislative power as was required should be exercised by the Governor acting with an appointed Council. The normal state of constitutional deadlock in the older American colonies, which had resulted from the dependence of the Governor on a recalcitrant Assembly for supply, had decided the British authorities to strengthen the executive. When legislative assemblies were granted to the northern provinces, the British Parliament provided revenues for the Governor to support the costs of government and reduce his dependence on the legislature.

Meanwhile, the northern provinces gradually acquired representative legislatures. The first Assembly in Nova Scotia was summoned in 1758, and in Prince Edward Island in 1773. The end of the American War of Independence led to a substantial wave of immigration into the northern provinces. The Loyalists who fought for the British connection against their fellow-Americans disapproved of revolution, but they were determined to retain their rights to representative institutions. The settlers who had come to that part of Nova Scotia lying north of the Bay of Fundy were given a separate provincial government in 1784. This legislation, which set up the province of New Brunswick, included in it the normal representative assembly. Finally, in 1791, representative government was extended to Canada.

The constitutions of the Maritime provinces conformed to the old colonial pattern. They were grants from the Crown under the royal prerogative. Each province possessed, in addition to the elected Assembly, an undifferentiated Council which performed the dual function of advising the Governor and of acting as a legislative second chamber.

6. Similar guarantees for the exercise of the Catholic religion in Nova Scotia were contained in the Treaty of Utrecht in 1713.

The constitutional provisions for the colony of Canada differed from the older constitutions in two respects. In the first place, they were created by a different constituent power—the Parliament of the United Kingdom. With the passage of the Quebec Act in 1774, the power of the Crown to legislate for Canada under the prerogative lapsed. Henceforth the constitution of that province lay in the gift of the British Parliament. The act of 1791, commonly referred to in Canada as the Constitutional Act, departed somewhat from the old colonial model, producing a constitution superficially similar to that of Great Britain. The Governor was to be advised by a small Executive Council, while a separate and larger body, the Legislative Council, together with the Legislative Assembly, made up the legislature. At the same time the colony was divided into two, each province with its own legislature. Lower Canada included all of the colony east of the Ottawa River, while Upper Canada took in the new settlements lying to the west along the upper St. Lawrence and the Great Lakes. Since almost all of the French Canadians lived in Lower Canada, it alone retained the French civil law. Upper Canada, with its English-speaking settlers, joined the ranks of the common-law provinces.

PARLIAMENTARY GOVERNMENT

John Graves Simcoe, the first Lieutenant-Governor of Upper Canada, claimed that the system of government over which he presided was indeed a facsimile of the British constitution, adapted to suit the needs of a backwoods colony. There was more truth in this claim than either the early reformers or the later historians have ever been prepared to admit. It requires an effort of imagination to grasp the context of the politics of another age. The fact that there did not exist in Canada, at the beginning of the nineteenth century, a constitution which was the same as the British constitution at the time of Mr. Gladstone's first ministry (1868-74) is less cause for complaint if we remember that such a constitution also did not exist in the United Kingdom in 1791. Similarly, there is as much difference between the position of Lord Dufferin and Mr. Michener as Governor General as there is between the position of Queen Victoria and Queen Elizabeth II.

In theory the eighteenth-century English constitution was one in which the King was the head of an autonomous executive, the Lords represented the great landed interests and the Commons represented a smaller but substantial property interest in the community. As described by Sir William Blackstone, the system depended in part on a legal separation of power between the executive and the legislature. It also depended on the fact that the King operated as a check on the power of the legislature, and Parliament acted as a check on the power of the Crown, to produce a system of countervailing power which resulted in constitutional government. But the overriding veto of the Crown in legislation was too closely associated with the memory of the Stuarts to be an effective check on the power of Parliament. The Crown's power was still real, but becoming more subtle and indirect. No sovereign after Queen Anne refused to assent to legislation. It was to be a long time before anyone noticed that by the last half of the eighteenth century the underlying reality was changing.

The change taking place was the emergence of Cabinet government, though it was not a part of the literary theory of the constitution until the days of Walter Bagehot. Before the accession of Queen Victoria it meant that the Crown's business was conducted by ministers who retained office through their ability to control and manage the House of Commons.Thus emerged a government continuously responsive to the majority in the House. This was not the separation of powers in the classic sense, but Bagehot's "close union, the nearly complete fusion of the executive and the legislative powers."[7] We may say, in short, that the British constitution in the last half of the eighteenth century worked in spite of, rather than because of, the separation of powers.

The real reason why the models of the British constitution broke down first in the old American colonies and later in British North America was that they failed to represent the realities of political and economic power in North America. In Great Britain the system worked, not because the interests of King, Lords and Commons were different, but because they were the same. The great landed families were not only an agricultural interest, for their wealth had been invested in trade and transportation. They controlled the rotten borough seats in the House of Commons, and a complex system of party management left them a decisive voice in the executive. The British system, in its turn, was to approach the brink of collapse before the Reform Bill of 1832 admitted the rising

7. Walter Bagehot, *The English Constitution*, World's Classics Edition (London, 1928), p. 9.

middle classes to a share in political power appropriate to their stake in the country.

The North American counterpart of this system provided no such neat behind-the-scenes combination of interests. The local elected Assemblies, with a wider franchise and a wider distribution of property, came to be the voices of the agrarian frontier. The Legislative Council in the Canadas represented a combination of large-scale wealth in land and trade. The Governor became the focus of a serious conflict of interest between the local communities and his imperial masters. Under such conditions harmony was only achieved by astute political management by the Governor. He, in his turn, suffered under the double disadvantage of strict control from Downing Street and (in most cases) a military background from which the arts of compromise and political management were notably absent. The result was collision without compromise, stiff-necked and unimaginative administration confronted with extremist and irresponsible legislative leadership.

Responsible government was finally achieved in the eighteen-forties. As H.A. Innis suggested, it was necessary to have responsible local politicians managing the administration of the provinces in order that the combined resources of the community be mobilized to underwrite the great developmental undertakings on which growth and prosperity of the colonies depended.[8] The repeal of the Corn Laws and the Navigation Acts, and the revolution in British commercial policy from mercantilism to free trade weakened the vested interests in the old colonial system and removed one of the major obstacles to responsible government as a means of local autonomy.[9]

The question of colonial responsible government had been debated many times. In Canada, prominent members of the Reform Party like the Baldwins, had urged it. Lord Durham had seen it as the one vital principle of British constitutionalism whose lack had turned the whole system of colonial government sour. A dispatch from Lord John Russell is the classic statement of the old Colonial Office view that no Governor could be put in the position of acknowledging two masters.[10] The Colonial Office was unimpressed by Durham's breezy assertion that there was no real

8. H.A. Innis, *Political Economy in the Modern State* (Toronto, 1946), p. 188.

9. Ibid., p. 222.

10. Russell to Thomson, October 11, 1839. Quoted in Arthur Berriedale Keith, ed., *Selected Speeches and Documents on British Colonial Policy, 1763-1917,* Vol. 1 (London, 1918), pp. 173-8.

difficulty since it was perfectly possible to separate things imperial from things local, that the Governor could render unto his ministers the things that were the colonies' and render unto the Queen's ministers the things that were the Queen's. Perhaps the Colonial Office was right, but it is the genius of the British constitution to avoid logical dilemmas.

For years colonial reformers had argued that the only way to ensure harmony between the executive and the legislature was for the Governor to appoint to his Executive Council those who had the confidence of, and were responsible to, the Assembly. This was how constitutional government worked in Great Britain, and this was how it must work in British North America. But this was a practice which the British government, impaled on the horns of its logic, could not accept. Nothing could arrest the drift to a constitutional crisis in all of the British North American provinces. The outbreak of armed rebellion in the Canadas in 1837 galvanized Whitehall into action.

The constitutions of the two Canadian provinces were suspended and Lord Durham was sent out to investigate and deal with the situation in the whole of British North America. In what was to live as one of the great state papers in British colonial policy, Durham made two major recommendations. He had found in Lower Canada a constitutional struggle which was also a struggle for mastery between two races. He therefore recommended a union of the two colonies to submerge the racial conflict. Secondly, he recommended the granting of responsible government.

But on this issue the British government was not prepared to yield. In 1840 the two provinces were reunited but the old framework remained. However, the pattern thereafter was very different, for the first Governor of the new united colony was to be the real founder of Cabinet government in Canada. It was Lord Sydenham who, as Adam Shortt said,

> boldly introduced the British parliamentary system into Canada, thus completely revolutionizing the previous system of colonial government. This he accomplished by personally undertaking its introduction, directly combining in himself the duties of governor-general, prime minister and party leader. He initiated his personally selected cabinet into the mysteries of cabinet government, dependent for its life upon retaining the support of the majority of the legislature including the assembly and the council. To accomplish this, he organized and maintained for the first time in Canada a government party, of which he was the recognized leader and upon which he depended for getting his

numerous and important bills through the legislature, for voting the necessary supplies, and supporting his executive government.[11]

Neither Sydenham nor his successors were able to make this system work effectively, and it led within a decade to the granting of responsible government. But we should recognize that the Sydenham system was not such a constitutional monstrosity as it has appeared to some later historians. It was a necessary stage for which there are historical parallels. For the British constitution in the eighteenth century passed through just such a phase—a "mixed" form of government in which ministers were dependent on the King, and also on their ability to manage Parliament. It was, in both British and Canadian constitutional history, a period of "essentially unstable equilibrium." "It would be difficult to think," wrote Professor Butterfield of the early years of the reign of George III, "of a situation which could have been more burdened with tensions, more clouded with ambiguities, more pregnant with the varied possibilities of development."[12] The result in both cases was Cabinet government.

CABINET GOVERNMENT

The emergence of Cabinet government in Canada illustrates the flexibility of the British constitutional system. Far more than any other single stage in Canadian constitutional development, it constituted the "great leap forward" which brought about genuine self-government by conferring initiative and power on the Canadian élite operating through the Canadian party system. This was not the result of a change in the formal constitution, but of a gradual change in the arrangements of the executive government.

Two important steps by Lord Sydenham were essential prerequisites to the granting of responsible government. He put into practice Lord Durham's recommendations for improving the organization of the executive by creating departments, placing each under a single political head, and making his Executive Council a genuine policy-making body of ministers. Without this, as Professor

11. Adam Shortt, "The Relations between the Legislative and Executive Branches of the Canadian Government," *American Political Science Review* VII, No. 2 (May 1913), p. 187.

12. Herbert Butterfield, *George III and the Historians* (London, 1957), p. 254.

Hodgetts says, "any grant of responsible government would be dangerous," because there could be no effective and coherent executive leadership.[13]

Sydenham's second step was equally important. He created a government party to sustain his ministers in the legislature. He was the head of the executive, presiding over his Council and using his powers and patronage to ensure support in the legislature for his ministry.

To the modern eye this may have a somewhat unseemly look, yet it should be remembered that it did not differ significantly from the Cabinet system in England under George III. But by the middle of the nineteenth century Cabinet government in England had changed considerably, and the incongruity of Sydenham's system was apparent to any well-informed observer. A change of government in England in 1846 made it possible to grant the concession of responsible government which had been so adamantly refused five years before. The new Colonial Secretary, Lord Grey, made it plain to the two new Governors appointed in 1847—Sir John Harvey in Nova Scotia and Lord Elgin in Canada—that in future they should choose their Councils from the leaders of the majority party in the Assembly.

The first test of this principle came early in 1848, when a non-confidence vote was carried against the government in Nova Scotia on January 25. Two days later the ministry resigned and Harvey called upon the leader of the majority to form a new government. Within a few weeks similar changes of government had taken place in Canada and in New Brunswick, and thus the principle of responsible government was firmly established in British North America. Henceforth the government was to be constituted from the group able to gain the support of a majority of the elected legislature, and the principle of ultimate control of the government by the electorate was established.

This fundamental change in constitutional practice was based on no formal alteration in constitutional documents. It did not even require a change in the Governor's official instructions. All that was necessary was a dispatch from the Colonial Secretary to the Governor. As the great Nova Scotian reformer Joseph Howe had written: "You have no Act of Parliament to define the duty of the Sovereign when ministers are in a minority; we want none to enable us to suggest to a Governor when his advisers have lost the confidence of

13. J.E. Hodgetts, *Pioneer Public Service: An Administrative History of the United Canadas, 1841-1867* (Toronto, 1956), p. 26.

our colonial Assemblies. But what we do want, my Lord, is a rigid enforcement of British practice, by the imperial authorities, on every Governor; the intelligence and public spirit of the people will supply the rest."[14]

The development of Cabinet government in Canada took place in three distinct stages, each of which was necessary to create the conditions favourable to the one that followed. Lord Sydenham's system of ministerial government, in which the Governor was still the effective leader of the administration, proved to be unworkable, but it did create the administrative foundations of Cabinet government. When responsible government came in 1848, Canadian politicians had had over six years experience as ministers, there was an administrative system accustomed to ministerial direction and a two-party system accustomed to the responsibility of power. This second stage required that the Governor should retain his advisers only so long as they, as a group, were able to maintain a majority in the lower house of the legislature. As long as a ministry remained in office the governor must, except where imperial interests were at stake, adhere to its advice. There followed a third stage—the introduction of true Cabinet government—which required the withdrawal of the Governor from direct participation in the deliberations of his constitutional advisers. This did not come about until at least six years after the introduction of responsible government. What happened in effect was the separation of the Cabinet from the Executive Council. What Sir William Anson had called the deliberative and the executive functions were already quite clearly divided between two different bodies, the Committee of Council and the Governor-in-Council. "The Council," wrote Sir Edmund Head in 1858, "...discuss *in committee*, the Governor not being present, the various measures or questions with which they have to deal."[15] The Committee of Council was simply the ministers meeting in the absence of the Governor. Its conclusions were given legal sanction by becoming formal actions of the Governor-in-Council. If the submissions were routine they were usually transmitted to the Governor for his signature at leisure in his office. But the Governor reserved the right to go into Council to discuss measures and to approve them in formal Council. For the Governor to attend regularly at meetings of ministers would, as Head wrote to the Colonial

14. *Novascotian*, January 4 and 11, 1847.

15. Quoted in D.G.G. Kerr, *Sir Edmund Head: A Scholarly Governor* (Toronto, 1954), pp. 174-6

Secretary in 1853, "check all freedom of debate and embarrass himself as well as his advisers."[16]

The third stage, in which the Governor did not normally participate in the discussion which led to decision-making, created a shift in the balance of power in the executive from the Governor to the political leaders of the Cabinet, and this contributed to the distinctive position of the First Minister. The union of the two parts of the Province of Canada as a result of the Act of Union of 1840 did not completely fuse the politics of its constituent parts, and there was indeed a *de facto* federalism which made coalitions essential. As a result there were always two Premiers (or First Ministers, as they were called), one from each part of the province. Only after Confederation did a single First Minister emerge. This had the effect of further diminishing the role of the Governor. As long as there were two First Ministers, he retained a degree of initiative by being able to hold the balance between them. But after Confederation, the single Prime Minister left the political head of the executive in a dominant position and the Governor General in the increasingly passive role of a constitutional head of state.

By 1867, the transformation of the Governor General from Colonial Governor to personal representative to the Sovereign had gone more than halfway. But the Governor General still possessed far more formidable powers than the Sovereign. In addition, the normal prerogatives were enhanced by the prestige of his position as an imperial officer. In those early years the Governor General consciously engaged in presiding over the birth of constitutional government in Canada. As Lord Dufferin somewhat grandly put it in a letter to Sir John A. Macdonald, "my great desire is to enhance the prestige and authority of Canadian statesmen, and teach the Canadian people to believe in and to be proud of their public men."[17] In an age when party leaders were not selected by any regular process of intra-party democracy, the choice by the Governor General of a Prime Minister was much more important than it is today. His ability to resist policy

16. Public Archives of Canada, *Secret and Confidential Despatches, Colonial Secretary 1856-1866,* Series G 10, Vol. II, and *Guide to Canadian Ministries since Confederation,* Ottawa, 1957. On the development of the Cabinet out of the Governor's council see J.R. Mallory, "Cabinet Government in Canada," *Political Studies* II, No. 2, pp. 142-53; "Cabinets and Councils in Canada," *Public Law,* Autumn, 1957, pp. 231-51; W.E.D. Halliday, "The Privy Council Office and Cabinet Secretariat in Relation to the Development of Cabinet Government," *Canada Year Book,* 1956.

17. Sir Joseph Pope, *Correspondence of Sir John Macdonald* (Toronto, n.d.), p. 203.

decisions of which he did not approve was far greater in the nineteenth century than it is today, and the correspondence of Prime Ministers with the Governor General in that period shows that on many issues there was a battle of wills between the Governor General and his ministers. In the end, of course, he had to yield because he could not afford to force their resignation, for "he would do so with the full knowledge that he would be compelled to find successors who would be prepared to take constitutional responsibility for his action."[18] In fact, no Governor General was ever driven to the actual dismissal of his ministers.

An open refusal of advice always endangers the political neutrality of a constitutional ruler. Thus Lord Aberdeen, in 1896, was successful in refusing to approve a number of appointments by the Tupper ministry after it had been decisively defeated at the polls, because in this case the Governor General was protecting the rights of the newly elected majority. On the other hand, Lord Dufferin apparently did not feel justified in demanding the resignation of Sir John A. Macdonald over the Pacific Railway scandal in 1873, though the subsequent resignation of the government relieved him of further embarrassment.[19]

Even where imperial interests appeared to be at stake it was not always possible for the Governor General to prevail over an intransigent ministry with a strong majority. For example, in 1900 there developed a difference of view between Lord Minto and the Laurier administration. Differences had arisen between ministers and the Officer Commanding the Canadian Militia (an officer then appointed by the government of the United Kingdom). The Cabinet submitted an order-in-council demanding that the United Kingdom should recall the offending officer, General Hutton. Lord Minto felt that this constituted political interference in purely military matters, and submitted a lengthy memorandum to the Cabinet arguing against the recommendation for dismissal. However, the Cabinet persisted in its recommendation, and Minto signed the order because he had become convinced that a refusal would lead to the

18. W.P.M. Kennedy, *The Constitution of Canada, 1534-1937,* 2nd ed. (London, 1937), p. 382.

19. Sir Charles Tupper claims that Lord Dufferin did in fact ask Macdonald to resign, but that he (Tupper) dissuaded him. Sir Charles Tupper, *Recollections of Sixty Years* (London, 1914), pp. 156-7. This incident is not corroborated in any contemporary document.

resignation of the Prime Minister, and in due course to a general election on the issue.[20]

As an imperial officer the Governor General possessed a number of specific powers which could be employed to protect imperial interests against the actions of the government and Parliament of Canada. Some of these powers were statutory. Section 55 of the British North America Act empowered him to withhold royal assent, or to reserve the bill for consideration by the government of the United Kingdom. This power was discretionary, but subject to the provisions of the act and to his instructions. In 1867 the powers of the Governor General were largely contained in the instructions issued to each Governor General on his appointment. In 1878 the powers of the Governor General were put on a more permanent basis by the issue of letters patent constituting the office. The instructions had enumerated classes of bills which should automatically be reserved.[21] There were also some doubts in the early years after Confederation about whether the prerogative of pardon should be exercised by the Governor General in his discretion or whether it should be based on ministerial advice and responsibility. The ambiguities which had emerged in practice were made more serious by proposals from the Colonial Office which would have had the effect of requiring the Governor General to preside in person over all meetings of his Council and which would have enabled him to act in certain circumstances without consulting his ministers or even against their advice. As a result of representation by Edward Blake, Minister of Justice, the Colonial Office proposals for the new letters patent were considerably modified. The enumerated list of bills on

20. John Buchan, *Lord Minto* (London, 1924), pp. 144-52. A better account of this issue is in H. Pearson Gundy, "Sir Wilfrid Laurier and Lord Minto," *Canadian Historical Association, Annual Report,* 1952, p. 28.

21. Under his instructions the Governor General should not give royal assent to certain kinds of bills, but reserve them for final decision by the Queen-in-Council, that is, by the British government. Under the instructions before 1878 the following bills had to be reserved: bills (a) for divorce; (b) for granting land or money gratuity to the Governor General; (c) for making paper or other currency legal tender; (d) for imposing differential duties; (e) contrary to treaty obligations; (f) interfering with discipline or control of H.M. forces in Canada; (g) interfering with the royal prerogative, the property of British subjects outside Canada, or the trade or shipping of Great Britain or her dependencies; (h) containing provisions to which royal assent had already been refused or disallowed. As a consequence of these instructions, twenty-one bills had been reserved. W.P.M. Kennedy, ed., *Statutes, Treaties and Documents of the Canadian Constitution, 1713-1929* (Toronto, 1930), p. 672 (hereafter cited as *Constitutional Documents*).

which assent was to be reserved was dropped, and it was provided that the prerogative of pardon was to be exercised on ministerial advice.[22]

Blake's memorandum made it clear that the limits within which the Governor General's reserve powers could be brought to bear in defence of imperial interests were too narrow to be based on a form of words:

> As a rule the Governor does and must act through the agency of Ministers, and Ministers must be responsible for such action. . . . Upon the argument that there are certain conceivable circumstances in which, owing to the existence of substantial imperial interests, it may be considered that full freedom of action is not vested in the Canadian people, it appears to me that any such cases must, pending a solution of the great problem of Imperial Government, be dealt with as they arise. . . . The effort to reconcile by any form of words the responsibility of Ministers under the Canadian Constitution with a power to the Governor to take even a negative line independently of advice, cannot I think, succeed. The truth is, that Imperial interests are, under our present system of Government to be secured in matters of Canadian executive policy, not by any such clause in the Governor's instructions (which would be mischievous); but by mutual good feeling and by proper consideration of Imperial interests on the part of His [*sic*] Majesty's Canadian advisers; the Crown necessarily retaining all its constitutional rights and powers, which would be exercisable in any emergency in which the indicated securities might be found to fail.[23]

Blake's memorandum served to emphasize how far the facts of constitutional government in Canada had already outrun the forms of the constitution, even at that time. For while it was true that the Governor General retained the reserve powers so jealously guarded by the United Kingdom government, these powers were no longer of substantial importance. It was no longer possible to contemplate an open clash in which the advice of Canadian ministers could be rudely overridden on the grounds of imperial interest. If imperial interest were to be protected through the Governor General's office, it must be through influence rather than overt action. For in the last analysis a Canadian government could make a constitutional issue

22. The proposed letters patent had originally been circulated to the Canadian government. Edward Blake, then Minister of Justice, presented a memorandum in August 1876, objecting strongly to a number of proposals. In the result they were considerably revised. The letters patent, together with the new instructions, are in Kennedy, *Constitutional Documents,* pp. 672-5.

23. Ibid., pp. 669-70.

of the matter. In such a case a Governor General would find it difficult, if not impossible, to find an alternative government, and if he did so he would certainly bring his office into politics--a situation above all to be avoided.

Blake had objected to the Governor General's reserve powers as an imperial officer. He correctly pointed out that the normal reserve powers of the Crown were in themselves a powerful means of restricting hasty, unfair, or undesirable measures by Canadian governments. However, over the years the Governor General's reserve powers had come to be so closely identified with his function as an imperial officer that it finally became doubtful how far he could exercise discretionary powers appropriate to the Sovereign in the constitution of the United Kingdom without arousing undue and misinformed controversy. Such was the case with Lord Byng's refusal of a dissolution of Parliament to Mackenzie King in 1926. We now know that the Sovereign is not bound automatically to grant a dissolution when it is requested by a Prime Minister, though there was some reason to be less certain in 1926 that any such discretion existed.[24] In the event, what was essentially a problem of the relationship between the head of state and the Prime Minister was perceived by a great many Canadians at the time as a struggle between a Canadian government and an arm of the British government.

At the height of the crisis Mackenzie King had demanded that the Governor General seek direction from the Secretary of State for the Dominions before refusing to grant the dissolution. Whether or not King knew that his request was constitutionally outrageous, it was a shrewd political move. But Lord Byng sensibly kept his own counsel. As L. S. Amery, who was Secretary of State for the Dominions at the time, said:

> This was a pretty obvious trap. If I took Mackenzie King's view Byng would be held clearly in the wrong, and would have to give way. If I supported Byng, I should provide all the ammunition required for raising the issue of Downing Street interference. Byng refused, on the sound constitutional ground that this was a matter for his own personal judgment of his duty to the people of Canada, and no concern of anyone outside—the answer I should certainly have given if I had been consulted.[25]

24. See below, Chapter II.

25. L.S. Amery, *My Political Life,* Vol. II (London, 1953), p. 378. Reprinted by permission of Hutchinson and Co.

The outcome of this incident was that it strengthened King's resolve to join with some of the other Dominion governments in pressing to strip the Governor General of his functions as an imperial officer. The question was raised at the Imperial Conference of 1926, and circumstances were propitious for the change. The great military contributions of the Dominions in the First World War, and the recognition of a greater degree of autonomy in their external as well as their internal affairs after the war, indicated that the constitutional structure of the British Empire was due for an overhaul. Canada was not the only Dominion anxious to modify the position of the Governor General, and the British government was sympathetic to such a modification. As a consequence the Governor General ceased to be in any sense an imperial officer and, necessarily, ceased to be the channel of communication between the United Kingdom and Canadian governments. What advantages this method of communication had possessed were, by this time, outweighed by its disadvantages. In the period of transition from purely local self-government to full nationhood it had been a useful method of transmitting the decisions of the imperial government on matters of imperial policy, and had served as a means of keeping the two governments in reasonably close touch with one another.[26]

The dual status of the Governor General had been outmoded by events, and the Imperial Conference of 1926 resolved to end the ambiguity in its declaration that

> It is an essential consequence of the equality status . . . that the Governor General of a Dominion is the representative of the Crown, holding in all essential respects the same position in relation to the administration of public affairs as is held by His Majesty the King in Great Britain, and that he is not the representative or agent of His Majesty's Government in Great Britain or of any Department of that Government.

It followed as a necessary consequence that the Governor General's documents, which (apart from a minor revision in 1905) were still in the form in which they had been made in 1878, should be

26. "In more recent years it had still served, more informally, to keep Dominion Ministers to some extent in touch with general Imperial policy. At the same time the Governor-General in his private letters could give the Colonial Secretary an intimate and detached view of the political affairs of his Dominion. But the practice was inconsistent with the theoretical conception of equal status, according to which the Governor-General had ceased to be in any respect an agent of the British Government, but was an integral part of the Dominion constitution with an undivided responsibility to the nation concerned. What is more, as the issue between Byng and Mackenzie King had just shown, it could lend itself to serious misrepresentation." Ibid., pp. 386-7.

amended to reflect his altered status. New letters patent and instructions were issued on March 23, 1931, at the request of the Canadian government. These removed the most obvious anomalies, including the clause empowering the King to give instructions to the Governor General by imperial order-in-council or through a United Kingdom Secretary of State, and required that leave of absence to a Governor General should in future be on the authority of his own Prime Minister rather than that of the Secretary of State.[27] A number of anomalies remained. The instructions, for example, still required the Governor General to transmit to the United Kingdom copies of all acts of Parliament and of all bills reserved by him, although the power of reservation had been formally declared to be obsolete by the Imperial Conference of 1930.[28] In certain other respects, the Governor General was not in the same position as the Sovereign since substantial parts of the royal prerogative were not exercised by the Governor General but remained with the Sovereign acting on the advice of the Canadian ministers.

These incongruities, and others, were finally removed by the issue on September 8, 1947, of new letters patent under the Great Seal of Canada, replacing the old letters patent and instructions.[29] This instrument empowered the Governor General to exercise, on the advice of his Canadian ministers, all of the powers of the Sovereign in relation to Canada; and the portions of the superseded instruments which were inappropriate to current constitutional practice were omitted. The effect of these changes is that the Governor General is now governed by wholly Canadian instruments in regard to his office, and may exercise, on the advice of Canadian ministers, all of the powers of the Sovereign in relation to Canada. The effect of the letters patent of 1947, as regards the exercise of those matters which normally are submitted to the Sovereign (such as the appointment and issue of letters of credence

27. Cf. Keith, *The Dominions as Sovereign States,* p. 210.

28. The practice of transmitting copies of all acts of Parliament to the United Kingdom was quietly dropped in 1942. Canada, *House of Commons Debates,* April 5, 1943, p. 1829. In 1947, the Canadian statute requiring transmission of copies of all acts of Parliament to the Governor General for transmission to the United Kingdom was amended (11 Geo. VI C.44).

29. Instead of assimilating the relevant part of the instructions to the letters patent, the Union of South Africa followed the rather incongruous course of issuing new letters patent and instructions over the signature of the Prime Minister of the Union as submitting officer. The Governor General of South Africa thus became bound by instructions emanating from his own Prime Minister. See Nicholas Mansergh, *Documents and Speeches on Commonwealth Affairs, 1931-1952* (London, 1953), pp. 71-6.

to ambassadors), is more apparent than real. There seems to have been an understanding at the time that the letters patent were approved that no change in existing practice was contemplated, and the Governor General has not in fact dealt with any of the submissions which are normally laid before the Sovereign.

Thus there has been a full emancipation from the United Kingdom in the Canadian executive. This has developed first through the gradual erosion of the power, and the constitutional right, of the British government to interfere in any way with Canadian matters. Secondly, it has been brought about by the disappearance of the Governor General's functions as an imperial officer, and by the wasting away of his influence in the process of government. Thirdly, it has come about by the development of a direct constitutional relationship between Canadian ministers and the Sovereign, so that in Canadian matters they are dealing with the Queen of Canada and not the Queen of the United Kingdom.

LEGISLATIVE AUTONOMY

The British North American colonies were given the power to legislate in local matters when they were granted legislatures. These powers of local legislation were subject, however, to a number of limitations. In the first place, they could not make laws having effect outside their own territories. In the second place, colonial legislatures could not make laws which contravened the law of England. But what was the law of England? If it meant the whole statute and common law applicable in England, then the things a colonial legislature could do were restricted indeed. This question gave rise to serious difficulties in the nineteenth century, and it was only settled by the Colonial Laws Validity Act, 1865. By virtue of this act, it was declared that the only laws of England which stood in the way of colonial legislation were those statutes which specifically or by implication applied to the colony. In the context of its time, then, the Colonial Laws Validity Act was a liberating statute, since it reduced the number of colonial laws which could be held null and void to those which were repugnant to such English statute law as applied to the colonies. This act marks a stage in the gradual rise of local colonial institutions to ultimate full equality with those of the United Kingdom. The British North America Act of 1867 did not increase the powers of self-government of British North America, but it did widen the area covered by a single colonial Parliament, and subtly enhanced the status of the new Dominion by describing its legislature as a Parliament and its lower house as a House of Commons.

In addition to the above, the legislative restraints on Canada were the following: matters reserved exclusively for the British Parliament (such as legislation having extra-territorial effect, legislation respecting the constitution, and legislation dealing with other reserved topics, such as copyright).[30] If the Governor General had doubts about colonial legislation he could reserve it for consideration by the British government, which could then give assent to it by imperial order-in-council if it had no objection to the bill's becoming law. In addition, the British government could disallow any act of the Canadian Parliament within two years of its enactment. There was no limit in law whatever on this last power; it could be used to nullify any act whatsoever. An act which was disallowed became null and void from the date of its first passage.

The powers of reservation and disallowance of Canadian legislation still remain, superficially unimpaired, in sections 55 and 56 of the British North America Act. However, both are constitutionally obsolete: reservation because the Governor General is no longer an imperial officer and therefore has no constitutional right to reserve a bill; and disallowance because the Queen-in-Council in the United Kingdom has lost the constitutional right to deal with Canadian matters.[31] In any event the powers of disallowance and reservation, except as theoretical limitations of Canadian sovereignty, had ceased to be of any practical importance long before they were declared to be obsolete by the Imperial Conference of 1930. Most of the bills reserved had been dealt with in accordance with the detailed instructions to the Governor General regarding numerous classes of bills which had been superseded by the letters patent of 1878. Thereafter reservation was no longer important. The last Canadian act to be disallowed had been in 1873. The true safeguard of British imperial interests had turned out to be, as Edward Blake had argued in 1876, not the exercise of imperial veto in Canadian affairs, but mutual respect and consideration.

The restraints on Canadian self-government which depended on the positive exercise of British powers of veto disappeared by a

30. The Governor General was required in his instructions to reserve bills in a number of enumerated categories for consideration by the British government. Cf. fn. 21, *ante.*

31. Cf. statement of the Prime Minister, Mr. St. Laurent, in Canada, *House of Commons Debates,* 1949, p. 287.

process of constitutional evolution. The restraints which flowed from the limited powers which the Canadian Parliament possessed in constitutional law presented greater difficulty, because they could not be modified by changes in the conventions of the constitution but only through a change in the substance of British constitutional law.

The right to legislate beyond the limits laid down by the Colonial Laws Validity Act and the British North America Act was conferred by the Statute of Westminster, 1931. This step had been agreed to in principle at the Imperial Conference of 1926, but the technical problems involved in the transfer of power were considerable. A great deal of merchant shipping and similar legislation had to be carefully scrutinized to prepare the way for Canadian enactments to repair the gaps which would be opened in the law. A committee reported on the question in 1929, and its report was accepted by the Imperial Conference of 1930. Agreement was there reached on the outstanding questions of detail, and the Statute of Westminster was passed in the following year.

In effect the Statute of Westminster was a declaratory act that removed the previous limits on the legislative power of the Parliaments of the Dominions. At the same time, it laid down that the Parliament of the United Kingdom could not in future legislate with regard to the Dominions, except at the request and with the consent, of the Dominion concerned. It further declared that in future all laws relating to the succession to the throne and the royal style and titles would be enacted only with the assent of all Parliaments of the Dominions as well as the Parliament of the United Kingdom. Of course, theoretically, it would be possible for the United Kingdom Parliament to repeal the Statute of Westminister, since no Parliament has, in English constitutional law, the power to bind a subsequent Parliament. However, this is a sufficiently unlikely contingency that it need not be a cause of serious apprehension. As Professor Wheare argues, "section 4 [which restricts the application of future United Kingdom acts to the Dominions save with their consent]. . . is not a rule restricting power; it is a rule of construction. It is not directed to the United Kingdom Parliament; it is directed to the Courts. . . . But it does not render it legally impossible for the United Kingdom Parliament to legislate for a Dominion without the request and consent of the Dominion."[32] The important thing is that,

32. K.C. Wheare, *The Statute of Westminster and Dominion Status,* 5th ed. (London, 1953), p. 153.

as far as the constitutional law of Canada is concerned, the power of Parliament is no longer restricted to the areas it occupied before the passage of the Statute of Westminster. It might be neater, in a thorough attempt to domesticate the entire Canadian constitution, if Canada, following the practice of South Africa, re-enacted the Statute of Westminster as part of an act of the Canadian Parliament. However, nothing would be gained in practice by this and in any event our constitutional law would still depend on a large body of English constitutional law which no one has seen fit to touch for centuries.

There was one question regarding the new powers of the Dominions which could not be resolved in 1930. This was the question of amending procedure for the British North America Act itself, so that it was excepted (by section 7) from the general operation of the Statute of Westminster. The reason for the difficulty was that no agreement could be reached in Canada on a method of amending the Canadian constitution, and so it was still necessary to secure certain constitutional amendments by recourse to amending acts passed by the United Kingdom Parliament at the request of the Parliament of Canada.

It may seem odd that in providing Canada with a constitution in 1867 the British Parliament did not insert in the British North America Act some machinery for its amendment. However, in this we have paid the price for having the first Dominion constitution. In the nineteenth century the British Parliament was jealous of delegating its legislative powers to subordinate bodies. It still regarded itself as the supreme constituent power in the British Empire and it would not lightly have been persuaded to grant an entirely Canadian procedure of amendment. The Quebec Resolutions of 1866, upon which the B.N.A. Act was based, made no mention at all of a general amending procedure for the constitution of Canada. The act did enable the provinces to amend their own constitutions, but this was significantly safeguarded by the protection of the office of Lieutenant-Governor as well as by the existence of the federal power of disallowance.

The most significant fact is that it did not seem to the Fathers of Confederation that the inclusion of an amending power was either desirable or necessary. Dr. Gerin-Lajoie was led to the conclusion that the amending provisions were deliberately left out to avoid dissention in the negotiations, and more important, "because the Imperial authority [was] thus considered as the ultimate safeguard of the rights granted to the provinces and to minorities by the constitution."[33] Whatever the original reason for the omission, the system of seeking amendments through the United Kingdom Parliament was to remain until the final achievement of patriation in 1982, as successive efforts after the passage of the Statute of Westminster in 1931 failed to achieve general agreement. However, a partial patriation of the amending power, relating to the institutions of the central government, was achieved in 1949, so that relatively few matters, notably those relating to the distribution of legislative power between the two levels of government, still required the old procedure.[34]

AUTONOMY IN JUDICIAL POWER

Final control by "imperial" agencies over Canadian affairs lasted longer in the machinery for appealing judicial decisions than in any other part of the constitution. Furthermore, this imperial control was more independent of Canadian influence than any other part of the machinery of the constitution. Why did this alienation of such an important part of the constitution persist for so long? Perhaps two reasons may be adduced. The first is that in the Anglo-American world judicial institutions are by long tradition completely free from political influence by the government of the day, and the regard for the independence and autonomy of the judiciary is based on deep respect and long experience. The second reason is that there are genuine practical advantages to having what is in effect a single system of law binding on a large part of the civilized world. The basis of our legal system is essentially the common law—the discovery and declaration by judges of the principles which are to be applied in particular cases. The advantages of a system of law in which a single decision at the summit of appeal would automatically bring into line the operation of the law in a large part of the trading

33. Paul Gerin-Lajoie, *Constitutional Amendment in Canada* (Toronto, 1950) p. 38. Alexander Brady's view is that the omission of the amending power was "conscious and deliberate, and so grounded in conviction that the Founding Fathers hardly took pains to explain it." They assumed that the Canadian Government and Parliament could get on request any needed amendment from Westminster, and that a more formalized amending procedure "might only detract from the unitary nature of the federation." "Constitutional Amendment and the Federation", *Canadian Journal of Economics and Political Science.* XXIX:4 (November, 1963) pp. 486-7. In the absence of conclusive evidence, Professor Brady's views must be regarded as authoritative.

34. A full discussion of constitutional amendment will be found in Chapter 10.

world were obvious and great. Such a system enormously simplifies the problems which confront international business transactions and the transfer of property. When a single judicial decision can clarify a long-standing muddle in the law of at least six countries, the task of law reform is greatly simplified. From the point of view of the practising lawyer, such a system represents a large step in the direction of rationalizing the private municipal law of the world.

Against such a unified system of law for the whole British Commonwealth there have been two objections. The first is that it is a derogation of the sovereignty of the Dominions if their own courts are not the final custodians of the law. The second argument is that, while in general such a unified system could be defended in private law, it was open to serious objections in certain fields of public and constitutional law. In Canada this objection bears particularly on the role of the courts in interpreting the meaning of the federal constitution, and thus in assigning a balance between the central and the provincial legislatures.

A further problem arose from the fact that the highest court of appeal for the British Commonwealth was not, in form, a court at all but a Committee of the Privy Council, which, although made up of judges, did not render judgment in the usual way with the usual dissents and varying opinions of judges sitting *en banc*. Instead it gave only one *per curiam* opinion which was, technically, advice to the Crown. The panel from which members of the committee were constituted was fairly large, its business fascinating in its variety, and it was seldom that the same body of judges would be found through the years dealing with the same kind of case from the same country. This system was thus open to criticism on two serious grounds. In the first place the absence of dissenting opinions, which often reveal the real difficulty in cases of serious complexity, made it more difficult for the court to recover from a bad decision once it had been made. Where dissents are recorded and separate reasoned judgments given, it is much easier in later cases to adhere to the most workable and desirable development of legal doctrine. Where only one opinion, which represents a compromise of conflicting views, has thoroughly muddled the real issue in the case, it is much more difficult for subsequent courts to gain clear guidance from an important leading case. The second difficulty is that the varying composition of the Judicial Committee decreases the familiarity with local conditions which is essential for a sound interpretation of constitutional law. The occasional bizarre *obiter dicta* thrown out by members of the committee and the inconsistency which flowed from lack of continuity of personnel were frequently exasperating to constitutional lawyers in Canada.

The principle that appeal lies from the courts in the colonies to the King-in-Council is an old one in English constitutional law. This prerogative right to appeal was made statutory in 1844, after which, of course, it could only be abrogated or modified by an act of the British Parliament. In general, an appeal could be brought to the Judicial Committee in the following cases: (1) where the matter in dispute was a question of property or civil right of substantial value (the usual minimum value was 500 pounds sterling, but the amount varied from one jurisdiction to another); (2) by special leave of the colonial court where the matter seemed to be of great general or public importance; (3) by special leave of the Judicial Committee itself.[35]

The panel from which judges who served on the Judicial Committee were chosen consisted of the Lord Chancellor of England and ex-Lords Chancellor, the Lord President of the Court of Session of Scotland, present and past members of the Supreme Court in England, and the Lords of Appeal in Ordinary, if Privy Councillors. The panel was subsequently widened to include also judges or ex-judges of the superior courts of the Dominions provided that they were Privy Councillors.[36] Thus, from about the beginning of the present century, the practice developed of appointing the Chief Justice of Canada to the Privy Council, and he frequently sat, particularly when Canadian cases were under consideration.

As early as 1888, the Parliament of Canada sought to curtail the jurisdiction of the Judicial Committee of the Privy Council by abolishing appeals in criminal cases. However, this act was held to be *ultra vires* in 1926 on the ground that only the British Parliament could modify the jurisdiction of the Privy Council.[37] However, after the Statute of Westminster this barrier was removed, and the Canadian Parliament again abolished appeals in criminal cases.[38] Appeals in civil cases presented more of a problem. In the first place, a good many such cases turned on important points of constitutional law dealing with the jurisdiction of the provincial legislatures or of the Parliament of Canada. There was some reason to believe that an

35. Keith, *The Dominions as Sovereign States,* pp. 385-6.

36. Ibid., pp. 392-3.

37. *Nadan* v. *The King* [1926] A.C. 482.

38. Sustained by the Privy Council in *British Coal Corporation* v. *The King* [1935] A.C. 500.

external body, totally disinterested in the result of its decisions, would be a better protector of the rights of the provinces against the Dominion than the Supreme Court of Canada, whose members are all appointed by the federal government. This has always been an ungenerous attitude towards the Supreme Court of Canada, and in the end it gave way to a growing feeling of impatience with many Privy Council decisions and a sense of national pride. The second difficulty was more serious. The British North America Act gives the Parliament of Canada complete jurisdiction of criminal matters, but the provinces are given jurisdiction in questions of the organization and procedure of the civil courts. It was therefore open to doubt whether the Parliament of Canada possessed the power to abolish such appeals.

However, this doubt was removed by the Judicial Committee in an opinion in 1947,[39] and Parliament proceeded to abolish the last vestige of appeals to the Privy Council. By the Supreme Court Act of 1949 no cases instituted after that date could be carried on appeal beyond the Supreme Court of Canada. The law's delays are such that almost a decade was to elapse before the last case had wound its way to the Privy Council. With it, the Canadian constitution became entirely domesticated in judicial matters.

FEDERALISM AND POLITICS

A long evolutionary process has created in Canada what the reformers of the eighteen-forties had sought: a constitution "similar in principle to that of the United Kingdom." But it is not an exact facsimile of the British constitution. At every point it bears the strong marks of Canadian experience. In one important respect it differs from the British constitution, which has grown up within the framework of a homogeneous community and a unitary state. Canada from the beginning has had the characteristics of federalism.

A federal form of government was inevitable in 1867 for two reasons. Poor communication and the deep-rooted tradition of local self-government would have made it almost impossible to bring the Maritime provinces into a legislative union with the Canadas in 1867. It is possible that the coming of the railway and the integration of the economy would have produced, as Macdonald had hoped, an eventual legislative union. But the political situation in Canada itself

39. *Attorney-General of Ontario* v. *Attorney-General of Canada* [1947] A.C. 127.

made this impossible. The united province had been a failure as a unitary state. It operated in many matters a system of implicit federalism, and barely escaped formal recognition of the concurrent majority principle as a governing rule of the constitution. Cartier and the other leaders of French Canada made it clear that, for them, a federal rather than a legislative union was a *sine qua non* for the new Dominion.

Under the protection of the federal constitution strong local interests have strengthened their hold, and in particular French Canada has survived as a distinct and separate entity in the system.

The pervasiveness of the federal principle has meant that almost all political institutions are representative in character and operate through a consensus which is based on a concealed system of concurrent majorities. The prevalence of landslide elections in some provinces—with the virtual disappearance at times of any effective parliamentary opposition—is another reflection of the same phenomenon. The Canadian voter is inclined to vote for different parties in federal and provincial elections. This may be an instinctive recognition that the real system of countervailing forces is Dominion-provincial and not government-opposition.[40]

In the chapters which follow the focus of the discussion will be on the institutions of the central government. One reason for this is my own ignorance. While a fair amount is known about the actual machinery of government in the Canadian provinces, systematic treatises are lacking on a significant number of them. The second reason is easier to defend. The differences in the actual machinery of government between the provinces and Ottawa are not great. Within limits, what is true of the central government is also true of any given provincial government.

The reasons for this are obvious. Parliament and Cabinet in Ottawa are direct descendants of the institutions of the United Province of Canada before Confederation. The same rules operated in the same chambers before and after Confederation. The majority of members were the same, and most of the officials of the Province of Canada then in Ottawa took service with the new Dominion government. The re-created governments of Ontario and Quebec carried on as before in the old province. Some of the western provinces were "colonial" creations which grew out of territorial governments set up under the auspices of Ottawa, and the early Lieutenant-Governors of the western provinces were experienced

40. This idea was first expressed by Professor F.H. Underhill. See, for example, his *In Search of Canadian Liberalism* (Toronto, 1960), p. 237.

politicians from Eastern Canada who played a decisive role in setting the political institutions of the provinces in motion.[41]

The differences then, are not great but are worth noting. The first is the relative unimportance of the extreme form of sectional representation which is necessary in Ottawa. Provincial Cabinets usually govern relatively homogeneous and unified communities, and this leads to less diffusion of power in their Cabinets. In all provinces there is considerable concentration of power in the Premier, or in a small group of ministers. In some of the smaller provinces even Cabinet office may be a part-time job and ministerial salaries may be relatively low. Full-time ministers may hold several portfolios, and the influence of part-time ministers is proportionately slight.

The second difference is accounted for by time-lag. Two major wars and the new responsibilities of twentieth-century government forced the pace of reform in Ottawa. Since the early nineteen-forties the major executive departments and the House of Commons have taken on the air of urgency and importance that go with the grave and rapidly changing concerns of a modern state, while their opposite numbers in the provincial capitals continued for nearly a generation to exhibit a somnolent Victorian atmosphere. Civil service reform was slow, and the quality of even the senior members of the public service was not high, advanced management techniques were unknown, and government—as far as legislators and even some ministers were concerned—was very much a part-time affair. This state of affairs persisted even into the nineteen-fifties.

Since then the pace of modernization in provincial governments has been such that in some cases they have surpassed the efficiency of the federal government itself. Initially this was the result of the growth of shared-cost welfare plans which compelled the provinces to develop efficient bureaucracies of their own. In addition, there was developed a lateral mobility of highly skilled civil servants between provinces and between the provincial and federal governments. The government of Quebec in the early sixties was able, for special reasons, to lure a number of able civil servants from Ottawa to Quebec. By the middle sixties, the superior competence and knowledge of some provincial delegations over their federal opposite numbers had become clearly visible at several of the federal-provincial conferences. Bureaucratic mobility in itself was bound to

41. See John T. Saywell, *The Office of Lieutenant-Governor* (Toronto, 1957) especially Chapter III.

encourage the spread of improved management techniques and lead to standardization of procedures.

Provincial legislatures have been the slowest to change. They are, in all cases, significantly smaller than the House of Commons in Ottawa. None has much more than a hundred members, and a number get along with half as many. Their procedure is therefore less formal; the pressure on parliamentary time has usually not been such that they have needed to make many modifications in procedure since the time when responsible government began. They have less to do than the Parliament in Ottawa, and generally do it in comparatively short annual sessions. Only Ontario and Quebec have been compelled to operate at a pace equal to that of the Parliament of Canada.[42]

Partly because provincial legislatures met for comparatively brief periods they have less often appeared to be concerned with major issues. The greatly expanded role of the provincial state in recent years will tend to minimize this difference and increase the similarities between provincial legislatures and the Parliament at Ottawa. While some provinces must reconcile the differences between two distinct communities, which enhance the saliency of their politics, most of them comprehend fairly homogeneous communities so that a blanket of consensus politics leads to large majorities in the legislatures, long tenure of governments, and ineffective political control of the executive.

The most important difference between provincial and federal government lies essentially in informal political organization. There are extremely wide variations in the character of the politics of different provinces; their party systems differ considerably; and the authority relationships of provincial parties tend to carry over into the more formal structure of provincial government.

42. See J.M. Beck, *The Government of Nova Scotia* (Toronto, 1957); Frank MacKinnon, *The Government of Prince Edward Island* (Toronto, 1951); H.G. Thorburn, *The Politics of New Brunswick* (Toronto, 1961); M.S. Donnelly, *The Government of Manitoba* (Toronto, 1963); Fred Schindeler, *Responsible Government in Ontario* (Toronto, 1969); Donald C. MacDonald (ed.) *Government and Politics of Ontario* (Toronto, 1975); S.J.R. Noel, *Politics in Newfoundland* (Toronto, 1971); Evelyn Eager, *Saskatchewan Government: Politics and Pragmatism* (Saskatoon, 1980).

2

The Formal Executive

QUEEN AND CROWN

The government of Canada is carried on in the Queen's name,[1] but the Queen herself does not govern. The Crown is the legal entity which embodies the Government. As a legal entity the Crown owns property, has legal rights and obligations and may be involved in lawsuits. The Crown is the institution which encompasses all of the powers of executive government, whether exercised by ministers or by other officials.

Originally, the executive power in England was in the hands of the monarch personally, but constitutional evolution has transferred these powers to responsible officials who exercise them in the name of the Sovereign. It is a fundamental axiom of the constitution that the Queen can do no wrong. "This . . . means that by no proceeding known to the law can the Sovereign be made personally responsible for any act done by her; . . . In the second place, no one can plead orders of the Crown . . . in defence of any act not otherwise justifiable by law."[2] Ministers, who exercise the lawful powers of government, are themselves responsible for the legal consequences of their acts. The Crown, as the legal abstraction representing government, is not. This is the general rule, but there are now important exceptions to it. In practice, many "emanations of the Crown," which are essentially commercial operations, are set up as legally separate entities apart from the Crown and their immunity from

1. "The Executive Government and Authority of and over Canada is hereby declared to continue and be vested in the Queen." The British North America Act, 1867, section 9.
2. A. V. Dicey, *Introduction to the Study of the Law of the Constitution,* 10th ed. (London, 1961), pp. 24-5.

suits at law is waived by statute.[3] Furthermore, since the passage of the Crown Liability Act, 1952, the Crown in the right of Canada can be sued in the courts in the same way as any other litigant.

In legal theory the Crown was regarded as indivisible, but in practice it manifests itself in what are essentially separate legal personalities, as for example the executives of the United Kingdom, Canada, Australia and so forth. Similarly, the powers and legal rights of the Crown within the Canadian federal system inhere in either the province or the Dominion, according to the division of powers under the British North America Act.[4]

The powers of the Crown derive from two sources: statute and common law. As we shall see, Parliament confers very wide powers on the Crown both to administer the law (executive power) and to make it (legislative power). The Crown's power to legislate is a delegated power, subject to change or removal by Parliament. In addition, the Crown retains some residue of common-law powers to legislate, which are the prerogative powers. Dicey defines the prerogative in this sense as "the residue of discretionary or arbitrary authority, which at any given time is legally left in the hands of the Crown."[5] The prerogative power to legislate is a wasting asset, since once Parliament has occupied the field, the prerogative power has been displaced. But there are still a few occasions when it is possible to legislate under the prerogative power, for example in making provision for the administration of conquered territory. In addition to the prerogative power to legislate, which is of slight importance, the Sovereign possesses certain "personal prerogatives," that is, powers to act independent of ministerial advice, which are still important reserve powers in the constitution. The significance of these will be considered later in this chapter.

A large and important part of the constitutional history of the British Commonwealth consists in the gradual transformation of the executive power from the personal government of the Sovereign to a legal abstraction which describes government by a variety of accountable officials. We still use the archaic phraseology to describe the process, but we know that the essence of the situation

3. See below, *Crown Corporations,* Chapter 4.

4. "The Lieutenant-Governor, when appointed, is as much the representative of Her Majesty for all purposes of provincial government as the Governor-General himself is for all purposes of Dominion government." *Liquidators of the Maritime Bank* v. *Receiver-General of New Brunswick* [1893] A.C. 117, at p. 132.

5. Dicey, *Law of the Constitution,* p. 424.

has changed. We speak of ministers "advising" the Sovereign, but we mean by this phrase that a minister or the Cabinet is assuming responsibility for a decision which they have taken. This is not "advice" in the same sense that Cardinal Wolsey was an adviser to Henry VIII, but rather a way of saying that the ministers have taken the decision and are prepared to be held accountable for it.

It is customary to think of the Sovereign as holding office by hereditary right, but this is only part of the truth. For the Sovereign really holds office at the will of, and under rules laid down by, the supreme constitutional power, which is Parliament. We need not inquire into the whole history of this process but it should be noticed that the succession to the throne and the conditions under which it may be retained are laid down in the Act of Settlement, 1701. In that act the succession was settled on the heirs of the body of the Electress Sophia of Hanover, provided that the holder is a Protestant. In addition to this limitation an act of the reign of George III, the Royal Marriages Act, 1772, limited the right of the children of the Sovereign to marry without the Sovereign's consent. It is equally clear, from the "abdication" of James II and the abdication of Edward VIII, that a Sovereign's right to remain on the throne persists only so long as ministers and Parliament are prepared to support it.

These are matters which do not rest exclusively with the Parliament of the United Kingdom. The preamble of the Statute of Westminster affirmed that "any alteration in the law touching the Succession to the Throne or the Royal Style and Titles shall hereafter require the assent as well of the Parliaments of all the Dominions as of the Parliament of the United Kingdom." Since that time, the only major piece of legislation affecting the succession to the throne was the act confirming the abdication of Edward VIII, His Majesty's Declaration of Abdication Act, 1936. This act was preceded by consultation among the governments of the Commonwealth and stated, in accordance with the provisions of the Statute of Westminster, that with Canadian consent it applied to Canada. Subsequently Canadian assent was given parliamentary sanction by the Succession to the Throne Act, 1937.

Similar rules governing common action apply in the case of the royal style and titles. The first such change after the Statute of Westminster occurred when the granting of independence to India made it necessary to drop the words "Emperor of India" from the royal titles. This had been incidentally provided in the Indian Independence Act. The change was brought about in Canada by the Royal Style and Titles Act (Canada), 1947. This act provided that the change should take place on a date to be designated in the *Canada Gazette*, and the notice was published on the same date as the change was brought about in the United Kingdom by royal proclamation. A further change was made in the royal style and titles in 1953, and was implemented by a somewhat different procedure. While Canada took little part in the 1947 change, except to approve it, the later change was the result of discussions at the Prime Ministers' Conference which met in London in December 1952. Agreement could not be reached on a uniform title appropriate to all countries, but "there was a general desire to have the royal style and title accord with the constitutional position of the various members of the commonwealth and to have it, in so far as might meet the conditions of the various members of the commonwealth, as uniform as possible."[6]

It was therefore left to each country to take appropriate steps to bring into force the style and title which had been agreed upon at the conference. This could not be done simply by legislative concurrence in a single title—which had been the procedure followed in 1947 and contemplated by the Statute of Westminster. Parliamentary provision in Canada was given by the Royal Style and Titles Act, 1953, which provided that the new title for Canada should "come into force on the day the Royal Proclamation authorized by section I is issued." Thus the implementation of the royal style and titles was left in the realm of the prerogative. A proclamation was therefore passed under the Great Seal of Canada, signed by the Prime Minister as submitting officer, and signed by the Queen on May 28, 1953.

Canada is also able, if required, to provide machinery for the exercise of the Sovereign's functions in relation to Canada in the event that they cannot be discharged in person, as a result of illness, infancy, or other causes. At present the United Kingdom legislation on the subject is the Regency Act, 1937 (as amended in 1943 and 1953.) These acts do not, however, apply to Canada. They were passed subsequent to the Statute of Westminster and could have been extended to Canada only with Canadian concurrence and assent. The reason why this was not done was stated in the British House of Commons by Sir John Simon who, as Home Secretary, was the minister responsible for legislation dealing with the Sovereign. He recalled that the question had been discussed with representatives of the Dominions at a Prime Ministers' meeting in London in 1935, but that it had been agreed that no legislation applicable to the Dominions was necessary because "A Dominion which has a Gover-

6. Canada, *House of Commons Debates* (unrevised), February 3, 1953, p. 1566 (Mr. St. Laurent).

nor-General gets its ordinary day by day business done in the name of the Crown by the executive action of the Governor-General. The state of health or absence of the Sovereign does not hold up the machinery at all."[7]

The letters patent of 1947 conferred on the Governor General "all powers and authorities lawfully belonging to Us in respect of Canada." Legally, therefore, the Governor General can exercise any of the Queen's powers in Canada. The converse is not true, however; the Queen cannot exercise the Governor General's powers because they are conferred on him, and not on the Queen, by the British North America Act. Where the function in question is purely ceremonial and does not require the production of some instrument of lawful effect, the Queen can officiate; where it is otherwise she cannot. Thus King George VI gave a royal assent to legislation in 1939, Queen Elizabeth II opened the Twenty-fourth Parliament on October 14, 1957, and held a Privy Council earlier on the same day. Unless Parliament were to pass a Royal Powers Act similar to the Australian Royal Powers Act, 1953, she could not, however, approve an in-council or in other ways effectively replace the Governor General during a royal visit.

In fact the amount of Canadian business which was dealt with by the Sovereign personally increased substantially in succeeding years, essentially because of the great increase in the number of Canadian missions accredited to foreign countries since the nineteen-forties, which meant a steady flow of ambassadorial appointments. While the letters patent of 1947 purported to delegate all royal powers in relation to Canada to the Governor General, there was an understanding at the time that all matters which prior to that time had been based on direct advice to the Sovereign would not be transferred to the Governor General without the consent of the Palace.[8]

7. Great Britain, *Parliamentary Debates* (Commons), 319H.C.Deb.5s., February 2, 1937, pp. 1452-3.

8. The press release of October 1, 1947, describing the significance of the letters patent contains the following passage: "the Governor General is authorized to exercise, on the advice of Canadian Ministers, all of His Majesty's powers and authorities in respect of Canada. This does not limit the King's prerogatives. Nor does it necessitate any change in the present practice under which certain matters are submitted by the Canadian Government to the King personally. However. . . . it will be legally possible for the Governor General, on the advice of Canadian Ministers to exercise any of the powers and authorities of the Crown in respect of Canada, without the necessity of a submission being made to His Majesty. . . . There will be no legal necessity to alter existing practices. However, the Government of Canada will be in a position to determine, in any prerogative matter affecting Canada, whether the submission should go to His Majesty or to the Governor General."

Since the remaining prerogatives of the Sovereign are jealously protected by the Private Secretary to the Queen any substantive change is likely to be achieved after prolonged and delicate negotiation. In fact, two changes have taken place since 1947, the most recent being the arrangement, reached late in 1977, which related to diplomatic appointments and the various exchanges connected therewith. It was agreed that in future the Governor General, not the Queen, would appoint and recall ambassadors accredited to foreign states (High Commissioners to other Commonwealth countries have always been appointed by the Governor General). Furthermore, the Governor General would also deal with the acceptance of Letters of Recall of foreign ambassadors and the approval of the establishment or severance of diplomatic relations between Canada and foreign states. It was agreed, however, that the Queen should continue to issue Letters of Credence to Canadian ambassadors, since this was a direct communication between heads of state.

These changes, described rather ineptly by an External Affairs spokesman as "removing one more little vestige of colonial status and putting the trappings of sovereignty in Canada," reflect a certain tension in the relations between the Palace and Ottawa which have characterized the prime ministership of Pierre Trudeau. In a parliamentary question to the Prime Minister on January 23, 1978, Mr. Diefenbaker described the changes as an evisceration of the Queen's rights. Mr. Trudeau's reply was simply to relate the changes to the letters patent of 1947. Nevertheless there were signs, from time to time, of the latter's government to enhance the role of the Governor General at the expense of the Sovereign. This was illustrated in the aborted Constitutional Amendment Bill of 1977 which *inter alia* sought to declare the Governor General to be head of state, while leaving the position of the Sovereign somewhat ambiguous.

The second significant change related to the grant of honours and awards. All such awards in the past, both military and civil, were purely British awards, submitted to the Palace on Canadian advice in accordance with the general rules of eligibility. Purely military awards, particularly those for valour, have never been a serious matter of controversy in Canada. On the other hand civil honours, particularly if they conferred titles, had for many years been objected to as inappropriate to a democratic society in North America. The profusion of knighthoods bestowed during the First World War strengthened this feeling and led the House of Commons to pass a resolution deploring the practice. Thereafter none was recommended except during a brief period in 1934-35 when a number of knighthoods were conferred at the behest of Mr. Bennett. At the end of the Second World War the award of honours was revived, no doubt partly out of a need to recognize the services of the large number of business people who had served as wartime civil servants. These did not include knighthoods and the practice stopped once the honours for wartime service had been conferred.

Nevertheless all countries feel the need to find some way of conferring a mark of public distinction on outstanding citizens and there became evident a growing desire to create a purely Canadian honour for this purpose. This was finally done in the Centennial Year. On April 17, 1967, Prime Minister Pearson announced the creation of the Order of Canada to replace the purely British honours and awards for which Canadians had hitherto been recommended by the Government of Canada. The letters patent issued by the Queen which created the order were amended in 1972 to enlarge the category of honours and awards in the Order of Canada and to provide for additional military awards.

There are now three levels of membership in the Order: Companions of the Order, Officers of the Order, and Members of the Order. The Military awards are the Cross of Valour, the Star of Courage, and the Medal of Bravery, all of which can be awarded to both civilians and military personnel. The awards of the Order of Canada are made by the Governor General, who is Chancellor of the Order, on the advice of an advisory council consisting of the Chief Justice of Canada (chairman), the Clerk of the Privy Council, the Undersecretary of State, the Chairman of the Canada Council, the President of the Royal Society of Canada, and the President of the Association of Universities and Colleges of Canada. Other committees such as the Armed Forces Decorations Committee and a bravery awards advisory committee advise the Governor General on the awards for bravery. The first awards were announced on July 1, 1967, and subsequent awards have been announced on January 1 and July 1 of each year.

There are still awards for which Canadians are eligible in addition to the Order of Canada. The most important of these are in the personal gift of the Sovereign, such as the Order of Merit and the Royal Victorian Order which is given for personal service to the Sovereign. When such awards are given the Sovereign informs the Prime Minister. Some Canadians may also receive British Awards which have been recommended by the British government, of which there have been a few. Between 1947 and 1973, according to an answer to a parliamentary question put down by Mr. Diefenbaker, six Canadians had received awards in the personal gift of the Sovereign, while eighteen had received British awards. In 1976 Mr. Diefenbaker was designated a Companion of Honour, which is one of the most prestigious and distinguished of British honours. Mr. Diefenbaker was quoted in the press on January 6 of that year as saying that "It is a designation by the Queen herself and is not based on a recommendation by the Prime Minister." This, as the Prime Minister's Office was quick to point out, was not the case. The award had been initiated by Mr. Trudeau but there was no further explanation of how the recommendation had been made.

The Sovereign's functions in relation to Canada have been somewhat attenuated by the 1977 changes which eliminated much of the paperwork connected with diplomatic appointments. In any event, they were a matter of routine most of the time, and the Queen is still more than just a ceremonial figure–aloof from Canadian affairs and appearing intermittently on royal visits. She is still an essential element in the appointment of the Governor General, is still involved with important foreign policy questions which arise out of the decision to appoint or withdraw ambassadors, and retains an ultimate role in the field of honours, since what Canadian honours there are must be constituted by royal letters patent.

Perhaps the best description of her position in the process of constitutional government in Canada is contained in a letter from her Private Secretary which sought to explain how matters stood in Australia:

> ...As we understand the situation here, the Australian Constitution firmly places the prerogative powers of the Crown in the hands of the Governor-General as representative of the Queen in Australia. The only person competent to commission an Australian Prime Minister is the Governor-General, and the Queen has no part in the decisions which the Governor-General must take in accordance with the Constitution. Her Majesty, as Queen of Australia, is watching events in Canberra with close attention, but it would not be proper for her to interfere in matters which are so clearly placed within the jurisdiction of the Governor-General by the Constitution Act.[9]

The position and influence of the Sovereign in the affairs of the United Kingdom is, of course, much greater than in Canada, where

9. From Sir Martin Charteris to the Speaker of the Australian House of Representatives, November 17, 1975. Quoted in Geoffrey Sawer, *Federalism under Strain* (Melbourne, 1977) p. 211.

day-to-day business is conducted by the Governor General. But even in such routine matters the Sovereign is kept informed of the general state of affairs by regular private letters from the Governor General. On the limited, but important, amount of business which is submitted directly to the Sovereign by her Canadian ministers, her information is as full and her influence as important as in the United Kingdom.

Modern government consists very largely in the transmission of files, documents and other pieces of paper through elaborate and intricate channels. The holder of any office could not retain effective participation in the process of decision-making without an expert staff to sort out the significant from the unimportant, to digest lengthy documents and to keep the wheels running smoothly by steady contact with other officials. To this bureaucratic necessity the Sovereign is no exception. The "departmental" functions connected with the Sovereign's position are dealt with by the Private Secretary to the Queen. The Private Secretary, who is appointed by the Queen, is therefore one of the most important officials in the government hierarchy. A succession of very able men, from the time of Queen Victoria's great Private Secretary, Sir Henry Ponsonby, have provided the Sovereign with skilful and discreet assistance without crossing the invisible line which divides their function from that of the Sovereign's confidential advisers under the constitution, the ministers in office at the time.

In addition to the decisions in which, under the constitution, the Queen must participate, as head of state she exemplifies what Walter Bagehot called the "dignified" functions of government. He argued that, in the conditions of Victorian England, the monarchy made democracy "safe" by diverting the attentions of the masses towards contemplation of the glamour and pomp of royal personages, while unglamorous politicians were left in an atmosphere of comparative calm in which they could run the country. Bagehot had seen the French Republic collapse and give way to the Third Empire, and he was highly sensitive to the danger which ambitious politicians who wish to play Caesar pose to a constitutional order. He felt that a democratic monarchy, which weakened the charismatic role of politicians by diverting public emotion to royalty, was likely to be more safe and stable than a republic. Thus, a head of state, totally divorced from political associations, would be able to act as a symbol of national unity presiding over the solemn occasions whose historic significance helps to cement national unity.

Even in Canada, where the atmosphere is essentially egalitarian, the effect of monarchical institutions cannot be entirely dismissed.[10]

It is, however, not possible to use Bagehot's Victorian arguments to justify the role of the monarchy in Canada today. The effectiveness of the monarchy in his time was that it could be understood by a public not sophisticated enough to understand responsible government. In Canada the reverse is the case. After a century of tradition the public does understand how the political side of government works, and probably has a somewhat disillusioned affection for it. The monarchy, on the other hand, is less real. The social system of which it is the apex never had strong roots in Canadian soil, and Canadians have seldom understood the emollient and therapeutic value of deference and protocol. The visible person of the Sovereign, even in an age of swift air travel, is still a rare and somewhat puzzling phenomenon.

While the monarchy may still have a strong emotional appeal, particularly to older persons in some parts of the country, this fact of itself is to some extent divisive rather than unifying. For to many an ardent monarchist, what is symbolized is not an integral part of Canadian government, but an emotional reminder of the past glories of the British Empire. For this reason it may be repugnant, because to those in search of authentic Canadian symbols of unity, it seems to be a surviving symbol of British colonial rule. These conflicting emotions were fully exposed in the debate, both in the House of Commons and in the country in 1966, over the Canadian flag.

The justification for the monarchy in Canada must rest, in the end, not on its symbolic and emotive value, but on its practical place in a rational system of government. Its real virtues are therefore twofold. In the first place, it denies to political leaders the full splendour of their power and the excessive aggrandizement of their persons

10. "The crown under the monarchical principle also lends, I think, stability and dignity to our national life, and I am sure we all agree that that is important in a democratic system based on the free and active play of party controversies. The crown as head of the state and as represented in our country standing above all such controversies, commanding and deserving the respect and loyalty and affection of us all, ensures a more solid and secure foundation for national development than might otherwise be the case under some other form of democratic government." Mr. L. B. Pearson in Canada, *House of Commons Debates* (unrevised), February 3, 1953, pp. 1576-7. One should note that this somewhat fulsome statement, for a Liberal Cabinet minister, was made in Coronation year. His successor as Prime Minister has shown little public enthusiasm for the institution of monarchy.

which come from the undisturbed occupancy of the centre of the stage. The symbolic value of the face of the leader on the postage stamp, the open and undisguised role of leader and redeemer of the people, are hints of the threatened presence of the one-party state. These are dangers which still lurk for even the most civilized and stable democracy. In the second place, the physical presence of the head of state (or her personal representative, the Governor General) in the process of ratifying great decisions is in itself a check on the ultimate power of elected politicians, against whom the checks of periodic elections and imperfect parliamentary scrutiny are not always sufficient. With this prudent separation of roles we are unlikely to share the agonizing trauma felt by many Americans during the Nixon years. To them impeachment of a president seemed perilously close to regicide. In Canada we can accept the necessary removal of a Prime Minister without such qualms.

The Queen no longer serves as a symbol of an imperial connection and of uncritical colonial loyalty to the British Empire. Nevertheless, the Queen, as head of the Commonwealth, still serves as a tenuous legal thread which holds the whole system together. The Prime Ministers' Conference of 1949 reached an ingenious compromise with the emergent republicanism of the Asian countries in a formula which stated that the several Commonwealth countries were "united as Members of the British Commonwealth of Nations" and accepted the King "as the symbol of the free association of its independent nations and as such the Head of the Commonwealth."

THE GOVERNOR GENERAL

The fourth of the Quebec Resolutions of 1866 stated hopefully that "the Executive Authority or Government shall be vested in the Sovereign of the United Kingdom of Great Britain and Ireland, and be administered according to the well-understood principles of the British Constitution by the Sovereign personally, or by the Representative of the Sovereign duly authorized." But at that date it was premature to suggest that Queen Victoria could be Queen of Canada, administering the government in person. The parliamentary draftsmen primly edited this aspiring clause into the briefer and more ambiguous form in which it appears in section 9 of the British North America Act, where "executive Government and Authority of and over Canada is and hereby declared to continue and be vested in the Queen."

Resolution four, with its emphasis on the "well-understood principles of the British Constitution," was intended to stress the essential fact of Cabinet government, that the Governor General should exercise his office as a constitutional monarch. The Queen, immobilized and unapproachable in her widow's weeds at Windsor, obviously could not be expected to have any direct connection with the government of Canada. Nevertheless, the point was made that the Governor General was above all the Queen's representative. "It is too much to expect," said John A. Macdonald, "that the Queen should vouchsafe us her personal governance or presence, except to pay us, as the heir apparent to the Throne, our future Sovereign has already paid us, the graceful compliment of a visit. The Executive authority must therefore be administered by Her Majesty's Representative. We place no restriction on Her Majesty's prerogative in the selection of her representative. The Sovereign has unrestricted freedom of choice. . . . But we may be permitted to hope, that when the union takes place, and we become the great country which British North America is certain to be, it will be an object worthy the ambition of the statesmen of England to be charged with presiding over our destinies."[11]

It was part of Macdonald's genius that he saw instinctively the way that the executive government of Canada was to develop, for there was as much of the future as of the present in resolution four and in his exposition of it. For just as the constitutional history of Britain consists largely in the gradual bringing of the royal prerogative under the control of ministers answerable to the House of Commons, the constitutional history of Canada has involved a similar operation with the office of Governor General. In his discussion of the executive power under the new Dominion, Macdonald stressed the aspect of the Governor General's dual personality which was to survive, and passed over in silence the role of imperial officer which was finally to disappear exactly sixty years later.

Legal and Constitutional Position

Constitutionally the Governor General bears the same relationship to his ministers as the Queen bears to ministers in the United

11. *Confederation Debates,* 1865. Quoted in W. P. M. Kennedy, ed., *Statutes, Treaties and Documents of the Canadian Constitution, 1713–1929* (Toronto, 1930), p. 559.

Kingdom. In general he is bound to act on their advice, and practically every act of the government requires ministerial responsibility. This position was affirmed by the Imperial Conference of 1926. As a consequence it is not the Governor General but his ministerial advisers who are legally responsible for all official acts done through him. "The Minister or servant of the Crown who thus takes part in giving expression to the Royal will is legally responsible for the act in which he is concerned," says Dicey, "and he cannot get rid of his liability by pleading that he acted in obedience to royal orders."[12]

It might seem to follow from this that the Governor General enjoys the same absolute legal immunity from any suit in the courts as does the Sovereign. This, however, is not so. The Governor General continues to have normal liability in civil and criminal matters when acting in a private capacity, though clearly, liability for official acts would fall primarily upon the ministers responsible. The position is, in this respect, anomalous, but the possibility of liability being a matter of inconvenience is so remote that no question seems to have arisen as to the need to remedy it.[13]

Appointment

The Governor General is appointed by the Queen by commission under the Great Seal of Canada on the advice of the Prime Minister of Canada.[14] The term of office, said Professor Dawson, "May be

12. Dicey, *Law of the Constitution,* p. 326.
13. Arthur Berriedale Keith, *The Dominions as Sovereign States* (London, 1938), p. 214.
14. The appointment of a native Australian, Sir Isaac Isaacs, as Governor General of Australia was the first occasion on which ministers in the Dominions had advised the King directly on anything, and was, in fact, the reason why the question was brought up at the Imperial Conference of 1930. The Australians became entangled in the toils of palace etiquette by allowing the information about the appointment to leak out prematurely, and this incensed the King. The normal practice in recommending such appointments is to submit several names informally and confidentially to make sure that the King has no personal objection, and only thereafter to submit a formal recommendation. The Australians, by omitting this courtesy, so annoyed the King that at one point he refused to accept their submission. Apart from the fact that the appointment had aroused political passions in Australia, the King did not like the idea of a representative who was personally unknown to him. In the end the appointment was made, but in subsequent cases the courtesies of palace etiquette have been more scrupulously observed. Sir Harold Nicolson, *King George V, His Life and Reign* (London, 1952), pp. 478-82.

simply, if somewhat ambiguously, stated as being officially recognized as six years, customarily treated as five years, while on occasion it has been seven years."[15] The letters patent of 1947 made provision for the succession to the office of Governor General "in the event of death, incapacity, removal, or absence," but failed to provide specifically for the possibility of voluntary resignation prior to the end of the term. Accordingly, new letters patent were issued in 1952 to enable Lord Alexander to resign office before the term of his commission had expired.

The actual removal of a Governor General is a different matter, since it implies the existence of conduct which is inappropriate to the office. It is an unlikely event, but one that is constitutionally possible. It was a possibility that was taken seriously during the constitutional crisis in Australia in 1975, and was, in fact, one of the reasons which led the Governor General, Sir John Kerr, to dismiss the Prime Minister. In his anxiety to keep the Queen from being involved in the crisis, he considered it necessary to win the race to the telephone ahead of his Prime Minister. He feared that if the Prime Minister knew that the Governor General contemplated dismissal, "he would instantly, whilst still Prime Minister, seek my recall" and advise the Queen to appoint a more complaisant Governor General.[16] His fears, while not totally groundless, were exaggerated. Mr. Whitlam claims that he had no such intention. In any event, it is difficult to believe that the Queen would acquiesce in such an important matter on the basis of a telephone call in the middle of the night. A proper decorum is required in such matters and it would be several days at least before the deed could be done. If the question arose in the middle of a crisis the delay would almost certainly leave time for the crisis to be resolved in some other way. Nevertheless, the fact remains that the Governor General's tenure of office is governed by the will of the Prime Minister.

The Governor General is appointed as "Governor General and Commander-in-Chief," but this double title should confuse no one who remembers that the Queen possesses the same honorific title under the constitution and that "the Command-in-Chief of the Land and Naval Militia, and of all Naval and Military Forces, of and in Canada, is hereby declared to continue to be vested in the Queen" as section 15 of the B.N.A. Act puts it. The only occasion on which any difficulty arose was during the term of office of Field Marshal

15. R. MacGregor Dawson, *The Government of Canada,* rev. ed. Norman Ward (Toronto, 1963), p. 163.

16. Sir John Kerr, *Matters for Judgement,* (Melbourne, 1978), p. 345.

H.R.H. the Duke of Connaught who, as Sir Robert Borden wrote, "laboured under the handicap of his position as a member of the Royal Family and he never fully realized the limitations of his position as Governor-General. Nominally he was Commander-in-Chief of the Canadian Military Forces, but only in the same sense as the King is Commander-in-Chief of the Military Forces of Great Britain. But he could not divest himself of the impression that this command was actual and not purely nominal."[17]

Statutory Powers of the Governor General

The British North America Act confers a number of powers on the Governor General which must be understood in the context of his constitutional position. Some have been rendered obsolete because they related to his now defunct position as an imperial officer. The others have to be read in conjunction with the long-established doctrine of responsible government which is now expressed in Clause II of the letters patent constituting his office, which enjoin him to exercise his powers "with the advice of Our Privy Council for Canada or of any members thereof." In other words these are powers which, though nominally conferred on the Governor General, are in effect vested in ministers. The first of these statutory powers is the power to summon senators (section 24) and to "summon and call together the House of Commons" (section 38). He appoints the Speaker of the Senate (section 34).

Section 55 of the British North America Act provides that the Governor General may assent to bills which have passed both Houses of Parliament; refuse assent to such bills; or reserve such bills for the signification of Her Majesty's pleasure. The section further provides that he shall exercise these powers subject to his instructions. Since the instructions have been abolished and the Governor General is no longer subject to control by the British government, the provisions of this section have become inoperative, although the section has never been repealed. If the Governor General has any power at all to refuse assent to bills, it is a power

17. *Robert Laird Borden: His Memoirs,* Vol. II (London, 1938), p. 604. The real cause of the mischief was the Governor General's Military Secretary, Colonel Stanton. The Canadian government, in 1921, appears to have raised the question of abolishing the Governor General's title as Commander-in-Chief, but no change was made. The office of Military Secretary was, however, discontinued at the time that Lord Byng was appointed Governor General in 1921.

which is part of the prerogative powers which he exercises in the same way as the Sovereign.

Section 90 of the British North America Act provides that the Governor General may exercise, in relation to provincial legislation, the same powers as those vested in the Sovereign and a Secretary of State in the United Kingdom by section 56. This power is always exercised on ministerial advice and in practice takes the form of an order-in-council recommended by the Minister of Justice. Thus the powers of disallowance and reservation in provincial legislation are powers which belong to the government of Canada, and are not part of the discretionary powers of the Governor General.

For the exercise of the various powers of his office the Governor General possesses two seals. The first of these is the Great Seal of Canada, which is used for sealing almost all important executive instruments such as proclamations, commissions of ministers of the Crown, etc. In addition to the Great Seal, the Governor General possesses a Privy Seal, which bears the impression of his own personal coat of arms. It is used for sealing the proclamation which is issued on his assumption of office, although other proclamations are sealed with the Great Seal. The Privy Seal is also used for sealing military commissions.

Prerogative Powers of the Governor General

The transformation of the office of the Governor General to the same position, in relation to the government of Canada, as that of the Sovereign in relation to the government of the United Kingdom means that, like the Sovereign, he has certain important prerogative powers under the constitution which he may exercise on his own initiative. The conditions under which he may act in relation to ministers on his own initiative are rare and the precise scope of the powers is undefined, yet such powers are generally acknowledged by the authorities to exist.[18]

18. H. V. Evatt, *The King and His Dominion Governors* (London, 1936), p. 286. These powers in the United Kingdom have never been defined by statute, and are part of the common law. In Canada they are, strictly speaking, no longer powers based on the prerogative but have a statutory base in the British North America Act. Section 11 provides for the Queen's Privy Council for Canada who "shall from Time to Time [be] chosen and summoned by the Governor General...and Members thereof may from Time to Time removed by the Governor General," while section 50 confers on him the power of dissolution

The most important of these powers is the appointment of the Prime Minister.[19] The decision of the Governor General "to commission a public man" (the phrase is Sir John Bourinot's) to attempt the formation of an administration is his alone, and not one in which he acts on the advice and responsibility of one of his ministers. "It is now well recognized," says Sir Ivor Jennings, "that in forming a Government the Queen acts on her own responsibility."[20]

In finding a Prime Minister the Governor General must, of course, recognize the working principles of parliamentary government. Normally he must call upon the recognized leader of the party capable of gaining the support of a majority in the House of Commons, so that in most cases his choice is, in effect, made for him. However, circumstances may arise, for example the death of a Prime Minister or an electoral stalemate, in which the Governor General enjoys real freedom of choice.

In the choice of ministers to make up an administration he is entitled to be consulted, and may influence the composition of a ministry and the nature of other appointments. There are numerous examples of the Sovereign's influencing the composition of a ministry in the United Kingdom,[21] but none of which we can be certain in Canada. It is known that Lord Grey objected unsuccessfully to the appointment of Sir Sam Hughes as Minister of Militia in the Borden government, and that he had reservations about some of the other proposed ministers. In the end, however, he was unable to prevent the appointment of ministers to whom he objected.[22] Influence, of course, must in the end yield to advice unless the Governor General is able to find another Prime Minister. Nevertheless, such influence might be decisive.

The right and the duty to find a Prime Minister if that office becomes vacant is the most important single function of the Governor General. It means that there can always be a legitimate government in office with full authority to act, for it is the constitutional duty of the Governor General to take the initiative in finding a Prime

---

of Parliament, and section 55 deals with his power to give or withhold royal assent to bills passed by the two Houses of Parliament. While these powers are assigned to him the extent to which he exercises them on advice or in his discretion is governed by the conventions of the constitution.

19. Sir Ivor Jennings, *Cabinet Government,* 3rd ed. (London, 1959), p. 20 ff.

20. Ibid., p. 89.

21. Ibid., pp. 61-6.

22. *Borden: Memoirs,* 1, p. 330.

Minister if the one in office dies or becomes incapable of performing his responsibilities. In this our constitution is distinctly to be preferred to the American. There the constitution not only combines in one man the often incongruous functions of head of state and head of government, but also makes ambiguous and uncertain provisions for the carrying on of the government in the event of the incapacity of the president. A serious and paralyzing illness, such as that of President Wilson, essentially brought the whole government to a standstill, and there was no effective legal way of preventing the wife of the president from carrying the government. There have been attempts to deal with this problem informally, such as the agreements made by President Eisenhower in 1958 and President Kennedy in 1961 with their vice-presidents, which empowered the vice-president to become acting president during periods of presidential disability. This has now been formalized in the 25th Amendment which enables a president to communicate a declaration of disability to the President *pro tempore* of the Senate and the Speaker of the House, whereupon the Vice-President becomes acting President. But these arrangements do not go to the heart of the difficulty. Vice-Presidents are not often chosen for their capacity to succeed to the presidency but rather to "balance the ticket," and in the event of the death or disability of a President the government may devolve on a successor entirely lacking in the capacity to discharge his responsibilities.

Under our system the matter is very different. The head of state is free to find a Prime Minister who can govern and who is backed by a body of disciplined followers. In his task he not only has constitutional right on his side, but he is entitled to the full support of the party leaders in his choice. As Jennings put it, his "primary duty is to find a Government. It is no less the duty of political leaders to assist him to find one. In the Duke of Wellington's famous phrase, 'The King's service must be carried on.'"[23]

It is necessary to recognize, however, that not all authorities are agreed that the discretion of the head of state in this matter is in modern times a valuable or a necessary constitutional device. Professor Edward McWhinney succinctly put the case of those who would like the head of state to be the exerciser of purely automatic functions. In choosing a Prime Minister, he argues, the Governor General is really picking the next leader of the party. He may choose the wrong man, and thus become involved in "partisan political issues." To make the succession to the prime-ministership auto-

23. Jennings, *Cabinet Government*, p. 51.

matic (by recognizing the rule that it should go to the next senior minister as a "caretaker" until the party has chosen its own new leader) would be "in line with contemporary constitutional trends towards the limitation or elimination of discretionary powers in non-elective organs of government."[24] Under Canadian conditions this argument has little force, except to a slavish believer in the superior virtue of elected over non-elected persons. But in that case why not elect judges? To have followed the rule in this country would have led to the selection of Sir Hector Langevin to succeed Macdonald in 1891, and it was the senior surviving minister, Sir Mackenzie Bowell, who was a disastrous choice as Prime Minister in 1894. Further, as Dr. Forsey pointed out, the way in which Canadian political parties select their leaders can only mean that there must be a delay of several months in which there is a caretaker government. On balance it is probably better, in the rare cases where the succession is not clear, to recognize that the initiative of the head of state is a necessary and useful device for ensuring the succession to government. "Cabinet government," as Professor Dawson put it, "...presupposes some central, impartial figure at its head which at certain times and for certain purposes supplements and aids the other more active and partisan agencies of government."[25]

More controversial than the right to choose the Prime Minister is the Governor General's right, under certain conditions, to refuse to grant a dissolution of Parliament. As Sir Ivor Jennings said, there are three distinct questions raised by the exercise of the prerogative of dissolution. The first relates to the advice upon which it is exercised, the second to whether this advice must be followed, and the third to whether the Governor General can dissolve Parliament without advice. The first question is answered clearly enough in Canadian practice, because ever since 1896 the sole right to recommend a dissolution to Council has been one of the "prerogatives of the Prime Minister."[26] Since the Prime Minister is likely to discuss such

24. See Edward McWhinney, "Prerogative Powers of the Head of State (The Queen or Governor General)," *Canadian Bar Review* XXXV, No. 1 (January 1957), pp. 92-6; J. R. Mallory, ibid., XXXV, No. 2 (February 1957), pp. 242-4; Eugene A. Forsey, ibid., XXXV, No. 3 (March 1957), pp. 368-9; Edward McWhinney, ibid., XXXV, No. 3 (March 1957), pp. 369-71.

25. Dawson, *The Government of Canada,* p. 165. See also J. R. Mallory, "The Royal Prerogative in Canada: the Selection of Successors to Mr. Duplessis and Mr. Sauvé," *Canadian Journal of Economics and Political Science* XXVI, No. 2 (May 1960), p. 314.

26. See, for example, Order-in-Council P. C. 3374 of October 25, 1935. A copy of an earlier version is in R. MacGregor Dawson, *Constitutional Issues in Canada, 1900–1931* (London, 1933), p. 125.

an important question informally with the Governor General first, the initiative is very much in his hands. In the United Kingdom the request for a dissolution seems to have been a Cabinet matter until the First World War, but since that time it has been recognized as a right which the Prime Minister can exercise without consulting his Cabinet.[27]

The third question is also easy to settle. A dissolution involves the acquiescence of ministers. The reason for this is that there must be a proclamation dissolving Parliament, and the proclamation must issue under the Great Seal of Canada. The Great Seal is in the custody of the Minister of Consumer and Corporate Affairs and he would have to accept political responsibility for its use in sealing the proclamation. Furthermore, the issue of a proclamation and the use of the Great Seal customarily require the authorization of an order-in-council, so that other ministers would also necessarily be involved in the implementation. Therefore, the Governor General cannot dissolve Parliament without the aid and advice of ministers.[28]

Only the second question remains. Does the Governor General have a negative discretion in deciding whether or not to grant a dissolution requested by the Prime Minister? Over the existence, or non-existence, of this personal prerogative a great deal of controversy, both in Canada and elsewhere, has raged.[29] In recent years both Sir Winston Churchill and Lord Attlee have affirmed that, while a Prime Minister may ask for a dissolution, it need not necessarily be granted by the Sovereign.[30] There are also some recent precedents which help to clarify the extent of the discretionary power in

27. Jennings, *Cabinet Government,* pp. 412-3.

28. The position in the United Kingdom rests on the same grounds. Cf. Jennings, *Cabinet Government,* pp. 412-3.

29. For the principal arguments in the debate see Arthur Berriedale Keith, *Responsible Government in the Dominions,* Vol. I, 2nd ed. (Oxford, 1928), pp. 146-52, 173-4; Eugene A. Forsey, *The Royal Power of Dissolution of Parliament in the British Commonwealth* (Toronto, 1943); Evatt, *The King and His Dominion Governors.*

30. Churchill in Great Britain, *Parliamentary Debates* (Commons), 5th Ser., Vol. 398, Col. 1516, March 29, 1944; Attlee in *Life* magazine, February 18, 1952, p. 31. Also in *Globe and Mail* (*London Observer Service*), August 26, 1959, p. 7: "The two principal constitutional powers remaining to the Crown are the selection of the person to whom a commission to form a new administration should be entrusted and the granting or refusing a dissolution to a prime minister. . . . It is rare now for a request by a prime minister for a dissolution to be refused, though there was a case in Canada where Lord Byng, the governor-general, the representative of the Crown, refused to give one to Mr. Mackenzie King. It might well have arisen had the Labour Government been defeated in the House of Commons when there was a majority of only six. The King would

granting a dissolution. In 1939 the Governor General of South Africa, Sir Patrick Duncan, refused a dissolution to General Hertzog when the latter's Cabinet had split over the issue of declaring war. As a result General Smuts was able to form a government and to retain his parliamentary majority in the subsequent general election. It has been asserted, on the other hand, that in the United Kingdom the Sovereign is nowadays required automatically to grant a dissolution on the request of the Prime Minister.[31] The basis for this view was that in 1924, when no party had a majority in the House of Commons, the King nevertheless "immediately" granted the dissolution which Ramsay MacDonald sought without considering whether other party leaders were able to form a government. It is now clear, however, that this statement of the facts was mistaken, and the doctrine it was thought to support cannot therefore be maintained. In fact the King did ascertain that no other party leader was willing to form a government before he acceded to MacDonald's request.[32]

The circumstances in which the Governor General may hesitate to grant a dissolution will only arise when a Prime Minister who has been defeated in the House of Commons—or who anticipates defeat—may decide to ask for a dissolution instead of submitting his resignation. This he might do if he anticipates, as Mackenzie King did in 1926, that the party situation in the House is such that the leader of the opposition cannot form a government. Judging merely by numerical party strength, the situation in 1926 would have made it possible for either the Liberals or the Conservatives to govern with support from the Progressive members, though neither could govern alone. Lord Byng's refusal of Mackenzie King's request for a dissolution was based on his view that "Mr. Meighen has not been given a chance of trying to govern, or saying that he cannot do so, and that all reasonable expedients should be tried before resorting to another election."[33] When his request for a dissolution was rejected Mr. King thereupon resigned, and Lord Byng sent for

have been within his rights in sending for the Leader of the Opposition if he thought that a working majority in the House could have been obtained by him. King George V might, had he chosen, have refused a dissolution to Ramsay MacDonald in 1924, but I fancy it was thought impolitic to refuse the request of the first Labour prime minister." In fact, both other party leaders were sounded out and refused. No doubt they thought it impolitic to accept office at that time.

31. Keith, *Responsible Government,* I, p. 172.

32. Nicolson, *King George* V, p. 400.

33. Quoted in Roger Graham, *Arthur Meighen: a Biography,* Vol. II. *And Fortune Fled* (Toronto, 1963), p. 415.

Arthur Meighen. Subsequent events showed that the Governor General had not sufficiently taken into account a factor on which Mr. King had relied, namely, that the Progressives were unable to give consistent and unbroken support to a Conservative government. Thus Mr. Meighen was forced to ask for, and was granted, a dissolution, which had previously been refused to Mr. King.[34]

The result of Lord Byng's miscalculation of the political situation was that both his position and his motives were misunderstood. The Governor General had felt he was performing his constitutional duty in trying to avoid, under the unusual party circumstances which then prevailed, a second general election within a year. As he said, in writing of the incident to the King on June 29, "I had three interviews with Mr. King, at each one of which I appealed to him not to put the King's representative in a position of appearing unconstitutional, and that another election was at the moment unwarranted by the state of affairs. He refused all pleadings and took the line that he was entitled to it (the dissolution) and to my support in having it. I still refused. Thereupon he resigned and I asked Mr. Meighen to form a government."[35] It was then easy for the Liberals to argue that Lord Byng, by refusing a dissolution to Mackenzie King which

34. Both Dr. Forsey and Professor Graham have argued that Meighen was as likely, on the evidence, to have governed as King. He did survive several votes after assuming office and a number of factors, such as the Robb amendment (regarding the validity of the expedient of having a government made up, save for the Prime Minister, of acting ministers) and a government defeat as a result of a broken pair, could hardly have been foreseen. But surely it was not a combination of bizarre circumstances which brought Meighen down (superficially, of course, this is so) but the fact that it was at best foolhardy, given the implacable hostility to Meighen of J. S. Woodsworth and certain other Progressives, and the unreliability of others, to expect that a Conservative government would have survived in that Parliament. Mackenzie King played very skilfully, and in the end successfully, on the old western distrust and even hatred of Meighen. Professor Graham points out the damning fact that Meighen had not been consulted about the possibility of having to take office in these circumstances, hesitated about it, and took office in part because he felt he could not in honour let the Governor General down. Others saw the danger but Meighen, supported by Borden, felt that it was his "inescapable duty to try to form a government." Ibid., p. 20. One is forced to the conclusion that Byng would have been in a better position if he could have prevented King from resigning outright until Meighen had a chance to decide what he wanted to do. In that sense, Byng did not move with sufficient skill, and by his action forced Meighen to assume office. But all of Meighen's actions after the election, as Dr. Graham makes clear, made it plain that he felt he was entitled to office at the first opportunity.

35. The letter is quoted in Nicolson, *King George* V, pp. 476-7. The date given there, June 29, 1925, should, of course, be June 29, 1926.

he subsequently granted to Meighen, had used his position to favour the Conservatives over the Liberals. It was almost equally easy for unsophisticated persons to believe that this was either the unconscious bias of a British Governor General in favour of the more "imperialist" of the Canadian parties or, worse still, the long arm of the Colonial Office interfering in the balance of Canadian parties.

Lord Byng's defence of his position rested, as he explained to the King, on "these salient features":

> A Governor-General has the absolute right of granting or refusing a dissolution. The refusal is a very dangerous decision. It embodies the rejection of the advice of an accredited Minister, which is the bed-rock of constitutional government. Therefore nine times out of ten a Governor-General should take his Prime Minister's advice on this as on other matters. But if the advice offered is considered by the Governor-General to be wrong and unfair, and not for the welfare of the people, it behoves him to act in what he considers the best interests of the country.[36]

Lord Byng's statement of his constitutional position is clearly literally correct. But he overstated it. The occasions on which a Governor General may consider disregarding the advice of his constitutional advisers are much rarer than one in ten; they are very infrequent indeed. They do exist, but they are so rare as to elude precise formulation, and at best have a pragmatic sanction. The Governor General can employ his discretionary powers only in those circumstances where he can get away with it, and where the alternative is something close to constitutional chaos. On that basis Lord Byng was mistaken, though not unconstitutional.

Every unsuccessful use of power is an adverse precedent. While it is impossible to agree with those who say that the 1926 affair disposed forever of the Governor General's supposed discretion in granting a dissolution, it is clear that the future discretion of a Canadian Governor General has been somewhat narrowed. If the circumstances arise again, the King-Byng controversy becomes a part of the total constitutional situation which the Governor General will have to consider.

It is important to remember that the situation in which no party has a majority and a dissolution of Parliament may be a means of ending a state of unstable equilibrium is rare, but it does happen. General elections in recent years have produced minority govern-

36. Ibid.

ments, notably in British Columbia in 1952 and Manitoba in 1958.[37] The federal elections of 1957, 1962, 1963, 1965, 1972, and 1979 were equally indecisive. Elections which returned governments with a clear majority in this period became the exception rather than the rule.

In at least one case (that of British Columbia) there was serious discussion of the possibility that the new government might seek to break the deadlock by a second dissolution without meeting the legislature at all. This is an action so utterly at variance with the theory of responsible government that it is not even discussed by most authors on the constitution. Mackenzie King did say, in a speech at Erindale during the 1925 election campaign, that if the result were indecisive he "would not hesitate to again call upon the Governor-General to dissolve Parliament and would continue until some party secures a majority to enable it to carry on the affairs of the country."[38] This extraordinary belief that a new election could be called without the assembling of Parliament was reiterated in a statement which he issued after the result of the election became known.[39] It has been effectively and rightly condemned by Dr. Forsey.[40]

37. On the British Columbia affair see H. F. Angus, "The British Columbia Election, June 1952," *Canadian Journal of Economics and Political Science* XVIII, No. 4 (November 1952), p. 518; on the Canadian election of 1957 see J. R. Mallory, "The Election and the Constitution," *Queen's Quarterly* LXIV, No. 4 (Winter, 1958), p. 465.

38. Quoted in Graham, *Arthur Meighen,* II, p. 353.

39. Ibid. Professor Graham also quotes a memorandum, dated January 18, 1926, prepared by Arthur Sladen, Secretary to the Governor General, which summarized an interview between Byng and Mackenzie King:

    "His Excellency again tried to persuade him to take the dignified course of resigning...but told him that there was no constitutional reason against his continuing in office.

    "Several more interviews took place but the Prime Minister did not again change his mind. The only course open to the Governor General was:—

    (1) To insist on the Prime Minister calling the House of Commons to meet at the earliest possible moment.

    (2) To make the Prime Minister understand that no political appointments (Senators, Judges, etc.) could be made in the interim—and that no contracts should be made for any public works.

    "His Excellency also gave the Prime Minister to understand that he would not grant another dissolution." Ibid., pp. 353-4.

40. "Mr. King and Parliamentary Government," *Canadian Journal of Economics and Political Science* XVII, No. 4 (November 1951), pp. 451-67.

The public memory of these matters seems to be short, for there was speculation in the press in 1957 that Mr. Diefenbaker upon taking office might demand another election at once to break the stalemate. As it happened he revealed no such intention, but even if he had sought a dissolution in the first weeks of the Twenty-third Parliament, he might have placed the Governor General in an awkward position had the Liberals been anxious to take office again. In such a case the Governor General would clearly have been entitled to refuse Mr. Diefenbaker's request if it appeared that Mr. St. Laurent was capable of carrying on without another general election.

The discretion of the Governor General in such cases must be seen in its proper light as part of the balancing mechanism of the constitution. When the party system works normally so that general elections return governments with working majorities, there is little reason to question the right of a Prime Minister to seek the verdict of the people at what seems to him the most advantageous time. However, there are cases when a request for a dissolution is an abuse of power and an attempt to evade the verdict of the House or the electorate, as in 1926. In such a case, the Governor General is in a position to protect the interests of the public and the rules of the constitution. Lord Balfour once remarked that the constitution cannot stand a "diet of dissolutions" and the duty of the Governor General is clearly to use his discretionary power to prevent a Prime Minister from making a farce of parliamentary government.

The right of the Governor General to dismiss a ministry is more disputable than his right to refuse a dissolution. No government in the United Kingdom has been dismissed in well over a century. There are only five cases since Confederation where provincial governments have been dismissed, and these occurred when the political situation was highly fluid and the party system less developed than it is today. In 1878 Lieutenant-Governor Letellier of Quebec dismissed the de Boucherville ministry, and in 1891 Lieutenant-Governor Angers dismissed the Mercier ministry, while in British Columbia three ministries—Turner (1898), Semlin (1900) and Prior (1903)—were dismissed.[41] Lord Dufferin did consider the possibility of dismissing the Macdonald ministry during the Pacific

41. The authoritative account of the office of Lieutenant-Governor, which deals fully with the above cases, is John T. Saywell, *The Office of Lieutenant-Governor: A Study in Canadian Government and Politics* (Toronto, 1957).

Scandal crisis in 1873, but he did not feel that he had sufficient evidence to justify a dismissal.[42]

Dismissal is clearly the ultimate weapon, to be employed only if the alternatives are certain to be worse. While the Governor General of Pakistan could dismiss a ministry on April 17, 1953, it would seem almost inconceivable that this could happen in such countries as Canada or the United Kingdom. Nevertheless, on November 11, 1975, the Governor General of Australia did dismiss the Whitlam government on the ground that, while it possessed a majority in the lower house, it was unable to pass its supply bills in the Senate and would soon be forced to resort to expedients of questionable legality in order to carry on, and that the Prime Minister nevertheless refused to advise a dissolution of the House of Representatives. There can be no question that Sir John Kerr possessed, under the constitution, the legal power to act as he did. His action has been criticised because it appeared to introduce a novel and hitherto unheard of convention in the Australian constitution, namely that responsible government involves a government having to have the continued confidence of *both* houses of parliament. Furthermore Kerr himself had earlier taken the position that a Governor General ought to accept the advice of his ministers even if he believes that advice to be wrong in law because the courts could ultimately provide a remedy against an illegal act of government. At the time when the dismissal occurred no illegal acts had taken place and there was also good reason for the government to believe that the Senate would yield at the last minute and pass the supply bills. Sir John Kerr's action in dismissing his Prime Minister was ill-advised but it serves to remind us that this prerogative power, long thought to be obsolete, is in fact real. It is probable that the Governor General could have managed the crisis with greater skill and success if he had been backed up by the same quality of advice and support staff as that possessed by the Queen.[42A]

42. "He did not consider it his duty to intervene until Parliament should have dealt with the matter, but that inasmuch as the decision of Parliament might itself be partially tainted by the corruption exposed, he should hold himself free to require the resignation of the Ministers in the event of their winning by anything short of a very commanding majority." *Letters of Queen Victoria,* 2nd ser., pp. 288-9, quoted in Jennings, *Cabinet Government,* p. 406.

42A There are numerous accounts of the dismissal of the Whitlam government, including Sir John Kerr's *Matters for Judgment* and Geoffrey Sawer's *Federation under Strain.* Other important books are Gough Whitlam, *The Truth of the Matter* (Ringwood, 1979) and L. M. Cooray, *Conventions, the Australian Constitution and the Future* (Sydney, 1979). See also J. R. Mallory "The Office of Governor-General Reconsidered" *Politics* XIII: 2 (November, 1978) p. 125.

The Australian crisis raises a further question. The powers of the Governor General in such constitutions as those of Australia and Canada seem, in their unabashed legal form, to be those of an English sovereign before the reign of Queen Anne. The fact that responsible government exists, and the rules governing how the head of state powers are generally exercised are contained in legally unenforceable conventions of the constitution. The courts generally have been reluctant to enforce constitutional conventions or to define them. As Sir Lyman Duff said "We are not concerned with constitutional usage. We are concerned with questions of law."[43] Because there may be a good deal of uncertainty about what the conventions actually are -which can be disconcerting in a crisis—it has often been argued that whatever discretion a Governor General has to act without advice should be clearly defined. It is not enough to say that our constitution is governed by the conventions of responsible government as defined by the preamble to the British North America Act, which gives us a "constitution similar in principle to that of the United Kingdom." This is no help when one is not sure what the rules are.

An attempt was made to arrive at a more precise definition in the Trudeau government's Constitutional Amendment Bill of 1979. There were a number of ambiguities and infelicities in the bill, which was later withdrawn, but the bill itself illustrates some of the problems of definition. The bill asserted, in section 35, that "the Constitution of Canada shall be the supreme law of the Canadian federation, and all of the institutions of the Canadian federation shall be governed by it and by the conventions, customs and usages hallowed by it, as shall all of the people of Canada." This is no clearer than the B.N.A. Act. Furthermore, if it is more than pious rhetoric, it may be an invitation to the courts at some future date to reduce to clear and unambiguous language the insubstantial rules which govern the relations between government and Parliament.

No mention was made in the bill of the Governor General's power to appoint the Prime Minister, and his power in section 49 (1) of the bill to appoint and remove ministers is not qualified by any statement as to whether this power is discretionary or not. A clumsy attempt was made to define the vexed question of dissolutions in section 53 (2) so as to ensure that a Prime Minister who has lost the confidence of the House of Commons (which the House itself must define) will advise a dissolution, resign, form another administration, or make way for someone else who can. This attempt to define

43. *Re Disallowance and Reservation* [1938] S.C.R. 71 at p. 78.

all of the possibilities is not only inadequate, but raises the possibility that the actions of all concerned might have to be reviewed by the courts.

There are two problems which flow from too strict a definition of what have hitherto been matters which were governed by convention. The first is that problems of this sort arise at time of crisis. Judicial review is by no means swift and the prospect of the whole process of government being held in suspense while the judges make up their minds is not alluring. Furthermore, it is not easy to see what effective remedy the courts can provide, and a mere declaratory judgment is not enforceable. Lastly there is considerable doubt as to whether these matters should be justiciable at all. Conventions are not free from ambiguity, and this may be a virtue since it permits an adaptation of the rules to suit changing values and circumstances. The whole method of legal interpretation is to impose clarity on apparently conflicting legal principles. Clarity and precision may be too high a price to pay in the one area where the constitution is flexible enough to respond to changing circumstance.

"The existence or absence of a monarch does not in itself," says Sir Ivor Jennings, "make a fundamental distinction in a constitution. In a Cabinet system the Cabinet governs."[44] And yet, he warns, we must be careful not to underestimate the influence of the head of state on the course of events. Put briefly, while the head of state must, in the last resort, accept the decisions of his Cabinet, he may have a considerable influence on those decisions. It is necessary at this point to make a distinction between what is true of British politics and what is true of Canadian politics. Necessarily, the influence of a Sovereign is immensely greater than that of a Governor General, for a Governor General has neither long tenure nor the same prestige. While a constitutional monarch is essentially free from political associations, a Governor General is less likely to be so. Since he is a public man who has achieved his high office after other service to the state, he is likely to have some past identification with a political party. While he himself may have transcended his past political associations, others will not forget them. A nineteenth-century Governor General had behind him the prestige of an imperial conception of good government which he was recognized, even in Canada, to embody. A modern Governor General has nothing to fall back on save the Sovereign, and the Sovereign's prestige would not lightly be committed to support a Governor General who had pressed his powers too far.

44. Jennings, *Cabinet Government,* p. 328.

Where, then, can a Governor General exert influence? He has a right, in a general way, to know the course of public business and to be told what is in the Prime Minister's mind. The very fact that so many government decisions, great and small, are taken in Canada by order-in-council or minute of council means that they must have the formal approval of the Governor General. However, the introduction of Cabinet minutes, which he does not necessarily receive, has contributed in a large measure to shutting him off from a whole range of policy decisions.[45] But even after the introduction of Cabinet minutes, the earlier practice of using Privy Council instruments to record and recommend a number of important matters, such as appointments, was continued. The Governor General has a right to know—and he will often make certain of finding out—the reasons behind a decision which is laid before him for his approval. On a great many matters, of which high appointments and resignations are an example, he is bound to know what is at stake. Nothing is more indicative of policy than resignations and appointments. Where the resignations are those of ministers, the consent of the Governor General is required for any statement by way of justification or clarification in which the minister is likely to disclose matters discussed in Cabinet.

Beyond the Prime Minister's constitutional duty to inform the Governor General of the course of public business, there is further incentive to confide in the Sovereign's representative. The Prime Minister occupies a lonely eminence at the top of the political hierarchy. While he will confide a great deal to his more intimate colleagues and must discuss most things with his Cabinet, the Prime Minister will not always find there the kind of confidant to whom he wishes to turn. There are often problems which can be partly eased just by talking about them to a sympathetic listener. A Prime Minister may upon occasion find it a solace and an aid to unburden himself to a listener who is both above political interest and a proper recipient of the most intimate secrets of the government. Thus a Prime Minister may seek an interview with the Governor General, as Mackenzie King occasionally did with the Earl of Athlone, simply because expounding a difficult problem sometimes helped him to clear his mind on it.

45. During the war years the minutes of the War Committee of the Cabinet were sent to the Governor General, the Earl of Athlone, but the minutes of Cabinet (which were started on a regular basis after the appointment of his successor) were not sent. Information on these matters is not easy to come by, but the decision on whether to circulate Cabinet minutes to the Governor General rests with the Prime Minister, and not all Prime Ministers seem to have followed the same practice.

In such cases a Governor General may be able to advise or to influence his Prime Minister. Sometimes he may play the role of a passive listener. However, his influence can never be merely negative, for the constitutional necessity of explaining a proposed course of action to an independent and non-political person outside the party in power is in itself some restraint on men of decency. One does not go *too* far in pushing a political advantage when one's actions must be expounded (even in confidence) to a political outsider.

There may be occasions when a Governor General may play more than a passive role in a difficult political situation. Lord Dufferin's intervention in 1876 to compose the public and acrimonious difference between the Canadian government and the province of British Columbia over the agreement to build a Pacific railway achieved no concrete result, but it undoubtedly lowered the political temperature. In a later and more severe political crisis the Duke of Devonshire summoned Sir Robert Borden, Sir Wilfrid Laurier and others to Government House to discuss the deteriorating political situation at the time of the conscription crisis. In 1935 Lord Bessborough was able, after much patient effort, to persuade R. B. Bennett and Mackenzie King to agree on the appointment of John Buchan as the next Governor General. Had he failed, the political consequences would have been extremely serious, for Mr. King had let it be known that as soon as he came into office after the pending election, which he correctly assumed that he would win, he would seek the removal of any Governor General whose appointment Mr. Bennett might recommend. This was carrying political partisanship rather far and roused the indignation of King George V. Mr. King's attitude, if persisted in, would have raised a number of awkward constitutional issues at a time when direct Canadian advice to the Sovereign was just being put on a regular footing. Lord Bessborough's protracted and ultimately successful effort to bring about agreement between the two party leaders is the best recent example of the role of the Governor General in composing party differences.[46]

The Governor General's position is one of influence, not power. As Walter Bagehot wrote of the Sovereign, he "has... three rights—

46. For an account of the whole incident see J. R. Mallory, "The Appointment of the Governor General: Responsible Government, Autonomy, and the Royal Prerogative," *Canadian Journal of Economics and Political Science* XXVI, No. 1 (February 1960), p. 96. It was from this affair that the belief grew up that the opposition is normally consulted before a Prime Minister recommends the appointment to the Queen. There is no evidence to suggest that such consultations have taken place except in the peculiar circumstances of 1935.

the right to be consulted, the right to encourage, the right to warn. And a king of great sense and sagacity would want no others."[47]

The Administrator and the Governor General's Deputies

The succession to the throne is a more or less automatic process, depending on the operation of known rules. There is, however, no hereditary continuity in the office of Governor General; therefore some provision has to be made for the automatic assumption of the Governor General's powers until a successor can be appointed. Article VIII of the letters patent constituting the office of Governor General provides that the office devolves upon the Chief Justice of Canada as Administrator "in the event of the death, incapacity, removal or absence of our Governor General out of Canada," with the proviso that if the Governor General is absent from Canada for less than one month he retains all of his powers as if he were still in Canada.[48]

The Administrator is vested with all of the powers of the Governor General. A commission does not issue appointing him, since his

47. Walter Bagehot, *The English Constitution,* World's Classics Edition (London, 1928), p. 67. Sir Wilfrid Laurier's opinion of the role of the Governor General was this: "The Canadian Governor-General long ago ceased to determine policy, but he is by no means, or need not be, the mere figure-head of the public image. He has the privilege of advising his advisers, and if he is a man of sense and experience, his advice is often taken." O. D. Skelton, *Life and Letters of Sir Wilfrid Laurier,* Vol. II (Toronto, 1921), p. 86n. Sir Robert Borden agreed, "It would be an absolute mistake to regard the Governor-General . . . as a mere figure-head, a mere rubber stamp. During nine years of Premiership I had the opportunity of realizing how helpful may be the advice and counsel of a Governor-General in matters of delicacy and difficulty: in no case was consultation with regard to such matters ever withheld; and in many instances I obtained no little advantage and assistance therefrom." "The Imperial Conference," *Journal of the Royal Institute of International Affairs,* July 1927, p. 204. An illuminating account of the Governor General's role can be found in the evidence of Rt. Hon. Roland Michener before the Special Committee of the Senate on the Constitution, Tuesday, November 21, 1978. pp. 2:5-2:32.

48. Before the letters patent were amended in 1905 the office of Governor General devolved on the Officer Commanding H. M. Forces in Canada as Administrator. Since Halifax was a long distance from the seat of government, and the rank and importance of the officer commanding the British forces was waning rapidly, the British government finally yielded to Canadian requests to substitute the Chief Justice. If the Chief Justice is unable to act, the letters patent provide that the office of Administrator shall devolve upon the next most senior available Justice of the Supreme Court of Canada.

power to act is conferred upon him *ex officio*. Before he assumes office he must, like the Governor General, take oaths of allegiance and office, and as Keeper of the Great Seal of Canada. He then issues a proclamation of his assumption of office in the same manner as the Governor General. His tenure is indefinite, and comes to an end only with the assumption of office of a new Governor General, or when the Governor General whom he has replaced is able to resume his duties.

It would be impossible for the Governor General to deal with the steady flow of routine matters requiring his approval and at the same time to travel extensively from Ottawa on the numerous formal occasions which require to be graced with his presence. Accordingly, provision is made for the appointment of a deputy so that the Governor General's periodic absences from Ottawa will not interrupt the conduct of government business. The letters patent authorize the Governor General to appoint deputies to exercise his functions when he is unable to act. One of the first acts of the Governor General after his installation in office is to appoint the Chief Justice and such of the puisne judges of the Supreme Court of Canada as may be required as his deputies.

The deputies of the Governor General so appointed are vested with "all the powers, authorities, and functions" of the Governor General, save that of dissolving Parliament, which is specifically excepted in their commissions. Their appointment ensures that the powers and functions of the Governor General can be exercised at any time even though the Governor General himself is prevented—by reason of absence, illness or constitutional convention—from exercising them himself.

Whenever the Governor General is unable by reason of absence or illness to act he will designate whichever of his deputies (in order of seniority in the Supreme Court) may be available to carry out his functions. By long-standing convention in Canada, the Governor General does not enter the precincts of Parliament except for the purposes of opening, proroguing or dissolving it. One of his deputies acts for him when the House of Commons is instructed to elect a Speaker and when bills require assent while Parliament is in session. The latter is merely a matter of convenience, not an immutable constitutional practice. Not only did George VI give royal assent in the course of a parliamentary session during the Royal visit in 1939 (though there was some initial objection from the Palace at this departure from British practice—which led Mackenzie King to cause the British practice to be adopted in Canada), but Jules Leger did so in 1974, Roland Michener did the same in 1973, as did Georges

Vanier in 1963. It is now also customary for his deputy to act for the Governor General in proroguing Parliament. For reasons of custom and convenience the Administrator also appoints deputies to act for him on the same occasions as does the Governor General.

It is not necessary for the deputy of the Governor General to be sworn as such, although it was the general practice prior to 1940 for the deputies to be sworn when new commissions were issued to them. In addition to the deputies who exercise the normal powers of the Governor General, the Governor General also appoints deputies for limited purposes. The Secretary to the Governor General and, upon occasion, other members of his staff are appointed to sign warrants of election, writs for the election of members to the House of Commons and letters patent of lands issued by the Governor General.

It will be noticed that the major discretionary prerogative of the Governor General—the granting of a dissolution of Parliament—is reserved to him alone (or to the Administrator if the office of Governor General is vacant). Similarly, there is no doubt that in other situations of major constitutional importance, such as the appointment of a Prime Minister, the Governor General would act himself and not leave action to one of his deputies. When a deputy has been designated, the Governor General still remains clothed with his full powers and thus may act himself in any matter which he deems of sufficient importance to require his personal attention.

INSTRUMENTS OF ADVICE TO THE CROWN

"There is hardly anything official which the Sovereign can do," says Anson, "without the intervention of written forms."[49] The powers of the Sovereign and of the Sovereign's representative, the Governor General, are almost without exception exercised on the advice and responsibility of ministers of the Crown. The employment of written forms, therefore, serves the purpose of fixing responsibility for acts done by the executive. Some kinds of instruments require authentication by seals, and in that case the signature and seal of the minister who is the constitutional custodian of the seal necessarily make him politically responsible for the act done under his seal. The forms employed vary with the purpose to be accomplished and the instrument needed to serve that purpose. In many cases, the

49. Sir William Reynell Anson, *The Law and Custom of the Constitution,* Vol. II, Pt. 1, 4th ed. (London, 1935), pp. 59-60.

form is dictated by the instrument; for example, where a statute empowers the Governor-in-Council to do something, an order-in-council is the necessary instrument. In other cases, custom and convenience have led to the adoption of a particular form, such as a minute of council, to provide an authoritative basis for actions by departments of government, such as the payment of official salaries.[50] In cases where all that is required is the formal evidence of political responsibility for the exercise of power, a letter from a minister has become the accepted form, as in the advice by the Prime Minister to the Governor General to authorize the disclosure of confidential matters.

The appointment of ministers and Privy Councillors was traditionally recommended by minute of council. In this way formal authorization was secured for the issue of the minister's commission under the Great Seal, and the Department of Finance found it convenient to date the minister's salary from the date of the minute of council recommending his appointment. However, this procedure was constitutionally incongruous, for it made the appointment of ministers seem a recommendation of the Cabinet, whereas in strict constitutional procedure such appointments rest solely on the advice of the Prime Minister.[51] To correct this procedural defect "a new instru-

50. The distinction between an order-in-council and a minute of council is one of both form and substance. An order begins "His Excellency the Governor General in Council, on the recommendation of the Minister of..., is pleased to order and doth hereby order as follows..." A minute of council usually begins "The Committee of the Privy Council, on the recommendation of the Minister of...advise that..." Orders-in-council are employed for the exercise of powers either inherent in the executive by virtue of the royal prerogative, or powers conferred on the executive by prerogative instrument or by statute. Minutes of council have traditionally been used to record advice tendered to the Governor General by his ministers. A minute of council is used, for example, to advise the making of appointments and, in the past, was employed to record the reception of dispatches from the imperial government and to set forth the views of the Government of Canada for transmission by the Governor General to the imperial government. With the creation of the Department of External Affairs in 1909 the handling of dispatches was gradually transferred from the Privy Council Office to the Department of External Affairs. With the introduction of the Cabinet Secretariat and the employment of Cabinet minutes, the use of minutes of council has further tended to decline.

51. The use of a minute of council to recommend the appointment of Privy Councillors and ministers was an example of the overly literal-minded theory of responsible government. It is based on the following syllogism: under responsible government the Governor General cannot act except on advice formally tendered by ministers; ministers formally tender advice as Privy Councillors in the form of Privy Council minutes or orders; therefore every act of the Governor General must be authorized by a Privy Council minute or order. Actually, the three first ministries after Confederation—Macdonald in 1867, Mackenzie in 1873, and Macdonald again in 1878—were not appointed

ment of advice was designed to indicate more clearly the constitutional position of the Prime Minister and the Governor General with regard to the appointment of Ministers and Privy Councillors and the summoning of Parliament.... The instrument is a formal letter to the Governor General signed by the Prime Minister wherein certain actions are recommended. The Governor General writes the word 'approved' above his signature."[52]

The difference in the form in which advice is tendered also results from whether the advice is tendered to the Governor General or to the Sovereign. Advice to the Governor General is cast in forms which are the result of long-standing practice in Canada, while advice to the Sovereign is generally cast in forms already in use in the United Kingdom. Advice to the Sovereign is usually tendered in the form of a submission, which is really a formal letter. It is then implemented by sign manual warrants, letters patent or proclamations which carry the signatures of the Sovereign and the Prime Minister and are sealed by the Great Seal of Canada.

With the exception of the "instrument of advice" noted above, formal advice to the Governor General is recorded in the form of minutes of council or orders-in-council. Most formal advice to the Governor General is tendered by ministers as a group and takes the form of a report on a matter of state from the Committee of the Privy Council.

---

by formal minute. The ministers were simply summoned to the Privy Council by the Governor General and there took the necessary oaths. Sir Wilfrid Laurier attempted to escape this dilemma by a document cast in the form of a minute of council, but without the necessary quorum of four ministers required to transact business. The only Privy Councillor present was described quite simply as "Present: The Honourable Wilfrid Laurier in the Chair." This in general was the procedure, though after 1930, the form was improved by the substitution of the phrase "the Prime Minister advises" for the incongruous and misleading "the Committee advise." Sir Robert Borden was confronted by an even more formidable dilemma when he became Prime Minister, for he was not even a Privy Councillor, and therefore technically not entitled to submit advice as such. He solved it by the following: "The Honourable Robert Laird Borden, the Prime Minister, submits for your Excellency's pleasure, that Robert Laird Borden LL.D, K.C. be a Member of the King's Privy Council for Canada." Except that Borden was not entitled to refer to himself as "the Honourable" until his advice was implemented and he had taken the oath, this unique instrument served the purpose. He was then able to advise, in a Privy Council minute, the appointment of his colleagues to office. This was all, of course, constitutionally unnecessary, but the formal letter which is now used is in accord with the correct constitutional relationships and preserves a document for the record.

52. Public Archives of Canada, *Guide to Canadian Ministries since Confederation,* Ottawa, 1957, p. 62. The instrument of advice here described was first used in 1953.

THE GOVERNOR-IN-COUNCIL

Executive government in Canada is vested in the Governor General, acting "by and with the Advice of the Queen's Privy Council for Canada." As everyone knows, however, the phrase "the Governor-in-Council" is a term of art. There are about one hundred persons on the roll of the Canadian Privy Council. Nearly all of them were summoned to the Council board on their appointment as ministers of the Crown. In recent years appointment to the Privy Council has been occasionally used as a signal mark of public recognition. Such distinguished persons as the Duke of Edinburgh and the Duke of Windsor were made Privy Councillors, as was Earl Alexander of Tunis at the conclusion of his appointment as Governor General. Others appointed have included the Chief Justice, and occasionally prominent political figures such as Mr. M. J. Coldwell, who was appointed after he had retired from active political life. Mr. George Drew was made a Privy Councillor while leader of the opposition, apparently to ensure for him a proper place in the order of precedence at state functions. As a Centennial gesture, all provincial premiers were made Privy Councillors in 1967. But, of course, these persons as a body do not in fact "aid and advise in the government of Canada." The real executive is the Cabinet, but about the Cabinet the law of the constitution maintains silence. The Privy Council, accordingly, is usually regarded simply as a piece of anachronistic legal flummery. Thus Professor Dawson said "the Privy Council would..., if active, be a large and politically cumbersome body with members continually at cross-purposes with one another; but it has saved itself from this embarrassment by the simple device of holding no meetings.... The Cabinet, lacking any legal status of its own, masquerades as the Privy Council when it desires to assume formal powers.[53] While not an entirely accurate statement, this does contain much of the essential truth, but it glosses over an important constitutional distinction between executive power in constitutional law, and the conventional arrangements by which power is exercised under Cabinet government.

It is important to distinguish between the Privy Council and the Governor-in-Council. The Privy Council as such has no constitutional function to perform, since it is a body "to aid and advise" the formal head of the government, the Governor General. The powers of government are conferred, by law and practice, on the Governor-

53. Dawson, *The Government of Canada,* pp. 184-5.

in-Council. Statutory references to the Privy Council are rare. It is mentioned in section 11 of the British North America Act and in section 35(8) of the Interpretation Act (R. S. 1952, C. 158), and there are some statutory bodies such as the Treasury Board and the Committee of Internal Economy of the House of Commons which are required to be composed of Privy Councillors.

The role of the Queen's Privy Council for Canada is best understood by recalling Walter Bagehot's distinction between the "dignified" and the "efficient" parts of the constitution. The dignified parts are no longer at the centre of decision in the process of government—they are surviving formalities which represent the realities of power of a much earlier age. The efficient parts are those in which the real process of decision-making takes place. The essence of the evolution of responsible government in Canada was that the Governor-in-Council—which was the true executive in the period before 1848—was gradually replaced by the Cabinet as the true executive. Lord Dufferin, writing to Macdonald on February 11, 1873, describes what had happened:

> I am rather inclined to favour than otherwise the tendency which is taking place, of the Governor-General's Council to transmute itself into the Prime Minister's Cabinet, at whose deliberations it would be inconvenient for the head of the Executive to be present. On the other hand, I do not think it would be desirable that the Governor-General should allow his right of presiding over his council to lapse altogether into desuetude.[54]

A failure to notice this distinction was evident in the Constitutional Amendment Bill of 1979. This would have provided in section 52 that the Cabinet should have all of the powers, duties and functions of the Council of State (which was the new name given to the Privy Council) "other than on and for occasions of ceremony of state when all of the members of the Council of State are summoned together with the Governor General of Canada." "Together with" sounds odd. One would have thought that it was the Governor General who summoned such a meeting, as is suggested in section 49(1) of the Bill. It has always been the practice for the "face" or cover of every batch of orders-in-council to contain a list of those present, including, needless to say, the Governor General. Of course on all but special occasions he is not actually present, but only "deemed to be present." Perhaps the confusion was caused by

54. Sir Joseph Pope, *Correspondence of Sir John Macdonald* (Toronto, n.d.), p. 203.

inadequate information on the workings of the Privy Council on London, as well as a failure to consider the meaning of our own documents. In the British system the Privy Council, presided over by the Queen, discharges a purely formal function of giving legal sanction to certain legal acts. For this purpose the practice is to summon enough Privy Councillors to satisfy a quorum. The only occasion when *all* Privy Councillors are summoned is for an Accension Council when a new Sovereign assumes the throne. When there have been "occasions of ceremony" such as a Privy Council when the Queen is in Canada, the practice has been to limit the summons to ministers. An exception appears to be made on other ceremonial occasions, such as when the Sovereign communicates approval of the marriage of an heir to the throne as required by the Royal Marriages Act, 1772. The first of these council was held in 1947, at the time of the engagement of the Princess Elizabeth, when former ministers were among those summoned. Similarly, in 1980, the marriage of the Prince of Wales to Lady Diana Spencer was approved by the Queen and this approval formally communicated at a Privy Council presided over by the Chief Justice as Deputy Governor General and attended by Privy Councillors from all three parties in the House of Commons.

The way in which this transmutation had taken place was by the splitting of the business of the Council into two distinct stages and two distinct bodies, a process which had emerged clearly by the eighteen-fifties.[55] Sir Edmund Head, in a dispatch written in 1858, drew a distinction between the Governor-in-Council when he was present and in the chair, and the Committee of Council, which is the members of the Council meeting in the absence of the Governor.[56] Head left a full description of the process in a memorandum which he prepared for the Administrator when he went on leave in 1857. After noting that the Council discussed business "*in committee* [italics in original], the Governor not being present," Head says that "the result of such discussion is embodied in a memorandum. Such memoranda when copied out fair by the clerk, filed and tied together are countersigned by the President of the Committees of Council. They are in this shape laid before the Governor. My practice usually is when there is no press of business out of the

55. See J. R. Mallory, "Cabinet Government in Canada," *Political Studies* II, No. 2 (June 1954), pp. 142-4; "Cabinets and Councils in Canada," *Public Law*, Autumn, 1957, pp. 231-4.

56. P.A.C., *Secret and Confidential Despatches, Colonial Secretary 1856–1866*, Series G. 10, Vol. II.

Parliamentary Session to approve the minutes and affix my initials to them *in the Council Room* [italics in original] at that table with the members (four being a quorum). During the session however and if there is nothing in such minutes which seems doubtful, or if they appear mere matters of course, I often initial them without going into Council."[57]

By the Confederation period the Governor-in-Council (that is, the Governor General presiding over a Council) had been relegated to the position of a dignified part of the constitution, while the Committee of Council had become the efficient part. Confederation itself made no change at all in the structure of the central government. Lord Monck continued as Governor General, many of the same ministers who had held office in the Province of Canada were in the first federal Cabinet, and the officials of the provincial Executive Council (including the Clerk) were carried over into the service of the new Dominion. The summoning of a formal Privy Council, presided over by the Governor General, continued for many years after Confederation. It was the practice for ministers and others such as provincial Lieutenant-Governors and Chief Justices to be sworn in "before His Excellency the Governor General in Council." Apparently every minister to take oath before 1878 did so in Council, but no ministers after 1887 seem to have done so. Thereafter the Privy Council *Oath Book* records that they took the oath before the Governor General alone. The last entry in the *Oath Book* showing that an oath had been taken in Council is that of Chief Justice Strong of the Supreme Court of Canada on December 5, 1892. The swearing-in of the Chief Justice is unique in that it is the only occasion governed by a statutory requirement. Accordingly, when the Governor General administers the oath to the Chief Justice it is always done in the presence of a quorum of ministers who are present as Privy Councillors. A new administration is sworn in in order of seniority by the Governor General, with the Clerk of the Privy Council in attendance with the Oath Book. Such occasions could be regarded as formal Privy Councils. The swearing-in of the Clark government on June 4, 1979, was unique in that it was carried out before the television cameras and transmitted live.

In summary, the occasions upon which the Governor General

57. Quoted in D. G. G. Kerr, *Sir Edmund Head: A Scholarly Governor* (Toronto, 1954), pp. 175-6. The Governors of the Province of Canada were empowered to appoint a President of the Committees of Council to preside in their absence. After Confederation the office was continued, but became, by a silent elision of the constitution, the President of the Privy Council.

presided at Council after Confederation were the following: the communication of the Governor General's instructions to his Council on his assumption of office; the installation of a ministry (the first three ministries were certainly installed at a Council presided over by the Governor General); the administration of oaths to ministers and certain others; and in a few cases the approval by the Governor General of minutes or orders-in-council.[58] There is definite evidence that Lord Dufferin met with his Council before agreeing to prorogation of Parliament in the summer of 1873, and there may have been other cases.[59] The formal Council presided over by the Governor General seems to have fallen into desuetude before the end of the nineteenth century.[60] Only in recent years has the formal Privy Council been revived so that it performs some of the ceremonial functions of its namesake in the United Kingdom.[61]

This is in accord with the intentions of Lord Monck and Sir John A. Macdonald, who wished to make the Canadian Privy Council as much like its British counterpart as possible. Together they were able to secure the provision that Canadian Privy Councillors, unlike colonial executive councillors in general, should hold office for life. They attempted to make the procedure as similar to that in the

58. It is difficult to be certain about whether the Governor General attended Privy Councils since the form of Privy Council records has always carried on the "face," or cover, "Present: His Excellency the Governor General in Council." The Privy Council *Minute Book* and *State Book*, which were not kept after 1882, provide more definite evidence, as does the Privy Council *Oath Book*.

59. Canada, *House of Commons Journals,* 1875, p. 35. Dufferin to Kimberley, August 15, 1873.

60. In the early days after the outbreak of war in August 1914, the Duke of Connaught attended Council, but whether this was to hasten the approval of urgent measures or for other reasons is not entirely clear. *The Canadian War History,* Vol. I, Appendix 23(a) says: "On August 4th, 1914, and on several other occasions during that month the Governor General on the Prime Minister's invitation joined the Ministers in conference, when the benefit of his experience was sought upon military plans and preparations."

61. On the early formal Councils see J. R. Mallory, "Cabinets and Councils in Canada," *Public Law,* Autumn, 1957, pp. 233-4, and Eugene A. Forsey, "Meetings of the Queen's Privy Council for Canada, 1867-1882," *Canadian Journal of Economics and Political Science* XXXII, No. 2 (November 1966), pp. 489-98. Dr. Forsey concludes there were a good many Councils, mostly formal, attended by the Governor General down to 1882, that they seem to have become considerably rarer in the nineties, but then obscurity descends. On the recent Councils see also W. E. D. Halliday, "The Executive of the Government of Canada," *Canadian Public Administration* II, No. 4 (December 1959), p. 230. It now seems usual to hold one or more Privy Councils presided over by the Queen when she is in Canada, e.g. the one in Halifax on August 1, 1959, at which she approved the issue of the commission to General Vanier as Governor General.

United Kingdom as possible. However, they were unsuccessful in their attempt to have Canadian Privy Councillors designated "Right Honourable."[62]

Compared to the Canadian Privy Council, the United Kingdom Privy Council is less important as an instrument of government because it is uncommon for Parliament to confer power on the government to make regulations by order-in-council. Consequently, the need to approve such orders is comparatively infrequent and ordinarily a Privy Council is not summoned more than twice a month. It is unusual to summon a large number of Privy Councillors to attend a Council in the United Kingdom. The only occasion of a wholesale summons is an Accession Council, which is required to meet when a new Sovereign succeeds to the throne, and the only occasion when a large number of ministers is summoned is when a new administration is sworn in. Normally only a quorum is summoned, so that the usual Council will consist of the Lord President and three or four others meeting in one of the royal palaces and presided over by the Sovereign. Usually those summoned are ministers, although the quorum may be made up by some non-political Privy Councillor from the royal family or the royal household.[63]

The Canadian Privy Councils of the nineteenth century conformed fairly closely to the United Kingdom practice. Councils might range in size from most of the ministers in the government to a bare quorum, but the latter was the usual size.[64] It does not seem to have been the practice to summon to Council any but ministers of the Crown. An exception to this is the Accession Council, although it was intended that the Council summoned in 1947 at which the King gave his assent, as required by the Royal Marriages Act, 1772, should

62. See the letter from Macdonald to Adams Archibald in Sir Joseph Pope, *Memoirs of the Right Honourable Sir John Alexander Macdonald,* Vol. II (London, 1894), pp. 3-4. It was announced on April 2, 1968, that the Queen had approved a recommendation of the Prime Minister of Canada that the Governor General, the Prime Minister, and the Chief Justice of Canada should be designated "Right Honourable" for life, and that this designation would no longer, in these cases, be associated with membership in the Privy Council of the United Kingdom.

63. Lord Samuel, "What is the Privy Council?" *The Listener,* April 26, 1945, p. 367. Rt. Hon. Herbert Morrison, "The Privy Council Today," *Parliamentary Affairs* II, No. 1 (Winter, 1948), pp. 10-18.

64. Originally the Governor General's instructions provided that the quorum of the Privy Council for the transaction of business should be four, but this requirement was omitted after the issue of the letters patent in 1878. The quorum, therefore, no longer rests on a firm legal foundation, though it is laid down in the minute of council which enumerates the "prerogatives" of the Prime Minister. See Chapter 3.

include representatives from other Commonwealth governments in order to emphasize the fact that the King was the head of all of them. After some discussion it was decided instead to have the form of consent read at "Councils (Privy or Executive)" in each of the Commonwealth capitals. In Canada consent was intimated at "a meeting of his Majesty's Privy Council for Canada summoned by His Excellency the Governor General, on His Majesty's instructions." Since this occurred in the middle of the Ottawa summer, His Excellency was represented by the Deputy Governor General, Mr. Justice Patrick Kerwin, and, in addition to ministers of the Crown, two senior Privy Councillors, not of the Cabinet, were summoned to attend. On November 14, 1958, a Privy Council was held in Government House, Ottawa, presided over by the Queen. On that occasion a minute of council recommending the approval of a taxation agreement with Belgium was laid before the Queen for her approval. Then the Governor General and Prince Philip were admitted and His Excellency administered the Privy Council oath to Prince Philip.[65]

What is the relationship of the Governor-in-Council as a formal body to the actual process of government decision-making? In essence, formal actions which require to be actions of the Governor-in-Council are dealt with by ministers acting as committees of the Privy Council, and the draft minutes or orders are then transmitted to the Governor General for him to signify his approval in his office. The most common of these actions is for the Cabinet to resolve itself into the Committee of Council, as the phrase goes, for the purpose of approving submissions to the Governor General of draft orders and minutes. A great many of these are of a minor and routine character, and it leads to a serious waste of valuable time for them to be considered by the full Cabinet. Accordingly, in recent years, purely routine minutes and orders do not go to Cabinet at all, but are laid before the Special Committee of Council, which is a body of four ministers, presided over by the senior minister present, to deal with the large number of routine submissions to Council which involve no new considerations of policy.[66] This may be because the policy is already clear from statutes or other orders-in-council, or

65. See P.C. 3037 of July 31, 1947. At the Council held in 1958 the Governor General's presence was necessary because the Queen is not empowered to administer the Privy Councillor's oath.

66. See A. D. P. Heeney, "Cabinet Government in Canada: Some Recent Developments in the Machinery of the Central Executive," *Canadian Journal of Economics and Political Science* XII, No. 2 (August 1946), p. 287; J. R. Mallory, "Delegated Legislation in Canada," ibid. (November 1953), p. 462.

because the matter has already been dealt with by a Cabinet committee or by the Treasury Board. The Special Committee has a quorum of four, and there is no doubt that its labours have greatly reduced the burdens on the Cabinet as a whole. With the increasing use of Cabinet committees, consideration of submissions to Council in many cases simply meant that the same rather small piece of routine business might come before a body of ministers two or three times before the requirements of consideration and implementation had been met.[67]

In addition to the above Committees of Council there have been from time to time statutory committees. The most important of these, and the only one which still survives, is the Treasury Board, which consists of the President of the Treasury Board and five other ministers. It has wide powers over the financial and personnel administration of the government and, since the passage of the Financial Administration Act, 1951, has the power of final disposition of a large number of matters.[68]

67. It was the Special Committee of Council that Hon. R. H. Winters had in mind when he informed a bemused House of Commons that "The governor in council is a committee of the cabinet and not a full cabinet, as some hon. members seemed to think." Canada, *House of Commons Debates* (unrevised), June 18, 1956, p. 5126.

68. See Mallory, "Delegated Legislation in Canada," and below, Chapter 4.

3

The Political Executive

The unchallenged centre of power in the government of Canada is the Cabinet. This body may be defined as those of the Crown's confidential advisers who are summoned to meet with the Prime Minister to formulate the policy of the government, to prepare for parliamentary consideration new legislation and the financial measures to meet the costs of government, and to administer the government. The Cabinet is a body of responsible politicians: responsible to the Governor General before whom they took the oath of allegiance and of office as Her Majesty's Canadian government; responsible to the Prime Minister and to one another in a bond of solidarity because they know that their strength depends on their unity; responsible to the House of Commons to whom they are politically accountable. "The House of Commons," says Walter Bagehot, "lives in a state of perpetual potential choice: at any moment it can choose a ruler and dismiss a ruler." But governments do not come and go with the passing whims of the House, because the House is organized into disciplined parties. The parties are the instruments through which the electorate brings its will to bear on a government, and the relatively fixed composition of parties between elections is the element of stability which keeps the government in power. Party is essential for the House of Commons to play its role. It is, in Bagehot's words, "inherent in it, is bone of its bone, and breath of its breath."[1]

The essential thing about the Cabinet is that its life is linked to a single human will and a single human life—that of the Prime

1. Walter Bagehot, *The English Constitution,* World's Classics Edition (London, 1928), p. 125. When Bagehot wrote this, party discipline was far less strict than it is today. The last Canadian government to fall, with a majority in the House, was that of Macdonald in 1873. Once elected with a secure majority, a government is normally safe until the next election. The chance of a party split so serious that it brings down a government is remote, but not impossible. Only when there is a minority government is the House of Commons really "in a state of perpetual potential choice."

Minister. On that slender thread depends the constitutional right of ministers to exercise the powers of government.

THE PRIME MINISTER

The office of Prime Minister, the most important single office in the government, is, while not unknown to the law, entirely lacking in a legal definition of its powers. The notion that it is unknown to the law is a consequence of paying too much attention to the British constitution and not enough to our own. The Salaries Act and the statutory list of offices exempted from disqualification from the House of Commons begin by listing "the person holding the recognized position of First Minister," and there are other statutory references, notably in the Prime Minister's Residence Act. However, the law does not tell us what his powers are, although the powers and duties of his colleagues have some statutory definition. There is, indeed, a minute of council which defines some of his unique powers but this is by no means an exhaustive description and it is somewhat out of date in form. At best, this document can be regarded as a reinforcement of conventional powers.

The Prime Minister is the First Minister—his former title, still used in the Salaries Act—in two senses. He is the link between the body of ministers composing the Cabinet on the one hand and the Sovereign's representative on the other. He is the first to be appointed and he remains pre-eminent. The right of his colleagues to office depends on him, and his death or resignation automatically places their offices at the disposal of his successor. This pre-eminence has always had special implications in the Canadian constitution. It was the Prime Minister who represented Canada at the Imperial Conference. He was usually made a United Kingdom Privy Councillor, and it was this fact, at a somewhat later date, which was used to justify his right to advise the Sovereign on Canadian matters long before the Queen's Privy Council for Canada came to be recognized in any real sense as the Sovereign's advisers. Today, as a member of the Commonwealth Conference of Heads of State and Heads of Government, he is a member of that headless body which meets from time to time to discuss Commonwealth matters.

Appointment of the Prime Minister

A primary constitutional duty of the Governor General is to designate a Prime Minister and commission him to form a government. The appointment of the Prime Minister is an exceptional constitutional action in which the normal rules of constitutional advice do not apply. The Governor General acts on his own authority. In most circumstances, of course, the choice of a Prime Minister is simple enough. A Prime Minister, to be able to form a stable government, must be able to command a majority in the House of Commons. Therefore he must, as a rule, be the leader of the majority party. Since political parties today choose their own leaders, it would be quite improper for the Governor General to choose any one other than the elected party leader.[2] The choice of a Prime Minister becomes important in two cases: where no party has a clear majority and a new government must be found; and where the Prime Minister dies or becomes incapacitated and the party has not already chosen a successor. Usually, a Prime Minister who is nearing retirement may ensure the succession by having the party choose a new leader before he retires. It is much easier for a party to choose a leader when it is in opposition, since the distractions of the leadership campaign and the temporary divisions created in the party by the contest can be quite embarrassing to a government in office, particularly when Parliament is in session. On the other hand, the risk may be worthwhile, since the retiring Prime Minister may exert some influence on the choice of his successor and a change of leaders may be highly desirable before the next election. Mackenzie King, on the eve of his retirement, was able to arrange a leadership convention which in effect ratified his own choice of Louis St. Laurent as his successor. Mr. St. Laurent, after his defeat in 1957, was able to exercise a decisive influence on the party's election of Lester Pearson to succeed him. Mr. Pearson was less fortunate. He announced his intention to give up the leadership at the beginning of 1968, and subsequently presided over a distraught and harried government in which most of the candidates to succeed him were members of the Cabinet. He exerted no overt influence in the choice of Pierre Trudeau as his successor.

The death of a Prime Minister in office is probably the most difficult situation, because continuity of government is essential and there is little time for a party leader to be found by any easy process. The classic Canadian case occurred in 1891, when, on the

2. On the death of Prime Minister Curtin in July 1945, the Governor General of Australia commissioned Mr. Francis Forde to form a new government. Shortly afterwards the Labour party caucus chose Mr. Joseph Chifley as their new leader. Mr. Forde then resigned as Prime Minister and the Governor General sent for Mr. Chifley.

death of Sir John A. Macdonald, Lord Stanley conducted negotiations over a period of ten days before a successor could be found. The paralysis which struck Macdonald left him unable to speak for several days, or do more than "signify his consent by a slight pressure of the hand." The primary concern was what could be done in the meantime. "I have been informally consulted on behalf of Council as to their duty under the circumstances and as to what business they can properly carry on," wrote Stanley to the Colonial Secretary. "I have answered that I see no difficulty in their asking the H. of C. to proceed with estimates and indeed with other business which Sir John Macdonald had previously sanctioned, but that they must not introduce any new measures and that they would do well to agree with the leaders of the Opposition that all contentious questions should be postponed or avoided." The most obvious choice for the succession was the senior member of the Cabinet, Sir Hector Langevin, but "I regret to say that his department is somewhat gravely compromised in course of a Parliamentary inquiry which is now going on, and unless, or until, he is personally cleared, I could not look to him alone."[3] Stanley would have preferred Sir John Thompson, but he was relatively junior and reluctant to be considered. In the end the choice fell on J. J. C. Abbott. Abbott's tenure was brief and he was succeeded by Thompson. Unfortunately, the latter died while on a visit to England, and organizing the succession under these circumstances was not easy. Stanley's successor, Lord Aberdeen, spent an anxious ten days before he was able to commission Sir Mackenzie Bowell to form a new government.

The problem was, in some ways, simpler before political parties had developed regular procedures for the election of leaders, either by the parliamentary caucus or—the method now established—by a leadership convention. The impact of this transition is illustrated by the procedures followed in the Province of Quebec upon the deaths in office of three leaders of the Union Nationale. Premier Duplessis died in 1959 and Paul Sauvé in 1960. In both cases the formal summons of the Prime Minister-designate by the Lieutenant-Governor was preceded by a "petition" from the party caucus requesting him to commission the leader whom the caucus had chosen.[4] A similar procedure was followed on the death of Daniel Johnson in

3. Stanley to Knutsford, Public Archives of Canada, *Secret and Confidential Despatches,* Series G. 12, Vol. LXXXV, pp. 194-5.

4. See J. R. Mallory, "The Royal Prerogative in Canada: the Selection of Successors to Mr. Duplessis and Mr. Sauvé," *Canadian Journal of Economics and Political Science* XXVI, No. 2 (May 1960), p. 314.

1968. In this case, however, the new Premier, Jean-Jacques Bertrand, felt it necessary to have his "mandate" to lead the party confirmed in a leadership convention in June 1969. It is now likely that a Prime Minister chosen by the exercise of the royal prerogative in similar circumstances would regard himself as not fully confirmed in his office until he had gained the ratification of a leadership convention.

The designation of a Prime Minister is the clearest case in which the Governor General has a positive, rather than a negative, discretion. In other cases his discretion is basically confined to the possibility of resisting or refusing advice. In the appointment of a Prime Minister no one—not even a retiring Prime Minister—has the right to tender advice. If such advice is sought it may be given, but it need not be sought from the retiring Prime Minister. The fact that the appointment of the Prime Minister does not require the issuing of any documents or instruments simplifies the problem, since it does not even indirectly involve the responsibility of ministers whose participation might otherwise be necessary for the use of seals or to make up a quorum for the issuing of a minute of council. The advice tendered in such a situation is not "advice" in the strict constitutional sense, since the giver is not held politically accountable for it.[5]

5. Sir Robert Borden, who left nothing to chance, caused the following memorandum to be prepared for the press on the eve of his retirement. It is dated July 5, 1920:

"Much confusion and misunderstanding seem to prevail in the press regarding the power and responsibility of a retiring Prime Minister in respect of the selection of his successor.

"The selection of a new Prime Minister is one of the few personal acts which, under the British constitution, a Sovereign (in Canada the representative of the Sovereign) is required to perform. A retiring Prime Minister has no right whatever to name his successor nor has he any responsibility with respect to the selection of his successor, except as follows:

"The Sovereign or his representative may not see fit to ask his views of the retiring Prime Minister with respect to the selection of his successor. For example, the Queen, on the final retirement of Mr. Gladstone, did not ask his advice or his views on the question. In such a case, the retiring Prime Minister has no right whatever to express his views or to tender any advice on the subject. If, however, the Sovereign or his representative asks the views of the retiring Prime Minister, he has a right to express them, but they need not necessarily be followed. In expressing such views he does not tender advice as a Prime Minister, because he has already retired from office. His advice is to be regarded simply as that of a person holding the position of Privy Councillor who has acquired a wide experience in public affairs, which would give a certain value to his opinion on such a subject." P.A.C., *Borden Papers,* O.C. 607 (2) 65303.

It is said that King George V was much incensed to read in the press that in

The constitutional rules and the manner of the Prime Minister's appointment were summed up by Sir John Bourinot in a letter he wrote on March 20, 1895:

> The Premier is the choice of the Crown or Governor-General and the members of the Ministry, practically of the former. . . . The Governor-General, on the retirement or or dissolution of a Cabinet, sends for a member of either House, and commissions him with the task of forming a new Cabinet. Should he accept the task, he is nominally the Prime Minister, but his position is conditional on his formation of a government. Should he fail, someone else would be commissioned. As a matter of fact, there is no appointment in the legal sense: the Governor-General authorizes a public man to assume the responsibility of forming a Cabinet. Only when the Premier takes a departmental office is there an appointment. The Premier is chosen under the conventions of the constitution. When he accepts the command of the Governor-General he is Premier theoretically. From a strictly legal point of view, I should say the moment the new ministers are accepted, and are sworn in, there is a legal ministry, and a first minister.[6]

To this statement one qualification should perhaps be made. While it is theoretically possible for a senator to become a Prime Minister (both Sir John Abbott and Sir Mackenzie Bowell led their administrations from the Senate), it should be noted that the modern practice of having all important ministers in the Commons, allied to the fact that the opposition may scarcely be represented in the Senate at all restricts, for all practical purposes, the Prime Minister to the Commons. Just as it is very unlikely that a member of the House of Lords would become Prime Minister in the United Kingdom, the chances of a senator's becoming Prime Minister of Canada are slight. A senator does have one advantage, however, over a member of the House of Lords: it is easier for him to resign his place in the Senate and seek a seat in the House of Commons. It is true that under the Peerage Act of 1963 it is possible for a peer to renounce his title and thus become eligible to sit in the House of Commons. However, this is only possible at the time he succeeds to the title (or, if he is a minor, when he attains the age of twenty-one)

1930 "Mr. Mackenzie King has issued a statement to the effect that he has advised the Governor General to send for Mr. Bennett." In the circumstances, his annoyance was justified. See J. R. Mallory, "The Appointment of the Governor General: Responsible Government, Autonomy, and the Royal Prerogative," *Canadian Journal of Economics and Political Science* XXVI, No. I (February 1960), p. 96.

6. N. O. Côté, *Political Appointments in the Dominion of Canada, 1867–1895* (Ottawa, 1896), p. 31n.

and cannot be invoked at any other time. The act did provide that existing peers, within one year of the coming into force of the act, could renounce their titles. This enabled Lord Home to return to the House of Commons when he became Prime Minister in 1963. It is significant that when Arthur Meighen resumed the leadership of the Conservative party in 1942 he resigned from the Senate and sought a seat in the House of Commons. On his defeat in a by-election, he gave up the leadership of the party.

Changes of Government

Underlying the rules and procedures governing the selection of the Prime Minister is an important constitutional principle—the principle that it is the duty of responsible political leaders to see that the Queen's government is carried on. When a government has been defeated at the polls or in the House of Commons, it becomes an obligation of all party leaders to assist in the formation of a new government. Until a new government can be formed, it is the duty of the old one to remain in office. While in office it still has the duty and the authority to govern, though a government which has lost the confidence of the people or of the House of Commons can only make routine decisions until a government which has the support of the House can be formed. This situation becomes difficult only in a case where a general election has left no single party with a clear majority, as occurred in 1925, 1957, and again on several occasions in the sixties and seventies.

In the first two cases, the Liberal governments had a choice of waiting to meet Parliament or of resigning as soon as a new government could be found. This choice has not always been permitted by the established practice of the constitution. In the nineteenth century it was thought that a defeated government should never resign until the House of Commons had had the opportunity to act as what Walter Bagehot called an "electoral chamber" by defeating it on a vote of confidence. Normally, the modern practice is that "the defeated government would not meet Parliament at all, but would resign as soon as the result of the general election was known."[7] But when the result of the election is known, but unclear, as in 1925, a government may do as Mackenzie King did and remain in office in the confident expectation of enough third party support to avoid

7. Sir Ivor Jennings, *Cabinet Government,* 3rd ed. (London, 1959), p. 25.

defeat in the House. Mr. Diefenbaker followed this course in 1962, as did Mr. Pearson in 1965 and Mr. Trudeau in 1972. In 1979, Mr. Trudeau resigned since he had no reason to expect that he could win a vote of confidence when the House met. However, to continue in office as a minority government creates the appearance of clinging to office at all costs, and it was partly for this reason that Mr. St. Laurent decided to resign as soon as he could after the election of June 10, 1957.[8]

A Prime Minister who has decided to resign is equally bound by the obligation not to create a needless hiatus in government. He should remain in office, contenting himself with purely routine decisions, until such time as his successor has assured himself that he is ready to form an administration. A defeated Prime Minister should not emulate Mackenzie King who, in 1926, simply announced that he had resigned and that there was no government at all.[9]

A government which has been defeated in a general election should not abuse its caretaker status by taking irrevocable decisions which its successors would not be free to change. This, essentially, was the issue which led Lord Aberdeen to refuse certain appointments recommended by Sir Charles Tupper in 1896. A defeated government is not absolutely barred from taking decisions and making appointments, because many of these may well have been agreed to in principle before the government's defeat, and consequently only the formal action remains to be taken after the Cabinet has lost its moral authority to act. Most governments are more circumspect than that of Sir John A. Macdonald, which appointed two Lieutenant-Governors on the day of its resignation,[10] but nearly all of them have held meetings of Cabinet and Council and made submissions to the Governor General. The Meighen government, defeated in the general election of 1921, aroused much criticism

8. In 1929 Baldwin "informed the King that the public might regard it as 'unsporting' of him if he did not resign immediately, and might suspect that he was contemplating some deal with the Liberals to keep Labour out." Sir Harold Nicolson, *King George V, His Life and Reign* (London, 1952), p. 435. Mr. St. Laurent, unlike some of his colleagues, evidently agreed with Baldwin, who later explained his resignation in the House by remarking that the verdict of the electorate meant "that whether they wanted the hon. members opposite or not, they certainly did not want me, and I was going to get out as soon as I could." 261H.C.Deb.5s., p. 535.

9. Canada, *House of Commons Debates,* June 28, 1926, pp. 5096-7.

10. William Leggo, *History of the Administration of the Earl of Dufferin in Canada* (Montreal, 1878), pp. 197-8.

because, on the day before its resignation was accepted, an order-in-council had been passed directing that a writ be issued to call a by-election to enable Meighen (who had been defeated in his own constituency) to seek a seat in the House of Commons.[11]

Though there is bound to be a substantial delay in the expedition of public business while the new government is being formed and new ministers are finding their feet, the normal procedure is to avoid any serious break in the continuity of government. Even after a Prime Minister has tendered his resignation, or after the death of a Prime Minister in office, ministers continue to be responsible for the conduct of the affairs of their departments, and do not yield authority until their successors have been sworn to office. Where there has been a complete change of government, a new administration may take office with only half the portfolios filled, even though all of the former ministers have vacated office. Thus, when Macdonald formed his second government, six ministers (including himself) were appointed on October 17, 1878, five more on October 19, one on October 26 and the last two on November 8. On June 29, 1926, Meighen formed a "temporary ministry composed of seven ministers," and most of the portfolios were not filled until July 13.[12] When the British Labour government took office in 1945, only Clement Attlee and six of his senior colleagues were sworn to office on July 28, after which the Prime Minister and the Foreign Secretary immediately flew to Berlin for the Potsdam Conference. It was not until August 4 that the remainder of the ministerial appointments were completed.[13]

In these circumstances the new ministers can assume full authority, in Canadian practice, by appointing from among their number acting ministers to administer the vacant departments. In this way undivided authority over all departments can be assumed by the new government.

Offices Held by the Prime Minister

In Canadian practice it was standard, until recently, for the Prime Minister to hold a department portfolio, partly because until the

11. P.C. 4675 of December 27, 1921.

12. P.A.C., *Guide to Canadian Ministries since Confederation,* Ottawa, 1957, pp. 12-13, 47-8.

13. Sir John Wheeler-Bennett, *King George VI: His Life and Reign* (London, 1958), p. 639.

Salaries Act was amended in 1920, there was no salary provided for the Prime Minister as such. When the responsibilities of government were much simpler the burden was not excessive, and departmental officials could afford the Prime Minister what support staff he needed. In other countries, Australia for example, there is a Prime Minister's Department, but there is no special reason why there should be one in Canada. The fact that there is not may have been one of the reasons the Prime Minister has usually held another department to which his essential support staff could be attached. The practice in recent years has been for the Prime Minister to hold no other office.[14]

At one time or another nearly every long-established portfolio has been held by the Prime Minister. Sir John A. Macdonald held, among other portfolios, that of Justice, while Alexander Mackenzie showed his determination to lay down his own standards of economy and integrity in public life by becoming minister of Public Works. R. B. Bennett was, for over a year, his own Minister of Finance, but even he found this a burden beyond the strength of one man. In the Union Government, Sir Robert Borden held office as Secretary of State for External Affairs, a portfolio which he himself had caused to be attached by statute to the Prime Minister in 1912. With the exception of the Union Government (1917-21), in which both Borden and Meighen held office as Secretary of State for External Affairs, every Prime Minister from 1896 to 1957 held office as President of the Privy Council. In fact these two departments, the Privy Council and External Affairs, have had close historical associations with the Prime Minister. There are reasons for this in both cases.

The first, and most important, reason is that, while the Prime Minister should not be burdened with departmental responsibilities which would constitute a serious drain on his time and energy, there must be some department to which his officials and advisers can be attached. Most of the Prime Minister's time is taken up with his

14. Mr. St. Laurent was the first Prime Minister to hold office as such when he transferred the Presidency of the Privy Council to Mr. Chevrier on April 25, 1957. Mr. Diefenbaker first took office as Prime Minister and Secretary of State for External Affairs, but later relinquished the latter post. Mr. Pearson was content to hold office as Prime Minister only. When Mr. Trudeau first became Prime Minister he continued to hold the Justice portfolio, but when he reconstructed his administration on July 5, 1968, he transferred Justice to Mr. Turner. Similarly Mr. Clark held office as Prime Minister only. When the Prime Minister gave up the Presidency of the Privy Council he nevertheless retained ministerial responsibility for the Privy Council Office, which, since 1940, has contained the Cabinet Secretariat.

duties as head of the government, and there is something to be said for having a department whose functions are in some degree related to the functions of the Prime Minister. This is true of both External Affairs and of the Privy Council Office.

The Department of External Affairs had grown up, in Sir Joseph Pope's words, as "in a special sense, the Prime Minister's Department." As long as Canada's window on the world was the British Foreign Office, Canada's relations with the outside world were concentrated at the summit in the Prime Minister. Sir Robert Borden rightly saw, at its inception, that External Affairs was a department which must belong primarily to the Prime Minister. It was only when Canada began seriously to conduct her own foreign policy and have her own diplomatic contact with the world that it became essential to have a full-time minister responsible for that department. It then became necessary to make other administrative arrangements for the "Prime Minister's Office."

Meanwhile the growth of the Cabinet Secretariat with the Privy Council Office had made it inevitable that the latter become the home of the Prime Minister's establishment. This could be defended on strong grounds of convenience. The close articulation of Cabinet and Privy Council in Canadian constitutional history has been reinforced by the growth of the Cabinet Secretariat as part of the Privy Council Office. This, together with the substantial growth of the Prime Minister's private office staff, under the direction of his principal secretary, have added considerably to the establishment of the Privy Council Office. The Prime Minister's Office, like other minister's offices, is comprised of advisers who are outside the regular public service, and is carried on the estimates of the Privy Council Office, but is distinct from the regular establishment of the office. The fact that the President of the Privy Council may be a minister other than the Prime Minister does not interfere with these arrangements. The Secretary to the Cabinet and Clerk of the Privy Council necessarily must serve the Prime Minister directly, and there is no constitutional barrier to this arrangement.[15]

15. A somewhat similar arrangement exists in Great Britain, where a comparable role is played by the Treasury. The political head of the Treasury is the Chancellor of the Exchequer, but the Permanent Secretary to the Treasury (or sometimes a Joint Permanent Secretary) is also Head of the Civil Service, and as such adviser to the Prime Minister, who also holds the sinecure office of First Lord of the Treasury. The Cabinet Secretariat is also attached to the Treasury, although it is for all practical purposes a separate organization and the Secretary to the Cabinet is, of course, one of the very small top group in the civil service. The creation of a Civil Service Department with a separate minister, which took over from the Treasury responsibility for the civil service, has somewhat altered these arrangements.

Cabinet-making

"The choosing of Ministers is, I think, the most difficult of all the tasks which fall to the lot of a Prime Minister, while their dismissal is the most distasteful," observed a former British Prime Minister.[16] It is the Prime Minister who recommends, by an "instrument of advice," the appointment of ministers to the Governor General, and it is the Prime Minister who has the right to recommend their dismissal or the acceptance of their resignation. Cabinet-making is never easy in Canada, for a good minister must have a number of qualities rarely found together in the same person, and the complex calculus of political representation may deprive a promising candidate a place.[17]

Ministers of the Crown are not required by law to have seats in Parliament, but when Parliament is in session it is impossible, in practice, for them to discharge the responsibilities of their office without a seat in the House of Commons or the Senate. For example, General McNaughton, who was appointed Minister of National Defence on November 2, 1944, sought a seat in the House of Commons on February 5, 1945, was defeated and, after being defeated again in the general election of 1945, resigned from the ministry on August 20, 1945. Similarly, Pierre Juneau resigned as Minister of Communications after being defeated in a by-election in 1975.

There is no constitutional requirement that any member of the Cabinet should be a member of the Senate. However, the necessity of introducing legislation and of debating and defending government policy in the Senate make it desirable for at least one person familiar with Cabinet business to sit in the Senate. Since Confederation, nearly every major Cabinet post, except that of Minister of Finance, has at one time or another been held by a Senator. There were even two Prime Ministers—Sir John Abbott (1891–92) and Sir Mackenzie Bowell (1894–96)—who were Senators. Sir John A. Macdonald's first administration contained five Senators (out of a Cabinet of thirteen), but the tendency over the years was for the number and proportion of Senators in the Cabinet to decline to the minimum. With the exception of Meighen's first ministry (1920–21) and the early part of the Bennett ministry (1930–35) the only members

16. C. R. Attlee, *As It Happened* (London, 1954) p. 155.

17. For a succinct discussion of the complexities of Cabinet-making see R. M. Punnett, *The Prime Minister in Canadian Government* (Toronto, 1977) Chapter Four.

of the Senate, except for a few brief periods, have been the Government Leader in the Senate or Ministers without Portfolio (or in some cases both). Since 1947, the Government Leader in the Senate has been paid an allowance in addition to his indemnity as Senator. The office is now regarded as a portfolio and its holder is accordingly sworn to office in the same way as ministers without departments. In 1954 a Senator was appointed Solicitor-General, and in 1963 Senator McCutcheon held the post of Minister of Trade and Commerce in the dying days of the Diefenbaker government. These appeared to be temporary aberrations. Mr. Diefenbaker managed for some time without even a Government Leader in the Senate in the Cabinet.

However, the vagaries of the Canadian electoral system have, in recent years, made it necessary to have several Senators in important Cabinet posts. A governing party with little or no representation in an important section of the country may be able to correct this deficiency by appointing Senators to the Cabinet. Thus, when Mr. Clark took office in 1979 his representation in the Commons from Quebec was so modest that he found it necessary to appoint Senators to two prestigious offices, Justice and Industry, Trade and Commerce, in order to increase francophone representation in the Cabinet. Similarly in 1980, Mr. Trudeau was returned with a majority but with no seats from western Canada, except for two from the Winnipeg area. He was forced to accord representation to the three most western provinces by naming Senators to the Cabinet. This is clearly an expedient of limited value, for no important section of the country is content to be denied adequate representation in the Cabinet from the House of Commons.

In fact sectional representation has always been one of the major characteristics of Canadian Cabinets. This political necessity is as old as Canadian self-government:

> The device of sectional equality (in the allocation of representation in the Senate) in fact gave to each province almost the same legislative representation as if representation in both houses had been based on population. This made it necessary in Canada to devise a system for making the cabinet federally representative. It has become the invariable practice of the Canadian constitution to have provincial, as well as certain racial and religious, interests represented in the cabinet. To a large extent this has merely pushed the process one step further back, so that the political party in power is the real federalizing element, and the secret caucus is the place in which federal conflicts are resolved. This last has been possible only since the rise of real national parties.[18]

18. W. Menzies Whitelaw, "American Influence on British Federal Systems" in Conyers Read (ed.) *The Constitution Reconsidered.* (New York, 1935) p. 305.

Underlying the whole structure of Canadian politics is, as Professor W. L. Morton argued, the principle of sectional balance which is necessary in a transcontinental state and a democratic society. There are three principles:

> the first is that of sectional representation in the executive as well as the legislative branch of the government. The second is the principle of sectional balance, exemplified not only in the equal representation of sections in the Senate and the weighted representation of sections in the federal Cabinet, but also in the careful equating of the sectional incidence of national policies.... The third principle is that of the communal representation of various religious and national groups, one of the greatest importance in the functioning of Canadian government.[19]

Representative government, in this rather general sense, is the dominant characteristic of the government of Canada. Nowhere is it more fundamental than in the case of the Cabinet. It goes back to the beginning and has been persistently reaffirmed. Speaking on the bill which set up the Department of Marine and Fisheries, Sir John A. Macdonald said:

> It was true that the theory of the constitution made no such requirement, nor prohibited the selection of the Cabinet altogether from any one particular district, but in the example of the United Kingdom, where England, Ireland and Scotland were each invariably represented at the Departments, it was thought advisable that the confidence of every section of the Confederation should be invited and secured by the recognition of its right to Cabinet representation.[20]

It was typical of Macdonald that he should justify an essentially Canadian practice by reference to an alleged British principle of government which in fact did not exist. Nevertheless the basic formula has remained. In Macdonald's time it already meant that Ontario and Quebec, in view of their "greater population and wealth," would require at least twice as many members in the Cabinet as New Brunswick and Nova Scotia. The addition of new provinces has had the effect of pushing up the size of the Cabinet in order to ensure at least one minister from each province, although Prince Edward Island has occasionally been left out. The increasing size and wealth of the western provinces has also pushed British Columbia's representation to as high as three and occasionally larger representation from the others.

19. W. L. Morton, "The Formation of the First Federal Cabinet" *Canadian Historical Review* XXXVI:2 (June, 1955) p. 113.

20. P. A. C. *Canadian Parliamentary Debates, 1866–1870,* April 3, 1868.

on his return to office Mr. Trudeau reverted to a single-tiered Cabinet.[23]

How are Cabinet ministers recruited? The most obvious source of talent in a parliamentary country is of course the House of Commons. However, it has not been the only, or perhaps the most important source. The politics of federalism in the early years after Confederation brought many important recruits straight from provincial politics. A provincial premier had a very strong claim to any vacancy to which his province was entitled. This was particularly important when a general election led to a change of government, and an incoming Prime Minister found in provincial politics many potential colleagues with experience as well as strong claims to office. Thus Laurier brought into his Cabinet three provincial premiers—Mowat, Fielding, and Blair—in 1896. Borden's first Cabinet contained a number of members with considerable experience in provincial politics. The number of provincial politicians anxious to make the leap into federal politics has declined in recent years, except perhaps in the case of aspirants to the party leadership. Even there, for every Robert Stanfield who chose the route, there have been several others who have openly spurned it. Neither Mr. Diefenbaker nor Mr. Clark made any effort to find room in the Cabinet for aspirants from provincial politics. The House of Commons remains a major source of Cabinet material. Even prominent recruits from the outside do better to get elected first and serve at least a brief apprenticeship in the House, as did Mackenzie King and Pierre Trudeau.

What is remarkable about Canadian Cabinets is the amount of room at the top which is open to outsiders with little or no direct experience in politics. There is a long tradition of recruiting ministers from the business world. In this group are numbered, among others, Sir Thomas White and C. C. Ballantyne (brought in by Borden); Murray MacLaren, Vincent Massey and C. D. Howe (brought in by Mackenzie King); and Wallace McCutcheon (brought in by Diefenbaker). More recently the federal bureaucracy has become an important source of Cabinet material. Mackenzie King, even while serving as Deputy Minister of Labour, was already clear in his own mind that his ultimate career was in the political

23. A two-tiered Cabinet may produce severe internal strains between Ministers who are "in" and Ministers who are "out", since all are equally bound by collective decisions in which all have not participated. See P. M. Weller "Inner Cabinets and Outer Ministers: Some Lessons from Australia and Britain." *Canadian Public Administration* XXXIII:4 (Winter, 1980) p. 598.

élite, and it is perhaps not surprising that it has been the Liberal party which has increasingly found an important part of its leadership in the civil service. Mr. St. Laurent "promoted" into the Cabinet both the Under-Secretary of State for External Affairs (Mr. Pearson) and the Clerk of the Privy Council (Mr. Pickersgill). Mr. Pearson himself, when he came to form his ministerial "team," relied heavily on such former civil servants as Mitchell Sharp, C. M. Drury and Maurice Lamontagne. Another class of political outsiders has been the academic power élite of university presidents. Mr. St. Laurent brought Milton Gregg into his Cabinet, and Mr. Diefenbaker sought out Sydney Smith.

This tendency to recruit the political élite from outside formal politics has been criticized by a number of observers. John Porter, for example, finds in it another example of "administrative politics" and sees it as a contributing factor in the lack of clarity in the political system.[24] Furthermore it undermines the separation of politics and administration, the combination of politically sensitized ministers and politically neutral bureaucrats, upon which so many of the rules of the game in Cabinet government depend.

The Prime Minister and Other Ministers

The Prime Minister is not an undisputed head of government: in matters of government policy he must carry his colleagues with him. If he does not they can destroy him by uniting against him. But his authority is very great—much greater than that of a single minister or mere chairman. It must be remembered that Cabinets on the whole do not reach decisions by voting, but by consensus, and they achieve this consensus under the leadership of the Prime Minister.

The Prime Minister's pre-eminent position over his colleagues is buttressed by rights which they do not possess. It is he who advises the Sovereign on the appointment of the Governor General. He, and only he, can advise the Governor General to appoint a minister or to accept his resignation. By resigning himself, a Prime Minister brings his ministry to an end. His right to advise on the dissolution of Parliament is a threat which he can hold over his colleagues and followers, for no politician welcomes the trouble and expense of fighting an election. He possesses the undoubted right to issue orders in any department without consulting the minister, and he

24. John Porter, *The Vertical Mosaic* (Toronto, 1965), pp. 386 ff.

may assume the administration of a department himself, as Sir Robert Borden did of the Department of Militia during the period when a Royal Commission was investigating allegations against the conduct of Sir Sam Hughes in 1916.[25] Finally, only the Prime Minister can advise the Governor General that the normal secrecy surrounding the Crown's confidential business may be relaxed. This is of great importance when there has been an irreconcilable difference of opinion in the Cabinet, and a minister who has been driven to resignation may wish to explain to Parliament the basis of his disagreement with his colleagues. If he is to do so without violating his Privy Councillor's oath, he must have the consent of the Governor General to disclose, as far as may be necessary, the proceedings of the Cabinet. Only the Prime Minister can accede to a request of this kind, though he will normally be willing to do so in order to make his own position clear.

No resigning minister can claim a right to reveal Cabinet discussions. According to Anson, "it is the practice that this permission should be obtained through the intervention of the Prime Minister and that the disclosure should be strictly limited by the terms of the permission granted."[26] The rule of Cabinet secrecy depends not only on the Official Secrets Act and the Privy Councillor's oath, but also upon the grounds that a Cabinet decision is advice to the Sovereign, whose consent is necessary for its publication. This consent applies only to the particular occasion and the particular disclosure for which the sanction is given, and can be obtained only through the Prime Minister, even if the disclosure relates to proceedings in a previous administration.

The resignation of J. L. Ralston from the Cabinet of Mackenzie King in November 1944 illustrates the operation of these principles in Canada. In requesting that their correspondence be made public in order to clarify the issue which had arisen, Ralston had written to the Prime Minister: "The whole question was discussed at very considerable length both at meetings of the Cabinet and of the War Committee." In his reply King had said that he would not be justified in advising "the publication of those portions of your letter relating to the deliberations in Council or of those portions of my reply referring to what you have said respecting these discussions." To this, Ralston made the apt rejoinder that the speeches by the Prime Minister, the Minister of National Defence and the Minister of

25. *Robert Laird Borden: His Memoirs,* Vol. II (London, 1938), p. 564.

26. Sir William Reynell Anson, *The Law and Custom of the Constitution,* Vol. II, Pt. 1, 4th ed. (London, 1935), p. 121.

Justice had left little of the story unrevealed. "Regarding Privy Council Secrecy," he wrote, "I feel I ought to point out that your own speech of November 8th contained references to matters treated, debated and resolved in Council discussions, and I am sure these references would not have been made had you not considered that they were permissible. Furthermore, you had no hesitation in May 1942 in publishing the correspondence regarding Honourable Mr. Cardin's resignation, which contained references to Council discussions."[27] He then formally requested that the Governor General be asked to consent to the release of the correspondence. This was done and the request granted on November 18.

Sir Ivor Jennings quotes a statement of Gladstone's that the Prime Minister "had no powers, properly so-called, over his colleagues."[28] In terms of constitutional law this statement is equally true of the Canadian constitution. However, certain of the Prime Minister's powers have been crystallized in written form in a minute of council. "The Committee of the Privy Council," it runs, ". . . submit the following Memorandum regarding certain of the functions of the Prime Minister." It states that "a Meeting of a Committee of the Privy Council is at the call of the Prime Minister," that the quorum for the transaction of business is four and that no minister can make recommendations to Council affecting the discipline of another minister's department. It lists certain "special prerogatives of the Prime Minister," which include the recommendation of the dissolution and convocation of Parliament, a number of appointments (including those of Privy Councillors, ministers, senators, sub-Committees of Council, Chief Justices of all courts, deputy heads of departments, and certain other official appointments) and "recommendations in any Department."

This minute normally used to be passed as one of the first acts of a new administration, but the most recent is P.C. 3374 of October 25, 1935. Mackenzie King once stated in the House of Commons, "I may say there is nothing unusual about this particular order. It is one that

27. King's letter to Ralston on November 10 had contained the statement (which is of course quite accurate) that "The Privy Councillor's oath is not less binding upon the Prime Minister than upon all other members of the Privy Council." Dr. Forsey rightly condemns King for propounding the "novel theory" that "the Prime Minister is entitled to reveal what took place in Council without the consent of the Crown, but other Ministers are not." "Mr. King and Parliamentary Government," *Canadian Journal of Economics and Political Science* XVII No. 4 (November 1951), p. 453. The correspondence between King and Ralston was tabled and published in Canada, *House of Commons Debates,* Nov. 27, 1944; Nov. 29, 1944, pp. 6600ff.

28. Jennings, *Cabinet Government,* p. 179.

was first adopted by Sir Charles Tupper when he came into office. . . . I have been told to be sure to inform the House that this list does not include all the prerogatives of the Prime Minister."[29] In 1896 Tupper assumed office with a Cabinet which had been seriously divided. The party had been demoralized by the death of Sir John A. Macdonald, and it could not be said that effective leadership had been given by Macdonald's successors, Abbott, Thompson and Bowell. Subsequent Prime Ministers have found it useful to reintroduce the minute, or at least to circulate a copy to each minister on his appointment.

The preservation by the Prime Minister of his position depends on the exercise of the highest qualities of leadership.[30] Among the endowments of the successful leader is the ability for "pattern-setting"—the ability to symbolize in himself the special qualities of an age which will evoke a response of recognition from his followers. Thus Macdonald evoked the romantic boldness and somewhat raffish character of a country still very close to the frontier; Laurier's dignity, charm and elegance appealed to a more settled age of optimism; Borden's earnest manner was clearly right for the grim trials of the First World War; Mackenzie King, in his cautious and superficially colourless way, succeeded in capturing the earnest concern of the middle classes in a world which seemed beyond control or understanding. After Mackenzie King—after the great victory, not only over the enemy in war, but apparently over the previously intractable problems of economics—the country was ready for the bland, avuncular and magnanimous St. Laurent. Televi-

29. Canada, *House of Commons Debates* (unrevised), March 23, 1936, p. 1436.

30. "Some Prime Ministers have been little more than chairmen of a committee concerned only with securing the greatest possible measure of agreement between more forceful colleagues. Others have been determined to get their own way, it might be by directly dominating the situation at the Cabinet, or it might be as a result of quiet talks outside with those whose opinions carried most weight. Some have been businesslike, have read all the papers up for discussion, and been mainly concerned to get decisions. Some have believed in letting everybody ventilate their troubles and in the value of desultory conversation. Some have been natural listeners disposed to lie low and say nothing, either waiting to see what others thought or in order to come in with their own decisive intervention to conclude the debate. Others have been inclined towards government by monologue. Some have tended to be wet blankets and some have been an inspiration. Some have made a point of seeing something of all their colleagues, and even of junior Ministers, individually. Some have mainly confined their talks to an informal 'inner Cabinet.' Others have seen little of their colleagues except at Cabinet meetings. Some Cabinets have been happy families, others have not." L. S. Amery, *Thoughts on the Constitution* (London, 1947), pp. 73-4.

sion has, it seems, greatly enhanced the political importance of the Prime Minister's *persona.* Mr. Diefenbaker's messianic manner undoubtedly possessed a remarkable appeal to large sections of the electorate. However, Mr. Pearson's public image, which was at great variance with his charm and effectiveness in small groups, became a grave electoral handicap. Mr. Trudeau, in his early years of triumph, gained a great deal of political advantage from his image of youthful informality, which appealed to an electorate which was mainly young, urban, and impatient of tradition. Subsequently he also came to suffer electorally by another aspect of his complex personality, that of the clear-headed intellectual, apparently unable to suffer fools gladly and frequently unable to avoid giving offence to those less articulate than himself.

Electoral style must be differentiated from managerial style of which the two most obvious are, in Malcolm Punnett's terminology, that of "chairman of the board" and "managing director."[31] The one is the skilful consensus-seeking chairman who leaves his colleagues a great deal of freedom in their own areas of responsibility and crystallizes agreement out of full discussion of major issues. The other is the firm leader who dominates his colleagues in the proconsular manner of R. B. Bennett. But even the chairman of the board needs to reinforce tactical skill with ruthlessness when necessary. It is not easy to first isolate a contentious colleague and then, in Gladstone's phrase, "be a good butcher." The important thing is to find formulas which dissipate or postpone conflicts which might tear at the vitals of the precarious unity of Canada. Macdonald is remembered by the fond nickname "Old Tomorrow." The following is a good, but unspectacular example. On October 7, 1879, he wrote to the Governor General, the Marquess of Lorne:

> Council will agree to take the ship [*H. M. Corvette Charybdis*] and fit her up. I am sure I could have carried it yesterday but as there were some dissentients I thought it well to allow it to stand over for a day. Persuasion is better than force and by six o'clock this evening Council will be persuaded.[32]

Mackenzie King will perhaps be best remembered for his handling of the extremely delicate issue of participation in European wars ("Parliament will decide", though when Parliament met the decisive steps had been taken and there were few who would

31. See R. M. Punnett, *The Prime Minister in Canadian Government and Politics,* Chapter 2.

32. Quoted in W. Stewart MacNutt, *Days of Lorne* (Fredericton, 1955) p. 199.

oppose them) and military conscription ("Not necessarily conscription but conscription if necessary").

In most countries under the Westminster system it is now common to designate, in the published list of ministers, the Prime Minister's second-in-command as Deputy Prime Minister. This title and the overt recognition of a Deputy Prime Minister have not, on the whole, extended to Canadian practice, although Pierre Trudeau has conferred this title on Allan MacEachen. Whether this practice will be followed in the future is uncertain. There has, however, been a persistent myth in Canada that English-Canadian Prime Ministers have normally had a "Quebec lieutenant" who occupied a position of such special eminence as to possess exceptional powers of veto and rights of consultation. This notion has been carefully examined by F. W. Gibson and as a result has been largely exploded. He says,

> ...two French-Canadians—Sir George Cartier and Ernest Lapointe—were singled out from their cabinet colleagues by English-Canadian prime ministers and given positions of quite special influence in the making of the cabinet and, subsequently, in the councils of the government; and one English-Canadian minister, C. D. Howe, was assigned a role of comparable authority under a French-Canadian prime minister. Yet none of these eminent ministers attained a position of full and recognized co-ordination with the prime ministers under whom they served; and the difference, in power and status, between each of them and his prime minister simply underscores the fact that the political executive of the government of Canada, since 1867, has not had more than one head.[33]

It is necessary, however, to provide for the exercise of the functions of the Prime Minister during his absence by appointing a minister "to act as Prime Minister." This is done by minute of council at an early point in the life of a government. A recent example is P. C. 1981-2707 of September 25, 1981 which provides "that in the absence from Ottawa of the Prime Minister or in the event of his being unable to perform the functions of his office, the next senior minister who is in Ottawa and is able to perform the functions of the office of Prime Minister, be authorized to act for the Prime Minister." The minute also designates Acting Ministers in order to provide for the exercise of the powers of the various ministers when they are, for similar reasons, unable to perform

33. F. W. Gibson (ed) *Cabinet Formation and Bicultural Relations.* Studies of the Royal Commission on Bilingualism and Biculturalism. (Ottawa, 1970), p. 155.

these functions. The Acting Prime Minister cannot, of course, act except in the circumstances mentioned, and of course the death or resignation of the Prime Minister would terminate the appointment.

THE CABINET

The Cabinet is the body of confidential advisers to the Sovereign (or the Governor General) who meet, on the instance of the Prime Minister to "advise" the head of state collectively on policy. Since the powers of the Crown are, with rare exceptions, exercised on the advice and responsibility of ministers—either individually or as the Cabinet—the Cabinet is the centre of the executive government. The Cabinet's functions are not, however, confined to executive acts. "A Cabinet," said Walter Bagehot, "is a combining committee—a hyphen which joins, a buckle which fastens the legislative part of the state to the executive part of the state."[34] Its special function in this respect arises from the fact that its members individually are members of Parliament, responsible to the House of Commons. As a body which leads the majority party in the House of Commons, it is able to act as a ruling committee which controls the business of the House of Commons. Nearly all legislation which is passed through Parliament today originates with the Cabinet. Thus, the Cabinet formulates and introduces the legislation which represents the policy of the ruling party in the House of Commons, and also shapes and supervises the execution of the acts which are the laws enacted by Parliament.

In general, Cabinet decisions are reached by consensus (which explains the length of Cabinet meetings when difficult questions are on the agenda), but a Prime Minister may sometimes impose a policy on his colleagues, or even act first and inform his colleagues afterwards. In any case, ministers are expected to publicly support the decisions which have been taken, or leave the Cabinet. The proceedings of the Cabinet are secret, for the constitutional reason that the Crown's business is confidential and is protected by the Privy Councillor's oath and the Official Secrets Act, and for the practical reason that full discussion and mutual confidence are possible only in an atmosphere of secrecy. As Lawrence Lowell put

34. Bagehot, *The English Constitution,* p. 12.

it, "Men engaged in a common cause who come together for the purpose of reaching an agreement usually succeed, provided their differences of opinion are not made public."[35]

While the Cabinet is made up of ministers theoretically equal to one another in position and power, one of them—the Prime Minister—occupies a special position which he shares with no one. Not only is he personally responsible for the appointment and removal of his colleagues, but he also determines who shall attend Cabinet, how its business is organized, and what ministerial offices are entitled to Cabinet rank. Although the practice in Canada has been to include in the Cabinet all of the major political offices in the administration, it would be quite possible for a Prime Minister to exclude one or more of them. Upon occasion in the past the Solicitor-General has been left out of the Cabinet, and during both world wars the Prime Minister created a small war committee of the Cabinet which took nearly all of the major decisions, while the full Cabinet met only on rare occasions. It is within the Prime Minister's power to decide, if he feels that the Cabinet is getting too large, that the holders of certain ministerial posts may have to be left out of the Cabinet.

The problem of size has already led to two different methods of removing the major policy decisions from the full Cabinet to smaller bodies. The first of these methods, adopted initially by the Davis government in Ontario and subsequently by the Levesque government in Quebec, has been to create a small inner group of "policy ministers" who have no operating departments of their own but whose role consists of deciding major policy questions under the chairmanship of the Prime Minister and exercising control over their policy areas through their chairmanship of Cabinet committees. The other alternative was adopted by Mr. Clark, who created an Inner Cabinet of twelve, who were at the same time departmental ministers. The first device has been less successful than was expected. In the case of Ontario, it has been difficult for senior and ambitious ministers to accept the low political profile which goes

35. Lowell argued that it was incorrect to base the obligation of Cabinet secrecy on the Privy Councillor's oath. This, he said, "would seem to be another case of confusion between the law and the conventions of the constitution. Although the permission of the sovereign must be obtained before proceedings in the cabinet can be made public, yet in fact the duty of secrecy is not merely a legal obligation towards the sovereign which he can waive under advice, for example, of a ministry of the other party. It is a moral duty towards one's colleagues, which ceases when by lapse of time, or otherwise, the reason for it has been removed; and the secrets must be kept from other privy councillors, the Leader of the Opposition for example, as well as from the rest of the world." Lawrence Lowell, *The Government of England,* Vol. I. (New York, 1914), pp. 65-6.

with the absence of large departmental budgets and the attendant publicity which goes with being identified with popular programs. The Quebec experience has been of shorter duration, but it appears that the "super ministers" have been more successful at integrating the process of policy initiation than they have been at controlling policy once it has been implemented. The Clark innovation of an Inner Cabinet had too brief a life for its effectiveness to be judged. Because it continued to play a major policy and co-ordinating role in addition to the major departmental responsibilities of most of its members, the burden must have been unbearably heavy.

There have been four kinds of ministers: the holders of offices defined by statute; Ministers Without Portfolio; and—in recent years—two different kinds of Ministers of State. First of all there are the political heads of departments. Normally they are designated "the Minister of . . .", but a few carry other titles. The President of the Privy Council has always been a minister. He does not, of course, preside over the Privy Council. On the rare occasions when there is a formal Council it is presided over by the head of state, and it is the Prime Minister who presides over the Cabinet. The President of the Privy Council does not even have ministerial control over the Privy Council Office, which comprehends the support staff of the Prime Minister and the Cabinet. Since the post is no longer held by the Prime Minister it was, for a time, used as a prestigious sinecure, but in recent years it has become a convenient ministerial post for the Leader of the House. The Secretary of State for Canada holds an office whose title goes back to the "secret-aries" of the distant past—the keepers of the secrets of their masters. The essential survival of this relationship in Canada was that he, like his predecessor, the Provincial Secretary before Confederation, was the custodian of the Great Seal of Canada. An unimaginative rearrangement of responsibilities in 1966, however, transferred this function to the Minister of Consumer and Corporate Affairs who is now responsible for the issue of corporate letters patent. There are also the two law officers of the Crown, although the Attorney-General also carries the title of Minister of Justice. The office of Solicitor-General was the junior of the two, with a limited number of statutory duties, and no department of his own. However, the Government Reorganization Act of 1966 created a separate Department of the Solicitor-General, under which fell the Royal Canadian Mounted Police, the Penitentiary Service and the National Parole Board. That act also formally created a separate ministerial post in the form of the President of the Treasury Board, which had hitherto been one of the responsibilities of the Minister of Finance.

The Cabinet has also contained Ministers Without Portfolio, who do not draw full ministerial salaries. This device was commonly used in the past as a means of "balancing" representation in the Cabinet or sometimes of retaining in the Cabinet senior ministers who may no longer be able to carry the burden of departmental responsibility. If these ministers are charged with special responsibilities a ministerial salary is usually provided, as in the case of the Government Leader in the Senate. Sometimes a Minister Without Portfolio was given responsibility for policy planning in a specific area, as was the case with Mr. Herb Gray at the beginning of the Trudeau administration.

The illogicality of having a Minister Without Portfolio who nevertheless had a specific job to do was removed in 1971 by the invention of a new and more appropriate title. Part IV of the Government Reorganization Act of that year brought into being two different kinds of Ministers of State. The first group were to assist Ministers whose responsibilities were too large to be effectively handled by a single minister. This had previously been done by appointing Associate Ministers, an example of which was the Associate Minister of National Defence who functioned from the beginning of the Korean War until the Diefenbaker years. The Clark Cabinet initially had no less than seven Ministers of State, each responsible for specific tasks in another minister's department. Examples were Minister of State for Federal-Provincial Relations (Prime Minister); Minister of State for Social Programs (Health and Welfare); Minister of State for Small Business (Industry, Trade and Commerce).

The second category of Ministers of State are those who are heads of separate structures, called Ministries of State for Special Purposes. These posts and agencies can be created by the government when, in the words of section 14, "it appears to the Governor-in-Council that the requirements for formulating and developing new and comprehensive policies in relation to any matter coming within the responsibility of the Government of Canada." The phrasing is important. These "Ministries" are to develop policy, not to administer it. Their number is limited at any one time to five and their purpose apparently was to be limited and transitory, as Mr. Drury explained to the House:

> Ministers of state for designated purposes would...be charged with responsibilities for developing new and comprehensive policies in areas where the development of such policies is of particular urgency and important; have a mandate effectively determined by the prime minister which would be of such duration as to enable them to come to

> grips with the policy problems assigned to them; . . . they would preside over ministries which would eventually either become parts of new or existing departments or whose existence would be terminated.[36]

One of the first of the new Ministers of State, explaining the role of his Ministry of State for Urban Affairs, enlarged on the role which was conceived for him and his officials:

> [The Ministry] is not a department. It will not take directly unto itself any program delivery capability. I think the very nature and complexity of the issues we are facing argues against the concept that policy emerges only from those entrusted with its administration. It embraces the concept that objective policy development across a broad range of activities and authorities can emerge when unfettered by the vested interest that grows from administering programs. . . . The Ministry. . . is so named because its policy mandate is unrestricted and as wide as possible while its direct operational role is non-existant [sic].[37]

There are some legal and administrative ambiguities here. Ministry is a new term in Canada and it is not clear whether this implies a difference in legal status between a ministry of state and a department. The matter was made more ambiguous because the Department of Transport, at the same time, had begun to call itself a Ministry for a totally different reason. To the people in Transport the "ministry concept" embraced not only the department, but also the autonomous crown agencies, such as the St. Lawrence Seaway Authority, which reported to Parliament through the minister.[38]

The Ministries of State involve a novel method of solving the perennial problem of policy co-ordination through the creation of co-ordinating ministers unencumbered by heavy operational responsibilities. The earlier experiments with this type of ministry did little to suggest that the problem had been solved. The ministers who held the first two portfolios (Urban Affairs and Science and Technology) were either relatively junior or else were senior ministers who at the same time held another and more important portfolio. On the rare occasions when their deputy heads (dubbed Secretaries of the Ministry) have been senior and powerful officials they have been moved rapidly onward to more prestigious departments. Thus ministers and officials did not hold a strong position in the

36. Canada. *House of Commons Debates.* January 26, 1971. p. 2772.

37. *Ibid.* June 28, 1971. p. 7146. See also G. Bruce Doern and Peter Aucoin (eds.) *The Structures of Policy-Making in Canada* (Toronto, 1971) pp. 57-8.

38. See John W. Langford, *Transport in Transition* (Montreal and London, 1976)

decision-making hierarchy. Thus their capacity to co-ordinate either inter-departmental negotiations or exert authority through the Cabinet committee system has been questionable, and the Treasury Board was quite unwilling to give up its own process of policy analysis to them.[39]

Nevertheless, if the Minister of State's position is reinforced by the chairmanship of the relevant Cabinet committee, and his position is politically strong and backed by first-class administrative support, his position in the Cabinet can be a very powerful one. The creation of what is now called the Ministry of State for Economic Development in the last days of the first Trudeau government and the Ministry of State for Social Development, initiated by Clark and carried on by the second Trudeau government, seem to have led to a more effective definition of roles. Under Clark such ministers (who were also chairmen of policy sub-committees) were members of the Inner Cabinet. Under Trudeau they are members of the Committee on Priorities and Planning, which is looking more and more like an inner Cabinet. As Senator Murray said "...decisions are, in fact, taken by the Committee on Planning and Priorities (sic) which, of course, binds the whole government and for which, according to the conventions of cabinet solidarity, the entire government takes responsibility. In other words, what we have under another name is an inner Cabinet and an outer Cabinet, the only difference being that with the present government we do not know who the members of the inner Cabinet are."[40]

If there are super-ministers beginning to be discernable at the top, there may be mini-ministers becoming visible at the bottom. These are the second class of Ministers of State provided in the 1971 reorganization. They are simply in charge of particular programs within another minister's department and in the end subject to his

39. This point is forcibly argued by Bruce Doern in his *Science and Politics in Canada* (Montreal, 1972) pp. 200-5. See also J. R. Mallory "Restructuring the Government of Ontario: A Comment." *Canadian Public Administration* XVI:1 (Spring, 1973) pp. 69-72. In spite of what Mr. Drury said in introducing the Bill, it should be noted that both of the first two Ministries of State (Urban Affairs and Science and Technology) were in fields which are largely in provincial jurisdiction. Urban Affairs was terminated in 1979. The most useful discussion of the Ministry of State problem is in Peter Aucoin and Richard French, *Knowledge, Power and Public Policy* (Ottawa, Science Council of Canada, 1974).

40. Canada. *Senate Debates.* April 24, 1980, p. 117. In fact we now know who they are. After initially refusing to do so, on the ground that how the Cabinet does its business is a matter domestic to the administration, the Trudeau government now publishes membership lists of Cabinet committees. See, e.g. Canada. *House of Commons Debates.* October 14, 1981. pp. 11801-3.

final authority. In the Trudeau Cabinet before 1979 they were clearly less important than departmental ministers but they appeared to retain all of the other advantages of Cabinet rank such as membership of Cabinet committees and access to all Cabinet documents which were not specially restricted (such as those of Priorities and Planning and Security and Intelligence). Under Clark however, these Ministers of State were at first put in a more clearly subordinate position, excluded from both the inner Cabinet and the main Cabinet committees. This exclusion from committees did not last more than a few months. Nevertheless, in the long run it is hard to see how these ministers can continue to claim real equality with departmental ministers.

Parliamentary secretaries (or parliament assistants, as they were called when these offices were introduced by Mackenzie King in 1943) are not, properly speaking, members of the administration. Under the provisions of the Government Organization Act of 1971 their number cannot, at any one time, exceed the number of Ministers as described in the Salaries Act (that is, not including Ministers of State or Ministers Without Portfolio). They are not required to take an oath of office. New appointments may not be made until the writ of election of the appointees has been returned following a general election.[41] Upon dissolution of Parliament the appointments lapse. Parliamentary secretaries are appointed by minute of council, and authority for payment of their salaries is provided by appropriate items in the Estimates. Ministers' salaries, on the other hand, are provided for in the Salaries Act.

It remains to be seen how far parliamentary secretaries will fit fully into the Cabinet system. To a certain extent, they are an apprentice-system for the Cabinet, given an occasional opportunity to demonstrate their "ministerial" skill in the House. Pierre Trudeau developed a consistent policy of rotating back-benchers through these posts so after two years they would find themselves relegated to the back-benches again as a new group was appointed.[42]

41. They do not have to be appointed even then. Mr. Diefenbaker did not appoint any parliamentary assistants at all in the first session of the Twenty-fourth Parliament. When he did so, in the subsequent session, he returned to the former designation of them as parliamentary secretaries.

42. This was explained by Mr. Trudeau, "If the hon. member wishes to refer to the practice established in the previous parliament, he will see that it was to give parliamentary secretaries what I call a double term so they would be in office for a period of approximately two years. It figures that this would permit the rotation of a large number of our talent within a given parliament. . .and at the same time to permit a stint in office which should be long enough to allow a member to acquire a good experience as a parliamentary secretary." Canada. *House of Commons Debates.* January 8, 1974. p. 9144.

A parliamentary secretary occupies a peculiar position at the same time connected with, and distinct from, the administration. He is often the spokesman for departmental policy, both in the House and in public speeches. A minister may, if he wishes, delegate to his parliamentary secretary some of his responsibilities in the department (this is a matter of internal departmental administration, which does not affect the overall responsibility of the minister). On the other hand, a parliamentary secretary is not a member of the government and is not bound by the same degree of administrative solidarity as a Cabinet minister. Thus, there have been instances of parliamentary assistants putting questions on the order paper addressed to other ministers, and of parliamentary assistants making statements in the House as private members.

Although a minister has primary and undisputed authority over his department, his absence, or inability to act, in no way interferes with the smooth running of the machinery of government. The appointment of acting ministers enables departments to operate in the absence of ministers. The Governor-in-Council has the power by statute to appoint an acting minister, and such appointment gives the acting minister full power. Acting ministers may be appointed with the right to act in the absence of a particular minister, or when a portfolio is vacant through the death or resignation of a minister, or in the formative stages of an administration while the Prime Minister is completing the process of Cabinet-making.[43]

The Cabinet at Work

The Cabinet is, above all, a committee to negotiate.[44] That is to say, its primary purpose is to reach agreement on what the policy of the government is to be. It is the policy-making organ of government. While it is true that Parliament gives legal effect to policy by legislating and by appropriating funds for specific programs, it is the Cabinet which decides what Parliament is to legislate about. The

43. The second Meighen ministry (1926) consisted largely of acting ministers, but this was to avoid the necessity of ministers vacating their seats in the House of Commons on assuming office, as was then required by the Dominion Elections Act. This situation lasted until July 13, when the Cabinet was re-constituted in the normal manner after Parliament had been dissolved.

44. K. C. Wheare, *Government by Committee* (London, 1955) *passim*.

second function of the Cabinet is to co-ordinate the separate departments of government into which the executive has been divided. The third function is to supervise the administration of policy which has been laid down by the legislature.[45]

These three functions require, for optimum efficiency, different kinds of Cabinets. For decision-making, the smaller the Cabinet the better.[46] For co-ordination the Cabinet should be large so that every aspect of administration is represented in it. The increase in the number of provinces and of interests to be represented, together with the great growth of demands on government in the last generation, have increased the size of the Cabinet from Macdonald's original thirteen ministers to the present size of over thirty.[47] As a consequence there have been substantial organizational changes within the Cabinet in order that its various functions can be discharged in an appropriate way.

It is sometimes argued that a minister in charge of a department should be above all a first-class administrator. But a minister must be many things. It is equally important that he be a good committee man and a good parliamentarian. It has also been argued with force that the common sense of the layman is a necessary balance to the specialized view of the expert. "The truth is," said Walter Bagehot, "that a skilled bureaucracy is, though it boasts an appearance of science, quite inconsistent with the true principles of the art of business. . . . One of the most sure principles is that success depends on a due mixture of special and non-special minds—of minds which attend to the means and of minds which attend to the end."[48]

The place where the Cabinet works and the time of meeting have changed in response to changes in the needs of government. Originally it met, as it had in the Province of Canada before Confederation, in the Privy Council Chamber in the East Block. There the ministers sat around the table which had been provided for formal meetings of the Privy Council. When the number of ministers increased after the Second World War the table became oval by a

45. See *Report of the Machinery of Government Committee.* Cd. 9230 (London, 1919).

46. "the Cabinet should be smaller in number—preferably ten, or, at most, twelve." *Ibid* p. 5.

47. As Sir John A. Macdonald said, "the great object of securing a full Cabinet, was that each province of the Dominion might be fully represented." P. A. C. *Canadian Parliamentary Debates,* 1866–1870, April 3, 1868.

48. Bagehot, *The English Constitution,* p. 174.

skilful addition in the middle. Then that table became too small and more and more meetings were shifted to the larger room near the Prime Minister's room in the Centre Block, which had normally been used when the House of Commons was in session. Finally, in 1979, it was moved again, along with the Privy Council Office and the Prime Minister's Office, across Wellington Street to the Langevin Building. Frequent, often daily, meetings were standard through the Diefenbaker years when the Cabinet seemed overwhelmed by detail. Thereafter the revival and refinement of the Cabinet committee system removed much of the business from the Cabinet room into committees so that the full Cabinet has now come to meet once a week, usually on Thursday. During the brief Clark ministry, full Cabinet met even less frequently, about every two or three weeks.

There has been an equally great change in the atmosphere. While Macdonald's Cabinets appeared from the early records to have sent out for food and liquid refreshment, later Cabinets became more formal. When Borden permitted smoking in the Union Government after 1917 it was noted that the atmosphere was more relaxed. However, neither Bennett nor King permitted smoking in the Cabinet, except on the occasion when Winston Churchill was provided with cigars. Nevertheless, Cabinet meetings retain a degree of formality unlike Cabinet committees where ministers will be "entering and leaving, taking phone calls, eating lunch, reading correspondence, and passing messages to one another."[49]

One of the nineteenth century traditions about British Cabinets was that the discussion was carried out with a complete absence of paper of any kind, although the Prime Minister was sometimes permitted to make a note of important topics of discussion. This was never possible in Canada, since the Cabinet was also acting as "the Committee of the Privy Council," recording its decisions in minutes and orders in council. For this purpose there was a box on the table in front of the Prime Minister. On one side of the box were draft submissions. If Cabinet approved a submission it was signed then and there, and placed in the other side of the box. After the meeting had concluded the Clerk of the Privy Council prepared the approved submissions for transmission to the Governor General, and sought the Prime Minister's direction as to whether those not approved

49. Richard D. French, "The Privy Council Office: Support for Cabinet Decision Making." in Richard Schultz, Orest M. Kruhlak, and John C. Terry, *The Canadian Political Process.* Third Edition. (Toronto, 1979) p. 366.

should be regarded as withdrawn or should be sent back for modification and re-submission. Almost all business before Cabinet took the form of draft minutes or orders, though occasionally the Cabinet discussed business which did not require formal submissions and therefore was not a matter of record at all. There was no systematic requirement that such submissions should have prior discussion among affected ministers or departments, although such prior discussion, in many cases, smoothed the passage of proposals.

There was no agenda. In Mackenzie King's time he alone had a folder in front of him, which he would occasionally consult. Generally he would allow ministers to bring up matters by permitting them to speak in order of seniority. Therefore, there was no direct way of ensuring that urgent matters could be dealt with quickly. The representative nature of the Cabinet reinforced the tendency for it to be swamped with detailed questions which were bound to reach it because they were politically sensitive to some minister preoccupied with the management of the political details in his district.

The principle of "diffusion of power"[50] which underlies the operation of central government in the Canadian federal system gave to the operation of ministerial responsibility a special structure. This was clearly set out in an order-in-council of June 14, 1904, relieving the Earl of Dundonald from his duties as General Officer Commanding the Canadian Militia:

> In the case of members of the Cabinet, while all have an equal degree of responsibility in a constitutional sense, yet in the practical working out of responsible government in a country of such vast extent as Canada, it is found necessary to attach a special responsibility to each Minister for the public affairs of the province or district with which he has close political connection, and with which his colleagues may not be so well acquainted.[51]

In short, in matters referring to a particular district, even the responsible minister deferred to the wishes of the minister from that district. This federalization of responsibility applied even to the

50. For the "diffusion of power" see W. L. Morton, "Formation of the First Federal Cabinet." *Canadian Historical Review* XXXVI:2 (June, 1955) p. 122.

51. Canada. *Sessional Papers.* No. 113, 1904, p. 2. The issue in this case was the General's action in seeking to raise a militia unit in the Eastern Townships which was an area of political responsibility for the Minister of Agriculture. Being innocent of the close connection between political patronage and militia commissions, Dundonald had ignored the fact that such appointments were intended to go to the political friends of the government of the day.

Prime Minister.[52] It was this crossing of lines of responsibility, between the minister's legal responsibility for his department and his conventional responsibility for his district, that had made it necessary for so many detailed matters to be brought to Cabinet. This tendency was reinforced by the requirement, either by statute or custom, that so many executive acts should be by order-in-council. Only in recent years has this tendency begun to weaken, and in the 1952 revision of the statutes a conscious attempt was made to reduce the number of matters requiring action by the Governor-in-Council rather than by the minister alone. An extreme example is contained in a letter from Lord Grey to Laurier which lists some prize examples of trivia submitted from Council for his approval, including the appointment of three police constables, dispensing with the services of a veterinary inspector, the removal from the effective list of veterinarians of the name of a dead man, and two leases of land belonging to the Intercolonial Railway for respectively five and six dollars per annum.[53]

Sir George Murray, who was commissioned by Sir Robert Borden in 1912 to make a study of the organization of the public service, stressed the same point: "nothing has impressed me so much in the course of my inquiry," he wrote, "as the almost intolerable burden which the present system of transacting business imposes on Ministers themselves."[54] Senator McLennan, the Chairman of the Senate Committee on the Machinery of Government, referred to the same problem in a speech to the Senate on March 21, 1919:

> Consider the work of a Minister holding an important portfolio. He attends Council daily probably over two hours or more on the average; he spends part of his time there in passing routine orders-in-council. He attends meetings of committees; he carries on the work of his

52. Laurier once had occasion to remind a supporter of this rule. He wrote: "I have had for some time your letter concerning the Senate. The time is approaching when we must make an appointment, and I will confer immediately with my colleagues from the Province of Ontario...but, as you know and I have already told you on several occasions, this appointment is one which chiefly belongs to my colleagues from your Province. It is true that I have the supreme word in all these matters, but you know those things as well as I do. The one who has supreme word has always to rely upon his advisors. In so far as my own Province is concerned, I am the first and the last judge; but in the other provinces, though I am the last, I am not the first judge, and with all this, you are quite familiar..." P.A.C.. *Laurier Papers* March 6, 1899 (30594).

53. P.A.C. *Laurier Papers* (207164-8).

54. Canada. *Sessional Papers.* No. 57A, 1913, para. 5.

> Department—there is scarcely any caller to whom he can deny himself. He has to look after the interests of his district and his constituency and the applications of everyone therein who wants anything from the government. He has his Parliamentary duties. The day for the Minister or for ordinary people is only twenty-four hours. Where in it is his time for deliberations?[55]

Sir George Murray's solution was for the "division of labour and devolution of power." By this he meant, first, that for the consideration of routine business a special quorum of ministers should be summoned instead of bringing such business before the whole Cabinet, and second, that more power should be delegated to individual ministers. Both recommendations were to foreshadow the development of forty years later, but no direct action was taken on them in Sir Robert Borden's time, except as temporary wartime expedients. The government's difficulties in pushing its controversial naval policy through Parliament in 1913, the mounting danger of war and the general difficulties which confront a new government, inhibited action. The use of the Special Committee of Council to handle routine orders-in-council, which became a regular procedure after the Second World War, precisely met Sir George Murray's recommendation for a quorum of ministers. His second proposal, a devolution of authority from the Cabinet as a whole to individual ministers, was also a development which was to follow the Second World War rather than the First. It finally came in an age when patronage was less important to ministers and when the growing complexity of government business had moved a very wide range of decisions downward so that they came to be settled by officials, simply because Cabinet could not deal with a fraction of them. Nevertheless, even in the Trudeau years, the last item on the weekly agenda, dealing with order-in-council appointments was still a Cabinet matter which was frequently time-consuming and contentious.

The Modernization of the Cabinet

If Sir George Murray's proposals were made before the time was ripe for their adoption, there was one modification of Cabinet procedure which was made necessary by the First World War. This was the

55. Canada. *Senate Debates.* March 21, 1919.

beginning of the Cabinet committee system. This had been urged on Canada and the other Dominions at a special conference on imperial defence in 1909 when, at the instigation of Sir Maurice Hankey, the Secretary of the Committee of Imperial Defence, the Dominions were urged to create Cabinet defence committees and to prepare "war books" of detailed plans to deal with a war emergency.[56] Sir Joseph Pope returned from the conference with plans for the war book, and it was from such plans that the emergency measures of 1914 were prepared.[57]

There was, however, no defence committee set up until October 6, 1917, when the Union Government was divided into two committees, a War Committee and a Committee on Reconstruction and Development, with ten members each.[58] These two bodies do not seem to have outlasted the war period, and it was not until 1936 that the Cabinet Defence Committee was organized, "at the earnest solicitation of the Canadian General Staff. This committee included the Prime Minister and the Ministers of Justice and Finance, in addition to the Minister of National Defence. It was, in effect, a small commiteee of the Cabinet, without executive authority like its counterpart in Great Britain, but which, supported by the expert advice of the service chiefs, exercised important advisory and consultative functions."[59]

The outbreak of war in 1939 led to an unprecedented flowering of Cabinet committees. Ten were functioning by the end of 1939, and the end of the war led, not to the disappearance of committees, but simply to an adaptation of the system to the responsibilities of postwar government. The wartime system of Cabinet government had two unusual features. The War Committee, while it nominally reported to the full Cabinet, virtually displaced it for the duration of the war. This has been a characteristic of the adaptation of Cabinet government to war conditions. The War Cabinets of Lloyd George and Winston Churchill, like that of Mackenzie King, not only displaced the full Cabinet for most purposes during the war, but also wielded such exceptional authority that they represented something very close to dictatorship by the executive for the duration. A

56. Amery, *Thoughts on the Constitution.* p. 116.

57. Borden. *Memoirs.* I. pp. 453-5.

58. *Ibid.* pp. 758-9.

59. George F. G. Stanley. *Canada's Soldiers.* rev. ed. (Toronto, 1960) p. 347. See Also C. P. Stacey *Arms, Men and Governments.* (Ottawa, 1970), who notes that until the outbreak of war the committee was neither very active nor very important.

second notable characteristic of the wartime committee system was that the distribution of responsibility into Cabinet committees became a matter of public knowledge and record. After the war, governments reverted to the practice of regarding such matters as "domestic to the administration" and refused to disclose the details of the internal operations of the Cabinet. However, in recent years it has become normal to disclose the names of Cabinet committees but not their composition. This practice was abandoned by the Clark government, which announced the composition of all Cabinet committees. The returning Trudeau government, after initially resisting, finally gave way and now tables in the House both the minute of council designating acting ministers and a full list of the membership of Cabinet committees.

The reasons given in the past for cloaking the operations of Cabinet committees in secrecy was that all decisions of this sort are the collective responsibility of the Cabinet, whether particular ministers had primary responsibility for initiating a decision or not. As Mackenzie King once said, "Because of the general principle of collective responsibility it has always been recognized that matters [relating to the proceedings and organization of the Cabinet]...are necessarily secret....The responsibility of the Cabinet, however, remains a collective responsibility and organization into committees is merely a matter of procedural convenience."[60] As a consequence, it was not considered appropriate to inform the public or Parliament of the composition of Cabinet committees, or whether a particular decision was taken by a Cabinet committee or by Cabinet as a whole. This position was supported by a ruling by Mr. Speaker Michener, who ruled that "an inquiry into the method by which the government arrives at its decision in cabinet is entirely out of order....As I understand the situation the decision of the government is one and indivisible. Inquiry into how it was arrived at and particularly inquiry into the cabinet process is not permitted in the house."[61] The general principle of collective responsibility still stands, but no harm to the polity seems to have come from making the process more open.

These quotations suggest the relationship of Cabinet committees to the process of Cabinet government. They are not a substitute for the Cabinet, but an elaboration of it. To facilitate the conduct of business, much of the preliminary and some of the final discussion

60. Canada. *House of Commons Debates.* February 10, 1947, pp. 251-2.

61. *Ibid.* November 6, 1957, p. 813.

is carried on in committees. Cabinet committees act as screening and filtering devices for the consideration of questions which are not, for one reason or another, in a form suitable for disposition in Cabinet. They may be brought directly to the committee or referred to it by Cabinet. In this way business reaches the attention of Cabinet at a time and in a form which permits of effective disposition.

In the overriding interest of wartime efficiency it was possible to impose an effective committee system on Cabinet government in Canada, but it represented a major structural modification of the time-hallowed federal nature of decision-making. Even in wartime it is probable that a number of Cabinet committees had little more than a paper existence. As Gordon Robertson pointed out, "the very fact of having committees meant more discussion of at least designated subjects." But C. D. Howe, J. G. Gardiner and other monarchs of sovereign areas brooked little interference with what was theirs. "The evolution did not go far."[62] While the Cabinet committee system was at least nominally in full operation from the early months of World War II, the work of Cabinet committees was much of the time ephemeral and *ad hoc. Ad hoc* committees to deal with particular problems sometimes enjoyed a brief and active life. Standing committees, in the St. Laurent years and even more under Diefenbaker, were prone to atrophy.

Although inevitable, the transition from informality to a structured decision-making process was slow and intermittent. It depended in part on the personal style which the Prime Minister brought to the Cabinet. In Mackenzie King's time, as Mitchell Sharp recalls, "the tradition was an oral one, and the recommendations of ministers were seldom rejected. Cabinet agenda were reasonably flexible so that matters could be raised of which notice had not been given. Very few records were kept. . . . Proposals by ministers came before cabinet in the first instance and only in the event of disagreement were they referred to ministerial committees which were more often than not *ad hoc.*"[63] Things became somewhat more formalized in Mr. St. Laurent's time. Business had become more complex and the Prime Minister was "a well co-ordinated chairman." King normally left his ministers to take the lead and only intervened to settle disputes, except where questions seemed to

62. Gordon Robertson, "The Changing Role of the Privy Council Office." *Canadian Public Administration.* XIV:4 (Winter, 1971) p. 498.

63. Mitchell Sharp. "Decision-making in the Federal Cabinet." *Canadian Public Administration.* XIX:1 (Spring, 1976). p. 3.

him to be politically sensitive or to concern his own department of External Affairs. St. Laurent, on the other hand, "would hold private discussions with ministers, then take the initiative, invite discussion, sum up the case pro and con, express his preference, and ask if there was any difference of view." Things did not change much under Mr. Diefenbaker, and decision-making was centred, to a large extent, on the Prime Minister, though Cabinet meetings were frequent, long, and often inconclusive.

All this began to change during the Pearson administration. On January 20, 1964, a radical restructuring of the Cabinet committee system was announced. The essence of the change was that "rather than being oriented towards specific *ad hoc* problems or operations, they were for the first time directed towards defined areas of the total government process."[64] Whereas before matters went first to Cabinet and then were referred to committees if need be, the new procedure required that most matters needing Cabinet decisions must first be brought by the minister concerned to the appropriate standing committee. A further important change was the creation, in January, 1968, of the Committee on Priorities and Planning, chaired by the Prime Minister. The need for a better decision-making process was clearly evident.

Up to that time continued economic growth had made it possible for governments to finance new programs out of a steadily growing gross national product. From that time onwards slow growth and periodic recession made this steady expansion no longer possible. If expensive new programs were demanded in future it must be at the expense of old and less desirable ones. Hard choices had become inevitable and continued to be a major problem of governments ever since.

One of Mr. Trudeau's first acts as Prime Minister was to extend and improve the Cabinet committee system, and to provide regular meeting times. The committees were in effect given the power not simply to recommend action, but to take decisions. Nevertheless, this had to be done in a way which protected the rights and interest of ministers not on the committee, or not present when the decision was taken. This was done by sending them the agenda and documents of all committees, except those of Priorities and Planning. Then they could decide if they had an interest to assert and whether they wished to attend the committee. All committee decisions of this type were then circulated as an annex to the next Cabinet

64. Robertson. "The Changing Role..." p. 490. See also Doern and Aucoin. *The Structures of Policy-Making in Canada*.

agenda. If a minister did not notify the secretariat in advance of his objection, the decision was deemed to be approved as a Cabinet decision.[65]

The first effect of the re-structuring of the Cabinet was to tilt decision-making further in the direction of being functional and managerial and less politically sensitive to the political pressures of federalism. Ministers were compelled to look at decisions, particularly in Cabinet committees, in terms of their departmental responsibilities in relation to the broad functional areas of government. Since in the past proposals usually reached Cabinet in a form in which inter-departmental differences had previously been worked out by consultation within the higher public service, the opportunity to consider alternatives at the ministerial level was thereby diminished. This was a trend which Mr. Trudeau sought to reverse when he became Prime Minister. This he sought to do by having senior officials present at Cabinet committee meetings and requiring that policy alternatives and departmental differences should be considered at that point rather than by prior negotiation among deputy ministers. "If ministerial responsibility were to be meaningful, something had to be done." After much intense thought it was decided "to change the system, to allow cabinet committees chaired by ministers to do the assessments and make the subsequent judgment which formerly had been done in full Cabinet. This would allow Cabinet to focus on final alternatives, knowing that the basic work and discussion had already taken place." This had not been easy to institute because of "ingrained method," but the attempt had been made.

> First, we wanted more decisions to be taken at the ministerial level. Second, we wanted to ensure that ministers had soundly researched alternatives from which to choose. Third, we wanted to aid ministers to make a conscious choice of priorities in the full knowledge of the real

65. The standing committee structure comprised five "functional" committees which dealt with areas of government activity—External Policy and Defence; Economic Policy; Social Policy; Science, Culture, and Information; and Government Operations (a catch-all for matters not covered by the others). A further four committees had a co-ordinating role—Priorities and Planning; Treasury Board; Legislation and House Planning; and Federal-Provincial Relations. "Other special committees," wrote Robertson, "deal, at irregular intervals, as required, with questions relating to security and intelligence, the public service, and a few other matters." *Ibid.* p. 490. The documentation of the committee on security and intelligence was highly restricted in circulation, being kept on a "need to know" basis. Priorities and Planning and Federal-Provincial Relations, which had the same membership, had become by 1978, virtually the same committee.

pressures which were being placed on their colleagues. Fourth, we wanted to extend dialogue between ministers and officials, and not just officials from their own departments. What we wanted was to let departmental concerns cross the border of one department, with officials from other departments being subject to questions and participating in the discussion with ministers of other departments.[66]

Cabinet Secretariat

The need for a comprehensive record of Cabinet decisions became clear in Canada much later than in the United Kingdom, where the problems of wartime administration led to the creation of the secretariat as early as 1915. No such organization was introduced in Canada until 1940, unless one takes into account the somewhat vague provisions for a secretariat to the Committee on Reconstruction in 1917. The reasons lay both in the small number of issues of major policy and in the existence of machinery that already recorded many Cabinet decisions in written form. Because the Cabinet had developed as "the" Committee of the Privy Council, and the practice had grown up of embodying a great many important decisions in orders-in-council or minutes of council, it was possible for a long time to get along without a secretariat. However, while most decisions were embodied, in a somewhat ungainly form, in Privy Council instruments, there were many that were unrecorded, except perhaps in the uncertain form of a manuscript note by the Prime Minister.[67]

The recognition that some sort of support agency was needed for the Prime Minister in his role of leader of the Cabinet was at first muddled because it was seen as part of the problem of getting

66. Canada. *House of Commons Debates.* May 22, 1975. p. 6013. See also J. R. Mallory "The Two Clerks: Parliamentary Discussion of the Role of the Privy Council Office." *Canadian Journal of Political Science.* X:1 (March, 1977), p. 3.

67. W. E. D. Halliday. "The Privy Council Office and Cabinet Secretariat in Relation to the Development of Cabinet Government." *Canada Year Book*, 1956. The problems that can be created by the absence of records are illustrated by what happened in Nova Scotia in the nineteen-sixties. "When the cabinet finished the agenda, it turned to other matters, often matters with sensitive political overtones, and Stanfield kept a record of the decisions taken in a little book he carried with him. That practice distressed the Liberals when they returned to office and could not find Stanfield's little book. 'We could never be certain what had been decided in cabinet before,' complained Premier Gerry Regan." Geoffrey Stevens, *Stanfield* (Toronto, 1973) p. 110.

adequate support for the Prime Minister in his position as party leader with a heavy burden of correspondence and the need for political intelligence on his behalf. A Prime Minister's department as such had never developed in Canada and successive Prime Ministers had to make do with a private secretary and a small ancillary staff together with whatever additional staff could be utilized from whatever portfolio the Prime Minister held. However, as early as 1927, Mackenzie King had begun to feel the need for a sort of political chief of staff to assist him both in his political role and to assist in keeping a closer hold on the operation of Cabinet business.[68] What he appeared to have in mind was a sort of unobtrusive political *eminence grise* to perform the functions which he fancied were performed in the United Kingdom by Sir Maurice Hankey and Thomas Jones. For this purpose he sought out Burgon Bickersteth, Warden of Hart House. Bickersteth, who had taken the trouble to talk to both Hankey and Jones while on a visit to England tried hard to make clear to King the different roles played in British government by the Cabinet secretariat and the Prime Minister's official and personal staff. In the end Bickersteth refused the appointment and the matter was not revived for almost ten years.

The growing burdens of government on the eve of war brought the matter forward again. King in the meantime solved some of his own staffing problems by treating his Undersecretary of State for External Affairs as a sort of chief of staff for domestic as well as external problems, and by seconding promising young officers from that department as his personal staff. This had the further advantage of giving to the Prime Minister the image of frugality in his personal staffing arrangements since their salaries were borne on departmental estimates. It has even been said that his personal stenographer who had served him since his days in the Department of Labour was paid until her retirement by her original department. But there was still far too much to do and the Prime Minister still needed someone to work under him on the organization of Cabinet business. He sought the advice of the Governor General, Lord Tweedsmuir, who told him essentially what he had heard from Bickersteth. Although King had started his public life as a civil servant, he did not have the typical civil servant's fondness for tidy organization to improve the conduct of business. It was people, not organizations, on which he relied. However, the man he found, Arnold Heeney, was determined to create an office and a role for himself on the model of the

68. See J. R. Mallory. "Mackenzie King and the Origins of the Cabinet Secretariat." *Canadian Public Administration.* XIX:2 (Winter, 1976) p. 254.

British system. In spite of King's obtuseness, he succeeded where a lesser man might have failed, but the real reason for the development of the Cabinet secretariat in its modern form was that the needs of wartime government made it indispensible.

Early in 1940, Heeney was appointed Clerk of the Privy Council and Secretary to the Cabinet. His duties were defined as (a) to prepare, for the approval of the Prime Minister, such agenda for Cabinet meetings as might be required; (b) to keep notes of Cabinet meetings and conclusions thereof as might be required; (c) to prepare and submit to members of the Cabinet, in advance, information as might be necessary for their deliberations; (d) to communicate to ministers, departments and others concerned the decisions of the Cabinet; (e) to maintain a liaison between the Cabinet and committees thereof; and (f) such other duties as might from time to time be assigned to him by the Governor-in-Council.[69] In fact the assumption of some of these duties was a gradual process. Heeney regularly attended the War Committee, but not the Cabinet, though he began to be in attendance of the latter by the end of the war. It was not until Mr. St. Laurent became Prime Minister that Cabinet itself was attended regularly by members of the secretariat and all ministers regularly received Cabinet minutes.

The Secretary to the Cabinet has under his direction a small staff of officers who are on the establishment of the Privy Council Office. The creation of the secretariat is a striking example of the flexibility of the central executive machinery under Cabinet government, for this revolutionary change was accomplished quite simply by order-in-council. The Governor-in-Council possesses by statute the power to impose upon deputy heads of departments duties in addition to those prescribed by statute, so that it was only necessary to graft the new title (Secretary to the Cabinet) onto the ancient office of Clerk of the Privy Council and to set forth the additional duties required in the order-in-council. This arrangement persisted until 1974. However, late in that year the government brought in a bill to create the new office of Secretary to the Cabinet for Federal-Provincial Relations and, for reasons of administrative tidiness, the earlier office of Clerk of the Privy Council and Secretary to the Cabinet was given a statutory base as well. However the bill made no specification of the

69. P. C. 1121 of March 20, 1940. Heeney's own authoritative account of the genesis and role of the office is contained in his "Cabinet Government in Canada: Some recent Developments in the Machinery of the Central Executive." *Canadian Journal of Economics and Political Science* XII:2 p. 282. He tells some more of the story in his autobiography, *The Things that are Caesar's* (Toronto, 1972.)

latter's duties, which are still based on their original formulation.[70]

The role of the Cabinet secretariat will naturally vary with the style of government which suits the taste of the Prime Minister and Cabinet of the day. Its role will be greater or less depending on the inclination of its political masters. As Arnold Heeney pointed out over thirty years ago, "under our Cabinet system the machinery of executive government must serve and not hamper the freedom of action of the political authority. Cabinet procedure and organization must in large measure be of an *ad hoc* nature, capable of rapid change and development to meet the needs of the hour, sensitive in these matters as in all else to the requirements of the day."[71]

The presence of the secretariat in Cabinet and committee meetings, the keeping of records of decisions together with a summary account of the discussion, and the elaborate documentation required before a proposal can be considered, have, to a degree, transformed these meetings into a form which is much more structured than the studied informality of the past. This process was carried a stage further under the Clark administration. In an interview published in *Le Devoir* on November 9, 1979, Mr. Roch LaSalle revealed that simultaneous translation had been introduced in the Cabinet and the Treasury Board. The reason for this was that Mr. LaSalle, who was the only elected francophone minister from Quebec and a member of the Inner Cabinet, was insufficiently fluent in English while many of his colleagues had even less command of French.

While the primary function of the secretariat is to serve the Cabinet, it is also in a "gatekeeper" role between the Cabinet and ministers seeking approval for proposals. It is important that it should not constitute itself as a sort of elite body in relation to the rest of the public service. It is not healthy, as Sir Winston Churchill once observed, to spend one's life in exalted brooding over the work of others. For this reason it is settled policy, as far as possible, to limit the time which civil servants spend attached to the secretariat. According to Gordon Robertson, "The term of appointment is purposely kept short, three to five years with personnel on loan from all departments. Vigor and integrity are maintained, but an elite with any sense of separateness or difference is not permitted to form."[72] Nevertheless the secretariat, by its very nature, is one of the

70. See J. R. Mallory, "The Two Clerks: Parliamentary Discussion of the Role of the Privy Council Office"....

71. "Cabinet Government in Canada..." p. 282.

72. Robertson, "The Privy Council Office..." p. 506.

major co-ordinating agencies, along with the secretariat of the Treasury Board, and a more extended discussion of the key central agencies in the bureaucracy will be dealt with in the next chapter.

A Cabinet secretariat, like any other form of organization, is simply a means of ensuring the efficient conduct of business. It is subordinate to the purposes of the Prime Minister who, with the consent of his colleagues in the Cabinet, is charged with the responsibility for the efficient conduct of public business. Necessarily, the Prime Minister must retain wide freedom of determination. He

> must be the master of the Cabinet in matters of organization and procedure. With the assent of colleagues, but on his own initiative, Cabinet committees are established, their terms of reference defined, and their membership determined. In any question as to the method by which business is to be dealt with, by what Minister, by what Cabinet committee, the decision must be that of the Prime Minister. Upon his authority the sequence in which matters are to be discussed is determined, the agenda settled. For any reason which he deems sufficient, he may alter the order of business, even set aside completely an agenda already settled, in favour of other subjects of greater importance and urgency. He may suspend meetings, summon additional meetings, dispense with or extend the normal record kept by the secretary or modify or set aside in any particular the normal rules of procedure.[73]

There is a double problem of security in Cabinet discussion. The first problem is to keep matters secret until decision has been reached and can be announced in appropriate form. The second, for a government going out of office, is to ensure that the record of its most intimate discussions is not made freely available to its successors for purely political purposes. At the same time the continuity and conduct of government business require that such records as are appropriate be available to a successor government. Accordingly the decision of Mr. St. Laurent and Mr. Diefenbaker in 1957 during the transfer of administration was an important milestone.

> One of the questions which they had to decide—for the first time—was that of the disposition of Cabinet records. We may count ourselves fortunate that they agreed that the British tradition should be followed, and that the Secretary to the Cabinet should now be accepted as the custodian of Cabinet papers, responsible for determining what communication should be made thereof to succeeding administrations.

73. Heeney, "Cabinet Government in Canada..." p. 282. The essence of the procedure was once described by Mr. St. Laurent during consideration of the Privy Council Estimates by the House. Canada. *House of Commons Debates*. March 23, 1956. p. 1436.

> With that agreement, the Cabinet secretariat became a permanent institution of Canadian government.[74]

This agreement has now become fully established, and most recently confirmed by Mr. Clark in reply to a parliamentary question. He said, "There is an arrangement in place, as has been the case for some time now, in the event of a change of government where a senior official of the public service of Canada is custodian of documents and will refer back to the Prime Minister and the senior ministers of the former government with regard to the release of any such documents."[75]

The Prime Minister's Office and Ministers' Exempt Staff

Just as the Cabinet secretariat represents the continuity of the state as well as the essential support agency for the Prime Minister and the Cabinet in controlling the business of government, there must also be, as Mackenzie King perceived, a strong capability in a support agency for the Prime Minister as party leader. This is not a role which can be assumed by the Privy Council Office without compromising the neutrality of the public service.[76] Sir Maurice Hankey, who moulded the British Cabinet secretariat in its modern image, was careful never to appear publicly in the company of the Prime Minister. In Canada the only personal staff for the Prime Minister was, until the end of the King period, the provision of one or more private secretaries to write the less important letters and keep track of the files.

There is not only the business of arranging travel, speaking engagements for political party occasions and the like, and dealing with the mail which now amounts to several bags per day, but there are also other roles. A Prime Minister needs to keep in touch in some way with not only the mood of the party caucus but also have antennae out to sense the feeling of the grass roots of the party in the country. In a more leisured age, Mackenzie King was able to personally conduct an enormous private correspondence with countless

74. A. D. P. Heeney, "Mackenzie King and the Cabinet Secretariat" *Canadian Public Administration.* X:3 (September, 1967) p. 373.

75. Canada. *House of Commons Debates.* October 10, 1979. p. 25.

76. For the gradual clarification of the distinct roles of the Cabinet secretariat and the Prime Minister's personal staff see J. R. Mallory, "Mackenzie King and the Origins of the Cabinet Secretariat."

people all over the country, but this is no longer possible. There must be machinery for keeping in touch with the party militants across Canada. This is all the more necessary since national party organizations are basically electoral machines which go into cold storage between elections. There is also need for policy advice so that the Prime Minister has alternatives to the views of his departmental ministers and the bureaucracy. The Prime Minister's Office, which had played a modest role under previous Prime Ministers, began to play all of these additional roles under Pearson and reached its greatest expansion during the Trudeau years.

Marc Lalonde, who served as Principal Secretary in the early Trudeau period, has given an account of the role of the Prime Minister's Office. The distinction between it and the Privy Council Office, in Gordon Robertson's words, is that the Privy Council Office is "non-partisan, operationally oriented, yet politically sensitive" while the Prime Minister's Office is "partisan, politically oriented, yet operationally sensitive."[77] Lalonde adds, "What distinguishes PMO from the rest of the political process is that it serves the prime minister personally, that its purpose is not primarily advisory but functional, and that it is fully accountable to the prime minister."[78] The Prime Minister's Office is carried on the estimates of the Privy Council Office and it is, for obvious reasons, located physically in the same place. While the support staff, such as clerks, typists, and so forth are part of the regular public service its senior members are political appointees in the same way as the private office staffs of other ministers.[79]

Much of the work of the Prime Minister's Office is the purely service function of "budgetting the Prime Minister's time on a daily, weekly, and monthly basis; the provision of press services; the preparation of speeches and other public statements to be delivered by the prime minister himself; the briefing of the prime minister in advance of House question period, press interviews, meetings, conferences, etc.; the planning of the prime minister's travel, the scheduling and arrangement of the travel plans; the daily processing

77. Robertson, "The Privy Council Office..." p. 506.

78. Marc Lalonde, "The Changing Role of the Prime Minister's Office" *Canadian Public Administration* XIV:4 (Winter, 1971) p. 520.

79. See J. R. Mallory "The Minister's Office Staff: An Unreformed Part of the Public Service" *Canadian Public Administration* X:1 (March, 1967) p. 24. and, for a recent and fuller account Blair Williams "The Para-political Bureaucracy in Ottawa" Harold D. Clarke, Colin Campbell, F. Q. Quo, and Arthur Goddard (eds.) *Parliament, Policy and Representation.* (Toronto, 1980) p. 215.

of a large volume of mail and the writing of replies; the processing of material to and from the prime minister each day—mail to be signed, cabinet documents to be studied, reports and memoranda to be read, etc.; the preparation of statements and messages for publication, of anniversary messages, of messages of condolence, etc.; the handling of constituency mail, letters of invitation, requests for appointments and interviews, enquiries of all kinds from the public, the press, party officials, members of parliament, ministers' offices, etc."[80]

Apart from these necessary housekeeping duties, what does the PMO do? The Principal Secretary is "the Prime Minister's chief of staff and main personal political adviser." The Prime Minister's day normally begins with a meeting which includes the Clerk of the Privy Council and the Principal Secretary, along with one or two of their senior officers. In Marc Lalonde's time at least, the Principal Secretary, with the Prime Minister's approval, attended Cabinet committee meetings. One of his most important roles is to act as a link between the Prime Minister and the party caucus and with the extra-parliamentary party. This perhaps went too far in the early Trudeau years when M.P.s complained that the setting up of "regional desks" in the PMO represented an interference with their own role as the principal channel of communication with the party in their own regions.

One of the important roles, though one which must be assumed circumspectly, is to render policy advice to the Prime Minister without intruding on the constitutional and political roles of departmental ministers. The purpose of this role is to set up a sort of counter-bureaucracy so that the Prime Minister has alternative sources of policy advice to the established departmental policy positions. It would be impossible to do this across the whole range of government without setting up what in effect would be an alternative government to the Cabinet itself. Nevertheless, some degree of non-departmental policy advice opens up ways to bring in new and creative policies from outside the regular channels. Accordingly, the emphasis on policy advice has been selective, largely ignoring at any one time most policy areas. Thus, when Tom Kent was Principal Secretary to Mr. Pearson, the emphasis was on innovation in social policy. For part of the Trudeau years the concentration was on a review of defence and foreign policy and, subsequently, on economic policy. At the start of Mr. Clark's term, the emphasis seems to have been on appointments to senior posts in the

80. Lalonde, "The Changing Role...." pp. 520-1.

bureaucracy and the various crown agencies, as well as on economic policy.

The development of the Prime Minister's Office as a necessary part of the process of government must be seen as inevitable. It is important that a Prime Minister's time—which is a very scarce commodity—should be effectively planned and used, that letters should be answered, that the lonely summit of government should not be insensitive to the feelings of the party and the electorate. The existence of politically-oriented policy advice, in a political system based on party government, creates a healthy tension between the party which happens to be in office and the continuing machinery of the state which operates through the bureaucracy.

For somewhat similar reasons, private office staffs of an essentially political sort are needed by ministers. They have important political responsibilities to the party and to their region. Staff support for these activities is not a function appropriate to the departmental bureaucracy. It is not a function which they can or should perform with either skill or enthusiasm. Ministers also need sources of advice which come from other than their own officials. It is better that these activities are carried on openly, out of public funds, than have them supported clandestinely or out of the minister's own pocket.

4

The Administrative Machine

"The Government," writes Professor J. A. Corry, "is not merely imposing restraints; it is acting positively to accomplish a wide range of purposes. . . . This task requires vast resources of energy, foresight, and initiative which, in the negative state, were largely supplied by individuals operating on their own account."[1] In other words, more and more of our everyday actions are limited by the actions of the government and by the rules and prohibitions laid down by its agencies. Before 1939 the number of decisions made by the government in Ottawa was small enough that it was still possible for an able and energetic minister to know about every action taken by officials in his department. This is no longer true. The centre of gravity in making decisions has shifted from Cabinet ministers to the large staff of anonymous officials who, from day to day, exercise the powers of government. These officials are, of course, subject to the authority of ministers, who in turn are responsible to Parliament. But today, officials deal with so many decisions, many of which are highly complex and technical, that ministers are no longer the intimate part of the process of government they once were.

GOVERNMENT DECISION-MAKING

Under a system of Cabinet government, as Lawrence Lowell put it, the administration is divided into two great classes: political officers who must have seats in Parliament, and non-political officers who must abstain altogether from politics.[2] In spite of political biographies and memoirs, as well as the diaries and voluminous papers of

1. J. A. Corry and J. E. Hodgetts, *Democratic Government and Politics,* 3rd ed. (Toronto, 1959), p. 119.
2. Lawrence Lowell, *The Government of England,* Vol. I (New York, 1914), p. 145.

departed statesmen which good luck sometimes leaves in the path of the student, we can never know very much about how decisions at the summit are taken under the Canadian system of government. "It is unfortunate, from a research point of view," as Professor Hodgetts says, "that the most fateful decisions affecting the public weal should be made by the cabinet."[3] A cloak of solemn secrecy surrounds the transaction of Cabinet business and we can never know how a decision was reached or on what grounds. The same holds true in describing the decision-making activities of officials. Though some official, or committee of officials, made a particular decision, the notification of the decision will be made in the name of the minister, or possibly of the Cabinet, and these latter are the only agencies which, in a public constitutional sense, are accountable for the decision.[4]

In theory, the business of the official is simply to serve his political master by sorting out the day's business, relating it and the governing statutes and directives of higher political authority to what has been done in similar cases in the past, singling out the important from the unimportant, and then saying, if effect: "Here is the relevant data out of which you must decide. I have marshalled the arguments for and against and it seems that you should adopt course A rather than course B—but you may have other good reasons of your own to reject my advice and take another course." In part, this theory of the role of the civil servant comes from Walter Bagehot's distinction between the intense perception of the specialist mind, and the wider vision of the non-specialist mind. Theoretically, the expert is "on tap" and the layman (the minister) is "on top." This is the theory; the facts are necessarily different. A minister who found his desk piled high each morning with carefully marshalled alternatives would soon wrathfully demand more competent subordinates who knew his mind well enough to anticipate what decision he would make if he dealt with the question himself, and act accordingly. As long as his subordinates are alert enough to anticipate when he must know details in order to defend his administration of the department to Parliament and to the public, the minister can safely trust them to take decisions on his behalf. This is

3. J. E. Hodgetts, "The Civil Service and Policy Formation," *Canadian Journal of Economics and Political Science* XXIII, No. 4 (November 1957), p. 467.

4. "It is the established and general practice to preserve the anonymity of civil servants serving on the interdepartmental committees. It has already been indicated that this panel [the security panel] is made up of senior officers of those government departments and officers most concerned with security matters." Canada, *House of Commons Debates,* March 11, 1954, p. 2881.

not to say that the minister has merely become a figurehead and that the "real" government is the bureaucracy, but that there should exist a mutual confidence and comprehension between the minister and his officials, and that both must have a sense of proportion about their respective roles.[5]

Canadian senior civil servants, of very different generations, have summed up the work of the senior official:

"An Administrator is appointed as a matter of necessity to do things which must be done, and he should do those things which are necessary as quietly and unostentatiously as possible."[6]

"At the top level, the public administrator must be able to work closely with and loyally for his minister. He must be able to harmonize conflicting views and competing interests. He must be able to advise on, and, on occasion, participate in, the determination of policy and to interpret policy in general terms; and he must be able to create the conditions in which policy can be decided. He must direct the implementation of the administrative program; under his minister, he must assume responsibility for administrative organization and reorganization when necessary; and he must co-ordinate the administrative machine. To be able to do these things, he must have the capacity for abstraction and generalization. He must have intelligence, imagination and judgment, and a sense of purpose and direction. He must have skill in negotiation, facility in communication, and an ability to judge men. He must be willing to accept responsibility and be decisive yet flexible, and he must be able to delegate."[7]

5. "Many years ago there was a Labour Minister without previous ministerial experience who suddenly discovered that enormous numbers of letters were going out commencing 'I am directed by the Minister, & c.,' which he had not seen. The Minister was very indignant and said, 'Why do you send out letters saying that I have directed you to say so-and-so when I have done nothing of the kind?' It was politely explained that life would be impossible for him if he were to see every one of these letters in draft. But he was insistent that he would not permit his name to be taken in vain and gave direct instructions that all such letters should be submitted to him for approval. Within a few days his room was impossibly crowded with files and draft letters. The Minister learnt his lesson and had to give way. In view of the enormous number of communications of this character which leave Departments, the fact that very few subsequently prove to be contrary to the minister's ideas is in itself eloquent tribute not only to the loyalty of civil servants but also to their ability in stating what the Minister would wish them to say." Herbert Morrison, *Government and Parliament* (London, 1954), p. 335.
6. Sir Joseph Pope, *Public Servant: The Memoirs of Sir Joseph Pope* (Toronto, 1960), p. 159.
7. Herbert R. Balls, "The Qualities of an Administrator." *Canadian Public Administration* IV, No. 2 (June 1961), p. 166.

On the close relationship which must exist between the minister and his senior officials, and in which policy and politics cannot be totally disentangled, we have the views of Mr. Mitchell Sharp, written in the interval between his career in the public service and his entry into politics. His views, originally presented in the *Toronto Star*, July 27, 1961, are considered by Professor Denis Smith in his discussion of the 1962 campaign in Eglinton, where Mr. Sharp ran against Mr. Donald Fleming:

> He [Sharp] thought that civil servants should not concern themselves with party politics ("Indeed, with one or two exceptions, I hadn't the slightest idea of my colleagues' political persuasions, if they had any"), but emphatically that they should be consulted and should play a major role in the initiation and formation of policy. A good public servant would loyally support his minister, and try "to keep his minister out of trouble," and this would involve offering advice about the political implications of policies; so a senior civil servant, though formally non-partisan, must be interested in "politics," in that sense. If the civil servant is encouraged to offer advice, a close relationship of mutual respect and friendship is bound to arise between him and his minister, but this will have "nothing to do with party politics."
>
> Mr. Sharp believed that this non-political friendship was demonstrated in 1957. "...The present permanent heads of Departments in Ottawa..., from my observation, behaved in a most exemplary manner when the change of government occurred."[8]

James Eayrs has shown, in his lucid discussion of the role of the higher civil servant in the making of foreign policy, that the Canadian senior civil servant's "involvement in the policy process has been as close and continuous as anywhere in the world."[9] He attributes this in part to the longevity of governments, which has led to prolonged and easy familiarity with his political masters, and in part to the uninhibited participation of government in taming and harnessing the resources of a large and difficult country which has demanded the utmost from the administrative talent of the civil service. Recent periods of brief and unstable governments have, in all likelihood, strengthened the civil servant's role, since the show must go on even if the politicians are too distracted by other cares to devote adequate attention to the process of government.

8. Denis Smith, "The Campaign in Eglinton," in John Meisel, ed., *Papers on the 1962 General Election* (Toronto, 1964), pp. 87-8. A sensitive discussion of the role of the official in reconciling his own values with decisions which emerge in the process of government is Escott Reid, "The Conscience of the Diplomat," *Queen's Quarterly*, Vol. LXXIV, No. 4 (Winter, 1968).

9. James Eayrs, *The Art of the Possible* (Toronto, 1961), p. 32.

This concentration of power in the hands of the bureaucratic élite should, however, be recognized for what it is. The handful of senior administrators in the few departments which are at the centre of high policy are intimately acquainted with one another and circulate in appointment rather freely among the key departments; they are thus bound to have a unique knowledge and authority in major decisions. "At this exalted level the gaze of the civil servant sweeps across the whole horizon of public policy,"[10] says Eayrs.

When we speak of civil servants "making policy" we at once create ambiguity through the use of a deceptively simple term. As Professor Hodgetts says, "we speak...of agricultural, foreign, or fiscal policy, and indiscriminately use the same term when we refer to the Treasury Board policy on travelling expenses."[11] Obviously some kinds of policy need to be made by subordinate officials, and some kinds of policy should never be made without full and careful consideration by ministers. It is part of the business of officials to sort these issues out, and this throws a great burden on the sense of professional responsibility and integrity of the civil service. Civil servants are often called upon to make decisions in such matters as the licensing of businesses or the allocation of scarce materials. Such decisions can mean either financial ruin or enormous profits to private business firms, many of which may not be averse to attempts to influence the makers of the decisions. The question of how civil servants are controlled in the exercise of their powers, and the quality and morale of the civil service accordingly assume growing importance.

The fact that such decisions are made by officals may be ignored in the theory of responsible government, but it is well known to the interests affected by these decisions. The result is that the enormous growth of state activity has worn away some of the insulation which was supposed to separate the civil servant from the public. It is no longer possible to believe that ministers make all of the decisions; therefore time is wasted in making representation to a member of Parliament or to the minister, when one could deal directly with the official concerned. Thus officials are, to some extent, emerging from their anonymity, sometimes even allowing themselves to be identified in the newspapers with a particular policy. This tendency is strengthened by the unslakable thirst of service clubs, professional bodies, and similar organizations for persons to deliver speeches to them of an elevating character. The supply of speakers

10. Ibid., p. 33.

11. Hodgetts, "The Civil Service and Policy Formation," p. 469.

is limited by nature. Government departments may too easily reach the conclusion that the publicity which attends such a speech will help them in informing the public of what the departments are trying to do, and so civil servants find themselves quite frankly expounding policy in public places. Thus, the civil service becomes more and more exposed directly to public pressure and public view. The consequences of this may, in the long run, generally be bad. In the first place, the constitutional doctrine that the minister is the one responsible for policy and for policy pronouncements is undermined. In the second place, by identifying individual civil servants with particular policies which they have so eagerly expounded in public, the independence of the civil service may be endangered. Not unnaturally, a new government coming into office and wishing to change the policies of its predecessor, may feel it the better part of discretion to get rid of those officials who have so vocally espoused the policies which it now wishes to alter.

The close connection between "politics" and "policy" means that the distinction between the minister who takes decisions for political motives, and the official who advises him in complete innocence of the political facts of life, is artificial and can no longer be maintained. A good official cannot help but be aware of the political pressures under which his minister operates, and must advise him accordingly. Thus the official becomes, whether he wants to or not, a political partisan who is part of the apparatus of maintaining the government of the day in power by the skilful timing of advantageous policies. There was, for example, a fairly widespread opinion in Canada that many senior officials who had grown up under twenty-two years of continous Liberal administration had become "an outpost of the Liberal party," and as such would be a problem for the Conservative government that came to power in 1957. There was some cause to support, at least in part, this belief. The Conservatives had last been in office in Ottawa in 1935. Since that time the responsibilities of government had expanded enormously, and along with the expansion had grown an able and dedicated civil service which believed in the system of government management of the economy that had worked so well during and after the war. Many senior officials had reason to believe that the Conservative party was unsympathetic to the objectives of many of the government policies which they considered essential, and they regarded, with something like horror, the prospect of a change of government. The result might have been that some of them would have been frozen out of positions of responsibility or have resigned in despair so that the whole apparatus of government might have suffered damage which it could not easily have sustained. As it happened, there were few resignations and few drastic changes in policy. The new ministers soon discovered that a good civil servant conceives it his duty to serve his political master to the best of his ability, and that the higher civil service was as effective at advising the new government as it had been the old.

There is only one danger in this situation: it further tips the scales in favour of the government in its running battle of wits with the opposition, which is intended to serve as the main check on the irresponsible use of power under parliamentary government. When ministers have at their elbows experts who are not only first-class administrators but also astute political tacticians, the critic of government becomes dangerously handicapped when it comes to exposing mistakes and abuses.

Government in a modern democracy is largely in the hands of a bureaucracy, using the term in its neutral sense as meaning a body of professionally competent, hierarchically organized administrators. The major problem in modern constitutional government is to retain an effective control, by public opinion and by legal restraints, of the apparatus of the state which constantly expands with the increased public demand for more social welfare services and with the growing burden of national defence in a world of increasing peril. Liberty in such a world can be nourished only by the full and effective functioning of the political and legal restraints on abuse of power.

Effective political control of the bureaucracy is further hampered by the fact that the balance of information and operational skill is heavily tipped against its political masters. One of the first things that new governments discover is that the machinery of the state has a momentum of its own which is extraordinarily difficult to alter in speed or direction. As Lord Zuckerman points out, "It has been said that a new Minister appointed to a Government Department has only a limited period of freedom before he becomes a slave to a past within which his civil servants are inevitably working, and which automaticaly constrains his room for manoeuvre."[12] Fresh ideas and new policies do not commend themselves to deputy heads and other senior administrators who have a vested interest in the survival of attitudes and policies which have evolved out of the accumulated wisdom of the department.

It is not without significance that the Clark government removed

12. Solly Zuckerman *From Apes to Warlords 1904–1946* (London, 1978) p. 357.

several key deputy heads and replaced them with appointees thought to be more sympathetic to the policies of the new government. Within nine months the Trudeau government was back, the new Deputy Minister of Finance was replaced and the Clerk of the Privy Council reinstated in the office from which he had been removed. To a degree these events can be perceived as a threat to the non-political and neutral character of the higher civil service. On the other hand, it must be remembered that deputy heads are not included in the protection which the Public Service Employment Act extends to most civil servants but are order-in-council appointments which fall under the discretionary control of the Prime Minister. There is nothing in our constitutional usage or tradition which prevents a Prime Minister from ensuring that his most immediate and senior advisers in the public service are congenial to his managerial style and outlook on life. Nor should there be.

It will be recalled that when Pierre Trudeau became Prime Minister in 1968 he attempted to offset the power and inertia of the bureaucracy in several ways. He tried to avoid having ministers confronted with no choice but to accept or reject a previously arranged bureaucratic compromise by having deputy heads sit as direct participants in Cabinet committee meetings so that ministers could evaluate for themselves conflicting official advice. He further began to rotate deputy heads from department to department so that they would be less likely to become set in departmental habits of thought. The result was that deputy heads were in position on average less than three years before being shifted. One unfortunate result of this was that deputy heads were strongly tempted to ignore problems in the hope that they would not be noticed until a successor was forced to deal with them. His most striking attempt to overcome bureaucratic inertia was to seek to build up, in the Prime Minister's Office, an alternate source of advice to that emanating from the bureaucracy.

Ministers' Personal Office Staff

It is generally assumed that civil service reform created a completely nonpolitical bureaucracy with only the minister and his parliamentary secretary as political officers above the apex of the administrative pyramid. This is not entirely the case, since the minister has an office staff of his own—appointed on his nomination and paid out of public funds—which to some extent insulates him from his department and provides a small nucleus of politically appointed officials who become part of the decision-making process. This exception to the merit-based and non-political structure of the public service has a long history and may represent, in part, the price that had to be paid to persuade ministers to give up their right to nominate candidates to the public service.

In any event, a minister has always had the right to appoint a private secretary. This arrangement has ensured that there will be one person close to the minister who can be expected to understand his political responsibilities. No doubt the necessities of federalism, which impose on ministers vague but important responsibilities for the section which they "represent" in the Cabinet, have heightened the importance of the political responsibilities which must be dealt with in a minister's office.

The exemption of the minister's office from the civil service system has been enshrined in successive acts dealing with the public service, and contains a provision that the minister's private secretary might, after three years service, transfer with equivalent rank into the public service. A significant number of higher civil servants over the years have entered the service through this back door, including Sir Joseph Pope, the creator of the Department of External Affairs and its first Undersecretary.

Since the nineteen-fifties, the size of the minister's private office has expanded greatly and changed in character. The former title of private secretary has been abandoned and replaced by the more stylish designation of executive assistant. In addition, the staff may include special assistants and administrative assistants, with duties that include speech-writing, cultivating the goodwill of the press gallery, and handling the bulk of the minister's correspondence and contact with the political world around him. There are also minister's offices in their constituencies, a privilege which has also been extended to members of Parliament.

It must be realized that, in certain respects, this development was inevitable and possibly even desirable. Ministers often feel the need to surround themselves with politically ambitious lawyers and bright young men and women from the universities, the world of journalism and public relations. Such people may be a source of fresh ideas for a politician anxious to make his mark on a department, and at least they can be expected to give him a professionally polished public image and enhance his political career. It could hardly be expected that such duties would be congenial or well executed if left in the hands of departmental officials. It is also just as well that these operations are paid for out of public funds, for the minister to pay from his own pocket would give rise to suspicion and uncertainty.

As long as the activities of the minister's office are confined to their proper sphere no great harm is done to the public service. However, they are open to abuse. Nevertheless, a strong-minded deputy head will not permit himself to be insulated from his minister by the private office organization, and will ensure that there is no interposition of this group in the decision-making flow in the department. Sometimes it has appeared that the minister's private staff lacks the experience and the sense of professional dedication to the public service which are required for the transaction of public business. In the British system, the core of the private office is drawn from the civil service, and service as a minister's private secretary is an exacting test for an ambitious young civil servant. Even in Canada, some ministers have deliberately chosen their executive assistants from the ranks of the public service, and some members of this group have made distinguished careers.

What is the proper role of the minister's private office? It might have been expected that it could be a source of alternative policy advice, but this does not seem to have happened. What it has done is strengthen the minister's political capacity. A recent account, which is authoritative because it is based on his own experience, by Professor Blair Williams, suggests that this is its principal role. The necessary work which stems from both his constitutency responsibilities and his role as a regional minister is usually accomplished by his "exempt staff." It handles the minister's liaison not only with his own and other executive agencies, but with the numerous private and semi-private groups with which his portfolio is concerned. Its "research" function lies not in generating policy ideas but rather, as Williams says, "is less on a question of orginial analysis and field work than it is a matter of compiling data and information from existing sources for use in speeches, press releases, briefing memos for Parliament and so on." A far from insignificant role is that of recruitment of "militants, managers, executives and candidates for the governing party." Minister's staffs attract young, well-educated, and politically motivated people whose taste for politics is likely to be enhanced by the experience.[13]

13. Blair Williams, "The Para-political Bureaucracy in Ottawa" in Harold D. Clarke, Colin Campbell, F. Q. Quo, and Arthur Goddard (eds.) *Parliament, Policy and Representation.*" For an account of abuses in the system see the Dorion Report, *Report of the Commissioner* (Ottawa, June 1965), and J. R. Mallory, "The Minister's Office Staff: An Unreformed Part of the Public Service."

Ministers and Deputy Ministers

For the sake of administrative convenience the executive, which as the Crown is a legal entity, is divided into separate departments each of which is normally subject to the authority of a single minister of the Crown. "A Department," wrote Sir John Salmond," at least in its normal and typical sense, may be defined as a branch of the Government Service separately organized under the control of a Permanent Head who is not himself under any control except that of a Minister in Charge."[14] Except where otherwise provided by statute, a department does not have an independent legal existence which enables it to enter into legal relations with other departments; it is merely one of a number of separate agencies of the Crown.

All formal acts of government officials are done on the authority and in the name of the minister. Accordingly, any act by an official of the public service, within the scope of his duties, is one for which the minister must assume responsibility.[15] The particular application of this rule is the responsibility of the minister to the House of Commons. He alone is accountable for the policy of his department; the civil servant cannot be called to account for policy statements which he may make, nor should he enter public controversy with regard to a departmental matter. If there have been mistakes the minister may take disciplinary action, but this does not absolve him from political responsibility. If the situation is serious enough it may lead, as it did in the case of the Crichel Down affair in the United Kingdom in 1954, to the resignation of the minister.[16] If the minister's officials are criticized in Parliament, it is his duty, as far as he

14. J. L. Robson, ed., *New Zealand: The Development of its Laws and Constitution* (London, 1954), p. 88.

15. Sir Robert Borden summed up the position in this way: "A Minister of the Crown is responsible, under the system in Great Britain, for the minutest details of the administration in his department;he is politically responsible, but he does not know anything at all about them. When anything goes wrong in his department, he is responsible therefore to Parliament; and if he comes to Parliament and points out that he entrusted the duty to an official in the ordinary course and in good faith, that he had been selected for his capacity, and ability, and integrity, and the moment that man has gone wrong the Minister had investigated the matter to the full and punished the man either by degradation or dismissal, he has done his duty to the public. That is the way matters are dealt with in Great Britain, and it is the way, it seems to me, that our affairs ought to be carried on in this country." Canada, *House of Commons Debates,* May 15, 1909, p. 6723.

16. No civil servant was dismissed for any action he had taken, but several were quietly transferred to other departments. The full account of the affair is contained in the report of the *Public Inquiry Ordered by the Minister of Agriculture into the Disposal of Land at Crichel Down,* Cmd. 9176, London, H.M.S.O., 1954.

can, to defend them, for an official cannot publicly reply to criticism.[17]

The civil service is presumed to be politically neutral, the minister essentially political. His officials act in his name, and on his responsibility. The power of the official is derivative, that of the minister inherent in his office. The minister is constitutionally responsible for the department and he therefore has the right to make the final decision, even if it is against the advice of his officials. If they cannot persuade him to change his mind they may resign in order to bring their difference with the minister out into the open. If they remain, it is their duty to carry out the minister's policy to the best of their abilities. If the policy does lead to severe criticism the minister will have to defend himself as best he can in Parliament and accept the consequences.

An official who resigns because he feels that his minister is disastrously mistaken thus makes his difference with the minister a matter of public knowledge. This will happen only in extreme circumstances, for officials are permanent while ministers come and go. A wise official usually prefers to bide his time until events prove him right by bringing about a change of his minister. Although officials are permanent, they do not have a protected right to any

17. Canada, *House of Commons Debates* (unrevised), August 22, 1958, pp. 3955, 3986. In this case the civil servant in question had been directly quoted in a newspaper article. This was unfortunate, and by his remarks the minister tried to restore the situation to its proper constitutional position. He said, "I am convinced that somewhere along the line there has been a misunderstanding as to how a certain write-up got into a certain Montreal paper and I do not lay any blame whatsoever on this particular employee for the interpretation, or for the quotations, whatever they may have been, that appeared in the Montreal *Star.* I am convinced that this man acted in the best of good faith. He is very understanding of the peculiar situation, one might say, in which a civil servant finds himself. His hands are tied; his tongue is tied and I am quite convinced that certain remarks apparently attributed to him were not uttered by him. I wish it to be understood completely that I have every faith in the way in which he conducted himself. Aside from that, I would also like the hon. member to understand that I am completely in accord with his over-all thinking concerning the problem." When civil servants, who often must necessarily brief newspaper correspondents on policy questions, find themselves quoted in the newspaper the result is bound to be constitutionally embarrassing, and it takes a courageous minister to be willing to assume the responsibility for the resulting criticism of the views expressed by his official.

An interesting problem was created by the summoning of civil servants before the Public Accounts Committee of the House of Commons in the 1958 session. The Chairman of the Committee, Allan Macnaughton, drew attention to the fact that the Public Accounts Committee in the United Kingdom holds closed sessions and that it was difficult for civil servants when they were compelled to testify in public. He said, "I don't know whether the civil servants who testified were pilloried. But you can see how civil servants might be embarrased to speak freely in public." Montreal *Gazette*, September 8, 1958.

particular post, and where an official and a minister do not get along well, the official may find himself transferred to a post where he is no longer likely to bother the minister by coming in contact with him.

The overall and ultimate responsibility of the minister for his department is clearly recognized in the statutory definition of his relationship with the deputy head of his department. Section 7 of the old Civil Service Act provided that "The deputy head of a department shall, subject to the directions of the head of the department, oversee and direct the officers, clerks and employees of the department, have general control of the business thereof, and perform such other duties as are assigned to him by the Governor in Council." Unfortunately, this definition was dropped in the general revision of 1969. Apparently it was not thought to be a useful or necessary description.

The permanent head (as distinct from the political head) of a department in Canada is called the "deputy head," and is in most departments styled the deputy minister. This term is confusing to outsiders because it implies that the deputy head has the power to act in place of the minister. This, of course, is not so, but several deputy ministers complained to a Royal Commission in 1890 that they had found it embarrassing that the public apparently believed they had this power. The difficulty is not only in the misleading sound of the title but also in the fact that the permanent heads of departments elsewhere in the Commonwealth generally go by the title of "secretary" or "permanent secretary," while the term "deputy minister" is used for what in Canada is called parliamentary secretary. However, this is not to say that the title of deputy head should be abandoned. It has existed in Canada for well over a century, and there is no reason why Canadians should change it to agree with a terminology which exists in other countries.[18]

The duties and responsibilities of the deputy head of a department are all-embracing. His principal duty, however, is to be the

18. The origin of the title is somewhat obscure. It was first given statutory recognition in the Civil Service Act of the Province of Canada in 1857. Hodgetts suggests that the reason for the title *deputy minister* arose because the Province of Canada took over, in the 1850s, certain departments up to that time controlled from Whitehall, such as the Post Office. The Post Office had a Deputy Postmaster General for British North America who was regarded as a permanent official. When the Post Office came under Canadian control, there was appointed a Canadian Postmaster General who was of course a political officer, and his permanent department head retained the title of Deputy Postmaster General. J. E. Hodgetts, *Pioneer Public Service: An Administrative History of the United Canadas, 1841–1867* (Toronto, 1956), pp. 92ff.

right-hand man of the minister; he must advise his chief on all of the numerous responsibilities which the minister has assumed with his portfolio. Deputy heads operate at the summit of the civil service in an intimate relationship with members of the government of the day. Their appointment is therefore of moment to that government. A great degree of mutual compatibility and confidence must exist between the minister and his deputy, and if this is lacking, it may be necessary for the government to find another deputy in whom the minister has confidence. Nevertheless, it should be noted that changes of ministers, and even changes of government, have occurred without any noticeable shifting of deputy heads.

The appointment of deputy heads, unlike that of other civil servants, is vested, under section 2 of the Public Service Employment Act, in the Governor-in-Council. The recommendation of these appointments to Council is one of the long-recognized special rights of the Prime Minister.

ADMINISTRATIVE ORGANIZATION

Government Departments

The executive departments are carved out on no coherent principle of organization. The British Committee on Machinery of Government found only two principles upon which the functions of departments should be determined and allocated. These were according to the classes of persons to be served (what the textbooks in public administration call clientele), and according to the services to be performed (or functions). They disliked the former principle because it led to "Lilliputian adminstration," and commended the latter.[19] In Canada both types exist: Veterans Affairs is one of the last of the clientele departments, while the majority of departments are functional, such as National Health and Welfare. But other types exist as well. There have been departments, such as the old Department of the Interior and Northern Affairs (now merged into Indian Affairs and Northern Development), which were essentially territorial in organization. While most departments have some kind of administrative responsibility for some part of the total area of government, there are a few which are not essentially administrative

19. *Report of the Machinery of Government Committee,* Cd. 9230, 1918, pp. 7-8.

at all, but perform servicing functions for other agencies of government. Thus the Department of Public Printing and Stationery is essentially a servicing agency, as is the Department of Public Works, which is responsible not only for the construction but also for the custodial and other services of government buildings. The Privy Council Office provides secretarial services for the Cabinet and numerous Cabinet and official committees, as well as the expert services of draftsmen for orders-in-council. The principal duty of the Law Officers of the Crown (that is, the Department of Justice) is to provide legal advice to the government, although departments also have legal staffs of their own.

Within the departments, officials are organized hierarchically with a clear chain of command running from the minister through the deputy head down to the lowest level of official. Most departments are large enough to be further subdivided into divisions. Some large departments are divided into branches (for example, the Indian Affairs Branch of Indian Affairs and Northern Development), while a very large department such as Transport is initially divided into Air Services and Marine Services, each of which is further subdivided into divisions.

Only a small fraction of the total strength of the public service is directly engaged in carrying out administrative decisions. Officers of the public service engage in this kind of administration carry out *line* functions, that is, they are part of the direct chain of command. The rest of the public service is engaged in *staff* functions, that is, they do not themselves take direct part in the process of decision-making, but they perform services necessary for those who do. Staff personnel may range from the legal and technical staffs whose expert advice is necessary in making decisions, to the many more persons who are necessary to the administrator in keeping records and providing the clerical and custodial services which all office establishments require. The administrative "brain" requires a "memory" in the form of well-organized records, as well as a variety of other organs to transmit its decisions to their destination.

Crown Corporations

A great deal of the business of government is not done by ministers and departments at all but has been entrusted to a variety of specialized agencies which are not headed by responsible ministers and are not directly accountable to Parliament. The reasons why this has happened are various. In some cases the government has found itself the owner and operator of an essentially commercial undertaking, which should be run relatively free from government and political interference and with the same managerial freedom as similar undertakings in private hands. In other cases it has seemed desirable to place some essentially regulatory functions in the hands of an independent body to ensure that political interference is kept to a minimum.

As their name implies, Crown corporations are legal entities in their own right, separate from the rest of the executive which has a collective legal existence as "the Crown." While they are separate from the Crown, they nevertheless, as "emanations of the Crown," enjoy certain rights and privileges, such as freedom from liability for municipal taxes. Because Crown agencies of various sorts may comprise a substantial part of the taxable property in many municipalities, it is now the policy of the federal government to pay annual grants in lieu of taxes in all cases where Crown property is a significant part of the ratable property in a municipality. While these grants are substantially the same as local taxes would be if they could be levied, the government still maintains the principle of immunity from taxation.[20] It was customary, however, even before the passage of the Crown Proceedings Act which removed the traditional immunity of the Crown from lawsuits, to waive this immunity in the case of Crown corporations.

The Crown corporation has been adopted in the interests of managerial flexibility, to free the agency from the somewhat cumbersome civil service methods of appointment and tenure, which are less appropriate to a business undertaking than to the public service itself. In addition, the Crown corporation is freed from political interference in day-to-day managerial decisions, though sufficient ministerial and parliamentary control is retained so that the objectives of national policy are carried out. Finally, the device of setting up a Crown corporation frees the agency to some degree from Treasury control. Thus the Crown corporation is freed from the strict control of parliamentary appropriation for specific purposes and from the pre-audit of the Comptroller General, and operating agencies are free to retain their surpluses instead of paying them

20. Section 125 of the British North America Act provides that "No Lands or Property belonging to Canada or any Province shall be liable to taxation." Prior to 1952, Crown corporations did not pay corporate income tax. However, the Income Tax Act has now been amended so that proprietary Crown corporations pay income tax in the same manner as privately owned corporations. This has the effect of making their financial statements more comparable to those of private industry and facilitates the measurement of their relative efficiency.

into the Consolidated Revenue Fund. However, their accounts are audited and laid before Parliament, and their affairs are subject to scrutiny from parliamentary committees, including the Public Accounts Committee.

The Crown corporation is characteristic of a mixed economy, in which the provision of most goods and services is in the hands of private persons or organizations, but the government interferes with private economic activity for the purpose of regulation or for the provision of goods and services required in the national interest which would not be adequately provided by private endeavour. The Crown corporation is not a new device in Canada. It has been employed for many years. Sir Robert Borden said of the first Crown corporation, the Canadian National Railways, incorporated in 1919, that it was set up in that form to ensure businesslike management, financial autonomy and freedom from political interference. The model which inspired him was the Suez Canal Company.[21]

The Financial Administration Act classifies Crown corporations in three main types: "departmental corporations," "agency corporations" and "proprietary corporations."[22] The classification used in the act is based on two considerations: the extent of financial independence, and the general nature of the activity carried on by the corporation. *Departmental corporations* carry on administrative, supervisory or regulatory functions and are financed by appropriations from Parliament in the same way as ordinary government departments. *Agency corporations* engage in trading, service and procurement operations and are usually given controlled revolving funds for this purpose. *Proprietary corporations* engage in lending, industrial or commercial operations and are normally expected to pay for their operations out of their revenues.[23] The division into three categories is somewhat arbitrary, since the activities of a single corporation may fall under more than one classification. An example of the difficulty of classification is the Northwest Territories Power Commission (now the Northern Canada Power

21. *Robert Laird Borden: His Memoirs,* Vol. II (London, 1938), p. 653.

22. Not all Crown corporations are subject to the provisions of the Financial Administration Act. Some, such as the Bank of Canada and the Wheat Board, are, because of their unique functions, excluded from the operation of the Financial Administration Act and are governed instead by detailed provisions in their own acts of incorporation.

23. See W. Friedmann, ed., *The Public Corporation* (Toronto, 1954); the special article on "Crown Corporations," *Canada Year Book,* 1955, pp. 98-105; and C. A. Ashley and R. G. H. Smails, *Canadian Crown Corporations* (Toronto, 1965).

Commission), which was subsequently transferred from the list of proprietary to the list of agency corporations by order-in-council as a result of an expansion of its functions.

The classification of Crown corporations imposed by the Financial Administration Act does not bear any relationship at all to their legal structure, which depends chiefly on the time and circumstances under which each agency was originally set up. In general, Crown corporations have been set up in one or other of the following forms: a board or commission set up by act of Parliament (for example, the Maritime Coal Commission, the National Harbours Board and the National Research Council); a public corporation set up by act of Parliament (for example, the Canadian Broadcasting Corporation, the Bank of Canada, and the St. Lawrence Seaway Authority); and a company incorporated under the Canada Business Corporations Act (for example Atomic Energy of Canada Limited, Polymer Corporation Limited and Eldorado Aviation Limited). The first two methods of setting up Crown corporations are slow and cumbersome, giving an opportunity for full public consideration and parliamentary debate while the legislation is under consideration. Such a course of action is appropriate in setting up a major undertaking of government which is likely to be operating for a long time. On the other hand, there are some activities of a more temporary character or of less importance, and these can be launched by the less formal methods of the Crown company. In this case all that is necessary is for a minister to apply for letters patent to set up a limited company in the same manner as would be done by private individuals. The whole of the capital stock of the company is held by the government, and the directors and officers of the company are thus, in effect, the nominees of the minister. Such undertakings have a maximum flexibility, since it is easy to have their powers amended or expanded, their capital increased or decreased, or simply to wind them up when their objectives have been accomplished.

All Crown corporations are subject to some degree of public control. What freedom they have from control is justified because it gives them greater managerial flexibility and freedom from the rigid framework of government financial and personnel controls. This independence is also necessary for Crown agencies such as the C.B.C. which are engaged in providing news and political commentary, and also for the protection of the cultural and artistic standards of the C.B.C., the National Film Board and other "cultural" agencies from political interference. They still, however, are amenable to final control by Parliament and the public since they are the instruments of public policy. All of them are to some degree under the control, formal or informal, of a minister of the Crown, whose wishes on general policy are bound to be of consequence to the corporation. Since the directors of Crown companies and the governing boards of other Crown corporations are appointed either by the minister or by the Governor-in-Council, the government retains one kind of influence over policy. The actual degree of independence of such bodies can be measured roughly by the tenure of their directing officers. Most of them are appointed "during pleasure" so that the government retains ultimate control by its power to alter the composition of the policy-making organ. When the members of the board are appointed for a term of years (as with most boards and commissions) they enjoy a greater degree of independence.

The relationship between the independence of an agency and the tenure of its principal officers is clearly illustrated by the Coyne affair in 1961. There had been a growing difference of opinion between the government and the Bank of Canada (chiefly with the Governor of the Bank, James Coyne) which came to a head at that time—ironically within a few months of the end of Mr. Coyne's seven-year term as Governor. For reasons which must remain somewhat inexplicable, the Minister of Finance, Donald Fleming, summoned Mr. Coyne on May 30 and demanded his resignation. Mr. Coyne refused, perferring to seek public vindication of his difference with the government over monetary policy.

Under the Bank of Canada Act, the Governor is appointed for a seven-year term and holds office "during good behavior." It is commonly assumed that the holder of a "good behavior" appointment can be removed only after a joint address of both Houses of Parliament, as is the case with judges and the Auditor General. This is not so. Indeed, it was discovered that the Bank of Canada Act made no provision at all for the removal of the Governor from his post. The government, balked by Mr. Coyne's refusal to resign, then sought to amend the Bank of Canada Act with a new clause which would declare the office of the Governor to be vacant. It is difficult not to regard this singular action as anything but a sort of bill of attainder, and it is to the credit of the Senate that the bill was defeated in committee. At that point, Mr. Coyne felt that his integrity and honour had been vindicated by his appearance before the Senate committee, and he thereupon tendered his resignation.

Long before the open collision between the minister and the

Governor, there had been serious and widespread doubts, not only as to the wisdom of Mr. Coyne's actions as Governor of the Bank, but also as to how far a central bank should go in opposing the considered policy of the government of the day. Both Mr. Graham Towers, Mr. Coyne's predecessor, and Mr. Louis Rasminsky, who succeeded him as Governor of the Bank, have made it clear that it should be the duty of the Bank to conform to the policy objectives of the government. This has now been written into the Bank of Canada Act. The decennial revision of the act in the 1966-67 session of Parliament contained a new provision in section 14 to ensure regular consultation on monetary policy between the Governor and the Minister of Finance. If these consultations fail to produce agreement "the Minister may, after consultation with the Governor and with the approval of the Governor-in-Council, give to the Governor a written directive concerning monetary policy, in specific terms and applicable for a specified period, and the Bank shall comply with such directive."

A second kind of control by the government is exercised through the power of the Minister of Finance and the Governor-in-Council to approve or authorize the more important financial operations of Crown corporations. Even where a corporation has full control over its operating budget it may still require approval by the Treasury Board or some other body for its capital program.[24]

In addition to control by the executive, which is of course responsible to Parliament, Crown corporations are also subject to some degree of direct parliamentary control. The prime source of this control is that only Parliament can authorize the existence, or alteration in the powers, of an agency (other than a Crown company), and that only Parliament can withdraw rights which Parliament has created. Moreover, the annual reports of Crown corporations are laid before Parliament, which thus has an opportunity to discuss their operations. There are three opportunities for parliamentary oversight of Crown corporations: they may be discussed in

24. The interest of the Treasury Board in such scrutiny is to keep the standards of financial propriety and judgment in Crown agencies as close as possible to that in the departments. "Often the plea of flexibility and freedom from control will produce such marked disparities of standards that criticism both internal and external to the public service will occur. Our Treasury scrutiny, therefore, is concerned not so much with the operating details of these agencies as with their standards of judgment, their choices of priorities and their general concern with the public interest." G. G. E. Steele, "The Treasury Board as a Control Agency," *Canadian Public Administration* IV, No. 2 (June 1961), pp. 203-4.

Standing Committee on the Estimates of the minister who reports to Parliament on their behalf; their reports may be referred to select or standing committees; and members may ask parliamentary questions. In general, questions and debates on Crown corporations are confined to matters of structure and policy, and do not extend to interference in the details of management.

Crown corporations are a form of quasi-political agency which represents a compromise in the normal pattern of government. To a greater or less extent, political direction and political accountability have been sacrificed for independence from the normal agencies of control. In the case of most Crown corporations the reason for this is an apparent contrast between businesslike management and democratic control. The managers of ordinary business enterprises have very wide discretionary powers over the resources at their command, and they are chiefly judged by results. In other words, if they can make a business pay without breaking the law, the stockholders should have no complaint. In a democracy we could not possibly give that much freedom to politicians and civil servants because it is as important that they achieve their objectives in the right way as that they achieve them at all. A minister and a civil servant operate in a world of procedural red tape because they are strictly accountable to the public for both the ends and the means of policy.

However, when the state is forced to "go into business," to buy or sell goods or services, it becomes important that it does so in an economically efficient way. The red tape of constitutional accountability creates extra costs and inflexibilities which are the price the public is prepared to pay for controlling the power which government must exercise. When the government is "in business" it is easier to measure efficiency by criteria of cost and service, and some of the democratic restraints on freedom of action are removed in the interests of efficiency.

Treasury Control

Cabinet government implies parliamentary control over the executive through ministers accountable to Parliament. In financial matters the accountability of the executive departments and agencies is subject to a series of detailed controls. The regulations governing the spending of public money and the accounting for expenditure are currently founded in the Financial Administration Act, 1951, and various amendments to it since.

Many of the powers of financial co-ordination and control in Canada are vested in a statutory committee of the Privy Council called the Treasury Board. For most of its history the Treasury Board was presided over by the Minister of Finance, with a support staff drawn from that department. As a result of recommendations made by the Royal Commission on Government Organization (the Glassco Commission) in 1962, the Treasury Board was moved from the control of the Department of Finance and given full departmental status, with a separate minister, called the President of the Treasury Board.[25] The reasons for this recommendation will be considered later but essentially, the change was made partly because of the demanding responsibilities of the Minister of Finance and partly to transform the Treasury Board from a negative controlling agency and to give it a more imaginative planning and co-ordinating role in government. The Board itself consists of a President and five other ministers, one of whom is the Minister of Finance. It is doubtless the federalization of the Canadian Cabinet system, referred to previously, which led at Confederation to placing the functions of financial control in a committee rather than a single minister.

The powers of the Treasury Board were revised, in accordance with the recommendations of the Glassco Commission, by amendments to the Financial Administration Act in 1967. "The effect of the amended act," the President of the Treasury Board told the House of Commons, "was to establish the Treasury Board even more clearly than before as the agency of government chiefly responsible for formulating central management policy including the financial management functions of short and long range expenditure forecasting, program analysis, estimates preparation, supervision and control of expenditures, leases, contracts, and financial commitments."[26] While it now has a "responsibility for providing leadership and stimulus to improve management performance," it operates within the general framework of policy laid down by the Cabinet. Policy decisions of the Treasury Board are made by minute

25. The new role of the Treasury Board was given statutory foundation by an amendment to the Financial Administration Act in 1967. However, the government was able, under its general powers in the Government Organization Act of 1966, to designate George McIlraith as President of the Privy Council and Vice-President of the Treasury Board and to appoint a senior deputy minister of long experience as Secretary of the Board on January 21, 1964. On this interim basis, the Treasury Board assumed a separate departmental status three years before the permanent legislation was passed.

26. Canada. *House of Commons Debates,* November 18, 1968, p. 2854.

of the Board itself, which has a quorum of three and meets regularly; the assembly of data for decisions is done by the officers of the Treasury Board Staff, who also make many minor and preliminary decisions.

Every service provided by a department of government costs money, and the funds for programs are appropriated annually by Parliament in a series of Votes. The money thus provided can only be spent for the purposes specified in the Vote. Thus the long-established practice was for each department to budget for the funds it required and submit these requirements to the Treasury Board. "The most important single function of the Treasury Board," said a former senior officer, "is that of rationalizing the requirements of all the departments of government and fitting them into the budgetary picture as a whole. If these requirements cannot be made to fit within the framework of government policies, the issues involved are referred to the Cabinet for decision."[27]

Nevertheless, one of the consequences of the Glassco recommendations was that the Privy Council Office and the Treasury Board emerged as strong central control agencies, interposed between the Cabinet and the departments. The Treasury Board saw its role as one of continuous review of the allocation process, well beyond the mere scrutiny of the expenditure budget, and including program evaluation in close consultation with the "policy" Cabinet committees through all the various stages of the decision-making process. It saw itself functioning as a "management committee" for the Cabinet as a whole. In this capacity "the Board is concerned with leadership or guidance or regulation respecting the several inputs which enter into program administration, and the manner in which they are combined or organized."[28] In this role the Treasury Board has attempted to reconcile the guiding principle of the Glassco Commission that the managers, i.e. the departments, should be free to manage without being restricted by needing to seek the consent of the central agencies for almost every decision. Hence the tendency to reduce the number of matters which required affirmative approval from the Treasury Board, and the trend to decentralize as much of recruitment and personnel policy as possible to the depart-

27. G. W. Stead, "The Treasury Board of Canada." *The Institute of Public Administration of Canada, Proceedings of the 7th Annual Conference,* 1955, p. 86.

28. A. W. Johnson, "The Treasury Board of Canada and the Machinery of Government of the 1970's." *Canadian Journal of Political Science.* IV:3 (September, 1971) p. 359. For a more critical discussion see Michael Hicks, "The Treasury Board of Canada and its Clients: Five Years of Change and Administrative Reform." *Canadian Public Administration.* XVI:2 (Summer, 1973) p. 182.

ments. What the Treasury Board has sought to develop in its central management function is the creation of guidelines rather than rules. While the departments strive to combine the most effective quality and quantity of personnel, as well as equipment and services, they cannot be left to do these things entirely on their own.

The nature of Cabinet and parliamentary government imposes important restraints. Thus the fair and equal treatment of public servants, the kind and quality of government service, and the prudent handling of public funds, are all matters on which the Cabinet as a whole is responsible to Parliament. This overall collective responsibility must be reconciled with individual ministerial responsibility which is the constitutional basis for departmental autonomy.

The budgetary process which had continued until the early sixties involved the preparation by a department of its expenditure budget, protracted negotiation with the Treasury Board over its details, and final submission to Cabinet, was significantly altered as a result of new managerial techniques in the sixties. The introduction of Planning, Programming, and Budgeting Systems (PPBS) and more refined managerial techniques meant that departmental proposals were no longer related to the old "vote" system which in effect listed a separate Vote for each statutory duty. Instead proposals were related to the total resources needed for whole programs, and the Vote structure of the Main Estimates was restructured accordingly. The Treasury Board reviewed departmental proposals as to whether they fell within the "A" budget of programs already sanctioned, the "B" budget of new programs which must be related to their effectiveness in terms of government objectives, and "X" items which represented programs deemed to be failing to meet their objectives. While the "B" and "X" items were scrutinized with care, "A" items tended to receive less scrutiny when the Treasury Board, meeting with the Minister, made its final allocation of resources to the department. Dissatisfied ministers could, and sometimes did, appeal such decisions to the full Cabinet.

There were a number of defects in this system. Departments, naturally unwilling to admit that programs were failing and unwilling to yield bureaucratic territory, showed little inclination to designated "X" budget items. These largely became a dead letter, though a belated attempt was made to revive them as a measure against the huge budget deficits of the late seventies. Furthermore, ministers and departments had two expedients to minimize Treasury Board control. One was to put forward a program on an emergency basis after the Main Estimates had gone through and then defend it for the next fiscal year as an established program. The other was to make a public announcement of a program before it had been approved by Cabinet in order to generate enough public support to overcome opposition by the Treasury Board and Cabinet. Perhaps the most serious flaw in the system was that decisions on new programs were taken in one place (the appropriate "functional" committee of Cabinet), while the decision on available resources was made in another (the Treasury Board).

The management control system gave to the Treasury Board the responsibility to lay down general personnel policies, including pay and classification, across the public service. The Board became the government's principal bargaining agent with the unions in the public service. It made general policy decisions regarding the use of expensive items such as computing and data processing equipment. The direction in which the Board sought to move in the seventies was to develop guidelines and delegate widely to departments, but this movement was limited by the need to impose common government policy from which departments would otherwise be too easily tempted to depart.

Effective control through program budgeting was strengthened by three important steps since 1977. In that year the powers of the Auditor General were considerably strengthened by an amendment to the act defining his office. In the following year, largely at the insistence of the Auditor General, the office of Comptroller General was revived. This ancient office, whose visible presence was evident in the person of his Treasury Officers located in each department to verify that each departmental charge on the Consolidated Revenue Fund was in accordance with the intentions of Parliament as expressed in the Vote, had been abolished on the recommendation of the Glassco Commission. The reasoning was that this essentially routine task was made unnecessary when all government transactions were handled by data processing systems. In his revised role, the Comptroller was installed in the Treasury Board with a status equal to that of the Secretary of the Board, and was made responsible for the rules and systems which govern and document the flow of money, and with the responsibility to prescribe systems of financial management and control. The third stage in making program budgeting effective was the development of the "envelope" system introduced by the Conservative government in 1979 and continued and elaborated by their successors. Under this system a sum is allotted for a particular program area, and the appropriate Cabinet committee then has the duty of allocating resources to particular programs within this limit. This has led to a significant change in the role of the Treasury Board. Under the old Trudeau system the Treasury Board had the final authority for evaluating programs, but the approval of new programs rested with the functional committees of Cabinet. Under the new system the work of the two bodies has been more closely integrated. "On the basis of Committee directions and planning guidelines, departments and agencies prepare and submit strategic overviews and operational plans to the Policy Committee and the Treasury Board for review. The Treasury Board carries out a review of the operational plans to determine the cost of carrying out those policies and programs which have to that point, been approved by the Committees. With this up-to-date costing, and within the context of the multi-year envelope ceilings, Policy Committees decided upon the policy proposals and program reviews to be undertaken."[29] What appears to have happened is that the role of the Treasury Board in policy committees is to advise on the state of available resources within the "envelope," but the decision on how far to support a particular program is vested in the "policy" committee.

The machinery of stern financial control goes far to secure strict adherence to what has been authorized by Parliament. However, this is not a certain safeguard that public money will be wisely spent. It is the executive which finally decides questions of financial priorities and what the objects of governmental expenditure shall be. For any decision which has behind it the political responsibility of the Cabinet and the authority of Parliament, which the Cabinet can command through its parliamentary majority, there can be no effective control. Governments frequently make decisions which may be financially wasteful even if they are politically necessary. Very often they have to risk that a very large expenditure may be completely wasted. Two of the largest financial commitments of the government in 1958 were the South Saskatchewan Dam, which even a royal commission had not found economically feasible, and the development of a new type of fighter aircraft by A.V. Roe, the aircraft manufacturers. Each of these involved large sums of money and neither could be justified on strict grounds of prudent economy. However, where major regional developments or national security are concerned, governments are not expected to follow the rules of a prudent financial administrator. They must take bold risks and if necessary bear the blame if things go wrong. Equally illustrative of

29. Privy Council Office. *The Policy and Expenditure Management System.* (Ottawa, 1981) p. 13. See also *Guide to the Policy & Expenditure Management System* issued by the Department of Supply and Services in 1980.

this difficulty was the government Printing Bureau which occupied so much of the time of the Public Accounts Committee in the 1958 session. The building had cost more than three times the original estimate, partly because of unforeseen difficulties in construction and partly because of changes in design. Much of the high cost was attributable to the site. However, the site itself was part of the national capital plan, though the decisions to rush the project and to adhere to the site were clearly based in part on political considerations.

There is always some "waste" in government decisions and some of this will be of large sums, since government entails much more than prudent estate management. Governments are expected to take political decisions, and governments which elevate rigid economy into a major principle of policy are not long for this world. To be fair to "extravagant" governments, there are many decisions which must be made in which financial prudence is far less important than national or regional welfare. Defence expenditures are the most "wasteful" of all because all professional military advisers are insatiable in their demands for more and bigger weapons and establishments. Governments have to balance the claims of military security against other claims on their limited resources, and they must often make difficult decisions against professional military advice. They can never be sure that such decisions will not gravely endanger military security. Similar, and almost equally pressing, claims are made for all kinds of government expenditures. Accordingly, such decisions are always difficult and they are decisions which can only be made by the government of the day. No matter how strict the financial controls are, it is not possible to take away from the government the responsibility for the magnitude of expenditure and the allocation of priorities. Such decisions are necessarily political and cannot be otherwise.

Parliament provides money for the purposes of government in specific Votes, and the money so appropriated can be spent only for the purpose consistent with the Vote. Since the financial planning of the government must be made as much as a year ahead, it is obvious that some provision must exist to take care of situations which cannot be foreseen but which must be dealt with when they arise. One way of doing this is for the government to ask Parliament for additional money in the form of Supplementary Estimates. For lesser amounts and in cases where Parliament is not in session there are other methods of providing emergency funds. In the first place a department may, with the sanction of the Treasury Board, transfer unexpended funds from one item to another *within* a Vote (but it is not possible to transfer money from one Vote to another). In the second place there is also a Vote for "unforeseen contingencies" which may, with the consent of the Treasury Board, be applied to such expenditures. Finally there are the Governor General's special warrants, under which it is possible to spend money without prior parliamentary appropriation, but under the general authority of the Financial Administration Act.

In general only Parliament can sanction the expenditure of public funds, but under certain circumstances expenditures can be authorized by a special warrant of the Governor General. This is a power which the British constitution does not contain but which appears to have been common practice in constitutions granted to British colonies. As presently provided in section 28 of the Financial Administration Act (as amended in 1958), where some expenditure "not foreseen or provided for by Parliament is urgently required for the public good," the Governor-in-Council may, on the recommendation of the minister concerned and the Minister of Finance, authorize such expenditure by a Governor General's warrant. Such warrants may be used only when Parliament is not in session or when it has been adjourned and will not assemble for at least two weeks. The Minister of Finance is required to lay before the House of Commons, within fifteen days of its reconvening, a statement showing the amounts of warrants issued since the previous session. In addition, it is now laid down that the amount of such warrants shall be included in the amounts provided in the next appropriation act so that there will be an opportunity to debate them in Parliament.[30]

For a government to employ warrants to authorize expenditure is usually a confession of miscalculation or failure, and such warrants are rarely used because they give rise to the criticism that the government is usurping the functions of Parliament. They are not normally necessary unless a government either has had difficulty in getting its supply bills through or has, for some other reason, been forced to dissolve Parliament before supply has been voted for the fiscal year. Warrants are, of course, a perfectly constitutional device which make it possible to provide interim authorization for expenditure until full parliamentary approval can be obtained. It was necessary to resort to a Governor General's warrant to provide additional money for the Department of Citizenship and Immigra-

30. Canada, *House of Commons Debates* (unrevised), July 29, 1958, p. 2823. The act previously did not have this requirement, though in most cases an opportunity to debate the warrant had been provided. There was considerable criticism of the government for not doing so in the 1957–58 session.

tion in August 1957, because the Hungarian refugee problem had constituted an undue drain on that department's Vote. Similarly, when the Twenty-third Parliament was dissolved in February 1958, full supply had not been voted for the fiscal year 1957-58, and no supply at all had been voted for the fiscal year beginning April 1, 1958. Consequently, the government was forced to employ three Governor General's warrants to carry it over until the new Parliament had assembled and was able to vote further supply.[31]

LEGISLATIVE AND JUDICIAL POWERS OF THE EXECUTIVE

The powers of the executive to legislate on its own account are twofold: prerogative and delegated. The prerogative power is the last vestige of the Crown's power to make law in its own right. The courts have made it clear that this power is gone forever once Parliament has legislated on a particular topic.[32] It is thus of declining importance, and there are very few matters on which the prerogative power to legislate still exists. It remains, to a limited extent, free from invasion by parliament in matters which deal directly with the personal powers of the Sovereign. There is, for example, no statutory definition of the reserve powers of the head of state; and the office of Governor General is regulated by royal letters patent rather than by statute. Regulations made to deal with conquered or occupied territory still fall within the realm of the prerogative. For example, the legal basis for the occupation government in the British zone of Germany after the Second World War was a number of regulations made under the prerogative.

Although Parliament has completely won the battle with the prerogative for constitutional supremacy, nevertheless acts of Parliament within the last century have more and more delegated extremely wide legislative powers to the executive. Why has this happened? The answer is simply that the responsibilities of modern government for the close and detailed regulation of a wide variety of normal everyday relationships are so great that no legislature would have the time to deal with a fraction of them. Furthermore, many of these regulations are so highly technical that there is nothing which

31. Ibid., May 13, 1958, p. 12.

32. *Campbell* v. *Hall* [1774] 20 St. Tr. 239; *Attorney-General* v. *De Keyser's Royal Hotel* [1920] A. C. 508.

could be intelligently debated on either side in a legislative chamber. The only judgment of any importance is that of experts, and only other experts understand what is being done.

It has been argued that Parliament has thus abdicated its legislating function to the executive. Around this fact much learned controversy has raged for nearly forty years. It now seems clear, however, that much of this controversy is quite unreal. We must accept the fact that governments are expected to do things which in the past were regulated in the private sector of the economy, and nothing is gained by a nostalgic yearning for the return of *laissez-faire* days that are gone forever. Parliament is no longer at the centre of the law-making process. The results of this we cannot foresee, but they are not likely to be totally beneficial.[33] It is necessary to accept delegated legislation as one of the consequences of modern democracy, for it is an essential instrument for greater equality and for a larger quantum of social justice, but it is not necessary to blind ourselves to some of its defects. We should recognize, in the first place, that the making of regulations by officials and the promulgation of these regulations by ministers or the Cabinet have one grave political defect. They are not discussed critically in the way that every bill that goes through Parliament is discussed. There has been no public debate before they become enforceable law, and there is very little opportunity to discuss their merits at any time. In the second place, it is obvious that there are some kinds of delegated legislation which are worse than others. In 1932, a committee set up in the United Kingdom to consider the whole question of the growing legislative power of ministers recognized the necessity of delegated legislation, but laid down certain instances when delegated legislation could be justified only in exceptional and emergency circumstances. These instances were (1) conferring on the executive the power to legislate on matters of principle, and even to impose taxation; (2) conferring the power to amend acts of Parliament, either the act by which the powers are delegated, or other acts; (3)

33. "It can thus be said that with regard to this vast new field of State activity Parliament no longer acts as the ordinary law-giver, but only as a sort of *constituante,* though it still exercises some form of control. The task of legislating and of defining the broad principles of public policy has devolved upon the Minister, while the public corporation has become the main executive agency. This new division of power retains the democratic method of law-making for the constitution only, while ordinary legislation is achieved by an autocratic method. The different councils which have been set up for the purpose of advising Ministers do not alter this fact, as they act in an advisory capacity only. So far they represent only a new type of *concilium regis;* but they may in time develop into a new type of Parliament." M. A. Sieghart, *Government by Decree* (London, 1950), p. 114.

conferring on the executive so wide a discretion "that it is almost impossible to know what limit Parliament did intend to impose;" and (4) where Parliament, "without formally abandoning its normal practice of limiting delegated powers, has in effect done so by forbidding control by the Courts."[34] If these criteria are taken as a means of evaluation, then there are a great many Canadian statutes which do serious violence to them. Naturally, the conferring of wide and discretionary rule-making powers on some government agency—nominally the Governor-in-Council, or a Minister, or some Board, but in practice on a host of subordinate officials—is more prevalent in time of emergency. Notable examples are the War Measures Act which during both World Wars placed most of the law-making powers of Parliament in the hands of the executive, the Relief Act of 1931 and the Defence Production Act of 1955, all perhaps justifiable in giving government the power to deal with a situation of crisis, but each representing a further erosion of the rights and powers of Parliament. However, there are a host of others which no crisis can explain, such as the wide powers of government marketing agencies, or the persistent claims of the Post Office to raise postal rates without the sanction of Parliament. Such powers raise serious issues of constitutional principle. As Professor Corry said of the Defence Production Act:

> [The opposition] had no difficulty in showing that powers of this kind are dangerous and not readily reconcilable with constitutional principle. Parliament was being asked to delegate extensive power to make rules and regulations which would take effect as part of the laws of the country without approval by parliament of the regulations so made. While such delegation has been of common occurrence in the last thirty years, it remains objectionable and should not be used except where it is indispensible for the protection of vital interests. Parliament was being asked to empower without limit of time the Minister of Defence Production to make orders altering the rights and obligations of persons without the persons affected having any appeal to the courts or elsewhere. Again this is nothing new in our recent experience. Nevertheless, it is another inroad on the rule of law.[35]

34. *Report of the Committee on Ministers' Powers.* Cmd. 4060, 1932. p. 31. The most judicious discussion of the whole issue of delegated legislation is Professor John Willis' *Parliamentary Powers of the English Government Departments.* (Cambridge, Mass., 1933). A more recent discussion of these matters, in both the United Kingdom and Canada, is John E. Kersell, *Parliamentary Supervision of Delegated Legislation.* (London, 1960).

35. J. A. Corry, "Arms and the Man." *Queen's Quarterly.* LXII: 3 (Autumn, 1955) p. 320.

That particular debate was a memorable one. In it the tireless speakers of the opposition kept the House of Commons in session through the heat of the Ottawa summer until the government gave way and accepted a time limit on the minister's extraordinary powers. But this lengthy use of the powers of obstruction did not appear at the time to have much impact on the public. Its most important effect was that the public was probably more receptive to the opposition case in the Pipeline debate the following summer. Clearly, if parliamentary criticism has value, it will persist only because members of Parliament stubbornly continue to practice it, and not because the public appears concerned about it.

Parliamentary criticism is of the greatest importance. The chief defect of delegated legislation is precisely that it is passed without public debate and without serious opportunity for subsequent parliamentary review. Furthermore regulations, unlike acts of Parliament, are not always published or collected in accessible form so that the citizen can know what the law is that governs him. Adequate parliamentary scrutiny and adequate publication of regulations have therefore become recognized as necessary accompaniments to the growth of delegated legislation in well-run communities. In the United Kingdom these requirements are met by provisions for the tabling, and in some cases necessary parliamentary approval, of orders; by the provision of a Select Committee of the House of Commons to scrutinize "statutory instruments" to make sure that they do not violate the criteria laid down in the Report of the Committee on Ministers' Powers; by the existence of time set aside in the House of Commons when members can move to annul a particular order; and, finally, by provision for the systematic publication of all orders in convenient form.

Progress in dealing with these matters in Canada has been slow. For historical reasons most delegated legislation emanated from the Cabinet itself, in the form of orders-in-council. Prior to the Second World War there was no general statutory requirement that subordinate legislation be either published or tabled in Parliament. The great volume of wartime regulations made it necessary for the government at that time to table in the House and to publish most regulations dealing with the war. The practice having been established, it was continued after the war. But the process went no further. The mere fact of tabling was, in itself, as Brooke Claxton said in the Throne Speech debate in 1943, "for all practical purposes, an empty form." He urged that orders having legislative effect should be referred to a committee of the House. The committee should be concerned with both the form and purpose of such orders. "In this way," he said, "there would be an opportunity of improving the drafting of orders, which sometimes leaves a great deal to be desired; there would be exercise of control over the executive, opportunity for ventilating grievances, and also observance of the important principle of the supremacy of Parliament."[36] The matter was not pursued. Claxton himself was to achieve high office but nothing further of significance was heard of the matter until after the war. In fact, almost forty years were to elapse before a parliamentary scrutiny committee was created.

The main episodes in the long road to reform were as follows. After the war the opposition in the House of Commons found a convenient theme in criticising "order-in-council government." In an attempt to disarm that criticism the government of Louis St. Laurent introduced, in 1950, a Regulations Act which provided for the systematic publication and tabling of all orders having legislative effect, whether emanating from the Governor-in-Council, from Ministers, or from other Crown agencies. The Act further provided that all such orders should undergo preliminary scrutiny in the Privy Council Office to ensure clarity and conformity to common standards of draftsmanship. Subsequently, there was included in the Bill of Rights, 1960, a requirement that all such orders should be examined by the Minister of Justice to ensure their conformity to the Bill of Rights. While these provisions may have had some deterrent effect on departmental draftsmen, scrutiny by both agencies seems in fact to have been perfunctory.

No provision was made for parliamentary scrutiny by the Regulations Act, on the somewhat surprising ground, adduced by the Prime Minister, that since most subordinate legislation was enacted by the Governor-in-Council rather than by individual ministers it received careful scrutiny before the fact. The matter did not surface again until 1964, when the Fifteenth Report of the Special Commons Committee on Procedure and Organization recommended the establishment of a standing committee on delegated legislation which would report to the House any abuse of delegated legislative power, but whose "terms of reference should exclude it from considering the merits of or the policy behind delegated legislation." Many of the substantial reforms in parliamentary procedure brought about in the sixties arose out of the recommendations of

36. See Kersell, *Parliamentary Supremacy*. . . " and J. R. Mallory "Parliamentary Scrutiny of Delegated Legislation in Canada: A Large Step Forward and a Small Step Back." *Public Law* (Spring, 1972) pp. 30-42, for a fuller account of these developments.

that committee, but the proposal for a scrutiny committee was not followed up. Instead in 1968, the House set up a Special Committee to consider and report on "procedures for the review by this House of instruments made in virtue of any statute of the Parliament of Canada." The Committee reported to the House on October 22, 1969.

It made the following recommendations: the same requirement should apply to all regulations of a legislative character, whether made under statutory authority or under the prerogative (save that regulations affecting national security should be exempted from the requirement for publication); criteria were recommended to ensure that enabling statutes should prescribe the precise limits of delegated authority, which should not permit either the making of retrospective regulations or the exemption of regulations from judicial review; regulations by independent agencies should be subject to disallowance by the Governor-in-Council, which should be the only body empowered to make regulations having substantial policy implications; delegated legislation should not extend either to the power to tax or to amend statutes; and tribunals with power to decide policy should not be created by regulation. The Committee also urged that internal procedures for reviewing draft regulations should be strengthened. A small committee of the House, to which all regulations should stand permanently referred, equipped with adequate staff should be instituted. To emphasize the objectivity of the committee, there should be some method of rotating its chairmanship among the parties. Regulations should be examined on the basis of six criteria:

(a) whether they are authorized by the terms of the enabling statute;
(b) whether they appear to make some unusual or unexpected use of the powers conferred by the statute under which they are made;
(c) whether they trespass unduly on personal rights and liberties;
(d) whether they have complied with the provisions of the Regulations Act with respect to transmittal, certification, recording, numbering, publication, or laying before Parliament;
(e) whether they
    (i) represent an abuse of the power to provide that they shall come into force before they are transmitted to the Clerk of the Privy Council, or
    (ii) unjustifiably fail to provide that they shall not come into force until published at some later date;

(f) whether, for any special reason, their form or purport call for elucidation.

In order that scrutiny should go not only to form but to merit, it was proposed that the committee should have the power to refer regulations to the appropriate "subject-matter" committee of the House. Parliamentary review should be implemented by a resolution referring an impugned regulation to the government for reconsideration but that where statutory provision now exists for affirmative or negative resolutions this procedure should continue.

In due course the government responded. A new statutory instruments act was promised, Cabinet directives would be issued to strengthen internal procedures, and standing orders would be amended to permit the establishment of a scrutiny committee. "All regulations," the Leader of the House announced, "with the single exception of regulations the disclosure of which would be injurious to international relations, national defence, security or federal-provincial relations, will stand permanently referred to such a committee."[37] This was a large and ominous exception, much broader than the Special Committee's exemption on the grounds of "national security." All efforts to persuade the government to yield on this point were unavailing.

Six months later the promised Statutory Instruments Bill was before the House. In moving the Bill at second reading, the Minister of Justice, Mr. John Turner, referred to a directive he was laying before Cabinet which would set out criteria which his department would enforce on departments and agencies. They would not sanction regulations which excluded the jurisdiction of the courts, which purported to amend the parent act or any other act of Parliament, which were retrospective, which sub-delegated regulation-making authority, imposed a charge on the public other than by way of fees for service, which trespassed unduly on personal rights and liberties, or power to make regulations involving important matters of principle or policy.[38] He referred to concern among Members of Parliament and the public about "the increase of legislative powers being given to the executive without any realistic form of parliamentary control." The Bill itself, together with other steps to which he referred, was "an attempt to restore a measure of Parliamentary control over the executive and to redress the balance in the relationship between the individual and the state." One of the main features

37. Canada. *House of Commons Debates.* June 16, 1970. p. 8156.

38. *Ibid.* January 25, 1971. p. 2734.

of the Bill would be to protect the public from the "improper or unusual" exercise of power which had been delegated by Parliament. In one way the Bill was much wider than the Regulations Act, which had applied solely to regulations of a clearly legislative nature. It would now cover statutory instruments in general, including rules governing practice before federal judicial or quasi-judicial bodies, as well as regulations made by federal Crown corporations and federally incorporated companies where a fine or imprisonment is provided. While not all regulations would be published in the *Canada Gazette*, the public would nevertheless have the right to inspect and obtain copies of such regulations except where considerations of security or the rights of the individual would preclude this. Examples would be orders that revealed the location or equipment of the armed forces, and parole and mandatory supervision certificates under the Parole Act. "Most" statutory instruments would stand referred to a parliamentary scrutiny committee which would be set up in due course.

The debate centred on two issues. The first was the wide exemption clause previously referred to. The second was the provision that instruments "stand referred" without any provisions which would enable the House to reject, amend, or vary them. In resisting further change, Mr. Turner suggested that he had already gone much further in the Bill than his colleagues in the Cabinet realized, and that it would not be prudent to embrace all of the Special Committee's recommendations without jeopardizing the Bill itself. He could not accept that the executive could yield its right to reject or amend a regulation to a parliamentary committee. The committee could recommend to the House, the House could deal with the recommendation as it saw fit. It is not easy to imagine that a government in control of the House would permit the House in the end to seek to overturn a regulation. Nevertheless, there was some comfort to be derived from the Minister's final assurance that he and his officials would be in a stronger position to enforce the spirit of the act if they could point to a report from a strong and independent committee.

In the end it was decided that the scrutiny committee should be a joint committee of both Houses. Standing Orders were amended accordingly on October 14, 1971, the Act itself was brought into force by proclamation on January 1, 1972, and the Joint Committee began to function in that year. How has it fared? The first thing to be said is that, with the aid of a conscientious and competent staff, it began the hard and dreary business of combing through vast quantities of statutory intruments and reporting regularly thereon to both

Houses. It was fortunate that its co-chairman on the Senate side in its formative years was Senator Eugene Forsey. As a publisher's reader and a frequent contributor to scholarly journals, he had long been the scourge of his fellow-scholars whom he found guilty of sloppy thought and cloudy writing. He was now, on a larger stage, to have what must have been his finest hour. The Committee was to have long, and not always successful, battles with departments and agencies over dubious orders. Forsey once asked a departmental official whether a particular order, for which there did not appear to be any statutory authority whatsoever, was based on the prerogative? That was not the case, replied the somewhat horrified official, the order was based on "the inherent powers of the state." Further comment is unnecessary.

In addition to its routine duties, the Committee undertook a full review of the Trudeau government's Green Paper on Freedom of Information as well as a full review of the statutory instruments problem with a view to recommending improvements in parliamentary control. As a result of the work of the Committee so far, two problems seem to have emerged. A questionable statutory instrument most often raises rather abstract problems of constitutional propriety. These are seldom easy issues for a parliamentary opposition, anxious to arouse public support and indignation, to turn into effective political issues. The public, unfortunately, seems to have little taste for such matters. The result is that the reports of the Committee are seldom considered in the House, either at question time or in debates. Occasionally they are debated in the Senate. Such debates rarely find space in the press. The second problem is a related one. Members of Parliament are political men whose time is scarce. It turned out to be extremely difficult for the Committee to muster a quorum, and most of the delinquents were from the House. As a result it now operates under skeletal quorum rules: for a vote or decision of the Committee, five members must be present and both Houses represented; for meetings and the authorization of the printing of evidence, the quorum is three with both Houses represented.

Over the years it has concluded that the criteria need to be refined. In its First Report to the Thirty-Second Parliament (tabled in the Senate June 3, 1980) it recommended the following criteria for judging adversely on regulations:

> Whether a regulation or other statutory instrument within its terms of reference, in the judgment of the committee:

1. (a) is not authorized by the terms of the enabling statute or, if it is pursuant to the prerogative, its terms are not in conformity with the common law; or
   (b) does not clearly state therein the precise authority for the making of the instrument;
2. has not complied with the provisions of the *Statutory Instruments Act* with respect to transmittal, recording, numbering or publication;
3. (a) has not complied with any tabling provisions or other conditions set forth in the enabling statute; or
   (b) does not clearly state therein the time and manner of compliance with any such conditions;
4. makes some unusual or unexpected use of the powers conferred by the enabling statute or by the prerogative;
5. trespasses unduly on the rights and liberties of the subject;
6. (a) tends directly or indirectly to exclude the jurisdiction of the courts without explicit authorization thereof in the enabling statute; or
   (b) makes the rights and liberties of the subject dependent on administrative discretion rather than on the judicial process;
7. purports to have retroactive effect where the enabling statute confers no express authority so to provide or, where such authority is so provided, the retroactive effect appears to be oppressive, harsh or unnecessary;
8. appears for any reason to infringe the rule of law or the rules of natural justice;
9. provides without good and sufficient reason that it shall come into force before registration by the Clerk of the Privy Council;
10. in the absence of express authority to that effect in the enabling statute or prerogative, appears to amount to the exercise of a substantive legislative power properly the subject of direct parliamentary enactments, and not merely to the formulation of subordinate provisions of a technical or administrative character properly the subject of delegated legislation;
11. without express provisions to the effect having been made in the enabling statute or prerogative, imposes a fine, imprisonment or other penalty, or shifts the onus of proof of innocence to the person accused of an offence;
12. imposes a charge on the public revenues or contains provisions requiring payment to be made to the Crown or to any other authority in consideration of any license or service to be ren-

dered, or prescribes the amount of any such charge or payment, without express authority to that effect having been provided in the enabling statute or prerogative;

13. is not in conformity with the *Canadian Bill of Rights*;
14. is unclear in its meaning or otherwise defective in its drafting;
15. for any other reasons requires elucidation as to its form or purport.

This all seems clear and reasonable. However, there are two problems. In the first place there is no certainty that the offending department or agency will pay heed to the Committee, and no evidence that either House has the will or the means to back the Committee up. The second difficulty is the Committee must deal with regulations after they are made, and that the fault may lie in sloppy drafting of the parent legislation which permits regulations which offend some of the Committee's criteria.

These difficulties might have been mitigated if the Conservative government's proposals for parliamentary reform, tabled in the house on Novemeber 23, 1979, had been implemented. These included an improvement in the opportunities to have the Committee's reports debated on the floor of the House, either in the proposed new arrangements for Private Members' time or on allotted days. For this to happen it would be necessary for opposition members and parties to use scarce time for this purpose, which so far they had been reluctant to do. A more promising proposal would have required that the enabling clauses of all bills be referred to the Statutory Instruments Committee at the same time as the bills are being considered at the normal committee stage. This would enable the Committee to review legislation before it is passed, instead of spending all of its time on regulations under old legislation. The pressure on legislative time is so great that it is very difficult to get a loosely-worded act amended. Under this proposal the Committee would have an opportunity to engage in some preventive medicine.

The Conservative proposal also included a suggestion, although not spelled out in detail, which would have provided a further opportunity for the House to address itself to delegated legislation. At the moment there are very few statutes that contain provisions which require regulations made under them have either an affirmative resolution of the House to confirm them, or provide that a negative resolution may be moved against them. It was recommended that Standing Orders be amended to provide for both affirmative and negative resolutions. This of course would not make it any easier for the House to annul a regulation, since a government with a majority could always muster enough votes to defeat an opposition motion. However the attendant publicity would be likely to shame the government into withdrawing or modifying the offending regulation.

Delegated Judicial Power and the Rule of Law

The exercise by the executive of the delegated power to legislate has never been regarded as a serious violation of the separation of powers under our system of government. Cabinet government involves, as Bagehot pointed out, a fusion of executive and legislature, and it is not difficult to combine ultimate parliamentary control with a good deal of power in the executive. With the exercise by the executive of judicial power, however, the matter is not quite the same. The independence of the judiciary from the executive is one of our basic principles of government, and we tend to look with much less enthusiasm on executive power in this area than in any other. However, even here the matter is not clear-cut. Originally the courts of justice were offshoots of the Crown, and it was only in the seventeenth century that the prerogative courts were swept away. Even now there are areas in which prerogative courts theoretically are accepted without question. One example is the Judicial Committee of the Privy Council, though in fact it has come under the control of statute and by virtue of this is staffed only with judges of the regular courts. Until recently, colonial constitutions in British North America still retained a residue of judicial power in the executive in the provision, in some of the older provincial constitutions, for the exercise of certain appellate powers by the Governor-in-Council.[39]

In modern terms the problem of judicial power by the executive is somewhat different. It stems from the needs of the welfare state. The regular courts have perfected a system of justice the high standard of which in part results from an arrangement that is highly expensive for the litigant and may involve considerable delays. This is quite proper when life and liberty are at stake or where the property interests in question are of substantial value. When, however, Parliament began to confer rights of relatively small monetary value on large classes of persons, the ordinary courts were not

39. Prince Edward Island resurrected the jurisdiction in divorce cases of the Lieutenant-Governor-in-Council as late as 1945. See Frank MacKinnon, *The Government of Prince Edward Island* (Toronto, 1951), pp. 262-5.

always the best instruments for settling questions of the application of the law. Those who may be eligible for worker's compensation or unemployment insurance are not able to afford the expense of litigation, yet the whole value of such rights is that they can be exercised at once before the beneficiary has died of starvation, or become an object of charity. But in many of these cases, complicated legal questions may arise which can only be settled by the use of skilled legal techniques. Thus the state has had to balance the advantages of a high standard of justice against the advantages of immediate determination of claims, and has tended to take such questions away from the ordinary courts and place them in the hands of administrative tribunals.

There are two main arguments used to justify the use of administrative tribunals: the argument of speed and cost and the argument of expertise. In the first place, it is clear that the courts are now overloaded with litigation and the creation by Parliament of further kinds of legal questions to settle would swamp the courts. It is also argued that most of the beneficiaries of recent legislation are unable to afford the cost and delay of resort to the courts, and so in case of a dispute would simply have to forego their rights. Secondly, it is argued that these new branches of law created by statute, such as unemployment insurance and worker's compensation, are highly technical and the courts are no more competent than anyone else to understand them. Only tribunals which have built up experience with this specialized and exotic branch of the law can be expected to apply it sensibly. The result is that the ordinary courts are barred, and aggrieved persons are compelled to bring their cases before special administrative tribunals.

There are, however, objections to administrative tribunals. The first objection is that in many of these disputes the state is both party and litigant. The state may appoint the tribunal and it may not completely relax its hold over the members. Judges, whatever their faults, enjoy security of tenure and can be intimidated by no one. On the other hand, many members of administrative tribunals hold office during the pleasure of the Crown and in some Canadian provinces this can speedily change to displeasure at an official who shows signs of independence. Sometimes the legislature deliberately tips the balance heavily in favour of the government. This was the case with the Income War Tax Act of 1940 which gave the Minister of National Revenue the power not only to determine assessments, but also to hear appeals from his own decisions. The present Income Tax Act, which provides a Tax Appeal Board, avoids a situation in which the minister has been virtually a judge in his own case.

Where administrative tribunals exist, it is therefore important to ensure that they are impartial and free from pressure, and that they follow a procedure which is in accord with our traditions of a fair hearing. They should find only on the evidence before them, they should give written opinions, and on questions of law there should, in the end, be some opportunity for final determination by someone with expert legal qualifications. The Canadian Unemployment Insurance Act is almost a model in this respect. When an insured person is denied a claim he may appeal to a referee who possesses legal qualifications, and a final appeal on matters of law can be made to an umpire who is defined in the act as a judge of the Federal Court of Canada. Decisions are thus in accord with the practice and tradition of judicial fairness, but at the same time they are speedy and inexpensive.

A second problem created by administrative tribunals is that they are often called upon to settle questions which are not questions of pure law, but also of policy. Their decisions are thus quasi-judicial.[40] Such, for example, are the decisions, grouped under the Canadian Transport Commission, on such matters as rate discrimination cases; and the public utilities commissions regulating the franchises of what are in effect chartered monopolies are as frequently making the law as applying it.

The essential question is perhaps this: in applying the law in novel fields, how much discretion should be granted to administrative tribunals? Even the courts have some discretion in applying the law where there is ambiguity, but in the case of administrative agencies this discretion is often positively conferred by statute. The statute may at the same time make it difficult or impossible to appeal the decision of an administrative agency to the courts.

> There are [as Professor Dawson argued]...serious risks involved in this erection of barriers between the citizen and the courts of justice, and few can contemplate with equanimity any substantial interference with so fundamental a constitutional principle as the rule of law. For while discretionary power does not necessarily result in arbitrary power in

40. See *Report of the Committee on Ministers' Powers.* Sir Ivor Jennings claims that the term quasi-judicial is meaningless, and that it is difficult to distinguish between "judicial" and "administrative" functions in terms of the nature and substance of what courts and administrative authorities do. "The most that can be said," he states, "is that the courts are much more concerned with questions of law, and the administrative authorities with questions of discretion." *The Law and the Constitution,* 4th ed. (London, 1955), p. 277.

> the sinister sense..., it does introduce the possibility of ill-controlled authority; it will always raise a strong suspicion of abuse; and on many occasions the inabiliy of the injured party to appeal to the courts cannot fail to convert suspicions into apparent certainties. The mere willingness of a Cabinet minister to accept political responsibility for administrative decisions is in the vast majority of cases not nearly as real or as effective a safeguard as that which a review of the courts would provide.[41]

At the base of all misgivings about administrative tribunals is Dicey's idea of the rule of law, "of legal equality, or of universal subjection of all classes to one law administered by the ordinary courts."[42] We have come a long way from the simple and universal application of Dicey's principle. The need for curbing large aggregations of corporate power, for conferring effective legal remedies on the many and not just on those able to afford legal advice, or for giving the executive special powers where the national interest is deemed to be at stake, have all combined to curtail the jursidiction of the ordinary courts and have left the determination of many legal questions either to adminstrative tribunals created for the purpose, or, in some cases, to a minister of the Crown or of the Cabinet. These are all inroads on the rule of law. They need not be inroads on constitutional liberty provided that the tribunals themselves are genuinely independent of the executive, possess professional competence in dealing with legal questions, and determine questions of law with the same respect for evidence and the same impartiality as the ordinary courts. Administrative tribunals and the exercise of judicial powers by the executive are increasing and are now so general that it would be hopeless to try to reverse the trend. The positive advantages of administrative tribunals are such that they are probably unavoidable. Nevertheless they need constant critical review if the remedy is not to be worse than the disease.[43]

Another important aspect of the problem is the spectacular growth of regulatory agencies, both federal and provincial, which carry out both regulatory activities of an administrative character and enjoy considerable powers of both a legislative and a judicial

41. R. MacGregor Dawson, *The Government of Canada* rev. ed. (Toronto, 1963) p. 296.

42. A. V. Dicey, *Introduction to the Study of the Law of the Constitution*. 10th ed. (London, 1961) p. 193.

43. See John Willis and H. F. Angus, "Administrative Decision and the Law." *Canadian Journal of Economics and Political Science* XXIV: 4 (November, 1958) p. 512.

nature. The process of regulation itself, in relation to giant industries of a monopolistic character, not only imposes a tremendous load onto busy ministers but is always vulnerable to the charge that decisions are open to abuse, and possible corruption. Not only the enforcement of regulations, but the making of regulations themselves inevitably raise questions of both politics and policy. It was no doubt for this reason, as Professor Hodgetts has pointed out, "that a new type of administrative agency was required that could take on the impartial and independent stamp of the judiciary and could be entrusted with subordinate law-making functions that would have to be delegated to it."[44] Thus we can see the Railway Committee of the Privy Council, which flourished as a Committee of the Cabinet, being transformed into the Board of Railway Commissioners and emerging in the sixties as the Canadian Transport Commission, an independent agency with wide policy-making as well as enforcement powers. It has since been joined by a number of other powerful agencies of the same sort, such as the Canadian Radio and Telecommunications Commission and the Atomic Energy Control Board.

All of these agencies have a number of characteristics in common. Parliament has left them with power to make the law, as well as enforce it. Many of their decisions are subject to final appeal to the Cabinet, thus preserving final political control to the executive. When they make a decision of a judicial character their procedures are subject to review by the Federal Court to ensure that they have conducted a fair hearing, for that Court can review on procedural grounds a wide but uncertain area where the law has conferred a discretionary power on the executive or a regulatory agency.

The same process has gone on apace in the provinces, which have entrusted the regulation of public utilities, highway transport, the marketing of natural products and many other activities to regulatory agencies. In all cases, the weakening of normal political control over the activities of government has been justified by a variety of considerations, such as the minimizing of "political" interference in basic technical matters, the introduction of greater procedural fairness into decisions, and the need to reduce the burden on ordinary ministers and departments. One consequence has been to hive off important policy areas from normal political control. Another has been an awkward side-effect on inter-governmental relations.

44. J. E. Hodgetts, *The Canadian Public Service* (Toronto, 1973) p. 144. See also, for a fuller discussion of the whole matter, G. Bruce Doern (ed.) *The Regulatory Process in Canada.* (Toronto, 1978).

The growth of the role of government has meant that both the federal and provincial governments and their agencies are constantly making decisions which affect one another's operations. This has been an important source of federal-provincial conflict which has one peculiar characteristic. Most inter-governmental conflict is in the end resolved by continuing negotiations between ministers at the two levels of government, and these conflicts can usually be resolved by negotiation and compromise. Such settlements are possible when ministers and Cabinets are involved. When one or both of the actors in conflict is a powerful but autonomous agency it becomes much more difficult for differences to be resolved.[45]

The existence of agencies, great empires in their own right, also severely hampers the achievement of coherent and effective national policies. For example, both Ontario and Quebec Hydros are huge borrowers on international money markets and are little disposed to brook control by others on their activities. This imposes severe constraints on the ability of the Bank of Canada and the Department of Finance to manage an effective monetary policy which controls the money supply and the value of the dollar. Similarly, such independent bodies are able to have considerable effects on the achievement of industrial strategies by both levels of government.

THE PUBLIC SERVICE

There are, apart from the employees of Crown corporations, about three hundred thousand employees in the public service of Canada. Theoretically, they hold office during the pleasure of the Crown and have no right to any tenure. However, unless they are temporary or casual employees, they can only be dismissed for cause. Where an employee has been dismissed by a deputy head for incompetence or incapacity, he has a right of appeal to a tribunal appointed by the Public Service Commission to ensure fairness and equity in each case. When employment has been brought to an end by layoff because of lack of work or discontinuance of a function, an employee enjoys a priority right of re-employment.

Since a civil servant, once appointed, is not as easily dismissed as the employee of a private employer, the selection process in the

45. See Richard J. Schultz, *Federalism and the Regulatory Process.* (Montreal, 1979)

public service is important because mistakes in hiring are not easy to correct. Accordingly, the machinery for personnel recruitment and management is of considerable significance.

The traditional attitude to public employment in Canada was to encourage the development of a kind of "spoils system," though one with important differences from that which prevailed in the United States. In summary, the Canadian position was that governments appointed their political friends to office, though they did not follow the process through to the point of removing all of the officials appointed by their political enemies—unless these officials had abused their positions by active political partisanship. As Sir John A. Macdonald wrote to an importunate follower in Prince Edward Island:

> It is a principle long settled in Canada that the British and not the American system should prevail as to office, and that a man once appointed should not be removed on account on his political proclivities so long as he performs the duties of his office, and does not use his position or influence ostentatiously against the Government of the day. It is but right that each party as they get possession of the Government should appoint their friends. The present government is doing so, and cannot object to its predecessor having done the same thing. When vacancies occur... as a matter of course our political friends will get the preference.[46]

It is perhaps not unfair to the old civil service to say that the only offence justifying dismissal was political partisanship. To support openly the political enemies of the government was intolerable; incompetence or scandalous behaviour was a human condition which could more readily be forgiven. Even today, when the bad old system is far behind us, the law imposes severe restrictions on overt political action.[47] Meanwhile, although the regular public service is

46. Sir Joseph Pope, *Correspondence of Sir John Macdonald* (Toronto, n.d.), pp. 270-1. The Governor General, the Marquess of Lorne, gives a slightly different view of the situation at that time: He protested to Macdonald that the number of dismissals recommended on grounds of political partisanship after the election of 1878 was excessive, and a great many such recommendations were withdrawn "because nothing could be alleged against him save that the new minister at the head of his department wanted him removed to provide for some political friend of his own." The Duke of Argyll, *Passages from the Past,* Vol. II (London, 1907), p. 414.

47. A certain nineteen-year-old stenographer in the Public Works Department, whose beauty had previously won her acclaim as Miss Ottawa Rough Rider of 1956, hastily resigned the position of Miss Young Liberal when it was pointed out that this was a grave violation of the Civil Service Act. Montreal *Gazette,* May 28, 1957.

insulated from political influence over appointments and dismissals, many M.P.s and defeated candidates still assert a prescriptive right to demand the dismissal of employees who are not protected by the act. When a temporary employee is accused of political partisanship by an M.P., he is dismissed without any investigation of the charge. In other cases an investigation is held.

Patronage was a natural consequence of responsible government, for the first fruits of power were opportunities to use government patronage instead of its remaining the monopoly of a privileged minority. The abuse of political patronage was, of course, condemned—but by parties in opposition with no access to the fruits of power. Their first task on gaining office was to ensure that political appointments went to worthy persons, who had demonstrated this by open adherence to the right party. Only after the essential needs had been met did parties think seriously of reforming the system. The electorate was small in the nineteenth century, and in many constituencies government employment was sufficient not only to keep the nucleus of the party machine on the public payroll, but also to influence what could be a significant number of votes. As the electorate increased in size, the number of disappointed seekers after government jobs became proportionately large compared with the number that could be accommodated; as a result even hard-headed politicians came to see some virtue in civil service reform. Only in the twentieth century did the question of civil service reform assume a new dimension. As the problems and responsibilities of government became more complex, it began to be important to have a civil service capable of meeting the more exacting demands of the new age. Sir George Murray, in 1912, found that one of the greatest weaknesses of the public service was that the quality of deputy heads and other senior officials was so uneven that far too many decisions remained with ministers. Only by developing a higher civil service, one capable of relieving ministers of the routine burdens of office, could the Canadian public service cope with the growth of government responsibility. It thus became possible to link civil service reform not only with civic purity but with efficiency.

Thus the pace of civil service reform was slow because there was no strong vested interest in it. The great landmarks of civil service modernization in the United Kingdom ran a whole generation ahead of similar progress in Canada.

The beginnings of the discussion of the problem of civil service reform in Canada were in a committee of the House of Commons in 1877. An amendment to the Civil Service Act in 1882 required that candidates for a large number of positions in Ottawa pass qualifying examinations set by an examining board. But the minister could still appoint the candidate of his own choice from an eligible list created by the examination. The results of this appear to have been negligible, for in 1907 a Royal Commission ruefully reported that the quality of the public service had actually declined in the twenty-five years during which the system had operated.[48] By this time, however, public opinion was more ready for reform. The imminence of an election precipitated action, partly because Robert Borden, as leader of the opposition, was finding reform of the public service an excellent piece of ammunition, and the Civil Service Act was accordingly amended in 1908.

The 1908 act created a Civil Service Commission, which was to set examinations for many posts in the "inside" service (employees in the departments in Ottawa), although similar reform in the "outside" service was to come much later. The Civil Service Commission was given independent tenure similar to that of the judiciary, and recruitment by examination in future was to be based on competitive examinations. In the 1918 act, the tenure of the three commissioners was reduced to ten years, but the provisions protecting them from removal were left unaltered.

Of all the Prime Ministers of Canada, only Sir Robert Borden displayed any serious interest in the cause of civil service reform. In and out of office he was a tireless advocate of the introduction of method and sound principles into the public service. He found it an antiquated structure distinguished by no discernible operating principles. He left it a service modelled on scientific methods for the government of a modern democracy. That the principles of organization sold to his government by high-powered American consultants were based on theories of organization no longer accepted as valid, and that the recommendations of the consultants were unsuited to the conditions of the public service at the time are perhaps beside the point.

The decision to call in American consultants to apply the principles of the 1918 act may itself have been sound. Sir George Murray's proposals had little impact because, as Borden later ruefully admitted, Murray had "an imperfect conception of the difficulties that would confront any administration in the attempt to put into force some of his recommendations however valuable they appear to

48. See, for an account of the early years of civil service reform, R. MacGregor Dawson, *The Civil Service of Canada* (Toronto, 1929).

him."[49] Murray had wished to introduce into Canada something very much like the administrative class of the British civil service. He did not realize that it would have been impossible to make the Canadian higher civil service the preserve of a distinct social and educational élite. The idea of such a closed administrative élite was alien to the North American tradition of democratic equality.

The old Canadian civil service, with all its faults, had in fact developed a class of administrators who, though uneven in quality, were qualified for higher posts by general ability of a high order. The 1919 regulations attempted to get rid of the old system and replace it with one in which each post was to be filled by competitive tests which would inevitably disclose the best available man for that particular post. To make this arrangement possible, the civil service had to be broken up into a very large number of classes, each one corresponding to some unique combination of duties and abilities. This system, which reflects the ideas then dominant in the field of scientific management, does promote equality of opportunity and its signal virtue is that it finds exactly the right man for a particular vacancy. While this is the principal virtue of the system, it is also its principal fault from the point of view of developing a career service in which young men of ability can be recruited with the prospect of increasing status and responsibility. For instead of recruiting potential administrators for the few but very important top posts, the government personnel agencies are bound to live within a rigid and inflexible system in which every vacancy is expected to be filled by competitive promotion.

The new system was radically flawed by the fact that it was unlikely to produce first-class administrtors from within the ranks of the civil service. It was also, for a country with a small number of public employees, excessively elaborate. These weaknesses, serious as they are, should not blind us to its virtues. It was probably necessary to have such a system in order to establish a tradition of fairness, equality of treatment, and efficiency in a civil service only emerging from the full bloom of patronage.

Actually, the Canadian civil service suffered less from the rigours of the 1918 reforms than might have been expected because there was a limit to their application. For all the paraphernalia of open competitive examinations, there were some side entrances to the civil service. A generous provision giving preference to war veterans gave them an absolute advantage in any competition for which they

49. Sir Robert Borden, "The Problem of the Efficient Civil Service," *Canadian Historical Association, Annual Report,* 1931, p. 15.

were qualified. The old provision that the private secretary to a minister of the Crown who had served for three years was entitled to an established post in the civil service was retained.

A peculiarity of the Canadian system which flowed from the 1918 act was the wide range of responsibilities given to the Civil Service Commission. In this it differed from the Civil Service Commission of the United States (which has very limited responsibilities for organization and classification) or the British Civil Service Commission (which is little more than an examining body for posts in the public service). The importance of the merit system, together with a prevailing belief in the scientific objectivity of an examination system, dictated that the commission should be an independent agency with considerable freedom from control by the government of the day. In accordance with the constitutional necessity for ministerial responsibility for financial matters, the commission reported to Parliament through the Secretary of State for Canada, who laid its Estimates before Parilament. As its spokesman in the House, the Secretary of State had significant influence, but, since the commission was an independent agency, he had influence rather than authority over the functions exercised by the commission.

The chief functions of the commission were indicated by the titles of its two main branches, the Investigation and Organization Branch and the Examination Branch. Under the 1918 act, the Examination Branch dealt with recruitment, examination and placement, and to an extent with promotions. The Investigation and Organization Branch dealt with such questions as the need for new positions and replacements, the classification of positions, rates of pay, and procedural methods and organization. Since an economic use of public personnel is an important personnel function, it became one of the concerns of the commission to survey the way departments used their human resources. The organization and methods officers of the commission could, by suggesting improvements in lighting, layout, or work allocation, enable a department to increase its efficiency without additional employees.

In spite of the breadth of its responsibilities, the commission lacked undisputed authority in almost all fields except recruitment and certification. In matters of pay it was subject to final decision by the Cabinet, advised by the Treasury Board, and in a wide range of matters concerned with establishment and personnel policy, authority was shared in a somewhat uncertain fashion with the Treasury Board. An expert foreign observer, Professor Taylor Cole, noted that "One outstanding characteristic of the Canadian public service has been the absence of arrangements for co-ordinating the personnel policies and procedures."[50] This problem, and the more general question of modernizing the whole system, was the subject of inquiry and debate for twenty years, and its resolution began to emerge with clarity only with major legislative change in 1967.

Personnel Management in the Public Service

The apparently massive changes brought about by the three important measures in 1967 were initiated by an announcement by the Prime Minister on August 7, 1963, "reaffirming the determination of the Government to establish in the Public Service an appropriate form of collective bargaining and arbitration," and setting up a committee of senior officials "to make the necessary preparations." It was obvious that such a step would require legislation of some kind, since collective bargaining for the public service was outside the scope of the Industrial Relations and Disputes Investigation Act. At the same time it was both natural and desirable to consolidate the personnel management functions relating to salaries and conditions of work in a single authority, and to provide some measure of managerial flexibility by delegation to departments so that the bargaining units on both sides would match one another.

As it happened all of these moves fitted into a lengthy debate over the readjustment of public personnel management functions which had been working towards a conclusion for nearly half a century. The long period of severe austerity during the depression had brought out again the need for tight financial controls, and led to the endowment of the Treasury Board with strong powers of veto over establishments, wage and salary policy, and expenditures generally. In order to protect the merit system there grew up a complicated divided jurisdiction between the Civil Service Commission and the Treasury Board, which made action difficult and often led to the sacrifice of personnel development policy for financial exigencies.

When the labour market for the public service changed as a result of the Second World War and the post-war boom this system became intolerable. It was no longer a matter of the Civil Service Commission playing the dual role of acting as a barrier against politically motivated appointments and of picking off the cream of the applicants by a leisurely method of competitive selection. It is

50. See. Taylor Cole, *The Canadian Bureaucracy* (Durham, N.C., 1949), pp. 34-51, and *passim*.

now necessary to seek out energetically the good candidates needed from a tight labour market with a speed and efficiency hitherto unknown. Also the experience of the war had revealed a radical flaw in the system created by the 1918 act. Its provision for upward mobility was slow and uncertain, and it possessed an original bias against direct recruitment of specialists and top administrators. The pre-war civil service just did not have within itself the resources to operate the expanded wartime bureaucracy, and the major needs of the public service were met by borrowing administrators and experts of all kinds from industry, the universities and even the provincial civil services.

The first attempt to break through this difficulty was in the Report of the (Gordon) Royal Commission on Administrative Classification in the Public Service, in 1946. This commission found that the principal defects of the Canadian public service were:

1. A lack of "enough men of high calibre in the senior and intermediate grades." This placed too great a burden upon ministers and deputy heads, who could not delegate responsibility to officers of senior and intermediate grade (this, it will be recalled, was also a criticism made by Sir George Murray in 1912).

2. There was no clear-cut assignment of responsibility for "the overall management and direction of the service." Consequently, there was no systematic training, seeking out, developing and transferring of promising officers within the service.

3. No machinery existed for making decisive and prompt adaptations in organization to meet changing needs or to deal with the problem of "redundant, unsuitable, or incompetent personnel."

4. Serious delays existed at all levels in making appointments and promotions.[51]

The major change recommended was that the functions of the Civil Service Commission be confined in future to recruitment and appointment. Establishment and personnel should be placed completely under a newly created division of the Treasury Board, headed by a director-general with broad powers over "organization of departments including establishments and rates of pay." At the same time, greater authority in personnel matters should be given to departments, for the deputy head was to be given final authority, with the concurrence of the director-general, over promotions of administrative, scientific, technical and professional employees. In

51. *Report of the Royal Commission of Administrative Classification in the Public Service*, 1946, p. 11.

addition, the disciplinary powers of ministers over their departments were to be strengthened.

The main proposal of the Gordon Commission did not command wide support, and was never carried out. The idea of centralizing public personnel policy in a "czar" (as he was called in the press reports) in the Treasury Board did not commend itself to the mass of civil servants and also encountered strong opposition from French-Canadian members of Parliament. They felt that the Treasury Board, which contained few French Canadians, would be less sympathetic to the conventionally established "balance" in civil service recruitment and allocation of personnel between French- and English-speaking civil servants than had been the Civil Service Commission. Similarly, because the Royal Commission had somewhat unwisely recommended a modification of the veterans' preference, its report was opposed by the Canadian Legion.[52]

While the main proposal of the Royal Commission for a re-allocation of powers and functions of the civil service failed to command public support and was not adopted, nevertheless important modifications in procedure after 1946 went a long way towards meeting the major criticisms which the report had made of personnel administration in the public service. Recruitment and promotion procedures were greatly simplified and speeded up, in-service training was developed, and close co-operation in practice between the Civil Service Commission and the Treasury Board led to much greater efficiency in many directions. The Civil Service Commission embarked on a deliberate policy of recruiting and developing what was in effect an administrative class through the Administrative Trainee Program. Furthermore, it appeared in the fifties that official opinion was veering in the direction of enhancing the powers, not of the Treasury Board, but of the Civil Service Commission itself.[53]

The 1918 act had governed the civil service for forty years when the government directed the Civil Service Commission to review the act and make systematic proposals for bringing it up to date. At the same time they appointed A.D.P. Heeney, a senior civil servant with long and varied experience, as chairman of the commission. It could hardly be expected that the Civil Service Commission would seek to preside over the liquidation of its own empire. However, its chief task was to recognize that the object of public personnel policy

52. Cole, *The Canadian Bureaucracy,* pp. 54-7.

53. See. A. D. P. Heeney, "Civil Service Reform, 1958," *Canadian Journal of Economics and Political Science,* Vol. XXV, No. 1 (February 1959).

was no longer largely to stamp out the evils of patronage, but the more positive aim of seeking out, developing, and making the best use of the skilled human resources in the civil service.[54]

The commission proposed a thorough revision of the Civil Service Act, and the regulations which had been under it. In essence it recommended that, while the distribution of authority between the government (through the Treasury Board) and the commission should be clarified, the special and large role played by the commission had justified itself and should be retained. In order to strengthen the independent role of the commission, especially in pay determination, it urged that the commission be divested of managerial functions with strong policy implications, while retaining those functions essential to its role as the guardian of the merit system and the efficiency of the service.

It rejected the transfer of classification and personnel policy to the Treasury Board because of the danger of political patronage. In keeping with its desire to avoid responsibility for major policy matters, the commission recommended the transfer of control over organization to deputy heads of departments subject to overall supervision of the Treasury Board. Personnel functions should, as the Gordon Commission had recommended, be decentralized to the departments, but the standards should be set by the Civil Service Commission, which would then delegate authority to departments. The commission would still retain strong appellate functions and itself take over the right of dismissal from the government, acting on the recommendations of deputy heads.

The boldest and most original of the Heeney Report's proposals dealt with the machinery which was to provide a system of co-determination of salaries and conditions of work. In this matter little had changed since Confederation, even though the government of Canada was no longer the master of a handful of clerks but a major employer of industrial labour as well as technical specialists. In an age when employers are compelled by the necessities of large-scale operation as well as by the consensus of public opinion to bargain in some form with representative organizations of employees, it would be only natural to expect that the government would also find itself in some kind of normal collective bargaining relationship with its employees. This, however, was not the case. Except for the employees of Crown corporations, who could be exempted from this provision (and in most cases were), employees of the federal

54. *Personnel Administration in the Public Service* (Ottawa, 1958).

government were debarred by section 55 of the Industrial Relations and Disputes Investigation Act from bargaining through recognized trade unions.

The principal reason given for this anomaly was that the sovereign position of the state made it impossible for it to put itself into a bargaining posture with its employees. It was alleged that constitutional theory made honest bargaining impossible because the authority to grant wage increases and thus an increase in public expenditures belongs exclusively to Parliament, and could not be assumed by the government.[55] This is a somewhat transparent argument, since it does not inhibit governments from making other contingent commitments to spend public money, and in any event a government which has a majority in the House of Commons can always honour any undertakings so made. Nevertheless, the government clung stubbornly to its position in resisting collective bargaining on grounds of high constitutional principle.

As a consequence, alternatives to collective bargaining were canvassed. The first of these was modelled on the British system of Whitley Councils in which a joint council of representatives of associations of employees and of the government was set up to discuss and recommend changes in employment conditions. In Canada this took the form of the National Joint Council of the Public Service of Canada, set up by order-in-council P.C. 3676 of May 16, 1944.[56] The two sides of the council must reach agreement before reporting their recommendations to the appropriate authority.

It must be said that the experience with this machinery has not been particularly satisfactory. In the first place, the council has been characterized by long periods of inactivity and by exasperating and

55. "From the very nature of employment in the public service, there can be no bargaining agent for the nation comparable with the employer in industry who has at his disposal funds derived from payments for goods or services. The funds from which salaries are paid in the public service had to be voted by parliament and parliament alone can discharge that responsibility." Canada, *House of Commons Debates,* February 21, 1951, p. 542 (Mr. St. Laurent). For a full discussion of staff relations in the public service see Saul J. Frankel, *Staff Relations in the Civil Service* (Montreal, 1962).

56. Its functions were then defined as follows by the Minister of Finance: "The National Joint Council will act in an advisory capacity to the Treasury Board in all matters affecting the conditions of work in the public service....The Council will, of course, have no executive powers which would impair the responsibility of the Cabinet or Treasury Board or Civil Service Commission, or possibly infringe upon the authority of Parliament." Canada, *House of Commons Debates,* February 24, 1944, p. 778. See also Frankel, *Staff Relations in the Public Service,* pp. 70 ff.; and Cole, *The Canadian Bureaucracy,* pp. 123 ff.

inexplicable delays in the implementation of such recommendations as it has made to the government. Secondly, by a rather odd evolution in its practice, the subjects it was empowered to discuss did not include salaries, although its constitution included "remuneration" among its terms of reference.

In spite of its manifest defects, the National Joint Council was an important advance. By recognizing a form of participation in joint decision-making, it led to a distinct improvement in the morale of the public service. While it was far better than nothing at all, it had signally failed to become a useful machine for the joint discussion of salary issues. "This issue," Professor Frankel concluded, "would not be very important if more direct means of negotiation, or even consultation, were available. But, since they are not, the pressure to extend the Council's functions, or to establish separate facilities for collective bargaining can be expected to grow."[57]

An obvious solution would have been to repeal section 55 of the Industrial Relations and Disputes Investigation Act to allow direct trade union bargaining between the government and its employees. However, this was not an acceptable solution at that time to either ministerial or official opinion. Furthermore, the civil service associations themselves were deeply divided on the issue. An alternative solution would have been to provide some machinery for binding arbitration where deadlock in negotiation had been reached. This solution, too, was unacceptable in the conditions of the time.

It was in this unpromising stalemate that Mr. Heeney and his fellow civil service commissioners sought to put staff relations in the public service on a new and more promising footing. They visualized, for the Civil Service Commission, the role of an independent third force standing between the government and the civil service associations in developing a staff and salary policy acceptable to both. Their proposals to divest the commission of its management functions were part of a general attempt to put the commission in a position in which its role would be accepted by civil servants as independent of the government. They explain, in some detail in Appendix B of the report, how they conceive the role of the commission. They argue that public and private employment are sufficiently different that the normal industrial pattern of collective bargaining is not directly applicable, but that it is necessary to seek other ways to reach a solution which makes genuine consultation possible. The recommendation of salary rates for the classified civil

57. Frankel, "Staff Relations in the Canadian Public Service," *Canadian Journal of Economics and Political Science* XXII, No. 4 (November 1956), p. 522.

service by the Civil Service Commission should continue, and its role should be conceived as "in no sense an agency of Government, but...as fully independent in status as any special arbitral tribunal which might have been set up by Parliament to resolve conflicts between employer and employee." Thus the commission would "provide the independent auspices under which representatives of the Government...and representatives of the organized staff associations...could discuss in systematic fashion questions of salaries and wages in government employment."[58]

Joint discussions would be held between representatives of the government and of the staff associations under the chairmanship of the commission. In addition to the argument presented by both sides, the commission would have the data prepared by the Pay Research Bureau, which had been set up within the commission in 1957 but with an advisory committee made up of a representative from each of the three major staff associations, three members representing the government, and a Civil Service Commission chairman to oversee its work and give it an appearance of impartiality. The commission, having heard all of the evidence in this procedure of joint discussion, would then deliberate and make its recommendation to the government, but would communicate it simultaneously to both sides.

This would have been a heroic remedy. It is just possible that the prestige of the commission might have been great enough for it to have worked. But there were serious difficulties. A rejection by the government of a commission recommendation would seriously undermine its position for the future. On the other hand, if the government felt bound to accept the commission's recommendations, this "would imply submission to *compulsory* arbitration in its least desirable form—arbitration without prior negotiations."[59]

In fact this perilous and intriguing proposal was never put to the test. A few hours after the Heeney Report was tabled in Parliament, the government announced that Mr. Heeney was leaving the commission and returning to his former post as Ambassador in Washington. The government later announced that it was not prepared to accept the recommendation on pay determination.

The revised Civil Service Act, in the form in which it passed through Parliament in 1961, embodied three main features.[60] In the first place, it carried forward the independent role of the commis-

58. *Personnel Administration in the Public Service*, p. 132.

59. Frankel, *Staff Relations in the Civil Service*, p. 156.

60. S.H.S. Hughes, "A Comparison of the Old and New Civil Service Acts," in Paul Fox, ed., *Politic's: Canada,* 1st ed. (Toronto, 1962) pp. 165-72.

sion, and preserved unimpaired its responsibility for the merit system, including the sole right to classify positions. Secondly, it clarified the role of the commission in areas of personnel administration which do not bear on the merit system. Thirdly, it conferred on the staff associations the right to be consulted on all matters relating to remuneration and the conditions of employment. It introduced a meaningful distinction between the terms "civil service" and "public service." The former term applied only to employees under the Civil Service Act, the latter also included employees of departments and agencies listed in Schedule A of the Public Service Superannuation Act.

The act conferred two substantial rights on civil servants. Under the Public Service Superannuation Act, the only right which civil servants possessed was to their pension. The revised Civil Service Act added to this the legal right to their pay, and the right to appeal against a number of administrative actions which affected their welfare. The latter had already existed in the Civil Service Regulations, but was now enshrined in the act. Thus an aggrieved civil servant could go to court if he felt that his pay had been wrongfully denied, or if he believed that an appeal board which dealt with him had been improperly constituted. Provision was made for appeals by aggrieved employees against decisions involving promotion, transfer, demotion, suspension, dismissal and denial of statutory increase.

The act failed to follow the Heeney Report in two respects: it did not modify the preference for veterans with overseas service, and it did not extend the authority of the commission to other branches of the public service not covered by the Civil Service Act.

Government as Management: From Glassco to Lambert

There is a sense in which government and business are involved in comparable activities. Governments now collect and spend a substantial part of the gross national product, and those responsible for executing the activities of government are confronted with accomplishing the same operations as those in comparable roles in large businesses: controlling operations through accounting procedures, accumulating and regulating the flow of large inventories, and achieving timely and effective operations with efficiency and at minimum cost. The process of rational management is now largely a matter of rapidly changing systems of data processing which are able to process outputs and control operations far more effectively than the bookkeepers of the past. Management and organization thus become problems for government in much the same way as they do for other large organizations.

There has always been a substantial body of opinion that has regarded government as inherently inefficient and has urged that it would be better for everyone if government operations followed "businesslike" methods. There is a large assumption contained in this point of view that government and business—as administrative processes—are identical and that what is good for one is equally good for the other. Setting this questionable assumption aside for the moment, there is also the undeniable problem that the revolution in administrative techniques—from cost control to policy analysis—is bound to have a profound effect on the way in which government organizations operate.

Even before the full implications of this administrative revolution were understood, the sheer growth of government operations had led to demands for importing the managerial techniques of mid-century big business into the process of government itself, which now appears to have operated on a comparable scale. The first full-scale study of the problem from this perspective was the work of the Royal Commission on Government Organization, created by the Diefenbaker government in 1960. While the government was concerned chiefly with the point, which the party had repeatedly made in opposition, that government operations were badly in need of being placed on a more "businesslike" basis, the commission seemed to have conceived its function to be that of a management consultant.

The Commission's reading of its terms of reference led it to concentrate its attention on the management function in the public service. Government organization was reduced in their eyes to a problem in management—the political controls such as Cabinet and Parliament were outside their purview, and there is little reference to them except as they seem relevant to the assumptions of the Commission. It was assumed that management is the same in business as in government, that owners and directors are the same as legislators and ministers, and that the subordinate processes can be deemed identical. Presumably directors (who are part-time) are the same as full-time ministers, and salaried top managers are the same as deputy heads. Hence one could apply the concepts of managerial flexibility and types of managerial organization appropriate to business. The Commission did not ask itself whether the analogy was a good one: to a considerable extent it was given to them in their terms of reference. Their method of work was not likely to cause them to question it. They held no public hearings. They considered the views of senior civil servants, and they commissioned research and management studies, few of which were ever published. The views of the public, the politicians, and anyone else not employed by the Commission were never sought.

The report begins by emphasizing the underlying unity of what government does: that departments, though primary operating units, are only segments of a single entity. From this useful but often forgotten observation should flow a recognition that higher administrators should be interchangeable within the system and that high management posts should be equally open to skilled specialists. The 1961 Civil Service Act, they noted, was a partial recognition of the "proper role of departmental management" since it enabled the Civil Service Commission to delegate some of its powers to the permanent heads of departments. Nevertheless, these changes were "marginal" and the general system of control, in their view, remained undiminished.[61] Here we can detect a theme which runs through the report and one which was to recur fifteen years later in the Lambert Report: a distrust of the old-fashioned mandarin who, whatever his education, had become a generalist, skilled in the arts of negotiation and dealing with his political masters, but apparently lacking in the managerial skills of the project engineer.

The heavy hand of the Civil Service Commission over appointments and promotions and the detail-obsessed scrutiny of the Treasury Board over the smallest transactions were making the effective management of the government machine nearly impossible. "The costly, frustrating and unproductive character of the existing system has been most strikingly acknowledged in the frequent use of semi-autonomous boards, commissions and corporations." The experience of these agencies, formed more closely on the model of the private sector and free of elaborate controls, suggested that the whole system was unnecessary for the achievement of efficiency and conformity to public policy. In the same way departments should be free to manage programs, be accountable for results, and only subject to such controls as were necessary to protect the general interest of government or which transcended departmental interests.

The principal function of central government, the commission thought, should be to relate what the public wants to what it will, and should, pay for through the budget; to allocate resources and priorities in existing and proposed programs; to frame general

61. *Report*, p. 50.

policies for the use of staff, money, and other resources throughout government; to ensure strong leadership and effective use of human resources in all departments; to develop effective management practices for control and improvement of operations; to assess the effectiveness of departmental operations; to maintain accounts which inform Parliament and government of the sources and uses of public funds; and to adapt the machinery of government to changes in objectives. These tasks are subordinate to the supreme task of political leadership, and are the role of the general manager in the private sector. But "the Government of Canada has not, and probably cannot have, a single chief executive in this sense."[62] Other than the Prime Minister, no minister—and, of course, no official—could perform this role. The Minister of Finance, through the budget, had exercised some of these functions, and there had been a growing tendency, ever since Confederation, to give an important role in central administration to the Treasury Board.

However, the Treasury Board laboured under two handicaps. It was made up of ministers who had departmental responsibilities and it was presided over by the Minister of Finance, who was also responsible for fiscal and monetary policy, public borrowing, cash management, international economic policy, the state of the domestic economy, and so on. It was therefore necessary to strengthen the Treasury Board by placing a full-time minister at its head, even though the Minister of Finance would necessarily need to maintain a close and continuing relationship with it. The second handicap under which the Treasury Board toiled was its continuing responsibility for approving an immense number of transactions, which involved something like sixteen thousand submissions from the departments each year. Much of this needed to be abandoned in order to leave the departments free to manage, and to free the Treasury Board to carry out a role of central direction. The location of the Treasury Board in the Department of Finance tended to give it a preoccupation with the details of expenditure. It should therefore be transferred to the Privy Council Office, and the Secretary of the Treasury Board should, along with the Clerk of the Privy Council, occupy a pre-eminent position among deputy heads. There were inherent dangers in centralizing authority in a single department. These could be minimized by keeping the staff of the Board to a minimum and rotating its members with the departments so that its officers should have a closer appreciation of the problems of line management and program delivery.

62. *Ibid.* p. 53.

While the thrust of the report was towards getting rid of irritating control systems which clog initiative and delay decision, the Commission recognized that there must be controls and safeguards. But these must be conceived differently, within a framework that would foster rather than frustrate good management. The best guarantee of administrative integrity would be a new concept of management defined more sharply in relation to authority and responsibility, and one which encourages strong administrative leadership. This would be reinforced by the balancing of functions between the Treasury Board and the departments, and between the Secretary of the Treasury Board and the Clerk of the Privy Council. It would be further strengthened by the rotation of senior officers. Finally, it would depend on the creation of a Treasury Board "presence" in the departments, whose Chief Financial Officer and Chief Personnel Officer would be part of a managerial pool that would rotate among the departments and the Treasury Board. On the other hand, the functions of the older control agencies, such as the Civil Service Commission and the Comptroller of the Treasury, would be considerably curtailed.

Under the Cabinet, the new role of the Treasury Board would be the co-ordination of programs and the general management of the public service. A Program Division of the Board would analyze programs, review estimates, and frame general standards of administration; a Personnel Division would be responsible for general personnel policy and standards of personnel administration; while an Administrative Improvement Division would stimulate and guide continuous improvements in operating systems and procedures. The central accounting needs of government would be met by the Comptroller of the Treasury, "more suitably called the Accountant-General," who would also provide related services to departments. The existing control functions of the Comptroller of the Treasury would no longer be needed, and be abolished.

The Civil Service Commission was to be left with only those functions which require independence from executive authority: certification of appointments, final appeals against disciplinary action, pay research, recruitment for common grades at the lower levels of the public service, and the operation of training programs. It would assist departments in the conduct of competitions, but staff recruitment to higher and specialized posts would be conferred on the departments.

Sweeping and exhaustive as the recommendations of the Glassco Commission were, it is not surprising that they were not received on all sides with unqualified enthusiasm. The general tone of the final report is perhaps best conveyed by the assertion that "Government in modern society is often burdensome and restrictive. Consequently, it will seldom be viewed as better than a necessary evil—and it is a sign of national vigour that this should be so."[63] This statement, combined with a preoccupation with "the curse of bigness" in government, carries a tone of covert hostility to government activity as such and is a theme which recurs throughout the report, giving rise to the suspicion that it pre-determined conclusions which should have been reached on more scientific grounds. It prompted one critic, with considerable experience of high office in the public service to say:

> Whether or not this remains either a useful or justifiable image of government is at least a debatable issue, but one to be settled in another realm of debate. What its relevance may be to a study of administrative management in the public service, other than to create an *a priori* judgment in favour of any stricture concerning the conduct of that management, eludes me completely.[64]

He goes on to raise a further question. The job of the Commission was—in the words of its own executive director—"much more analagous to the job of a management consultant firm called in to look at the operation of an organization, public or private."[65] Yet the Glassco enquiry lacked the characteristics of a management survey—a clear-cut definition of objectives and direct and confidential relationships with the client. A royal commission is hampered by the broad and vague nature of its mandate, the "shock therapy" effect by which its highly publicised criticisms are likely to antagonize most of those who should take them to heart, and, lastly, because once a commission has reported it has come to an end, so that the responsibility for carrying the desired reforms will fall upon others.[66]

Nevertheless a very large proportion of the recommendations of the Report were, in due course, implemented. While the Treasury Board was not placed in the Privy Council Office, it was separated from the Department of Finance and was to emerge, along with the PCO, as a powerful central agency of a new sort exercising, under the Cabinet, new kinds of management control which flowed from

63. *Ibid.* p. 25.

64. T.H. McLeod, "Glassco Commission Report". *Canadian Public Administration* VI:4 (December, 1963) p. 395.

65. Ronald S. Ritchie *et al.* The Glassco Commission Report: A Panel Discussion". *Ibid.* V:4 (December, 1962) pp. 386-7.

66. McLeod, "Glassco Commission Report" pp. 387-94.

the greatly expanded capabilities of electronic data processing and the new management techniques associated with PPBS and its successors. The introduction of collective bargaining greatly enhanced the role of the Treasury Board as representing the management side of the process. The method of committee decision-making which characterized the Trudeau Cabinet system further enhanced the roles of both the Privy Council Office and the Treasury Board. Shorn of much of its previous role in personnel policy, the Public Service Commission was nevertheless able to develop new roles in relation to executive development training, an aggressive and on the whole successful attempt to increase the participation of French-Canadians in the higher posts of the public service, and in the development of language training. The office of Comptroller of the Treasury was abolished, but a number of his functions were continued in the new Department of Supply and Services, which was also intended to strengthen the provision of common services for all departments.

The prescription was applied to the patient, but apparently the malaise continued. For much of the intervening period the government was frequently embarrassed by the annual reports of the Auditor General, who seemed to delight in emphasizing "horror stories" of waste and mismanagement. The government, in its turn, argued that it was not the business of the Auditor General to criticize policy, but to scrutinize the public accounts for accounting failures. In the end a new Auditor General Act in 1977 widened his powers somewhat to enable him to use the criterion of "value for money" in scrutinizing the public accounts, though he was still not to concern himself with policy questions. It was perhaps the failure of government departments to respond to criticism from both the Auditor General and the Public Accounts Committee of the House of Commons which led to the revival in 1978 of the office of Comptroller General. In his reincarnation the Comptroller General was placed under the Treasury Board, with a status equal to the Secretary of the Board. His responsibility was primarily to impose accounting and information procedures across the public service which would enable program analysts to evaluate program performance.

However useful these measures were, they were not enough. It was time for a fresh attempt at diagnosis. Again the method was the same, and the consulting physicians were of similar character. The Royal Commission on Financial Management and Accountability (called the Lambert Commission after its chairman) was set up late in 1976 and reported in March, 1979. While it was more receptive than the Glassco Commission to the views of the public, of Members of both Houses, and of provincial governments, the burden of its report was not greatly dissimilar to its predecessor. In both cases the rhetoric is similar and one suspects that both commissions, in their detailed recommendations, were seeking to give force and legitimacy to organizational changes which were already in the minds of some senior members of the public service.

The Lambert Commission's terms of reference were wider than its predecessor so that they were able to address themselves not only to the perennial search for accountability in departments, and the development of controls and information needed by central agencies, but also to the wider question of giving Cabinet and Parliament the means to judge how effective policies actually are. Central to effective government, they argued, was the collective responsibility of the Cabinet, both for determining priorities and policies and for the oversight of management systems to control the delivery of programs. Such a role requires effective leadership from the Prime Minister, the Minister of Finance, and the Treasury Board.

Essentially, the recommendations of the Commission are aimed at increasing the flow of information, not only to assist better management and planning, but also to inform Parliament and the public so that the objectives of government planning can be better understood, and informed judgment can be made as to whether program objectives can be achieved. The management systems generated since the early sixties had generated information, but much of it was not properly timed in relation to the budgetary cycle and therefore not used effectively, and there was overlapping of jurisdiction among the control agencies with considerable duplication of information. In the end, at the Cabinet committee level, decisions on policy were not made in conjunction with decisions about resource allocation, which appeared to be one reason for ineffective expenditure control. Some critics have wondered whether the proposals for increased ministerial and parliamentary control take adequate account of the essentially political character of Cabinet and Parliament, and also whether it is realistic for governments to be expected to adhere to fairly strict five-year fiscal plans in the face of so many political and environmental variables. One of the harshest criticisms came from a former senior member of the federal public service. He said, "Too much in the document under review, as with the earlier Glassco Commission Report, is not relevant enough or appropriate enough in the context of public business."[67]

67. Stanley H. Mansbridge, "The Lambert Report: Recommendations to Departments." *Canadian Public Administration.* XXII:4 (Winter, 1979) p. 540. See

The Lambert Commission argued that the first essential step is for government to develop a forward plan which allocates resources within the constraints of available revenue and total expenditure according to established priorities. This would involve the adoption by Cabinet, and the submission to Parliament, of a five-year fiscal plan. This plan would necessarily have to be modified from time to time, in light of changing circumstances, but modifications would have to be clearly conveyed to Parliament at appropriate times, such as through the budget or with the introduction of supplementary estimates. To avoid the fragmentation between policy and resource allocation the plan should be jointly prepared by the Treasury Board, the Department of Finance, and the Privy Council Office. With such sponsorship it would carry great weight in Cabinet.

One of the major weaknesses of fiscal planning in the past had been that the fiscal plan was considered by the Committee on Priorities and Planning at a time when departments had already completed their program forecasts in ignorance of government priorities. Furthermore, the plan dealt only with total levels of expenditure, and left the Treasury Board to allocate resources at a time when departments were already heavily, and sometimes publicly, committed to particular programs. Thus departmental planning was done without the need to make hard choices, which were left to the Treasury Board. This had led to acrimonious disputes between the Board and departments. There was no close link between the estimates and the public accounts, so that it was difficult to measure departmental performance from year to year.

The Commission's proposals were aimed at curing these various weaknesses. The proposed Fiscal Plan should indicate not only priorities, but how they should be funded so that they could form a basis for medium- and long-term planning by departments and agencies. The Plan should indicate whether last year's objectives had been successfully met and whether an appropriate balance had been struck between expenditures and revenues. In the preparation of the Plan, a key role would be played by the Department of Finance, which would apportion total expenditures among the

---

also in the same issue, J.R. Mallory, "The Lambert Report: Central Roles and Responsibilities"; Andre Gelinas, "Le Rapport Lambert: Les organismes de la Couronne."; Paul Thomas, "The Lambert Report: Parliament and Accountability."; and R.B. Bryce, "Reflections on the Lambert Report"; and Douglas G. Hartle, "The Report of the Royal Commission on Financial Management and Accountability: A Review." *Canadian Public Policy.* III.3 (Summer, 1979) p. 366.

broad functions of government, and reconcile these with the priorities for managing the economy. The functional ceilings would be refined into departmental and agency limits by the Comptroller General's office in the Treasury Board. The Privy Council Office would see that the Plan conformed to the Cabinet's priorities. Once the Plan had been communicated to departments they would have a strong incentive to manage their resources within the limits assigned, and to weed out ineffective programs in order to support more urgent and successful ones.

While it would appear that the Department of Finance would be given a much stronger role in overall financial planning at the expense of the Treasury Board, the latter would be given much greater staffing responsibilities by a further diminution of the role of the Public Service Commission, which would be reduced to one of monitoring the merit system. The Treasury Board (to be rechristened the Board of Management) would operate with twin deputy heads, one chiefly concerned with personnel management and the other (the Comptroller General) responsible for estimates preparation, accounting procedures, and program evaluation. The responsibilities of the two would still overlap, but the Commission seemed to think that a common secretariat attached to both would be able to reconcile differences between them.

It has seemed to some critics of the Lambert Commission that its recommendations, taken as a whole, were still vitiated by a remarkable naivete about the operation of government generally, and the federal government in particular. Business decisions taken in the private sector can be reasonably based on balancing results against costs—"the bottom line." However government decisions are much more complex. For all of the precision of economic modelling, it is extremely difficult to anticipate the behavior of an economy with so many variables a year in advance, let alone five years. The process of government planning is based on political rationality as interpreted by ministers, and compounded by the complex politics of interagency rivalry and bureaucratic empire-building. To speak of parliamentary scrutiny without taking account of the fact that the government of the day controls the House of Commons, and that opposition politicians are informed by political rather than fiscal rationality seems to be another example of the Commission's naivete.

Furthermore, the Commission—like most would-be reformers of the fiscal system in the last twenty years—seems to believe that much can be accomplished by better management techniques. If all of the expenditures of the federal government were discretionary and could be readily altered from year to year this would be the case.

Money could be saved by cutting the size of the public service as programs which required staffing were cut back. How far is this the case? In 1977–78, as the Commission noted, 56 percent of public expenditures did not require parliamentary approval at all because it was based on continuing legislation. Nearly all of this is made up of transfer payments to the provinces. The labour costs involved are slight, since program delivery is in the hands of provincial agencies. Service to the national debt costs almost as much as the administrative costs of all non-defence departments and agencies. Cutting or even limiting payments to the provinces is a political decision, likely to be extremely painful, and involving major political decisions outside the assumptions on which most proposals for reform of fiscal management are based. Greater cost-effectiveness in the management of the public service is no doubt a goal in itself, but its overall effect on the fiscal malaise of the federal government is likely to be slight.

Tighter fiscal restraints in recent years has led to modest decreases in the size of the public service. This has largely been achieved by attrition, so that the service as a whole is older, probably tired, and overburdened. New recruitment has generally been confined to auditors and program evaluators, rather than those whose duty it is to plan and deliver programs. The result will be more chiefs and fewer Indians.

The Public Service in a Bicultural Community

An effective political system must adequately represent the many divergent sections of the community. In Canada the most basic of these sectional differences arises from the co-existence of two cultures, and two language groups. The political system, in the Cabinet, the courts, the usages of Parliament and in other ways, has developed mechanisms of representation and accommodation. And so it should be with the bureaucracy. If a country is to be administered in a manner satisfactory to its citizens, the bureaucracy itself must be representative of these accepted differences. There are two ways in which this representativeness is important. In the first place, it should be reasonably possible for citizens of both languages, when they come in contact with the margins of government, either face to face or by written communication, to be able to express themselves and be understood in their mother tongue, whether French or English. This requires the staffing of departments with clerks and the like who, if not bilingual, are at least fluent in the language of those with whom they have to deal. It also requires the provision of translators to ensure that notices and correspondence can be addressed in the language of the recipient.

This is a minimal requirement. There is a second which is of equal importance, and that is there should be adequate numbers of the minority language group, which in Canada is French-speaking, in the senior posts of the public service. Furthermore, if these officials are to work effectively they must be able to work in their own language. Only the most fluently bilingual are unaware of the severe mental strain of expressing one's thoughts with clarity and precision in a second language. Under this handicap, not a few French-Canadian civil servants, unable to express themselves with the nuance and clarity of their own tongue, appeared to be less than bright, and spent their lives in dreary jobs in minor departments. Nor should one neglect the sacrifice imposed on a French Canadian of civilized taste condemned to live in Ottawa. For in the public service English was, until recently, the only working language, anglophone Ottawa the only environment. It is not so many years ago that a senior Canadian diplomat at the United Nations was instructed to deliver a major policy speech in French. He himself was a French Canadian. His minister was fluently bilingual, several of the senior officials in Ottawa who assisted in preparing the speech were French Canadians. But the speech was written in English, transmitted to New York in English, and the delegate delivered a text translated by his translation staff into French. Such were the absurdities of the Canadian public service.

It is true that as early as 1882, the Civil Service Act provided that "all examinations under this act shall be held in the English or French language or both at the option of the candidate."[68] The Civil Service Commission has always contained one French-Canadian commissioner, and this no doubt has been some insurance that there should at least be a proportionate number of clerks, typists, messengers and the like in the public service. However, for reasons fully and sensitively developed by David Kwavnick,[69] French-Canadian representation in the past was less than adequate in positions in the service where policy was made. It was perhaps natural that the development and improvement of the Canadian bureaucracy was largely in response to the interest in efficiency and professionalism

68. *Statutes of Canada*, 45 Vict., ch. 4, s. 28, 1882.

69. D. Kwavnick, "French Canadians and the Civil Service of Canada," *Canadian Public Administration* IX, No. 1 (Spring, 1968), p. 97.

which was a characteristic of the urban English-speaking business and professional class. It was equally natural that the more intellectual among them should be the predominant majority among the senior officials of the Departments of Trade and Commerce and Finance, where most major government policy is made. It was equally natural that the traditional training of the French-Canadian élite—the *collège classique* and the "respectable" professions of law and medicine—should provide them with neither the training nor the inclination to take their due place in the centres of economic power.

It was not surprising that the major recommendations of the Royal Commission on Administrative Classification in the Public Service were buried in the late forties because of the opposition of French-Canadian politicians who would not trust public personnel policy to the Treasury Board. But it was ominous that a member of the Glassco Commission, Eugène Therrien, was impelled to file a separate statement additional to the main report of the commission because he felt that it should have addressed itself to the question of bilingualism and biculturalism in the public service, and had not. He pointed out that "the number of French Canadians holding key positions in the government administration is insignificant, save for a few district offices in the Province of Quebec. In several key departments, not a single high official is French-speaking."[70] This was in 1962, when the quiet revolution in Quebec society was plainly visible, and more than a generation after an industrial and urban revolution had created in Quebec a new and modern middle-class élite no longer willing to tolerate second-class status based on language alone.

The Preliminary Report of the Royal Commission on Bilingualism and Biculturalism encapsulated the problem in a poignant passage:

> In Sudbury, one French Canadian, in answer to an English-speaking Canadian who had insisted that competence should be the requirement for admission to and promotion within the Civil Service replied, "First of all I want my language to be respected in public places, particularly in federal offices. I am a French Canadian, I am entitled to my language and I want to be able to speak it whenever I think I should, throughout Canada and in everything belonging to Ottawa, and I demand that respect.[71]

70. *Report of the Royal Commission on Government Organization*, Book I, p. 69.

71. *Preliminary Report of the Royal Commission on Bilingualism and Biculturalism*, (Ottawa, 1965), p. 74.

Explicit in this quotation is an anglophone value-judgment, widespread in the public service and not uncommon in the country at large, that to require language competence in the federal public service is a direct challenge to the merit system. It would not be too much to say that this failure of imagination has been the greatest single fault of the Canadian bureaucracy.

But things are changing. The "B & B" Commission, in the course of its inquiry, was able to assume the role of a moderate but forceful educational device by drawing attention to appalling anomalies at a time when public opinion was sensitive to the need for long-overdue changes. There was little surprise at, and little disposition to oppose, the recommendations in Book I of its report, "that English and French be formally declared the official languages of the Parliament of Canada, of the federal courts, of the federal government, and of the federal administration."[72]

One cannot impose bilingualism by fiat, particularly in a vast bureaucratic structure of several hundred thousand persons, the great majority of whom are unilingual and whose initial condition of service made no such requirement. The only remedy is to bring about gradually, but as rapidly as possible, a more bilingual régime through greatly increased translation facilities, voluntary language training programs, and incentive plans. There are now signs that the ponderous government machine is beginning to respond to the challenge. Much of the responsibility for bringing these changes about has fallen on the Public Service Commission.

In April 1966 the new policy was enunciated by the Prime Minister in the House of Commons. This statement asserted as the goals of the policy

> that it should become common practice for English- and French-speaking public servants to express themselves in either official language in the course of their work, knowing that they will be understood;...that Canadians of either official language should be able to communicate in their own language with federal public servants; that the linguistic and cultural values of both groups should be taken into account in public service recruitment and training, and that a climate should be created which would permit English- and French-speaking public servants to work together towards common goals, in a mutual understanding of their respective languages and cultures and a full appreciation of the contributions they could make to their country.[73]

72. *Report of the Royal Commission on Bilingualism and Biculturalism*, Book I, (Ottawa, 1967), p. 91.

73. *Public Service Commission of Canada, Annual Report*, 1967, p. 18.

Language training courses run by the commission since 1964 enabled about one thousand English-speaking public servants to achieve working fluency by 1967. But such resources are limited and the commission's first priority is still executive, administrative, and foreign service officers, with supervisory personnel in scientific and technical grades still in second priority. One sign of progress is the commission's report that thirty percent of senior officers entering the executive category in 1967 were bilingual.

It is not yet possible to evaluate this effort. One index of its apparent success was a spectacular rise of over one hundred percent in the number of both applicants and appointees in the French-speaking group in the competitions for administrative trainees and foreign service officers between 1965 and 1966, and 1966 and 1967. A more useful piece of evidence will be the retention and promotion rate of this group, for the only pay-off that matters is in the long run. The object is to ensure, in the words of one of the senior civil servants responsible for the program, that "the public service of Canada will be assured, in some fifteen to twenty years from now, and permanently thereafter, of sufficient resources from which to appoint truly bilingual senior officials likely to react with greater sensitivity to the cultural outlook of their colleagues."[74]

Politically, the belated effort to give the public service a bilingual appearance may yet turn out to be too little and too late. But there can be no doubt that it is an accurate reflection of a change in the political system.

74. Sylvain Cloutier, "Senior Public Service Officials in a Bicultural Society," *Canadian Public Administration* XI, No. 4 (Winter, 1968), p. 403.

5

The Electorate

> "No one can have had some years' experience of the conduct of affairs in a legislature or an administration without observing how extremely small is the number of persons by whom the world is governed." Lord Bryce, *Modern Democracies.*
>
> "The limit of direct action is for all practical purposes the power to say Yes or No on an issue presented to the mass." Walter Lippmann, *Public Opinion.*

Essentially, the government of Canada is representative government. A gradual broadening of the franchise since colonial times has made it, at the same time, democratic, so that ultimate political power is vested in the people as a whole. Nevertheless this power is indirect and intermittent, since it consists only in the right to vote for one representative in one geographical area at such times as an election in that constituency may be held. In constitutional theory, it is the sum of such local elections that determines the composition of the House of Commons, which in turn decides which of a limited number of possible alternative governments to sustain. In fact, the issues at stake in a particular constituency are more likely to be national than local, so that the voter, in casting his ballot, is more concerned with the choice of a government than with the choice of a particular member of Parliament. However, a majority of voters across the country may vote for one particular party and not succeed in giving that party power. The rationale being the wide variation in the number of voters in different constituencies, and the fact that large majorities may be "wasted" in safe seats. The real determinant of government is a majority of seats, not a majority of the popular vote.

THE FRANCHISE

Originally the right to vote was thought of as a direct consequence of property interest, rather than one adhering to the person as a political right. This theory still survives in the government of joint-stock companies and, to a limited extent, in local government. It was only by gradual steps that the vote was altered from a property right to a political right. The first franchise in British North America was based on property, and its last symptom—plural voting based on a vote where property is held—was not removed until 1920.

No uniform franchise for voting in national elections was provided at Confederation. Section 41 of the British North America Act had provided that, until such time as Parliament was able to set up a uniform franchise law, the provincial franchise would prevail. It was not until 1885 that a federal act was passed. In that year the Macdonald government introduced a bill which set a low property qualification. The government had been impelled to introduce this bill in part by a conservative dislike of a tendency towards manhood suffrage in certain provinces, and in part by the fact that some provincial legislation had disfranchised federal employees (it should be remembered that a majority of provincial governments were Liberal, while that in power in Ottawa was Conservative). The Liberals swept away the federal franchise in 1898, in effect restoring the provincial franchise except that provincial disqualifications were not to apply in federal elections. The Union government carried two measures through Parliament in 1917, the Wartime Elections Act and the Military Voters Act, which as Professor Ward puts it, "could hardly fail to return a majority in Parliament for the party which enacted it."[1] Subsequently, in 1920, in the Dominion Franchise Act, the basis for the present electoral law was laid. In essence the act provided for adult suffrage in Canada. Later amendments have gradually removed anomalies by which certain classes of persons disfranchised by provincial law, such as Orientals in British Columbia, were also disfranchised in Dominion elections. It was not until 1960 that Indians residing on reservations were given a vote, although the previous law had enfranchised those in this group who had served in the armed forces.

The franchise law, with minor rectifications, remained for fifty years within the broad principles of the 1920 act. The exclusion of Indians on reservations had been based on the nineteenth-century notion that persons in a tutelary position should not vote. Indians on reservations are wards of the Crown; therefore they should be excluded from full citizenship. On somewhat similar logic, minors, lunatics, inmates of penal institutions and persons convicted of

1. Norman Ward, *The Canadian House of Commons: Representation* (Toronto, 1950), p. 227.

illegal practices at elections are still excluded. But these exclusions, with the exception of those under age, are minimal.

In 1970, however, Parliament enacted a thorough revision and consolidation of the Canada Elections Act. Of the several changes made the most important were the following: the voting age was lowered from twenty-one to eighteen; the format of the ballot was changed to minimize spoiled ballots; increased opportunities were made for voting by those unavoidably absent on polling day; and the electoral law for the first time took account of the existence of political parties by providing that party designations could be printed on the ballot.

The ancient provision, dating back to colonial times and made obsolete since 1948 by the introduction of separate citizenship in each country of the Commonwealth, that the primary voting qualification was to have the status of "British subject" has been replaced. The law now states that only Canadian citizens are qualified to vote, although British subjects, other than Canadian citizens who were qualified to vote on June 25, 1968, and have not ceased to be Canadian residents, are deemed to be qualified voters.

The redesigned ballot paper has a small circular space opposite the name of each candidate for the elector to indicate his choice. This no longer need be by a cross, nor must the mark be made by black lead pencil only.

A proxy voting system, exercised only on polling day, has been introduced for fishermen, mariners, prospectors, and full-time students, whose occupations make it impossible for them to be in their ordinary places of residence on polling day. The provisions by which members of the Canadian forces serving abroad and their dependants are enabled to vote is now extended to public servants posted abroad and their dependants, but not to others whose normal occasions require them to be abroad on polling day.

Political parties wishing to endorse candidates at an election for the House of Commons must register with the Chief Electoral Officer. A new party wishing to be identified on the ballot paper must have candidates officially nominated in seventy-five constituencies on the twenty-eighth day before polling day. The ballot paper will no longer give the address and occupation of the candidates, but only political affiliation for candidates qualified to have it.

The invidious privilege previously given to Returning Officers of voting only in the case of a tie vote is abolished. Instead, it is now provided that where there is an equality of votes, the Returning Officer will apply to a judge for a recount.

ELECTIONS

If Parliament is dissolved there must be a general election to fill all of the seats in the House of Commons. The dissolution of Parliament is a prerogative act of the Governor General, acting on the advice of ministers. A Parliament may be dissolved at any time, although there is no known precedent for the dissolution of a Parliament which has not even met after a general election. If Parliament is not otherwise dissolved, it may come to an end by the efflux of time, as provided by section 50 of the British North America Act, five years from the date of the return of the writs of election.[2] As soon as Parliament is dissolved, it is the duty of the Chief Electoral Officer to issue writs of election to Returning Officers in the various constituencies.

Until 1920 the duty of issuing such writs lay upon an official called the Clerk of the Crown in Chancery, who had the further duties of revising voters' lists and of participating in the pronouncement of royal assent to bills in the Senate chamber. As a consequence of division of authority and general inefficiency, the conduct of elections had become chaotic. The last Clerk of the Crown in Chancery was such a classic example of inefficiency that the Speaker of the House, under whose jurisdiction his office fell, was driven to asking the Prime Minister to initiate an investigation by the Civil Service Commissioners. The report of this investigation was so damning that when the office fell vacant it was not filled, and it was swept away completely in the electoral reform of 1920.[3] The Dominion Franchise Act of 1920 placed the conduct of elections in the hands of an independent officer of Parliament called the Chief Electoral Officer. He is chosen by resolution of the House of Commons, holds

2. Parliaments seldom expire by the efflux of time, since this deprives a Prime Minister of the choice of a strategic moment to call an election. When a Parliament is allowed to run its course, this is usually an indication of grave weakness in the government of the day. The Parliament of 1891 expired by efflux of time. The conditions of near party truce in the early years of the First World War made it difficult to bring about the dissolution of the Parliament elected in 1911 at a "normal" time, and its life was extended for one year by constitutional amendment in 1916. The Parliaments elected in 1930 and 1974 were dissolved shortly before they had run their course. In each case (as in 1896) the government was defeated.

3. See J. R. Mallory, "The Clerk of the Crown's Tale," *Canadian Bar Review* XXXIV, No. 1 (January 1956), p. 60. For a full discussion of Canadian electoral law and practice see T. H. Qualter, *The Election Process in Canada* (Toronto, 1970).

office during good behaviour and may only be removed by the Governor-in-Council if this is demanded by a joint resolution of both Houses.

The Chief Electoral Officer appoints a Returning Officer for each constituency, who in turn must appoint Deputy Returning Officers and Poll Clerks for each poll. Upon receipt of the writ of election it is the duty of the Returning Officer to publish the date at which nominations close, and make all necessary arrangements for the conduct of an election. At the close of the poll on election day the ballots in each poll are counted by Deputy Returning Officers, sealed in their ballot boxes again and sent to the Returning Officer, who will issue an official return declaring the candidate with the largest number of votes to be elected. The dates for nomination, polling and declaration of returns are now uniform throughout the country. In order to prevent the publication of early unofficial returns from eastern time zones from influencing voters still going to the polls in the west, the Elections Act prohibits the publication of these returns until the polls have closed in each time zone.

Except for the new provision by which political parties may endorse candidates and have their political affiliation listed on the ballot, nominating and balloting are divorced from party politics. A candidate may be nominated by twenty-five electors, though in practice political parties have their own nominating procedure for their own candidates. The nomination paper of a candidate must be accompanied by his written consent to nomination, together with a deposit of two hundred dollars. The latter provision is to discourage frivolous candidates and is returnable if the candidate polls not less than half as many votes as the winning candidate. This deposit has the double effect of discouraging independents who might wish to run in opposition to the party machine, and of imposing a severe financial handicap on third parties.

A seat in the House of Commons which has become vacant for any reason may be filled at a by-election if the government directs the Chief Electoral Officer to issue a writ of election. In this case the Returning Officer for the constituency will need to conduct an election in the same manner as described above.

Sometimes the announced result of a poll is very close, or there may be allegations of irregularities in the voting or in the counting of ballots. In such cases the election may be controverted, the ballots recounted and the election either confirmed or voided as the case may be. Until 1873, the trial of controverted elections was one of the privileges of Parliament which was dealt with by the House of

Commons itself, and there were many unseemly wrangles in House committees over controverted elections. It was common in those days for a large number of elections to be challenged on grounds which were—given the political conditions of the time—probably quite valid. Then the managers of both parties would agree to drop most of the challenges. In 1873 the Canadian Parliament followed the practice which had been adopted in the United Kingdom in 1868, and provided that controverted elections should be dealt with by the judiciary. Two superior court judges in the province where the election has been challenged now conduct an inquiry, scrutinize the ballots for irregularities and report their finding to the Speaker of the House of Commons. An appeal from such findings lies in both law and fact to the Supreme Court of Canada.

REPRESENTATION

For the purpose of representation in the House of Commons, Canada is divided into a number of geographical constituencies which return a single member to Parliament.[4] The basis of representation in the House is the principle of "representation according to population." This was a major political issue in the politics of the Province of Canada prior to Confederation, and its inclusion in the terms of union (balanced by equal regional representation in the Senate) was one of the major questions settled in the Confederation negotiations.

The principle of representation according to population in the constitution applies only to the provinces as such, and does not imply any idea of equalization as applied to the size or composition of individual constituencies. Section 51 of the British North American Act laid down the original basis for the allocation of seats to each province, and further provided that after each decennial census, beginning with that of 1871, Parliament should reapportion seats assigned to each province according to a prescribed formula. The 1867 arrangement was essentially this: sixty-five seats were allocated to Quebec, and each of the other provinces were entitled to as many seats in proportion to its population as sixty-five bore to the popula-

4. In the period 1872-92 there were as many as ten two-member constituencies. See Norman Ward, "Voting in Two-Member Constituencies," *Public Affairs*, September 1946, pp. 220-3. The last two—Queen's (Prince Edward Island) and Halifax (Nova Scotia)—were swept away by the redistribution of 1965.

tion of Quebec. There were some qualifications to the rule, such as the one which protected a province from losing seats if its population increase was substantially at the same rate as the rest of the country, and the one introduced in 1915 (section 51A) that no province could have fewer seats in the Commons than it had in the Senate.

It was implicit in this arrangement that the fixed number of seats given to Quebec would assure that province of a permanent and substantial share of the seats in the House of Commons. Professor Ward adduced evidence to show that "a legislature based on a scheme that gave Quebec 65 members would not be a large one, a point which seems to have weighed heavily with some Lower Canada leaders; the larger the legislature, they argued, the larger would be the absolute majority that Upper Canada would have over Lower Canada."[5] There was a further advantage to this arrangement. Canada East already had sixty-five seats in the legislature of the United Province of Canada. These could be retained unchanged, while an application of the formula to New Brunswick and Nova Scotia gave each province one seat for each county, with two extra for the cities of Saint John and Halifax. Thus, only in Ontario was it necessary to make any substantial change in seats, and there it was arranged without difficulty.[6]

Unfortunately the actual, and probably the character, of population growth reduced Quebec's share of seats from one-third to one-quarter and threatened to reduce it further. The addition of new provinces, together with population growth in the country as a whole, meant that the House increased in size at each decennial census, while Quebec representation remained constant. In 1867 the House consisted of 181 members, and by 1946 it had risen to 245. Furthermore, the various exceptions to the straight population formula mean that only four of the nine provinces actually had representation in strict accordance to their populations. In addition, the redistribution based on the 1941 census would have had a further distorting effect on some provinces because of substantial, and in part temporary, shifts in population as a result of the war. For that reason, redistribution was postponed by an amendment to the British North America Act, and a new formula was introduced by amendment in 1946.

This formula set a definite number of seats for the House of

5. Ward, *The Canadian House of Commons,* p. 20.

6. *Ibid.* p. 21.

Commons (though the number varied slightly as a result of the operation of clarifying and safeguarding rules) and provided that each province was entitled to as many members in proportion to its population as the total number of seats bears to the population of the province. A further modification was introduced in 1952 to protect a province against undue loss of seats at any one redistribution.[7] The total number of seats (after the accession of Newfoundland to the union in 1949) thus became 263, of which one each was assigned to the Yukon and the Northwest Territories. Each province would then have its representation calculated by dividing its total population by 261. If at the end of the exercise not all seats are allocated the additional seats would go to the provinces with the largest remainders. If this results, as it inevitably did, in some province getting less seats in the Commons than in the Senate, its representation would be raised accordingly and the exercise repeated for the remaining provinces.

In spite of this and the other safeguards, the end result at every redistribution would be to lead to a reduction of seats for some provinces. This is a difficult business, since it involves tearing up old constituency boundaries and leaving some members of Parliament with the awkward problem of seeking another seat, either in hostile territory or at the expense of a sitting member of their own party. The fixed size of the House of Commons in a country with a rapidly growing and shifting population was thus bound to cause a good deal of resentment. The difficulty was compounded by a worse problem in that urbanization had caused a drastic decline in the birth rate in Quebec which was not made up by immigration. It therefore seemed that each decennial census would lead to further erosion of Quebec's share of seats.

In the wake of the 1971 census the federal government, no doubt with some reluctance, grasped the nettle. A bill was introduced in 1973 to halt the redistribution process until January, 1975, and on January 11, 1974, the House ordered "that the system of readjusting representation in the House of Commons, including the method of determining the number of Members for each province established by Section 51 of the British North America Act be referred to the

7. The effect of this amendment was that no province could lose more than 15 percent of its seats at any one redistribution, nor could it have less seats than a province with a smaller population. This amendment was introduced after the amending procedure for the B.N.A. Act was modified in 1949, and was the first British North America Act Amendment passed by the Parliament of Canada. Representation in the House of Commons thus was removed from the entrenched clauses in the constitution.

Standing Committee on Privileges and Elections." The intention was that the Committee should reconsider the matter thoroughly, hear expert witnesses, and come up with a new formula before the end of the year. In fact, the dissolution of Parliament prevented serious committee study and subsequently, the government brought forward its own proposal.

In the end this was substantially accepted, perhaps because a continuation of the old system was repellent to almost everyone concerned, since no less than five provinces would have their representation reduced in spite of an increased population, and Ontario with an absolute increase three times that of British Columbia would receive only the same number of additional seats (three). Basically, the government sought to attain three objectives: (a) no province should lose seats and the small provinces should continue to have "equitable" representation; (b) there should be better representation by population among the provinces; and (c) Quebec should remain the pivotal element in the redistribution process.[8] Accordingly the provinces would be classified into three groups:

Small Provinces: Those with less than 1.5 million population, which comprise Newfoundland, Prince Edward Island, Nova Scotia, New Brunswick, Manitoba, and Saskatchewan. If the population of one of these provinces increases during the decennial period, the total number of seats to which it is entitled is determined by dividing its population by the average constituency population of the small provinces in the previous redistribution.

Medium Provinces: Those with populations between 1.5 and 2.5 million, at present British Columbia and Alberta. In subsequent redistributions it is probable that British Columbia will move up into the next category. A population increase will lead to one additional seat for every two the province would have received if treated as a small province with the largest average constituency.

Large Provinces: Those with more than 2.5 million population, that is to say Ontario and Quebec, and subsequently British Columbia. Quebec is attributed 75 seats in the redistribution following the 1971 census and four more at each decennial census thereafter. The number of seats assigned to the others in this group will be based on the average constituency population of Quebec.

In the calculation remainders are to be disregarded, and the proviso was added that no province would have a lesser number of

8. For the details, complete with calculations, see *Canada. House of Commons. Standing Committee on Privileges and Elections. Minutes of Proceedings and Evidence.* No. 3. April 9, 1974. pp. 3:27-3:145.

seats than another province with less population. One effect was that the old safeguard of a floor based on the number of Senate seats was discarded. This had been a source of irritation both to the Western provinces which have less Senate seats than New Brunswick and Nova Scotia, and to those who were opposed to the Senate on principle, like the Hon. Stanley Knowles. As initially proposed, the House would have increased immediately to 276 and would be likely to raise to 352 by the year 2001.

The bill was introduced on December 2, 1974, and received Royal Assent on December 20. Perhaps because of the season the bill received only perfunctory debate and aroused little public interest. To meet some opposition resistance the bill increased the representation for the Northwest Territories to two, and increased representation for Alberta and British Columbia by one each, to give them 21 and 28 respectively.

Two problems remain. One is Quebec. The warning came from Mr. Rene Matte, who said, "Mr. Speaker, by virtue of the underlying principles of the legislation, it could happen, in theory, that the French-Canadian element of the country, for example, would have almost no representation in this House . . . it could happen that the number of members from Quebec in this House would drop alarmingly, and we would thus be admitting that those who no longer believe in Canada are completely right."[9] The minister in charge of the bill, Mr. Sharp, had stressed that the position of Quebec was "pivotal" in the whole scheme. He said: "Should these assumptions prove to be wide of the mark, parliament may choose at some later date to add fewer or more seats to Quebec, which is the pivot of the whole system, as it was until the law was last amended."[10] It is doubtful if this half-promise is sufficient to reassure Quebec. Senator Martial Asselin echoed an old theme when he said:

> I say that the amalgamation formula, which other members of the House of Commons and myself did study does not live up to the expectations of the people of Quebec at the present time. Quebec cannot put up with such an unbalanced representation as compared with the representation of Ontario in the years to come. I am saying that, and I repeat it, because Quebec has a particular character, because it is not a province like the others—even though other senators and other members of the House of Commons believe that there should be a melting pot, and Quebec should be blended with the rest of Canada, and I think Quebec deserves particular treatment.

9. *Canada. House of Commons Debates.* July 9, 1973. p. 5438.
10. *Ibid.* December 2, 1974. p. 1864.

> I am not asking for any favours from other provinces of Canada. But if that Canadian Confederation is to be kept alive Quebec should have the same number of members as the largest province, Ontario.[11]

For some of the western members on the other hand the essential element in the whole matter is the principle of representation by population. For them arithmetical democracy is basic and overrides those historical and constitutional arguments which are most comforting to the Maritime Provinces and, above all, to Quebec.[12] It is not unlikely that, as the demographic and economic centre of gravity of the country shifts westward, their sense of grievance will be enhanced. The next debate on the redistribution formula is likely to be a much more difficult matter.

The British North America Act lays down the rules for the apportionment of seats among the provinces. It left to the Canadian Parliament the decision on each occasion how these seats were to be allocated within particular provinces. Sir John A. Macdonald told the House in 1872 that "While the principle of population was considered to a very great extent, other considerations were also held to have weight; so that different interests, classes and localities should be represented, that the principle of numbers should not be the only one."[13] In this statement he reflected an eighteenth-century view of representation that while seats may be assigned on a territorial basis, the ultimate purpose of representation is to take account of the various interests in the community.

In the beginning, proposed boundary changes were incorporated in a bill introduced by the government and put through in the same manner as any other government measure. It was thus possible to redraw constituency boundaries in order to confer political advantage on the government. The redistribution bills of 1872, 1882 and 1892—all of which, as it happened, were introduced by Conservative governments—contained a large number of "gerrymanders." The most famous of these was that of 1882, in which forty-six Ontario constituencies were gerrymandered. The Liberals, who first presided over a redistribution in 1903, introduced a new system which certainly eliminated the large-scale gerrymanders of the past. This system nevertheless left open the possibility of a limited amount of

11. *Canada. Senate Debates.* December 17, 1974. pp. 423–4.

12. For a discussion of some of the issues, see J. R. Mallory *Amending the Constitution by Stealth. Queen's Quarterly.* LXXXII: 3 (Autumn, 1975) pp. 22-27.

13. Canada, *House of Commons Debates,* 1872, p. 926.

skillful butchery. The detailed determination of constituencies' boundaries was referred to a select committee of the House. On this committee, of course, the government had a majority. However, much of the detailed work was done in provincial sub-committees and here there was room for close in-fighting among the parties which happened to be strong in that particular province. Thus, in the redistribution of 1947 the boundaries of Cartier, a constituency in the east end of Montreal which had returned the Communist Fred Rose to Parliament, were re-drawn in a very elaborate manner. In the next general election the constituency returned safely to the Liberal fold. In Saskatchewan, Prince Albert, which had turned its back on Mackenzie King in 1945 and elected a C.C.F. member, was re-drawn, as was Lake Centre, then the constituency of the only Conservative member in the province, John Diefenbaker. Neepawa, then held by Conservative leader John Bracken, was tacked onto the neighbouring constituency of Portage la Prairie, which was already a safe Conservative seat. Having been "hived" out of Neepawa, Bracken ran next time in Brandon, where he was handily defeated by the sitting Liberal member. To complete the tale, Muskoka in Ontario was added to a neighbouring safe Liberal seat. This compelled the chief financial critic of the Conservative opposition, J. M. Macdonnell, to run against the Liberal member, Wilfrid Macdonald. This was an unequal contest, for "Bucko" Macdonald had played hockey for many years for the Detroit team in the National Hockey League. When his professional playing days were over he was able to build up a strong local political following against which his Conservative opponent could make no headway.

In 1952 the main problem in redistribution was Saskatchewan, which lost three seats and would have lost more if the then Minister of Agriculture, Mr. James G. Gardiner, had not persuaded his colleagues to insert the 15 percent rule by way of amendment to section 51 of the B.N.A. Act. In the group of Saskatchewan members, the C.C.F. was the largest group and the Conservatives the smallest. It is perhaps not surprising that two of the seats to be abolished were Mr. Diefenbaker's Lake Centre, and Moose Jaw, which had been represented by the rebel C.C.F. member Ross Thatcher.

It should be understood that in all of the cases noted above—with the exception of Montreal Cartier—it could be plausibly argued that the seat which was abolished should have been done away with. In all cases they had relatively small electorates, and attaching them to neighbouring seats preserved a degree of community affinity. The only remarkable thing about them is, in each case, the identity of the sitting member at the time the seat disappeared. Accordingly, to argue that the system was a substantial reform over its predecessor is to exaggerate; there was still room for undercover work in the committee room. As examples of successful political spite, the kind of boundary change noted above reflected little credit on our political system.

Past redistributions were generally limited to those cases in which an increase or decrease in the number of seats allotted to a province had changed.[14] The boundary alterations were then usually sufficient to accomplish this objective, and were made in such a way as to confer some party advantage to the government of the day. Inevitably the reduction of seats provided the best opportunities for party spite.

Lurking behind this process were two grandiloquent principles which were used as excuses for inaction, though occasionally disregarded if the political motives were strong enough. The first of these was a deference to the boundaries of existing areas which have some claim to being historic communities, such as counties, city wards and the like. The second principle was a deliberate over-representation of rural constituencies out of deference to the political myths of agricultural fundamentalism: that the urban areas were the centres of articulate and influential sinister interests like big business, the trade unions and so on, while the farming interest was unorganized and weak; that the country dweller is an embodiment of Jeffersonian virtue because he is close to the soil, while the urban crowds are rootless and politically unstable.

As the population became more urbanized, the imbalance in representation was increasingly anomalous and the need to correct it harder to ignore. The proposal to place the question of representation in the hands of a non-political commission and set out rational rules for its operation has been made many times. In 1933 Mackenzie King, then in opposition, suggested that there should be a commission of six judges, three nominated by the government and three by the opposition.[15] A bill had already been drafted in 1940 which would have set up a commission composed of a superior court judge as chairman, assisted by two commissioners from each

14. Thus Sir John Thompson said in introducing the 1892 bill: "We have been guided by the principle almost exclusively...that we should only interfere with the representation in those districts where additional representation for increased population had to be provided." Quoted in Ward, *The Canadian House of Commons,* p. 368.

15. Canada, *House of Commons Debates,* May 25, 1933, pp. 5468-9.

province to deal with the constituencies in that province.[16] Unfortunately nothing further came of the bill, and when the time arrived for the next redistribution, the House went back to its old ways.

From time to time thereafter proposals have come forward for setting up independent boundary commissions. One of the most elaborate of these was contained in a private member's bill introduced by Mr. Douglas Fisher.

In introducing his bill, Mr. Fisher urged, first, that "no province shall lose any more seats," and second, "the old idea of there being two kinds of constituencies in Canada, rural and urban, is no longer valid." In his view there were at least four kinds of constituency: metropolitan (for example, Toronto-Trinity); suburban (York West or Scarborough); "the proper rural constituency" (Dufferin-Simcoe); and the frontier constituency (Churchill). Some of these last are extremely large, more than thirty being over eleven thousand square miles in area. Each of these different types, he argued, presented a different problem of representation. There was need for Parliament to set out the principles of representation, and then set up an independent commission to carry them out. He continued:

> I think we need an independent commission because of the very complexity of drawing boundaries. I suggest that on the commission we need a geographer, a demographer, a jurist, and then someone who has had experience in political life. I know it is going to cost a certain amount, but it seems to me it is necessary to guarantee to people what we really want basically from our electoral system, namely that each Canadian's vote is roughly, with some degree of tolerance, equal in value.[17]

In 1962, Prime Minister Diefenbaker introduced a bill to set up an electoral boundaries commission. The dissolution of Parliament prevented the bill from being proceeded with, but his successor brought forward a bill which finally became law in 1964. Its progress was slow because of a long deadlock in committee over the question of who would appoint the provincial redistribution commissioners, and over the permissible percentage deviation from the normative size of constituencies.

In its final form the act embodies the following features. Redistribution is handled by ten independent commissions constituted as follows: the Representation Commissioner, who is a member *ex officio* of all commissions (the first commissioner was the former

16. Ibid., February 21, 1947, pp. 698-9.

17. Ibid., February 12, 1960, p. 1042.

Chief Electoral Officer, Mr. Nelson Castonguay), a judge of the provincial Supreme Court, who is appointed by the Chief Justice of the province, and two members appointed by the Speaker of the House of Commons. The commissions proceed as follows: after each decennial census each province is assigned a number of constituencies, according to the formula in the constitution. An electoral quotient is obtained by dividing the number of seats in the province into the population of the province. The commission then re-draws the electoral boundaries in the province in conformity with the quotient, allowing a variation from the quotient of not more than 25 percent less than, or more than, the quotient. The effect of this is to reduce the impact of redistribution on rural constituencies, and limit to some extent the number of changes which the new formula requires. Nevertheless the effect has been profound, particularly in increasing the representation of the new suburban areas at the expense of rural constituencies and the older constituencies in the centres of large cities.[18]

There can be no doubt that one of the effects of this act was to reduce the disparity which had existed between the results of the popular vote at a general election and the number of seats gained by the parties which contested it. Seldom does a party which wins an election poll as much as fifty percent of the vote. Fairly minor shifts in the total vote polled can bring about landslide reversals, such as those between 1930 and 1935 and between 1957 and 1958.

One of the principal causes of the disparity has been a very large increase in the number of candidates, which diffuses the vote and produces unpredictable results and an increase in the likelihood of a minority government. Ever since the Progressive party contested the general election of 1921 there have been substantial "third" parties in the lists, sometimes as many as three. One consequence is that the winner in a large number of constituencies is the choice of less than half of the electors who actually voted.

There have been proposals from time to time to make election results both fairer and more representative by the use of some form of proportional representation. The most cautious of these proposals for reform is the single-alternative vote in one-member constitu-

18. Statutes of Canada, 1964. It is probable that, if the election of 1964 had been fought on the same electoral map as that of 1968, the Liberal party would have gained a majority in 1964. Widespread boundary alterations greatly increased the number of "marginal" seats in 1968, and may have increased the effect of the Liberal swing.

encies. The use of this system would ensure that the winning candidate is at least acceptable to the majority of his electors.[19]

The single-alternative vote existed for many years for provincial elections in the provinces of Manitoba and Alberta, where at the same time a system of proportional representation was applied in the cities of Winnipeg, Calgary and Edmonton. The single-alternative vote was also introduced briefly in British Columbia, but was abolished at the first opportunity because it caused so much confusion to the electorate, and was also thought to have contributed to the inconclusive results of the provincial election of 1952.

At one time, its introduction was seriously considered in federal elections. It was referred to in the Speech from the Throne in 1924, and bills to authorize it were introduced, but not passed, in the 1924 and 1925 sessions. The connection of these events with the rise of the Progressive movement, which had been instrumental in introducing the single-alternative vote in the western provinces, is evident. A special committee of the Commons reported against both the single-alternative vote and proportional representation in 1936 and 1937. Since then interest in the question has died out. It is probable that resistance to the idea came chiefly from the major political parties, who feared that it would increase the likelihood of party fragmentation.

Actually, western experience with the single-alternative vote is inconclusive. Its existence seems in fact to have increased the size of the Social Credit majorities in Alberta, where the old parties were weak and their supporters tended to give second choices to Social Credit. The result was to weaken them and to minimize the chances of the C.C.F. It is probable that the fears of the fissiparous tendencies of the single-alternative vote were groundless, given the structure and discipline of Canadian political parties. Nevertheless, the reason that there has been no major change in the electoral system since the introduction of the secret ballot in 1874 is that the political parties themselves are content with the system as it is.

Nevertheless the electoral system seems to have created one serious problem which seems beyond the wit of political parties to solve. Despite the fact that the major political parties have significant support in all parts of the country, there are whole provinces,

19. Under the single-alternative vote the elector marks his choices in order of preference. If no candidate has a majority the bottom candidate is dropped and his second choices applied to the others. This process may be repeated until one of the candidates has an absolute majority of votes.

indeed regions, where one of them cannot translate votes into seats in the House of Commons. This was strikingly illustrated in the general elections of 1979 and 1980. In the former, the Conservative government was reduced to three seats in Quebec, while in the latter a majority Liberal government was unable to win seats anywhere in the western provinces except for two in Winnipeg, but won all but one seat in Quebec. This heavy regional imbalance, which seems to be more than a temporary phenomenon, has led to a revival of proposals for some sort of mixed system by which something like fifty seats would be added to the House of Commons and allocated to political parties in proportion to their share of the popular vote in a particular province. The acute embarrassment of having no elected ministers at all in an important part of the country may yet lead the political parties to adopt this expedient.[20]

POLITICAL PARTIES

Democratic politics begins with political parties. Indeed political parties are older than democratic politics, but a party system has become a necessary part of democratic politics. Originally, as the political power of legislatures grew, political parties arose as a means of giving a stable base to government. When government needed to depend on parliamentary majorities, rather than on the favour of the Crown, it became necessary to create a system which would ensure the continuity of authority. This process, which began in the middle of the eighteenth century in British politics, had become fully developed in the period between 1832 and 1867. In British North America, similarly, party government emerged in the eighteen-forties *pari passu* with the growth of responsible government. The result was what Maurice Duverger has called the cadre party, an organized group of parliamentarians held together by common objectives and expectations of benefit from the fruits of power.[21]

20. A full examination of the problem and a discussion of how it might be solved in this manner is contained in William Irvine, *Does Canada Need a New Electoral System?* (Kingston, Ontario, 1979). See also Government of Quebec. *One Citizen, One Vote: Green Paper on the Reform of the Electoral System* (Quebec, 1979). Adoption of this system is also recommended in *The Task Force on Canadian Unity* (the Pepin-Robarts Report): *A Future Together* (Ottawa, 1979) and suggested in *The Constitutional Committee of the Quebec Liberal Party. A New Canadian Federation* (the "Beige Paper") (Montreal, 1980).

21. See his *Political Parties* (London, 1954).

Because of their informal origins it has been commonly believed that political parties are entirely outside the framework of constitutional law. They were informal entities, not even legally incorporated bodies, and there was a general tendency to think this was a desirable characteristic which should be retained. It is true that some parties, such as the communist party, have from time to time been singled out by being declared unlawful organizations which have been proscribed, but that in a sense reinforced the argument. Recognition might well lead to regulation of a sort which would undermine the basic institutions of democracy. However, the fact of the matter is that the law in Canada has gradually encroached on political parties, as an incident to the regulation of political broadcasting, as part of a reform of party financing, or as part of the process of regulating the business of Parliament.[22]

The political party has now become the essential mechanism of democratic politics. The principal difference between oligarchic politics and democratic politics in a parliamentary system is that the source of legitimacy and the focus of operations have changed from Parliament to the electorate. In a parliamentary system it was the configuration of parties in the House of Commons alone that mattered. In democratic politics the ultimate arbiter is the electorate, and the interplay of politics becomes a sort of permanent electoral campaign. As Professor Crick puts it, "The theory which now best fits the facts is that Parliament influences the electorate which has the real power to control the Government."[23]

The kind of political parties and the type of party system which a country has will depend on its political institutions and the environment in which they operate.[24] Canadian parties will inevitably reflect the fact that Canada is a country of bi-ethnic culture with a federal system, and a country with "an American-style social and economic class structure."[25] It is of equal importance that political parties in Canada operate within a constitutional system of a parliamentary type, based on single-member territorial constituencies.

22. For a full discussion of what has happened see John C. Courtney, "Recognition of Canadian Political Parties in Parliament and in Law." *Canadian Journal of Political Science.* XL:1 (March, 1978) p. 33.

23. Bernard Crick, *The Reform of Parliament,* 2nd ed. (London, 1968) p. 28.

24. There is a substantial recent body of writing about Canadian political parties. Perhaps the most useful are F. C. Engelmann and M. A. Schwartz, *Canadian Political Parties: Origin, Character, Impact.* (Scarborough, 1975) and C. Winn and J. McMenemy, *Political Parties in Canada* (Toronto, 1976).

25. Leon D. Epstein, "A Comparative Study of Canadian Parties," *American Political Science Review.* LVI:1 (March, 1964) p. 47.

The last point is important. The politicians who have learned to work the system are generally content with it, and few political scientists have been disposed to ask whether its occasional hardships—such as weak minority governments or massive majorities and a decimated opposition—are really necessary. It is therefore refreshing to find that Professor Alan Cairns has argued forcefully that the electoral system, far from being unimportant in shaping the party system, has a major influence on it. Furthermore this effect is dysfunctional. Not only does it distort the results of an election by often over-representing the majority party, but it operates against the maintenance of an effective opposition.

The electoral system itself tends to strengthen the attachment which particular sections of the country have to political parties, so that within these sections purely party divisions are minimized. Thus the electoral system, instead of reflecting the differences between parties, exaggerates sectional divisions.[26]

Finally, this leads Professor Cairns to raise serious doubts about the effectiveness of Canadian political parties as nationalizing agencies, playing a brokerage function in reconciling diverse interests. "The party system," he argues, "importantly conditioned by the electoral system, exacerbates the very cleavages it is credited with healing."[27] There are plenty of examples in Canadian electoral history to support his point. The remarkable misrepresentations of the results of a Conservative victory put about by Liberal organizers in Quebec were clearly successful in defeating Arthur Meighen in 1921. The Conservative failure to be adequately rooted in Quebec has led that party to write Quebec off altogether in its election strategy, as in 1957, or to make unsuccessful and uncomprehending attempts to achieve an "instant" organization in Quebec, as it did again in 1968. This tendency for party strategy to be sectionalized is not confined to Quebec, and increases the balkanization of Canadian politics.

Given such built-in obstacles to survival, it is surprising that the country has endured so long, for one of the hardest things to change in a political system is the cluster of habits and laws which make up the electoral system. In the beginning there was not much choice, for the political framework was imposed, or perhaps graciously granted, by the British government. In any event, it is likely that earnest Canadian politicians and pamphleteers, looking to the Brit-

26. Alan C. Cairns, "The Electoral System and the Party System in Canada, 1921–1965," *Canadian Journal of Political Science* I, No. 1 (March 1968), p. 62.

27. Ibid., p. 64.

ish model in the middle of the nineteenth century, took the electoral and political system for granted.

Furthermore, it seemed more pleasing to believe that political parties were held together by a common devotion to doctrine and not merely by bargains among interest groups. A civilized political system *should* be divided into liberals and conservatives, for this was part of the conventional wisdom about politics, and it had much to commend it. There is bound to be, in any community, a difference between those who have a stake in things as they are, and those who stand to gain from change. There is also a temperamental difference between kinds of people, a matter of what used to be called disposition, which makes them stand-pat or innovating by nature.

Nevertheless, the model of a party system based on the division between liberal and conservative has never been easy to apply to Canada. There was a tendency in the nineteenth-century British ruling class to think that a pioneer community would be so poor in ideas that its government was unlikely to be based on considerations of principle. Such people, it was felt, were unworthy of self-government.[28]

Part of the difficulty about Canadians' developing good, sound parties of political principle on the English model stemmed from the problem of governing a very diverse and scattered country. The shaky coalitions of strange bedfellows, which were necessary to carry on any government at all in the Province of Canada, schooled Canadian politicians in a system which they used to meet the more arduous challenge of governing the new federation after 1867. If anybody were to construct a stable base of government at all, it would require an elaborate coalition of interests and a minimum of agreed principle. In any event a careful party leader was bound to be instinctively aware of Jefferson's warning against political differences which coincide with geographical boundaries. And while campaign tactics often roused those very interests, there was also a counter-tendency to preserve as far as possible a conspiracy of silence about the things that would be so divisive as to lead to the brink of civil war.

28. Shortly after his arrival in Canada, which occurred during an election campaign, Lord Dufferin wrote to the Colonial Secretary, "...although I have taken some pains to ascertain what may be the questions likely to divide public opinion at the Hustings, I cannot detect any that are not of a personal, municipal, or local character unless it be a dispute between Ontario and Quebec as to the direction of the Pacific [railway]." Dufferin to Kimberley, July 5, 1872, P.A.C., *Secret and Confidential Despatches,* Series G.12, Vol. LXXIII, p. 373.

There is a more fundamental difficulty about applying the conservative-liberal litmus test to politics in North America. Louis Hartz has argued that in the United States there is only one tradition—a liberal one—because North America escaped a feudal social order out of which European conservativism grew.[29] There may be reactionary or populist extremists on the margins of American politics but they can never dominate the broad central liberal stream. It follows that in the United States there can never be a viable conservative party or a viable socialist party, since the essential conditions out of which they might take root are absent.

However valid this thesis may be as an explanation of American politics, it can be argued that Canadian conditions are, in important respects, different. In the first place, French Canada does have precisely the feudal roots that Hartz claims are necessary to found a conservative political order, and it is also arguable that colonial societies created by the Loyalists after the American Revolution themselves represented the beginning of a conservative tradition. Thus the "organic" element which produces tory democracy (in, for example, the policies of Adam Beck in Ontario or the Bennett "New Deal") is present in Canada and creates the conditions for both a conservative and a socialist party.[30]

The fact of the matter is that the two major parties in Canadian politics describe themselves as Conservative and Liberal. Do these terms mean anything? It may be that they did mean something at the beginning, even if the differences that now exist seem as uninformative as the names of patent medicines. On such matters as the franchise, the tariff and the imperial connection, the Conservative party of Macdonald differed from the Grit and Reform elements of the Liberal party in a way that is consistent with the notion of conservative and liberal. Since these questions have been settled by a general consensus it has been difficult to find others which divide the parties on principles of this order.

More fundamental, perhaps, was the discovery by Macdonald of

29. Louis Hartz, *The Liberal Tradition in America* (New York, 1955). See also Bernard Crick, "The Strange Quest of American Conservatism," *Review of Politics* XVII, No. 3 (July 1955), p. 359; and note further Gunnar Myrdal's remark that "America...is...conservative.... But the principles conserved are liberal, and some, indeed, are radical." *An American Dilemma* (New York, 1944), p. 7.

30. See G. Horowitz, "Conservatism, Liberalism, and Socialism in Canada: An Interpretation," *Canadian Journal of Economics and Political Science* XXXII, No. 2 (May 1966), p. 143 (also reprinted in Hugh G. Thorburn, ed., *Party Politics in Canada,* 2nd ed. (Toronto, 1967)); and Samuel Beer, *British Politics in the Collectivist Age* (New York, 1965).

"the standard formula for the construction of a national party in Canada" which Dr. Hougham describes as "the development and pursuit of some unifying programme: the conciliation (if not the satisfaction) of opposing interests and attitudes; and, in an emergency, a not-too-high standard of political ethics—a readiness 'to buy love and purchase peace.' "[31]

Not all parties have been successful in making this formula work. And yet most of the time it is clear that party strategists understand it and seek to apply it. It can be argued that one important element of success is the capacity of the party—and above all of its leader—to project an image which fits the mood of the country at the time. The political character of a country is bound to change, and there is a strong likelihood that the electorate will yearn for the kind of leadership which matches its mood.[32]

It is also possible that the growth of urbanism and the decline of the small community, together with the development of radio and particularly of television, have magnified the importance of the personality of the leader as the image of the political party. This in itself may represent a substantial change in the structure of Canadian politics. Thus, the eminent Canadian historian, F. H. Underhill, found in the Conservative revival in 1957–58 confirmation of the erosion of the two-party system which began under Mackenzie King.

To explain this paradox he argues that "a two-party system in the classical sense of the term," in which two parties alternate in office with reasonable frequency, has not been restored. "As far as we Canadians are concerned, the two-party system in this classical sense is only a sort of political Garden of Eden towards which our newspaper editors and our university political scientists yearn nostalgically. But an angry God drove us out of this Eden after 1918, and it is mostly wishful thinking that sees us now being readmitted to it."[33]

"What Mackenzie King established," he says, "was a one-party domination at Ottawa with two or three splinter-parties posing as opponents of the leviathan in office." Mackenzie King's party, "which called itself Liberal," not only blanketed the centre in

31. George M. Hougham, "The Background and Development of National Parties," in Thorburn, *Party Politics in Canada,* p. 3.

32. J. R. Mallory, "The Structure of Canadian Politics," in Thorburn, *Party Politics in Canada,* pp. 28ff.

33. F. H. Underhill, "The Revival of Conservatism in North America," *Transactions of the Royal Society of Canada* LII, Series 3 (June 1958), pp. 1-19.

politics, but "spread out so far both to the left and to the right, that the opposition groups seemed to become more and more ineffective." He had thought that the meaning of the Liberal defeat in 1957 was that Mackenzie King was at last dead. But no. "Since March 31, 1958, we have had established at Ottawa another governmental party, calling itself Progressive Conservative this time, still more overwhelmingly blanketing the centre and spreading out to left and right."

In addition to the single majority governmental party, Underhill adduces the fact that the real opposition is not in Parliament at all but in the provincial capitals. He points out that before 1957 Social Credit governments in British Columbia and Alberta, the C.C.F. in Saskatchewan, Conservative governments in Ontario, New Brunswick and Nova Scotia, and the Union Nationale of Maurice Duplessis, formed our effective opposition. "Maybe," he suggests wistfully, "when the first fine careless rapture of the post-March 31 situation has passed, our provincial electorates will begin to move towards real opposition again." It is not clear what is meant here by "real opposition." There is a sense in which major cleavages in Canada are now expressed in federal-provincial conflict and reconciliation, but this ignores the role of a parliamentary opposition which acts as a check on government. And even the weakened opposition after 1958 was far from ineffective in this role. After 1962 it was, of course, a numerical majority in the House until 1968.

That the voters tend to act consciously to create a balance between the party in power in Ottawa and opposition governments in the provinces is disputed by Professor Denis Smith. It is more likely, he feels, that the electorate keeps the two political systems, federal and provincial, quite separate. They tend to vote, therefore, for the candidate or the party which is likely to win, and are not engaged in a sort of electoral calculus.[34] While it is increasingly true that many of the major questions of Canadian politics seem to be the subject of debate and negotiation in federal-provincial conferences, this may not be so much the result of a shift in the centre of gravity of politics as of a tendency in modern parliamentary systems for political leaders to reach over the heads of legislatures and appeal directly to the public. To this extent we are becoming more of a plebiscitary and less of a parliamentary democracy.

Professor C. B. Macpherson discerns, in his study of prairie politics, the emergence of what he calls a "quasi-party system"

34. Denis Smith, "Prairie Revolt, Federalism, and the Party System," in Thorburn, *Party Politics in Canada,* pp. 196-7.

which he thinks may become characteristic of the Canadian system as a whole.[35] This quasi-party system, which differs from both plebiscitary democracy and the party system of democratic theory, has arisen because the normal class basis for a political party system is absent.

The striking thing about Alberta has been that its politics have been dominated by a single party at a time, with change taking place by the massive overthrow of the party in power and the emergence again of single-party dominance. In Macpherson's view, the key factor has been the semi-colonial status of the province, producing for an outside market, and with the bulk of its resources owned by external interests. The most numerous and influential class in Alberta are independent agrarian producers, an essentially petit-bourgeois class. Their radical discontent is directed against the external forces which seem to exploit them, but as they achieve power they recoil from fundamental radical reform because they fear a destruction of the economic system.

It would be possible to apply a somewhat similar analysis to Quebec in the Duplessis era as well as to certain other provinces where parliamentary institutions seem to be weak. It may also be that as the Canadian economy becomes increasingly dependent on the United States, the same characteristics of huge majorities such as occurred in 1958, a weakness of parliamentary institutions, and long periods of one-party dominance, may conform more closely to the model of a quasi-party system for the country as a whole.

It is certainly true that one-party dominance is one of the enduring characteristics of Canadian politics, and it is a pleasing paradox that a highly determinist class theory of Canadian politics should be the explanation of the end of ideology.

In national politics, the shifts in power from a period of Liberal domination to one of Conservative domination appear to be less certain and less massive than those which take place in provincial politics. Part of the explanation for this may lie in the persistence of third parties which, since 1921, have proved strong enough to survive but never strong enough to displace one of the older parties.

The major parties, because they are delicate balances of interest, have a kind of rigidity in their programs and in their capacity to act which makes it difficult for them to be receptive to new ideas or to adjust to the needs of novel conditions. When political or economic conditions become very bad, a large number of voters will become disillusioned with the whole political process.

35. C. B. Macpherson, *Democracy in Alberta* (Toronto, 1953).

Thus the various protest parties, whose greatest strength was in the west, represented a revolt not only against the old parties but also against the rules of the political game. It was a kind of political fundamentalism which sought to remold the complex and unsatisfactory world into a simpler and more satisfactory pattern.[36] They shared with American populism the belief that man was essentially good, but had been corrupted by bad institutions and sinister interests. In their first blush of triumph the Alberta Social Crediters gladly embraced all of the reforms in the liberal canon. But their theory of the nature of man and of social change was always dangerously close to a conspiracy theory of history, and when they have been soured by their failure to create the New Jerusalem by a brief exercise of power it has been easy for them to turn to the pursuit of scapegoats, whether Jews, foreigners, bankers, communists or sometimes all of them together in some vast and improbable conspiracy to enslave the world.

But even Social Credit, among whose followers such nightmares are most likely to occur, has learned quickly from the responsibilities of power that life is complicated and survival depends on adopting the compromises, the methods and the organization of the old parties.

While third parties are the principal source of instability which inhibits the creation of broad-based majority governments, they may not be the dread symptom that they seem to editorial writers, pundits and other established alarmists. The fact they do not seem to wither and die like American third parties may be a sign that Canadian politics is not the same as politics in the United States, and not a sign that our society is sicker.

The received doctrine about third parties in American life is that they play the necessary role of innovators in the political system and then, having discharged their creative role, expire promptly like the male bee. The innovator role is explained by the state of monopolistic competition which confronts major political parties—similar to that facing the industrial giants which produce soap or motor cars. Like them, the parties adhere to the principle of minimum differentiation of the product, warily peddling the same set of ideas and policies which have worked for them in the past. They are disposed to be afraid of new ideas, for fear of making costly mistakes which may lose support they already have, without making compensating gains.

36. See S. D. Clark, "The Frontier and Democratic Theory," *Transactions of the Royal Society of Canada* XLVIII, Series 3 (June 1954), pp. 72-3; and Richard Hofstadter, *The Age of Reform* (New York, 1955).

Third parties, with nothing to lose, can afford to experiment with new ideas, for ideas are the only working capital they have. In the process, the public will be gradually educated to an awareness of the need for a new policy or a new program. Then, in the fullness of time, the larger parties will take over the more durable of the reforms advocated by third parties and enact them into law.

Third parties have a second beneficent effect on the political system. Since they are movements of protest they enlist the participation of many good and earnest people to whom conventional political activity is sordid and unattractive. Thus a third party may enlist large numbers of voters into political activity and help to rescue politics from the "professionals." The forces that divorce the average voter from politics are of increasing strength, and the evangelical politics of a new party may penetrate the alienation of the lonely urban crowds and bring them into meaningful political activity.

These cleansing and renewing activities would happen even if third parties had the short life assigned to them by the wise men of the editorial pages. What is so exasperating to them is that third parties fail to die, and seem to live in a state of perpetual young middle-age. Their survival needs explaining. The answer may lie in part in the nature of the Canadian political system. In the United States the presidency—which can only be held by one man—reduces to improbability the chance of success by a third party. In Canada, the Cabinet and parliamentary system gives an opportunity for manoeuvre which does not exist in the United States. Third parties have had some success in capturing power in some provinces. This gives them a power base from which to support federal election campaigns and the opportunity to gain power and experience in office, thus showing to the skeptical that they have the capacity to govern. And in a country of only ten provinces, rather than of fifty states, the road upward appears easier.[37]

While Professor Cairns has argued that the fragmentation of Canadian politics along sectional lines is dysfunctional since third parties tend to represent sectional interests,[38] it is possible that this argument is pressed too far. The sectional cleavages in Canada go very deep, and it may be that third parties take some of the strain. If no major party can gain a solid foothold in large parts of the country, it may not be entirely the fault of the electoral system or of the other institutional factors that strengthen third parties. It may simply be

37. See J. R. Mallory, *Social Credit and the Federal Power in Canada* (Toronto, 1954), Chapter VIII.

38. Cairns, "The Electoral System and the Party System in Canada."

that no consensus is possible on a number of major issues. In the past there have been several occasions where this has seemed to be the case. But each time this has happened, a change in program or leadership in one or other of the major parties has broken the stalemate. Thus, the sudden reincarnation of the Conservative party under Mr. Diefenbaker turned it overnight into a majority party of the classic type. Ten years later Pierre Trudeau was to have the same galvanic effect on the Liberal party.

However, in general the character of Canadian politics (at least in English-speaking Canada) is unique in one respect: it is "the only society in which the centre triumphs over left and right. In Europe the classless appeal of Liberal Reform does not work: the centre is decimated by the defection of high-status adherents to the right and low-status adherents to the left. In Canada, the classless appeal of King centrism is the winning strategy, drawing lower-class support to the Liberals away from the left parties, and higher-class support away from the right parties. This forces the left and right parties themselves to emulate (to a certain extent) the Liberal's classless strategy. . . . The liberal refusal to appear a class party forces both right and left to mitigate their class appeals and to become themselves, in a sense, centre parties."[39]

The behaviour of Canadian electorates has tended to respond more strongly to religio-ethnic-regional factors than to class factors because of the attempts of the parties to adapt to the pattern imposed by the tactics of the triumphant centre. So far these tactics, which tend to dilute the ideological content of politics, seem to have worked. But there are signs that the strains on the system are multiplying. The sheer explosive growth of great urban areas and the redistribution of representation, which increases the electoral importance of these areas, reduces the importance of the old symbols of religion, ethnicity and region in animating voting behaviour. Out of this development, it is often argued, must come a form of politics in which class issues become more important. The temporary effect of a charismatic politician—a Diefenbaker or a Trudeau—may arrest this trend, but in the longer run the shift in the party system seems inevitable.

What seems bound to reinforce it is the apparent change in Quebec politics, where for so long traditional values and a static social structure kept the Quebec voter out of the mainstream of politics, so that its leaders played something of the same role in the

39. Horowitz, "Conservatism, Liberalism, and Socialism in Canada," p. 170.

Liberal party as the Southern Democrats did in the Democratic party in the United States. The rise of a new urban middle class with a taste for ideological politics has broken up the party structure in Quebec and made it much more difficult to hold the majority of Quebec voters to a party system based on the old symbols.[40]

THE LEADER AND THE PARTY MACHINE

While political parties are informal groups which play a necessary part in democratic politics, they are not necessarily endowed with the apparatus of internal democracy. Nowhere is this paradox more apparent than in the way in which their leaders are chosen, and in the relationships between leaders and followers. In the nineteenth century the choice of a party leader was inextricably bound up with the constitutional arrangements for choosing a prime minister.

The choice of Sir John A. Macdonald as the first Prime Minister of Canada at the same time clothed him with the party leadership. The four leaders who succeeded him were designated in the same way by the exercise of the prerogative. This was deemed to be the natural way for a party leader to emerge.

If a party is in opposition, it cannot avail itself of the magic of the prerogative to legitimize a leader. The alternative, almost equally respectable in the nineteenth century, was for the leader to be chosen by the parliamentary caucus. These two methods, between them, were deemed adequate by both Liberals and Conservatives until 1919. In that year the Liberals introduced the special leadership convention—a vast assemblage of party satraps, parliamentarians and representatives from constituency organizations—which had for long been the method of choosing presidential candidates in the United States.

This innovation did not immediately commend itself to the Conservatives, for when Sir Robert Borden retired in 1920 they resorted to a process by which Borden "sounded the caucus," in a manner very similar to that which prevailed until 1964 in the British Conservative party,[41] before indicating to the Governor General that the prerogative should be exercised by calling on Arthur Meighen. It was only with the selection of R. B. Bennett in 1927 that the Conservatives adopted the leadership convention. They have fol-

40. See Hubert Guindon, "Social Unrest, Social Class, and Quebec's Bureaucratic Revolution," in Thorburn, *Party Politics in Canada,* pp. 182-8.

41. Cf. Robert McKenzie, *British Political Parties* (London, 1964).

lowed this practice ever since, except in the case of Meighen's brief resumption of the leadership in 1942.[42]

The practice with both Conservative and Liberal parties was to assume that the leader was chosen on an indefinite tenure, though by 1966 both parties were beginning to show concern with the need to review the leadership on a regular basis, and the constitutions of both parties provide a biennial opportunity for a leadership review.[43] The fact of the matter has been that as long as the party is winning, no question is likely to arise of renewing the leader's mandate. If he leads it to disaster there are likely to be attempts to "persuade" him to resign, but once a leader is chosen his power and authority are hard to shake unless he himself decides—like Mr. St. Laurent in 1958, and Mr. Clark in 1983—to give up his post. The five years of agony endured by the Conservative party after 1962, in which various attempts were made to bring down Mr. Diefenbaker, show how a wily and determined leader can hold out against persistent revolt.

The leadership convention has now become an important element in democratic politics. It is not merely the summoning of an unusually large and representative "parliament" of the party in order to ensure that the leader is the choice of the party as a whole. It is at the same time an opportunity to reshape party policy by the adoption of a "platform" which lays down a program ostensibly binding the party in the next election. Its third function is one of building up the morale of the party and generating enthusiasm in the party workers. Its fourth function is now perhaps the most important of all: that of exposing the party, its program and its leader to the public. No other method has been devised which, at such little cost, has such enormous impact.

The convention is not merely an intra-party affair. Television has made it possible for the whole electorate to be an audience of the proceedings. Since the convention itself is part of the party's propaganda campaign in the next election, it is obvious that one of the effects of television will be to impel the managers of the convention to make sure that it projects a healthy image, and that any evidence of acute division, of unseemly argument or of boring convention politics is suppressed. There will, therefore, be cause for regret that

42. After Meighen's defeat in the South York by-election, the caucus chose R. B. Hanson as temporary leader. An excellent account of the Conservative party in this period is J. L. Granatstein, *The Politics of Survival* (Toronto, 1967).

43. The most comprehensive study of this matter is John C. Courtney, *The Selection of National Party Leaders in Canada.* (Toronto, 1973).

the convention will become increasingly phony lest the public should be shocked by the sight of intra-party democracy in the nude. But it should be remembered that the television medium has no commitment to the party, and skillful television producers may be able to reveal much of what is supposed to be artfully concealed. In any event, says Professor Ward, "To blame television for converting the convention into a show...ignores the obvious fact that a leadership convention *is* a show, and is carefully arranged to be as good a show as possible."[44]

The preparation for a convention is necessarily elaborate, and the party organizing committee will be responsible for everything from accommodation for delegates and publicity arrangements to the main matters of business to come to the convention floor. The most important of these will be the reports of sub-committees on resolutions. These will be likely to bring about debates on party policy and on organization, on which discussion will be a mixture of debate on tactics and recrimination. Important decisions will have to be taken about such matters as a keynote speaker and the other details of the program. The keynote speaker, like so much of the apparatus of the convention, is borrowed straight from the American conventions. His role is a combination of invocation and electrification of the convention. It is not sufficient to designate a brilliant orator; it is desirable to be sure that he will utter the appropriate sentiments. It is worth noting that the Liberals in 1956 dispensed with a keynote speaker altogether because "the most logical choice..., Senator Power, had given the party a shrewd scolding in 1948, and it was feared by some that he might do it again."[45]

When the call has gone out for the convention, the focus of activity shifts to the constituencies. Local associations and other affiliated groups (the women, the university groups and the "young") will be preparing resolutions on various policy matters for the delectation of the main resolutions committee, which will have the task of scrutinizing them and producing some sort of consolidated version of party sentiment for the convention floor. In this task the party research department, afforced by available intellectuals, will play an important part.

44. Norman Ward, "The Liberals in Convention," in Thorburn, *Party Politics in Canada,* p. 98. In addition to Professor Ward's admirable account of the Liberal convention of 1958, see also Professor John Meisel's thorough discussion of the Conservative convention of 1956 in *The Canadian General Election of 1957* (Toronto, 1962).

45. Ward, "The Liberals in Convention," p. 99.

Meanwhile the candidates for the leadership will have embarked on their campaigns. They and their supporters will be in contact with every constituency and every group likely to produce convention votes.

The most exciting part of the show at a leadership convention is the contest itself. The candidates for the post will have armed themselves with buttons, flags, banners and all other means of creating an illusion of strength. There will be much handshaking, "hospitality suites" will be centres of good spirits, and a great deal of work behind the scenes will be devoted to mustering votes, especially those which become available in later ballots as the bottom candidates are dropped off. Attempts will be made, when the candidate speaks to the convention, to set off demonstrations by the use of bands, pipers, pretty girls and marchers in the aisles. The voting itself, in which each delegate casts a secret ballot, lacks the theatrical quality of open voting by delegations which characterizes the American convention. Before the introduction of voting machines, it was necessary to interpolate an awkward period of business to fill the time necessary for the scrutineers to count the ballots. When the result is finally announced after the last ballot, the winner will speak, the losers are expected to behave like good losers, and the show—as a show—is over. There may be a good deal more convention business, but the public and many of the delegates will have better things to do. For many of the delegates the main problem will be to decide whether to get much-needed sleep, or to travel home with a hangover.

Whatever the atmosphere of false bonhomie at the convention, the likelihood will be that the leader chosen will conform to the type of the party brass—a group of respectable figures who, with their circle of political friends, will have found the considerable sum necessary to conduct a leadership campaign. It goes without saying that the leader chosen is likely to be an established politician, and recent contests suggest that he is more likely to have a record of achievement in federal politics than in the limited arena of a province. In the Conservative party, where the problem of leadership has recurred with embarrassing frequency, it is significant that the choice of John Bracken was a disaster, and while George Drew proved to be energetic, he was unable to save his party. Provincial origins had also proved to be something of a handicap for Robert Stanfield.

Mackenzie King and his two successors to the leadership of the Liberal party were so clearly establishment figures that they almost parodied the type. Indeed Mr. Pearson, who embarked on the leadership endowed with few political instincts and little parliamentary skill, showed how far the establishment virtues of social grace, respectable origins, diplomatic skill and knowledge of the world outweigh political experience and earthy appeal. While he was clearly at home reading a book or in a senior common room, and certainly understood and enjoyed professional sporting events, he could not avoid looking embarrassed wearing an absurd hat at a stampede or striking up a rewarding conversation with his barber.

Mr. Diefenbaker was, of course, an exception to the pattern. He knew it and had considerable skill in exaggerating the difference. To the dismay of the Conservative establishment, he made his principal stock-in-trade an effective and open attack on those respectable forces who prefer to think that, whoever may be in office, they at least are still in power. A Prime Minister capable of campaigning as the champion of the little people against the bureaucrats, the newspapers and the articulate classes generally, is bound to be a cause of alarm in every respectable suburb from Victoria to Halifax. It is no wonder that the press was almost entirely against him by 1963 and that powerful forces inside his own party tried furiously to unseat him.

Mr. Trudeau's success in first capturing the leadership and then winning an election was largely due, in all probability, to the successful projection of an image of youth and unconventionality. He thus had a "Diefenbaker effect" of appealing to a large group of uncommitted voters (though probably a younger and more urban group), in spite of the fact that in education, social class and previous connection with public service, he was in many ways very much like his predecessors.

While the leader is the visible and articulate embodiment of the party in an election, the curious practice persists of trying to determine party policy at a leadership convention. One of the most prolific industries in the convention rooms is the creation of a platform and the definition of a policy for all conceivable issues. Since much of this has to be done before there is any clear indication of who is to become leader, much of this intense activity may be wasted. "In the final analysis," as Professor Meisel points out, "the leader of a party plays by far the largest part in presenting its views to the nation."[46] Whatever the platform may say, he will have his own ideas and surround himself with his own men. The candidates of his party will have every incentive to follow his lead.

With respect to party organization, there appear to be significant

46. Meisel, *The Canadian General Election of 1957*, p. 41.

differences between the Liberal and Conservative parties. In the former, the executive officers of the National Liberal Federation have effective control over the party organization and a good deal of autonomy in relation to the leader. This may be an inheritance from Mackenzie King, who preferred to leave the party organization to his trusted lieutenants and to concentrate on higher things. It may also be a consequence of the Liberals' having fought so many elections while in office, whereas the Conservatives have normally been in opposition. The Conservatives' main strength for electoral purposes, depended a great deal on strong provincial governments in provinces where their party was in power. In any event, Professor Meisel concludes:

> The powers of the national leader, the control imposed by the national office on the party organizations in the provinces and in the constituencies, and the virtual disappearance of local organizations in some provinces had conspired to make of the Conservative party a political machine largely dominated from the centre.[47]

In both parties a small central national office, expanded many times over during election campaigns, is an important element of continuity, a source of political intelligence and a strategic operational centre whose duty is to prepare for the campaign. As a source of influence on leadership and day-to-day tactics it naturally yields place between elections to the parliamentary caucus. It is the leader and his parliamentary followers who are on the firing line day after day when Parliament is in session, and it is natural that the leader is more sensitive to caucus as an indication of feeling in the country and the party than he is to a central office whose contacts with the country are far less effective than those of M.P.s.

While Canadian political parties must be organized to bring their weight to bear on the battlefield in Ottawa, they must also be effectively linked to the electorate. There must be both a command structure and some kind of democratic or consultative machinery by which the rank and file of a party can be integrated into the process of decision-making. The base of the pyramid in the party is the constituency organization where the party leadership must establish an effective relationship with its active supporters.

"The basic function of the constituency organization," says Professor Meisel, "is to select a suitable candidate and to get him elected."[48] But while the *raison d'être* of political parties is to win

47. Ibid., p. 74.

48. Ibid., p. 83.

elections, the electoral organization itself performs the essential function of bringing party members into active participation in party affairs. The constituency association is thus capable of being an instrument of democratic participation in its own right. The extent to which it does so varies greatly in different constituencies.

There are pronounced regional differences in the character of Canadian parties so that, for example, there is likely to be more similarity in the degree and kind of internal democracy in all parties in a particular region than there is between comparable structures of the same party in different regions. The important power centres within the parties are, moreover, likely to be the provincial organizations. National party organizations are to a large extent shadowy bodies with only intermittent life. This is a consequence partly of the size of the country and partly because smaller units are more manageable. Of perhaps equal importance is the fact that the range of activity of provincial governments gives such scope for participation and patronage that the provincial organization is able to offer the party worker most of the rewards and satisfactions which come from political activity.

The formal structure of party organization reflects these forces. In a federal country is it not surprising that political parties themselves are federalized, and that the provincial association has much greater reality than the national organization. The primary unit of participation is the constituency organization, and it is the representatives of these units which make up the provincial association, together with Privy Councillors, senators, members of the Legislative Assembly and defeated candidates of the two previous classes who ran in the last federal and provincial elections.[49] This body is responsible for party organization and, in a general way, for policy. Many years may elapse between the "annual" meetings of the association.

The functions of a provincial association are somewhat nebulous and when things are going well its powers are exercised by small bodies, such as the executive. The more important powers are, in any event, located elsewhere. A party leader, in both federal and provincial politics, has a good deal of freedom from control by the party rank and file. The bodies whose views he must take seriously are those of the Cabinet (when the party is in power) and the

49. The formal structure of Canadian parties is fully described in Dawson, *The Government of Canada,* Chapter 22. The composition of the provincial association described above is that of the Liberal and Conservative parties in Ontario. There are important differences in other provinces, notably Quebec. There the Conservatives have no provincial organization, and the federal and provincial Liberal parties are now formally separate.

caucus. Even the choice of the leader is not vested in the regular association but in a special convention.

Political observers from Michels and Ostrogorski to Robert McKenzie have pointed out that the fine Victorian ideal of a political party democratically controlled by the rank and file has never effectively prevailed against the problems of large size and the differences in political skill and available time between the party professionals and the ordinary membership. Canada has conformed to the generality of experience in this matter.

An exception of some importance is of course the New Democratic Party. Largely because of its heavy commitment to democratic ideology and mass participation, the organization of the N.D.P. is much more effectively democratic than that of its rivals. The most powerful democratic influence in its structure is its dependence on financial support from individual members and its reliance on unpaid volunteer election workers.

Its provincial associations, in areas where the N.D.P. is strong, still eagerly debate questions of policy and exert considerable control over the leadership. The national leader is much more closely controlled by the national council than any of his opposite numbers. The biennial national convention not only debates and lays down general policy, but also re-elects the leader on each occasion. It was very noticeable in 1966 that there were strong pressures in both the Liberals and Conservative parties for periodic reassessment of the leadership and for greater democratic participation. This may have been caused by dissatisfaction with the leadership in a period of party stalemate, but Mr. Trudeau, after his election to the Liberal leadership, showed strong interest in party democratization.

But complete democratization is difficult to sustain. Even in the N.D.P., strong tensions persist between the more ideological constituency parties and the party establishment, which has preserved a remarkable continuity in office and a considerable ability to get its own way. If it grows in size and gains power, the party will experience many of the same problems as any other political party.[50]

The growth of urbanization has seriously undermined the traditional democracy of Canadian political organization. When life was still largely rural, the leading positions in political parties fell inevitably into the hands of the natural leaders of the community. In small communities there was an instinctive system of selection in which people of ability almost unavoidably rose to the top in

50. See Leo Zakuta, *A Protest Movement Becalmed: A Study of Change in the C.C.F.* (Toronto, 1964).

community affairs. It thus did not matter much if the actual conduct of the affairs of a local party organization was a friendly arrangement among the recognized few who made their decisions informally in whatever manner they chose. A formal apparatus of constitutional government within parties would have led, in fact, to the same people taking the same decisions in much the same way.

This informal but essentially democratic process could not be expected to survive in a highly urban environment. No longer does everyone know everyone else in the community, for there is no longer a community in that sense. More and more community functions fall into the hands of those in key positions who have little direct contact with the constituents on whose behalf they run local organizations. What is true of the Community Chest is equally true of the political party. The consequence is the growing separation between an élite group and the mass of apathetic non-participators who need to be herded, by the most skillful available techniques of public relations, to do their civic duty, whether it be voting or donating blood. In the process the lumpen mass is being manipulated by a class of persons with whom they have no real contact.[51]

PARTY FINANCE AND THE COST OF ELECTIONS

There is an old saying that elections are not won by prayers. To mount the massive publicity campaign necessary to contest seats in all parts of the country, to move party speakers around in a large country, to keep on hand the experts to write speeches and press releases and prepare election material, is becoming an extremely costly enterprise. Until recently only a tiny fraction of this cost was met out of public funds, by the responsibility imposed on the Canadian Broadcasting Corporation to provide free time on radio and television on an equitable basis to national parties. The Committee on Election Expenses estimated, on the basis of confidential information from the political party organizations and its own researchers, "that the national parties' organizations spend in excess of eight million dollars in a national election campaign. This estimated figure includes funds which are given by the national parties directly to support their candidates. Supplementary to this

51. For a more sophisticated discussion of this point see John Porter, "Power and Freedom in Canadian Democracy," in Michael Oliver, ed., *Social Purpose for Canada* (Toronto, 1961), and the same author's *The Vertical Mosaic* (Toronto, 1965).

total should be added a similar amount raised and expended by or on behalf of the candidates themselves. The estimated total expenditures would approach $16 million inclusive of those funds expended by the state itself and its agencies."[52]

One of the largest elements of expense that confronted a candidate in the Liberal or Conservative parties was the accepted practice of paying electoral workers, at least for the work done on election day. Professor Meisel noted that drivers with cars would expect to be paid between ten and thirty dollars a day, and that canvassers, scrutineers and baby-sitters would cost between six and eight dollars a day each. It was possible to run a campaign in a rural constituency for $7500 to $12 500, but the cost per candidate in urban seats would run to $15 000, and amount to at least $25 000 in metropolitan seats. In fact, many candidates spent a great deal more.[53]

There does not seem to be any close connection between the amount of money spent and the results of the election. It is well known that the Conservatives fought in 1957 with very little money compared with the Liberals, and yet they were much more successful.

Where does all the money come from? In the case of the Liberal and Conservative parties, the money at the disposal of the central party organizations comes chiefly from businesses and wealthy individuals. Many firms now give money to both parties, and usually give larger amounts to the party in power—a fact which had some bearing on the Liberal rout in 1958. Dr. Harrill estimated that at least fifty percent of general party funds come from industrial and commercial firms, "and probably at least forty percent from businessmen who are so closely identified with particular companies that it is difficult to distinguish between them."[54] The remaining ten

52. *Report of the Committee on Election Expenses* (Ottawa, 1966) p. 32. The Committee was appointed by the Secretary of State for Canada in 1964. Its report was based on a large-scale research program directed by Professor K. Z. Paltiel. The report and its supplementary volume, *Studies in Canadian Party Finance,* was a uniquely valuable source of data on a hitherto mysterious matter. Excerpts from the report, and its recommendations, are reprinted in Thorburn, *Party Politics in Canada,* pp. 104-23. The first major study of the financing of a major political party is Reginald Whittaker's illuminating *The Government Party: Organization and Financing the Liberal Party of Canada 1930–58.* (Toronto, 1977).

53. Professor Meisel's figures are based on the *declared* expenses of the candidates. In many cases the actual figures are probably a good deal higher. Meisel, *The Canadian General Election of 1957,* p. 116.

54. E. E. Harrill, "Money in Canadian Politics," in Thorburn, *Party Politics in Canada,* p. 65.

percent, he thought, comes from smaller contributions from individuals.

In contrast with the larger parties, third parties have much more limited sources of funds, but are likely to have much smaller expenses because of their ability to get practically all work at the constituency level done by unpaid volunteers. Professor Meisel has concluded that in the 1957 election the C.C.F. could not have spent much in excess of $200 000 altogether, including constituency expenses.[55] By 1965 the N.D.P., with much greater support from trade union sources, was able to spend just under a million dollars.[56] The information available about the financing of the Social Credit parties is by no means complete, though a very useful study has been made of the ingenious methods of financing used by the Ralliement des Créditistes.[57] Mr. Caouette and his followers were particularly effective in using local television broadcasts. The money available for the Social Credit party in national elections seems to have been highly variable, and depends on the amounts that can be raised by provincial parties which are strong enough to get substantial contributions from business sources, that is to say, in British Columbia and Alberta.

The fact that so much of party funds is raised from business sources is not as clear evidence of corruption as it would have been in the nineteenth century, or even as recently as the Beauharnois Scandal. Business can no longer expect direct favours—at least from the federal government—since practically all government contracts are let by public tender. Nevertheless *quid pro quos* are undoubtedly expected. "Certainly what most givers want," says Professor Paltiel, "whether they give large or small amounts at the local or party level, is *access* to decision makers at various levels. In addition, donors may wish to define the parameters within which decisions are made and this helps to explain the often heard appeal for funds to preserve the 'two party' system."[58] It is therefore probable that most contributors to party funds have little expectation of direct benefit.

55. Meisel, *The Canadian General Election of 1957, p. 216.*

56. *Report of the Committee on Election Expenses,* p. 265.

57. Ibid., pp. 267-77, and Michael Stein, "The Structure and Function of the Finances of the Ralliement des Créditistes," *Studies in Canadian Party Finance* (Ottawa, 1966), pp. 405-57.

58. Khayam Z. Paltiel, "Federalism and Party Finance: A Preliminary Sounding," *Studies in Canadian Party Finance,* p. 16.

Nevertheless, the dependence of political parties on funds provided by wealthy donors raises questions about the sources of such funds, and the possibility that they may come from very dubious sources indeed. Efforts were apparently made to smooth the immigration application of a certain Mr. Stonehill by hints of his possibly generous contribution to party funds.[59] Only slightly more alarming is the eagerness with which the possibility of political contributions on behalf of Lucien Rivard, apparently an active party worker and contributor (as well as an accomplished drug smuggler), were received by certain Liberal politicians, such as Mr. Guy Rouleau.[60]

The Committee on Election Expenses was clearly aware of the dangers and ambiguities of the present methods of party financing. They recognized that political parties require substantial financial resources in order to play their proper role. Some of these expenses could probably be borne out of public funds. For the rest provision should be made, through income tax concessions and in other ways, to encourage voluntary support of political parties by as many individuals as possible. Equally important, there should be much more effective legislation to ensure the financial accountability of political parties for the funds they hold, and a maximum amount of publicity of their sources of funds. In summary, the committee made the following recommendations:

(1) Political parties should be legally recognized and made legally responsible for their actions in raising and spending funds.
(2) A degree of financial equality should be established among candidates and among political parties, by the extension of certain services and subsidies to all who qualify.
(3) An effort should be made to increase public participation in politics, by broadening the base of political contributions through tax concessions to donors.
(4) Costs of election campaigns should be reduced, by shortening the campaign period, by placing limitations on expenditures on mass media by candidates and parties and by prohibiting payment of poll workers on election day.
(5) Public confidence in political financing should be strengthened, by requiring candidates and parties to disclose their incomes and expenditures.
(6) A registry under the supervision of a registrar should be established to audit and publish the financial reports required, and

59. *The Dorion Report* (Ottawa, 1965), pp. 44ff.
60. Ibid.

to enforce the provisions of the proposed "Election and Political Finances Act."

(7) Miscellaneous amendments to broadcasting legislation should be enacted to improve the political communications field.[61]

The committee's proposals for public subsidy of election campaigns were principally directed towards reducing the cost of the use of communications media, which are clearly—notably in the case of television—responsible for the rapid escalation of election costs. Because the committee recognized that "the increasing use of broadcast media constitutes the greatest contributing factor to the rising cost of campaigning," it recommended that political parties be relieved of a substantial part of this burden and at the same time "limit the use of the media to reasonable proportions." This would be done by requiring broadcasters, as a condition of licence, to provide 50 percent of the broadcast time allocated to political parties without compensation. The other 50 percent would be reimbursed to the broadcaster by the Registrar of Elections and Political Finance.[62]

At the same time candidates should be reimbursed for the postage costs of mailing one item of literature to each elector in his constituency. They should further be reimbursed at a rate of two cents per elector for the costs of purchasing space or time in any communications medium, from newspapers and broadcasting to posters and brochures. This concession should be restricted to candidates obtaining at least 15 percent of the votes cast.[63]

As a result of the committee's recommendations an Election Expenses Bill to amend the Broadcasting Act, the Canada Elections Act, and the Income Tax Act respecting election expenses went through all of its stages in time to receive Royal assent in January, 1974. It is a somewhat improved version of the bill which had been introduced in 1972, but which had died on the order paper. The general purpose of the act is to increase political participation by encouraging financial contributions from individuals, to ease the financial burdens on political parties and candidates, to restrict excessive expenditures and to control the sources of campaign contributions.

Under the act, contributions by individuals to registered parties and candidates become deductible against income tax payable in

61. *Report of the Committee on Election Expenses,* p. 37.

62. Ibid., pp. 44-5.

63. Ibid., pp. 41-2.

the following manner: 75 percent of contributions not exceeding $100; $75 plus 50 percent of contributions between $100 and $550; $300 plus 33⅓ percent of contributions above $550, with a maximum deduction of $550. All contributions over $100 require the disclosure of the name of the donor.

The act further provides for the reimbursement out of the public treasury of the expenses of candidates who poll at least 15 percent of the vote. Reimbursement will be the lesser of the following: the amount of the candidate's expenses or the total of postage costs of one mailing to all electors in the riding or eight cents for each of the first twenty-five thousand and six cents for each name in excess of that number. Also refunded are the candidate's deposit, and up to $250 for the payment of the auditor required to audit the candidate's accounts. For very large ridings there is additional provision for travel costs—the least of actual costs, square miles multiplied by one cent, or $3000. Candidates who fail to get 15 percent of the vote qualify only for the payment to the auditor.

The act also imposes limits on the total permissible election expenses to one dollar for each of the first fifteen thousand electors, plus fifty cents for each elector between fifteen and twenty-five thousand, and 25 cents for each elector in excess of twenty-five thousand. For example, in a riding of forty thousand electors the maximum permitted expenditure would be $23 750—of which about $6100 would be reimbursible, so that the less a candidate spends the higher the percentage of his expenses would be recoverable. The personal expenses of the candidate up to $2000 and necessary travel expenses are not included in the above limits. Expenditures of political parties are limited to thirty cents for each name on the electoral lists. Registered parties are also entitled to a refund of half the cost of the radio and television time allocated to them by the CRTC. The amount of such paid commercial time is limited to 6½ hours for all registered parties and the rates charged must not exceed lowest commercial rates.

Each registered party is required to have a chief agent who is required to submit audited statements to the Chief Electoral Officer after each campaign, and at the end of each fiscal year. These accounts are available to the public and must be tabled in the House of Commons. Failure of compliance with the reporting and other aspects of the act is punishable by a fine not exceeding $25 000. Enforcement of the act is in the hands of a Commissioner appointed to work under the Chief Electoral Officer. In the course of the passage of the bill an amendment was added to provide that the provision of services supplied by a government or public organization in a campaign would constitute an election expense, e.g. transportation in government aircraft.[64]

These reforms will not work a miracle. But they provide a climate of elections in which candidates are on a footing of much greater equality in putting their case before the public, and the mystery, suspicion and temptation which had surrounded party finance has been largely removed.

64. An amendment to the Act, passed in 1983, raised these amounts by adjusting them in relation to the Consumer Price Index, and made some other minor changes.

6

Parliament: The Senate

"There shall be One Parliament for Canada, consisting of the Queen, an Upper House styled the Senate, and the House of Commons." British North America Act, 1967, Section 17.

THE SOVEREIGN LEGISLATURE

The ultimate centre of legal power under the Canadian constitution lies not in the people, but in the sovereign legislature. It is through the operation of certain ancillary provisions, which provide for the primacy of the House of Commons in financial matters, for annual Parliaments, for the dissolution of Parliament and new elections at least every five years, that the electorate remains in final control over the law-making process. "Parliament is not legally subject to any physical limitation," says Sir Ivor Jennings.[1] This is only true of the Parliament of Canada as long as it acts within its jurisdiction, as defined originally in the British North America Act as well as by the Charter of Rights and Freedoms contained in the Constitution Act, 1982. Under the latter act it also shares with the legislatures of the provinces the amendment of the most important parts of the constitution. Within the limits of its legislative authority Parliament is the supreme law-making body.

When we speak of Parliament in this sense we think of it as comprehending three elements: the Queen, the Senate and the House of Commons. Strictly speaking, as Jennings points out, Parliament consists not of three distinct bodies, but of "the Queen in Parliament," that is the Queen (or, in normal circumstances her representative, the Governor General) sitting with the Senate in the Senate chamber, and with the Commons standing at the bar.[2] This is a purely formal ceremony called for specific purposes, such as the giving of royal assent to legislation and the reading of the Speech from the Throne.

1. Sir Ivor Jennings, *Parliament.* 2nd ed. (London, 1957) p. 2.
2. Ibid., pp. 2-3.

As far as the functions of Parliament are concerned, the role of the three elements is very different. Responsible government has reduced the "efficient," as distinct from the "dignified," functions of the Queen and the Governor General to being almost entirely nominal and automatic. The Speech from the Throne is composed by the Prime Minister with the assistance of the Cabinet, and the other functions of the Sovereign in relation to Parliament are carried out on the advice and responsibility of ministers. Again, the functions of the two Houses of Parliament are in practice very different. Except for the primacy of the House of Commons in financial legislation, the powers of the two chambers are declared to be equal, but in fact it is the House of Commons which is the heart and centre of Parliament. So much is this so that when most people (and not only members of the House of Commons) speak of Parliament, they are thinking exclusively of the House of Commons.

ROYAL ASSENT

Section 55 of the British North America Act empowers the Governor General, when a bill has passed both Houses, and is presented to him "for the Queen's Assent," to "declare, according to his Discretion, but subject to the Provisions of this Act and to Her Majesty's Instruction, either that he assents thereto in the Queen's Name, or that he withholds the Queen's Assent, or that he reserves the Bill for the Signification of the Queen's Pleasure." To the extent that these discretionary powers are related to his functions as an imperial officer, they have of course been obsolete since the Imperial Conference of 1926. Thus the reservation of bills is now barred by constitutional evolution. The power to withhold assent altogether is not, in all probability, covered entirely by the same rule. There is probably a vestigial authority, which is part of the royal prerogative, to refuse assent to bills, but it is significant that assent has not been refused to a bill in the Canadian Parliament since Confederation, and in the United Kingdom royal assent has not been refused to bills since the reign of Queen Anne.[3] For all practical purposes, the royal

3. In fact in the provinces this particular royal prerogative is by no means dead. There are a number of cases of refusal of assent by Lieutenant-Governors, the most recent being in Prince Edward Island in 1945. In this case, and in many others, the Lieutenant-Governor was acting not as a Dominion officer, but on his own discretionary authority. See James McL. Hendry, *Memorandum on the Office of Lieutenant-Governor of a Province: Its Constitutional Character and Functions* (Ottawa, 1955).

veto of bills is, as far as the Canadian Parliament is concerned, constitutionally obsolete.

The ceremony of royal assent still retains the trappings of ancient parliamentary procedure. The short titles of bills are read out in the Senate chamber, with the Commons present at the bar, by the Clerk of the Parliaments. The formula of assent is then pronounced, not by the Governor General, but on his behalf by the Speaker of the Senate. According to constitutional custom, the Governor General does not himself attend Parliament to give royal assent to bills. The Deputy Governor General attends in his place.[4]

MEETING OF PARLIAMENT

Theoretically, the life and functioning of Parliament depend upon the royal prerogative. Parliament cannot meet unless it has been summoned by a proclamation of the Governor General issued under the Great Seal of Canada. When it has met, the first business of Parliament is to assemble in the Senate chamber to hear from the Governor General the "cause of summons," which is set forth in the Speech from the Throne.

If Parliament has been summoned to meet after a general election, there is a prior item of necessary business which must be transacted—the Commons must be directed to elect a Speaker so that they will have a recognized spokesman at the formal ceremony of Parliament. Accordingly, on the day when Parliament is first summoned to meet, the House of Commons will assemble in their chamber, sign the roll and take the oath administered by the Clerk of the House of Commons. Then there will be three loud knocks on the door of the chamber, and the door will be opened to admit an officer of the Senate called the Gentleman Usher of the Black Rod. He enters the chamber and announces, in English and in French, that the Deputy of the Governor General desires the presence of the Commons in the Senate chamber. There, the assembled Commons

4. This is a matter of practice only. In 1939, King George VI gave royal assent to bills in the middle of a parliamentary session in Ottawa. See Canada, *House of Commons Debates* (1st session), 1939, pp. 3708, 4322. In recent years, royal assent is sometimes given by the Governor General in the course of the Session. This was deliberate policy on the part of Jules Leger, as a means of making his role more visible and most likely to happen where one of the bills is of particular public importance.

will be informed by the Speaker of the Senate that His Excellency the Governor General "does not see fit to declare the cause of his summoning the present Parliament until the Speaker of the House of Commons shall have been chosen according to the Law."

When the Commons return to their own chamber they then proceed to elect a Speaker. The Clerk of the House, who presides on this occasion, then points to the proposer and seconder of the candidate for the speakership. By custom the proposer is the Prime Minister. Up until 1953 the seconder was always a minister of the Crown. In that year, it was arranged that the leader of the opposition should second the nomination of the Speaker. This agreeable practice continued through the next three Parliaments, but in 1963 Mr. Pearson reverted to the older practice of having the nomination seconded by another minister.

This done, the House adjourns and re-assembles in the afternoon. Again Black Rod appears, bowing thrice as he progresses into the chamber, and announces that the Governor General desires the attendance of honourable members in the Senate chamber. This time the members move in solemn fashion, preceded by the Sergeant-at-Arms bearing the mace, and the Speaker. On this occasion the Governor General will be seated on the dais, and about him at the sides will be the Prime Minister and senior officers and officials, and seated in chairs on the Senate floor will be the judges of the Supreme Court in their full-dress scarlet robes.[5]

The Speaker of the House of Commons, from his place at the bar of the Senate, will then announce his election to the Governor General, and claim, on behalf of the House, "all their undoubted rights and privileges, especially that they may have freedom of speech in their debates, access to Your Excellency's person at all reasonable times, and that their proceedings may receive the most favourable consideration." So far the proceedings are substantially similar to those in the British Parliament. There is, however, one significant omission. In Westminister the claim of privileges is preceded by a request for the royal confirmation of the election of the Speaker. In Lower Canada, Lord Dalhousie refused to confirm the election of Louis Joseph Papineau as Speaker in 1827, and this led to the dropping of this request altogether in the Parliament of the Province of Canada in 1841. The practices of the Province of Canada generally prevailed at Confederation, and as a consequence

5. They used to sit on a woolsack, as do the judges at Westminster. When the size of the Court was increased to nine in 1949 the woolsack proved to be too small, and was replaced by chairs.

the request for the Speaker's confirmation has never been a part of the ceremonial of the Parliament of Canada.[6]

The Speech from the Throne is then read by the Governor General. It used to be the practice to read it through first in English and then in French. In recent years, no doubt in conformity with the official bilingualism of federal institutions, some parts of the speech are written in English and some in French. Since the Speech from the Throne tends to be unconscionably long and the proceedings are now usually televised, this useful compromise helps to reduce the tedium of the ceremony. After the ceremony is over the Commons return to their own chamber. At the beginning of each session of Parliament the ceremony of summoning the Commons to the Senate Chamber will be gone through again, though in normal circumstances the Commons will not need to elect a new Speaker for the duration of that Parliament.

Back in their own chamber, the Commons will be informed by the Speaker that he has claimed their usual privileges, which His Excellency "was pleased to confirm." At this stage the Prime Minister rises in his place and moves for leave to introduce Bill Number One, "respecting the administration of oaths of office." This motion is agreed to, and in so doing the House has vindicated its ancient right to consider its own business before turning to the business of the Crown.[7] The Speaker then announces that he has provided himself with a copy of the Speech from the Throne "to prevent mistakes." He does not actually read it again, but it is printed in the report of debates at that point. Consideration of the Speech from the Throne will normally be the first order of business, and it will be debated on a motion to adopt an Address in Reply, moved and seconded by two private members on the government side. The address, when adopted, will be engrossed and presented to the Governor General, along with a similar address from the Senate, at a small ceremony at Government House.

Each session of Parliament must be brought to an end by the formal ceremony of prorogation. Like the summoning of Parliament, this is one of the powers of the Governor General, exercised on advice, and is thus one of the ways by which the Cabinet can

6. Sir J. G. Bourinot, *Parliamentary Procedure and Practice in the Dominion of Canada,* 3rd ed. (Montreal, 1963), pp. 184-6.

7. The Senate also has a bill introduced for the similar purpose, "a bill relating to railways." Neither bill is ever proceeded with, and in times of urgency they both may be dispensed with altogether. Thus, in the second session of Parliament called in 1950 to deal with the emergency created by the railway strike, Bill Number One was the bill to restore the railways to operation.

control a recalcitrant House. Prorogation has the effect of bringing all parliamentary business, whether completed or not, to an end. Thus any bill which has not gone through all stages in both Houses and received royal assent will die, and must be commenced again *de novo* at a subsequent session.[8] Similarly, prorogation will bring any committee business to an end. This was an important constitutional issue in 1873, when Lord Dufferin was waited on by a deputation of ninety Liberals urging him to refuse to agree to a prorogation requested by the Macdonald government. The effect of the prorogation, as everyone knew, would be to terminate abruptly the work of a parliamentary committee investigating certain matters connected with the Pacific Scandal. "I could not," said Dufferin, "have treated Parliament as a pregnant woman and prolonged its existence for the sake of the lesser life attached to it." He agreed to the prorogation over the summer with reluctance, after getting assurances from his ministers that parliament would be reconvened that year if necessary.[9]

Unlike the opening and prorogation of Parliament, which are stately ceremonials, for purely historical reasons dissolution is by proclamation only. Charles I is quoted as having said that it was better for a monarch to be seen doing pleasing things, and not to be seen when unpleasant things have to be done. Accordingly, dissolution of Parliament normally takes place after Parliament has been prorogued.

In considering the advice of a Prime Minister to dissolve Parliament, the head of state is exercising one of the few surviving discretionary prerogatives of the Crown.[10] The prorogation and dissolution of Parliament before a session has lasted a reasonable time is unusual, and rightly thought to show a lack of respect for parliamentary institutions. Mackenzie King, in 1940, caused Parliament to be summoned (he had promised to do so), and thereupon caused it to be dissolved.[11] Far more serious a breach of constitutional propriety would be the dissolution of Parliament before it had

8. In Prince Edward Island, the government sought to revive a bill which had been refused assent by having a newly appointed Lieutenant-Governor give assent to it after the legislature had been prorogued. The courts held, as might have been expected, that the bill was dead and could not be revived. See *Gallant* v. *R.* [1949] 2 D. L. R. 425.

9. Harold Nicolson, *Helen's Tower* (New York, 1938), p. 151.

10. See *ante* Chapter 2.

11. See Eugene A. Forsey, "Mr. King and Parliamentary Government." *Canadian Journal of Economics and Political Science* XVII, No. 4 (November 1951), p. 463.

even met. There was some talk of dissolving the Parliament of 1957 before it had met, but this does not seem to have been entertained by any responsible person.[12]

THE SENATE

The Senate plays the role of a senior but minor partner in the process of parliamentary government. The focus of parliamentary ceremonial in the Senate Chamber is a reminder of Walter Bagehot's distinction between the largely "dignified" functions of the House of Lords and the essentially "efficient" role of the House of Commons in the United Kingdom. The Senate inherited its place in the formal constitutional structure of the legislature from the Legislative Council of the pre-Confederation period and thus originally from the House of Lords. Its critics seem to suggest that it possesses most of the faults of its prototype and few of the virtues. Suggestions are frequent that it could, with advantage, be abolished since reform seems to be out of the question. It is not without significance that the first serious work on the Senate, Dr. MacKay's careful study, published in 1926, bears the title *The Unreformed Senate of Canada*.

And yet the Senate was intended at Confederation to play an important role in the Government of Canada. Its composition was the subject of much anxious negotiation, for it was considered to be the heart of the federal system. It is evident from the Confederation Debates that there was little discussion or concern about the division of powers between the federal Parliament and the provinces, but grave difficulty over the powers and composition of the Senate and the relations of the two Houses. No doubt this was in part because the Fathers of Confederation in the Province of Canada were trying to project their own experience of the quasi-"federal" structure of the Canadian Parliament into the future. But there was also, as Professor Waite argues, a deeper reason: the constitution which emerged from the Charlottetown, Quebec and London conferences

> . . . gave the central legislature and its institutions a preponderant role; it is also the answer to the puzzle of everyone's preoccupation with the Senate. The same problem had existed at Philadelphia seventy-seven

12. See J. R. Mallory, "The Election and the Constitution," *Queen's Quarterly* LXIV, No. 4, pp. 471-2.

years before, and the result was not dissimilar. The Senates of both Canada and the United States caused enormous difficulties, and the division of powers seemed relatively easy. One explanation is that government was neither so pervasive nor so complex in the nineteenth century as in the twentieth. Jurisdictional problems were anticipated by Dunkin and others, but the "difficulties of divided jurisdiction," to use the title of Professor Corry's work, were not very apparent. That the division of powers is the heart of the federal system is a modern proposition, not a nineteenth-century one.[13]

The Senate was to be a crucial balancing mechanism in the new federal system. It thus had to be based on equal representation between the two Canadas. The acceptance of this principle was enough to persuade the Lower Canadians to concede the demand of the Upper Canadians for representation by population in the lower house, and thus solved that intractable problem which had bedevilled the politics of the Province of Canada for so long. As George Brown said in the Confederation Debates, "On no other condition could we have advanced a step."[14] It is doubtful if, having conceded so much, the Lower Canadians would have accepted equal representation of all provinces in the Senate. In any event, agreement was achieved on a formula which gave the Maritime provinces as a group the same number of senators as Ontario and Quebec.

There was also general agreement that the Senate should be composed of appointed rather than elected members. In the mid-nineteenth century popular assemblies were still viewed with misgiving, and it was generally believed that a true parliamentary system needed a revising chamber to restrain the impulses of its more fickle partner.

It must be [said Macdonald] an independent House, having a free action of its own, for it is only valuable as being a regulating body, calmly considering the legislation initiated by the popular branch, and preventing any hasty or ill considered legislation which may come from that body, but will never set itself in opposition against the deliberate and understood wishes of the people.[15]

There is little doubt what Macdonald meant by "hasty and ill considered legislation." The interests of private property were

13. P. B. Waite, *The Life and Times of Confederation* (Toronto, 1962), p. 111. Quoted by permission of the University of Toronto Press.

14. *Confederation Debates* 1865, p. 88.

15. *Confederation Debates* 1865. p. 36.

always in a minority in a democratic society, and the Senate was expected to protect them. Few of the Fathers of Confederation can have viewed the rising tide of nineteenth-century democracy with much enthusiasm and the Senate must have seemed a natural obstacle to the excessive growth of democratic institutions, or of confiscatory legislation. And so it turned out to be.

CONSTITUTION OF THE SENATE

The total number of Senators provided for in the British North America Act is now 104. Originally, twenty-four were assigned to Ontario and twenty-four to Quebec, and these numbers have remained constant. Another twenty-four were given to the Maritime Provinces. At first New Brunswick and Nova Scotia received twelve each, but on the entry of Prince Edward Island into Confederation in 1873, four of these were allotted to that province, and the representation of the other two fell to ten each. The western provinces on entry were given variable numbers of senators, but by an amendment in 1915 they were given six each, thus providing for twenty-four for the whole region. The same amendment provided that Newfoundland would receive an additional six when it came into the union, so that its inclusion in 1949 raised the total to 102. A further amendment in 1975 added one Senate seat for each of the Yukon and Northwest Territories so that out of the present total of 104, eight are outside the basic regional number of twenty-four. Under this arrangement the four western provinces have argued that they are under-represented in proportion to their population and importance. For different reasons, Quebec, which now is represented by less than a quarter of the total, can argue that its special position is insufficiently recognized. Any re-arrangement of Senate numbers will have to take these difficulties into account.

Section 26 of the British North American Act provides for the appointment, in unspecified circumstances, of what are called "additional senators." When these additional senators are appointed, there must be either four or eight, drawn equally from each region. It is further provided that no ordinary vacancies in the Senate can be filled in any one of the four divisions, unless the total representation of that division has again fallen below twenty-four. This safeguard was inserted by the 1915 amendment, which at the same time increased the total number of senators.

This provision did not form a part of the proposals for the

constitution of the Senate agreed at the Quebec Conference. Its inclusion was pressed upon the Canadian delegates in London by the British government. The Colonial Secretary, Lord Carnarvon, argued that there was no mechanism to escape from a serious deadlock between the two Houses. The accepted method of dealing with a situation of this kind in the United Kingdom was the creation of additional peers by the Sovereign. But the appointment of additional senators could wreck the delicately balanced composition of the Senate, finally achieved after patient negotiation at the Quebec Conference. Macdonald set to work to devise a formula for appointing additional senators without, at the same time, violating the agreement on balanced representation.[16] As a result, the permitted number of extra appointments is so few that it is difficult to see what circumstances would be clarified by such appointments.

While the appointment of ordinary senators was vested in the Governor General, the appointment of additional senators was provided for in a way that left the final decision to appoint them—though not the appointments themselves—to the British government. The relevant words of section 26 are: "If at any Time on the Recommendation of the Governor General the Queen thinks fit to direct that Three or Six [now Four or Eight] Members be added to the Senate, the Governor General may by Summons" make the appointments. The effect of this was that, should the Canadian government wish the appointment of additional senators, it would have to transmit its recommendation through the Governor General to the Colonial Secretary who would then advise the Sovereign. Thus the final decision rested with a minister in the United Kingdom.

Additional senators have never been appointed under this section, but there have been at least three occasions upon which Canadian Prime Ministers have raised the question, at least informally, with the Colonial Office. On December 22, 1873, shortly after the dissolution of Parliament but before the pending general election, the Mackenzie administration advised the Governor General that it was "desirable in the public interest" that six additional senators be appointed. Though no reason was alleged in support, it was understood at the time that this was simply to reduce the preponderance of the Conservative opposition in the Senate.[17] In a confidential memorandum, Mackenzie argued that "the political

16. D. G. Creighton, *John A. Macdonald: The Young Politician* (Toronto, 1952), pp. 457-8.

17. A. Todd, *Parliamentary Government in the British Colonies* (Boston, 1880), p. 164.

complexion of this body cannot therefore be regarded with indifference by any Government, as a large and hostile majority in the Senate may affect the Government very seriously, acting in conjunction with a powerful minority in the Commons."[18] However, Lord Dufferin delayed transmitting the request to London until he was certain that it would arrive after the results of the election were known there. Lord Kimberley's reply from the Colonial Office was a flat refusal, in which he said that the power vested in the Crown should only be exercised "in the event of an actual collision of opinion between the two Houses."[19]

In 1900, Sir Wilfrid Laurier tentatively raised the question of appointing additional senators, but was given a reply that "satisfied him that he would not be accorded this favour."[20] In 1912 Sir Robert Borden informally explored the possibility of extra Senate appointments during the struggle over the Naval Bill, but no formal action was taken.

These past circumstances offer no guide to present practice, since the British government is no longer in a constitutional position to advise the Queen on a Canadian matter. In such a case the only person entitled to advise the Queen would be the Prime Minister of Canada. Accordingly, for what it is worth, the appointment of additional senators now lies as much with the Prime Minister as does the appointment of ordinary senators.

While a Prime Minister can exercise this power at any time he chooses, there are three possible sets of circumstances in which it might be desirable for him to do so, the first of these being if the opposition has a narrow majority in the Senate, and the appointment of additional senators would be sufficient to overcome opposition obstruction. Since the Senate on the whole has obeyed Macdonald's injunction not "to set itself in opposition against the deliberate and understood wishes of the people," this circumstance is unlikely to arise. A second possibility would be the situation in which a government has no representatives in the Senate at all, and there are no vacancies. A third possibility might be where an incoming government finds that its only supporters in the Senate are too old and ill to

18. Eugene A. Forsey, "Alexander Mackenzie's Memoranda on the Appointment of Extra Senators, 1873-74," *Canadian Historical Reviw* XXVII, No. 2, p. 191.

19. Eugene A. Forsey, "The Appointment of Extra Senators under Section 26 of the B.N.A. Act," *Canadian Journal of Economics and Political Science* XII, No. 2 (May 1946), p. 160.

20. A. B. Keith, *Responsible Government in the Dominions,* Vol. I, 2nd ed. (Oxford, 1928), p. 465.

bear the necessary burdens in the conduct of government business. Either or both of these last possibilities might have confronted the Conservative party had their return to power been delayed many years beyond 1957. As it happened, their predecessors had got into the habit of ostentatiously leaving Senate vacancies open on the eve of a general election, perhaps as evidence of their confidence in being yet again sustained in office.

The sober functions assigned to the Senate at Confederation suggested that senators be persons of maturity and substance, and such, in fact, was the case. The age of initial appointment was higher than that for other offices, and according to the standards of the time a senator needed to be a man of property to qualify. In brief, the qualifications for the Senate are as follows: a senator must be at least thirty years of age; he must be a natural-born or naturalized subject of the Queen; he must hold real property free of debt to the value of at least four thousand dollars, and have a net worth of at least four thousand dollars; he must be resident in the province for which he is appointed, and, in the case of Quebec, he must be qualified by residence or property in the district for which he is appointed. In Quebec, though not in the other provinces, there is one senator for each of the districts formerly represented in the Legislative Council. A senator may be of either sex, in spite of the fact that the statutory references in the British North America Act, passed before the emancipation of women, are all masculine.[21]

A senator is appointed by instrument under the Great Seal of Canada. The appointment is vested in the Governor General, but in practice has always been on ministerial advice. Once appointed, a senator used to hold his place for life, though he could resign by submitting his resignation in writing to the Governor General. In 1965 a bill was passed which in effect imposed a retiring age of seventy-five on all senators appointed thereafter. At the same time senators were brought under the provisions of the Members of Parliament Retiring Allowances Act to qualify them for pension on retirement. In the case of senators who had previously been appointed for life, provision was made that they would receive a pension equal to two-thirds of their parliamentary salary if they chose to retire at the age of seventy-five.

The seat of a senator may become vacant if (a) he fails to attend the Senate for two consecutive sessions of Parliament; (b) he becomes the subject of a foreign power; (c) he becomes bankrupt;

21. This was decided by the courts in the *Persons* case, *Edwards* v. *The Attorney-General for Canada* [1930] A. C. 124.

(d) he is attainted of treason or convicted of a felony or any infamous crime; and (e) he ceases to be qualified by residence or property, except that he is not so disqualified if he is required by reason of public office to reside in Ottawa. The Senate is the judge of any disqualification, and must take note of it in order for a seat to be declared vacant.

The Speaker of the Senate is appointed by the Governor General and may be removed at any time by him. In consequence this office is a government appointment which will certainly change with a change in government, and may be changed from time to time if the Prime Minister wishes. Indeed, the Speaker of the Senate remains an important political figure, since unlike the Speaker of the Commons he has no tradition of separating himself from active political and parliamentary duties while in office.[22] Unlike the Speaker of the Commons, the Speaker of the Senate has an ordinary, but not a casting vote. In the event of a tie vote, a motion is considered to be lost. A quorum of the Senate is fifteen.

In addition to these governing provisions in the British North America Act, the Senate has adopted its own rules of procedure. The rules are similar to those of the House of Commons, but the atmosphere in which they operate is rather different. The Senate is a smaller and more intimate body than the Commons, and in the conduct of its debates it has consciously imitated the more relaxed and leisurely manner of the House of Lords. A senator who rises to speak addresses himself not to the Speaker, but to the other senators.

Until the recent reforms in House of Commons organization, the most striking difference between the way in which the two Houses dealt with legislation lay in committee procedure. Legislation in the Commons was invariably dealt with in committee of the whole, while in the Senate bills normally went to standing committees.[23] The greatly enlarged role of Commons standing committees does not lessen the usefulness and importance of Senate committees in the legislative process. It is in these committees that much of the most valuable work of the Senate is done. In several respects Senate

22. The Speaker "is frankly a Ministerialist, sometimes a member of the cabinet and necessarily a supporter of the administration of the day." J. W. Lederle, "Party Forms in the Senate," *Queen's Quarterly* LVII, No. 1 (Spring, 1950), p. 28. According to Dr. MacKay, "He may still attend the party caucus; . . . he uses his personal influence in support of party measures." *The Unreformed Senate of Canada* (London, 1926), p. 29. See also F. A. Kunz, *The Modern Senate of Canada, 1925-1963* (Toronto, 1965), p. 105.

23. E. Russell Hopkins, *How Parliament Works* (Ottawa, 1957), p. 39.

committees enjoy advantages over Commons committees in discharging their responsibilities. One of the most important of these is that their "actions and utterances do not threaten the stability of the Government." Furthermore these committees have "the valuable element of continuity which is often difficult to maintain in the complexion of House Committees."[24] Finally it is worthy of notice that the chairmen of Senate committees do not necessarily change with a change of government. Thus, in 1960, the chairmen of twelve of the sixteen standing committees were carried over from the previous Liberal regime. These included two committees of major legislative importance, the Banking and Commerce Committee and the Transport and Communications Committee, and the hard-working and meticulous Divorce Committee.

There is one important respect in which the powers of the Senate are not equal to those of the House of Commons, though the extent of the Senate's powers in this matter are a cause of outstanding disagreement between the two chambers. This is in respect to financial legislation. One thing is certain: such legislation must originate in the House of Commons. Section 53 of the British North America Act states that "Bills for appropriating any Part of the Public Revenue, or for imposing any Tax or Impost, shall originate in the House of Commons." Accordingly, the Appropriation Bill is presented to the Governor General for royal assent in the name of the House of Commons only.

Following British practice, the House of Commons claims the exclusive right to grant supply, and claims that the Senate has no right to amend supply bills in any way.[25] This claim has been firmly rejected by the Senate, which argues that since the British North America Act omits any mention of such restriction on its powers, none can have been intended, and that if the Senate, as representing the provincial interest, cannot amend such bills, it cannot discharge its constitutional functions.[26] Accordingly the Senate has amended not only bills containing financial clauses, but even taxation bills.

24. John E. Kersell, *Parliamentary Supervision of Delegated Legislation* (London, 1960), p. 76.

25. Standing Orders of the House of Commons, No. 63. "All aids and supplies granted to Her Majesty by the Parliament of Canada are the sole gift of the House of Commons, and all bills for granting such aids and supplies ought to begin with the House, as it is the undoubted right of the House to direct, limit, and appoint in all such bills, the ends, purposes, considerations, conditions, limitations and qualifications of such grants, which are not alterable by the Senate."

26. Canada, *Senate Journals,* 1918, pp. 193-203.

For example, it made substantial reductions in the income taxes proposed by the Minister of Finance on the eve of the outbreak of war in 1939. When this happens the Commons is often in no position to fight. The government may need the legislation urgently, and so the Senate amendment is accepted, with the somewhat lame assertion that "while doing so it does not think it advisable at this period of the session to insist on its privileges in respect thereto, but that the waiver of the said privileges in this case be not however drawn into a precedent, that the clerk do carry back the bill to the Senate and acquaint their Honours that this house has agreed to their amendments."[27]

Since the passage of the Parliament Act, 1911, in the United Kingdom, which curtailed the power of the House of Lords so that they have no power to either delay or amend money bills, the exceptional position of the Senate in this matter has become even more anomalous. The incautious use of the Senate's power to interfere with money bills would expose it to the greatest danger of drastic reform. Senate reform was an important part of Liberal party policy in the nineteen-twenties. Any measure for reform would, of course, require the concurrence of the Senate, and to accomplish this Mackenzie King's nominees in that period were asked to agree in advance to support any measure he might put forward with respect to Senate reform. Fortunately for Their Honours, this project slipped out of the area of high priority before the King government went out of office in 1930, and did not again assume in Mr. King's mind the degree of urgency which might have brought decisive action.

The Senate has been a favourite butt of popular criticism since Confederation. It is said that as a non-elective body it has no place in a democratic society, that it is largely composed of the representatives of powerful business interests who are able to exercise a sinister effect on legislation, that it does very little work (it sits, as will be seen, less often than the Commons), that it represents a needless expense to the taxpayer without much visible benefit, that if it agrees with the House of Commons it is unnecessary, and if it disagrees it is violating the principles of democracy. As Dr. MacKay put it, the Senate represents

> nothing but itself and the Prime Minister or party leader who has appointed its members. Therefore, when it opposes the House of Commons its actions seem capricious and arbitrary. To the public such

27. *Canada. House of Commons Debates.* June 1, 1939, p. 4846.

> action is the antithesis of representative government, and the voice of the Senate is but the voice of the Minister who has appointed its members, "ventriloquising through his nominees." This is the chief explanation of its weakness and its unpopularity.[28]

A symptom of the decline of the Senate as an important part of the parliamentary process is the decline in the number of ministers who are senators. The first ministry after Confederation contained four senators (which in those days of small cabinets, meant one-third of the ministry). Two Prime Ministers, Sir John Abbott and Sir Mackenzie Bowell, were senators. But the decline set in at the end of the nineteenth century. Sir Robert Borden began the practice of having no ministers in the Senate who were heads of government departments, and the number of ministers since 1921 who have sat in the Senate has been small. Mackenzie King contented himself with a Government Leader in the Senate who was also a Minister without Portfolio. In 1954 Mr. St. Laurent appointed a senator to the post of Solicitor General. Mr. Diefenbaker completed the process of pushing the Senate out of contact with the centres of power by excluding even the Government Leader in the Senate from the Cabinet in 1958. He did not continue this practice, however, and on practical grounds it does not seem possible for long to have no competent and knowledgeable member of the Cabinet in the Senate. Nevertheless the Government Leader in the Senate is bound to know little of the details of departmental business, and few Senate Leaders in recent years have possessed the exceptional energy and ability to master the intricate details of government legislation in order to pilot it with authority through the Senate.

The awkward results of the general elections of 1979 and 1980, by which the Clark government had negligible representation from Quebec and the succeeding Trudeau government no seats at all west of Winnipeg, meant that it became necessary to appoint several senators to important ministerial posts. While this is not likely to be a long-term solution to the problem of effective regional representation in the Cabinet, it has made the Senate a much more important part of the parliamentary process.

Furthermore, the life term has militated against the effectiveness of the Senate because a large number are appointed to the Senate and remain in it well after they are able to contribute much to its effectiveness. In 1953, for example, seventy-two senators were over

28. MacKay, *The Unreformed Senate of Canada,* p. 192. See also Colin Campbell. *The Canadian Senate: A Lobby from Within.* (Toronto, 1978)

60, thirty-nine were over 70, and four were over 80 years of age. Professor Kunz feels that it is easy to make too much of this argument. During the period which his study covers, he found the average age of senators at first appointment was slightly over 58, while the comparable age for first entry to the Commons was 51.1. The "life tenure" of senators averaged out at about sixteen years, and on the average senators died at age 74, which is less than the present retiring age.[29]

The life term of senators was intended to strengthen their independence of the government of the day, and it is generally argued that the Senate should be, to a greater degree than the Commons, above partisan issues. In fact practically all appointments to the Senate have gone to political supporters of the government, who have remained active political partisans after their appointment. The Senate has turned out to be an invaluable means of pensioning off ministers, M.P.s and others whose health and fortune has been ruined by long service in the political wars. Prime Minister St. Laurent actually appointed one active political opponent to the Senate, and appointed one or two genuine independents, but these were notorious exceptions to the general rule. The introduction of a pension plan for members of Parliament has now provided an alternative means of looking after deserving M.P.s, but it does not seem to have had any noticeable effect on the quality of Senate appointments. A Prime Minister always has to consider many candidates with strong party claims and it is not surprising in the circumstances that he does not feel free to embellish the Senate even with a modest seasoning of the eminent scholars and professional men that ardent Senate reformers would prefer to see given places in the red chamber.

All of these factors militate against the effectiveness of the Senate. It should be said, however, that the Senate can rightly complain that much of the trouble is not its fault at all. Since there are normally few departmental ministers in the Senate, most government legislation is introduced first in the House of Commons. As a result there is not much that can usefully be done early in the session either on the floor of the Senate or in those of its committees which await the flow of legislation from the Commons chamber. Because the conduct of business in the Commons is slow and chaotic, few bills reach the Senate until the session is well advanced, by which time the most important bills have become urgent and there is little disposition to

29. Kunz, *The Modern Senate of Canada,* pp. 69-71.

encourage the Senate to consume further time by giving them serious debate.

In recent years this situation has been somewhat mitigated by a change in Senate rules, adopted in 1947, which enables a minister who is not a senator to appear on the floor of the Senate in order to introduce and conduct his legislation through the Senate. Thus, in the twenty-two years 1924-45 only 36 government bills were introduced in the Senate, while no less than 138 were introduced in the following eight years. For the whole period of 1945-59 the total was 201. It is true that in this period a large number of revisions and consolidations of complicated and non-contentious statutes, such as the Criminal Code, the Bankruptcy Act and the Citizenship Act, were taking place, and this may have furnished an unusual opportunity to draw the Senate into full participation of difficult, tedious and politically unrewarding work.[30]

Ministers have been somewhat reluctant to appear in the foreign atmosphere of the Senate, and as a consequence the effectiveness of the rule has been somewhat reduced. Nevertheless, it must be recognized that the introduction of even a few bills in the Senate in each session not only balances the parliamentary load more evenly, but gives the Senate an adequate opportunity to consider them. If bills reach the Senate late, then the upper chamber is under strong government pressure to rush legislation through without adequate consideration because the Commons has finished its important business and wants to go home.

Criticism of the Senate and proposals for its reform stem in part from a "tendency to expect too much from the Senate: much of the criticism has been based on a misunderstanding of its proper functions."[31] In any event, not all of the functions attributed to it at its inception were feasible. Because the central problems of the federal system have been focused elsewhere, it has not played much of a role as a guardian of provincial rights. While it has the dubious distinction of performing somewhat better as a protector of vested property rights, it would be difficult now to argue that this is one of its most necessary functions. Similarly, it is difficult to take it seriously as a check on the partisan passions of an uninstructed Commons. The only functions on which the Senate should now be

30. For a thorough discussion of the modern Senate as a revising chamber see Kunz, *The Modern Senate of Canada,* Chapters 6-9.

31. Hopkins, *How Parliament Works,* p. 21.

judged are those of a revising chamber and general watchdog on the details of administration.[32]

In complex and highly technical bills there are likely to be a number of unsuspected flaws, even when those bills have been drafted by skilled government draftsmen. Some of these flaws may only appear after the House of Commons and the public have had some time to digest them. Furthermore, the acceptance by the government of an amendment in the Commons may require unforeseen consequential changes. These changes can be inserted when the bill is going through the Senate without unduly delaying the progress of the bill. There is no way that this could be done without greater delay in a single-chambered legislature.[33] Nor should it be forgotten that the Senate contains a number of former ministers and M.P.s with long experience of public life and expert knowledge of many highly technical branches of law and administration. Their contribution to the consideration of legislation is not a negligible one, and is one well worth retaining.

The Senate is necessarily involved in the process of constitutional amendment. For over a century it was the practice to seek amendments to the British North America Act by resolutions of both Houses of Parliament, so that Senate concurrence had become a convention of the constitution. Usually it has concurred in such resolutions, sometimes with reluctance, but there are two occasions when it has substituted its own judgment for that of the other chamber by rejecting or modifying proposals. It is also no doubt understood by all concerned that the Senate possessed a veto over proposals to reform it, which explains in part why Senate reform has been more frequently advocated than acted upon.

In 1936 the Senate refused to concur in a proposed amendment which would have set up loan councils to consolidate the borrowing powers of the provinces and would at the same time have clarified their taxing powers. More recently, in 1960, it amended a proposed amendment to the British North America Act regarding the retiring ages of judges. The Commons had earlier passed a resolution seeking to impose compulsory retirement on all superior, county

32. Professor Crick argues that, in addition to its revising function, a second chamber's most important role is through its committees of scrutiny and investigation, whose work cannot now be effectively done in the overworked Commons. Bernard Crick, *The Reform of Parliament,* 2nd ed. (London, 1968), pp. 156-8.

33. This argument is advanced by Herbert Morrison in *Government and Parliament* (London, 1954), pp. 194-7.

and district court judges at the age of 75. In the course of the debate in the Commons, misgiving had been expressed at the inclusion of county and district court judges on the ground that Parliament could deal with them under ordinary legislation without any amendment to the British North America Act. The government refused to yield on this point, but the Senate deleted reference to district and county court judges from the resolution.

The situation before the passage of the 1982 Constitution Act was that the Senate possessed a veto over constitutional amendments to the "safeguarded" parts of the British North America Act (chiefly those amendments relating to provincial rights and powers and to certain minority rights) by virtue of the constitutional convention that such amendments must be preceded by a joint resolution of both Houses, and a veto by law over amendments enacted by the Parliament of Canada under section 91 (1) of the British North America Act as amended in 1949.

While the Senate retains a veto over amendments which only require legislation by the Parliament of Canada, the Constitution Act of 1982 has reduced the power of the Senate to a suspensive veto in relation to amendments which require provincial concurrence. Section 47 (1) of that act provides that such an amendment may be made "without a resolution of the Senate authorizing the issue of the proclamation if, within one hundred and eighty days after the adoption by the House of Commons of a resolution authorizing its issue, the Senate has not adopted such a resolution and if, at any time after the expiration of that period, the House of Commons again adopts the resolution."

Even its critics agree that the Senate does extremely useful work in its consideration of private bills, which necessarily must be given thorough consideration in committee. Most private bills which are introduced in the federal Parliament are those which confer rights on, or relieve from liability, a particular person or body of persons. Many of these "persons" are corporate persons, companies or charitable organizations which must be incorporated, or have their corporate powers altered, by private-bill legislation.[34] By far the most prolific source of private bills dealing with individual persons arose because, until 1968, the provinces of Quebec and Newfoundland

34. Most companies are now incorporated under and controlled by general legislation. Parliament has laid down the general rules to be followed in the Canada Corporations Act, and such matters as incorporation, change of powers or winding-up are dealt with by application to a minister of the Crown, the Registrar General. Railway, banking, and finance companies, and many charitable organizations, still, however, must be dealt with by private bill.

did not have divorce courts, and divorce by legislation was the only recourse open to persons in those provinces.

From the beginning, divorce bills had to be introduced first in the Senate, and it was the Senate's Committee on Divorce Bills, which dealt, with patience and fortitude, with the often unsavoury and saddening details of the private lives of petitioners for divorce. The comparable Commons committee was usually content to review the labours of its sister committee. Largely as a result of a filibuster by some members of the Commons, aimed at forcing divorce procedure into the courts of the reluctant provinces, a bill (originally introduced by a private member of the Commons) introduced a modified procedure in 1963, which relieved the Commons, and in part the Senate, of dealing with these bills. A Senate officer, known as the Divorce Commissioner, heard divorce petitions *in camera* in the first instance and then recommended appropriate action to the Senate Committee on Divorce. This committee then decided, on the basis of the commissioner's recommendation, which of the petitions would be embodied in Senate resolutions to grant divorce.

Four years later the whole process of parliamentary divorce was brought to an end. Beginning in 1968, all divorce petitions are now heard in provincial courts, and the two delinquent provinces of Quebec and Newfoundland have authorized their courts to deal with them. At the same time Parliament has broadened the grounds for divorce to include a number of sexual offences in addition to the old ground of adultery, as well as physical and mental cruelty, and to make it possible to obtain a divorce simply on the ground that a marriage has broken down.

Since the object of a private bill is certain to affect the rights of other individuals or legal persons, there is an important element of judicial procedure in private-bill legislation in order to protect the rights of third parties. "In dealing with private bills," says Professor Kunz, "the Senate is practically a court called upon to protect persons whose interests are affected by the proposed legislation and who appear before the Senate as suitors and adverse parties."[35] The petitioners are required to support their proposal with full information and to notify, through advertisements in the *Canada Gazette* and local newspapers, everyone concerned who may have an interest to be protected by putting in an appearance before the Senate committee. The debates on second and third reading of such bills have only nominal significance; the real and essential stage is the

35. Kunz, *The Modern Senate of Canada,* p. 209. For a detailed description of the stages of legislation, see the following chapter.

committee at which the parties, represented usually by counsel, appear.

The number of private bills which must go through Parliament, even with the elimination of divorce bills, is large. A great many of them do not raise serious questions of public policy, but they all require careful scrutiny to protect the rights of third parties who may be affected by them. This is important work, but work which is not likely to be done adequately in the hard-pressed Commons. It is done, and done well, in the Senate. While it is legally possible to introduce private bills in either House, it has long been recognized that the public interest is best served by encouraging the promoters of such bills to introduce them in the Senate. This was accomplished through a simple device. In 1934 the Commons raised the fee for introducing a bill there to five hundred dollars, while the fee for introducing a bill in the Senate was left unchanged at two hundred dollars. This has the advantage of giving the Senate a large amount of legislative work early in the session, when there is little general legislation yet ready for it from the Commons. In fact the impression often given that the Senate is idle early in the session while the Commons is busy is quite misleading. The Senate itself may not be sitting, but numerous standing committees and sub-committees may be very active indeed, doing the kind of unspectacular but careful work which the Commons would never be able to find the time to do adequately.

The process of parliamentary government under the Cabinet system tends to place policy initiatives overwhelmingly in the hands of the executive and, at the same time, make effective scrutiny of the process of administration imperative. Executive dominance can be mitigated to a considerable extent if Parliament itself can develop institutions for more effective policy initiation, scrutiny, and control.[36] These functions can be discharged by committees. Because the Senate is less overtly partisan, less directly concerned with day-to-day political issues which can affect the survival of governments, and generally less overworked than the Commons, its committees can potentially play a very important role in these matters. However, under our parliamentary system, committees cannot do these things on their own. They must be created and mandated by the parent chamber, which must also provide the funds for research, witnesses, travel, etc., which these activities require. Governments, which under the Cabinet system control such matters,

36. See Kersell, *Parliamentary Supervision of Delegated Legislation*, pp. 164 ff, and Crick, *The Reform of Parliament*, pp. 155 ff.

are never eager to encourage either rivals or critics. In spite of these handicaps the Senate Committees have managed to do well, and were most visible and effective during the seventies when the Government Leader in the Senate was Paul Martin, an energetic minister of unmatched experience and great influence in the Cabinet. The result was a number of major policy studies, such as those on poverty, science policy, and the plight of the aged.

Such enquiries in the past have generally been done by royal commissions or, in the modern jargon, task forces. The trouble with these bodies is that, having submitted a report, they disperse. The members of a parliamentary committee on the other hand are still in a position to watch over the results of their enquiries and continue to urge their acceptance.

In addition to inquiry, committees can devote their energies to scrutiny of executive operations, to see if they conform to the law and achieve the purposes for which they were intended. There is scope for a great deal of this activity. While there is some scrutiny of ministerial departments on a regular basis, Crown corporations—particularly if they do not depend on annual appropriation—are less likely to have any serious inquiry into their activities in Parliament. Some, which are politically sensitive like the CNR and the CBC, may indeed receive excessive—if not particularly well-informed—attention in Parliament. Others may escape systematic review for generations. Not all of this work can be done by the Commons, which has too much to do already. A significant amount of it, particularly if it involves rather hard and dreary work of a politically unrewarding kind, can be done by the Senate. An excellent example of this is the scrutiny of statutory instruments, already described previously in Chapter 4, where a joint committee (in which a great deal of the work is actually done by Senators) does important and invaluable work. Such activity could profitably be extended.

In summary, the functions that the Senate can most usefully perform are the following: to act as a revising chamber for general legislation originating in the Commons; to assume the main burden in the consideration of private bills; and to scrutinize the operation of executive agencies. These useful functions have been resolutely ignored by almost all those who have addressed themselves to the question of the Senate in the context of constitutional reform in the last ten years. But it is these very functions, according to Senator Jacques Flynn, which the Senate was intended to perform. He said

> This is essentially what the Fathers of Confederation had in mind. Traditionally throughout the world, second houses were to review the constitution, that is to exercise a role of sober second thought with

> respect to legislation. Implicitly, and obviously in 1867, because this was not in the Constitution,—it was said afterwards—the Senate was to protect minorities or regional expectations. But it is not so obvious that the Fathers of Confederation had this in mind. It was especially a matter of correcting the method of proportional representation of the House of Commons, of equalizing it somewhat and of checking the powers of the executive. That is what they had in mind.[37]

He went on to say that the Senate had been subject to criticism and requests for its abolition or reform since 1868. Nearly a century later the basis of this seemed to be, as he said, that "nothing happens in the Senate." However in the last five or six years, the Senate has assumed new roles "not foreseen in 1867" of enquiring into matters of general interest and drawing up reports which would help government in drafting remedial legislation. Since the Senate tended to fall for many years under the dominance of one party, it might be thought that it would be merely acquiescent under a government which a majority of members supported and a source of difficulty and embarrassment, because of its veto power, to one which lacked party control of the chamber. He said that had not happened because of the use of the "Hayden formula" by which a Senate committee "considers the bill and makes a report with recommendations often before it has passed second reading in the House of Commons." In this way the government and the House know what the Senate's reaction to the bill will be so that amendments can be introduced before the bill even reaches the Senate. This formula, he said, had been used with much benefit in such complex legislation as the Income Tax Act, the Bankruptcy Act, the Canada Corporations Act, and many others.

In spite of considerable testimony that the Senate performs a useful and necessary function as a legislative chamber, those eager to reform it doggedly persist in ignoring that role and seek instead to destroy it while demanding that the Senate fulfil a role for which it was probably not intended, that of a major vehicle of adjustment and decision within the federal system. As far back as February, 1969, the Trudeau government placed Senate reform among its major proposals to the federal-provincial constitutional conference. The object of the proposal was in part a response to the need for some indirect provincial participation in the carrying out of central government responsibilities for international relations and in the ratification of appointments to the Supreme Court.

Nearly a decade later, these ideas had been expanded and given

37. Canadian Study of Parliament Group. *Seminar on the Senate* (Ottawa, 1979) p. 1:18.

concrete form in the constitutional reform proposals contained in Bill C-60. Essentially, it was proposed that the Senate should be composed one-half of members chosen by the House of Commons, and one-half by members chosen by the various provincial legislatures. Thus it would reflect the party balance in any particular House of Commons, and the party balance in the various provincial legislatures at that time. In this way its membership would reflect more accurately the state of opinion in the country. The number of members would be somewhat altered and the new body would be christened the House of the Federation. It would have a suspensive veto and special provisions were inserted regarding the kind of majority necessary to pass "legislation of linguistic significance." It would also have the power to approve the appointment of judges of the Supreme Court.

Such a chamber would be a much more partisan house than the present Senate. It is doubtful if its members would possess the time or the experience which now make the work of its committees of inquiry and scrutiny of government operations so valuable. A further, and perhaps fatal, objection was pointed out by Mr. Mark MacGuigan.

> The great problem I see with Bill C-60 in this context is the lack of control a federal government would have over its legislation. I do not know how any federal government could carry on, even if its legislation was merely being delayed, when it had only one-third of the Senate as its permanent supporters. Senator Forsey, I think, has figured out that it would be 41 or 42 government supporters in the House of the Federation on that basis.[38]

It would, he was convinced, become merely a House of obstruction.

The bill, it will be recalled, was received with little enthusiasm in any quarter. Nearly all of its proposals struck a tender nerve somewhere, and the difficulty was compounded by the fact that the bill was so badly drafted that nobody knew what it really meant. To enlarge public discussion the government sent the bill to a joint committee of both Houses. The Senate also referred the bill to a committee of its own. One of the matters that became clear in these committee hearings was that there was considerable doubt as to whether Parliament had the power, under section 91 of the constitution, to abolish the Senate and replace it with another body without the concurrence of the provinces. It was of course true that Parliament had unilaterally made some changes in the Senate under this section, imposing a retiring age for Senators and providing for representation from the territories. But these were minor changes. What was in effect abolition, or at least fundamental change, might

38. *Ibid.* p. 1:24.

well be a different matter. For the time being the bill disappeared from view and the government, with great reluctance, referred the question to the Supreme Court for an advisory opinion on November 23, 1979.

The case was heard in March, and judgment was pronounced on December 21, 1979. In its judgment the Court noted that the purpose of the amending power under section 91 was to obviate the necessity of proceeding in certain amendments through the British Parliament. The amendments which had been made since that power was added to the constitution in relation to the Parliament of Canada had been essentially of a "housekeeping" nature. The powers of amendment in relation to parliamentary institutions were not analogous as between the federal and provincial governments. Under section 92 the power to make such amendments (under which several provinces had abolished their legislative councils) is conferred on "the Legislature." The federal power, on the other hand, was conferred on the Queen, "with the Advice and Consent of the Senate and the House of Commons. Thus, section 91.1 confers a power of amendment subject to specific exceptions which, as we have already pointed out, contemplate the continued existence of both the Senate and the House of Commons." Accordingly, Parliament cannot unilaterally abolish the Senate and replace it with another body under another name. Making the Senate a completely or partially elected body "would affect a fundamental feature of that body.[38A]

While the federal government was concocting its own proposals for constitutional change, which purported to deal essentially with matters other than the division of legislative power, it had also launched a more formal inquiry of a more fundamental kind into the nature of the union. To set up a royal commission was apparently not enough. This body was rather grandly christened the Task Force on Canadian Unity. It was initially set up by order-in-council under the Inquiries Act in 1977, and submitted its findings two years later under the title *A Future Together.* That report will be considered elsewhere in this text. Present concern will relate only to its views on the Senate.

It identified seven functions appropriate to a second chamber in a federal system. These are (1) the critical review and improvement of central government legislation; (2) the conducting of investigatory studies; (3) the protection of minority rights; (4) the provision of broader regional representation for political parties and the correc-

38A. *Reference re: Legislative Authority of Parliament to Alter or Replace the Senate* [1980] S.C.R. 54. Quoted in Peter H. Russell, *Leading Constitutional Decisions*. Ottawa, 1982, p. 418.

tion of imbalances in the first chamber created by the electoral system; (5) the provision of a legislative house less dominated by the executive and party discipline; (6) representation of constituent provincial governments on a more equal basis than in the popular chamber, thereby increasing their influence over central legislation bearing directly on regional or provincial concerns; and (7) the promotion of central-provincial consultation on those particular areas which are of joint concern.[39] The present Senate, they concluded, while its usefulness "has often been underestimated," is valuable only in "the first two of the seven functions listed above."

Accordingly, they proposed to get rid of it altogether and replace it by a second chamber, composed of provincial delegations appointed by provincial governments, and dubbed the Council of the Federation. This body "could combine the function of a second legislative chamber in which provincial interests are brought to bear, and [sic] a means of institutionalizing the processes of executive federalism (with their confederal character) within the parliamentary process." This, they added, had the additional virtue of being a proposal similar to those put forward by the government of British Columbia, the Ontario Advisory Committee on Confederation, and the constitutional committees of the Canadian Bar Association and the Canada West Foundation.

A somewhat similar proposal is contained in the proposals of the Constitutional Committee of the Quebec Liberal Party. It suggested a Federal Council whose "scope of activities would be limited to specific objectives and subjects. They would include the approval of certain extraordinary powers of the central government, the ratification of a certain number of laws and appointments and the examination of certain bills and decisions made by the central government from a regional perspective."[40]

What are we to make of these proposals? Mark MacGuigan fears that a heavily politicised second chamber which the federal government could not control (which in fact is true of all of these proposals) would make effective government in Ottawa a situation of constant stalemate and frustration seem all too plausible. Professor Smiley shares his misgivings. He says, "The proposal of a House of the Federation as proposed in Bill C-60 has received little support and is likely soon to be forgotten." This is probably true, except for those who found it conclusive evidence of a dangerous naivete and confusion of thought in the Department of Justice and the Federal-

39. *A Future Together.* p. 96.

40. *A New Canadian Federation.* p. 53.

Provincial Relations Office. Smiley concludes, "Furthermore, no one, it seems, has thought through carefully the relations between the new second chamber and the ongoing processes of executive federalism."[41]

The Senate itself, through a sub-committee of its Standing Committee on Legal and Constitutional Affairs, has come furthest in thinking the matter through. It rejects the various proposals recently put forward on the ground that they fail to meet the requirements for "genuine federation" by respecting the sovereignty of the two orders of government. While there is a legitimate provincial desire to exercise control over the extraordinary powers of the federal government, "any such arrangement would have to respect the federal character of Canadian political institutions and hence preclude the introduction of confederal elements into the Canadian Parliament."[42]

If there is a need for some kind of provincial participation in federal decisions which directly affect the provinces the Senators would prefer an institutionalization of the Conference of First Ministers. Such a Conference would (a) negotiate constitutional amendments and the possible delegation of powers, (b) it would provide a means of provincial approval for federal proposals directly affecting provincial areas of jurisdiction, and (c) perform a co-ordinating role in such areas as fiscal policy. In its second role it might proceed either through a majority of the provinces representing a majority of the population or with the assent of at least three of the four regions of Canada. Such decisions, once reached, would only be final if approved subsequently by Parliament and the appropriate number of legislatures.

The Report also goes on to provide a prescription for a continuing role for the Senate itself. It recites with approval the roles which the Senate has played as a revising body and an investigating body. While the Senate has always had a "regional" role, "it should be emphasized that the senators were intended to represent regions and provinces, not provincial governments or legislatures. They were not intended to play a significant part in protecting the jurisdiction of the provincial legislatures. The courts would do that."[43]

The sub-committee noted that there is a widespread belief that

41. D. V. Smiley, *Canada in Question: Federation in the Eighties*. Third Edition. (Toronto, 1980) p. 85.

42. Standing Senate Committee on Legal and Constitutional Affairs. *Report on Certain Aspects of the Canadian Constitution*. November, 1980. p. 10.

43. *Ibid.* p. 27.

restructuring the upper house would solve all of the problems of regional dissatisfaction and alienation. This is an illusion. However the Senate has in the past acted as a useful spokesman for regional interests and could do more in this role. Similarly, while the Senate in the past has played a minor role as a protector of linguistic and other minorities, this too could be subject of increased senatorial concern. Regional caucuses and additional committees could focus its efforts more clearly. Essentially, they stress that the Senate as a second chamber has a complementary role to the Commons. Compared to the Commons it has a low turnover so that its members are more experienced. It is less partisan, thus it is capable of a constructive role in both legislation and oversight of the executive.

They reject the idea of an elective Senate because it would be both more partisan and a rival to the Commons. It would be better balanced in their view if the representation of the western provinces was increased so that its total number be increased to 126. While Senators should still be appointed by the federal government, every second appointment should be made from a list submitted by the appropriate provincial or territorial government. The retirement age should remain the same, but senators should be appointed for an initial term of ten years, which may be renewed for a further five years on the recommendation of a Senate Committee set up for the purpose. The property qualifications should be dropped as should the now meaningless requirement that Quebec senators reside in a particular district.

There should be some alterations in the powers of the Senate. A suspensive veto of six months should replace the present veto, which is seldom used. "The very fact of its absoluteness makes the Senate reluctant to reject any bill, however bad, even temporarily. We believe that a six month's suspensive veto would give the Senate all the power it needs. The government, the House of Commons and the country would be compelled to think again. The Senate would have enough time to put its case before the public."[44]

The sub-committee endorsed a previous recommendation of the Standing Joint Committee on Regulations and Other Statutory Instruments that there should be both affirmative and negative powers over statutory instruments. This would enable the Senate to disallow such regulations. The Speaker of the Senate should be elected. When a province has no representation in the Cabinet, the practice of appointing a Senator from that province should be followed. There should be closer co-operation between committees

44. *Ibid.* p. 39.

of the two Houses considering the same bill, and the now rarely-used practice of conferences between the two Houses as a way of dealing with differences should be revived. Because important bills receive extended debate in the Commons while the Senate is expected to deal with them at excessive speed, it is urged that the practice now used by the Banking, Trade and Commerce Committee of giving lengthy study to bills while they are still before the Commons should be used more widely. In short, they argued, modest changes in present constitutional arrangements would create a much stronger Senate without threatening the present parliamentary system and at the same time greatly strengthen the institution of Parliament as a whole.

And yet the argument for enhancing the legitimacy of the Senate by making it, in some fashion, elective will not go away. Senator Roblin, for example, strongly dissented from the Lamontagne subcommittee's report on that ground and proposed that the Senate become an elective body, when he spoke in the debate on the Report on February 24, 1982. While he was somewhat vague on how this was to be done, his own inclination was to favour a single alternative vote with, presumably, each province being a single electoral district. The difficulty with such proposals is that the Senate would become a much more partisan House as a result and thus a serious rival to the House of Commons. The situation in Australia, where the elected Senate was able, in the constitutional crisis of 1975, to make the government as much dependent on the Senate as on the house, reveals the sort of problem which might be created. This matter is now the subject of a lively debate in Australia and proponents of an elected Senate should attend carefully the arguments now advanced there.

It is not clear why so many recent constitutional proposals require a radical alteration of the Senate as a centrepiece of reform of the federal system. Perhaps it is because, as long as anyone can remember, the Senate has been the least popular of our institutions—in both senses of the word. When political myths become deeply ingrained it is difficult to counter them. Because so few people seem to love the Senate, it seems all too easy to use it as a readily salable part of a constitutional reform package. And yet the Senate continues to make a place for itself in the constitutional structure, unhonoured and unsung. Perhaps it will be saved in the end, not so much by its own virtues as by that invaluable political trait, inertia.

7

Parliament: The House of Commons

"The most prominent if not the most important function of Parliament is legislation. . . . In making laws its control over conduct is direct and absolute." Sir William Anson.

Hon. Walter Harris: After all, if parliament meets for one thing only, I think it could be said that that thing would be to vote supply for the purposes of the government for the following year.

Mr. E.D. Fulton: Or, in the alternative, to withhold it. Canada, *House of Commons Debates* (unrevised). February 8, 1955, p. 937.

The Centre Block of the Parliament Buildings houses the Senate Chamber and offices in its east wing, the Parliamentary Library in a rotunda leading off the central entrance hall, and the House of Commons and members' offices (which have now spread to the West Block and the Confederation Building as well) in the west wing. Here, by common consent, is the central nucleus of representative democracy—where the government must confront in debate the people's chosen representatives. Members of the House of Commons are not alone in equating their own chamber with Parliament. The rest of the apparatus of Parliament, including the Senate, performs necessary functions, but the direct and necessary confrontation of representative and responsible government is connected with the Commons and the Commons alone.

Only a constitutional lawyer could have uttered the first quotation that appears above. In a purely formal sense Parliament makes law, but everyone knows that laws are drafted and decided on within the executive. Parliament is expected to dutifully ratify them. It neither initiates them nor has the capacity to make significant changes in government bills. Similarly, while government cannot spend the public revenues unless they are approved in some detail by an annual Supply vote, the existence of disciplined political parties makes it virtually impossible in modern times for the House of

Commons to withhold supply or to make significant variations in what a government has proposed.

The system of responsible government, which achieves its stability from the fact that Members of the House of Commons are organized into disciplined political parties, means in fact that the government controls the House of Commons rather than the reverse. Does this mean that the House of Commons is becoming a sort of constitutional vermiform appendix? As it was developed in Canada in the nineteenth century, it was based on a Victorian model which was made up of part-time and amateur politicians to deal with the problems of an age of limited government. How can it cope today when membership has become a full-time occupation requiring expert knowledge to cope with the endless demands placed on the modern state? The Hon. Robert Stanfield has been led to the gloomy conclusion that "We can accept the loss of parliamentary responsible government or we must accept a more limited role for our federal government."[1] Before we accept this, it is important to consider what the House of Commons does, how it does it, and how it might do it better.

The first function of the House of Commons is, as Bagehot pointed out, to act as an electoral chamber; to give a government authority; to sustain it and thus make stable government possible; and, lastly, to withdraw confidence from a government which no longer deserves to rule. But the House is not a body of uncommitted persons. Its members are grouped into organized political parties. Thus most of the time we know, as soon as the election results are in, which party is to govern and that this will not change until the House is dissolved and a new election held. Sometimes the voters do not get their sums right and no party has a majority. In that case the party which can negotiate the support of third parties can carry on as a government. When that third party support is withdrawn, as in December 1979, a government will be forced to either resign or, most probably, seek a new election to settle the matter. Most of the time a government can control the House through its majority so that it is an illusion to think of the House of Commons being able to make or destroy a government at any time. Members of the House of Commons are not players in this game: they are part of the scoreboard.

The second function of Parliament is legislation, but the role

1. Robert L. Stanfield "The Present State of the Legislative Process in Canada: Myths and Realities" in W.A.W. Neilson and J.C. MacPherson (eds) *The Legislative Process in Canada: The Need for Reform.* (Montreal, 1978) p. 47.

nowadays is not to make the law, but to approve what the government has proposed. This is not quite the mere formality that it sounds. Opposition parties can drag their feet, and obstruct progress until a government will either modify its proposal to get it through or abandon it. The rules permit a government majority to force its will on the House by limiting or stopping debate, but these are measures which cannot be employed too often for a government cannot allow itself to appear high-handed too often and the day-to-day business of Parliament moves most smoothly with the co-operation of opposition parties.

The third function of Parliament is to act, as John Stuart Mill said, as the nation's congress of opinions and committee of grievances. Ministers must answer on the floor of the House at question time, and defend in detail the operation of their departments against the criticism of opposition members. Governments today profess to pay a great deal of attention to opinion polls as a means of knowing what the public thinks, but inability to perform effectively before parliamentary criticism is still one of the most fatal faults in a minister.

The business of Parliament is not only the articulation of grievances, but the informed discussion of public issues before decision is taken. To Walter Bagehot parliamentary debate had a reciprocal function. Not only did it provide a full discussion of alternatives before Parliament acted, but, more importantly, it performed the educative function of making the voter aware of the general scope of issues confronting the country so that his contribution on election day would be better informed. This was no doubt true a hundred years ago when the newspapers printed full accounts of parliamentary debates, but the daily confrontation in the House is still what Professor Crick has described as a "permanent election campaign" in which the parties seek to establish their positions on issues which will be prominent when election time comes. What the opposition says or does in the House may not have much effect today, but it will matter at the ballot box. One could liken parliamentary debate to a sort of instant theatre seeking to reduce complex issues to simple moral propositions.

Above all, the House of Commons is a debating chamber, governed by a complex set of rules and procedures which have to be understood. Parliamentary discussion takes place within an elaborate regulatory system which, properly understood, can be used to provide effective democratic control of the government without permitting fractious and unnecessary obstruction. The essence of our whole system of government, according to Sir John Bourinot, is that it is a structure having at its base freedom of speech and thought.

Decisions reached in Parliament are the result of free discussion. But free discussion, unless governed by rules of order, may be disorganized and purposeless. The control of parliamentary discussion is the function of "parliamentary law". Bourinot's classic statement of the principles underlying parliamentary procedure is as follows:

> The principles that lie at the basis of English parliamentary law have, however, been always kept steadily in view by the Canadian Parliament: these are—to protect a minority and to restrain the improvidence or tyranny of a majority; to secure the transaction of public business in an orderly manner; to enable every member to express his opinion within the limits necessary to preserve decorum and prevent an unnecessary waste of time; and to prevent any legislative action being taken on sudden impulse.[2]

Canadian parliamentary practice, along with most other basic elements in our constitution, was derived from the United Kingdom Parliament. There are, however, important differences. Representative government in British North America is more than two centuries old. When introduced it was based on British parliamentary practice at the time, adapted and simplified for the needs of a small colony. Since then it has developed on its own, adopting or adapting from time to time new principles and practices which reflected British parliamentary government at the time at which they were introduced. While the seed of the plant was brought across the Atlantic and the growing tree has from time to time had new elements grafted onto it, it has grown and nourished itself in Canadian soil and become a distinctly Canadian tree.

The formal sources of Canadian parliamentary practice are: the British North America Act, certain acts of the Parliament of Canada, the standing orders of both Houses, the *Debates* and *Journals* of the two Canadian Houses and of the British Lords and Commons, the writings of recognized authorities on parliamentary practice such as Erskine May (the standard British authority), and Canadian authorities such as Bourinot and Beauchesne, and the rulings of Speakers. "When the formal rules are silent or obscure, resort is had to 'the practice'. This means the traditional practice of the House. If this does not cover the situation, then the House falls back on British practice."[3]

2. Sir John Bourinot, *Parliamentary Procedure and Practice in the Dominion of Canada.* 2nd. edition (Montreal. 1892) pp. 258–9.
3. E. Russell Hopkins *How Parliament Works* p. 30.

THE ROLE OF THE SPEAKER

The most important safeguard of the effective working of parliamentary procedure is the office of Speaker, who is the presiding officer of the House of Commons, its representative in all external matters and the one who decides disputed questions of procedure as they arise. These functions cannot be effectively discharged unless the Speaker knows his job, has the respect of the House and is impartial. These have been difficult conditions to meet in Canada, where it has been the custom for the majority party to choose a Speaker from among their own number, and to leave him in office as a rule for no more than a single Parliament. With few exceptions, the office has rotated between French- and English-speaking members, no doubt as a consequence of the requirement that the Speaker's deputy shall be of a different mother tongue from the Speaker and that turnabout is fair play.

The result is that few Speakers were in office long enough to learn the job properly, and the Speaker had not usually severed his ties with his party and his constituents, nor given up his hopes of a further career in politics. In this he differed from the Speaker in the United Kingdom Parliament, who severs his connections with his party on election, is not normally opposed in his constituency at elections, is normally left in office for several Parliaments until he wishes to retire, and retires to a peerage and a handsome pension on relinquishing office. Under these conditions his impartiality is assured, his rulings are final and from his august position he can effectively protect the rights of all members.

Until fairly recently the situation was very different in Canada. However in the fifties, opinion in the House began to move in the direction of strengthening the position of the Speaker.[4] One of the most important of these was the abolition of the rule which made it possible to appeal his decisions. As long as that rule was there, it was possible for a government to appeal a decision of the Speaker which it did not like and use its majority to overturn it. When the Opposition appealed, the appeal would be overturned, but this symbolic gesture illustrated the partisan nature of the office. To an almost alarming extent the rights, not only of minority groups in the House

4. Much of the impetus for reform of the office has come from academic critics. See, in particular, Denis Smith, *The Speakership of the Canadian House of Commons* (Ottawa, 1965), and J.H. Aitchison "The Speakership of the Canadian House of Commons" in R.M. Clark (ed.) *Canadian Issues: Essays in Honour of Henry F. Angus.* (Toronto, 1961).

of Commons, but of minority groups in the country which they reflect and represent, depend on the integrity, competence and independence of the Speaker. The cluster of traditions surrounding the office in Canada has done little to strengthen the Speaker's office and much to weaken it. The fact that the general record of Speakers was good was a tribute to the capacity of ordinary men to rise above what their circumstances might have made them.

Generally speaking, it has never been possible to disentangle the appointment of the Speaker from the process of Cabinet-making. It is true that no Speaker before 1891 successfully aspired to be appointed to the Cabinet, and in all only seven have been "promoted" to ministerial rank, the most recent being the Honourable Marcel Lambert's appointment as Minister of Veteran's Affairs after dissolution in 1963. No less than four of these examples have occurred since 1940, and it may be that the increasing size of the Cabinet has something to do with it.

The knowledge that the choice of Speaker is in effect made by the Prime Minister at a time when he is also engaged in the making or reconstructing of a Cabinet makes it inevitable that the office will be considered part of the complex of appointments. It is also likely that there will be times when failure to be appointed to the Cabinet will be compensated by election to the Speaker's chair. When Mackenzie King was unable to find room for Rodolphe Lemieux in his first Cabinet, he persuaded him to accept the Speakership,[5] and there can be little doubt that it was only the excessive Conservative front-bench strength from Toronto which placed Mr. Speaker Michener in the chair rather than in the Cabinet. The result of this tendency is twofold: the Speakership becomes a sort of consolation prize, although it is only in provincial legislatures that it is definitely regarded as a junior ministerial post. A Speaker reluctantly persuaded to accept the chair in lieu of office, will, secondly, retain his hopes of preferment and may ultimately succeed to the position of power and influence to which he originally aspired.[6] The fact that every Speaker since Michener has remained in office for more than

5. R. McGregor Dawson *William Lyon Mackenzie King: A Political Biography* (Toronto, 1958) p. 366.

6. This question, and the related one as to whether the Speakership underwent a sharp decline after 1940 as a result, is thoroughly canvassed in J.R. Mallory "Parliament and Pipeline" *Canadian Bar Review* XXXIV:6; Eugene A. Forsey "Constitutional Aspects of the Pipeline Debate" *Public Law* (Spring, 1957); correspondence between D. Forsey and myself in *Canadian Bar Review* XXXIV:7, and in Professor Aitchison's "The Speakership of the Canadian House of Commons." Cited above.

one Parliament, and that they have, thereafter, left the Commons for diplomatic or similar posts—Michener also served with distinction as Governor General—suggests that a qualitative change for the better has taken place in the office. It has come a long way from being a major political office to one that is essentially above politics. Before the days of responsible government the Speakership was the main prize of a majority opposed to the government. It has come a long way from the days of Papineau.

One way in which the role of the Speaker is emphasized is by his translation from the floor of the House, so that he never appears in the mortal guise of an ordinary member. Such in fact is the modern custom. The physical arrangements of the Canadian House of Commons (like that of all other legislatures in Canada) assign desks and chairs on the floor to individual members so that each has, quite literally, a seat in Parliament. By invariable custom the desks on the extreme upper end of the front row on the Speaker's right (the government side) are assigned to Mr. Speaker and his deputies. However, these desks are never used and Mr. Speaker does not appear on the floor of the House; he is, in any event, forbidden by Standing Order 10 from taking part "in any debate before the House". Nor, with one exception, did he ever appear in any of its committees.[7]

The exception was his yearly appearance in the Committee of Supply, when he took his seat for convenience in one of the ministerial seats and defended his estimates before they were voted in the same way as departmental estimates are presented by ministers. The reason for this was that the Speaker is chairman of a body called the Committee of Internal Economy, consisting of himself and four Privy Councillors (who are always ministers), which is responsible for the internal administrative arrangements of the House, such as the affairs of the clerks at the table, and other domestic arrangements which come under the control of the Clerk of the House and the Sergeant-at-Arms.

Useful as this little debate is, the appearance of the Speaker in a sort of ministerial position was an incongruity. In recent years the practice has been brought in line with that of the United Kingdom, where it is the Leader of the House (a member of the Internal

7. This was apparently not always so. Professor Ward described Mr. Speaker Anglin (1874–78) who "More than once during his career as Speaker. . . argued with members from the Chair, or engaged in controversy from his own desk on the floor of the House." Norman Ward "The Formative Years of the House of Commons, 1867–91" *Canadian Journal of Economics and Political Science* XVIII:4 (November, 1952) p. 439.

Economy Committee) who is responsible for the defence of the estimates for the House of Commons.[8]

The Speaker is not placed under the intolerable burden of having to preside over the House at all times. Standing Orders provide that the House shall elect for each Parliament a Deputy Speaker who "shall be required to possess the full and practical knowledge of the official language which is not that of Mr. Speaker for the time being." The effect of this is, as previously noted, to ensure that one of the two principal presiding officers of the House is French-speaking and the other English-speaking. The Deputy Speaker is also Chairman of Committees, and thus presides over the House when it is in Committee of the Whole. The House at the same time elects a Deputy Chairman of Committees and an Assistant Deputy Chairman. These officers are also available to preside over the House if the Speaker and his principal deputy are not available.

To some extent the cluster of practices which insulates the Speaker from political activity also govern his deputies. They do not normally take part in debate nor occupy their desks on the floor of the House. However these offices are not as clearly non-political as that of Speaker. Part of the reason, no doubt, is that they are not usually regarded as within the line of succession to the Speakership.

RECORDS OF THE HOUSE

The proceedings of the House and of its committees are normally public. To the extent that they are public they are also a matter of record. The records of Parliament fall into two categories: the purely formal record of business transacted, which is kept by the Clerk Assistant and which appears in *Votes and Proceedings* and the *Journals* of the House; and the verbatim record of every word spoken which is audible to the reporters. Both the *House of Commons Debates* (commonly called *Hansard*) and the formal records of the House are kept in both French and English, and there is now also a simultaneous translation of all debates with receivers connected to members' desks. The debates of the House are also televised.

The daily printed report of *Hansard* is as accurate as the short-

8. See J.R. Mallory "The Financial Administration of the House of Commons" *Canadian Journal of Economics and Political Science* XXXIII:1 (February, 1957) pp. 108–13.

hand reporters can make it. It includes, with the exceptions noted below, only what was actually said in the House. Thus it is not possible for a member to get the consent of the House to have incorporated into *Hansard* a speech or part of a speech which he did not deliver. However the House may give unanimous consent to the inclusion in Hansard of the Speech from the Throne (which is reported to the House by the Speaker) and of tables of figures and other technical matter such as may form part of the budget speech of the Minister of Finance. It is now usual to print as an appendix to *Hansard* the Minister of Finance's White Paper which is laid before the House the day before he brings down his budget. Occasionally copies of letters or other documents may be printed in the same way, but most documents tabled in the House are not printed in *Hansard.* If deemed to be of sufficient general interest they may subsequently be printed as sessional papers. *Hansard* thus includes what was said or what the shorthand reporters understood to have been said, though obvious errors may already have been edited out. Other errors will be corrected before the revised edition for the session is printed. A member may secure a correction by drawing it to the attention of the *Debates* editors, but he may wish also to place it on record, in which case he will have his correction recorded by bringing it up in the house at the next sitting.

Except for corrections to improve sense and correct grammar, *Hansard* is not tampered with and the House is very jealous of the integrity of *Hansard.* Only under grave circumstances would there be a substantial change in a *Hansard* report. On November 15, 1940, such an incident is recorded in Mackenzie King's diary. The Prime Minister felt that the leader of the opposition, then R.B. Hanson, had committed a grave breach of wartime secrecy by reading in the House messages which had been shown to him in his capacity as a Privy Councillor. There had ensued an angry exchange in the House, and it was strongly urged that the whole passage be suppressed in the interests of security. The Prime Minister was able to secure the agreement of the Speaker and the principals in the debate, as well as impose censorship on the press. The diary entry concludes, "It was going pretty far with the records of the House but I had to take a chance, and should a question be raised, will get the House to support my action by a vote. This, however, not likely to be necessary."[9] Thus, even Mackenzie King in wartime hesitated to tamper with a *Hansard* report.

9. J.W. Pickersgill *The Mackenzie King Record* Vol. I. (Toronto, 1960) p. 168.

When exceptional circumstances require it, the House may go into secret session when the public will be excluded from the galleries and there will be no report of the proceedings. Such might be done in a grave emergency, and there have been secret sessions held in wartime to enable ministers and members to speak more freely without endangering security. It is possible to clear the galleries and exclude the public by invoking a Standing Order, which empowers the Speaker to order strangers to withdraw, at the call of any member. Such action, however, would not exclude the *Hansard* reporters. Accordingly, the practice is to arrange the details of a secret session "behind the curtain" between the party leaders, and then have forty-eight hours notice given by the Prime Minister in the usual way. On the appointed day, the Speaker will read prayers but will not say "Let the doors be open." At the conclusion of the secret debate the Prime Minister will move that "the remainder of this day's sitting be open," the *Hansard* reporters will return and the galleries will be opened.

Order of Business

The procedure of the House, while highly formal, is capable of adaptation to provide for full discussion of any public question which lies within the jurisdiction of Parliament. A great many debates turn on points of procedure, rather than substance (for example, that a bill be read a second time), but the rules permit these procedure debates to deal with matters of substance. There may also be substantive motions, such as to approve a treaty or to express non-confidence in a government. One other point needs to be made. On the whole, the House does not take one topic at a time and follow it through to the end. To allow time for reflection, Standing Orders do not permit the House to deal with more than one stage of a bill in a sitting day, although if circumstances warrant, the parties may agree to suspend Standing Orders in order to do so. Furthermore each day is divided up on the clock so that, for example, at a given time the House will interrupt a debate on the second reading of a bill and turn its attention to private members' business. This apparently confusing attempt to deal with a number of matters on the same day is useful. In the first place it provides the opportunity each day for required business such as notices of motion, and in the second place it imposes a useful delay in proceedings to ensure full discussion. It is much easier to discuss a bill adequately if there is time to study previous speeches and to give adequate consideration to objections which have been raised.

Each day, as soon as the Speaker has called the House to order he reads prayers, after which the galleries are opened to the public.[10] The first item before the House is motions under Standing Order 43 which are moved by members for a period of fifteen minutes. Such motions only pass with unanimous consent, which is rarely given, and there is no debate. Such motions give members an opportunity to "blow off steam" by drawing attention to some pressing matter which is a cause for concern or possibly approbation. There follows the Oral Question Period of about forty-five minutes when members ask questions of Ministers. Such questions are asked without notice and accordingly all ministers are under the need to be present at this period. An attempt to introduce a "roster system" of a specific group of ministers each day, attempted in 1968, was quietly dropped after sustained criticism in 1973.

Question period, which begins at 2:15 in the first four days of the week and at 11:15 on Fridays, is immediately followed by an opportunity to give the Speaker notice of questions of privilege, and then a number of routine proceedings such as reports from Standing Committees, the tabling of documents, statements by ministers, first reading of Senate bills, and government notices of motion. Then come answers to questions on the order paper, which are essentially those which require fairly detailed answers of a factual nature from the departments. When these have been obtained the Parliamentary Secretary to the Leader of the House will indicate which questions will be answered and the answers are printed in *Hansard*.

Finally the House gets down to the main business of the day. This will be government business, arising out of bills or motions which have reached the order paper. The Leader of the House will choose which item to discuss on any day, though there will normally be discussion among the House Leaders of all parties as to what will be dealt with so that party spokesmen will be prepared. Normally the government House Leader will indicate on each Thursday what business he hopes to carry through in the following week. On four days a week, i.e. forty hours during the session on Mondays and Tuesdays and every Thursday and Friday, the House will devote an hour to bills and motions sponsored by private members. It is probable that this time was selected, just before the dinner break,

10. The authoritative and detailed account of a day in the House is to be found in John B. Stewart's the *Canadian House of Commons: Procedure and Reform* (Montreal and London, 1977) pp. 52–78.

because it is too late for the deadlines of afternoon newspapers and too early to retain much news value for morning newspapers. There is only one important restriction on a private member's right to submit a bill on any subject. The government alone has the right to introduce bills which have the effect of levying taxes or spending money. Accordingly, if a private member wishes to bring before the House a measure which is financial in character he can only do so in the form of a resolution urging the government to "consider the advisability of" introducing legislation for this purpose.

Private members' bills are seldom passed. If he is a member of the party in office, his bill has not been considered important enough to become part of the government's program. Otherwise it would be sponsored by a minister and introduced as a government measure. If he is a member of the opposition, the government majority will normally oppose it as a matter of policy. In any event, the time available is seldom sufficient for these bills to be passed. They can only be considered according to the precedence given them in Standing Orders and the daily order paper. Unless they can gain the active support of the government they are seldom brought to a vote. The easy way to dispose of them is to "talk them out", that is, the opponents of the bill continue the debate until the time is exhausted, thus preventing the bill from being voted on. If it does not pass second reading in the allotted hour it drops to the bottom of the list. Sometimes a bill may be seen as desirable in principle, and there may be an agreement that it be withdrawn from second reading and referred to a committee. An example of one of the rare private members' bills which did pass was one put forward by Hon. G.J. McIlraith on Tuesday, March 28, 1972. This was Bill C-78 respecting the use of the expression "Parliament Hill" to prevent its commercial exploitation. After second reading (which took about twenty minutes) the House went straight into Committee of the Whole, the bill was reported, read a third time and passed, taking in all about twenty-five minutes.[11]

Private members' bill and resolutions nevertheless serve a useful purpose. They enable a subject to be discussed and publicized and this helps to educate and mobilize public opinion in its favour. When it becomes apparent that there is strong public support, it is likely that the government itself will introduce a bill on the subject. Opposition parties are often able to make skillful use of private members' time to introduce bills or resolutions which embody parts

11. Canada. *House of Commons Debates* March 28, 1972 pp. 1224–26.

of their program, thus placing them on record and in the public eye. It would not be an exaggeration to say that practically every significant measure of reform in the last forty years has first been introduced in Parliament by a private member, usually, but not invariably, from the opposition.

The House will resume, after the dinner break, the consideration of public business. On Wednesday and Friday the Speaker will adjourn the debate without putting the question when the hour of adjournment has been reached—which on those days is before the dinner hour. However, on Monday, Tuesday, and Thursay there is a short debate beginning at ten o'clock ostensibly on a motion to adjourn. This procedure, first introduced in 1964, was to offset the curtailment of the question period, which previously had no fixed time limit. Under this new procedure, a member who is dissatisfied with an answer by a minister may seek the Speaker's permission to raise it on the adjournment. Up to three members will then have an opportunity to speak for seven minutes and the minister, or more usually his parliamentary secretary, will reply for three minutes. After this half hour, on a motion to adjourn, the House will automatically adjourn at 10:30.

Most of the time of the House of Commons is now devoted to government business, which is determined for it by the Prime Minister and the Cabinet. The detailed arrangements are left in the hands of a minister who has been designated as Leader of the House. In recent years it has been clear that this task is sufficiently exacting that it is not possible to combine it with heavy departmental responsibilities, so that it is now given to the minister who holds the prestigious but sinecure office of President of the Privy Council. He will decide what business will be taken up by the House, from his knowledge of what his colleagues in the Cabinet want done and the progress that has been made in preparing government legislation. His key role in the Cabinet, as Chairman of the Committee on Legislation, enables him to plan House business. He must consult on a regular basis with the House Leaders of the other parties to ensure their co-operation in the smooth operation of the business of the House. Each Thursday at the end of the Oral Question Period, he will announce to the House what he wishes the business to be for the coming week. Professor Stewart adds, "but given the inability of the other house leaders to make firm commitments—which varies from party to party, and from time to time—these forecasts always are highly hypothetical."[12] While it is true that a House Leader of a

12. Stewart, *op. cit.* p. 73.

governing party has normally more authority over his caucus—particularly if it is a Liberal caucus—no party is in a position to control its own back-benchers if they feel strongly enough, but about an issue to persist in debating it even if all of the party leaders would be content to see it disposed of.

It might be though, that, since the government controls its own time absolutely, these discussions of the House Leaders, while no doubt magnanimous, are unnecessary. In fact the opposition has in its power to create serious delays in the government program by taking full advantage of the opportunities to discuss each stage of legislation. Accordingly a great deal depends on the skill and persuasiveness of the Leader of the House if the government is to get through its business without difficulty. He must be reasonable and accommodating with the opposition if he expects them to co-operate with him. He must know when to be firm and when to give way. He must gain the trust and respect of the House if he is to do his job properly.

What has been said above sets out the context in which the rules operate to control debate in the House. "The House operates constantly in an atmosphere, if not of tension, at least of contention," says Mr. Russell Hopkins. He continues:

> The area of contention is pratically unlimited when a new session begins, but the rules of debate operate almost at once to restrict the area until finally all contentious matters have been disposed of or held over for the next session. This is because once an issue has been decided by a vote of the House it cannot be raised again (except by unanimous consent) during that session.[13]

The severe limitation imposed by the rule against reviving matters already decided is illustrated by a ruling given by Mr. Speaker Beaudoin on an amendment in the debate on the address in reply to the Speech from the Throne in 1955. He was warning members against the tendency which had been increasing since the change in rules in 1927 to allow subamendments to the address. As a result there had been a tendency to move lengthy amendments which greatly widened the area of debate. Shorter amendments would not only limit the area of debate, but would enable many topics to be debated more fully later in the session. Their inclusion in the Throne Speech debate gave the Speaker no choice but to rule them out of order on later occasions.

13. Hopkins, *How Parliament Works*, p. 36. Reproduced with the permission of Information Canada.

The rule against repetition is one of the most effective means of confining debate in the later stages of the session. There are other limitations which militate against successful obstructon by filibustering. The most effective of these is the rule that limits the length of speeches to forty minutes on the floor of the House, except in the case of "the Prime Minister and the Leader of the Opposition, or a minister moving a government order and the member making a motion of 'no confidence' in the government and the minister replying thereto," as Standing Order 31 puts it.

Furthermore, members must not indulge in repetitious or irrelevant remarks.[14] It is in the interpretation of the rules to expedite debate which challenges the inventiveness of the opposition and the judgment of the Speaker. In a debate in which a determined and aroused opposition is striving to delay a government measure, the Speaker must engage daily in a battle of wits with the procedural experts on both sides of the House and at the same time retain his reputation for firmness and fairness.

However, a member may exercise his right to speak on every motion, amendment or subamendment. While no more than two proposed amendments can be before the House at any one time (including the subamendment or amendment to the amendment), a new amendment may be moved as soon as the previous one has been disposed of. Since it requires a large number of separate motions to get even a simple bill through the House, it can be seen that members in opposition, who are fertile in imagination and heedless of the importance of time, may be able to make a long fight of any measure which they are determined to oppose.

It may appear to a public unfamiliar with the rules and traditions of the House of Commons that the often tedious debates and wrangles in the House are worse than a waste of time: they are a fractious attempt to obstruct the legally elected government from carrying out the people's will. This is not the case. The business of the opposition is to oppose, and it has both a right and a duty to use its legitimate rights in debate to put its own side of the question. If questions are not fully canvassed in Parliament, then the electorate will not have a chance to judge between the parties at the next election. A government, in return for the privilege of governing, must submit to the necessity of arguing its case step by step through the House of Commons.[15]

14. *Ibid.* p. 37.

15. "If the Opposition is to be given no moral case for obstruction, the government must 'play the game' and respect the principles of parliamentary democracy,

The opposition has a right to oppose, but it should not normally carry opposition to the point of obstruction. It must, in deciding to obstruct the completion of business, calculate whether the issue is important enough to justify its action. The public will become impatient of needless obstruction, while a government unable to carry its business through the House can resort to the dissolution of Parliament and appeal over the heads of the opposition to the people in a general election. Then it becomes important that the issue which brought on the election should be a good one. For example, the opposition did not press obstruction against the Defence Production bill in the summer of 1955 to the bitter end, but accepted modifications in the most criticised parts of the bill. They contented themselves with obtaining limited but important concessions because it became clear that the issue raised—wide and arbitrary powers conferred on the minister—was not understood by the public, so that there would not be good fighting ground if an election were forced.

Closure and Limitation of Debate

A government, confronted by obstruction in the House, is not forced to threaten dissolution in order to get its business through. Standing Orders provide means of curtailing debate through three procedures: closure, a motion called "the previous question," and the imposition of an allocation-of-time order through a procedure first introduced in 1965 as a sessional order and continued until 1968. In the following year, permanent provision was made for time allocation in Standing Order 75. In addition, the House has gradually placed other limitations on debate through the provision of a daily adjournment time, through limitations placed on such traditional set pieces as the debate on the Address in Reply to the Speech from the Throne (which in 1926 had to be carried by the imposition of closure after six weeks of debate) and the debate on the Budget, as well as the replacement of the once endless "supply days" by 25 "allotted days" for business initiated by the opposition.

Closure was first introduced by Sir Robert Borden in order to

---

otherwise parliamentary government will be endangered. However, the public interest comes first, and if action is necessary to protect it, action must be taken." Herbert Morrison, *Government and Parliament.* (London, 1954) p. 98.

overcome parliamentary obstruction to the Naval Bill in 1913. Closure may be invoked only by a minister of the Crown, and the procedure is as follows: the minister must give notice of his intention to introduce a closure motion; he may then, at the next sitting, move that consideration of the question before the House not be further postponed or adjourned (this is a procedural motion which takes precedence over the main motion under debate, and it must be voted on immediately without further debate); once the motion has been carried, debate resumes on the original question, but speeches are limited to twenty minutes each, and the question must be put not later than one o'clock the following morning.

Closure is more useful as a threat than an actuality. The knowledge of its existence gives a government a valuable reserve of power, and it has only been used on a few occasions. The reason for this is that closure is a double-edged weapon. A government forced to use it is admitting its inability to carry the House by reasoned argument. An opposition may try to manoeuvre a government to resort to closure in order to hold it up to the public as arbitrary and autocratic. This was deliberately done by the Liberal opposition in 1932 in order to call public attention to the extreme provisions of the Relief Bill of that year. Similarly, in the Pipeline debate of 1956, the use of closure enabled the opposition to exploit their accusations of contempt of Parliament which they later levelled at the St. Laurent government in the 1957 election campaign.

In addition to closure, there is an ancient procedural device called "the previous question" which may be used to end debate in certain circumstances. It is a modified form of closure. At any time during the debate on a motion, any member may move that "the question be now put." This procedural motion then becomes debatable and, when it is carried, the question on the original motion must be put at once. This is called the previous question because it is disposed of immediately before the vote is taken on the main motion. Its disadvantages are obvious and it is not now used. It cannot be moved when an amendment is before the House, but only on debate on the main motion. It can only be moved in the House, but unlike closure cannot be moved when the House is in committee.

These two methods of ending debate are crude and often arbitrary tactics. They may end debate but they do little to improve its quality by minimizing irrelevance. If anything, they tend to ensure that debate will deal not with the substance of the question but with the technicalities of procedure. A better approach has been to modify the rules of debate along lines developed in the British House of Commons. The first of these three changes relate to the closure rule itself; the other two require the adoption of time limits to debates and the granting of power to the Speaker to confine debate to the more substantial questions and refuse to permit debate on amendments of little substance.

The British closure rule differs somewhat from the Canadian one. Its most important difference is that a motion for closure is not mandatory—that is, the Speaker may refuse to accept it if he feels that there has been insufficient opportunity for debate. It is obvious that this difference in procedure between the two countries reflected the difference in the position of the Speaker. In the United Kingdom, general confidence in the fairness of the Speaker made it natural that the decision to apply closure should be left to his judgment. In Canada, where in the past the Speaker was less independent of the government, we have not thought fit to leave to his discretion the decision to limit debate. Yet this is to undervalue the Speaker who would, without doubt, take his responsibility seriously.

Another British rule aimed at curtailing debate on matters of little substance is called the "kangaroo." This is the power possessed by the chair in the committee stage of a bill, to select only certain amendments for consideration out of the total submitted. This cuts down the opposition's power to delay through proposing an excessive number of amendments.[16] The nearest to this in Canada is the power possessed by the Speaker, under the 1969 changes in Standing Orders, to combine similar amendments submitted at the report stage of a bill.

There is, finally, a modification of the closure procedure, known as "closure by compartments" (the "guillotine"), which in Britain is used to control the length of debate on a measure expected to be contentious. The purpose is to prescribe the time to be allotted to each stage of the debate in advance, to prevent the legislative program of the government from being thrown out of gear by a long debate on one particular bill. A resolution is passed allotting the maximum amount of time to be spent on each stage, and providing that when each of these periods comes to an end the Speaker shall put the question or questions necessary to complete that stage without further debate. The resolution will have several sections, according to the number of stages, and will lay down the number of sitting days to be devoted to, for example, second reading, the

16. Eric Taylor, *The House of Commons at Work* (London, 1951) p. 171.

committee stage, and the report and third reading. A guillotine motion itself may be debated fiercely and take some time to pass. However, it possesses certain advantages over closure. In the first place, an allocation-of-time order is passed before the contentious measure is itself before the House. On the other hand, closure can only be moved after a measure is actually under consideration, and in the heat of debate it is much more likely to be resented than the guillotine.[17] Furthermore, by planning the stages of debate in advance, the government can argue that time has been provided to consider the real points of substance in the bill.

In the procedure of the Canadian House of Commons, the principles of mandatory allocation of time were first effectively introduced in 1955. By 1960 the length of the Throne Speech debate had been further reduced from ten to eight days, and the debate on the budget from eight days to six. In 1965, the six debatable resolutions to go into committee of supply were reduced to four. At the same time an overall limit of "not more than 36 days" was placed on "the business of supply" in each session. The complete revision of supply procedure in 1969 included a further reduction, as will be discussed.

A form of guillotine procedure was introduced on a provisional basis in 1965, and continued through to the 1967–68 session. Rule 15A gave a kind of formal recognition to the meeting of House leaders and gave that body important new powers. If the Business Committee agreed unanimously on the timetable for a bill, that recommendation would be put before the House for agreement (or rejection) without debate. If the Committee could not agree, the government could propose its own timetable, provided that any such timetable had to allow at least two sitting days on the second reading, two sitting days in committee, and one sitting day for third reading.

In spite of its formidable appearance, Rule 15A was in fact only resorted to three times, and only once led to an allocation-of-time order.[18] In the autumn of 1968, as part of a large number of procedural reforms, there was introduced a new rule, 19A, which provided for a Proceedings Committee made up of the House leaders of the various parties. Like its predecessor it provided for a mandatory vote without debate on allocation-of-time orders which had been unanimously approved by the Committee. A two-hour debate was provided in the case of recommendations which were not unani-

17. *Ibid.* pp. 117–21.

18. Stewart, *The Canadian House of Commons.* p. 247.

mous. There was strenuous opposition to this proposal when it was introduced in December 1968, and in the end it was withdrawn so that the rest of the procedural changes could be adopted at that time. Much of the difficulty stemmed from the fact that the government, in combination with the minor opposition parties, could combine to overcome the official opposition. Essentially the Conservatives took the position that any Standing Order which permitted a time allotment motion which was not unanimous was unacceptable.

At the end of the 1968–69 session the government returned to the attack. It carried, by a majority of the Committee on Procedure and Organization, a proposal for a new group of rules, Standing Orders 75A, 75B and 75C. The first of these proposals enabled the government House leader to propose, with the agreement of all of the other House leaders, an allocation-of-time order governing one or more stages of a bill. The second provided that the House leader could propose allocation-of-time if a majority of the House leaders agreed, and such a proposal was debatable for two hours. Under the third proposal, Standing Order 75C, the government House leader could, after giving notice at a previous sitting that there was no agreement under the terms of Standing Orders 75A or 75B, propose an allocation-of-time order for a public bill. This order must allot at least one sitting day to each stage of the bill. The allocation order, like its predecessors in the earlier proposals, was debatable for two hours, no member being allowed to speak more than once or for more than ten minutes. It should be noted that these Standing Orders refer only to bills, and not to motions. This omission would have meant that such a procedure would not have ended the Flag Debate of 1964, which was on a motion to concur in a report of a committee, and was similarly unavailable to the government to move its constitutional package early in 1981. In that case, the only alternatives were closure, used in the Flag Debate, or compromise, which was the solution reached in the impasse over the constitutional resolution.

There can be few who dispute seriously that the will of the majority should prevail in the House of Commons against excessive obstruction by a small minority of members. The new Standing Order 75B might be seen to meet that situation in an appropriate way. However, it gives very strong bargaining power to third parties, and if used against the far more numerous official opposition, is open to the objection that it overrides a substantial part of the House. It is perhaps mainly for that reason that it has not been used. However 75C raises this difficulty in even more striking terms. Any government has a natural urge to see its legislative proposals advanced through Parliament as rapidly as possible. The fact that the government has a majority in the House is evidence that it has the approval of the electorate in preference to any other party. And yet governments are not always infallible. The existence of an opposition implies that legislative proposals should be thoroughly discussed before they become law. That is what Parliament is for.

Furthermore, an opposition party knows that it cannot press its opposition too far or the public, which has little patience with the complexities of parliamentary procedure, will turn against it. It must always find the fine line between opposition and obstruction. It should be realized that in the parliamentary struggle the main bargaining weapon is time. A government that wishes to push unpalatable proposals knows that its best chance to have them accepted is on the eve of a sessional adjournment when members are anxious to return to their constituencies. Similarly, an opposition party is in the strongest bargaining position when it can use up time to prevent the government from carrying out its program. Thus both sides are prone to engage in a certain amount of brinkmanship when time is on their side.

But this is not the normal parliamentary situation. These confrontations arise when the issue at stake strains the normal consensus to the breaking point. Usually, the business of the House of Commons goes smoothly because it is possible for the business to be arranged in good-tempered discussions "behind the curtain" in a spirit of give and take. Much can be accomplished when sweetness and light prevail. On the other hand a sour, bad-tempered House will accomplish little, no matter how much the rules appear to make it possible for business to be forced through. It is difficult to see the forcing through of Standing Order 75C by resort to closure as anything but a brutal use of majority power. In the end, it is likely that the occasions when a government will risk employing it will be few. Professor Stewart does not consider that these three Standing Orders have created "a satisfactory time-allotment procedure. The efforts made by the Liberals in 1969 to win agreement among the parties by including elaborate safeguards had the effect of making the rules too complex and cumbersome for that purpose. What happened was that, paradoxically, the emphasis on safeguards produced rules—the important one is S.O. 75C—that have far more the character of closure rules than time-allotment rules."[19]

The decade of the sixties had been a period of considerable change in Standing Orders to improve the flow of business in the

19. *Ibid.* pp. 257–8.

House. While some changes were made in the way of improving members' facilities in the following decade, there was a lull in making actual changes in Standing Orders until 1982. The extraordinary length and frequently acrimonious character of the first session of the Thirty-Second Parliament finally led to an all-party agreement on several significant changes, many of which had been advocated for some time, and which came into force for a trial period on the resumption of the session in January 1983.

In summary, the House adopted the following changes. For the first time the House adopted a permanent calendar with fixed times for adjournment at the end of the three planned semesters. The effect of this will increase the average number of sitting days to 175 over the previous 165, but will make it easier for the government and opposition to plan their use of the parliamentary timetable and also make it possible for members to plan more realistically for the time they spend out of Ottawa in their constituencies or for speaking engagements out of Ottawa.

It has long been argued that the time allotted for speeches is too long, providing too great a temptation for a member anxious to fill his allotted time to resort to long quotations and matter of dubious relevance. The reduction of speeches to twenty minutes will provide a strong incentive to stick to the point. Furthermore, motions under Standing Order 43 are abolished. These have been frequently frivolous and have baffled a public unable to appreciate the often schoolboy sense of humour displayed by members of these occasions. An important matter raised under Standing Order 43 is usually and more effectively followed up at question time. In the place of the resolution, members will instead have ninety seconds in which to raise points of importance during the fifteen minute period preceding question time. All private members' business will in future be taken on Wednesday afternoon. In addition, the quorum rule has been modified. The quorum remains at twenty but if the Speaker is required to notice that a quorum is lacking the bells will ring for fifteen minutes to enable members in committees or other parliamentary business to return to their places.

Another important change which critics have long advocated relates to committees. Their membership is reduced to ten from fifteen members. At the same time all reports which are required to be tabled in Parliament by statute will automatically be referred to committees, with the result that committees will have greater control over their own business.

Much more remains to be done. The House Leader, in introducing the changes, said: "I would have liked to mention an area which those who deal with parliamentary reform will have to examine during the next few months, namely supply procedure, budget confidentiality, budgetary bills, financial bills, and the delays involved as a result of our outmoded procedures. . . ."[20] It is likely that the renewed impetus for procedural reform will lead to other important innovations.

Parliamentary Questions

One of the most important means by which ministers are made regularly accountable to the House is through their obligation to answer questions put to them by members relating to matters under the jurisdiction of their departments. Parliamentary questions are, in the words of a former Clerk of the British House of Commons, "the one procedural invention of the democratic era."[21] They provide a means of finding out the acts or omissions of government departments reasonably quickly and with a great deal of publicity. The whole administrative machine can, by the best use of parliamentary questions, be kept in a state of anticipatory reaction not only to the questions which are asked, but for those that may be asked. For this reason governments have always sought to limit or discourage them if possible. In Canada they have been a part of parliamentary life since Confederation.[22] However, their operation is a striking example of the difference between what is permitted by Standing Orders and a procedure which, until 1965, was based on nothing more than the usage of the House.

Questions, as provided in Standing Orders, have to be submitted in writing forty-eight hours in advance. A minister may then have the answer printed in *Hansard*, or, if the answer is likely to be lengthy, he may ask that it be passed as an order for return which will be tabled in the House in due course. A member who wishes an oral reply will mark his question with an asterisk. What usually happens is that there are a large number of questions on the order paper for which, at some time, a department will provide an answer. There are frequent complaints at the long delays which may ensue before an answer is provided, and occasionally suggestions from ministers that some members abuse their rights by asking an excessive number of questions.

20. Canada. *House of Commons Debates.* November 29, 1982. p. 21071.

21. Lord Campion *et al. Parliament: A Survey.* (London, 1952) p. 165. See also for the fullest discussion of the whole matter, D.N. Chester and Nona Bowring *Questions in Parliament.* (London, 1962).

22. The evolution of Canadian practice is fully described in W.F. Dawson, *Procedure in the Canadian House of Commons.* (Toronto, 1962) pp. 147ff.

In addition to these questions, of which due notice has been given, the usage of the House has sanctioned the asking of oral questions. These questions are, in Mr. Speaker Michener's words, "a limited supplement to questions which may be put on the order paper, and are for the purpose of enabling members to get information on public affairs of urgent importance without delay and to bring such matters to the attention of the government." Mr. Michener further amplified the procedure for oral questions as follows:

(1) The question should seek information or press for action on matters "of such immediate urgency" that they could not appear on the order paper.
(2) Both question and answer should be "concise, factual and free of opinion and argument which might lead to debate."
(3) Explanation of government intentions may be sought but not "explanation or opinion upon matters of policy."
(4) Supplementary questions are a matter of grace.
(5) Since a minister is entitled to notice, a member cannot insist on an answer to an oral question.[23]

These questions in fact enable members to use their ingenuity in asking factetious, probing or embarrassing questions in hope of knocking the minister off balance. When a member is anxious for an answer he will telephone the minister's office so that the minister will come to the House prepared to reply.

This so-called "orders-of-the-day question period" grew up quite outside Standing Orders, and presented the Speaker with the extremely difficult task of controlling it. It had no effective time limit and so it consumed a great deal of time, often to little purpose. Nevertheless, it was treasured by members, and in its own way provided an opportunity to bring matters of immediate urgency to public attention.

The Special Committee on Procedure sought in 1964 to remedy, as far as possible, these defects and at the same time retain what was valuable in the institution. They recommended "a standing order to regularize the orders of the day question period and to give control over that question period to Mr. Speaker."[24] This Standing Order governs questions and gives the Speaker the right to direct that a question be transferred to the order paper if it is not, in his opinion,

23. Canada. *House of Commons Debates.* February 26, 1959. p. 1393. There are a number of other limitations, relating to the proper subjects for questions and similar matters, which apply to both oral and written questions.

24. Mr. Stanley Knowles in Canada. *House of Commons Debates.* April 20, 1964. p. 2342.

urgent. The daily question period since 1975 has been limited to forty-five minutes.

The Speaker has the difficult job of recognizing members who ask questions. The Leader of the Opposition is normally recognized first, followed by the other party leaders. Thereafter he attempts to recognize members from the various parties in an equitable way. Nevertheless there are fairly frequent complaints of members who have been unable to be recognized for several days and this no doubt will be a continuing problem as the House increases in size. The fact that there is a rotation in recognizing members tends to diffuse the impact of a particular line of questioning, though opposition parties can increase their impact by focussing their attention on a minister who may be particularly vulnerable at that time. Naturally, questions are important to opposition parties and there is the possibility of the limited time being abused if the Speaker recognizes too many questions from the government's own back benchers. The object of such questions is likely to give ministers the opportunity to smuggle announcements and other pleasing things into their answers. Naturally enough, ministers cannot ask questions of other ministers, but at one time parliamentary secretaries were allowed to ask questions as long as they did not ask questions of their own ministers. However, Mr. Speaker Jerome ruled that such questions would no longer be permitted.[25]

The Stages of Legislation

A bill is a proposed law in the process of consideration by Parliament. When it has passed all of its stages in both Houses and they are completely agreed upon its terms, it is presented for royal assent, whereupon it becomes an act of Parliament. There are several kinds of bills. First of all, there is the basic distinction between a public bill and a private bill. A public bill is simply a bill that changes the law in a way affecting the public in general. A private bill is one which confers special powers or rights upon individuals or corporations. In the Canadian Parliament, private bills are usually to incorporate or alter corporate powers of companies or certain religious or charitable organizations. While most companies are able to avail themselves of a simpler procedure, which consists of applying for letters patent under the Canada Corporations Act, certain of them, notably railways and banking and finance companies, must seek their charters from Parliament.

25. *Ibid.* November 5, 1974. p. 1060.

Public Bills

The majority of bills which take up parliamentary time are public bills. Public bills are further divided into (a) government bills and (b) private members' bills. The latter, as already noted, receive only a small amount of parliamentary time and very few of them actually reach the statute book. Except that they have a different place on the parliamentary timetable, they follow exactly the same procedure as government bills. There is a special class of public bills known as money bills to which special rules of procedure apply. These special requirements are contained in part in sections 53 and 54 of the British North America Act and their purpose is (a) to ensure the primacy of the House of Commons in financial legislation, (b) to confine the initiation of financial measures to responsible ministers, and (c) to provide, through a special committee procedure (committee of the whole), for the fullest discussion of the government's financial policy on the floor of the House. Until 1969 it was also necessary for these bills to be preceded by financial resolutions which were debated in one or other of the forms of committee of the whole as well.

The first requirement is that bills for the appropriation of public funds and for the raising of any tax or impost must first originate in the House of Commons. The second requirement is that the House may not adopt any financial measure unless such measure has been recommended to the House by the Governor General, acting through a minister. In the case of appropriations bills, the estimates must be considered in one or other of the standing committees before the bills are introduced.

Government bills will have gone through a number of preparatory stages within the administration before they are brought to Parliament. A decision in principle to introduce a bill, from among the many which the departments of government wish to bring before Parliament, will first be made by the Cabinet or in most cases the Cabinet Committee on Legislation and House Planning. The bill will then be sent to the parliamentary draftsmen in the Department of Justice to be prepared in the proper form. Then, at an appropriate time in the session, a minister will have the bill placed on the order paper. The procedural stages for public bills are as follows:

1. The first stage is a motion for leave to introduce a bill, specifying its title. This is not a debatable motion, though the member sponsoring the bill may give a short description of its purpose.
2. At a subsequent sitting a non-debatable motion will be presented "That this bill be read a first time and be printed."

3. The bill will then go before the House for the second of its three readings, each of which must be on different days. The second reading is the first major debate on the bill, and it must be passed at that stage before any amendments to it can be introduced. Opposition motions against it are therefore procedural—either that it be referred to a committee before second reading, which would delay it, or that it be read six months hence, which would in fact prevent it from being introduced again in that session.
4. Once a bill has passed second reading it is referred to a committee. Except for supply and ways and means bills, which go to Committee of the Whole, the bill will go to a standing committee for detailed consideration. The House may instead refer the bill to a special committee or to a joint committee of both Houses. In the committee stage each clause of the bill is considered separately, and members may move amendments to these clauses.
5. Once a bill has been passed by the committee, with whatever amendments may have been made, it proceeds, after a lapse of at least forty-eight hours, to the debate at the report stage. Until the change in standing orders in 1968 this stage was not debatable, but this was altered to give members an opportunity to debate and move amendments to a bill, detailed discussion of which up until then had been confined to a small committee.[26] For this reason the report stage of financial bills, which have had their committee stage in Committee of the Whole is not debatable. At least twenty-four hours before consideration of the report stage, members may give notice of amendments to the bill. At this stage, the Speaker has the power to select or combine amendments for debate. At the conclusion of the debate there will be a motion to concur in the bill, and it may be considered for third reading at the next sitting of the House.
6. Third reading is the last debatable stage of a bill, on the motion "that the bill be now read a third time and passed."
7. The bill will then be transmitted to the Clerk of the Parliaments, and will receive consideration in the Senate, if it has not already passed the Senate before being introduced into the House. If the Senate makes any amendments in the bill these must be reported to the House. The minister in charge of the bill will move either

26. Mr. Lewis:... "obviously, in view of the new set-up of our committees the intention of the report stage is to give all members of the house an opportunity to deal with a bill and to move amendments. In this way the collective wisdom of the house replaces the collective wisdom of a number of members of the house. This may not always be better wisdom but it does give wider representation." Canada. *House of Commons Debates.* June 18, 1969, p. 10321.

concurrence or rejection of such amendments. If there is a deadlock between the two houses the bill can proceed no further.

8. The bill will be presented, when it has passed both Houses, for royal assent in the Queen's name by the Governor General or his deputy. Unless the bill provides for a date of its coming into force, it will become effective on the day on which royal assent was given.

The changes effected in 1968 in procedure relating to public bills have struck at one of the most obvious inefficiencies of parliamentary procedure. Members of Parliament feel that they have been sent there to talk and it has been extremely difficult to persuade them to accept changes which curb their loquacity. The elimination of the financial resolution stage has at least cut out a piece of indefensible constitutional mumbo jumbo. The remarkable legislative achievement of the first session of the Twenty-eighth Parliament (elected in 1968) shows how effective the reforms were. But the Commons is not merely a legislative sausage machine for the government of the day. While it must have adequate time for effective discussion of legislation, it is necessary to keep its legislative activity within bounds so that adequate time is left for the necessary function of scrutiny and control of the government.

Private Bills

The procedure for the consideration of private bills, while similar to that for public bills, differs in detail. Because private bills may affect the rights of third parties, who might be ignorant of their provisions, elaborate procedures are followed to ensure that all affected interests have an opportunity to be heard. For this reason, there is more consideration in the preliminary stages of private bills. At the same time, since many of them do not involve any major public interest, there is usually little detailed discussion of them at the stages when a major debate occurs in public bills. As noted previously, private bills originate in the Senate, and only occasionally receive more lengthy consideration in the Commons than in the upper chamber.

The promoter of a private bill begins by filing a petition with the Clerk of the Senate and with the Clerk of the House of Commons. Some fees are required when the petition is filed, and others must be paid following second reading. Petitions for private bills must be filed within the first six weeks of the session. The petition must also be published in the *Canada Gazette*, and there must be notification directly or by advertisement to persons who might be affected by the bill. Since each private bill must be sponsored by a member, the promoter of the bill must enlist a senator and a member of the House of Commons to conduct it through its stages.

COMMITTEES

"The essence of a committee is, surely," said Sir Kenneth Wheare, "that it is a body to which some task has been referred or committed by some other person or body."[27] He goes on to consider the various roles committees play, which are to advise, to inquire, to negotiate, to legislate, to administer, to scrutinize and control. Not all of these functions are normal to parliamentary committees. Sometimes they may be said to advise, as in the case of a committee to study a government white or green paper. They do not normally administer, though some of the "housekeeping" committees such as those on the parliamentary restaurant, the parliamentary library, and on internal economy may be said to perform an administrative role. Sometimes they inquire, but this is a function usually given to bodies such as royal commissions whose work will not be abruptly terminated by the prorogation or dissolution of Parliament. The main functions of parliamentary committees are to legislate, to scrutinize and to control.

While the House of Commons since Confederation has had a full panoply of committees of various sorts, many of these existed only on paper. The fact of the matter is that in the system of Cabinet government, the existence of strong and active legislative committees is thought to be inconsistent with the operation of responsible government. Apart from some "housekeeping" committees, almost all of the committee work of the House of Commons was done in committees of the whole. Much of this was made necessary by the need to deal with financial resolutions before legislation in the Committee of Supply and the Committee of Ways and Means. The committee stage of all bills was then taken in committee of the whole as well. There were certain advantages to committee of the whole procedure. It was more informal, and members could speak more than once. The concentration of practically all parliamentary business on the floor of the House was time-consuming and inefficient. Gradually, efforts were made to get rid of much of the role of

27. K.C. Wheare, *Government by Committee* (Oxford, 1955) pp. 5–6. See also Bernard Crick *The Reform of Parliament* (London, 1964), particularly Chapter Four.

committees of the whole. In the extensive changes in Standing Orders introduced in 1968 a number of changes, some of which had been tried out on an experimental basis before—were introduced. The old Committee of Supply and the Committee of Ways and Means were abolished and in their stead the opposition parties were given twenty-five "supply" days called "allotted days" in which they could introduce motions of their choice. The committee stage of all bills (except finance bills) was in future to be taken in standing committees, which would also deal with the estimates. The new standing committees are "subject matter" committees corresponding to the main functions of government. Their size varied from twenty to thirty.

The relatively small size of the House has made it difficult for these committees to do their job properly. The party whips found great difficulty in providing enough members to ensure that the committees could function. A large number of members are simply unavailable for ordinary committee membership. These include the Speaker and his three deputies, the more than thirty ministers, and as many as twenty-seven parliamentary secretaries. In addition each committee requires a chairman, and many have a vice-chairman. There are always some members who are ill or absent on public business. There are some members who are lazy. One former minister has calculated that there were not more than sixty members who carry the bulk of the committee load.[28] To ensure adequate attendance the party whips have the power to substitute members, with the result that the turnover from day to day in any one committee is liable to be high. This can be particularly frustrating when dealing with the estimates, since members newly arrived on the committee may well ask the same questions as were answered at the last meeting. When the new committee system was introduced it was thought that it would greatly improve estimates procedure. In fact members seem to have worked better on bills and found the estimates procedure less than satisfactory so that attendance when committees are considering bills is considerably better than when they are dealing with the estimates.

A further difficulty was that committees can only deal with matters specifically referred to them by the House. This problem has been in part ameliorated by the new provision conditionally introduced at the end of 1982 which automatically refers all reports required to be tabled in Parliament by law to the appropriate standing commit-

28. John M. Reid, "The Backbencher and the Discharge of Legislative Responsibilities." in W.A. Neilson and J.C. MacPherson, *The Legislative Process in Canada*. pp. 139ff.

tee. Another change, introduced at the same time, may reduce the problem created by wholesale substitutions by reducing the size of standing committees to half their previous size.

The amount of work a particular committee may have to do is highly variable. During May and June there is a period of heavy work when it is necessary to rush through the estimates. At such times the consideration of bills has to be put aside. A committee which also has to deal with a long and complicated piece of legislation will have a heavy work load. It is perhaps not too much to say that the House—after ignoring the role of committees for so long—has now placed too great a burden on them. Not only have there been too few members to carry the load, but there have been other problems as well. A limited number of committees can meet at the same time, and there is a strong tendency to avoid, as far as possible, meetings on Mondays and Fridays when members have constituency and other business on their minds. Not all committee meetings can be held when the House is not sitting and Wednesday morning was pre-empted by the weekly party caucuses. In consequence at certain times of the day the House can be very thinly attended because members are absent on committee or other assignments. The new hours of sitting introduced in 1983 may alleviate this problem, but it is unlikely to solve it. Initially there were far too few committee rooms available and if a number of committees are meeting simultaneously the burden on translation staff becomes very heavy. The practice by which the right to speak or ask questions is rotated faithfully among the parties leads to discontinuity in the flow of business. Since public exposure is important to members who need to think of being re-elected it will not be easy to change this practice, which does not happen in Senate committees.

Another problem arises in connection with the management of committee business. Generally speaking since 1968 the tendency has been for the government's business on a committee to be in the hands of a parliamentary secretary. But not all ministers have parliamentary secretaries. In their absence the responsibility for ensuring that the government's business goes smoothly is bound to be felt by the chairman, who is thus cast in the ambiguous role of being at once an impartial chairman and to an extent the guardian of the interest of the government.[29] In fact the position of a committee chairman is an unenviable one. The practice of the Trudeau government seems to have been to use parliamentary secretaryships and committee chairmanships as a means of testing and rewarding

29. See Robert Jackson and Michael Atkinson, *The Canadian Legislative System.* (Toronto, 1980) pp. 145–46.

backbenchers. Normally each of these posts is held for about two sessions, and then there is a general change. Since parliamentary secretaries are paid an extra stipend and committee chairmen are not, it is liable to matter which of these posts an aspiring backbencher is given. Committee chairmen know that they are in a sort of probationary post in which their success is liable to be measured by their ability to run a committee to the satisfaction of the Prime Minister. They are seldom in a committee long enough to establish their authority and their impartiality is liable to be suspect. It should be noted however that an experienced committee chairman is sometimes able to exert a good deal of independent influence in quietly expediting legislation he favours and somehow slowing down business he does not like. Nevertheless the present position is not satisfactory.

Many would agree with Hon. Marcel Lambert, a former Speaker, when he said "If the Prime Minister wishes to share views on that, I can tell him that I would prefer to see a panel of chairmen from the House generally, as in Britain. You get a much more equitable and a much more effective operation of committees. . . ." The Prime Minister then suggested that what Mr. Lambert was advocating was something closer to the American Congressional system, but Mr. Lambert replied ". . . I said a panel of chairmen, selected by the Speaker for the particular jobs. . . . I am not in favour of the American system."[30] We may indeed come to something like that, but it should be recognized that there is a difference between the British standing committees which deal with legislation, perhaps half a dozen in number, and the very much larger number of Canadian committees.

A related issue is whether committee work would be improved if committees had staffs of their own, in addition to the committee clerks who perform routine duties. Certain committees have regular staff support, such as the Joint Committee on Regulations and other Statutory Instruments and the Public Accounts Committee which receives support from the staff of the Auditor General. Other Committees such as those studying white or green papers of a highly technical nature may receive expert staff for this purpose. It has been argued that all committees should have staffs of their own, like American Congressional committees. In the American system committees of both Houses play a central role as a sort of counter-executive in the preparation of legislation and supervision of the executive branch through the control of funding. Such a role for

30. Canada. House of Commons. Standing Committee on Miscellaneous Estimates. *Minutes of Proceedings and Evidence* Tuesday, May 26, 1981. pp. 58:25–6.

committees in Canada would profoundly alter a system which is based on executive dominance. It is not the business of Parliament to try and govern in place of the executive. When a government has a majority in the house, that majority conceives its role as one of supporting the executive, while the opposition parties raise grievances and set forth alternative policies which they hope will win the next election.

Would committee staffs enhance their capability? Apart from constitutional objections, there are some practical difficulties. Committee loads are highly variable and staff activity would vary greatly. Assembling a pool of expert staff would be very expensive and might not contain the skills required at any one time. Relying on outside consultants means relying on experts who are often unfamiliar with the nature of the parliamentary operation. There is a danger that staffs would be more interested in making work for themselves than helping the committees do their jobs and might lead to staff members usurping the role of members. There is an ambiguity about committee staffs since it is not clear to whom they are responsible. Is it the chairman, the majority on the committee, or individual members? In any event the increasing size of the research staff of the Parliamentary Library provides much of the expert services which members may require.[31]

Committees are a microcosm of the House of Commons. They are small groups capable of becoming fairly expert in the subjects confided to them. In that sense they can do much more and do it better than the House itself could achieve. To an extent, they develop some of the characteristics of small-group behaviour in that members develop close personal ties from working together so that intra-party partisan feeling will tend to be lowered. That is why governments are somewhat suspicious of committees since partisan control of the majority may be eroded. For a different reason, members themselves often have limited enthusiasm for committees. However valuable the work of committees is, it tends to be largely invisible since committees receive little coverage in the media. Members of Parliament are political men, ever conscious of the need to be re-elected, and generally reluctant to devote much time to politically unrewarding work. So, while committees enhance the work of the House, too much cannot be expected of them as long as the realities of politics inhibit their fullest development.

31. See Peter Dobell, "Committee Staff—what else is needed?" paper presented to the Second Legislative Studies Conference, Simon Fraser University. February, 1979.

THE MEMBER OF PARLIAMENT AS OMBUDSMAN

Besides their collective role as part of the organized contest of political parties in the House, members play an important role individually. They represent all of the people in their constituencies. Individual voters have problems with governments on which they need advice and help. This is an activity which members of the House are happy to perform because it enhances their role in the constituency and contributes to a degree to the support they can expect at election times. Furthermore, the life of a backbencher is in many ways frustrating. In the eyes of party managers, the member is seen primarily as a vote in a committee or on the floor of the House. He must go where he is bidden by the whips and do what he is told. In contrast, the task of helping a troubled constituent gives a sense of achievement. Members have always known this, but recent improvements in members' services have made it a more effective role.

Members now have individual offices, adequately staffed, as well as offices in their constituencies. To some extent these staffs provide some kind of support for the legislative duties of members, but to a large extent they make it possible to hear and seek to redress individual grievances of constituents.[32] Few members have been willing to sacrifice a staff position devoted to constituency service for a staff member who is primarily a policy adviser. To a considerable extent, such needs are already met by the research service of the Parliamentary Library and by a small cadre of parliamentary interns. The latter, who are university graduates serving in the House for a year, may lack the experience and knowledge of seasoned servants of Parliament, but their training in the rapid and clear exposition of complex material makes them a useful adjunct to the resources available. There are also caucus research staffs, which do not appear to be thought of highly by the officers of the House. Nevertheless they do provide the partisan research which enables party spokesmen in the House to maximize the political effect of parliamentary questions and the like.[33]

One of the most enduring problems for the average member of Parliament is information. Only a part of the problem is the difficulty which opposition members have in gaining access to informa-

32. See Alistair Fraser "Legislators and Their Staffs" in Harold C. Clarke, Colin Campbell, F.Q. Quo, and Arthur Goddard (eds.) *Parliament, Policy and Representation* (Toronto, 1980) p. 230.

33. See Edwin R. Black "Opposition Research: Some Theories and Practice" *Canadian Public Administration* 15:1 (Spring, 1972) p. 24.

tion because of the obsessive secrecy which surrounds the working of Cabinet government. Within limits, that difficulty may be ameliorated by Freedom of Information legislation. The larger part of the problem is that the individual member has not too little information, but too much. In addition to *Hansard* itself, in which he will read his own speeches and seek to obtain political advantage by a close reading of the speeches of his opponents, hundreds of documents reach his office. Most of these he will not have the time, or perhaps the inclination, to read. Many of them are intelligible only to experts. The Member of Parliament of the future will need to have skills uncommon in past members, most of whom came from small towns with limited or no experience of how to use the resources of large and complex organizations.

Most of the reforms of the House of Commons in the seventies were aimed at moving more business off the floor of the House and making it more efficient. To a degree this has been successful. There is much more to be done. Professor Franks has argued for a much more rational and orderly use of time on the floor of the House, and a reduction in the size and number of committees. He would prefer a few much larger committees dealing with bills, rather on the British model, thus freeing the smaller committees for scrutiny and control functions related to consideration of the estimates and departmental and agency reports.[34] The Clark government introduced a useful package of reforms in 1979, which unfortunately died with the dissolution of parliament and the subsequent defeat of the government.[35] These changes included reducing time for speeches in the House from forty minutes to twenty, a positive and negative resolution procedure which would have strengthened the House's control over delegated legislation, and the reduction of the number of allotted days from twenty-five to twenty. There were suggestions for reducing the size of committees and improving their performance in other ways. The reduction in the number of allotted days, together with the provision for bringing back some of the Estimates to the floor of the House on such days, accords with the recommendations of a former House Leader, Hon. Mitchell Sharp.[36]

Other proposals, which have been made by Professor John Stewart, would include drastic curtailment of second-reading debates, as

34. C.E.S. Franks, "Procedural Reform in the Legislative Process" in W.A.W. Neilson and J.C. MacPherson, (eds.) *The Legislative Process in Canada*. p. 249.

35. Hon. Walter Baker, *Position Paper: The Reform of Parliament.* (Ottawa, 1979)

36. See. J.R. Mallory "The Two Clerks: Parliamentary Discussion of the Privy Council Office" *Canadian Journal of Political Science* 10:1 (March, 1977) p. 12.

is done in the United Kingdom. The purpose of the second-reading debate is to consider the principle of a bill, and allowing this debate to drag on leads merely to repetition. Similarly, there would be advantage in sending contentious bills to committee for public hearings straight from first-reading, as is frequently done in the National Assembly of Quebec. In this way a government, before being too heavily committed to the details of a bill, may be more willing to accept modifications of it in detail.[37]

The object of reform should be to make the House, or to be accurate, the opposition parties better able to make effective criticism. The Lambert Commission argued that neither Parliament nor the public now have adequate information to understand government policy.[38] Central to their proposal was that Parliament should annually debate the general fiscal plan of the government over the next five years. In this way it should be possible to know where the government is going, and whether it seems to know where it is going. They were also very critical of the way in which the Estimates were presented, and the government in 1981 began the process of improving them to be more informative and useful in relating programs to performance.

Efforts to reform the House of Commons must keep steadily in view that its members are political men organized into political parties which are seeking power. Proposed changes which seem to be incongruous with members' perceptions of the imperatives of their existence will fail. Changes which seem to them to fit are likely to be adopted. Their adoption will depend on a reconciliation of the views of a government party and its opponents in opposition. Neither is inclined to make life easier for the other. In general, the object should be to make opposition more constructive and less obstructive.

Parliamentary Privilege

The purpose of parliamentary privilege is to enable members of both Houses of Parliament to be as free as possible from external restraints and pressures in the transaction of public business. Both Houses are given wide powers to protect their members against anything which might disturb the free and orderly conduct of their business, and their proceedings and the members themselves have certain immunities from the normal legal consequences of their

37. John B. Stewart, *The Canadian House of Commons*. pp. 269–71.
38. Royal Commission on Financial Management and Accountability. *Final Report*. pp. 369 ff.

actions. Any interference with the business of the House or the freedom of a member to attend it constitutes a breach of privilege, or in other words, contempt of the House. Parliamentary privilege is thus somewhat similar to the protection which the law of contempt of court affords to the courts of law. This similarity is not accidental, for much of the original *lex et consuetudo Parliamenti* derives from the claim of the English Parliament to be a court of law. In Canada these legal immunities do not derive directly from this ancient form of law, but were conferred on the Canadian Parliament by statute. Section 18 of the British North America Act, as amended in 1875, confers on the Parliament of Canada the right to define its privileges, immunities and powers, but these powers cannot exceed those at the same time possessed by the Parliament of the United Kingdom. Even this limitation on the power of the Canadian Parliament to define its own privileges has now been removed by the passage of the British North America (No. 2) Act of 1949.[39]

The Independence of Parliament provisions of the Senate and House of Commons Act take elaborate, though rather ineffective, precautions against a member of either House having a conflict of interest through financial involvement in public business. Thus no member, save the enumerated ministers of the Crown and their parliamentary secretaries, may accept "an office of profit under the Crown." This curious provision reflects the original intention of the Act of Settlement to exclude "placemen" from Parliament and thus to prevent the domination of either House by the executive. In addition, a member who derives profit from a public contract is disqualified from sitting—a provision which in 1874 temporarily unseated Mr. Speaker Anglin. The protection of the purity of members of Parliament which this section affords is less sweeping than would appear, since it does not apply to profits derived from shares held in a company which has contracts with the Crown, except in the case of public works contracts. Similarly, it does not apply to professional fees, so that in fact very few members are now inconvenienced by it. However, if the independence of members of Parliament depended merely on legal prohibitions, there could be little confidence in the institution. The real protection of the independence of Parliament is the integrity of the members themselves.

An important part of parliamentary privilege historically was the legal immunity from arrest, detention and other restrictions on freedom of movement which might prevent a member from attend-

39. See. W.F. Dawson, "Parliamentary Privilege in the Canadian House of Commons," *Canadian Journal of Economics and Political Science* XXV, No. 4 (November 1959), pp. 462–70.

ing parliamentary sessions. There was never a period in Canadian history when this privilege was of major importance. In Canada it extends only to civil actions, and does not include treason, felony, breach of the peace or any indictable offence. A member can be arrested, even during the parliamentary session, if charged with an indictable offence, though he cannot be arrested if actually on the floor of the House when it is sitting. It was for this reason that Fred Rose was arrested on the eve of a new session in 1946. The only other comparable case is that of Louis Riel who, while a member of Parliament, stood attainted of treason and a fugitive from the law in 1873. Had he been caught his arrest would have been perfectly legal and not a breach of parliamentary privilege.[40] However, if a member is arrested it immediately becomes the duty of the magistrate concerned to notify the Speaker of the cause of the arrest.

In addition to the immunity from arrest, a member also has an immunity from certain legal duties which would equally limit his freedom to attend Parliament. A member is excused from jury service if it interferes with his attendance in the House. Similarly he can resist a subpoena to appear in court as a witness, though in this case there are examples of the House being prepared to waive this immunity in the interests of justice.[41]

The most important of the parliamentary immunities is freedom of speech. A member speaking in the House cannot be held legally responsible for what he says. He cannot be sued for slander, nor for libel on the basis of the printed proceedings. This is a wide, and in some respects dangerous, immunity if it is abused. An unscrupulous member could blacken the characters of defenceless persons, and destroy reputations at will without being restrained by considerations of either truth or the law of libel. Fortunately this has not happened in Canada. In spite of its inherent danger to innocent individuals, this particular parliamentary privilege is valuable and necessary. The Canadian law of libel is strict, and it would seriously hamper a zealous member who ventured to attack a powerful and wealthy vested interest. More important still, the government itself may think twice before succumbing to the temptation to silence criticism by resort to the Official Secrets Act. This actually occurred in the United Kingdom in 1938, when the government of the day threatened Duncan Sandys with prosecution under the Official Secrets Act because he persisted in pressing an awkward parliamentary question.[42]

40. *Ibid.*, p. 464.
41. *Ibid.*
42. Sir Ivor Jennings, *Parliament*, 2nd ed. (London, 1957), p. 109.

Control by the House over the freedom of speech of its members extends to control over the reproduction or publication of debates. The House publishes its verbatim debates in *Hansard*, and freely allows their reproduction by newspapers and other media. However, for a long time it did not show any enthusiasm for allowing its proceedings to be broadcast or televised. Suggestions that this should be done were strongly resisted, no doubt on the sound ground that they would not enhance the public image of the House. State openings of Parliament have been shown on television, and the proceedings in both Houses were televised when the Queen opened the 1957–58 session; the Speech from the Throne was also televised on other occasions. But these were ceremonial occasions, not open to the same objection as normal parliamentary business. In 1954 the opposition severely criticized a parliamentary committee for making a tape recording of its proceedings. This had been done with the consent of the Speaker in order to assist the accuracy of committee reporters. Again, in 1958, the Prime Minister, Mr. Diefenbaker, without even consulting the Speaker, installed a loudspeaker connection between his office and the House. Both of these relatively innocuous procedures were criticized primarily on the ground that the permission of the House itself had not been gained before they were set up. It is significant that the Prime Minister's private wire was removed before the next session.[43] It was not until 1977 that the house finally agreed to have its proceedings televised.

However strongly the House may feel about interference with its proceedings by outsiders, it has effectively retained the right to discipline its own members. This, of course, is justifiable in order to preserve order and decorum in debate. A member who refuses to be called to order from the chair may be named by the Speaker and then suspended from the service of the House. The motion for suspension is moved customarily by the leader of the House. When it is carried, the member is removed by the Sergeant-at-Arms and cannot again take his seat until he has apologized. A recent case of "naming" a member who refused to sit down when ordered by the Speaker was that of Mr. Donald Fleming during the Pipeline debate in 1956.[44]

The House has, on a few occasions, imposed even more severe penalties on members whose conduct seemed to warrant it. Louis Riel was twice expelled from the House, once for refusing to attend

43. Dawson, "Parliamentary Privilege," p. 466.

44. Canada, *House of Commons Debates*, May 25, 1956, p. 4352. A recent example was the naming of Mr. Svend Robinson in 1983. *Ibid.* October 19, 1983. pp. 218129-30.

in his place and answer charges brought against him and on a second occasion after he had been judicially declared an outlaw. Thomas McGreevy was expelled from the house for his connection with the public works scandals of 1891 and Fred Rose was expelled as a consequence of his arrest on charges of espionage in 1945.[45] Members of Parliament and others, including among them no less a person than Sir John A. Macdonald, have on a number of occasions public works scandals of 1891 and Fred Rose was expelled as a consequence of his arrest on charges of espionage in 1946.[45]

Lastly, the House of Commons has seldom indulged itself in its undoubted right to punish breaches of privilege as a form of contempt and to punish them by committal to prison. There is no doubt that the House has the power to do this, though a member committed to jail on the order of the house would have to be released on the prorogation of Parliament since such an order is only valid for the session in which it is made. The House of Commons is not a body endowed with judicial temperament. Its procedure is necessarily partisan and lacking in judicial flavour. When the liberty of a person who might have offended its touchy dignity is possibly at stake, opinion nowadays would no doubt prefer that such matters be left to the courts.

The most objectionable feature is that, while there is no settled procedure for raising breaches of privilege, the general tendency has been for the House to deal with them itself, and the process of summoning persons to the bar to purge themselves of contempt is less dignified than might be thought. Professor W. F. Dawson notes that unlike its British counterpart, the Canadian house of Commons has made little use of the Committee on Privileges and Elections, a smaller body which might be able to deal with these matters with more dignity and decorum.[47]

While they seem largely irrelevant today, the privileges of Parliament, taken as a whole, are a body of legal principles whose purpose is to protect the House from potential interference with its necessary business. The history of the Canadian Parliament since Confederation is largely free of issues of moment and substance in the matter of parliamentary privilege. That this is so means that parliamentary institutions thus far in our history have not been seriously threatened. Long may it be so.

45. Dawson, "Parliamentary Privilege," pp. 467–8.

46. Norman Ward, "Called to the Bar of the House of Commons," *Canadian Bar Review* XXXV, No. 5, May 1957, pp. 529–46.

47. Dawson, "Parliamentary Privilege," p. 468.

8

The Courts and the Administration of Justice

The third of the classic threefold divisions of the functions of government is the judicial process. The executive and the legislative branches of government are, under Cabinet government, inextricably intermingled. The judicial branch is distinct and independent, and its independence has become a matter of fundamental constitutional principle. This was not always so. The courts of law grew up as part of the apparatus of the executive. When King James I objected that as King by divine right he could not be subject "to any man," Sir Edward Coke replied that the King "is not subject to any man, but to God and the Law." The struggle between the King and Parliament in seventeenth-century England led to a recognition of the independence of the judiciary in the Act of Settlement of 1701. This principle was not carried over automatically in the British North American colonies, but was achieved gradually as a result of constitutional reform in the first half of the nineteenth century.

The legal system is the part of a constitutional order which particularly promotes and preserves liberty and justice. The purpose of law is to make explicit the rules which reconcile liberty with order, and it is the business of the courts to apply the law where there are disputes about legal rights. These disputes may involve an apparent conflict between the rights of individuals, they may arise out of conflicts between the citizen and the government or they may arise, particularly in a federal state, out of conflicts between governments. The courts therefore act both as the arbiters of private rights and as the interpreters of the constitution.

Law is the rules of conduct on which the political order of our society is based, and it is concerned with those rules which will be enforced by the ultimate sanction of the organized force of the state. Canada is a federal state, and the law-making power as well as the machinery of the courts are divided between the two levels of government. Since the capitulation of New France, French Canadians in Quebec have been guaranteed the preservation of the system of private law which they knew before. Therefore in Quebec an important part of the law is based on what is called the civil law, while in the rest of Canada the legal system is based on the English common law.

Civil law in this sense is based on the Roman civil law which prevails generally in continental Europe. At present, Quebec law is derived from a codification of that law contained in the Civil Code and the Code of Civil Procedure, which were assembled over a century ago in a form modelled on the Code Napoléon of France. There are important differences between the civil law and the common law in the concepts and forms of action in relation to personal and property law, particularly regarding the status of minors, the succession to estates and the transmission of property.

The English common law arose from the principles applied by English judges in early medieval England as they developed a system of law for the whole country. In essence the common law is not based on any codification or act of legislation, but is what is known as judge-made law. That is to say the judges, after an examination of a particular case and the consideration of earlier precedents, declared what the law was. An important ingredient in this process is the rule of *stare decisis* by which previous decisions are binding on the court in subsequent cases.

Of course, most modern law in Canada has been made by the legislature so that little of the original common law still remains. Nevertheless our legal system is founded on the common law, and the importance of judicial interpretation of what the law means, as well as the survival of the logic and method of the common law in the judicial process, still creates important differences between the legal systems of Quebec and the rest of Canada.

Whatever their origins, however, the legal systems that operate in the Anglo-American world have one distinctive characteristic: law is a highly technical and specialized branch of knowledge, only understood by experts trained in it. The law has built up over the centuries a language and a logic of its own which is a highly sophisticated method of getting at certain important kinds of truth. With one major exception the operation of law is confined to the experts who understand it. This is true both of the principles which still survive from the common law and also of the most recent enactments of the legislature. For while the electorate and the members of the legislature may know what they want in the form of a new law, only a highly trained statutory draftsman can put it into language which will enable the courts to give it full effect. The only role which laymen play in the operation of the legal system is as members of juries, because of the very old English tradition that where a man's life or liberty are at stake the facts of the case shall be decided by a jury of his peers.

The rise of popular democracy in North America has sometimes been accompanied by a populist distrust of law and lawyers, who are regarded as part of a conspiracy of vested interests. In the United States the popular election and recall of judges, the transfer of law-making functions from the legislature to the people through initiative and referendum have been a part of this process. Even in Canada these ideas have had some effect. They led to the attempt to introduce in the province of Manitoba both initiative and referendum in 1916. They explain the belief of the late William Aberhart of Alberta that no lawyer could be trusted to hold the office of Attorney General of the province.

The legal process and the legal profession enjoy an extraordinary degree of autonomy in the community, in spite of the pressures of a democratic age. Furthermore, the courts and the judges seem to be insulated both from democratic control and from normal liability to an extraordinary degree. The reason for this needs to be understood in order to grasp the central role of the courts in a constitutional order.

Coupled with the autonomy of the courts is the fundamental constitutional doctrine of the rule of law. As defined by Dicey, the rule of law has three "distinct though kindred conceptions."[1] The first of these is that no man may be punished except for a distinct breach of law established before the ordinary courts of the country. The second meaning of the rule of law is that every man, whatever his rank or condition, is subject to the ordinary law and to the jurisdiction of the ordinary courts. The third meaning of the rule of law is that the basic general principles of the constitution, such as the right to personal liberty and to public meeting, have come about as "the result of judicial decisions determining the rights of private persons in particular cases brought before the courts," rather than by constitutional definitions of the rights of man.[2]

1. A. V. Dicey, *Introduction to the Study of the Law of the Constitution,* 10th ed. (London, 1959), p. 188.

2. Ibid., p. 195. The relationship of this proposition to the Canadian Bill of Rights and the Charter of Rights and Freedoms will be considered below.

THE LEGAL PROFESSION

The first thing to be noted about our courts is that they are at the apex of a legal profession consisting of what in the middle ages were sometimes called pleaders, that is, learned persons who argue cases before the courts. In some countries the judiciary is part of a career civil service, in the sense that trained lawyers either join the staff of a Ministry of Justice and work their way up by promotion to high judicial office or embark on the private practice of law. The anglo-American system is different in that judges are appointed from among lawyers in private practice.

While the legal profession is now a single body (or rather ten single bodies since each province has its own separate legal profession) it was originally divided, as it is today in the United Kingdom, into two distinct branches. The broad division between these branches is between the pleaders or advocates (commonly called barristers) who represent clients in court, and the solicitors who advise clients on such business and property matters as land titles, wills, estates, etc. The division between the two branches in England is furthered by the customary arrangement that a barrister does not deal directly with a client, but has to be briefed by a solicitor. These elaborate arrangements proved uneconomical in a pioneer country, so that in the Canadian common law provinces all members of the bar normally secure qualification also as solicitors and notaries. An exception to the general North American pattern is Quebec, where a separate body of notaries deals with questions of titles, wills, estates and similar matters. The rest of the legal business—representation in court, legal opinions, etc.—is carried on by advocates.

In each province the legal profession, as an organized corporate body, is given wide powers by the legislature governing the admission, training, discipline and even expulsion of its members. The traditional method of legal training used to be a form of apprenticeship, which still survives in rudimentary form although formal training in law is now mainly the work of law schools. While the law schools can teach law, they cannot license to practise, and the organized legal profession still retains tight control over admission to the profession and exerts a strong influennce on the curricula of the law schools. Only in the case of the sister professions of medicine and divinity does the hand of public regulation rest so lightly on a body of persons who live by the sale of their services. How can this autonomy of the profession be justified?

Part of the answer lies in the nature of the ancient professions. Their practice is concerned with the vital processes of the citizen—his life, health, liberty and welfare—and public policy has had to recognize that the citizen has neither the knowledge nor the ability to be able to suffer the results of *caveat emptor*. The only alternative to close regulation by the state has been to rely on the professional tradition and self-regulation of the profession.

The fact that judges are drawn from those engaged in the private practice of law is one of the more important characteristics of the Anglo-American legal system. It has tended to emphasize the deep-rooted individualism of judges and given them a natural scepticism in evaluating the claims of the state against the citizen. This is a bias of some significance in the atmosphere of constitutionalism. For it has often been argued that in countries where the judicial hierarchy is a professional career service, judges are inclined to accept the argument of administrative convenience more readily than the right of the citizen to assert his rights to the limit, and to be more concerned with the purely police problems of public order than with the need to protect the rights of the individual. By the time a judge is appointed to the Bench, however, his habits of mind are fixed, so that he continues to regard the state and public officials as equal claimants with the individual when their rights appear to be in conflict. This argument is easy to exaggerate, but it possesses enough truth so that it creates a judicial attitude which reinforces Dicey's emphasis on the proposition that officials are as much subject to the law as private persons.

JUDICIAL INDEPENDENCE

The independence of the judiciary has two aspects: the autonomy of the courts from the other branches of government, and the immunity of judges from the normal consequences of their acts. It was perhaps an accident of history that judges in the middle ages, while servants of the King, were drawn from the legal profession. The result of this was, as Professor Lederman has said, that "Henceforth judicial competence and integrity would depend in a large measure on the quality of the legal profession—upon its training, learning and experience."[3] In practice judges were able to develop the principles of private law with impartiality from the early days of the common law courts in England. Until the eighteenth century, the pressure which the King could bring on judges through the power of dismissal was considerable in public law questions which affected the power or position of the Crown. In the seventeenth century this issue came to a head during the long struggle between the Stuart kings and Parliament. The reform of the judiciary and of judicial tenure was one of the major questions in the revolution settlement. It was not one of the terms of the Bill of Rights (although such a provision was contained in the Scottish Claim of Right of 1689)[4] but the omission was rectified in the Act of Settlement of 1701. This act provided that "judges commissions be made *quamdiu se bene gesserint*, and their salaries ascertained and established; but upon the address of both houses of parliament it may be lawful to remove them." Thus the three basic requirements of judicial tenure were established: that judges be appointed during good behaviour; that their salaries be fixed so they could not be penalized indirectly; and that they could be removed for cause only on the request of both Houses of Parliament.

While these principles were firmly established in English law by the beginning of the eighteenth century, they were not carried over to the colonies. Since the other terms of the Act of Settlement determining the succession to the throne applied generally to the colonies, it is surprising that the establishment of judicial independence did not also apply.

The reason for the anomaly is that the origins of the early colonial constitutions lay in the royal prerogative. The constitutions themselves were based on royal charters or other instruments, and colonial governors operated within the context of royal instructions and other powers based on the prerogative. Only in the case of Quebec did the British Parliament provide for the constitution of a colony, and the Quebec Act is a special case based on the unusual circumstances of the colony. Thus it was natural for English law officers and ministers to act on the assumption that the Act of

3. W. R. Lederman, "The Independence of the Judiciary," *The Canadian Bar Review* XXXIV, No. 7 (August-September 1956), p. 779, on which much of this section is based. Quotations, unless otherwise acknowledged, are from this source.

4. D. O. Dykes, *Source Book of Constitutional History from 1660* (London, 1930), p. 7.

Settlement dealt only with English judges and was not intended to apply to the details of colonial government. Accordingly, the original power of the Crown to issue judicial commissions during pleasure was still exercised in the case of colonial judges. Furthermore, this power was jealously protected by the disallowance of colonial statutes which interfered with the royal prerogative.

Colonial governors, with the assent of their councils, could create local courts to administer the common law, though this power was also claimed by colonial assemblies. In some colonies the Governor, or the Governor-in-Council, acted as a court of exchequer, as a court of probate, and as a court of matrimonial causes. In a number of colonies the Governor-in-Council constituted the highest court of appeal in the colony, and sometimes acted as a court of chancery as well.[5]

Appeals in important cases lay from colonial courts to the Judicial Committee of the Privy Council in England. Colonial judges were usually appointed by the Governor-in-Council through the Governor's power to exercise the royal prerogative under his commission and instructions. A frequent exception was the Chief Justice of the colony, who was appointed and paid by the British government. In addition to the regular colonial courts, there were colonial courts of admiralty which came under the direct jurisdiction of the British government. The Lords of the Admiralty appointed the colonial Governor by commission as Vice-Admiral and as such empowered him to appoint deputies to act as judges and officers of the vice-admiralty courts. In addition to normal admiralty jurisdiction, these courts were empowered to enforce the Imperial Acts of Trade and such imperial revenue statutes as the Stamp Act. Subsequently, these were involved in the complex constitutional struggle which broke out in the American colonies—a struggle which concerned the same constitutional principles which had been at issue in England in the seventeenth century.

Since the need for local revenue required the exercise of taxing powers by local assemblies, it happened that in most cases colonial judges were dependent on the assemblies for their salaries. In the struggle to curb the royal prerogative, the colonial judges became involved as "either pawns or partisans of the governor" in his

5. Sir William Holdsworth, *A History of English Law,* Vol. 11, 3rd ed. (Boston, 1922), p. 59. The power of the Governor-in-Council in Prince Edward Island to act as a divorce court in the island has survived into modern times. See Frank MacKinnon, *The Government of Prince Edward Island* (Toronto, 1951), pp. 262-4.

struggle with the assemblies. The Governors and the British government tried to assert control through the power of appointment and dismissal, while the assemblies resorted to stopping judicial salaries or imposing conditions on the grant of them.

After the American Revolution, this constitutional problem continued to exist in the British North American colonies. However, the tenure of judges was perhaps more secure than appeared on the surface, for tenure at the pleasure of the King was not the same thing as tenure at the pleasure of the Governor-in-Council, and "the development of this distinction in post-revolutionary British North America brought a significant measure of secure tenure to colonial judges." Judges in the colonies could not be dismissed without "good and sufficient Cause," which must be signified "in the fullest and most distinct Manner" to the Secretary of State and the Lords of Trade. Furthermore, as a result of Burke's Act in 1782, colonial officers appointed under patent from the Crown could not be removed by a colonial Governor-in-Council except for persistent absence without leave from the colony, neglect of duty or other misbehaviour. An officer who had been suspended or removed was entitled to a fair hearing in the colony, and could appeal therefrom to the King-in-Council in London.

After the division of Canada and the granting of representative government to the two colonies in 1791, the struggle between the assembly and the Governor—in which the role of the judiciary became an issue—developed on much the same lines as it had in the older American colonies before the Revolution. In part this struggle was an attempt to separate the judges from the executive and legislative organs of government. In 1814, and again in 1817, there were attempts in the Lower Canadian Assembly to impeach judges. There were doubts about the power of colonial assemblies to impeach, and in fact these cases were ultimately decided by the Prince Regent-in-Council.

Gradually, in their efforts to separate judges from their close connection with the official oligarchy, colonial legislatures were driven in the direction of giving them security of tenure. By 1834 an important landmark was reached when the imperial authorities raised no objection to a statute of the Upper Canadian legislature which provided that the judges of the King's Bench of that province were to hold office during good behaviour, though they could be removed after a joint address of both Houses of the legislature, subject to appeal to the King-in-Council. Somewhat earlier, in 1830, the imperial authorities had made it plain that they would not appoint Upper Canadian judges to the Executive or Legislative Councils.

One of the recommendations of Lord Durham's Report which was implemented in both provinces was his proposal that "The independence of the judges should be secured, by giving them the same tenure of office and security of income as exist in England." A Canadian act of 1843 extended to the King's Bench in Lower Canada the same tenure as already existed in Upper Canada. An act of 1849 extended the same principle to the remaining superior courts in both parts of the province, and the process of exclusion of judges from the Legislative and executive Councils was completed. The removal of the judges from these bodies made it necessary to create courts of appeal in both provinces.

A similar development took place in the Maritime provinces. The Supreme Court of Nova Scotia was created in 1754, with a Chief Justice whose commission had been issued in England. An act of 1789 fixed the salaries of the judges, and provided that they could be removed either at the pleasure of His Majesty, or upon a joint address of the Council and the Assembly. By 1830 all of the judges, except the Chief Justice and the Master of the Rolls, had been barred from sitting on the Council. The latter was barred by local statute in 1836, and in 1837, as a result of the efforts of Joseph Howe, the Colonial office removed the Chief Justice from the Council. An act of 1848 made general provision for the security of tenure of judges, subject to removal on the resolution of both Houses, and subject to an appeal to the Queen-in-Council.

Thus before Confederation, and in part as a consequence of the struggle for responsible government, judges had acquired a security of tenure similar to that guaranteed to English judges in the Act of Settlement. It was a simple matter to carry over these provisions in their present form into sections 99 and 100 of the British North America Act which provide that judges of the superior courts shall hold office during good behaviour, but shall be removable by the Governor General on Address of the Senate and House of Commons; and that their salaries "shall be fixed and provided by the Parliament of Canada."

Judges are in one important respect different from all other public officials. Generally speaking, public officials are accountable for their acts both politically and legally. The fact that judges hold office during good behaviour means in effect that they cannot be removed except for misbehaviour, so that political accountability, which may lead to the removal of political officers, does not apply to them. In addition, judges enjoy a legal immunity, so that no action will lie against a judge for anything which he does or says in his judicial capacity in court. As long as he is acting within his jurisdiction he cannot be made legally accountable, even if he acts maliciously. This immunity also extends to the whole of the court proceedings, including the verdicts of juries, the words spoken by parties, witnesses and counsel. The reason for this extraordinary freedom is the public interest in judicial independence, which overrides the rights of individuals who may suffer from a corrupt or malicious judge. On balance, the public benefits from this system because it enables the judge to act without fear or favour. Since he cannot be harassed by the fear of legal actions being brought against him, he can act in an atmosphere completely free from pressure. His removal is so difficult to accomplish that he can afford to offend the most powerful in the land. Only in rare cases do judicial indiscretions provoke a Minister of Justice to launch an inquiry which would lead to the removal of a judge.[6]

This high and privileged position can only be justified by results. Essentially, it depends on the integrity of judges, on their sense of professional pride in high office and on the sense of competence that a great profession can engender. In every community there will be great concentrations of power, sometimes in the hands of private individuals, sometimes in the hands of governments. It is true that the relations of men, one with another, are governed by law. But law is a dead letter unless it can be applied. The method we have evolved for securing freedom under law is to entrust enormous and literally irresponsible power in the hands of the courts. We have found by experience that this system works, and it is improbable that any other system would work as well. As Professor Lederman succinctly puts it, "historical evidence suggests that judicial independence is a distinct governmental virtue of great importance worthy of cultivation in its own right."

THE STRUCTURE OF THE COURTS

In the Canadian federal system the division of executive and legislative power between the central and provincial units is fairly complete. There is no similar federalizing of the judicial branch. While

6. A recent example of this rare situation is the case of Mr. Justice Leo Landreville of Ontario, and these charges related essentially to his actions before his appointment to the Bench. See *Inquiry Re: The Honourable L. A. Landreville* (Ottawa, 1966).

jurisdiction over various parts of the judicial function is divided between the two levels of government, the effect has been to produce a single structure of courts. The provinces had long been in existence at the time of Confederation, and the obvious course was to maintain the provincial courts also. This was done by section 129 of the B.N.A. Act, but in other parts of the act, power and responsibility over the courts were allocated between the provinces and the new federal government. The main grant of power to the provinces is section 92 (14) which confers "exclusive" legislative power over "the Administration of Justice in the Province, including the Constitution, Maintenance, and Organization of Provincial Courts, both of Civil and of Criminal Jurisdiction, and including procedure in Civil Matters in those Courts."

At the same time very considerable powers were conferred on the federal authorities. In the first place, to balance the grant of exclusive power of civil procedure given to the provinces, Parliament was given exclusive power over criminal procedure by section 91 (27). Secondly, the appointment, tenure and salary of all judges of "the Superior, District, and County Courts" in each province was given to the central government. These powers were only limited in the following ways: judges of provincial courts must be appointed from the Bar of the province; life tenure and removal procedure were laid down in the act, and therefore changeable only by constitutional amendment. Thirdly, Parliament was given the power to constitute and maintain a "General Court of Appeal for Canada," and to establish any other courts "for the better Administration of the Laws of Canada."

While the provinces have exclusive jurisdiction to establish and maintain courts, they do not possess the power to appoint judges or pay their salaries in the case of superior, district or county courts. Thus, it is important to have co-operation between the provinces and the federal government. Any expansion or reorganization of courts to improve their efficiency requires the two governments to act in step. Mr. St. Laurent, when Minister of Justice, said:

> [The provinces] are the ones who determine what courts they will have and how many judges constitute the bench of each court. Of course we have something to say in the matter. We do not admit that they can provide for any number of judges, a number that would be out of all proportion to the number required to handle the judicial business. But we try to meet the desires of the provincial authorities in providing sufficient judges for the courts which they organize as being the ones required for their local needs.[7]

7. Canada, *House of Commons Debates,* Vol. IV, 1946, p. 3732. Sometimes it was

The provision in section 99 of the British North America Act for the appointment of judges of the provincial superior courts during good behaviour was regarded as a constitutional guarantee of life tenure for them. This limitation was not deemed to apply to the judges of federal courts created under section 101. Thus, when it became desirable to provide for the compulsory retirement of judges at the age of seventy-five, it was possible for Parliament to impose this provision on judges of the Supreme and Exchequer Courts, but not on the others. This anomaly persisted for a number of years.

The difficulty was overcome by a section of the Judge's Act which enabled the Governor-in-Council to withhold the salary of a judge who was found, on a report of the Minister of Justice, to be incapacitated through age or infirmity. Before such report was made a commission of inquiry, composed of one or more judges of federal or provincial courts, conducted a hearing at which the judge whose appointment was affected could be represented. It appears that this procedure, or a threat of its use, was sufficient in a number of cases to bring about the resignation of a judge who was alleged to be incapacitated.[8] Nevertheless, the procedure was not a nice one in the sense that it enabled the executive to terminate the tenure of a life appointee other than by the method provided by the constitution. Professor Lederman doubts whether it is "constitutionally permissible," since the stoppage of salary and pension rights, while not outright removal, is "removal by subterfuge." A constitutional amendment, passed in 1960, now fixes the same retiring age for judges of the provincial superior courts as for the federal judiciary.

Part of the security of a judge's tenure has always been related to his right to enjoy his full salary. Professor Lederman notes Blackstone's view that the judges' "full salaries are absolutely secured to them during the continuance of their commissions," and feels that the provision of section 100 of the B.N.A. Act which requires parliament to fix and provide the salaries means the same as the corresponding English provision, the effect of which is to protect

---

the provinces which were obstructive. In spite of numerous complaints from Bench, Bar and public, it was very difficult to bring about agreement between the government of Quebec and the federal government during the lifetime of Maurice Duplessis to increase the number of superior court judges in Quebec. A shortage of judges, combined in some areas with a shortage or inadequacy of courtrooms, created an atmosphere of delay and frustration in the courts. This did not, however, arouse the sympathy of Duplessis.

8. R. MacGregor Dawson, *The Government of Canada,* rev. ed. Norman Ward (Toronto, 1963), p. 439.

judges against diminution of their salaries during the force of their commissions. This does not mean that judges are not liable for income tax or any other tax which applies equally to all others. However, the government of Canada, when it imposed a 10 percent cut in civil service salaries in 1932, did not feel that it had the legal right to impose a similar cut on judicial salaries. Instead, it imposed a special income tax with a special impost for one year on judicial salaries. While this was not challenged at the time, it would appear doubtful if such a discriminatory tax was any more justified than the proposed salary cut. Thus, the roundabout method of forcing judges off the Bench by limiting their salary or pension rights is at least constitutionally undesirable. The uniform retiring age may remove the more objectionable features of this provision.

As was noted above, the division of power in the constitution between the provinces and the central government is not so complete as to preclude some overlapping of jurisdiction between the federal and provincial courts. However, taken together, the courts of Canada form a hierarchical structure.

Federal Courts

Under the general power to create courts, Parliament has set up two of major importance, both first provided for in 1875. The Supreme Court of Canada is a "general Court of Appeal for Canada." It now consists of a Chief Justice, who is the Chief Justice of Canada, and eight puisne judges. The court sits in Ottawa and exercises general appellate jurisdiction in civil and criminal cases. It is also required to render advisory opinions upon questions referred to it by the Governor-in-Council. The Court has the right to hear appeals from the provincial courts on any matter which it considers to be of legal importance, whether those courts have granted leave to appeal or not. Questions that may be appealed include matters either of law or of fact, or both.

Until 1949, appeals from the Canadian courts could be carried to the Judicial Committee of the Privy Council in England. In that year the Supreme Court Act was amended, ending such appeals, except for cases then before the courts. The Judicial Committee played a significant role in the evolution of the Canadian constitution, and the importance of its contribution will be considered below in the section dealing with the courts and the constitution.

As with all major organs of government, the Supreme Court is constituted, both *de facto* and *de jure*, on representative principles. The Supreme Court Act provides that at least three of the judges shall be appointed from the Bar of the province of Quebec. This is a minimal and necessary provision, but it is reinforced by a customary recognition of other sectional and minority groups in the country. One of the three judges from Quebec is normally an English-speaking Protestant, the two others from that province are French-speaking Catholics. Two or three judges are normally drawn from Ontario, at least two from the Prairie provinces and British Columbia, and at least one from the Atlantic provinces. Just as the English-speaking Protestants of Quebec are represented, so also are the English-speaking Catholics from outside Quebec.

The full Court does not hear appeals, unless it considers them to be of such importance that they should be dealt with in this way. A large number of appeals are heard by smaller panels, made up of an uneven number of judges to ensure a majority decision. In the case of appeals in civil matters from the Quebec courts, for example, it is usual for all but the most important cases to be heard by a panel of five judges, three of them from Quebec so that a majority of the judges are familiar with the nuances of the Quebec codes. All applications for leave to appeal, except for cases involving the death penalty, must be heard by a panel of three judges.

Until a recent and important change in the law, the Supreme Court as the ultimate custodian of the law was severely hampered in its work by a serious overload of cases which led to long delays and a less than optimum use of Court time. This problem was remedied by legislation introduced and passed late in 1974. Three matters were dealt with, the first two of which were relatively minor. The provision that judges and the Registrar and Deputy Registrar of the Court should live in Ottawa was amended to provide that they must live either within the National Capital Region or within twenty-five miles thereof. The second provided that, in the case of awards made by the Supreme Court in appeals where no award of money is made, interest will run from the time of the original application to the lower courts.

The third change was the most substantial. It restricts appeals to cases in which leave has been granted. This applies to civil cases only and not to either criminal cases or reference cases. This decision was reached after the Minister of Justice (then Mr. John Turner) requested the Canadian Bar Association in 1972 to study the matter of case overload and make recommendations. The Association set up a strong committee with Professor W. R. Lederman as research director. In essence, the legislation adopted the committee's recommendation.

Various solutions were considered, such as enlarging the Court, and a comparative study of the United States Supreme Court and the House of Lords was undertaken. The identifiable cause of the overload was the burden of cases which the Court was bound by law to hear. This meant that about two years elapsed from notice of appeal to the date of hearing and about six months from the date of hearing until judgment was rendered. Eighty percent of the cases were appeals as of right under S. 36 of the Supreme Court Act, which consist of civil cases where the amount in issue exceeds ten thousand dollars, as well as cases of habeas corpus and mandamus. The committee noted that this provision enabled a well-funded litigant to "terrorize" (in Lord Atkin's words) an opponent with the threat of a further appeal. These cases had already been heard in the lower courts and in the provincial courts of appeal so that the likelihood of a further appeal succeeding was slight. What should be done? The size of the Court could be increased, the amount could be raised to some larger sum, or the rule governing appeals to the Supreme Court of the United States by which appeals could only be heard by leave could be adopted. The last course was adopted and the relevant clause (now section 41 (1)) is "that [in the opinion of the Court]. . . any question involved therein is, by reason of its public importance or the importance of any issue of law or any issue of mixed law and fact involved in such question, one that ought to be decided by the Supreme Court or is, for any other reason, of such a nature or significance as to warrant decision by it, and leave to appeal from such judgment is accordingly granted by the Supreme Court."

Before submitting the report, the Canadian Bar Association had overruled its committee and recommended that this new provision not apply to cases inscribed and pending rather than forthwith on the ground that it would have retroactive effect. However, the government and Parliament rejected this and provided that the new provision come into force on proclamation. This was done because the alternative would delay the application of the reform for as much as five years, as had been the case with the abolition of appeals to the Privy Council in 1949.

The second major court created in 1875 was the Exchequer Court, which was gradually increased in size from one in 1887 to eight, including a President. Its jurisdiction covered suits against the Crown in the right of Canada, as well as suits in relation to patents and copyright, and admiralty law. In 1971, the Exchequer Court was abolished and replaced by a new court with a substantially larger jurisdiction, called the Federal Court of Canada.

The Federal Court operates in two divisions, a Trial Division presided over by an Associate Chief Justice and an Appeal Division presided over by the Chief Justice of the Court. Both divisions may sit throughout Canada. The Appeal Division, which acts as a Federal Court of Appeal, consists of four judges, including the Chief Justice, while the remaining judges, up to eight in number, comprise the Trial Division. At least four of the judges must be appointed from the Bar or Bench of Quebec. Judges already appointed are governed by the then existing retiring age of seventy-five, but newly appointed judges to the Court retire at the age of seventy.

In the past, appeals from federal boards and agencies lay to the Supreme Court. Their transfer to the Federal Court freed the Supreme Court to devote itself to its proper role of an appeal court of last resort. The Federal Court now has exclusive jurisdiction to review all decisions and orders of a judicial or quasi-judicial nature rendered by federal boards or other tribunals on questions of error in law, excess of jurisdiction, or failure to apply the principles of natural justice. Previously, the superintending jurisdiction over such agencies lay with the various provincial courts by means of the ancient prerogative writs of prohibition, *certiorari*, and *mandamus*. The intent of this reform was both to speed up such proceedings, and to encourage—through the use of a single court—a more coherent body of administrative law.

The jurisdiction of the Trial Division includes a concurrent jurisdiction with provincial superior courts over matters within Parliament's field of legislative competence, such as bills of exchange and promissory notes, aeronautics, and works and undertakings of an interprovincial character. The Court also has jurisdiction over matters outside the competence of provincial courts, which may well be important in relation to the expansion of Canadian jurisdiction in the North and off the coast of Canada.

The Federal Court Act repealed the Admiralty Act, transferring this jurisdiction to the Trial Division of the Federal Court. Also repealed was the Petition of Right Act, and a new and simplified procedure for bringing suits against the Crown was introduced, which put the Crown on a more equal footing with other litigants. The Act further empowered the Court to determine, by examining the documents in question, whether a refusal to produce them in court on the claim of crown privilege by the executive is justified. By having a court determine whether or not to order disclosure has the effect of strengthening the rights of individuals involved in litigation with government agencies. The Federal Court's power to act in this way does not extend to documents affecting national security, international relations, or federal-provincial relations, where a simple declaration by a minister will prevent disclosure. The removal, or at least narrowing, of the minister's power in such matters is generally thought to be a necessary part of effective legislation to provide for freedom of information.

There are also several special courts or boards which are designated by statute as courts of record. The Court Martial Appeal Court, established in 1959, consists of not less than four judges of a superior court of criminal jurisdiction appointed by the Governor-in-Council. This court, as its title implies, is the court of appeal from courts martial. The Tax Review Board (formerly the Tax Appeal Board) is made up of qualified lawyers and is empowered to hear appeals instituted by taxpayers from assessments made under the Income Tax Act. Certain other administrative agencies exercise some judicial powers and have also been designated as courts of record, such as the Tariff Board and the Canadian Transport Commission.

Finally, there are the territorial courts of the Yukon Territory and the Northwest Territories, each of which at present has one judge. They exercise both civil and criminal jurisdiction, as well as appellate jurisdiction over certain decisions of justices of the peace and police magistrates. The judges of these courts hold office during good behaviour and cease to hold office at the age of seventy-five years. Unlike judges of the Supreme Court of Canada and the Federal Court, their removal for cause does not need to be initiated by a joint Address of both Houses of Parliament. In 1960, provision was made for a territorial court of appeal consisting of a Chief Justice and justices of appeal of Alberta and judges of the two territorial courts.[9]

Provincial Courts

Provincial courts may be divided into three classes, depending on the method of appointment and tenure of their judges. In the first class are judges of the provincial superior courts whose tenure is

9. For the federal courts see *Organization of the Government of Canada* (Ottawa, 1962), pp. 47-57; and *Canada Year Book,* 1961, pp. 75-7.

defined in section 99 of the British North America Act, as amended in 1960. They are appointed by the federal government and hold office during good behaviour until they reach the age of seventy-five. They cannot be removed except on a joint Address of both Houses of Parliament. The nomination of provincial Chief Justices, it will be recalled, is one of the "prerogatives" of the Prime Minister, while that of other provincial judges is at the insistence of the Minister of Justice. The second class of provincial courts is the district or county courts, the tenure of whose judges differs from that of superior court judges in the fact that they may be removed for cause by the Governor-in-Council without the necessity of a parliamentary resolution. However, the papers relating to the dismissal must be tabled in Parliament. The third class is made up of various provincial inferior courts, whose members are usually appointed during good behaviour (sometimes for a probationary period) by the Lieutenant-Governor-in-Council.

The provincial superior courts are variously named, but they all have two principal parts: a court of appeal made up of several judges sitting together, and courts of original jurisdiction in which a single judge will sit, sometimes with a jury, as in criminal cases and libel cases. In Ontario, for example, the Supreme Court of Ontario embraces all superior court judges and has two divisions, the Court of Appeal for Ontario, and the High Court of Justice. The Court of Appeal, presided over by the Chief Justice of Ontario, has appellate jurisdiction in both civil and criminal cases from the High Court. It also may hear appeals from decisions of individual judges of the Supreme Court, and from inferior courts such as county courts. It may sit in two or more divisions of three or more judges (the number of judges must be uneven to facilitate decision since each judge renders his own decision and the majority will prevail).

The High Court is a court of original jurisdiction in both civil and criminal cases, and all cases of substance are likely to be heard there. The only matters outside its jurisdiction are certain admiralty questions and other matters which are the exclusive jurisdiction of the Federal Court. Both the High Court and the Court of Appeal are governed in part by federal and in part by provincial law. The provincial legislature has exclusive jurisdiction over the constitution, organization and maintenance of the courts, as well as over procedure in civil causes. Parliament not only provides the salaries of the judges, but also has exclusive jurisdiction in criminal law and procedure. Most legislation dealing with property and civil rights is provincial in character, so that most of the civil causes before the courts will be based on provincial legislation. However, Parliament has exclusive jurisdiction over some aspects of property and civil rights under the enumerated heads of section 91 of the British North America Act in such matters as, for example, bills of exchange and bankruptcy.

Following an English legal reform of the nineteenth century most Canadian provinces also established what were called County or District Courts. The original purpose of these courts was to provide a less expensive system of courts for minor causes. As Dicey put it, "Every man, for example, has a right to be paid the debts owing to him, but until the creation of the County Courts it was often difficult, if not impossible, for any poor man to obtain payment of even an admitted debt."[10] The high cost of litigation in the superior courts is a necessary part of the process for deciding questions which involve very substantial property interests, but a less expensive system is necessary to extend equal rights to the poor. In Ontario, for example, the County Courts have jurisdiction in civil suits of less than five hundred dollars, and if the parties agree, cases involving larger amounts may be decided in County Court. A number of matters under a variety of federal and provincial statutes may also be dealt with in County Court. In minor criminal cases a County Court judge may either sit with a jury as a Court of General Sessions, or may sit without a jury acting as a Criminal Court of summary jurisdiction.

All provinces have created a variety of lesser courts. In Ontario there are surrogate courts which deal with deceased persons' estates. Judges of these courts may be appointed by the Lieutenant-Governor-in-Council, holding office during good behaviour. The normal practice is to appoint a County Court judge for this purpose and to pay him an additional stipend. Similarly, divisional courts, which are civil courts with jurisdiction over minor personal actions, are usually staffed by County Court judges who are paid an additional stipend for the work.

Lastly there is a large class of what were formerly called magistrates' courts. The name has now been generally changed to provincial courts because the magistrates were thought to be too close to the police. In the past many of these courts were staffed by laymen, especially in less populated areas. These courts hear petty offences, conduct preliminary hearings, issue warrants and the like. Nowadays such courts are staffed by qualified lawyers. In Ontario they are appointed by the Lieutenant-Governor-in-Council and must retire at

10. A. V. Dicey, *Law and Opinion in England During the Nineteenth Century.* 2nd ed. (London, 1914) p. 175n.

the age of seventy. For the first two years they hold office at pleasure; thereafter they can only be removed for cause after an enquiry at which they may be legally represented. Furthermore, all the relevant documents in the event of removal must be tabled in the Legislative Assembly within the first fifteen days of the next session.

For various reasons, no doubt in part with the increased competence and growing jurisdiction of the provincial courts, a number of provinces have now amalgamated their County Courts with their Superior Courts. An amendment to the Judge's Act in 1979 provided for the amalgamation of the District Courts of Alberta and Saskatchewan and the Country Courts of New Brunswick with their respective Courts of Queen's Bench. Apparently, Prince Edward Island had already done that at an earlier date, and a Law Reform Commission Report in Ontario in 1973 had made the same recommendation, but strong resistance from the High Court Judges had prevented similar action in that province.

The Quebec courts, while they conform to the general pattern, are different in some important particulars, partly as a result of the different system of civil law which prevailed in the province. Until recently there were two separate "superior" courts in Quebec, the Court of Queen's Bench and the Superior Court. The Court of Queen's Bench functioned both as a court of appeal and as a court of original jurisdiction in criminal matters. Some of its judges were designated to preside in the cities of Montreal and Quebec as assize courts in criminal matters. Outside of these two cities, criminal matters were heard by a Superior Court judge for the district, who held a commission to sit there in assize court. The Superior Court was a court of exclusively civil jurisdiction for matters arising out of the Civil Code as well as for such federal statutes as the Bankruptcy Act. This had led to a great deal of unnecessary confusion since prerogative writs may be either civil or criminal according to the nature of the original proceedings to which they relate. In many cases, a litigant had to make a difficult decision about the nature of his application and the difficulty was more irritating because it might be the same judge involved—exercising different jurisdictions—but the action would fail if the wrong choice was made.

A major change in the system was made by legislation introduced late in 1974. The Court of Queen's Bench was abolished and the Superior Court was given jurisdiction in both civil and criminal cases. At the same time a Court of Appeal was created. This court sits in Quebec City under the Chief Justice and in Montreal under an Associate Chief Justice. Quebec now conforms much more closely to the general Canadian pattern.

Quebec has never had county or district courts, but Provincial Courts, staffed by judges appointed by the provincial government, have a comparable jurisdiction. Civil suits involving less than a thousand dollars must be brought in this court rather than in the Superior Court. The Provincial Court has also recently introduced a Small Claims Court at which litigants appear without counsel, thus considerably reducing the cost of litigation over minor claims. There are also four social welfare courts in the districts of Montreal, Quebec, Trois Rivieres, and St. Francis. There are nine judges in each social welfare court, including a chief judge. These courts deal with juvenile delinquency, children's welfare, and similar matters. Then there is the Court of Sessions of the Peace, which is primarily a court for preliminary and summary criminal proceedings, but it has a number of special jurisdictions as well. Lastly there are courts of summary jurisdiction, such as recorder's courts, which are set up by city and town councils, staffed by magistrates appointed by the provincial government.

JUSTICE AND THE LEGAL SYSTEM

The judicial process is a social mechanism both complex and expensive. The courts have developed a highly sophisticated means of getting at the truth, of reducing the general phraseology of the law to fit a thousand individual circumstances, and of defining and disentangling the complex web of rights which may attach itself to a single piece of property. The courts employ a vocabulary and a logic of their own and a method of handling evidence which, though highly artificial, is heavily weighted with safeguards for the unwary. But for this vast mechanism to work properly a dialectic between the skilled advocates of the parties at issue is required. To them, and to the community, it is very expensive in both time and money. There can, however, be no doubt that as a social expenditure it is well worth while since the result is both sophisticated and just.

The system has, however, one disadvantage. It would break down at once if it were compelled to deal with the vast majority of cases where the liberty or property of the citizen is in jeopardy. In most cases the value of the property at issue is too small, or the alleged offence too minor for the question to be brought before the full majesty of the major courts. For these cases something much cheaper and quicker will have to serve. The landlady or the laundress who wishes to collect a small debt will be advised to resort to a minor and local court, and the labourer facing a charge of assault will prefer to invoke a speedy trial before a magistrate rather than either raise bail or languish in jail until his case can be heard before one of Her Majesty's judges.

In the nature of things, the kind and quality of justice meted out by inferior courts will be inferior. There is an inescapable hypocrisy in any system of law which prices most people out of the market for the best-quality justice. The real measure of the justice of the system rests in considerable part on the quality of the inferior courts. Are the magistrates in these courts, who do not enjoy the prestige and security of tenure of Superior Court judges, both impartial and competent? Are there enough of them, or is their work obstructed by overcrowding and delay? Do provisions for legal aid for the poor and the welfare and rehabilitation agencies make it possible for the poor to have even a minimum of justice and protection of the law? It is doubtful if the answers to any of these questions would provide comfort to a Canadian of tender conscience.

One of the answers to these social problems has been the gradual spread of collective benefits to the poor and the provision by administrative agencies of their own machinery for settling claims. Thus the hypothetical right of the workman injured on the job to collect damages from his employer through expensive and hazardous litigation has been systematically replaced by a system of worker compensation administered by a board. The rights of a person under unemployment insurance are determined not by individual resort to the courts, but by a system of administrative tribunals internal to the unemployment insurance commission. Gradually, in adjudicating the rights of the public to social benefits, the courts have been superseded by administrative tribunals.

This has seemed objectionable to legal purists to whom resort to the courts, however out of the question in practice, is the ultimate right of the citizen and should not be taken away. The growth of administrative tribunals free from effective control by the courts has seemed an ominous development in a constitutional system founded on the independence of the judicial process from the executive. These complaints cannot be dismissed lightly. But the answer lies not in abolishing the administrative tribunal which settles claims quickly and without expense, but in ensuring that the standards and procedures of these tribunals meet the essential tests of a fair hearing, and that the courts are still able to intervene where there has been excess of jurisdiction, abuse of power or essential error in procedure.

One of the curious anomalies of our judicial system is that for all the security of tenure which surrounds judicial appointments, the method by which judges and lesser magistrates are appointed would seem to undermine the very possibility of independence—at least from the government of the day. For such appointments are made by ministers, and there can be little doubt that judicial appointments, like Crown appointments, are frequently patronage appointments. Political parties not only appoint from among their own, but judicial appointments are a useful way of rewarding former Cabinet ministers. Both the provincial and the federal courts are studded with former ministers and others whose political services no doubt strengthened the claim of the appointee.

But what are the alternatives? The election of judges in the United States is generally recognized to have been one of the least successful devices of democratization, for election at once makes the choice more highly political and the appointee less independent than before. Appointment by government is at least a considered choice by experienced and responsible persons to know that on them might ultimately rest responsibility for removal. However, while it can be said that the Canadian system of appointing judges is surprisingly satisfactory, it probably accounts for both the major weaknesses as well as the major strengths of the Canadian judiciary.

The major weakness is evident to all who must at some time read any considerable number of high court judgments. Most judges have not been trained as legal scholars; they seem to lack both the art of subtle legal reasoning and the scholarly apparatus which attained its greatest flowering in such outstanding American jurists as Oliver Wendell Holmes, Jr. They lack, in short, a real theoretical grasp of the law and the literary and forensic skill to handle it. On the other hand, Canadian judges, as experienced and tough-minded men of affairs, prefer practical workability to legal subtlety. In a federal country where even questions of private law have overtones of public policy, the experience of a significant number of judges in the problems of statecraft is bound to influence the creation of law by the courts.

Judges are drawn from the legal profession itself, and will reflect the prevailing values and standards of that profession. It is significant that the profession has shown sufficient interest in legal appointments to make it likely that the trend in Canada will be towards the British system whereby judges—though appointed by the government—are in effect pre-selected by the profession, so that the majority of appointments to the Bench are effectively outside politics. The present practice in Canada is for the Minister of Justice to send a short list of names of possible appointees to a judicial vacancy to the Canadian Bar Association. This list is returned to the minister with the candidates divided into three categories: well qualified, qualified or not qualified. The final decision is made from the candidates in the first two groups, and political affiliation is not a deciding factor.

THE ADMINISTRATION OF JUSTICE

While the judges who sit in Canadian courts are appointed by the federal government and Parliament has exclusive jurisdiction to enact criminal law, the British North America Act, section 92 (14), gives to the province the exclusive jurisdiction over the administration of justice in the province. This means that a large part of the police power of the community is vested in provincial law officers, and constitutional responsibility for police functions and law and order fall mainly on provincial and local authorities.

In the provinces, the maintenance of law and order fell in the beginning on local police and peace officers, while the prosecution in the courts of persons accused of offences under the criminal law fell to the Attorney General of the province.

The growing complexity of crime in big cities in the twentieth century and the need for larger and better integrated police organization for the prevention and detection of crime made it necessary to create police agencies which were not hampered by the limited size and often limited resources of local police forces. In addition to this general and universal problem, the need to provide police and traffic control over highways and to enforce provincial liquor laws led to the creation of provincial police forces in most of the provinces (after the end of the First World War all provinces except Quebec introduced prohibition with its attendant problems of law enforcement). The difficulty of maintaining these provincial forces at a high standard of efficiency led, in the decade following the Depression, to the absorption of most of these provincial forces into the Royal Canadian Mounted Police. Now only Quebec and Ontario maintain separate provincial police forces.[11]

11. For a discussion of the reorganization measures taken to restore the Quebec Provincial Police to a proper standard of efficiency and impartiality after the defeat of the Union Nationale régime in 1960, see J. P. Dessureau, "Reorganization Problems and Selection of Personnel: Quebec Provincial Police," *Canadian Public Administration* V, No. 2 (June 1962), pp. 180 ff.

The R.C.M.P. had its origin in the North West Mounted Police, formed in 1873 to deal with public order in the territories. Subsequently, the force was amalgamated with other federal police agencies and assumed a number of special functions throughout Canada involving the investigation of matters under federal jurisdiction. The principal of these are customs and excise, Indian affairs, narcotics, merchant marine, security against subversive organizations and the protection of government property.

In addition to these matters the force also carries out police duties under contract with the provinces. Under a provision of the Mounted Police Act the minister may, with the approval of the Governor-in-Council, enter into an agreement with the government of a province for the use of the force to aid in the administration of justice and the enforcement of the laws of the province.[12] Eight provinces now have such agreements, under which the Royal Canadian Mounted Police carry out duties in the province which would otherwise be undertaken by provincial forces.[13] The force is thus placed in the difficult position of serving two masters, and while it has done this with commendable efficiency within its resources, there have been a few cases where this conflict of authority over the force has created serious difficulties with the provinces, notably in the role of the force during the strike in the Newfoundland forests in 1958 and at the time of the public disorder in certain Doukhobor communities in British Columbia in 1962.

It could be argued that by contracting out police functions to the R.C.M.P. a province is sacrificing a certain degree of control over its constitutional responsibilities. However, in the few cases where differences have come to light, there does not seem to have been intentional or undue influence on provincial authorities. On the other hand there are great advantages of efficiency and economy in these arrangements. In addition to "provincial police" functions in the eight provinces, the force also may carry out local police duties in municipalities that wish to contract for them. It is possible that these arrangements, however economical, may have gone too far. They not only impose a great strain on the resources of the force, but place too much responsibility for law and order in a single federal agency. It is likely today that all but the smaller provinces could

12. Until this duty was transferred to the Solicitor General by the Government Organization Act of 1967, the minister in charge of the R.C.M.P. was the Minister of Justice.

13. See J. R. Lemieux, "Esquisse de la Gendarmerie Royale du Canada," *Canadian Public Administration* V, No. 2 (June 1962), p. 186.

support provincial forces large enough to operate at a high level of efficiency.

Some of the most important duties of the force involve responsibilities which are not closely related to police work. Such is the work of the Security Service of the force, which is responsible for internal intelligence and security. Secret service work of various sorts has a long history in Canada, beginning before Confederation when the province of Canada employed secret agents to gather intelligence on Fenian activities in both Canada and the United States. The Dominion Police, which dates from 1868, was mainly for the purpose of protecting public buildings, but it maintained a small detective force against the Fenians. The North West Mounted Police used secret agents during both the Northwest Rebellion and the Yukon Gold Rush, when there were fears of American intrusion. During the First World War and the inter-war period, Mounted Police agents infiltrated "anarchist" and communist organizations. During the Second World War, security activity of the force was greatly expanded and extended to nazi and fascist organizations. In 1946 this activity was entrusted to what was then called the Special Branch, which in 1956 became the Security and Intelligence Branch of the force. By that time the principal activities of the Branch had become security screening for the public service, immigration, and security intelligence about "subversive" organizations.

One of the major problems associated with the security operations of the force is that ministerial responsibility for its work is not clearly defined. In general the responsible minister for the R.C.M.P. since 1967 has been the Solicitor-General for Canada, but it appears that in its role as a security service the R.C.M.P. is supervised by the Cabinet committee on security and intelligence, which is chaired by the Prime Minister. Because of the nature of intelligence work, the activities of the security service are clothed in a heavy veil of secrecy. It has operated on the "need to know" principle, which has apparently extended to the exclusion of ministers and their civil service advisers from information which might prove embarrassing.

Security work is not so much a matter of enforcing the law as of anticipating breaches of the law and thus becomes largely surveillance and clandestine activity. Sometimes the clandestine activity itself may involve breaches of the law by the security service. General criticism of some of the activities of the service has led to exhaustive enquiries by two royal commissions in recent years. The first of these was the Mackenzie Commission which recommended in 1969 that security work should be taken away from the R.C.M.P. and placed in the hands of a separate security service. The principal argument in favour of this change was the highly specialized nature of security and intelligence work which, in the Commission's view, should not be carried out by persons primarily trained for police duties. On the one hand, much of the work does not require many of the skills of a highly trained police force, and on the other, such a force is lacking in sufficient understanding of the nature of political ideas and international relations to distinguish what its targets should be. One consequence of this incomprehension was a good deal of futile and ill-informed sleuthing on university campuses.

The recommendation of the Mackenzie Commission for a separate civilian security and intelligence organization was not accepted at the time by the government, which however did appoint an experienced foreign service officer as the civilian director of the service. However, further criticism, arising mainly out of the activities of the security authorities during and after the F.L.Q. crisis in Quebec, led to the appointment of another Commission, chaired by Mr. Justice David McDonald, in 1977. After exhaustive enquiry, that Commission finally reported in 1981.[14]

The Commission found that the Security Service, in its enthusiastic, yet ill-conceived attempts, to counter subversion, had engaged itself in a number of dubious activities which included barn-burning and dynamite theft, surreptitious entry, and even sometimes mail-opening and access to confidential records in other government departments. Although some of these activities, such as the use of falsely registered vehicles and registering in hotels under false identities, might appear to be necessary expedients, they happen to be contrary to provincial or federal law. While the police and the responsible minister have frequently argued that such activities are justifiable in law in certain circumstances so that there is nothing to be alarmed about, the McDonald Commission did not agree, though it did suggest that some federal and provincial laws be amended to make it possible for the security authorities to take necessary measures but remain within the law. The Commission was equally certain that most of the security operations were unsuited to the training and organization of the R.C.M.P., and should be entrusted to a more appropriately trained and recruited civilian agency. This the government has begun to implement.

14. *Report of the Royal Commission on Security* (Ottawa, 1969) pp. 18-24; *Second Report of the Commission of Enquiry Concerning Certain Activities of the Royal Canadian Mounted Police* (Ottawa, 1981); see also Richard French and Andre Belliveau, *The RCMP and the Management of National Security.* Institute for Research on Public Policy (Montreal, 1979).

It should be noted that the Security Service—in careful observance of the "need to know" principle—seems to have shielded ministers and presumably their senior officials in the Privy Council Office and the Department of the Solicitor-General from all knowledge of these awkward episodes. This raises the central problem of how to create and sustain effective ministerial control of such operations. It may be the new civilian agency will be more willing to keep ministers informed, although this is less certain as long as control remains diffused in a Cabinet committee rather than subject to the undivided attention of a single minister. Nor can ministers—clothed in official secrecy—be completely trusted unless there is some kind of parliamentary scrutiny. One of the problems here is that the security authorities are not likely to trust the discretion of Members of Parliament, who may be tempted, for political or other reasons, to misuse highly secret information made available to them. There are thus problems with a parliamentary committee of scrutiny. Not least of these is that under present parliamentary practice the wholesale substitution of members on the committee will mean that a very large number of members would be involved. It seems likely that the service would not consent to such scrutiny unless they were satisfied that all potential members were free of the suspicion of being security risks. The distasteful prospect of full security screening of Members of Parliament is not one that readily commends itself either to Members or to the public.

The McDonald Commission sought to get around this difficulty by proposing both an Advisory Council on Security and Intelligence of three members, whose appointment should be confirmed by resolution of both Houses, and a Joint Committee of both Houses to review the activities of intelligence agencies. To disarm the fears of the security authorities this should be a small committee of ten, chaired by a member of the opposition, and composed of members selected by the party leaders and expected to serve on the committee for the duration of a Parliament.

LIBERTY AND AUTHORITY

"The law guards the liberties of each by limiting the liberty of all."[15] These words occur in the conclusion of a lecture in a series, "Law and Order in Canadian Democracy," prepared for the Royal Cana-

15. *Law and Order in Canadian Democracy* (Ottawa, 1949), p. 48.

dian Mounted Police. The lectures emphasize, quite properly, that individual freedoms must be reconciled with one another, and that there must be restraints in order to maximize freedom. However, not all freedoms are equally important. Some indeed are so important that any limitation of them at all is a matter of grave concern because they go to the heart of a free constitutional system. An obvious example is freedom from arbitrary detention, which is generally known as the habeas corpus rule. This means that no man can be deprived of his liberty unless he has been charged with a specific offence against the law. The days when this constitutional guarantee was a useful protection against authorities who imprisoned those whom they regarded as politically dangerous on frivolous or trumped-up charges have now gone. It is now understood, quite rightly, to be a restraint on the zeal of the police in arresting troublesome people on suspicion of crime and holding them until enough evidence can be turned up to justify a charge. In many countries there are constitutional provisions to enable the authorities to place persons suspected of subversive or revolutionary designs in preventive detention lest they should endanger the safety of the state by being at liberty. Such powers have in fact been used in wartime by the government of Canada but they have been granted with reluctance and distaste and promptly withdrawn in peace time.

How far are these basic rights and liberties safeguarded in the constitution? How far are they defined, or how far is their definition left vague until some urgent problem brings them to the fore? Are there, under our federal constitution, basic group rights which inhere in minorities, and what happens if the collective rights of minorities are in conflict with the basic rights of individuals?

The British North America Act does not set forth a declaration of human rights which are deemed to be above the ordinary law of the land. In Professor Scott's words, "It has been traditionally said among us that we were like the British in this as in so many other ways, and that any declaration of rights was incompatible with our kind of constitution. Does not the preamble of the B.N.A. Act say that we are to have a constitution similar in principle to that of Great Britain? And does not this mean that we leave the protection of our freedoms to the ordinary courts of law?"[16] In practice, the principles of British liberty "with Magna Carta in the background, and Dicey's rule of law in the foreground" seem to have left us in the enjoyment of liberties which compare respectably to other constitutions which

16. F. R. Scott, *Civil Liberties and Canadian Federalism* (Toronto, 1959), p. 12.

do have safeguarded liberties, even including that of the United States. But Professor Scott has some misgiving about the effectiveness of the protection of our liberties without a fuller definition of them in the constitution. He notes that the British system depends on three things of which we cannot be wholly certain in Canada: "parliamentary restraint in legislation, bureaucratic restraint in administration, and a strong and lively tradition of personal freedom among citizens generally."[17] One of the difficulties is that we must expect these standards from eleven legislatures and eleven administrations and not just one. The growing power and responsibility of the state increase the strain on the self-restraint of governments, and it is perhaps open to doubt whether our society is old enough and homogeneous enough to have developed a coherent spirit of liberty which will be an effective check on arbitrary government. "We have in Canada a very mixed population, drawn from different European and Asiatic societies, which has not yet been brought to a common understanding of the processes of parliamentary democracy by centuries of shared struggle and lively history."[18]

Scott notes that in fact our constitutional history is studded with examples of the entrenchment of particular rights or the specific provision for them in a form which is now difficult to interfere with by ordinary legislation. To begin with, the right to practise the Roman Catholic religion, which was not freely permitted under the law of England at the time, was guaranteed in Nova Scotia by the Treaty of Utrecht in 1713. The Quebec Act of 1774 entrenched the religious liberties of Roman Catholics in Quebec, and by modifying the oath of allegiance, enabled Catholics to exercise political and civil rights with good conscience; it also restored French civil law in matters of property and civil rights in the province. In 1785 habeas corpus was introduced into the province. All of these can safely be regarded as entrenched constitutional principles. The Freedom of Worship Act of the Province of Canada, passed in 1851, laid down that "the free exercise and enjoyment of religious profession and worship, without discrimination or preference" was extended to all of Her Majesty's subjects in the province. Since this act was never repealed, and the subject matter with which it deals is now within the exclusive jurisdiction of the Parliament of Canada, it is Professor Scott's view that it cannot be repealed or amended by the legislatures of Ontario or Quebec.

17. Ibid., p. 13.

18. Ibid., p. 14.

The history of the constitutional entrenchment of the two official languages is, curiously, much shorter than the history of the protection of freedom of worship. French was not specifically protected in either the Treaty of Paris or the Quebec Act, though of course French was, in practice, recognized equally with English from the beginning. The Act of Union of 1840, reflecting the hope expressed by Lord Durham that assimilation would be good for French Canadians as well as the feeling engendered by the Rebellion of 1837, prohibited the publication of the laws in French. In 1848 the act was amended, restoring French as an official language and the intent of this was extended in section 133 of the British North America Act. The protection accorded the French language in the B.N.A. Act went only so far as to guarantee its use in the federal Parliament and the federal courts. The transfer of the amending power over certain parts of the constitution to the Parliament of Canada in 1949 entrenched the guarantee of language rights to the extent that they then existed.

A considerable extension of the constitutional guarantees of rights to the use of the French language was proposed by the Royal Commission on Bilingualism and Biculturalism in 1967 and subsequently put forward by the federal government as part of an enlarged Bill of Rights at the 1969 constitutional conference.[19] These proposals would have had the effect of making French and English the official languages of Canada, and extended the same principle to the provinces of New Brunswick, Ontario and Quebec. The recommendations of the B. and B. Commission would also have applied the same principle to other provinces where the linguistic minority (English or French) reached ten percent of the population, and the recommended "bilingual districts" wherever the population of an appropriate administrative unit had a substantial number of persons of the minority language. While no constitutional change resulted at that time from these proposals, the federal government carried through Parliament in 1969 an Official Languages Act which sought to implement these objectives insofar as they lay within federal jurisdiction. The act conferred official status on the two languages, so that they are equally recognized not only in Parliament and the courts, but also in all administrative agencies. An official Languages Commissioner was created to report to Parliament on the performance of these agencies.

The British North America Act did not, with the exception of

19. *Report,* Book I (Ottawa, 1967), pp. 134-85. Pierre Elliott Trudeau, *The Constitution and the People of Canada* (Ottawa, 1969), pp. 54-8.

certain important minority rights essential to Quebec, specifically make provision for basic constitutional rights and liberties. It either took them for granted or dealt with them by implication, as for example in the phrase in the preamble about a constitution similar in principle to that of the United Kingdom. This could be taken to mean a great deal: "the United Kingdom at that time was a parliamentary democracy headed by a constitutional monarch who reigned but did not govern; it had a long tradition of civil liberties, and the rule of law was firmly established," says Professor Scott. Admittedly, the United Kingdom had a constitution of which the most obvious element was parliamentary sovereignty, which does not seem to be consistent with the idea of a higher constitutional law which restrains the complete freedom of action of the legislature. Nevertheless, it is possible to discern in the constitution some limitations on the right of a legislature to alter the basic institutions of parliamentary government. Thus Professor Scott points to the argument used by Chief Justice Duff in the *Alberta Press* case, that parliamentary government assumes full freedom of discussion and that it is therefore beyond the competence of a provincial legislature to "abrogate this right of public debate or to suppress the traditional forms of the exercise of that right."[20] Professor Scott points out that "this new line of argument opens a wide door to the discovery within the text of the Act of an inherent limitation on Canadian legislatures, both federal and provincial, deductible from the meaning the courts must give to words like 'Parliament' and 'Legislature.' "[21] In the *Alberta Press* case Chief Justice Duff applied this limitation only to provincial legislatures, implying that the suppression of free speech and assembly must belong to the national Parliament. Mr. Justice Abbott went further than this in the *Padlock* case, though clearly he was speaking *obiter* and alone, in suggesting that "Parliament itself could not abrogate this right of discussion and debate."

There are, of course, narrow limits beyond which the courts cannot go in stretching the words of the constitution to limit the rights of our legislatures to enact laws within their own general area of competence. Nevertheless it is interesting to find Canadian judges treating the notion of unlimited parliamentary sovereignty with such evident lack of respect in questions where fundamental

20. *Reference re Alberta Statutes* [1938] S.C.R. 100. While the Duff reasoning may have opened up a line of argument, the courts have not in fact clearly decided that freedom of speech and discussion are entrenched in the B.N.A. Act.

21. Scott, *Civil Liberties,* p. 19.

constitutional values seem to be at stake. It is not without significance that a prominent English legal scholar (who is, however, of American birth and origin) asserts the existence of basic constitutional principles which could not conceivably be violated by act of Parliament. He includes among these the rule of law, free elections, freedom of speech, thought, and assembly and the independence of the judiciary.[22]

There are also certain reserve powers in the constitution which enable the federal government to annul provincial legislation through disallowance or through the reserve powers of the Lieutenant-Governor.[23] These powers have, to a large extent, fallen into disuse, but their employment against Alberta Social Credit legislation in the nineteen-thirties shows that they can be revived if necessary. In the days of our subordination to the British government, similar reserve powers could be used against federal legislation. However, such reserve powers are not totally consistent with democracy and self-government, and accordingly are not the most useful kind of constitutional protection.

Freedom of speech and freedom of association have always raised acute difficulties of definition in democratic societies. It is obvious to all that both kinds of freedom are essential to the democratic process. Both, however, are open to abuse not only by those whose purpose is to create violence and disorder, such as fascist movements, but also by authorities, from Cabinet ministers to police officers, and even by the general public who wish to suppress unpopular opinions. Freedom is of no value if it is reserved only for those who have no call to use it. It is the critics of society and the nonconformists who invite suppression by those who are shocked by what they say. But if people cannot be protected when they say things that shock the authorities then free speech is a sham which is of no value in protecting our society from complacency, arrogance and folly. In short, freedom of speech usually concerns somebody who has said or done something which offends the good people around him. This is a point worth remembering in considering the following cases, all of which deal with civil and political liberties, though not always with freedom of speech.

The first case was the *Alberta Press* case, already referred to, in which the legislature of Alberta passed a bill which would have compelled newspapers to publish "corrections" at the direction of a

22. A. L. Goodhart, *English Law and the Moral Law* (London, 1953), pp. 55-60.

23. See Chapter I.

government agency to any news stories which were "inaccurate" and "misleading." The title of the act itself is worth remembering—it was the Accurate News and Information Act. Its purpose was to gag the press which, at that time, was thought by the Social Credit government of Alberta to be malicious and hostile. It was not malicious, though the Alberta newspapers were editorially hostile to the Aberhart government. This bill never passed the legislature, for it was reserved by the Lieutenant-Governor. However it was later reviewed by the Supreme Court, along with the other bills in contention, and the evident tenor of the bill led the court to spell out the constitutional protection of freedom of the press and of discussion.[24] Here, as in other cases, the righteous zeal of those who would suppress contrary opinions has led instead to a defence of liberty in the courts.

The Jehovah's Witnesses are a well-known sect who believe that all organized religion is the work of the devil. They therefore seek to proselytize all other sects, both Protestant and Catholic. Their efforts in Quebec in the years following the Second World War aroused a great deal of hostility in French-Canadian Catholic circles in Quebec, partly because for many years the uneasy tension between a Catholic majority and a Protestant minority had been muted by a tacit "gentleman's agreement" between Protestant and Catholic not to proselytize one another. This dissident sect thus appeared to be shamelessly violating the well-understood rules for the maintenance of social peace.

The first important case involving the Witnesses was the case of *Boucher* v. *The King.*[25] Boucher had been charged with seditious libel for the distribution of a pamphlet called "Quebec's Burning Hate," which in rather strong terms protested against the treatment of Witnesses in Quebec by officials of church and state, as well as by mobs. To the Quebec courts it was clear that the charge of sedition was well founded, since it seemed to accord with the old common-law notion of sedition which included statements that held not only the sovereign, but public and private authorities up to hatred and contempt. This argument was rejected by the Supreme Court of Canada. The Supreme Court, says Professor Scott, "removed a rather vague idea that merely saying or writing something that might stir up feelings of ill-will between different classes of subjects constituted

24. See J. R. Mallory, *Social Credit and the Federal Power in Canada* (Toronto, 1954), pp. 77-87.

25. [1951] S.C.R. 265.

sedition in itself, whether or not there was an intention to incite to violence."[26]

One of the principal dangers to the full freedom which the law allows is the zeal of administrative agencies and police officers to anticipate the desire of those in high authority in the community to be spared the annoyance of dealing with critical or "difficult" individuals and bodies. This well-known human desire to please was illustrated in the case of the *Alliance des Professeurs catholiques.* The *Alliance* was an association of teachers whose militancy had displeased the Catholic School Commission of Montreal, which firmly requested the Quebec Labour Relations Board to decertify it. On the day the request was made the board, sitting in Quebec City, obligingly granted decertification without a hearing or indeed without even waiting to receive the document seeking decertification. The *Alliance* was notified by telegram of its decertification. The Supreme Court found the action of the board to be invalid because the decision, taken without a hearing, denied the principles of natural justice.[27]

In another case, the *Chaput* case, two police officers were ordered by a zealous superior to break up a religious meeting held in a private house. The meeting was peaceful, but the officers broke in, seized religious books and pamphlets, and forcibly removed the officiating minister. In this case the Supreme Court was unanimous in awarding damages to Chaput against the police officers. They did not accept the theory that police officers acting under orders are immune from the consequences of acts which are themselves illegal. In another case also involving Jehovah's Witnesses, a certain Miss Lamb was illegally arrested, held over the weekend in police cells without being permitted to call her lawyer, and then offered her release if she would sign a document releasing the police from liability for their actions.[28]

A final example of administrative desire to please is found in the *Roncarelli* case.[29] Roncarelli operated a restaurant in Montreal. As a member of the Witnesses he had frequently offered to put up bail for

26. Scott, *Civil Liberties,* p. 38.

27. [1953] 2 S.C.R. 140. In the end the *Alliance* was frustrated because the Quebec legislature retrospectively amended the Labour Relations Act. "Provincial autonomy won over the power of judicial interpretation, and this will ever be the case in all matters falling within provincial jurisdiction if we do not have a true Bill of Rights in the constitution." Scott, *Civil Liberties,* pp. 39-40.

28. [1959] S.C.R. 321.

29. [1959] S.C.R. 121.

members of the sect. On the theory that he was abusing his rights as a liquor licence holder in doing an action so obviously displeasing to the authorities, Mr. Duplessis instructed the Quebec Liquor Commission to cancel his licence forthwith and announced that he could never hold another. Roncarelli brought an action for damages on the ground that his licence had been cancelled wrongfully and without legal justification. He won his case in the court of first instance, though with only a part of the damages claimed. The Quebec Court of Appeal reversed this decision and dismissed his action. The Supreme Court of Canada by a majority of six to three found that the action of Mr. Duplessis in ordering the cancellation of the licence was both malicious and beyond the powers of his office. Under the Quebec Civil Code he was liable for damages, which the Court fixed at twenty-five thousand dollars.

Mr. Justice Rand, in his judgment, noted that the deprivation of a liquor licence in these circumstances contained "the element of intentional punishment by what was virtual vocational outlawry." He said, further,

> that, in the presence of expanding administrative regulation of economic activities, such a step and its consequences are to be suffered by the victim without recourse or remedy, that an administration according to law is to be superseded by action dictated by and according to the arbitrary likes, dislikes and irrelevant purposes of public officers acting beyond their duty, would signalize the beginning of disintegration of the rule of law as a fundamental postulate of our constitutional structure.[30]

The abuse of administrative powers is easier for the courts to curb than is the absence of restraint on the part of the legislature, for as long as the legislature is acting within the scope of its powers it need not act either reasonably or in good faith. This is not true of subordinate legislative bodies, and the courts have found it easier to confine within narrow limits the powers of municipalities which, under the guise of regulating the cleanness of the streets, for example, have sought unduly to restrict the distribution of pamphlets.[31]

30. Ibid., 142.

31. *Saumur* v. *City of Quebec* [1953] 2 S.C.R. 299. This case was decided by a bare majority of five to four. Only four of the majority thought that the by-law went beyond the powers of the provincial legislature to authorize. The fifth thought that the province had jurisdiction, but that the Quebec Freedom of Worship Act protected Saumur from its effects. For an excellent discussion of all these cases, see Walter S. Tarnopolsky, *The Canadian Bill of Rights* (Toronto, 1966).

By a curious irony, legislative attempts by the provinces to curb freedom of speech and religion have been frustrated by the fact that jurisdiction over these matters has been held to be covered by the federal jurisdiction over the criminal law. This is not because the exercise of either of these freedoms is criminal in itself, but because the Criminal Code specifically protects the individual in the free exercise of his religion and because attempts to curb free discussion are difficult without creating a new species of criminal acts.

Two cases illustrate this point and show how provincial jurisdiction is rebuffed by the pre-eminence of federal criminal jurisdiction. In the first, the city of Montreal, acting under powers conferred by provincial statute, sought to impose compulsory store-closing on six Catholic holidays.[32] In this case the Supreme Court overruled the Quebec courts in holding that this law related to religious observance and not to the holidays of employees, and was therefore invasion of a field which did not belong to the provincial legislature.

The second case involved the notorious Padlock Act, which Ernest Lapointe, when Minister of Justice, had refused to disallow, although he had expressed the opinion that it was probably *ultra vires.* Perhaps for this reason the Quebec authorities had been extremely careful in using the act in order to avoid a test case. This act forbade the use of any property in Quebec for the purpose of disseminating communist propaganda, leaving, in effect, the definition of what constituted such propaganda to be determined by the Attorney General of the province. When satisfied that property was used for this purpose, the Attorney General could order the premises padlocked and thus effectively deny their use to the owner. Two views could be taken of the substance of the act. It could be argued that it dealt only with property and civil rights and was therefore a matter of provincial jurisdiction. In many of these sorry pieces of provincial legislation, from the Alberta Press Bill to the Padlock Act, there seems to run the argument that since the provinces have exclusive jurisdiction over property and civil rights, their purpose in legislating about them should be to take such rights away. On the other hand it could be argued that the Padlock Act deals in essence with the matter of political discussion—it is irrelevant that it deals with the discussion of "dangerous" ideas, for in any case the matter falls under the criminal law and is outside the legislative sphere of the provinces. When the constitutionality of the act was finally challenged in the courts in the *Switzman* case, eight of the nine judges of the Supreme Court of Canada were persuaded that the act

32. *Birks* v. *City of Montreal* [1955] S.C.R. 799.

was beyond the legislative power of the province and accordingly the Attorney General of Quebec could not lawfully order the padlocking of Switzman's apartment and thus deny its use both to him and to the owner from whom he had leased it. Again to quote Mr. Justice Rand,

> Parliamentary government postulates a capacity in men, acting freely and under self-restraints, to govern themselves; and that advance is best served in the degree achieved of individual liberation from subjective as well as objective shackles. Under that government, the freedom of discussion in Canada, as a subject-matter of legislation has a unity of interest and significance extending equally to every part of the Dominion.[33]

It must not be thought that it is only the provinces who are potential enemies of our democratic freedoms, although the fact that provincial law officers are responsible for the normal enforcement of the law makes it inevitable that problems of police power and civil liberties are likely to concern the provinces. But the federal authorities may also act in a way to cause concern in these matters. In the panic generated by the Winnipeg general strike the Union Government pushed through Parliament the notorious section 98 of the Criminal Code which greatly widened the definition of unlawful associations and provided for severe penalties for membership in such organizations. The section further provided that any person attending a meeting of such association was presumed to be a member unless he could prove otherwise. Importing and distributing the literature of these organizations was an offence which could lead to imprisonment for up to twenty years. At the same time another part of the Criminal Code, section 133, which contained a guarantee of free speech by providing that criticism of the government in good faith did not of itself imply seditious purpose, was repealed. It was not until 1936 that persistent criticism brought about the repeal of section 98.

In wartime, when emergency powers for national security are freely invoked by the federal government, far-reaching questions of freedom of the person and property of the subject are likely to arise. In such a grave emergency the scope of the powers of the federal government is greatly enlarged at the expense of the provinces so that Canada becomes, for the time being, practically a unitary state. Furthermore, in the War Measures Act passed during the First World War and employed again in the Second, Parliament conferred enor-

33. [1957] S.C.R. 285.

mous powers on the executive. As a consequence the federal executive had the power to legislate, by regulation, in practically every aspect of human life and conduct. Thus, under the war emergency the central government developed elaborate controls over prices and production so that government departments could decide who could own what commodities, whether they could be sold and to whom, and the price at which they were to be sold. In addition to this massive control over property, with which few would quarrel in conditions of total war, the government by regulation assumed wide powers over the liberty and persons of Canadians. It assumed, for example, the power to hold in preventive detention persons whose conduct was deemed to endanger the conduct of the war. This denial of habeas corpus covered not only persons of subversive and enemy sympathy, but also those who were considered capable of such sympathies. Thus preventive detention was applied to the mayor of Montreal. On a wider scale all persons of Japanese ancestry, whether Canadian citizens or not, were forcibly moved from their homes in British Columbia and relocated in detention camps while their property was disposed of at forced sale prices. There is, unfortunately, no doubt that this mass detention was a valid exercise of the powers which, in an emergency, inhere in the federal Parliament and that the action itself was within the scope of the War Measures Act.[34] The whole enterprise was the result of an unreasoning fear of fifth-column activity and invasion which seemed much more reasonable in wartime than it does in retrospect.

A similar example of the alarming powers which the state may assume in times of national crisis was illustrated by the Russian spy inquiry of 1946. There, as a result of disclosure made to the security authorities by a defecting member of the staff of the Russian embassy in Ottawa, the decision was taken to arrest and detain for interrogation a number of persons who seemed to be connected with the espionage apparatus.[35] They were held incommunicado, without access to legal advice, and interrogated by a royal commission appointed for the purpose. Subsequently, many of them were prosecuted for espionage or breaches of official secrecy on the basis of evidence obtained by the royal commission. The report of the commission shows with abundant clarity the sudden shocked awareness of Canadian authorities of the harsh realities of interna-

34. *Co-operative Committee on Japanese-Canadians* v. *Attorney-General for Canada* [1947] A.C. 87.

35. *Report of the Royal Commission Appointed Under Order in Council,* P.C. 411 of February 5, 1946 (Ottawa, 1946).

tional intrigue and the organization of espionage and subversion which is now part of the machinery of international politics.

While it was a chilling lesson in the elements of international politics, it was also a reminder that in times of crisis traditional liberties are among the first casualties. While it is of course important to take all essential measures for the safety of the state, it is equally important to preserve to the utmost the legal context of the traditional liberty. In the present world it is not enough to find that our law of treason has been little changed since the Middle Ages, and that it contains powers over the liberty of the subject which have been largely forgotten in the placid centuries of national growth. It is not surprising therefore that the period since the end of the Second World War has been one in which there has been an increasing agitation for a clearcut bill of rights.

A number of factors have combined to bring the question of the adequacy of the legal protection of the basic rights and freedoms of Canadians into the forefront of discussion in the post-war years. It is not quite true to say that this had not been a matter of concern in earlier periods of Canadian history. However, the focus of concern has shifted a good deal as a result of a change in the spheres of activity considered proper to government. In earlier periods there had been a noticeable preoccupation with the property values which inhere in the notion of liberty. Liberty and property are closely related in the *laissez-faire* theory of a liberal society. To protect these values the federal government was driven, from time to time, to use its overriding power of disallowance of provincial legislation to veto provincial laws which were unjust, confiscatory or in some other way subversive of vested property rights. The change in the character of Canadian federalism in the twentieth century gradually rendered disallowance a rusty and antiquated weapon which governments in Ottawa became more and more reluctant to use.

While it is true that the courts have developed an increasing sophistication in limiting attempts to restrict property rights as part of a general retreat from *laissez faire*, the whole agonizing problem of reconciling the legal order with a shifting emphasis on the definition of liberal values is in a less than satisfactory state. This problem, as it relates to the Canadian constitution, will be discussed in the next chapter.

The sudden mushroom growth of wide and discretionary powers of the federal government over both the liberty and the property of the subject during wartime galvanized the legal profession into a sudden and growing concern over the effect of these powers on the traditional liberties of even the most modest man of property. "It is interesting that at that time," notes Professor Tarnopolsky, "... members of the Canadian Bar attending the Annual Meetings seemed to regard the profusion of Orders-in-Council and regulations, and the broad executive powers, as the main encroachments on civil liberties."[36] It was not until after the war that the profession's main concern came also to embrace a concern for other than "economic" liberties.

And yet questions of freedom of opinion, of conscience and of expression had arisen before. The Defence of Canada Regulations, which made it possible for the authorities to employ preventive detention to those whose actions, or even views, might be considered subversive, were demonstration enough of how far things could go in wartime. In time the public conscience was aroused by what had been done, in a period of shameful panic, to Japanese Canadians. The middle-class conscience is only mildly sensitive to the plight of those whose words and actions express what seems to be a naïve and subversive view of society. It is hard to think, in the case of such troublemakers, that when they are mistreated by the authorities important constitutional principles are at stake. One of the most important catalytic agents in convincing influential segments of public opinion that the problem was real and significant was the long struggle between the Jehovah's Witnesses and the authorities in Quebec. However bizarre their beliefs, the fact was that they were being persecuted for *religious* beliefs, and this was something that the respectable middle-class Protestant had been conditioned to regard as a grave matter.

And it must be noted that the whole question of human freedom was in the air. Everyone knew by then what the Nazis had done in standing the values of a civilized legal order on their heads. The horrors of Belsen and Auschwitz were at last clearly revealed. The defeat of the Axis powers had removed one set of totalitarian states, but others, perhaps as fearsome, now stretched from Eastern Europe to China. It was a time to take seriously the Universal Declaration of Human Rights, which had been adopted by the United Nations in 1948.

A consequence of the growing awareness of the dangers of uncurbed executive power was the enactment of the Canadian Bill of Rights in 1960. This project had been, for a number of years, an enterprise close to the heart of Mr. Diefenbaker and it was only

36. Tarnopolsky, *The Canadian Bill of Rights,* p. 6.

natural that he should wish to promote it on achieving office. The act begins by declaring that "there have existed and shall continue to exist without discrimination by reason of race, national origin, colour, religion or sex" a number of human rights and fundamental freedoms, namely,

> (a) the right of the individual to life, liberty, security of the person and enjoyment of property, and the right not to be deprived thereof except by due process of the law;
> (b) the right of the individual to equality before the law and the protection of the law;
> (c) freedom of religion;
> (d) freedom of speech;
> (e) freedom of assembly and association; and
> (f) freedom of the press.

How are these provisions to be enforced? The Canadian Bill of Rights is a statute of the Parliament of Canada, and from this flow two important limitations on the effectiveness of the Bill of Rights. In the first place it does not apply to the provinces, which are not affected by it at all. The second limitation is that as an ordinary act of Parliament it can be modified by any other act of Parliament. It is not, therefore, a fundamental law of the constitution in the light of which all acts of Parliament would have to be interpreted and which would render null any provisions inconsistent with it. For example, the act does not have any visible effect on wide powers, such as those under the War Measures Act, which Parliament may confer on the executive. Indeed, except for adding a section to the War Measures Act making it possible for ten members of either House of Parliament to institute a debate on the proclamation of the War Measures Act, the Bill of Rights does little to ensure the protection of fundamental rights in an emergency. Indeed it does the opposite by exempting the War Measures Act from the operation of the Bill of Rights.

There can be no doubt that the weaknesses and difficulties of the present Bill of Rights would have been largely avoided if, instead of the present Bill of Rights, there had been a Declaration of Rights inserted by amendment into the British North America Act, applying to both the provinces and Parliament, and superior to the legislation of both. No doubt the reason why this was not done was the obvious difficulty of securing the assent of all of the provinces to a constitutional amendment of this magnitude. It was not really a choice between two kinds of bills of rights, it could be argued, but a choice between one that was unattainable and one that could be achieved.

The present Bill of Rights has been described by Mr. Diefenbaker himself as a first step. Professor Scott sensed the difficulty in this approach:

> It seems to be assumed that a first step is always a good thing. Presumably a first step is a good thing if it is taking us closer to a desired goal, and will be followed by a second step. But if the taking of the first step confuses the issue and discourages people from any further effort then it may not be a good thing. I am frankly afraid that that is the position we may be facing.[37]

If the achievement of a limited Bill of Rights exhausts the energies of those who have successfully promoted the question for a decade, then further necessary effort may be stultified. It may be, however, that the wide public discussion of the issue while the bill was before the federal Parliament had the effect of making public opinion more sensitive and more sophisticated about the issue of human rights. This no doubt was the hope of those who supported the bill without reservation.

Time will be required to find out how far the courts will go in applying the principles to the interpretation of Canadian statutes. Professor Tarnopolsky's lucid and thorough discussion of the first five years do not furnish much ground for hope. He finds that in most cases the guarantees in the bill, as specified in section 2, seem to add very little if anything to the safeguards which already exist in the law. The courts, so far, have been in the main wary of taking a strong stand on the guarantees in the Bill of Rights when they are able to take an acceptable stand on the specific guarantees for the protection of accused persons which already exist in such places as the Canada Evidence Act or the Criminal Code. In the end, "the ambit of the *Bill of Rights* will depend upon whether the judges are positivist and give it a narrow interpretation, or whether they are activist and interpret it widely."[38] There was ground for hope that this might happen when the Supreme Court, in the *Queen* v. *Drybones* case,[39] held that the Bill of Rights overrode and rendered nugatory a part of a previous act of Parliament. In this case the question at issue was whether section 19(b) of the Indian Act (which imposed penalties on an Indian, found intoxicated off a reserve, different from those imposed on other Canadians) infringed the

37. Scott, *Civil Liberties*, p. 52. Quoted by permission of the University of Toronto Press.

38. Tarnopolsky, *The Canadian Bill of Rights*, p. 98.

39. S.C.R. [1970] 282.

"equality before the law" guaranteed under section 2 of the Bill of Rights. It had been contended that the Bill of Rights merely laid down an interpretation and did not invite the Supreme Court to engage in what Mr. Justice Abbott called "judicial legislation" by in effect repealing acts of Parliament in force at the time of the passage of the Bill of Rights. It was further argued that as long as Indians as a class were treated alike, there was no infringement of the notion of equal treatment. However, the majority of the Court rejected these arguments, and held that the impugned section of the Indian Act was inconsistent with the Bill of Rights, and was therefore invalid.

Since that decision the Court has generally taken a more cautious view of the applicability of the Bill of Rights. Where there are specific statutory safeguards, as for example in the Criminal Code, it has been simpler to reach a decision on that basis, so that the more general provisions of the Bill of Rights do not need to be invoked. In some cases "the civil libertarian value could be recognized without holding any law to be inoperative. The existing laws did not deny a hearing or counsel or an interpreter—they were silent on these points—and the Bill of Rights employed as a rule of interpretation, enabled the court to supply the civil libertarian safeguard."[40] Thus the Bill of Rights has functioned in a number of cases as a rule of interpretation.

Since *Drybones*, the Supreme Court has generally taken an attitude of judicial restraint. This was illustrated in *Attorney-General of Canada* v. *Lavell*,[41] which dealt with the rights of an Indian woman who had married a non-Indian. The lower courts, including the Federal Court of Appeal, held that section 12(1)(b) of the Indian Act was inoperative by virtue of section 1(b) of the Bill of Rights as denying equality before the law to the respondent. Mr. Justice Ritchie, for the majority of the Court, overturned the lower decision. The Bill of Rights, he said, was not intended to overturn the B.N.A. Act and the jurisdiction over Indians "could not have been effectively exercised without enacting laws establishing the qualifications required to entitle persons to the status of Indians." He rejected the suggestion that the Bill of Rights makes the whole Indian Act inoperative. Equality before the law means what it did at the time when the Bill of Rights was passed, that is "to be read in context as part of the rule of law." What Parliament meant by equality before the law was not equal treatment but equality in the administration and enforcement of the law. The decision in

40. Peter W. Hogg, *Constitutional Law of Canada*. (Toronto, 1977) p. 443.

41. [1974] S.C.R. 1349.

Drybones, therefore, did not apply in this case because it in fact involved the question of denying equal treatment in the administration and enforcement of the law. The attitude of the Court in applying the Bill of Rights to the interpretation of existing statutes was summed up by Mr. Justice Laskin when he said "compelling reasons ought to be advanced to justify the Court in this case to employ a statutory (as contrasted with a constitutional) jurisdiction to deny operative effect to a substantive measure duly enacted by a Parliament constitutionally competent to do so, and exercising its powers in accordance with the tenets of responsible government which underlie the discharge of legislative authority under the British North America Act, 1867."[42]

The Bill of Rights could therefore be described as a useful first step. It has made the courts more conscious of procedural safeguards, but it has not opened a new avenue to challenge the statute law itself. It has not been an effective restraint on Parliament, although there is only one occasion on which Parliament has used a "notwithstanding" clause to exempt a statute from the Bill of Rights. This was the Public Order (Temporary Measures) Act at the time of the October Crisis in 1970. However, the obligation on the Minister of Justice to scrutinize draft bills for conformity with the Bill of Rights does not seem to have been taken seriously, as it might have been had there been a parliamentary committee to encourage him. The Bill of Rights does not, of course, apply to the provinces at all, so that further progress inevitably involved the more difficult question of entrenchment in the constitution.

This nettle was grasped in January 1968 by the government of Canada which published a paper entitled *A Canadian Charter of Human Rights* for discussion at a federal-provincial conference. This document not only faced the problems raised by the incomplete achievement of the 1960 Bill of Rights, but also enlarged the proposed area which such rights should cover. "At this time in their history," it was stated, "Canadians are not afforded any guarantees of fundamental rights which (a) limit government power *and* (b) possess a large measure of permanence because of the requirement that it be amended not by ordinary legislative process but only by the more rigorous means of constitutional amendment."[43] The 1960

42. *Curr* v. *R.* [1972] S.C.R. 889 at p. 899. Also quoted with approval by Mr. Justice Martland in R. v. *Burnshine* [1975] 1 S.C.R. 693 at p. 707.

43. Pierre Elliott Trudeau, *A Canadian Charter of Human Rights* (Ottawa, 1968). For the Constitutional Conference of 1969 these proposals were put in the context of constitutional reform as a whole in Trudeau, *The Constitution and the People of Canada* (Ottawa, 1969).

bill has served to "inhibit" Parliament from violating its principles but had provided no constitutional limitation to prevent such violations from happening. Furthermore, "the Courts have held that it does not expressly overrule any provisions inconsistent with it which may be contained in earlier federal statutes." Not only is the Bill of Rights subject to amendment or repeal by Parliament, but it has the further defect that its main thrust is against the invasion of human rights by individuals, "not by governments or legislatures." There thus arose the necessity of building into the constitution a limitation on the powers of both federal and provincial legislatures to protect rights deemed essential. The rights singled out fell into four classes: political, legal, egalitarian and linguistic.

The political rights included freedom of expression (subject to the existing laws of sedition, obscenity and defamation), freedom of religion and freedom of assembly and association. All three cut across the existing distribution of legislative power between the two levels of government. All of them now enjoy considerable protection under provisions of the Criminal Code, the Bill of Rights and other statutes, but they have important provincial aspects. The law of defamation is a provincial matter, and freedom of religious belief is to a degree affected by the fact that education is exclusively a provincial matter. Similarly, freedom of assembly and association is subject to the actions of both federal and provincial authorities. Provinces regulate a wide variety of commercial, charitable and educational organizations. The parks, roads and other places of public assembly are controlled by provinces and municipalities. Thus an effective protection of these rights must apply to governments and legislatures at both levels.

Legal rights, embodying adequate protection of the life, liberty and property of the citizen before the law "go to the very root of the concept of liberty of the individual." Like other rights, they fall under the responsibility of both federal and provincial authorities which can deal with deprivations of liberty and property, and with the administrative and judicial procedures related to them. Thus it is necessary to extend the protection of the Bill of Rights to the citizen who may be adversely affected by the actions of provincial authorities. Judicial interpretation has already disclosed anomalies in the Bill of Rights, and further guarantees must be added against *ex post facto* laws which create crimes retroactively, and also against unreasonable searches and seizures and for protection of the citizen from exile.

The Charter of Human Rights proposed in 1969 also added two new categories of rights which should be protected in the constitution. The first of these, "egalitarian" rights, is already referred to in the Bill of Rights, the first section of which is aimed at discrimination by reason of race, national origin, colour, religion or sex. Most of the legislative protection against discrimination was contained in a variety of provincial laws dealing with accommodation, employment and the like.

The second, and more novel, departure was the proposal to include linguistic rights along the lines recommended by the Royal Commission on Bilingualism and Biculturalism. In the main, these linguistic rights would fall into two broad categories: communication with government institutions in either official language; and a guarantee of the right of the individual to education in the official language of his choice.

The basic political rights, together with language rights in modified form, were included in the Victoria Charter, which the federal and provincial governments tentatively accepted at the Federal-Provincial Conference at Victoria, British Columbia, June 14-16, 1971.[44] Five provinces (Ontario, Quebec, New Brunswick, Prince Edward Island, and Newfoundland) accepted both French and English as the languages of both court and legislative proceedings, as well as communication with government departments. Provision was made for subsequent adherence by other provinces. The Victoria Charter also included, among other matters, the entrenchment of the Supreme Court of Canada in the constitution, and an agreed formula for constitutional amendment. For reasons to be discussed in Chapter Ten it was the last-named provision which prevented the ratification of the agreement by Quebec and the whole exercise was therefore nullified.

In the meantime, the October Crisis in Quebec in 1970 illustrated the fragility of generally accepted civil rights and indeed of the whole constitutional order. There had been bomb incidents and sporadic episodes of terrorism in Quebec since the emergence of the Front de Liberation du Quebec in 1963, but it had seemed possible to keep these activities under control by normal police action. However the kidnapping of the British Trade Commissioner in Montreal and the Quebec Minister of Labour, and the subsequent murder of the latter, made it appear that a new and more dangerous form of revolutionary action threatened. When it seemed that regular police measures were ineffective and the situation might get out

44. The text of the Victoria Charter is printed as an appendix to the *Final Report* of the Special Joint Committee of the Senate and of the House of Commons on the Constitution of Canada (Ottawa, 1972) pp. 106-10.

of hand, the federal government responded to the urgent appeal of the provincial and Montreal authorities by bringing into force the War Measures Act to deal with an "apprehended insurrection." Public Order Regulations were then issued to arm the authorities with additional powers to deal with the crisis.

In essence the regulations declared the F.L.Q. to be an illegal organization, enabled the police and the military forces assisting them to search and arrest without warrant and on suspicion, and provided for the detention of suspected persons for a period of seven days before they were charged with an offence. This period could be extended for a further twenty-one days on the authority of the provincial Attorney-General. The regulations also made it an offence to disseminate F.L.Q. propaganda or to permit premises to be used for this purpose. While strictly speaking the regulations did not impose censorship, they had the initial effect of creating a good deal of "self-censorship" in the media and a noticeable wariness on the part of the owners of halls and other places of meeting to allow their use for purposes which might be construed as violating the regulations.

While the regulations emanated from the federal authorities, it was not possible for Parliament to hold them accountable for the enforcement since under the constitution this responsibility falls on the provincial authorities. Because the Bill of Rights exempts the War Measures Act from its guarantees, the regulations had the effect of setting aside not only habeas corpus and the right to bail, but also in practice, access to counsel for many of those detained. It cannot be doubted that such widespread and obtrusive police action almost on the eve of a civic election in Montreal provided a most unsuitable climate for effective opposition to the party in power in Montreal. In the event the mayor and his supporters returned to City Hall without a single successful opposition candidate.

In laying the regulations before Parliament, the federal government said that in its view the War Measures Act was the only source of power available to deal with the crisis, and undertook to introduce less sweeping legislation at the earliest moment. When it did so, on November 2, it was explained that more permanent legislation would be better left over to a time when the matter of special powers to deal with civil emergencies could be considered more carefully and fully. Such time has not yet arrived. Governments, confronted with the perennial problem of scarce parliamentary time, are naturally reluctant to spare it for a debate which will be so much to the taste of the opposition.

The Public Order Temporary Measures Act was, on the whole, a re-enactment until April 30, 1971, of the Public Order Regulations then in force. It shortened the period of detention without charge, and required somewhat stronger proof of adherence to the F.L.Q., but it retained the provision outlawing the F.L.Q. and continued the retroactive provisions of the regulations, so that a person could be liable for acts which were legal at the time that they were committed. In fact, however, the subsequent prosecutions were all for offences under the ordinary law so that the whole exercise seemed mainly a psychological gesture to restore control of the situation to the authorities and the police.

The whole affair is a dramatic example of the difficulty of reconciling dissent with a constitutional order. The wide extent of freedom of speech and political action which a viable political system requires creates awkward problems of definition when dissent is pushed beyond the limits of ordinary debate. Dissent in extreme and disorderly form arises in part from the frustration of those who feel that they are neither heard nor answered, and is bound to be exploited by those who do not accept the legitimacy of the society in which they live. The response almost inevitably of the authorities is not only to seek to avert violent action but to suppress the opinions which are thought to set off the action. Governments which are responsible for peace and order cannot ignore the threat of escalating disorder.

When political systems are threatened either by war from without or by rebellion from within, they can respond effectively only by a drastic curtailment of freedoms. This produces a paradox: free societies are driven in resisting the violence of their enemies to themselves operating an unfree society. If they do not, they may succumb to those who would destroy them. In order to deal with this unpleasant necessity constitutional governments have, since the days of the Roman republic, resorted to some form of constitutional dictatorship. These powers of crisis government strictly limited as to duration and purpose, are sometimes provided for in the constitution, as is the case with most European countries. In the Anglo-American world, the tendency has been for the legislature to make provision for these emergencies either through permanent legislation or through emergency laws passed *ad hoc*.[45] It cannot be said that the present arrangements in Canada for reconciling liberty and order in time of trouble are the best that could be devised.

45. The best discussion of the whole matter is in Clinton L. Rossiter, *Constitutional Dictatorship: Crisis Government in Modern Democracies.* (Princeton, 1948).

The devotion to ad hoccery no doubt stems from the same roots as the reluctance to contemplate the entrenchment of basic rights in the constitution. In part it stems from Dicey's famous threnody on the advantages of a rule of law entrusted to the courts rather than to the inspiring rhetoric, often unforceable, of the rights of man in the constitution. This debate was to form an important part of the discussions which led up to the Constitution Act, 1982, and the inclusion of a Charter of Rights in it.

The failure of the Victoria Charter led to a long lull in discussions for constitutional reform, caused by the loss of momentum for change, a period of minority government, and a period of economic crisis in the middle seventies. However the election of the Parti Quebecois to power in Quebec in 1976 made it inevitable that discussion of major changes in the Canadian federal system could be no further deferred. Action was precipitated by the referendum in Quebec in 1980 which sought to give the Quebec government a mandate to negotiate "sovereignty-association" with the rest of Canada. In the course of that debate federal, and in some cases provincial, politicians made much of a promise of "constitutional renewal" should the referendum be defeated.

This was the great opportunity for Prime Minister Trudeau to resume his long battle for a Charter of Rights which would include language as well as the usual civil and political rights. While there were other important matters contained in what became known as the "Trudeau package," the proposed Charter of Rights was, for most provincial premiers, a major cause of contention. A draft charter was put forward by the federal government and was the subject of lengthy preliminary discussion with provincial ministers. To the provincial premiers, the issue created by the charter related to the political values of constitutional government. To their attorneys-general, mindful of their responsibilities for law and order and well briefed by the police, the object of the exercise was to resist any curtailment of police powers. While the original draft charter was not made public, the version which was subsequently laid before Parliament in the autumn of 1980 was so watered down that it would not be unfair to describe it as the "policeman's charter." The document was in fact to be considerably strengthened in committee at the Parliamentary stage.

Before the proposals were laid before Parliament there was a final First Minister's meeting in September to secure their agreement to the federal proposals. It was there that the issues of principle involved in the Charter received their last full debate. One of the elements of disagreement was the belief that an entrenched charter was incompatible with the sacred principle of parliamentary sovereignty, of which the principal protagonist was Premier Levesque of Quebec. He still held to the view of his predecessors, notably Jean Lesage, in refusing to infringe the sovereign powers of the Quebec legislature by curtailing them through a charter of rights. The fact that the charter threatened Quebec's jealously-guarded exclusive control over language and education no doubt strengthened his conviction, but on the question of the principle of legislative sovereignty he was at one with the vast majority of great English constitutional lawyers throughout modern history.

The second objection came from the western premiers, and was most fully articulated by Sterling Lyon, the Premier of Manitoba. The charter was, in his view, a direct challenge to the constitutional values set down by Dicey, that the rights of the citizen are best protected by the common law as enunciated by the courts, rather than by a charter which would put the courts in a position to erode the sovereign powers of the legislature on which the Westminster system is founded. It was not charters of rights which protected the citizen, he argued, since even when they are enforced they impose the values of a particular time in a form which cannot readily be changed. In his view it would be better to leave the judges to interpret the law and to leave the legislature the task of reflecting changing community values.

Other western premiers preferred to express the more populist view that an entrenched charter would transfer the power to define social values from the people's representatives in the legislature to non-elected judges. The issues at stake were simply the conflict between democratic and elitist values.

THE CANADIAN CHARTER OF RIGHTS AND FREEDOMS

The constitutional proposals put forward by the Trudeau government, after prolonged federal-provincial negotiation, a decision of the Supreme Court on their legitimacy, consideration by a parliamentary committee, and debate in both Houses, were finally adopted in December 1981, and transmitted to London for implementation. After the Constitution Act, 1982, had been passed by the British parliament, it was brought into force by a Royal Proclamation by the Queen in Ottawa on April 17, 1982. The first, and longest, part of the Act is the Canadian Charter of Rights and Freedoms.

The rights and freedoms contained therein are "subject only to such reasonable limits prescribed by law as can be demonstrably justified in a free and democratic society." They include fundamental freedoms (conscience and religion, thought and expression, peaceful assembly, and association); democratic rights (voting, limitation on the duration of Parliament and the provincial legislatures—which however may be extended in emergencies—and annual parliaments); mobility rights (subject to laws of general application and reasonable residence requirements for eligibility for provincial services, or to ameliorative programs when provincial unemployment is above the national average); legal rights (security of the person, except in accordance with the principles of fundamental justice, protection against unreasonable searches and seizures and arbitrary arrest or imprisonment, right to be informed of an offence and to have access to legal counsel, open and prompt trial, etc.); equality rights (equal protection and equal benefit of the law without discrimination); equal status of the two official languages in Canada and New Brunswick (Quebec and Manitoba are already protected in the constitution), minority language education rights (where numbers warrant); and aboriginal rights.

Section 15 regarding equality rights does not come into force until three years after the proclamation of the Charter, to enable Parliament and the provincial legislatures to make necessary amendments to existing law to eliminate discriminatory provisions. With regard to the minority rights to education in the English language in Quebec, the right is limited in the first instance to children of parents who have been educated in that language in Canada (the "Canada clause"), but may be extended with the consent of the legislature and government of Quebec. Furthermore, section 33 contains a "notwithstanding" clause by which Parliament or a provincial legislature may declare that an act may operate notwithstanding the provisions of the Charter regarding Fundamental Freedoms (section 2) or Legal and Equality Rights (sections 7 to 15). Such a declaration shall have effect for not more than five years, after which it may be extended for a further five years, or may be revoked at any time. Only Quebec has so far taken advantage of this provision by a general statute asserting that Quebec laws operate notwithstanding the above sections of the Charter. It is not certain whether the words of the Charter permit a general, as distinct from a particular, enactment of a notwithstanding clause.

How seriously should one take the "notwithstanding" clause as fundamentally weakening the Charter by allowing all legislatures to opt out of its provisions? Perhaps not as seriously as it appears. It is probable that neither Parliament nor most of the provincial legislatures will resort to it save in exceptional circumstances. The case of Quebec is of course peculiar. The provincial government is on the one hand assiduous in refusing to give up any jurisdiction which the Quebec legislature might have on the simple ground of legislative autonomy. On the other hand, it has at the same time asserted that Quebec has its own charter of human rights, which is claimed to cover the same ground. However that charter is contained in an ordinary statute which can be amended at will by the legislature.

It is probable that one of the most widespread effects of the Charter will be on administrative action, rather than in curtailing the law-making powers of legislatures. It is with regard to the actions of administrative officers and policemen, as Professor Russell points out, "that the Charter may have its greatest and most welcome effect."[46] The tacit recognition of the doctrine of legislative supremacy has had a powerful effect in impelling Canadian judges to exercise judicial self-restraint. They have not shown the same inhibitions in imposing standards of fairness and strict adherence to the limits of the law on boards and other government agencies. "Judges," he says, "who may be disinclined to second-guess decisions of elected legislators may feel much less restrained in assessing the reasonableness of actions or inactions of bureaucrats, policemen or security agents that are not clearly mandated by law. In applying the requirements of a constitutional charter in this context, instead of vetoing elected legislators, the judiciary is more likely to be compensating for the weakness of legislative bodies in our system of parliamentary government in monitoring and sanctioning the activities of the executive." Professor Russell also feels that the existence of the notwithstanding clause itself may strengthen the resolve of the courts to second-guess legislators, since it will still be possible for the legislature to overturn a judicial decision by resort to the notwithstanding clause.[47]

46. Peter H. Russell, "The Effect of a Charter of Rights on the Policymaking Role of Canadian Courts," *Canadian Public Administration.* XXV:2 (Spring, 1982) p. 21.

47. *Ibid.* p. 19. The Prime Minister, in a letter to Cardinal Carter, in which he explained why certain rights had been left out of the Charter in the necessary compromises with the provincial premiers, also said "Should a court decide on some future date that sections 7 to 15 do establish a right to abortion on demand, Parliament will continue to legislate on the matter by overriding the court's decision and the specific Charter right as interpreted by the court." Similarly Parliament could re-establish its authority on some matters on which the Charter is silent, such as abortion, capital punishment or euthanasia. The text of the letter is reproduced in Canada. *Senate Debates.* February 3, 1982. p. 3553.

All the evidence suggests that, at least initially, one of the effects of the Charter will be that the courts will play a much more important policy-making role in relation to social issues than in the past. Within weeks of the proclamation of the Charter there were more cases before the courts than there had been in the first five years after the passage of the Bill of Rights. The enlarged role of the courts has been further strengthened by a much wider interpretation of the *locus standi* rule, which greatly increases the access of individuals to challenge legislation in the courts. This can be traced to the landmark decision of the Supreme Court in the Thorson and McNeil cases.[48] In the past it was, generally speaking, only possible to challenge a law in court if one was directly affected by it. Now there is room for an action instituted by "concerned citizens." This, combined with the fact that the Charter has opened a new avenue for litigation by making it possible to argue that a contested law is not merely beyond the jurisdiction of the enacting legislature, but alternatively may be contrary to the Charter, may well shift the focus of constitutional litigation into a pattern more familiar under the constitution of the United States.[49]

Moving the courts into a much more central role in authoritatively deciding social values as a result of the Charter may not be without its disadvantages. Social differences on such issues as obscenity, Sunday closing, abortion, and so forth entail, Professor Russell feels, creating "the danger, however the courts resolve these issues, of transforming these matters into technical legal questions and of making the answers to these questions hinge on the outcome of a contest between legal adversaries rather than on a political process more likely to yield a social consensus."[50] He thinks that the legislative override, "that quintessential Canadian compromise," will mitigate the danger. What we may get is "legislative review of judicial review." He concludes, "Weird as such a system may seem to the purists on both sides, it just might help us wring the best that can be hoped for a charter of rights without totally abandoning our reliance on the processes of parliamentary government to settle difficult issues of social policy."

48. *Thorson* v. *Attorney-General of Canada* [1975] 1 S.C.R. 138; *Nova Scotia Board of Censors* v. *McNeil* [1976] 2 S.C.R. 265. See John M. Johnson "Locus Standi in Constitutional Cases after Thorson." *Public Law* (1975) p. 137, and J. R. Mallory "Constraints on Courts as Agencies of Constitutional Change: the Canadian Case." *Public Law* (1977) pp. 421ff.

49. J. R. Mallory, "Conflict Management in the Canadian Federal System." *Law and Contemporary Problems.* 44:3 (Summer, 1981) p. 231.

50. Russell, "The Effect of a Charter of Rights..." p. 32.

THE OMBUDSMEN

There are limits to the ability of the law to provide remedies to an aggrieved citizen whose relations with government have been marred by what seems to be neglect, injustice, or administrative insensitivity. Laws must be framed in general terms, and cannot take account of all circumstances. Even if the law provides a legal remedy, the aggrieved citizen is often hampered by inability to penetrate the secrecy which protects government operations in order to prove his case. In any event such legal action is often beyond the capacity or financial means of the ordinary citizen. To some extent, under our system of government, an aggrieved citizen can be rescued from the results of administrative delay or insensitivity by the intervention of members of the legislature who find this role politically and personally rewarding. Nevertheless this recourse is unsystematic and unorganized and there have been arguments for years that there ought to be some kind of public protector to carry out this function.

In Scandinavian countries, this role is played by an ombudsman, who is an officer of parliament with the power to investigate grievances of the public against the administration. Under our system it is necessary to insert the ombudsman between the courts, which supervise administrative agencies essentially on procedural or jurisdictional grounds, and legislators, who seek to remedy the grievances of their constituents by a combination of private pressure and parliamentary questions or similar means. Neither of these is ultimately effective, particularly against maladministration as distinct from illegal, malicious, or other remediable acts.

In countries where the Westminster system is established, the introduction of the ombudsman has been resisted on two grounds. The first is that it is inconsistent with the doctrine of ministerial responsibility to establish an office which can deal directly with administrative officers who are, by the law and practice of the constitution, solely under the authority of ministers.[51] The second source of resistance has come from members of parliament themselves, who have not wished to share their constituency obligations with someone else. So strong was this resistance that when the

51. See Donald C. Rowat, *The Ombudsman: Citizen's Defender.* (Toronto, 1965); *Ontario Royal Commission of Inquiry into Civil Rights.* (Toronto, 1968); V. Seymour Wilson, *Canadian Public Policy and Administration: Theory and Environment.* (Toronto, 1981) pp. 252-4.

office was introduced into the United Kingdom it was provided that the parliamentary commissioner, as their ombudsman was called, could only take up cases referred to him by Members of Parliament.

Nevertheless, the office has now been established in nine of the ten Canadian provinces. While no such office yet exists at the federal level, a number of specialized "ombudsmen" have been created to investigate and report on administrative maladministration in a number of specific areas. There are now a Commissioner for Official Languages, a prison ombudsman, a transportation ombudsman, a Human Rights Commissioner and a Privacy Commissioner.

The role of the office in the province of Quebec has been described by the Public Protector or Protecteur du Citoyen (as he is called) in his first annual report as follows:

> The Public Protector is an agent of the National Assembly whose duties are to hear complaints lodged by the public respecting government administration, to carry out investigations, and, if necessary, to make such representations as he deems appropriate to the authorities concerned in the form of recommendations and reports.[52]

His effectiveness thus depends not on his legal power to enforce his findings, but on his powers of persuasion supported by the publicity from his reports to the National Assembly.

The impartiality of the Public Protector is ensured by the fact that he is appointed by the National Assembly itself, and he can be removed only by a two-thirds vote of that body. As in the case of judges, the holder of the office is disfranchised and thus totally immunized from politics. He is immune from intervention through the supervisory role of the courts, and has the privileges and immunities of a superior court judge in carrying out his enquiries. Thus he cannot be sued for acts done in good faith. In his work he has access to any documents he considers necessary for an enquiry. Because he does not have the power to enforce his recommendations, but can only persuade, he does not breach the constitutional rule of ministerial responsibility. He and his staff are outside the public service, his assistant has the same immunities as he has himself, and cannot be removed without cause.

The advantage of the ombudsman function is that, unlike resort to the courts, it does not impose costs on members of the public seeking redress. Furthermore, since complaints can be made informally (though in writing, which means that if they are made by telephone or orally the office assists in drafting the complaint), the

52. (Quebec, 1969) p. 35.

aggrieved citizen does not suffer from the hazards of recourse through the courts. In that case it is essential that a complaint be formulated in the right legal form, and there is the further problem that discovery (compelling the production of documents deemed necessary) is difficult against crown agencies so that proof to satisfy the court may be difficult.

Is the ombudsman available only as a last resort when all legal remedies have been exhausted? The legislation in Quebec is not clear but the Protector has successfully interpreted his powers somewhat widely. The legal recourse must be reasonably available, and the Protector may, on grounds of equity, intervene even if all legal remedies have not been exhausted.

Members of the National Assembly seem not to have resented the fact that the Protector receives complaints directly. Members appear to have a generally favourable view of his role, though they have shown little interest in supporting his activities by debate, either within committee or on the floor of the House. In general where the office exists, as it does in all provinces except Prince Edward Island, it is favourably regarded by members of the public service, who do not perceive it as a threat. As a result, the recommendations of the ombudsmen are usually accepted.

One of the potential difficulties of the office in large jurisdictions is that, to be successful, it has to be an informal and essentially personal operation. In Quebec, where the Protector has one senior assistant, adequate staff, and offices in Quebec City and Montreal, this seems to have happened. On the other hand, there have been recent complaints in Ontario that the office has been so bureaucratized that its purpose is in danger of being lost sight of. It is not intended to be a large bureaucratic organization attempting to be a watchdog over even larger, but equally impersonal, bureaucracies.

In many provinces there are also Human Rights Commissions, whose main functions are the prevention of discrimination by members of the public against one another in such matters as employment, accommodation, and so forth. These commissions very often play a mediatory role, investigating complaints, seeking to settle the dispute between the parties informally, and only resorting to legal action in the courts when all other methods fail. How far the wide ambit of the Charter of Rights in the constitution will lead to more reliance on direct resort to the courts instead of resort to Human Rights Commissions remains to be seen. That will depend in part on how sensitive the courts will be in giving full and effective meaning to the rights newly embodied in the Charter.

9

The Federal Distribution of Power

INTRODUCTION

The constitution of 1867 created a federal union, consisting initially of four provinces. The British North America Act embraced New Brunswick, Nova Scotia, Ontario and Quebec (a re-division of the United Province of Canada). It also provided for the adhesion of the remaining provinces, British Columbia entering the union in 1871, Prince Edward Island in 1873, and Newfoundland finally in 1949.[1] The province of Manitoba was created in 1870, and those of Saskatchewan and Alberta in 1905.

While the preamble to the B.N.A. Act speaks of the provinces as being "federally united into One Dominion," the constitution that was contained in the act did not, in strict terms, create a true federation. It needs to be remembered that Canada was still a colony, and that its institutions combined the principle of local self-government with the retention of certain safeguards against the possibility that local autonomy might threaten the larger interests both of British North America as a whole and also of the British Empire. On the one hand the legal capacity of the Dominion and provincial governments was limited to essentially internal matters. The power to legislate with external effect, to deal with other states or with matters which were of concern to the British empire as a whole, was still retained by the government and Parliament of the United Kingdom. Certain of the powers of central supervision over the provinces were delegated to "the man on the spot," the Governor General. There may have been some doubt in 1867 as to how far

1. The first two were added by imperial order-in-council under the authority of the B.N.A. Act. When Newfoundland decided to adhere in 1949 this procedure was no longer regarded as constitutionally appropriate and the admission was brought about by formal amendment to the B.N.A. Act.

he was to exercise these powers on his own authority as an imperial officer, but with the enlargement of the authority of the Dominion Cabinet these powers of supervision in fact became part of the powers of the central government.

Dr. K. C. Wheare lays down, as a working definition of modern federal government, the proposition that "by the federal principle I mean the method of dividing powers so that the general and regional governments are each, within a sphere, co-ordinate and independent."[2] In the case of the B.N.A. Act there are important qualifications to be made as to how far the division of power is such that it meets the tests of his definition. For in certain important respects the central government is able to compromise the autonomy of the provinces, which led Wheare to describe the Canadian constitution, in its legal form in the B.N.A. Act, as "quasi-federal."[3]

It must be remembered that in the beginning the relationship between the federal government and the provinces could aptly be described as a "colonial" one.[4] There were two main reasons for this. In the first place, the grand coalition which had negotiated Confederation survived to form the basis of Macdonald's first government. It was a formidable collection of political talent which did not leave much political weight in provincial capitals. With the opening of the West, the creation or admission of new provinces added new "colonies" to the political tutelage of Ottawa.

2. K.C. Wheare, *Federal Government* (London, 1953), p. 11. Wheare's model is thought by a number of writers to be inadequate and excessively formal. See William H. Riker, *Federalism: Origin, Operation, Significance* (Boston, 1964). Wheare is said not to take sufficient account of the informal political institutions which are the real stuff of the system, such as parties, pressure groups and the effect of political attitudes on the system. The reality of federalism is to be found in the groups or communities which struck the federal bargain, and the analytically important matters are how these groups interpret, reinforce and reinterpret the federal bargain. See Michael B. Stein, "Federal Political Systems and Federal Societies," *World Politics* XX, No. 4 (July 1968), p. 721. Riker's is a useful and important way of looking at federal systems, and it is particularly helpful in understanding the relations between French- and English-Speaking Canadians, which are discussed later in this chapter. However, it may obscure the fact that Confederation involved more than some kind of a union between the two language groups. The formal structure of the constitution is important, otherwise so much energy would not have been expended in drafting it and arguing about it ever since. Men act within the framework of formal rules, and act as if they are important. The formal structure of the constitution shapes and limits the rules by which the political actors play.

3. *Federal Government*, p. 19.

4. See J.R. Mallory, "The Five Faces of Federalism," in P.A. Crepeau and C.B. Macpherson, eds., *The Future of Canadian Federalism* (Toronto, 1965), pp. 3–5.

This colonial relationship was a natural one which grew out of the political institutions of the time. Macdonald and his ministers had grown up in the period when colonial responsible government was finding its feet. They were accustomed to the idea of the dual role of the Governor who, in matters which affected the interests of the senior government, was expected to exercise powers independent of his ministers. In the terms of the British North America Act the Lieutenant-Governor of a province inherited this imperial role and was expected to play it in the interests of the federal government which appointed him. In its relationships with the provinces, Ottawa assumed the role of mother country, and the institutions of control over the provinces were the familiar ones of colonial rule.

However, after Macdonald's first ministry it was not possible for Canada to be governed from Ottawa as an almost unitary state, with the exception of the years of the two world wars. The development of a more genuine federalism was a consequence of the persistence of powerful centrifugal forces whose strength has not waned to this day.

The subordinate, rather than co-ordinate, status of the provinces in 1867 was made clear in three ways. First, through its power of disallowance, the central executive could disallow an act of a provincial legislature, whether or not the act fell within the powers assigned exclusively to the province in the B.N.A. Act. Secondly, the federal government appointed the Lieutenant-Governor of a province and could instruct him to withhold his assent to provincial bills or to reserve them for the consideration of the federal government, which itself could give or refuse royal assent. Thirdly, all judicial appointments to the superior courts of the provinces were made by the federal government.

Gradually, in the light of experience, successive Ministers of Justice developed principles of policy governing the circumstances in which the disallowance power might be used. While it is clear that the scope of disallowance is legally unlimited,[5] the role of disallowance has changed as a result of changing concepts of public policy and of the political factors which in the end will determine whether a government will use force or be content with persuasion.

Forty years have passed since the disallowance power was used to nullify a provincial statute. One has to go back to 1910 to find the power exercised against either Ontario or Quebec. It was always

5. *Reference re The Power of the Governor-General-in-Council to Disallow Provincial Legislation and the Power of Reservation of a Lieutenant-Governor of a Province* [1938] S.C.R. 78.

easier to invoke the power against a distant or peripheral province, and in any event a province in which the same political party was in power at both levels of government was usually amenable to some kind of negotiated settlement behind the scenes. There were petitions for the disallowance of the Prince Edward Island Trade Union Act of 1948, which sought to limit the activities of pan-Canadian trade unions, but in the end the act was amended as a result of intra-party pressure from Ottawa.

The ultimate weapon of disallowance was much more likely to be deployed against a hostile provincial government. This was particularly likely to happen if the provincial government was in the hands of a splinter party of unorthodox views whose legislative program attacked at some vital point a major national interest such as monetary policy. The classic example is, of course, Alberta, which had passed a number of acts threatening the banking system or the system of mortgage credit while William Aberhart presided over a Social Credit government.[6]

In more recent times the use of this ancient colonial device would gravely offend the democratic principles of the public generally and the consequent political risk would almost always be too great to justify it. The disallowance power of the federal government is just as legal as it was when the Supreme Court ruled on it in 1938. What has changed, probably irrevocably, is the political climate which would permit its use. Thus the federal government seems to have shown no disposition to disallow the Quebec Charter of the French Language in 1977, preferring to leave the courts to deal with the constitutional issues which it raised. The evidence suggests that the federal government would be only too willing to give up the disallowance power, but naturally prefers that it may be used as a trade-off in federal-provincial bargaining over larger constitutional change.

The Lieutenant-Governor's twin reserve powers of veto and reservation are generally coupled with disallowance as a technique of federal control over the provinces. While a case can be made for the preservation of disallowance as the considered exercise of power in very exceptional circumstances by a careful and responsible federal government, no such case can be made for the reserve powers of the Lieutenant-Governor. There are two reasons for this. The royal veto is an incongruous device which offends against the rhetoric of our constitutional tradition. Furthermore, these powers are prone to

6. See, for a fuller discussion of the above point, J.R. Mallory, *Social Credit and the Federal Power in Canada.* (Toronto, 1955); and G.V. LaForest, *Disallowance and Reservation of Provincial Legislation.* (Ottawa, 1955).

unskillful and inappropriate use by Lieutenant-Governors who, as a class, are not likely to be versed in constitutional law or rich in political experience.[7] Even in Macdonald's time the federal government was occasionally embarrassed by Lieutenant-Governors invoking their reserve powers unwisely. Consequently, Macdonald was prompted to lay down, in a minute of council in 1882, the doctrine that reservation should be used, except in the unlikely case of extreme necessity, only on the instruction of the federal government. Even in 1882 Macdonald felt that the "facility of communication" was such that extreme necessity should "seldom if ever arise."

The examples of reservation and withholding of assent in the last fifty years are almost frivolous and acutely embarrassing to the federal government. The one exception is the reservation of three Alberta bills in 1937, which we now know to have been on the initiative of the Minister of Justice.[8] In 1945 the Lieutenant-Governor of Prince Edward Island refused assent, on conscientious grounds, to an amendment to the provincial Prohibition Act. Fortunately his term was nearly up and his successor was more compliant.[9] In 1961, the Lieutenant-Governor of Saskatchewan telephoned the Under-Secretary of State in Ottawa on a Saturday to say that he had reserved a bill which gave the provincial government the power to alter certain mineral contracts. The federal government in due course itself assented to the bill.[10]

It must be admitted that the retention of the Lieutenant-Governor's power of reservation is a constitutional anomaly. Not only does it invite him to disregard the advice of his ministers so that the decision can be taken by the federal government—a reminder of inferior and "colonial" status that modern provincial governments properly resent—but it furnishes him with no guidance whatever in the use of his power. It is doubtful if Macdonald's minute of council of 1882 has been known to Lieutenant-Governors in this century. Had the Diefenbaker government been given any warning of Lieutenant-Governor Bastedo's reservation of Saskatchewan legislation in 1961, there can be little doubt that he would have been told not to

7. See John T. Saywell, *The Office of Lieutenant-Governor: A Study in Canadian Government and Politics* (Toronto, 1957).

8. See John T. Saywell, "Reservation Revisited, Alberta, 1937," *Canadian Journal of Economics and Political Science*, Vol. XXVII, No. 3 (August 1961), p. 367.

9. Frank McKinnon, *The Government of Prince Edward Island* (Toronto, 1951).

10. J.R. Mallory, "The Lieutenant-Governor's Discretionary Powers: The Reservation of Bill 56," *Canadian Journal of Economics and Political Science*, Vol. XXVII, No. 4 (November 1961).

reserve. Although Mr. Diefenbaker told the House after the event that consideration was being given to providing more explicit instructions to Lieutenant-Governors, nothing in fact was done.

At the Dominion-Provincial Constitutional Conference in 1950 the premiers of Quebec, Manitoba, Saskatchewan and Alberta proposed that the constitution should be amended to abolish the power of reservation. While no action was taken, no dissenting voice was heard, and it is likely that such a change would evoke general approval.

The third major non-federal characteristic of the Canadian constitution, in Wheare's terms, flows from the imperfect division of power between the two levels of government over the judicial structure of the country. The superior courts are provincial courts, but the judges of these courts are appointed and paid by the federal government. While this arrangement lacks logical neatness it is not easy to see that it seriously impairs the impartiality of the courts.

However, there are objections which can be made to it. The first is perhaps trivial. The power of appointment is a political act. To deprive provincial governments of the right to appoint their own judges is to deny them access to one of the highest kinds of appointment under the Crown in the province. The second objection is more substantial. The courts are not only arbiters of private rights; they are also the interpreters of the constitution. Within Canadian federalism the courts, in determining conflicts of jurisdiction between the federal government and the provinces, are able to tip the balance of forces one way or the other. Since the federal government appoints the judges, it may be suspected that its appointments—particularly to the Supreme Court—might go to judges who are likely to favour a strong central government. At the very least they might be unwilling to appoint judges with a known and pronounced bias in favour of provincial rights.

Furthermore, it can be argued that judges might show a subconscious cultural bias in constitutional cases where the assumptions of French and Catholic Quebec might not be the same as those of Protestants schooled in the English common law. It is impossible to forget that the long series of civil liberties cases were handled very differently in the Quebec courts than they were in the Supreme Court of Canada. From this it might be argued that Protestant common lawyers are incapable of seeing with imaginative sympathy the problems of order and propriety in French-Canadian society. There can be no doubt that numerous rebuffs which the Supreme Court administered to Quebec authorities in these cases caused exasperation to many French Canadians. It is equally true that the demand for a new court of final appeal in constitutional cases which is not open to the suspicion of "centralist" bias and lack of sympathetic grasp of Quebec law exists exclusively in Quebec.

This is a difficult question to deal with, because it proceeds from an assumption about the judicial system which is not readily admissible. For, while it is true that judges cannot divorce themselves entirely from the social pressures of their environment, the Anglo-American legal tradition is based on an acceptance of the impartiality of the judicial process, and it would be unfortunate to build judicial institutions on the assumption that judges are, in effect, delegates of the community from which they are drawn.

Human institutions are seldom perfect, but it is reassuring to note that there is little in the record of the Supreme Court of Canada to substantiate the idea that it is in any sense biassed in dealing with the rights of Quebec or of the other provinces. Even in the Quebec civil liberties cases the division of opinion of the court did not follow the cleavage lines of French-English, Protestant-Catholic, or even common lawyer against civilian.

Nevertheless, the Supreme Court of Canada—like that of the United States—is capable of playing the role of a "nationalizing" institution, which interprets and imposes the sense of the whole community even where that consensus is openly rejected by a part of the community. This has been strikingly true in recent years in the United States where the Supreme Court, and not the Congress or the President, has been the active agent in enforcing racial equality against powerful opposition and obstruction from the southern states. In so doing it has imposed grave strains on the unity of the country, but it is the one institution which is capable of asserting and imposing common values. It is possible that this example has not been lost on those French Canadians who fear that the sheer weight of English-Canadian society is inevitably crushing all that is distinctively French in Quebec.

THE DISTRIBUTION OF LEGISLATIVE POWER

The Macdonald Interpretation

The general intention of the British North America Act appears to have been to assign a limited number of explicit functions to the provincial legislatures, and to confer the remainder on the Canadian

Parliament. Thus the opening words of section 91 assert, "It shall be lawful for the Queen, by and with the Advice and Consent of the Senate and House of Commons, to make Laws for the Peace, Order, and good Government of Canada, in relation to all Matters not coming within the Classes of Subjects by this Act assigned exclusively to the Legislatures of the Provinces;" this would seem to be clear enough. The provincial legislatures have limited and explicit powers; the Parliament of Canada has general and residual authority over everything else. However, the sentence quoted does not end there. It continues with a modifying clause, "for greater Certainty, but not so as to restrict the Generality of the foregoing Terms," and enumerates twenty-nine (amendment has increased the number to thirty-one) specific items.

This is a formidable list which includes the regulation of trade and commerce; an unrestricted power to tax; the regulation of banks, credit and currency; jurisdiction over navigation, citizenship and defence. In contrast to these wide and general powers, the provinces were given, in section 92, a much more limited jurisdiction over local matters; taxation powers limited by type and by object (direct taxation within the province for provincial purposes), and property and civil rights. This last was a necessary provision to protect the power of the Quebec legislature to preserve the system of French civil law within the province. Since this power was given to Quebec, it was also given to the others. But there was further provision in section 94 (which has never been invoked) for the Canadian Parliament to make uniform laws in relation to property and civil rights for the other provinces with their consent.[11]

It is reasonably certain, from the historical evidence, that the Fathers of Confederation intended to create a strong central govern-

11. The *Tremblay Report* argues that "Lower Canada only consented to enter the Union on the express condition that it would conserve control over its civil and social organization." Hence the reservation to the provinces of exclusive control over municipal institutions and property and civil rights. Similarly, the exclusion of Quebec from the uniformity provisions of section 94 confirms this. The report quotes Lord Carnarvon in the debate on the British North American bill in the Lords: "Lower Canada, too, is jealous, as she is deservedly proud, of her ancestral customs and traditions; she is wedded to her peculiar institutions, and will enter this union only upon the distinct understanding that she retains them. . . The *Coutume de Paris* is still the accepted basis of the Civil Code, and their national institutions have been alike respected by their fellow-subjects and cherished by themselves. And it is with these feelings and on these terms that Lower Canada now consents to enter into this Confederation." *Report of the Royal Commission of Enquiry on Constitutional Problems*, Vol. II (Quebec, 1956), p. 142.

ment with exclusive and effective powers over economic policy for the purpose of building up a strong transcontinental economy which would be able to resist the powerful economic pulls that otherwise would suck the British North American colonies piecemeal into the United States. The union of the provinces and the determination to build a transcontinental state were agreed on as the only means of avoiding absorption by a powerful neighbour ambitiously determined to fulfil its "manifest destiny" on the North American continent. The Civil War had just ended, every day the American railroad builders were thrusting deeper into the empty plains towards the Pacific, and the United States had the most powerful battle-hardened army in the world, backed by the war-stimulated industrial might of the northern states.

The Province of Canada had been distracted to immobility with internal strife and deadlocked over local questions. It was hoped that these local questions could be removed from politics by giving them to the provinces. A. T. Galt, in speaking of the economic and financial aspects of the union, asserted that these concerned the "public at large" and bore "no reference to what may be the creed, nationality or language of portions of the people."[12] Professor Creighton summed up the new union in a sentence:

> Local and cultural matters could be confined to the provincial governments; but the great affairs which from the first had been associated with the St. Lawrence, the projects of territorial expansion and material development, would be entrusted to the new national administration.[13]

It was the prospect of westward expansion which made Confederation attractive. But westward expansion would be expensive. Out of the union, it was hoped, would come the economic strength to support such a spectacular enterprise. The union was necessary to mobilize economic strength. As Harold Innis pointed out, the Province of Canada had been unable to float a successful loan on the London market in 1866, even at the rate of eight percent. "The Dominion," he wrote, "served as a credit structure by which capital became available with government support."[14] The Canals and the railways had nearly bankrupted the old colonies, and even greater

12. *Confederation Debates*, 1865, p. 55.

13. "Conservatism and National Unity," in R. Flenley, ed, *Essays in Canadian History* (Toronto, 1939), p. 167.

14. H.A. Innis, *Political Economy in the Modern State* (Toronto, 1946), p. 191.

resources would be required. It was a case of go on or give up. The new national Parliament was to be the chosen instrument for nurturing the transcontinental expansion of a new nation.

The Canadian constitution-makers had American experience to draw upon. In particular, they knew that certain kinds of powers could not safely be left to provincial legislatures. American states had mismanaged their credit, had done violence to the rights of creditor interests, and had in some cases repudiated their debts. The United States was a rich country which could perhaps afford such vagaries. Canada was less attractive to the foreign investor; it could not afford to offend the providers of borrowed capital. Thus Parliament was given exclusive authority over banks, interest and currency. The central government possessed, and in the beginning widely used, reserve powers of disallowance over provincial legislation which attacked at any point the rights of property or contract.[15]

The allocation of financial powers was itself suggestive. Parliament was given an unlimited power to tax, while the powers of the provinces were restricted. The public debt of the old provinces was transferred to the new Dominion, so that the provinces started with a clean slate. The functions of the provinces were, in Victorian terms, limited and inexpensive, and could safely be supported by meagre and inelastic revenues.

Macdonald's first administration boldly embarked on a national policy of expansion which came ultimately to embrace transportation, settlement and industrial growth supported by the tariff. But it became clear, even in Macdonald's lifetime, that Canadian federalism was not to be so heavily centralized as he and his colleagues had intended. In part they underestimated the strength of sectional feeling, they did not foresee the extent to which the party system would operate through the federal structure, and they were unable to control the profound political convulsions which were unleashed by such questions as the Manitoba schools and the execution of Louis Riel. They failed, quite evidently, to foresee the profound sociological impact which modern industrial society was to make on French Canada. Finally, they failed to foresee either the role which the courts would play as the interpreters of the constitution, or the effect which judicial interpretation would have on the British North American Act.

15. See J.R. Mallory, *Social Credit and the Federal Power in Canada* (Toronto, 1954), Chapter II.

The Judicial Committee and Judicial Review

It is difficult in a federal system to avoid having some body which is able to stand as arbiter between the two conflicting jurisdictions, the federal and the provincial. Canada, like the United States, found that this task of adjudication was assumed by the courts. In the United States the court got off to a strong start with a pronounced bias in favour of national, rather than state powers. The great Chief Justice John Marshall reminded his fellow judges that it was a constitution they were interpreting. In each generation the court has re-interpreted the constitution to meet the requirements of a strong national government.

In Canada the courts professed to be interpreting not a constitution, but a statute. This was not essentially the fault of the Judicial Committee of the Privy Council, but of the English judicial system in the nineteenth century. On the whole, English judges have refused to admit that they were making law and have insisted that theirs was not a task of creative statesmanship. They interpreted the constitution as they found it, and in the same narrow, literal way that they would have interpreted a statute which required the carrying of lamps on bicycles. In a sense this is a part of the British constitutional system. Parliament is free to change any law by simple statute whenever it pleases, which makes the British constitution so flexible that it practically does not exist. So the courts have never been concerned much about the consequences of their decisions; Parliament could always change them if it wished. But in a federal system change is less easy, and amendment does not take place by simple statute.

The Judicial Committee of the Privy Council, which was to play a significant part in the development of the Canadian constitution, was in many respects an ideal court of constitutional appeal. It was free from Canadian influence, and divorced from Canadian affairs. In the distant fastness of Whitehall, it seemed to meet the criteria of absolute impartiality and disinterestedness. Its constitutional basis gave it a unique role in the development of constitutional government in the British Empire. It originated with the constitutional notion that British subjects in overseas colonies which owed their constitutions to prerogative grants had the right to bring grievances from the local courts to the foot of the throne for satisfaction. These legal disputes were referred to a Judicial Committee of the Privy

Council. By the nineteenth century the Privy Council had become the established court of last resort for a large empire. Its composition and jurisdiction were given regular statutory form in statutes of 1833 and 1844. In general the Judicial Committee was composed of the Lord Chancellor and such other judges as were Privy Councillors. Since all of its members had other judicial duties it became normal to appoint a number of judges as Privy Councillors in order to provide a pool from which a panel could be constituted in any particular case. Within the pool of available judges were not only those trained at the English Bar, but also Scottish judges trained in civil law. It was thus possible to create a panel which included members who were trained in the civil law when cases arose from those parts of the Empire—like Quebec and South Africa—whose legal systems were based on Roman rather than English law. In the twentieth century the Privy Council was made a more appropriate court of appeal for the British Empire by the decision to add colonial and Indian judges to it. With the exception of the last group, the judges on the Privy Council were essentially the same as those who sat in the House of Lords in its capacity as the highest court of appeal in the United Kingdom. Thus, in effect, there was a single court of appeal for the whole British Empire. In a mature and flexible legal system, such as the British, the refinement and clarification (and sometimes even the reform) of the law takes place through the decisions of appellate courts. Thus the legal system of a large part of the civilized world responded automatically to the precedents established at the summit.[16]

Such were the virtues of the unified appellate system of the British Empire in its heyday. Undoubtedly great benefits, which were of inestimable advantage to commerce, flowed from automatic inclusion in a highly sophisticated system of private law. It is also true that in colonies where public order and security were serious problems, the liberty of the subject was better protected than it would have been in local courts, for such cases in the last resort were decided by judges with the scrupulous respect for personal liberty which has always characterized British courts.

These benefits were great. But they were increasingly offset by objections which became more important as overseas communities matured. The most obvious objection stemmed from growing colonial nationalism. It became more and more intolerable that the final decisions of the courts—particularly in matters of public law—lay outside the sovereignty of a "self-governing" colony, in the hands of

16. See A. Berriedale Keith, *The Dominions as Sovereign States* (London, 1938).

judges of another country. In the end it was the rising tide of nationalism which was to sweep away, in most Commonwealth countries, the appellate jurisdiction of the Privy Council.

The second difficulty was structural. The Judicial Committee of the Privy Council, although composed of eminent judges, was not strictly speaking a court, and it departed in one important particular from the usual court of appeal. Because it was technically a committee of the Privy Council it rendered advice to the Sovereign. Such advice, by the nature of its parent institution, had to be unanimous and the grounds for achieving unanimity naturally were secret. Thus was lost one of the great procedural advantages of the appellate court structure in the Anglo-American system. Courts of appeal are always made up of several judges who render individual judgments. In these circumstances a unanimous decision has much greater force than one reached by a majority of one, especially if it is a decision in which the majority came to the same conclusion by different lines of reasoning. Such decisions will be regarded with some reserve in subsequent cases. While it is true that the *stare decisis* rule makes the decision of the highest court a binding precedent, a split decision may prompt a subsequent court to "distinguish" a later case in order to reach a more satisfactory precedent. In such circumstances the dissenting opinions are manifest to later courts, and a powerful dissent may in the long run be recognized as the better interpretation of the law.

This escape hatch from a bad precedent was not provided for the Judicial Committee. Indeed, there is reason to believe that unanimity was often reached by a policy of deference to the one member of the board thought to be most familiar with the law.[17] Thus in effect the advantage of a plurality of judges was lost and replaced by a system in which a single judge was decisive. In other cases, no doubt, the process of compromise so blurred the issues that the virtues of a clear-cut majority-minority difference were lost.

Furthermore, the Privy Council had a disturbing lack of continuity from the very variety and burden of its case load, which had to be adjusted to the other judicial duties of its members. Normally the highest court of appeal in a country is composed of a definite number of judges, who always sit together and whose collective

17. Cf. the interesting observations of Lord Wright on Privy Council procedure, in his obituary tribute to Sir Lyman Duff, *Canadian Bar Review.* XXXIII:10 (December, 1955) pp. 1123–8. In due course the difficulty created by the unanimity rule in the Judicial Committee was recognized in the United Kingdom. It was abolished by Order In Council in 1966, thus permitting individual and dissenting opinions.

experience with the law gives body and continuity to the work of judicial interpretation. This benefit was almost lost completely when a series of cases from one country on similar points of law were heard by what, in effect, were a series of different courts of appeal, since the panels from which the Boards were composed were made up of different judges. This led to an exasperating inconsistency. An editorial note in the Dominion Law Reports expresses this difficulty with admirable force:

> Such vacillation, without explanation, in a court having ultimate power to define the limits of legislative authority in a federal state, indicates a want of appreciation of the important stake that Canadians have in understanding what scope for legislation resides in the central and local legislatures respectively. It reflects a casualness about constitutional power in Canada that is more irritating because exhibited by a tribunal, the membership of which, generally speaking, does not have to live with the results of its own pronouncements.[18]

The above quotation also reveals a further weakness of the Privy Council in the field of public law. It is apparent from a study of the case law of Canadian federalism that few if any of the distinguished judges understood the constitutional difficulties of federalism, or even what federalism as a form of government is. Their minds were patterned in the legal system of a unitary state in which Parliament (one Parliament, not eleven) is sovereign and free to modify the law at will if the courts make a mess of it. This reinforced their natural reluctance to engage in "judicial statecraft" and inclined them to work on the narrowest and most literal construction of the law.[19] Those few who professed to understand it, like Lord Watson and Lord Haldane, acted as if they had never read the British North America Act through.

18. [1947] 1 D.L.R. 433.

19. Cf. Edward McWhinney, *Judicial Review in the English-speaking World*, rev. ed. (Toronto, 1961). The most recent, and important, contribution to the long debate on the question of whether the judicial Committee "distorted" the constitution by "imposing" a form of federal system which was different from that intended in 1867 is by G.P. Browne, *The Judicial Committee and the British North America Act, An Analysis of the Interpretative Scheme for the Distibution of Powers* (Toronto 1967). He presents a powerful and technically sophisticated argument to show that, given the nature of the judicial task as judges are trained to understand it, the Judicial Committee produced an interpretation of the meaning of sections 91 and 92 which was correct and consistent with the logic of federalism contained in the B.N.A. Act.

The jurisdiction of the Judicial Committee of the Privy Council was an inevitable limitation on Canadian autonomy in 1867. Because of the restrictions on Canadian legislative power, it was difficult to remove or limit it as long as the Colonial Laws Validity Act remained in force. However, as early as 1888 the Parliament of Canada had begun to limit the jurisdiction of the Privy Council by abolishing appeals to it in criminal cases. In 1924, the Privy Council ruled that this has been *ultra vires*, since only the British Parliament could modify the powers of the Judicial Committee.[20] The Statute of Westminster removed this limitation on Canadian sovereignty, and the Canadian Parliament again abolished appeals in criminal cases.[21] Because the provincial legislatures have exclusive jurisdiction over procedure in civil cases, some doubt existed as to whether appeals in such cases could be abolished except by an amendment to the British North America Act. The question was referred to the courts for an advisory opinion, and in 1947 the Judicial Committee ruled that there was no constitutional limitation on the power of the Canadian Parliament to limit appeals.[22] Accordingly, all appeals were abolished by the Supreme Court Act, 1949, which established the Supreme Court of Canada as the final court of appeal in Canadian cases.

Canada was the first federal system to be set up in the British Empire, and it was not immediately obvious that the courts were to emerge as the arbiters of the balance of the constitution. It was only in the 1880s, largely because of the persistence and ingenuity of Macdonald's great opponent, Premier Oliver Mowat of Ontario, that the struggle for power between the Dominion and the provinces shifted more and more into the courts.

The first important case on the distribution of powers turned in fact on the central question raised by the wording of sections 91 and 92 of the B.N.A. Act. Were the provincial powers limited to a number of enumerated heads and all the rest of the powers of legislation "residual" in the hands of the federal Parliament, or were both sets of powers strictly enumerated with perhaps a vague but unusual residual power left over for Parliament in some unspecified circumstance? The late W. P. M. Kennedy argued, along with many other

20. *Nadan* v. *The King* [1926] A.C. 482.

21. *British Coal Corporation* v. *The King* [1935] A.C. 500.

22. *Attorney-General of Ontario* v. *Attorney-General of Canada* [1947] A.C. 127.

constitutional authorities, that the former interpretation was the correct one.

> The federal powers are wholly residuary for the simple reason that the provincial powers are exclusive; and the twenty-nine "enumerations" in Section 91 cannot add to the residue; they cannot take away from it. . . . They have no meaning except as examples of the residuary power, which must be as exclusive as is the grant of legislative powers to the provinces. The enumerated examples of the residuary power cannot occupy any special place; they cannot be exalted at the expense of the residuary power, for that would "restrict the generality" of that power. It all looks reasonably simple, and Sir John A. Macdonald was perhaps justified as he looked at the scheme in hoping that "all conflicts of jurisdiction" had been avoided.[23]

But the law is never simple where substantial conflicts of interest are at issue. *Russell* v. *The Queen* arose out of an apparent conflict between the provincial jurisdiction over property and civil rights and a federal statute, the Dominion Temperance Act, permitting local areas to prohibit the sale of intoxicating liquor. The Privy Council was clear in supporting the jurisdiction of the federal Parliament. "Their Lordships cannot think that the Temperance Act in question properly belongs to the class of subjects, 'Property and Civil Rights,'" wrote Sir Montague Smith. The act was indeed a law more akin to legislation dealing with poisonous drugs or dangerous explosives. The fact that these things could be held as property and give rise to legal rights did not prevent Parliament from restricting or prohibiting their sale or use on the ground that they were dangerous to public safety. Such a regulatory law, making violation a criminal offence, was not a law relating to property and civil rights. "What Parliament is dealing with in legislation of this kind is not a matter in relation to property and its rights, but one relating to public order and safety."[24]

This was to imply that the Dominion had the power to legislate, under the general heading of "peace, order and good government" even over matters exclusively assigned to the provinces. Seldom again was the Judicial Committee to take a similar view. The danger inherent in it was that it gave to Parliament an indefinite and possibly wide power to legislate in fields assigned "exclusively to the provinces." The *Russell* case was a precedent which the courts

23. "The Interpretation of the British North America Act," *Cambridge Law Journal*, 1943, Vol. VIII, No. 2, pp. 150–1.

24. (1882), 7 App. Cas. 829.

were later extremely reluctant to follow, and at times the committee was driven to somewhat fanciful attempts to explain it away. Thus Lord Haldane thought that the rationale of the case could be understood only on the assumption that the country was succumbing to a national disaster of intemperance, similar in character to an epidemic or pestilence.[25]

A year after the *Russell* case, the Judicial Committee again was faced with an apparent conflict of jurisdiction. On this occasion they asserted that the provincial legislatures were not subordinate to the federal Parliament, but sovereign equals. Within the powers assigned by section 92, "the local legislature is supreme and has the same authority as the Imperial Parliament or the Parliament of the Dominion, would have in like circumstances."[26] The same principle of sovereign equality was conferred on the provincial executive as well in *Liquidators of the Maritime Bank* v. *Receiver-General of New Brunswick* in 1892. Despite the fact that the Lieutenant-Governor was a federal appointee and a Dominion officer, he was the head of an autonomous government possessing the royal prerogative and he was "as much the representative of Her Majesty for all purposes of provincial government as the Governor-General himself is for all purposes of Dominion government."[27]

While the relations between the federal government and the provinces at Confederation were essentially the "colonial" model of superior and subordinate, it was clear that the courts saw the relationship in a more "federal" form in which the provinces were, within their jurisdiction, the equals of the Dominion. To this generalization, with which few would now quarrel, they added a further gloss. The legislative powers of the provinces in their enumerated subjects were exclusive and Dominion legislation under the general power on these subjects was forbidden. Lord Watson, in upholding an Ontario scheme of liquor regulation similar to the Canada Temperance Act, said that while Parliament could, under the enumerated heads of section 91, enact legislation which affected the heads of section 92, it could not use the "peace, order and good government" power to encroach on any subjects enumerated in section 92. A construction which allowed Parliament, in supplement to its enumerated powers, to legislate "upon matters which in each province are substantially of local or private interest, upon the

25. *Toronto Electric Commissioners* v. *Snider* [1925] A.C. 396.

26. *Hodge* v. *The Queen* (1883) 9 App. Cas. 117.

27. [1892] A.C. 437.

assumption that these matters also concern the peace, order and good government of the Dominion" would practically destroy the autonomy of the provinces.[28]

Two things should be emphasized about the legal battles between Canada and its provinces before 1914. First, in practically no case was there a successful attack on the constitutional validity of an actual federal statute; the one notable exception was when the Judicial Committee cut down a part of the Railway Act towards the end of the period.

Second, the provinces were finding that their responsibilities for social and economic policy were much more important than anyone had suspected at Confederation. Such a growth of the welfare and regulatory functions of government is invariably resisted by those economic interests which find them inconvenient or expensive, or both. Dicey was not the only one to perceive in the nineteenth century a struggle between *laissez-faire* and collectivism, in which the social expectations of groups which became enfranchised by growing industrialism and prosperity led to demands for "collectivist" legislation to mitigate the effects of the free market on the economically weak.[29] Dicey was perceptive enough to see that the struggle over the delineation of the boundaries of government, which is confined in unitary states to a political struggle for and against particular pieces of legislation, will in federal states be conducted largely in the courts where the interests opposed to a particular law can argue that it is unconstitutional.[30] This is a better posture in a democracy than a political attempt to oppose the will of the majority.

One of the prevailing themes in the development of the Canadian constitution has been a constant litigious pressure against the growth of the powers of government. It did not matter which government was attempting to introduce workmen's compensation or regulate the insurance business. The correct tactic for those who would be hurt by this was to get the issue into court and argue that the power to deal with this particular matter lay with the *other* level of government, provincial or federal–whichever was not in fact seeking to do anything about it. A very large number of the cases on

28. *Attorney-General for Ontario* v. *Attorney-General for Canada* [1896] A.C. 348.

29. A.V. Dicey, *Law and Opinion in England during the Nineteenth Century*, Introduction to the Second Edition (London, 1914).

30. "Federalism substitutes litigation for legislation," quoted in Zechariah Chafee, Jr., "International Utopias," American Academy of Arts and Science, *Proceedings* LXXV, No. 1(October 1942), pp. 9–53.

the distribution of power in Canada arose in this fashion. The initial protagonists were not the Dominion and the provinces, but private interests seeking to protect themselves from the effects of legislation they did not like. As Lord Dunedin said of one of the earliest of these cases: "The case of the *Citizens Insurance Company* v. *Parsons* was not fought directly between the Dominion and the Provinces either as parties or interveners. It was an action by a private individual to recover money under an insurance contract for a loss by fire."[31] In this particular case, incidentally, the fire insurance company was trying to avoid payment on a policy by arguing that the Ontario statute which imposed a standard set of terms was *ultra vires*.

It should be noticed that most of the criticism by historians and legal writers of the judicial interpretation of the constitution was written from the perspective of the nineteen-twenties and thirties, when the important cases of the period before 1914 had become awkward precedents in determining the constitutional arrangements of an age when the problems of government were much different. In the pre-war period a somewhat loose federation, in which the provinces were slowly being pressed into welfare and regulatory legislation against a steady resistance in the courts from affected interest groups, worked reasonably well.

This situation did not endure, for the social dislocation caused by the First World War, followed by the grave economic problems of the inter-war period, created the need for vast and expensive systems of unemployment relief and social security, as well as for increased economic dirigisme, which were beyond the resources of all but the largest units of government. Thus although constitutional interpretation gave the provinces a wide jurisdiction in these matters, they did not possess the financial and administrative resources to control them effectively.

An apparent solution to this impasse had developed during the First World War. When the federal government was driven at last to control prices and commodities and generally to regulate the private property and rights of the citizen, the courts found a neat justification in Lord Watson's decision in the *Local Prohibition* case. There he had implied that the peace, order and good government clause could justify Dominion legislation within fields of exclusive provincial jurisdiction when conditions of grave emergency prevailed. Could this argument be employed for the post-war period?

31. *In re the Insurance Act of Canada* [1932] A.C. 41.

The Canadian government, anxious to retain some of its vast wartime powers, sought to embody some of the more important of these in permanent statutes. In the Board of Commerce Act, for example, some of the controls over the allocation of supplies and over excessive prices, originally set up under wartime orders, were now placed under a permanent government agency. The Judicial Committee, however, found that the act was *ultra vires* and in handing down this decision Lord Haldane gave a more precise statement of the emergency doctrine, which he had derived from Lord Watson:

> It may well be that the subjects of undue combination and hoarding are matters in which the Dominion has a great practical interest. In special circumstances, such as those of a great war, such an interest might conceivably become of such paramount and overriding importance as to amount to what lies outside the heads of s. 92, and is not covered by them.[32]

This decision appeared to contain one promising concept, which encouraged those who urged greater responsibilities on the federal government to meet the disaster of the Great Depression. Surely, it was thought, such a disaster must be an emergency. But they were to be sorely disappointed. The courts had now clearly grasped the idea that social legislation was a matter of property and civil rights and therefore lay outside the powers of Parliament. In the *Snider* case Lord Haldane found that the Industrial Disputes Investigation Act, unchallenged on the statute book for eighteen years, was *ultra vires*, and by this decision confined the jurisdiction of Parliament in the major field of collective bargaining to those undertakings, like shipping and railways, which fell specifically under federal jurisdiction. In all other undertakings jurisdiction was settled by the primacy given by the constitution to the provinces over property and civil rights.

Even in the case of the power to implement treaties judicial attrition wore away powers previously exercised by Parliament. While the Judicial Committee upheld the federal power to implement treaties in the *Aeronautics* case, the power was given such a narrow construction in the *Radio* case that in effect it meant that Parliament could give legislative effect to a treaty only if it could pass the necessary laws under its ordinary power to legislate under the constitution. Before the Statute of Westminster, no such restric-

32. *In re Board of Commerce*...[1922] 1 A.C. 191.

tion existed on the power of the Parliament of Canada to implement "British Empire treaties."[33]

The impact of the Great Depression made plain the unsuitability of the division of the responsibilities of government which had been worked out by judicial interpretation. Mass unemployment and widespread agricultural distress threw enormous burdens on all governments. In this grave social crisis thousands of families, without jobs or incomes, would have become homeless paupers without massive relief payments. The sluggish economy seemed in its death throes, and only the energy of government could revive it. The measures which then seemed urgent to the distracted governments of the day were chiefly subjects from which the constitution excluded the central government. The provinces, on whom the responsibilities fell, were hopelessly lacking in either revenue or administrative experience for such an enormous task, which had caused municipal governments to collapse at the first impact. Some provinces, such as Saskatchewan, were vast distressed areas. Even the more fortunate provinces were unable to finance the mounting demands made on them by the Depression.[34]

In the circumstances only the federal government could come to the rescue. But while it could provide funds out of the federal treasury, it lacked the constitutional power to take wider measures. At last, inspired by the example of the New Deal in the United States, Parliament began to act. A natural products marketing scheme was enacted in 1934, and in the following year social insurance, minimum wages and other measures were passed. No doubt the hope was entertained that the courts could not be blind to the desperate situation in the country, and on the analogy of wartime would permit an emergency jurisdiction to the federal Parliament. But an emergency is a temporary thing, and everyone hoped that the Depression would end, though it was not likely that the need for such measures as unemployment insurance would be any less. Accordingly, a number of these statutes were drafted in accordance with conventions of the International Labour Organization, which the government had ratified. The test of this device in the courts was not long to be delayed.

In 1935 the Bennett administration went down to humiliating

33. *In re Regulation and Control of Aeronautics in Canada* [1932] A.C. 54; *In re Regulation and Control of Radio Communication in Canada* [1932] A.C. 304.

34. For an admirably lucid account, see *Report of the Royal Commission on Dominion-Provincial Relations*, Book I, *Rowell-Sirois Report* (Ottawa, 1940).

defeat, and Mackenzie King led the Liberals back to power. One of his first acts was to refer his predecessor's "new deal" legislation to the courts for an advisory opinion on its validity. There is reason to believe that the government had little enthusiasm for the legislation.[35] In any event, the argument put up by counsel for the federal government did not prevail. In 1937 the Privy Council delivered itself of a number of decisions on the legislation referred to it.

> The result of the destruction by the courts of these statutes was practically to paralyse the Dominion as an agency for regulating economic activity. Specifically it had not the power to legislate regarding hours and conditions of labour (except in certain narrowly defined national undertakings such as railroads) even if such legislation was necessary to ratify obligations which had been entered into by the government; it lacked the power to set up a scheme of social insurance; it could not provide for the marketing of natural products; in short, the Dominion had practically no jurisdiction over labour, prices, production, and marketing except in wartime. All that survived the slaughter were an amendment of the Criminal Code in connection with combines and an extension of a form of bankruptcy procedure to farmers under the Farmers' Creditors' Arrangement Act.[36]

The courts had reached this constitutional impasse by favouring one theory of constitutional interpretation over another. They had been able to exclude Dominion jurisdiction by a rigid application of the "watertight compartments" theory—an unhappy metaphor of Lord Atkin's.[37] If the subject matter of the legislation falls within the enumerated heads of section 91, then the provinces are excluded from dealing with it. If the subject matter of the legislation falls within section 92, then Parliament can have nothing to do with it. This would not have been so serious if there had been a sort of safety compartment to take up fields of jurisdiction of urgent national concern which had not been thought of at all in 1867. This no doubt was the proper intention of "peace, order and good government."

35. "I believe," Mr. King had said in the House in the debate on the Natural Products Marketing Act, "that when this measure is properly studied it will be found that some of its provisions are also contrary to the provisions of the British North America Act," Canada, *House of Commons Debates*, Vol. III, 1934, p. 2343.

36. J.R. Mallory, *Social Credit and the Federal Power in Canada*, p. 51. The cases are in [1937] A.C. 368; ibid., 377; ibid., 391; ibid., 326; ibid., 355; ibid., 405. Quoted by permission of the University of Toronto Press.

37. *Attorney-General of Canada* v. *Attorney-General of Ontario [1937] A.C. 327.*

But no. Save in the single circumstance of war "emergency," the powers of the Dominion were strictly enumerated. What happened to the new functions of government? The answer, alas, was simple. Regulatory and welfare legislation are bound to deal in some way or other with the rights or property of the subject. Therefore, in pith and substance, such legislation deals with property and civil rights, and belongs exclusively to the provinces.

There was an alternative line of interpretation which the courts might have followed. It was laid down by Lord Fitzgerald in *Hodge* v. *The Queen* in 1883: "The Principle which *Russell* v. *The Queen* and the case of *The Citizens Insurance Company* illustrate is, that subjects which in one aspect and for one purpose fall within section 92, may in another aspect and for another purpose fall within section 91."[38] In the cases of the 1930s, the aspect doctrine held no appeal to the courts.

The consequences of the strict and narrow interpretation of the distribution of legislative power did, of course, give to the provinces powers of regulation over the economy which had been vainly asserted by Parliament. In some circumstances these were powers which were beyond the administrative and financial means of provincial governments, and they were sometimes powers which the provinces did not welcome. In addition to this, it became extremely difficult in practice to set up marketing schemes, either federal or provincial, which did not run foul of the artificial barriers which the courts had constructed in the constitution. What the courts had created was a legislative no man's land which neither level of government could effectively occupy.[39]

The truth of the matter was that they did not like the growing power of the state. The frustrating experience of Canadian federalism was not unique in this period. Both the United States and Australia found the same difficulties in extending the role of government into new areas of economic and social policy. But it is going too far to blame the courts alone. The legal system of the Anglo-American world, which had reached its maturity in the nineteenth century, was profoundly individualist. The courts do not impose constitutional doctrines in a vacuum. In each of these countries there were powerful interests which were able to resist with every legal means in their power the growing regulatory functions of the

38. (1883) 9 App. Cas. 130.

39. F.R. Scott, "The Privy Council and Mr. Bennett's 'New Deal' Legislation," *Canadian Journal of Economics and Political Science*, Vol.III, No. 2 (May, 1937), p. 240.

state. The courts were arbiters in a complex social adjustment, in which the methodology of legal interpretation and the courts' own subconscious predilections made it inevitable that they would lean in the direction of those who resorted to litigation to contain the extension of the role of government.

When it seemed that Canadian federalism was about to wither away in failure and frustration, deeper historical forces were already at work. The outbreak of the Second World War at once restored, under the emergency doctrine, all of the ample powers of government which had been lacking in the Depression. At the same time the desperate nature of the conflict restored a sense of urgency and national unity. The federal government was no longer trying half-heartedly to fulfil a role that was frequently unwanted. The boldness and daring innovation, so conspicuously lacking on all sides during the Depression, was now evident both in Ottawa and in the business world. It is a melancholy reflection that it took a war for survival to cure the economy of the ailments which had baffled the experts in time of peace. The war not only restored the economy to health, it laid the foundations for that prosperity and strength which had—throughout Canadian history—been the objective of the makers of national economic policy. Where the canals, the railroads, western settlement and massive immigration had all failed, the war finally succeeded.

Because of the unlimited federal powers during the war, the question of distribution of powers in the constitution was for the time being laid aside. But even during the war there was some evidence that the courts might be coming to a broader and more liberal interpretation of the constitution. The Privy Council itself, in *The Canada Temperance Federation* case, astonished constitutional lawyers by apparently abandoning completely the narrow and restrictive interpretation of federal power which had stemmed from the labours of Lord Watson and Lord Haldane. The Board had been invited, by the nature of the case before it, to consider whether *Russell* v. *The Queen* could now be regarded as rightly decided in the light of the substantial jurisprudence which for so long had sought to explain it away. Lord Simon's judgment refused to accept this invitation.

Instead, he rejected the notion that the B.N.A. Act "gives power to the Dominion Parliament to legislate in matters which are properly to be regarded as exclusively within the competence of the Provincial Legislatures, merely because of the existence of an emergency." The *Russell* case is no authority for such an emergency doctrine, for no emergency existed at the time of the Canada Temperance Act, and none was alleged as justification for the act. "The true test must be found in the real subject matter of the legislation: if it is such that it goes beyond local or provincial concern or interests and must from its inherent nature be the concern of the Dominion as a whole... then it will fall within the competence of the Dominion Parliament as a matter affecting the peace, order and good government of Canada, though it may in another aspect touch upon matters specially reserved to the Provincial Legislatures." Thus the Privy Council accepted the concept, which its predecessors had on a number of occasions found inadequate, that legislation which goes beyond local interests is inherently the concern of the Dominion as a whole. In place of Lord Atkin's watertight compartments, it was prepared to go back to the "aspect" doctrine first enunciated in *Hodge* v. *The Queen.*[40]

The Supreme Court's Interpretation: 1949 to the Present

Since the end of the war and as a result of the abolition of Privy Council appeals by an amendment to the Supreme Court Act in 1949, the final interpretation of the constitution has fallen mainly to the Supreme Court of Canada. It might be assumed that two important changes would follow. The Supreme Court might be expected to be more sensitive to the currents of Canadian political forces and less remote and aloof from the real political issues which underlie apparently abstract legal conflicts. Secondly, the court might be expected to give more consistency and continuity to the development of constitutional doctrine. How far this has been so can be inferred from consideration of the major cases on the distribution of power.[41]

40. [1946] 2 D.L.R. 1, at p. 5. This case is not lacking the deadpan humour which sometimes finds its way into the courts. In the *Snider* case, Lord Haldane had been driven to explain the rationale of the *Russell* case on the theory that the board had been convinced of the existence of a national disaster of intemperance at the time. This explanation, said Lord Simon, "is too narrowly expressed."

41. For a discussion of recent cases see V.C. MacDonald, *Legislative Power and the Supreme Court in the Fifties.* (Toronto, 1961); Peter H. Russell, "The Supreme Court's Interpretation of the Constitution from 1949 to 1960". and "The Supreme Court Since 1960." in Paul W. Fox (ed.) *Politics: Canada.* Fourth Edition. (Toronto, 1977) pp. 532–46; Peter H. Russell, *Leading Constitutional Decisions.* Third Edition. (Ottawa, 1982); and Peter W. Hogg, *Constitutional Law in Canada.*

The apparent erosion of the "watertight compartments" theory can be seen in several cases which relate to the administrative difficulty of setting up systems of regulation where jurisdiction is artificially divided by distinction between interprovincial and intraprovincial trade. A possible solution to this problem might have been the delegation of provincial powers to the federal level or vice versa in order to achieve uniform and comprehensive regulation. In 1948 a bill was introduced into the Nova Scotia legislature which sought to authorize the delegation to Parliament of authority to legislate in stated matters of provincial jurisdiction and to provide for the possibility of federal delegation to the province in a similar way. This bill was referred to the courts. Neither the Nova Scotia court nor the Supreme Court was able to uphold it. The Supreme Court, in a unanimous judgment, held that since Parliament and the provincial legislatures are sovereign bodies with regard to the powers assigned to them, neither has the power to delegate away the authority conferred on it by the constitution.[42] This case, while conclusive, may not have finally disposed of the matter. The Dominion-Provincial Conference of 1950 suggested in its recommendation for constitutional amendment that the question of delegation be considered, and a provision for limited delegation was included in the Fulton proposals for constitutional revision.

The year after the *Delegation* case the Supreme Court was able to find an escape from the difficulty in *P.E.I. Potato Marketing Board* v. *H. B. Willis Inc.*[43] Here the court upheld the provisions of the Agricultural Products Marketing Act, 1949, which empowered the federal government to delegate to a provincial board the power to make and enforce regulations under the act. This time there was no delegation of authority from Parliament to the provincial legislature, but the federal government had "adopted as its own" a provincial board to carry out the purposes of the act.

When, in the *Winner* case,[44] the Supreme Court ruled that Parliament alone had the power to regulate interprovincial bus lines, the difficulties of divided jurisdiction were avoided by the passage of the Motor Vehicle Transportation Act by Parliament. This act simply

42. *Attorney-General of Nova Scotia* v. *Attorney-General of Canada [1951] S.C.R. 31.*

43. [1952] 2 S.C.R. 392.

44. *Winner* v. *S.M.T. (Eastern) Ltd. and Attorney-General of New Brunswick* [1951] S.C.R. 887.

delegated back to provincial licensing boards the power to make the necessary regulations in the same manner as that previously upheld in the *P.E.I. Potato Marketing Board* reference.

Another problem of divided jurisdiction over trade and commerce was dealt with in the case of *Murphy* v. *C.P.R. and Attorney-General of Canada.*[45] A provision of the Wheat Board Act required that all grain shipped in interprovincial or international trade should be sold to the Wheat Board, and producers, railways, and elevators were required to conform to this regulation. The original suit was against the C.P.R., which had refused to accept grain when the shipper had not conformed to the board's regulations. The suit was an attempt to break the monopoly of the Wheat Board and divert the windfall profits from the control of the price of barley away from traders. The Supreme Court was unanimous in upholding the validity of the Wheat Board Act. This case and the *Potato Marketing Board* reference represent, said Mr. Justice MacDonald, "a maturing of opinion in the Supreme Court as to the process of trade and the problems inherent in its regulation, marking a great advance from the negative approach of the Privy Council cases, and . . . constitute good ground for hope that precise limits will be found for dividing Provincial and Dominion powers, upon such a functional basis as will enable their practical exercise by each, or by both in co-operation."[46]

An even wider scope to the power of the Wheat Board was given by the Manitoba Court of Appeal in *Regina* v. *Klassen*, where the powers of the board were held to apply to a feed mill whose business was entirely within the province. The intra-provincial aspects of the trade were held to be incidental to the orderly carrying out of the policy embodied in the act.[47] In spite of Lord Simon's acute and discriminating disposal of the old emergency doctrine in 1946, the courts have nevertheless continued to resort to it in a number of cases. In the first of these the Privy Council, in the *Japanese-Canadians* reference, upheld the measures taken to evacuate Japanese-Canadians in British Columbia, to dispose of their property, and in some cases to repatriate them, even where they were Canadian citizens and not Japanese nationals.

45. [1958] S.C.R. 626.

46. MacDonald, *Legislative Power and the Supreme Court*, pp. 15–16.

47. [1959] 20 D.L.R. (2d) 406.

However, the emergency doctrine was conceived by the board in less narrow and restricted terms than Lord Haldane had defined it in the *Board of Commerce* case. Lord Wright said:

> Under the B.N.A. Act property and civil rights in the several provinces are committed to the provincial legislatures, but the Parliament of the Dominion in a sufficiently great emergency such as that arising out of war has power to deal adequately with that emergency for the safety of the Dominion as a whole. The interests of the Dominion are to be protected and it rests with the Parliament of the Dominion to protect them. What these interests are the Parliament of the Dominion must be left with considerable freedom to judge.[48]

The Supreme Court also was unable to resist the emergency doctrine in the *Margarine* reference. A statute of considerable antiquity, the Dairy Industry Act, prohibited the sale and manufacture of margarine in Canada. When this provision was first enacted margarine may have been somewhat nasty and possibly unsafe. In any event its prohibition was bound to gratify the agricultural lobby. Experience of the wartime butter shortage had considerably reduced the patience of a large section of the urban electorate with the sanctity of the dairy industry. In addition, the terms of union with Newfoundland had included the legalization of the sale of margarine in the island notwithstanding its prohibition anywhere else. The only way out of this absurd anomaly, without offending the agricultural interests, was to get rid of the act without repealing it. Accordingly the federal government was suddenly assailed by doubts of the constitutionality of the act, and its lawyers ingenuously sought to assure the Supreme Court that the prohibition of margarine was founded on the emergency power to safeguard the health and taste of the country. The Supreme Court, not surprisingly, was unable to perceive the dimensions of the emergency with which the act purported to deal, and found the controversial clauses *ultra vires.*[49]

A year later, the court was given an opportunity to make it clear that the *Margarine* decision was not an outright return to the rigidity of the *Board of Commerce* conception of the emergency power. In the *Rentals* reference it restated the emergency doctrine and sought to clarify Lord Simon's position in the *Temperance*

48. *Co-operative Committee on Japanese Canadians* v. *Attorney-General for Canada* [1947] 1 D.L.R. 577, at p. 585.

49. [1949] 1 D.L.R. 433.

Federation case. The Chief Justice, in particular, referred to the reluctance of the court to deal with the question of finding out as a matter of fact when the emergency had passed away. Parliament, in transitional emergency legislation, and the government, in various orders-in-council made thereunder, had made it plain "that the exceptional conditions brought about by war, which made the *Wartime Leasehold Regulations* necessary, are still continuing, that the orderly transition from war to peace has not yet been completed, and that, in such circumstances, Parliament is entitled and empowered to maintain such control as it finds necessary to ensure the orderly transition from war to peace."[50] The emphasis here clearly means that the Supreme Court is most reluctant to set itself up as the arbiter between the two levels of government if the question is whether there is an emergency or not. Parliament has a responsibility to act which the court will not readily curtail.

Along with a more benign view of emergency powers, the court has shown some disposition to recognize federal jurisdiction over matters which have assumed such a dimension as to become of national concern. In the *Johannesson* case the question was whether aeronautics had in fact assumed such a dimension of national importance that could be recognized by the court. The original Aeronautics Act had been upheld in 1932 because it had been founded on a British Empire treaty. But the original treaty had been denounced and replaced by the Chicago Convention, which could not by any stretch of the imagination be described as a British Empire treaty. The court laid heavy stress on Lord Sankey's implication in the *Aeronautics* case that aeronautics fell under the residuary clause as a matter of national importance. They then took up Lord Simon's dictum that if a subject of legislation "must from its inherent nature be the concern of the Dominion as a whole," then it belongs to Parliament "as a matter affecting the peace, order and good government of Canada." They were unmoved by the fact that "national importance" had been rejected twice in 1937, and came to the conclusion that aeronautics was federal because it was outside section 92 and within the residuary clause.[51]

It is of course true that for the court to have found aeronautics outside federal jurisdiction would have created a situation so bizarre that it would have been necessary to remedy it by some other means, such as constitutional amendment. The difficulty created by the

50. [1950] S.C.R. 124, at p. 130.

51. *Johannesson* v. *Rural Municipality of West St. Paul* [1952] 1 S.C.R. 292.

chain of reasoning used by the Court is "how far we may consider that the Residuary Clause now applies to similar topics of demonstrable national importance, and which, unlike those covered by the Aeronautics Act, may normally lie within Provincial jurisdiction."[52] Mr. Justice MacDonald saw in this decision some hope that the "aspect" doctrine may confer on Parliament overriding power under the residuary clause to legislate on matters which are otherwise in provincial jurisdiction, even when they have become "matters of national concern" without the urgency of emergency conditions.

Indeed, such an approach to the matter seems to be implied in an Ontario case (which did not go to the Supreme Court) in which Mr. Justice McLennan upheld federal jurisdiction over labour relations in uranium mining on the ground that it was a matter which fell under the legislative authority of Parliament as legislation for the peace, order and good government of Canada. Having upheld the federal jurisdiction under the general power, he did not feel it necessary to consider whether the jurisdiction required to be supported on the two further grounds that it related to defence and that the uranium industry had been declared a work for the general advantage of Canada under the exceptional provision of section 92(10) of the B.N.A. Act.[53]

Even if the residuary power to legislate for peace, order and good government does not confer the broad powers to legislate even on aspects of the enumerated provincial powers, as the two cases above suggest that it might, there is another source of federal legislative power which potentially could remove many of the older restrictions on the power of Parliament. This is the defence power, contained in section 91(7). Before he was elevated to the bench, Professor Laskin (as he then was) quite properly asked why, since this head of jurisdiction is listed in section 91, it was necessary at all for the Judicial Committee "to develop an 'emergency' (in the main, a war) concept of the general power."[54] He noted that the defence power was used as a makeweight in the *Aeronautics* case, and wondered if it might have been raised in the *Board of Commerce* case. In any event, it is clear that the federal Parliament has been able to use the defence power not only in the lengthy transition from

52. MacDonald, *Legislative Power and the Supreme Court*, pp. 21-2.

53. *Pronto Uranium Mines Ltd.* v. *Ontario Labour Relations Board* [1956] O.R. 862.

54. Laskin, *Canadian Constitutional Law.* p. 242.

the end of the Second World War, but also in the cold war that followed. Laskin noted that the Essential Materials (Defence) Act, which conferred very wide powers over the production, distribution and use of materials regarded by the government as essential, was justified in Parliament by references to the defence power. The act was never before the courts, but the somewhat less sweeping Defence Production Act, 1951, which replaced the Essential Materials Act a year after its enactment, is still in force. The wide compulsory powers were allowed to lapse, but the act itself was transformed from temporary to permanent in 1955. This would appear to be a potentially substantial source of federal power which, by its very nature, is unlikely to be seriously challenged in the courts.

In the period since it became the final court of appeal the Supreme Court seems to have developed a more generous interpretation of the federal power than has existed, except in wartime, since the beginning of the ascendancy of Lord Watson. Nevertheless, this does not represent an abandonment of what Professor McWhinney calls judicial self-restraint and a clear move in the direction of judicial activism.[55] On the whole, the court has continued to manifest judicial self-restraint: it has kept its decisions on narrow grounds, it has avoided ruling on constitutional issues unless this has been unavoidable, and it has started out with a presumption of the validity of the legislation before it. This constitutes an increase in what Professor Russell has called judicial flexibility which has the effect of "adding to the areas of law in which the provinces and Ottawa have concurrent jurisdiction."[56] While it has added to the legislative capacity of both levels of government, it has left the boundaries of legislative jurisdiction less clear than before.

For a time, following the *Johanneson* case, the court seemed to be attracted by the use of the concept of "national dimension" to fill in the gaps in federal power where the constitution was not clear. Thus, in *Munro* v. *National Capital Commission*[57], Mr. Justice Cartwright asserted that it is "difficult to suggest a subject matter of legislation which more clearly goes beyond local or provincial interests and is the common concern of Canada as a whole than the

55. Edward McWhinney, *Judicial Review in the English-speaking World.* pp. 212 ff.

56. Peter H. Russell "The Supreme Court since 1960." in Fox. *Politics: Canada.* p. 541

57. [1966] S.C.R. 663.

development, conservation and improvement of the National Capital Region. . . ." Two years later, in the *Offshore Minerals Reference*[58], the court was to use the same argument to uphold federal jurisdiction over the sea-bed adjacent to the coast of a province. However, the court has been sparing in resorting to this basis for federal jurisdiction. Significantly, the majority of the court in the *Anti-inflation Reference*[59], did not accept the argument that the subject of inflation had assumed a national dimension, but preferred to uphold federal jurisdiction on the ground of national emergency.

A more important source of federal power has resulted from jurisdiction over trade and commerce, a power which had been almost completely destroyed by Lord Haldane. The American Supreme Court over the years has used the "flow of commerce" concept to extend the reach of the commerce power in the United States. The Supreme Court of Canada seems now to be moving in the same direction to give the commerce power a wider meaning than it had when that power was constricted by the artificial divisions created by the "watertight compartments" view of federal and provincial powers. A more liberal interpretation of the commerce power enabled the court to sustain the national energy policy in *Caloil Inc.* v. *Attorney-General of Canada.*[60] Similarly, in *Attorney-General for Manitoba* v. *Manitoba Egg and Poultry Association*[61], the court struck down a provincial scheme of regulation of trade in eggs on the ground that it had the effect of impeding the flow of commerce across provincial boundaries and thus infringed on the exclusive federal control over trade and commerce.

The most sensitive area, from a provincial point of view, was the extent to which the Supreme Court's revived interest in the commerce power threatened to undermine the powers of a province to regulate the production of its natural resources under section 109 of the British North America Act. Two cases which arose in Saskatchewan in the middle seventies illustrate this. Private companies had challenged the provincial potash conservation regulations and the taxation which sought to regulate the exploitation of oil. The provincial government was dismayed to find that the federal government had intervened in these cases to defend its own jurisdiction. In the

58. [1967] S.C.R. 292.

59. [1976] 2 S.C.R. 373.

60. [1971] S.C.R. 543.

61. [1971] S.C.R. 689.

end the Supreme Court ruled that the attempt to regulate the oil industry through taxation and to control the potash industry were invasions of exclusive federal jurisdiction over indirect taxation and trade and commerce.[62] Since most non-renewable resources are shipped beyond the boundaries of a province, provincial attempts to regulate resource exploitation have been seriously curtailed by overriding federal powers.

This has been a notable cause of provincial resentment which in part explains the intransigence of some of the western premiers at the constitutional negotiations in 1980. It led to the inclusion in the 1982 constitutional changes of a new section 92A (into what is now described as "formerly named the British North America Act, 1867"), which confers exclusive jurisdiction on provincial legislatures to make laws in relation to exploration, development, conservation and management of non-renewable natural and forestry resources, provided that these laws are not discriminatory. The section also safeguards the continuing right of Parliament to make such laws, which will prevail in case of conflict.[63]

In its role as arbiter of the jurisdictional boundaries between the two levels of government two things may be said about the role of the Supreme Court since it became the highest court of appeal. On the one hand it has on the whole been more sensitive to previously weak sources of federal jurisdiction, such as the general power and the commerce power. On the other hand it has generally been more sympathetic to the attempts of both levels of government to extend the reach of legislative control over economic activity. This is an attitude of judicial self-restraint in which the court has shown a disposition to assume that the legislature knew what it was doing and should not be frustrated by overly narrow interpretations of the constitution. The court, in other words, has come to accept the expanding role of government as legitimate. It remains to be seen whether the existence of the Charter will provide more opportunities for judicial activism which may modify that trend.

62. *Canadian Industrial Gas & Oil Ltd.* v. *Government of Saskatchewan* [1978] 2 S.C.R. 545; *Central Canada Potash Co. Ltd. and Attorney-General of Canada* v. *Government of Saskatchewan.* [1979] 1 S.C.R. 42.

63. Professor Russell's view is that the effect of the amendment will be modest. He says, "While this amendment would give the provinces some concurrent jurisdiction in relation to interprovincial trade, it would mean that the provinces were still excluded from regulating the marketing of products in international trade. Thus it is probably of little value to those provinces which seek to reverse the Supreme Court's decision in the Potash case." Peter H. Russell, *Leading Constitutional Decisions.* Third Edition. p. 258.

THE DISTRIBUTION OF FINANCIAL RESOURCES

Whatever the distribution of legislative authority in a federal system, the distribution of revenue sources will play a decisive role in the ultimate balance of power in the system. Enormous influence and authority will flow to the level of government whose surplus revenues give it the capacity to influence financially weaker governments. This has been true of Canadian federalism.

The larger and more flexible tax base of the federal government gave it very great leverage in the years after the Second World War when it could use the spending power to assert strong leadership in fields of provincial jurisdiction. However, the fact that the provinces did possess legislative jurisdiction gave them a source of countervailing power which in the end made it possible for them to bargain on equal terms with the federal government. In more recent years, as the fiscal balance shifted to the stronger provinces, the dominant position of the federal government began to weaken and the pressure for greater decentralization in the system has mounted.

In the negotiations that led up to Confederation, it had proved to be impossible to divide revenue sources in the same way as legislative responsibilities. Not only did the lion's share of apparent revenue sources go to the federal government, but there also emerged a marked and growing disparity in the financial strength of the various provinces. At the union the three original provinces found over 80 percent of their revenue from customs and excise duties. This rich and powerful source of revenue was given exclusively to the national Parliament. Since it was in practice impossible for some of the provinces to meet their costs of government from their own revenues, the new federation at the outset included the principle of federal subsidies to the provinces. It could be said that the responsibility for rectifying regional disparities of provincial revenue and equalizing the burden of taxation now enshrined in section 36 of the Constitution Act, 1982, has always been an implicit part of the constitution. It has been refined and strengthened, but it was always there.

The main lines of the financial settlement at Confederation are clear. Section 91(3) of the B.N.A. Act confers a simple and sweeping power on the Parliament of Canada to raise "Money by any Mode or System of Taxation." The provinces, on the other hand, are limited by section 92(2) to "Direct Taxation within the Province in order to the Raising of a Revenue for Provincial Purposes." In addition, the provinces are able (section 109) to raise revenue from the sale of natural resources. Section 121 ensures freedom of trade within the union by providing for the free entry into all provinces of the products of each. Neither the federal nor the provincial legislatures are permitted to tax the property of the other, since these are exempt from taxation by section 125. "It is clear from these initial provisions of the constitution," writes Professor Scott, "that the concept of provincial autonomy prevailing at Confederation was subject to two important financial restrictions: first in being limited to direct taxation, and secondly in being dependent on subsidies. On the other hand the taxing powers of Parliament appeared unlimited."[64]

The granting of the power of direct taxation to the provinces in 1867 was not as rich an endowment as it might now appear. The state of the economy at that time would have made an income tax costly to administer and probably unproductive. There was a deep-rooted objection to direct taxation which can be explained by the character of the times. It was in fact assumed that the power of direct taxation would enable the provinces to confer the power to levy such taxes—chiefly on real estate—on the municipalities. It was only towards the end of the century that the provinces began seriously to resort to direct taxation. Before 1914 the increasing need for provincial revenues was met partly by revenues from resource exploitation and from increases in federal subsidies. Only after 1918 did the provinces become seriously concerned with the search for new revenues.

By that time the taxation power had been clarified by a number of judicial decisions. As a result there was a slight limitation of the apparently wide taxing powers of the central Parliament. It was held that Parliament cannot levy a direct tax within a province in order to raise revenue for a provincial purpose.[65] There is some doubt as to the validity of social insurance schemes paid out of federal revenues, since if they have not been covered by constitutional amendments, they are likely to deal with the exclusive provincial legislative power over property and civil rights. This limitation, however, only applies to direct taxes: "indirect taxes escape its application, since the provinces cannot impose them at all."[66] Similarly, it is

64. F. R. Scott, "The Constitutional Background of Taxation Agreements." *The McGill Law Journal.* II:1 (Autumn, 1955) p. 2.

65. *Caron* v. *The King* [1924] A.C. 999.

66. Scott, "Constitutional Background..." p. 3. The question has been raised at a number of federal-provincial constitutional conferences to confer some powers of indirect taxation on the provinces, so far without result.

difficult to see how the courts can limit the expenditure of moneys which are simply a charge on the general revenues of Canada.

Meanwhile the provinces were able to enlist the support of the courts in enlarging the scope of their taxing powers. In an early case, the Judicial Committee of the Privy Council defined a direct tax in words found in J. S. Mill's *Principles of Political Economy*: "A direct tax is one which is demanded from the very persons who it is intended or desired should pay it. Indirect taxes are those demanded from one person in the expectation and intention that he shall indemnify himself at the expense of another."[67] Subsequently, the provinces were able to hit on the device of levying what are in fact indirect taxes by making the vendor a sales tax collector for the provincial government.[68] There are disadvantages apart from the one that large numbers of theatre operators, tobacconists and retailers become reluctant and not always reliable agents of government. These taxes are difficult to administer and it is sometimes difficult to recover them from the vendor. It is administratively impossible to recover the tax from residents who are able to do their shopping across the provincial boundary in a less heavily taxed jurisdiction. Furthermore, in spite of the benevolent attitude which the courts have taken, there always remains a nagging doubt that such taxes, which fly in the face of a common sense definition of a direct tax, are constitutionally valid.

Fiscal Transfers: From Subsidies to Tax-sharing

In spite of provincial ingenuity in searching for new sources of tax revenue, federal transfer payments in one form or another have always played an important part in provincial budgets. The original basis of these arrangements was contained in section 102-20 of the B.N.A. Act. Because of the transfer to the federal government of existing provincial debts together with jurisdiction over the assets, such as railways and other property, for which the debts had been incurred, an attempt was made to find a formula to relieve provinces with heavy debts without penalizing the more frugal and cautious provinces. Accordingly, a formula of twenty-five dollars per

67. *Bank of Toronto* v. *Lambe* [1887] 12 App. Cas. 575.

68. *Atlantic Smoke Shops* v. *Conlon* [1943] A.C. 550.

capita constituted "allowable" debt. A province under the debt limit would be entitled to a perpetual annual grant of five percent of the difference, while a province over the limit was expected to pay interest at the same rate on the excess. In fact the limits were subsequently raised, partly to remove the obligation of some provinces to pay the charge on "excess" debt and partly to justify payments to new provinces. There were also general grants in support of government for all provinces as well as grants to Alberta and Saskatchewan to compensate them for the retention of federal control over their lands and resources at the time of their creation. However, when control over their resources was returned in 1930 the grants continued to be paid. The most important of the federal subsidies to the provinces was the payment of 80 cents per head of population, based on the 1861 census. In 1907 this was revised to relate the payment to the most recent census, with the further proviso that the payments would be reduced to 60 cents per head for population in excess of two and one-half million.[69]

While it is clear from this account that substantial changes in the arrangements have taken place, the B.N.A. Act itself asserted that the original grants to the provinces were to be "in full settlement of all future demands on Canada." If this had been taken literally, any increase would have required amendment to the B.N.A. Act. However, when the federal Parliament first sought to revise the subsidies upwards they were advised by the Law Officers of the Crown in London that they had the power, under section 91, to increase subsidies as they chose. "The decision no doubt reflected," as Professor Birch dryly remarked, "the traditional British attitude to written constitutions; that if they appear to conflict with the demands of common sense too much attention should not be paid to them."[70]

While the subsidies continue to be paid, they have become a steadily decreasing portion of provincial revenues and are of little significance today. The steady growth of provincial spending responsibilities has forced the provinces to increase efforts to exploit new tax fields. They entered the fields of personal and corporate income, estate and natural resource taxes. They found a method of levying sales taxes. As a result federal subsidies, which

69. *Rowell-Sirois Report*, I pp. 42-6.

70. A. H. Birch. *Federalism, Finance and Social Legislation.* (London, 1955) p. 63.

amounted to almost three-fifths of provincial revenues in 1874, had fallen to one-quarter by as early as 1913.

The growing importance of highway construction, general electrification, which required heavy expenditures for power facilities, and other needs caused provincial expenditures to more than double between 1921 and 1930. Until the Great Depression broke, the provinces were able to keep up with their responsibilities although it was becoming obvious that the poorer provinces were less able to adjust than the wealthier ones. There were thus two distinct problems associated with the financial provisions of the constitution. The first was the unforeseen growth of provincial expenditures generally as a result of new responsibilities placed on governments. The second was the emergence of pronounced regional inequalities between the financial capacities of the richer and the poorer provinces.

The claims of the poorer provinces for financial help were largely based in the inter-war period on the need for compensation for the adverse effects of past federal policies. This was the basis of the land claims of the western provinces, which led to the settlement of 1930. "Whatever the dubious nature of their claims (Dominion management had been responsible for 'opening up' the West) the prairie provinces were placed on a somewhat more tenable financial footing. But the main point is that the new Dominion grants were based not on existing economic needs but rather on a supposed 'disadvantage' arising from past federal policy."[71]

A similar argument was used to increase subsidies to the Maritime provinces, which claimed to have suffered since Confederation from the adverse effects of the tariff and comparatively smaller federal expenditures on Maritime development. A royal commission of 1926 (the Duncan Commission) recommended that annual subsidies to the Maritime provinces be increased by $1.6 million until the matter could finally be settled. A second royal commission (the White Commission) in 1934 was compelled to look at the matter in the midst of the Depression when the situation was far more grave. They refused to see the question as one of fiscal need, and preferred to salve the conscience of the country with the admission that the Maritimes should be compensated because they had not "shared proportionately with the other provinces of Canada

71. J. Stefan Dupre, "Tax Powers versus Spending Responsibilities: An Historical Analysis of Federal-Provincial Finance." in Abraham Rotstein (ed.) *The Prospects of Change: Proposals for Canada's Future.* (Toronto, 1964) p. 85. This is an admirable summary of the problem.

in the economic advantages accruing from Confederation." Accordingly, the interim grants of the three provinces were to be increased to $2 475 000 in perpetuity as "a final equitable settlement."

Nevertheless, by the Depression of the 1930s the financial difficulties of the provinces were beyond the point where they could be solved by tinkering with the subsidy formula. The provinces had been saddled with crippling responsibilities for social welfare, and the failure in the courts of the Bennett "New Deal" had made it plain that their difficulties could not be alleviated by increased activity by the federal government. Accordingly, the Royal Commission on Dominion-Provincial Relations was appointed with a wide-ranging mandate to examine the economic and financial basis of Confederation, the distribution of legislative responsibility and the financial relations between governments.[72]

The Commission, whose findings were based in part on a massive series of special studies, which remains one of the finest collective efforts of Canadian scholarship, sought to relate the original plan for Confederation to the problems and needs of the twentieth century. They were convinced that the constitutional development which had given the provinces the primary role in social and welfare policy was right and healthy. "Provincial responsibility for social welfare should be deemed to be basic and general; Dominion responsibility, on the other hand, should be deemed an exception to the general rule, and as such should be strictly defined."[73] Even though these services were so massively expensive, and provincial resources so inelastic and unequal, they rejected the idea that they should be assumed by the federal government. Only in the case of unemployment insurance and responsibility for "unemployed employables" (the frightening and intractable problem of the Depression) were the grounds of administrative efficiency and financial burden sufficient to justify a constitutional amendment to transfer them to the authority of the federal government.

But the whole financial basis of inter-governmental relations would have to be drastically reorganized in the interests of efficiency and economy and to ensure adequate revenues to even the poorest provinces. The old subsidy system, a ramshackle structure propped up by special grants, loans, advances and inconsistencies, should be scrapped. To the federal Parliament would be given exclusive jurisdiction over the highly productive taxes on personal

72. Rowell-Sirois Report, II. pp. 9-11.

73. *Ibid.* p. 24.

incomes, corporation incomes and succession duties, where double (and even triple) taxation from federal, provincial and sometimes municipal authorities imposed a crippling burden on the economy. The federal government would assume the full burden of provincial debts. What sources of revenue remained to the provinces would be left to them undisturbed, and they would also receive a federal payment equal to ten percent of net federal revenue from mining and oil-producing companies. While the old system of provincial subsidies would be wiped out, a national adjustment grant, which would be recalculated every five years by an independent commission, would be paid to the provinces on the basis of fiscal need. On the initial calculations of the Commission, all provinces would qualify for this grant except Ontario, Alberta and British Columbia. In addition to the adjustment grants, which would be irreducible, there would also be emergency grants to meet the needs of provinces experiencing exceptionally serious economic conditions.

The report of the Commission was laid before a Dominion-Provincial Conference in May, 1940, but the determined opposition of the governments of Alberta, Ontario, and British Columbia, none of which were to receive the new grants, led to its proposals being abandoned. "In spite of the scope and quality of the commission's work," wrote Professor Smiley in a powerful defence of its recommendations, "its analysis of federal-provincial relations had surprisingly little influence on the direction that the theory and practice of Canadian federalism have taken since 1945."[74] Nevertheless, two of the Commission's most important ideas, provincial primacy in social welfare jurisdiction and the notion of revenue equalization to balance the burden of taxation at a roughly equivalent level of services, have become permanently embedded in the fabric of Canadian federalism. Only the method of achieving them which the Commission recommended has failed to gain recognition.

In the event it was not possible to wait on a more sober view being taken of the recommendations of the report. The federal government, with the tremendous bargaining strength which flowed from its formidable wartime power, was able to bring the provinces into a series of taxation agreements in 1941 by which they relinquished control over the income, corporation and succession duties tax fields for the duration of the war. In return, the provinces were to receive unconditional payments to compensate them for the reve-

74. D. V. Smiley, "The Rowell-Sirois Report, Provincial Autonomy, and Post-War Canadian Federalism." *Canadian Journal of Economics and Political Science.* XXVII:1 (February, 1962) p. 54.

nue lost. At that time the agreement stipulated that the federal authorities would reduce their rates of taxes sufficiently to enable the provinces to re-enter the income and corporation tax fields a year after the return of peace.

However, the experience of the war years and the anticipated needs of reconstruction convinced the federal authorities of the need to control the major tax fields in order to use fiscal policy as the major weapon of economic management. Accordingly, at the end of the war the federal government proposed that the transfer of major tax fields be made permanent in exchange for unconditional subsidies based on the gross national product, together with full federal jurisdiction over old-age pensions and most of unemployment relief, and a wide range of conditional grants to the provinces in a number of fields of development and social welfare. These proposals, first laid before the Dominion-Provincial Conference on Reconstruction in 1945, were not accepted. However, individual agreements were made with various provinces to perpetuate federal "rental" of the major tax fields for a further five-year period. These agreements contained escalator clauses to enable the provinces to benefit from upward changes in national income, and a number of different options and formulas were developed to meet the needs of particular provinces. Even so, Ontario refused to take part in the agreements which began in 1947, and Quebec remained outside as long as the rental agreements were in force. However, Ontario did agree in 1952 to rent personal income tax and succession duties, but, in the 1957 agreement, to rent only personal income tax.

Thus, because of their very flexibility, the taxation and expenditure powers of the federal Parliament and the provinces became the means by which the system adjusted itself rapidly to changes in circumstances and in political forces without substantial constitutional changes. Because the taxing powers of the two jurisdictions are independent of each other, no question arises about the constitutional validity of double taxation. It has sometimes been claimed that the provincial power to impose direct taxes gives the provinces a priority in these fields.[75] This is not so. The provincial jurisdiction in direct tax fields is exclusive for provincial purposes, the federal jurisdiction exclusive for federal purposes. In Lord Macmillan's words, "Both income taxes may co-exist and be enforced without clashing. The Dominion reaps part of the field of the Manitoba

75. This claim was once written into the preamble of a Quebec statute (2-3 Eliz. II, cap. 17), but subsequently repealed when Quebec taxpayers were allowed to deduct an allowance fot the Quebec tax.

citizen's income. The province reaps another part of it."[76] But what if, as Professor Scott put it in an extension of the image, "the poor Manitoba citizen is reaped right down to his bare stubble."[77] To this Viscount Dunedin in the Privy Council had already given the answer; the federal tax will prevail:

> The two taxations, Dominion and Provincial, can stand side by side without interfering with each other, but as soon as you come to the concomitant privileges of absolute priority they cannot stand side by side and must clash; consequently the Dominion must prevail.[78]

This doctrine has given the federal government a powerful lever in negotiating the taxation agreements with the provinces. A similar, though somewhat narrower, freedom in expenditure has provided the remainder of the foundation for the post-war system of intergovernmental financial relations. When a government imposes a license or levy as part of a special fund, then the levy will stand or fall depending on whether the scheme of regulation with which it is associated is within the powers of the legislature. This point was made clear in the numerous cases relating to schemes for the marketing of natural products, as well as in the *Unemployment and Social Insurance* reference. However, if the expenditure is not related to a scheme of regulation, these restrictions do not apply.

All public monies raised by federal and provincial governments—except those related to particular funds—are paid into the consolidated revenue funds of either the federal or provincial governments. These monies belong to the Crown, and as Professor Scott pointed out, "the Crown is a person capable of making gifts or contracts like any other person, to whomsoever it chooses to benefit. . . . Moreover, the Crown may attach conditions to the gift, failure to observe which will cause its discontinuance. These simple but significant powers exist in our constitutional law though no mention of them can be found in the B.N.A. Acts."[79] Accordingly, on the basis of the royal prerogative and the common law, governments can subsidize one another as much as they like, and can make gifts to individuals as well as to other governments. Thus the federal gov-

76. *Forbes* v. *Attorney-General of Manitoba.* [1937] A.C. 260.

77. Scott, "Constitutional Background . . ." p. 7.

78. *In re Silver Bros.* [1932] A.C. 514.

79. Scott, "Constitutional Background . . ." p. 6. See also The Right Honourable Pierre Elliott Trudeau, Prime Minister of Canada. *Federal-Provincial Grants and the Spending Power of Parliament.* (Ottawa, 1969)

ernment pays family allowances, and it has made a great variety of conditional grants to provincial governments.

This right of largesse has been the principal means by which the federal government has been able, with its preponderance of financial resources, to equalize the financial position of the provinces, and to initiate uniform policies for the whole country even in matters lying entirely within provincial jurisdiction. This largesse has taken a number of forms: the old statutory subsidies provided in the British North America Acts; the payments to the provinces under the tax-sharing arrangements, including certain equalization payments and special payments to the Atlantic provinces; conditional grants made on the understanding that the province pays an agreed share of the total costs and adheres to certain standards in the project; and, in the view of the federal government, "tax room" allowed to the provinces by the federal government in fields of shared taxation to meet the costs of joint programs.

This system, whatever its advantages in terms of economic efficiency and rational planning, was accepted with evident reluctance by a number of provinces and was objected to on various grounds. The effort of will required of the wealthier provinces not to levy taxes in some lucrative fields became almost unbearable. At the same time the demands of all provinces, rich and poor alike, for a larger share of federal transfer payments to meet rising costs of government made the task of re-negotiating the agreements more and more difficult in each five-year period. By the time the agreement was due to expire in 1962, the two sides were far apart. In addition, one province (Quebec) was levying a personal income tax and a corporation income tax of its own, and another province (Ontario) was also in the corporation income tax field. Political objections to the tax rental system were widespread. It was argued that in foregoing these taxes the provinces were giving up their constitutional rights and undermining their autonomy. It was further argued by many that for governments to spend large sums that they did not themselves raise by taxation promoted fiscal irresponsibility and an unhealthy attitude towards government expenditure on the part of the public at large.

In some combination, these arguments finally impelled the federal government to propose an end to the tax rental system, and to replace it by one in which the tax-sharing aspects were more apparent. New proposals were therefore laid before the provinces at a federal-provincial conference on February 23, 1961. The central feature of the federal proposal was to fix on the provinces their share of the responsibility for the principal shared-tax fields. As long as the tax rental system had operated, the federal Parliament had levied the main burden of taxes, redistributing an increasing proportion of them to the provinces for provincial services. Under the new arrangements the provinces would have to levy their own taxes, which meant not only the attentive taxpayer would discover how much of his tax was attributable to the province, but also that the provincial legislatures would again be the locus of debate on the taxation policies of the provinces.

In order to provide room for the new taxes, the federal government agreed to withdraw from the personal income tax field to the extent of 16 percent of its revenue from this source in 1962-63, with a progressive withdrawal of one further percentage point until a level of 20 percent was reached in 1966-67. In addition, the federal government agreed to withdraw to the extent of 9 percent from the corporation income tax field and 50 percent from succession duties. The federal government offered an arrangement by which the provinces could levy their own taxes, but designate the federal authorities as the collection agency. Consequently, all of the provinces except Quebec (which already collected its own income taxes), agreed to have their income taxes collected by the federal government, and all but Quebec and Ontario did the same for the corporation income tax. The federal government continued to pay equalization grants to the provinces on a modified formula which based them on the average *per capita* yield on income taxes and succession duties, plus an amount which would bring the natural resource revenue of a province up to the national *per capita* yield. Under the new arrangement, said the Minister of Finance, "the provinces would reassume their constitutional rights and responsibilities and vary their taxes as they saw fit."[80] All of these changes were embodied in the Federal-Provincial Fiscal Arrangements Act, which was passed by Parliament in September, 1961, and came into effect on April 1, 1962.

The tax-sharing arrangements retained a number of features developed during the tax-rental period. Decentralization of taxation power was not accompanied by as much decentralization of administration as might have been expected. Most provinces enacted income taxes based on exactly the same exemptions and rate structure as the federal government. Even in the corporation tax field the pressure of common administrative practice tended towards as much uniformity as possible. Quebec modified its corporation

80. Canada. *House of Commons Debates*. July 11 1961. p. 7911.

income tax to bring it substantially into line with the federal tax, and Ontario for years modelled its tax on the federal one. Thus, however much the political institutions of federalism tend to fragment the citizen, the requirements of administrative convenience and simplification in the ever-widening web of modern government tend to put him together again.

The arrangements solemnly concluded in 1962 were soon modified, partly as a consequence of the change of government in Ottawa. As a result of federal-provincial conferences in 1963 and 1964, the rate of federal withdrawal from the income tax field was accelerated so that it reached 24 percent by 1966-67, and the federal withdrawal from succession duties was increased from 50 percent to 75 percent. In addition, the equalization formula was modified by reverting to the 1957 basis (the average yield of shared taxes in Ontario and British Columbia).

Further changes were brought about by legislation introduced into Parliament in 1967. The tax abatements were increased from 24 to 28 percent in the case of income tax, and from 9 to 10 percent in the case of corporation income tax. The reason for these changes was an alteration in the means by which the federal government provided support for post-secondary education. Instead of the previous system of grants to universities, the federal government increased the tax room available to the provinces to help them meet the rising costs of education. Additionally, the legislation altered the equalization formula so that it was based on "a comprehensive index of the relative fiscal capacities of the provinces."[81]

The decades of the sixties and seventies revealed a number of difficult and increasingly grave problems associated with the regime of fiscal federalism, chiefly in connection with tax-sharing and shared-cost programs. Not only was the cost of government steadily rising but the pressure on the federal government to increase the provincial share of revenue fields was mounting at a time when federal revenues were no longer growing in real terms. The dramatic increase in world oil prices was accompanied by a general inflationary pressure felt by all. The principle of shared-cost programs in fields of primarily provincial jurisdiction was challenged, particularly by Quebec, as an interference in exclusive provincial jurisdiction as well as a distortion of provincial priorities. The desire of provincial governments to opt out of such programs with fiscal compensation, while it was tolerated in some cases, was resisted by the federal government because the only government likely to do so

81. *Ibid.* March 9, 1967. p. 13787.

was Quebec, which would tend to produce a *de facto* special status for that province. At the same time the provinces resented federal accounting controls in joint programs which they perceived as an interference in their proper constitutional jurisdiction. It was this last pressure in particular which led to one of the most important changes in the 1977 arrangements.

While the various governments wrestled with these problems, the 1967 fiscal arrangements had been extended twice, first to 1974 and subsequently to 1977. The federal government, with increasing pressure on its own resources and alarmed at the growth of its open-ended commitments to contribute proportionately to established programs had, since 1972, limited the increase in its contributions to not more than 15 percent over the previous year. Finally, an agreed program was submitted to Parliament, and on February 18, 1977, the Minister of Finance moved second reading of the Federal-Provincial Fiscal Arrangements and Established Programs Financing Act, 1977. The new fiscal arrangements, he said, would transfer to the provinces, in the form of cash transfers and tax points, an amount which represented more than a sixth of the federal budget. He said in part:

> Much of the discussion and debate over the past year and a half stemmed from obvious differences in perspective. We at the federal level believe that the national government must preserve enough fiscal resources to redistribute income to persons and regions, to stabilize the economy and to continue to help finance the services Canadians in all parts of the country need and deserve. Those at the provincial level have claimed that the federal government has in the past intruded into areas of provincial jurisdiction through the use of its spending power; that the shared-cost programs in particular have distorted provincial expenditure priorities; and that this, in turn, has forced the provinces to provide high-cost programs where equally effective but lower-cost alternatives would serve as well. Reflecting only a personal viewpoint as a member who was in the House through the decade of the sixties when a number of these significant measures came to their realization, I for one remain unrepentant about the use of the federal spending power for the purpose of providing better services to Canadians.... I would think there could hardly be any question that without the exercise of the spending power in the areas of health or post-secondary education we could not have had the good national standards in all provinces in the fields of health and education which have been supported in all corners of the House.[82]

In the case of these two programs the government had evidently concluded that they were so well established that it could dispense

82. *Ibid.* February 18, 1977. p. 3201.

with controls over expenditure by the provinces. The federal contribution would essentially be about half in tax points and half in per capita cash grants. Additional cash transfers on an interim basis would be made to provinces with an insufficient tax base, but these would eventually disappear. Federal payments would no longer be tied to provincial spending, nor would federal auditing of provincial accounts be required. The Prime Minister in a press conference made the following points: it benefits the provinces since the poorer provinces would not have to spend to get more federal funds; it is a step in the direction of decentralization of power since the provinces would now be able to manage their own financial affairs; the provinces would receive more than they would have under a fifty-fifty cost-sharing arrangement; "the possibility of distortion of provincial priorities is no longer an issue." He was to say, later in the House on December 14, that the federal government was in a sense gambling on the fact the provinces would be deeply committed to these programs, even if they were administering them without federal oversight. If after five years it appeared that serious disparities had developed because some provinces had reduced the quality of their program the matter would have to be reconsidered. Since federal contributions to the two programs were to be lumped together it would be impossible to determine how much federal money would go into each.

When the fiscal arrangements came up for renegotiation in 1982 one of the long-term trends in Canadian public finance had become clearly visible. The federal share of total revenues before transfers declined between 1960 and 1980 from 58 to 47 percent, while the provincial-local share increased from 42 to 53 percent. When federal transfers to the provinces were taken into account the federal share of total revenues declined from one-half to one-third.[83]

The second major factor, which affected all governments, was that slight or zero growth in the economy combined with rising inflation had steadily increased the cost of government services at a time when there was no corresponding rise in revenues so that nearly all governments were faced with continuing and intractable deficits. This was emphasized by the Minister of Finance when he moved the adoption of the bill to amend the Fiscal Arrangements and Continuing Programs Financing Act. He said:

> As I indicated in the budget, current circumstances require that the federal government apply restraint in all areas. Since transfers to the

83. Honourable Allan J. MacEachen, *Federal-Provincial Fiscal Arrangements in the Eighties.* A Submission to the Parliamentary Task Force on the Federal-Provincial Fiscal Arrangements, April 23, 1981. (Ottawa, 1981)

> provinces account for approximately 20 percent of total federal expenditures, they cannot be insulated from our restraint effort. However, the restraint which must apply to federal transfers to the provinces should be tempered with equity. I am convinced that the means whereby we propose to moderate the growth of these transfers is equitable. While the changes we proposed to established program financing would affect all provinces, except the richest, in more or less the same way, the new equalization system would be particularly beneficial to those with the lowest fiscal capacity. [Here he repeated the figures for changes in relative shares of public revenue]. . . . It is evident that the provinces now spend the largest share of public moneys raised in Canada. What these numbers indicate is that Canada is one of the most fiscally decentralized countries in the western world.[84]

The basic features of the proposal included a new equalization formula which would make it possible for provinces to provide reasonable standards of basic public services without unduly high levels of taxation. The formula is based on the taxable capacity of five provinces, which taken together comprise over eighty percent of the population of the provinces. Alberta is excluded at the top and the four Atlantic provinces at the bottom. The provinces eligible for equalization are the four Atlantic provinces, together with Quebec and Manitoba. For reasons of equity, the per capita value of total transfers under the Established Programs Financing arrangements will be equal as a result of changes in the computation of the cash transfers. The revenue guarantees in the previous program were terminated in 1982-83 but federal contributions will rise with increases in the gross national product over the five year period. Tax changes previously announced in the November, 1981, budget were expected to lead to increases in provincial revenues. The general effect of the new fiscal arrangements was to reduce federal contribution below the level which they would have attained under the 1977 agreements. This, of course, was viewed by the federal government as part of the policy of restraint, while critics of the proposal saw it as a cut in federal contributions.

Another aspect of the federal position was an attempt to retreat from the policy of non-interference in provincial program administration which had been a major characteristic of the 1977 Established Programs Financing. In negotiating with the provinces, the federal government held out the promise of increasing its share in exchange for provincial agreement to co-operate in certain federal initiatives, and in general to increase provincial accountability in their administration.

84. Canada. *House of Commons Debates.* March 22, 1982. p. 15678.

At the First Ministers Conference in March it had been proposed that the Established Program Financing remain unchanged until March 1984 to enable consultations on federal proposals, which included a provincial undertaking to increase overall funding for post-secondary education for the next two fiscal years by the same rate as the increase in EPF cash and tax transfers (over 11 percent); discussion of means to achieve major national objectives; no discrimination on entry based on province of origin (mobility); reasonable access to post-secondary and adult training (accessibility); accountability so that Parliament could assess effectiveness; joint planning; agreement to provide full opportunity for minority official language training; discussions leading to new training programs; discussions on new health care legislation to more clearly define national conditions and standards; and discussions on improving accountability to legislatures, especially Parliament.[85]

These proposals were not welcomed by provincial governments, which generally saw them as renewed attempts at federal invasion of their constitutional responsibilities. Actually the proposals involve two different but related issues—visibility and accountability. For some time federal politicians had complained that the federal government, while clearly perceived by the public as a tax gatherer, was receiving no recognition from the electorate for programs in which it was paying something like one-half of the cost. At a time when no government was very popular, this was causing considerable anguish among caucus members of the governing party. Furthermore ministers are accountable to Parliament for the expenditure of the funds raised by taxation, but Parliament is not able to specify the objects of expenditure nor ministers to control policy, so that serious questions are raised about responsibility and accountability in government. The legitimacy of both concerns was endorsed by the Parliamentary Task Force on Federal-Provincial Fiscal Arrangements, which said:

> Our simple principle is that responsible federal ministers must answer in Parliament of the disposition and use of funds transferred to provincial governments. Two requirements follow directly from that principle:
>
> 1. the arrangements governing transfer programs must provide a means to ensure that sufficient information is forthcoming from provincial governments to enable federal ministers to discharge the obligation to answer in the House of Commons for the disposition of the transfers; and
> 2. the arrangements must provide for a clear definition of the objec-

85. The text of the proposal is printed in *Senate Debates.* March 17, 1982. p. 3851.

> tives to be achieved through transfer programs along with criteria, where appropriate, against which the extent of achievement of these objectives, or of the satisfaction of program conditions, can be measured and, if necessary, enforced through withholding some portion of the transfer.

All of this is sound and unexceptional constitutional doctrine, even though it asserts norms which are seldom fully achieved in Canada. Since the Task Force was made up of political men it was also natural that they should give equal emphasis to the issue of increased visibility for the federal government. They said:

> The question of visibility is a little more difficult. It is not, as is sometimes alleged, simply a matter of political posturing, a search for the limelight and the ribbon-snipping ceremonies. It is also answerability to the electorate. Federal spending without federal presence, or participation in provincial programs without visibility in the provinces, is not just frustration for the politician, it is also a denial of the citizen's right to see the government's work and to judge it. When the federal role is not evident, it cannot be assessed. Visibility involves a search for the chance to take the credit, but at the same time, a willingness to shoulder the blame. As politicians, therefore, we reject the simplistic view that a concern for visibility is not more than public relations for its own sake. Answerability of federal MPs to the public is the other side of the coin from accountability of ministers to Parliament, and a government that is not visible cannot be answerable.[86]

The general problem of federal-provincial fiscal relations, with the accompanying difficulties inherent in the incongruity between constitutional responsibilities and revenue sources, and of regional inequalities, is in many ways similar to that of the inter-war period. A combination of hard times and fiscal restraint produces both a sense of desperation in governments seeking to carry out their responsibilities, and a widespread loss of faith in government itself, which is both unhealthy and dangerous to the survival of the Canadian political and constitutional system.

86. Canada. House of Commons. Parliamentary Task Force on Federal-provincial Fiscal Relations. *Fiscal Federalism in Canada.* (Ottawa, August, 1981). p. 196.

10

Stability and Change: Mechanisms of Adjustment in a Federal System

The object of a federal system is to stabilize political relationships in a community where lack of homogeneity makes it impossible to allow important questions to be settled by majority decision. Gunnar Myrdal remarked that "No important political problems can be solved by a minority vote." Nowhere is this more true than in federal countries, where preservation of minority values is of the essence. Federal constitutions attempt this in two ways. By making the constitution difficult to change they seek to preserve the "federal bargain" against political accidents which might otherwise inundate the special position of the parties at the time of the union. Furthermore, through a distribution of the powers of government between autonomous central and regional governments, they provide for appropriate majority decisions to be made. The central government is generally given such powers as defence and economic policy, which are necessary for the common welfare of the union. But those questions on which the regions so differ that no common policy acceptable to all is deemed possible are left to the communities in the regions.

Yet no political order can be permanent and immutable. The world in which it lives changes, and these changes will be reflected in its internal composition. There must be room for adaptation and change, room to adjust the constitutional clothing to changes in the outside climate and to allow for bodily change within. One kind of change which all federal systems must face is a revision in the terms of the original bargain. This may be brought about by constitutional amendment or, if the changes are gradual and involve the tacit approval of the whole community, they may be brought about by judicial modifications of the meaning of the constitution.

A further kind of change is a day-to-day response to the interdependence of the two levels of government in an age when the role of government has greatly expanded. The "classical" kind of federal system, in which the two levels of government operated in serene isolation from one another, was no doubt possible when the role of government was very limited, but this is no longer the case. Governments find themselves making decisions all the time which can be effective only if taken in concert with other governments. Accordingly, federal systems now must accept and develop machinery for the co-ordination and co-operation of the actions of central and regional governments.

CONSTITUTIONAL AMENDMENT

In a federal state the preservation of a stable distribution of power between the central and regional governments is crucial if the balance of the system is to be maintained. It is thus necessary for federal states to enshrine in an organic law those parts of the constitution which embody its federal character. Such arrangements are seldom considered necessary in unitary states. Thus Alexis de Tocqueville could write of the British constitution, "elle n'existe pointe."[1] For the British constitution was never a formal document embodying a dramatic break with the past; it was the consequence of prolonged and almost casual historical growth.

To the extent that many of the institutions of government in Canada simply grew out of the British constitution, the Canadian constitution is rooted in the obscure and remote sources of English constitutional law, supplemented by a number of more or less formal steps which established these institutions in Canada. Thus, in its broadest sense, the Canadian constitution has a number of sources, including royal letters patent, dispatches and instructions to colonial governors, and acts of the British and Canadian Parliaments. To these sources the provincial constitutions have added a substantial body of provincial legislation.

There is, accordingly, no Canadian constitution consolidated into

1. Quoted in A.V. Dicey, *Introduction to the Study of the Law of the Constitution*, 10th ed. (London, 1959), p.22. It is true that Great Britain is not a wholly unitary state, since the Act of Union with Scotland implemented a treaty which in some measure limited the power of the new United Kingdom Parliament to change it. The absence of a settled notion of a superior organic law in English constitutional law has meant that in practice the United Kingdom has functioned as a unitary state, whatever the intentions may have been in the eighteenth century.

a single basic document with its own rules of interpretation and a single uniform system of amendment. Some parts of Canadian constitutional arrangements can be amended by simple statute. Provincial constitutions, within certain limits, can be amended in this way. Only parts of the constitution considered to be basic to the whole system need to be amended by the various procedures contained in the Constitution Act, 1982.

Until the adoption of the act most of the provisions of the Canadian constitution were to be found in the British North America Act and the various amendments which have been made to it. New elements have been added by the new Constitution Act, but many of the constitutional provisions of the B.N.A. Act remain in force. A large part of that act provided for the formal machinery of government for the new Dominion, as well as for the provinces of Ontario and Quebec, which were recreated out of the united province of Canada. While many of the institutions of government are of major constitutional importance, their amendment in most cases poses no serious problem. Difficulty lies in the apparent scope of the federal government to amend its own institutions, since some of them—such as the Senate and the Supreme Court—so closely affect the interests of the provinces that unilateral amendment of them may seriously affect the balance of the federal system. It was not until 1980 that the constitutional amending powers of the federal Parliament, which were contained in the 1949 amendment to the B.N.A. Act, were seriously tested in the courts. One of the proposals in the federal government's Bill C-60 had been a fairly radical revision of the Senate which would have altered its powers and provided for its selection by a process of indirect election. A joint committee of both Houses, which examined the bill, voted to seek the Supreme Court's opinion on the validity of the proposals which dealt with the Governor General and the Senate. Accordingly, the federal government referred the question of the power over Senate reform to the Supreme Court, and the Court ruled that Parliament could not, under section 91(1), alter the fundamental character of the Senate.[2] Subsequently, the 1982 Constitution Act has entrenched the powers and method of selection of the Senate in section 42(1) and at the same time has provided in section 47(1) for overriding a Senate veto on constitutional amendments.

However, the central problem of amending machinery is concerned with those federal features which govern the disribution of

2. (1980) 1 S.C.R. 54.

power between the central and provincial governments, as well as the provisions which entrench minority rights against encroachment by provincial or federal authorities. The British North America Act, as a statute of the Parliament of the United Kingdom, could, in important respects, be amended only by that body. Unlike, for example, the Australian constitution, it did not contain a general amending clause or procedure for amendment. This strange lack was not the result of an unwillingness, at least for the last half-century, on the part of the United Kingdom to give up its rather peculiar power to amend the Canadian constitution. It stemmed rather from the difficulty of securing agreement in Canada on an appropriate procedure.

The development of the flexible techniques of co-operative federalism for a time reduced the urgency of the problem of devising an agreed amending formula, which had been so anxiously sought in the inter-war years. Nevertheless, considerations of status and constitutional tidiness made it important to "patriate" the Canadian constitution. In fact a gradual process of patriating parts of the Canadian constitution had been going on for a number of years. Important parts of it came to be based on Canadian instruments, such as the letters patent governing the powers and functions of the head of state, the Seals Act which provided for the sealing of prerogative instruments, and the Supreme Court Act which governs the appellate court. Only the British North America Act remained partly domiciled abroad.

These difficulties of repatriation and amendment stem from the fact that Canada was first in the field. The first colonial legislatures, such as those of the early American colonies, had the inherent right to amend their own constitutions. However, these early constitutions had been founded on various kinds of royal grant, and this dispensation was not thought to apply to those constitutions which were founded on acts of the British Parliament. Two of the Canadian provinces, Ontario and Quebec, fell into this second category. Consequently, unless the British North America Act contained an amending procedure, it was deemed that the power of amendment was still vested in the British Parliament.[3] It has only been in more recent times, when sovereign independence was accepted as a quick and natural outcome of self-government, that the ultimate constitutional power of the British Parliament was waived at the start.

3. See Martin Wight, *The Development of the Legislative Council*, 1606–1945 (London, 1946), p. 122.

It is not possible to be certain why the omission of a general amending power occurred. The power to amend their own constitutions was given to the provinces in the London Resolutions, but no such power either for the Dominion or for the federation as a whole was mentioned. The earlier Quebec Resolutions had conferred a general power on the Dominion Parliament to legislate for the "peace, welfare, and good Government," qualified by the phrase "saving the sovereignty of England." There was very little discussion of the question in the Confederation Debates in the Canadian Parliament in 1865. The most explicit reference to the amending power is that by D'Arcy McGee:

> We go to the Imperial Government, the common arbiter of us all, in our true Federal metropolis—we go there to ask for our fundamental Charter. We hope, by having that Charter which can only be amended by the authority that made it, that we will lay the basis of permanency in our future government.[4]

It is quite likely that the question of amending procedure was left deliberately ambiguous because it might have given rise to difficulties on which the whole agreement could have foundered. Or Macdonald may well have felt that leaving the matter ambiguous avoided a cumbrous procedure involving provincial participation which he did not want. One recalls his exasperation when the draftsmen inserted a provision for increasing the number of senators in case of disagreement.[5] It is also possible that the omission was deliberate because "the Imperial authority was . . . considered as the ultimate safeguard of the rights granted to the provinces and to minorities by the constitution."[6] However acceptable such a role may have been in the nineteenth century, it is one that is no longer either appropriate or possible.

It would have been natural to expect that the grant of full autonomy to the Dominions by the Statute of Westminister would have automatically severed the legal tie which kept the amending power in Westminster. However, on Canadian insistence (brought about by provincial resistance led by Ontario) the Statute of Westminster contained a saving clause excluding the British North America Acts from its liberating provisions. The reason for this was that otherwise

4. *Confederation Debates*, 1865, p. 146.

5. D.G. Creighton, *John A. Macdonald: The Young Politician* (Toronto, 1952), pp. 456–7.

6. Paul Gerin-Lajoie, *Constitutional Amendment in Canada.* (Toronto, 1950) p. 38.

the power to amend the B.N.A. Act would have been conferred on the Parliament of Canada alone. Thus decision on the amending procedure was postponed, to wait on the long process of negotiation until agreement between the provinces and the federal government could be reached.

Constitutional Amending Procedures

While it is true that, except where the B.N.A. Act otherwise provided, the sole amending authority was vested in the United Kingdom Parliament, it had long been Imperial constitutional practice to amend colonial constitutions only on colonial initiative. This practice became a matter of law as far as the Dominions were concerned with the passage of the Statute of Westminster in 1931. Some of the earlier amendments to the British North America Act were enacted at the request of the Canadian government, but the practice soon became established that amendments should not be requested without the consent of the Canadian Parliament. In 1871 the Canadian House of Commons passed a resolution by 137 votes to none, asserting that "no changes in the provisions of the British North America Act should be sought by the Executive Government without the previous assent of the Parliament of this Dominion."[7] Since that time the proper form of initiating desired amendments became an address of both Houses of Parliament to the Sovereign, praying that an amendment be laid before the British Parliament.

This procedure gave the Senate the power to modify or veto the proposal, and there have been occasions when the Senate has exercised this right. In 1915 it secured a modification in the proposed amendment dealing with parliamentary representation, and in 1960 it forced the Commons to accept an important change in an amendment dealing with the retirement of judges. On one occasion, in 1936, a proposed amendment which would have limited provincial borrowing powers by subjecting them to the approval of a loan council, and which sought to clarify the distribution of taxing power, failed because the Senate would not agree to it.

While the political difficulties which would be created by amendments affecting the rights and powers of the provinces being accomplished without their concurrence made it difficult to conceive such amendments taking place without provincial consent, it was gener-

7. Canada. *House of Commons Journals*, 1871, p. 148.

ally thought that provincial participation in the process was based merely on usage and convenience and not on either the law or conventions of the constitution. The provinces have no *locus standi* with either the British government or the British Parliament, either to promote or oppose an amendment. In practice, however, if their interests were deemed to be affected, they were invariably consulted and their agreement obtained before an Address was presented. As the Minister of Justice, Hon. Guy Favreau, put it when he was advocating an amending formula in 1965:

> The Constitution cannot be changed in a way that might deprive the provinces of their legislative powers unless they consent. The law does not say so, but the facts of national life have imposed the unanimity requirement, and experience since Confederation has established it as a convention that government or Parliament would disregard at its peril.[8]

There thus were three separate procedures of amending the British North America Act. The first was the "safeguarded" procedure in which the provinces participated, and which required action by the British Parliament. The second and third were already domiciled in Canada either by the original act itself, or by amendment to it.

Amendment of "Safeguarded" Provisions—These amendments had to be made by the British Parliament at the request of Canadian authorities. The preliminary step in Canada was negotiation between the federal and provincial governments until agreement was secured from all of the provinces. Much of the tentative discussion involved officials and Attorneys-General followed by an exchange of letters between the Prime Minister and each provincial premier. In recent years, particularly when the proposed changes were far-reaching, involving a new amending formula, the final phase of the discussion tended to be in a full-dress conference of first ministers. In the past it was not usual for provincial governments to secure ratification of the agreement by their legislatures but in recent years they have tended to secure legislative concurrence before final agreement. After agreement was secured, the federal government then moved the necessary resolutions through the Senate and the House of Commons. The joint resolution, with the text of the proposed amendment attached as a schedule, was then transmitted by the Governor General to the Queen for transmission to the British government, which then introduced the

8. Hon. Guy Favreau. *The Amendment of the Constitution of Canada.* (Ottawa, 1965). p. 47.

necessary legislation into the British Parliament. It was never certain how many sections of the British North American Act fell under this procedure, but it certainly governed those which covered fields of provincial jurisdiction, and those which were shared with the provinces.

Amendemnt of Provincial Constitutions by Provincial Legislatures—The whole of Part V of the British North America Act (sections 58-90), and a number of the Miscellaneous Provisions of Part IX, deal with provincial constitutions. Many of these provisions arose out of the need to provide for the governments of Ontario and Quebec, not only because they had to be extricated from the effects of the Act of Union of 1840, but also because both had constitutions based on earlier acts of the British Parliament. New Brunswick and Nova Scotia, whose constitutions were founded on prerogative instruments, were largely governed by provisions which continued their constitutions in force as far as they remained appropriate. Section 92(1) gives the provincial legislatures an exclusive power to amend their own constitutions "except as regards the office of Lieutenant-Governor." This stems from the Lieutenant-Governor's role as a Dominion Officer, which is spelled out in section 90 of the Act. There is some reason to believe that restriction may also be a bar to a province which might seek to divest itself of the forms of parliamentary government.[9]

A further restriction of provincial legislative power is that specific sections of the act may override this general power. Thus the province of Quebec found that a part of its Charter of the French language which abolished the equality of the French and English languages in the courts and legislature of the province was invalid because it conflicted with the terms of section 133 of the B.N.A. Act.[10] While the significance of this is generally taken by commentators to refer to the question of language rights, it would not be unreasonable to regard the decision of the Supreme Court as one restricting provincial powers of constitutional amendment.

Since the provinces are able to amend their own constitutions by ordinary statute, there is no certainty how many times they have in fact done so. However, examples are readily found. Ontario and Quebec have made a number of alterations in the composition of their Legislative Assemblies, and in their Executive Councils. New Brunswick, Nova Scotia, Manitoba and Quebec, which were the only

9. *In re Initiative and Referendum Act* [1919] A.C. 935.

10. *Attorney-General of Quebec v. Blaikie* [1979] 2 S.C.R. 1016.

provinces to have second chambers, have abolished them. Numerous changes in the machinery of government, which have been made by all provinces, must also be considered as constitutional amendments.

Amendment by the Parliament of Canada—The Canadian Parliament has always possessed a limited power to amend the British North America Act. A number of the original provisions of the act were transitional, and were intended to apply "until the Parliament of Canada otherwise provides." The power of amendment was substantially extended by the British North America (No. 2) Act, 1949, which added a new subsection (1) to the powers of Parliament enumerated in section 91, conferring the power to amend "the Constitution of Canada," except in relation to the exclusive legislative powers of the provinces, exclusive rights and privileges granted to the provinces, the rights of certain minorities with regard to schools, and rights to use the English and French languages. A further safeguard limited the power to extend the life of Parliament, or to modify the requirement for annual Parliaments by the provision that, in times of emergency, such changes could be made only if they were not opposed by at least one-third of the members of the House of Commons.[11]

THE SEARCH FOR AN AMENDING FORMULA

There have been a number of attempts to reach agreement on a procedure of amendment which would replace the cumbersome and constitutionally unseemly method of resorting to the British Parliament. All proposals have sought some acceptable combination

11. Mr. St. Laurent, when Minister of Justice, once allowed himself to be drawn into a position which became difficult for him to live down in Quebec. In defending the 1946 amendment governing parliamentary redistribution, he took the position that this was a matter which belonged exclusively to the federal Parliament, so that the provinces had no right to be consulted about it. When asked if this was also true of section 133, governing the use of the two languages, he said that "legally" this was also true. (Canada. *House of Commons Debate*, Vol. III. June 18, 1946. p. 2621.) There is some reason to believe that the 1949 amendment, coming so soon after he had succeeded to the prime ministership, was an attempt to cover up this slip by inserting a guarantee of language and minority rights. In any event, the whole amendment was loosely drafted, and has conferred on parliament the exclusive right to legislature regarding the redistribution of seats in the House of Commons, though its right to deal with the Senate was curtailed by the Supreme Court in the Senate Reference.

of sufficient flexibility to make amendments feasible, together with full protection of provincial rights. It has been possible to agree in principle on a formula which would accomplish this, but grave difficulties of definition over details led to stalemate and a fresh round of discussions. It was to take over fifty years to achieve some sort of resolution of issues which were both complex and changing in the process of constitutional renewal.

There was not even general agreement on the need for a new amending procedure until after the passage of the Statute of Westminster. Early in 1935 a special committee of the House of Commons was set up to consider the matter and it heard a number of proposals for a new amending procedure. Though invited to do so, the provincial governments did not respond to the invitation of the committee to submit their views. However, later in the same year a Dominion-Provincial Conference set up a subconference on constitutional questions under the chairmanship of the Minister of Justice and including the provincial Attorneys-General. This conference agreed that Canada should have its own amending procedure provided that one could be found that was acceptable to both the federal Parliament and the provincial legislatures. Its recommendation that a committee of federal and provincial representatives should further consider the matter in detail led to the setting up of a Continuing Committee on Constitutional Questions. From these discussions emerged agreement that there were in essence four categories of amendments that required in each case different means of implementation: matters which concerned the federal government only, the provinces only, the federal government and some provinces, and the federal government and all the provinces. They further emphasized that matters which affected the fundamental constitutional relationships between the federal government and the provinces, and those which dealt with the rights of minorities and the use of the English and French languages, were essential parts of the federal system and should be entrenched in the constitution.[12]

Thereafter the growing danger of war, and then the needs of the periods of war and reconstruction, thrust questions of constitutional reform into the background. The proposals for constitutional reform which had been made by the Royal Commission on Dominion-

12. The history of early proposals for constitutional reform are fully dealt with in Gerin-Lajoie, *Constitutional Amendment in Canada*, (1950), and the background of further discussions is adequately summarized in Favreau, *The Amendment of the Constitution of Canada*, (1965).

Provincial Relations in 1940 failed to commend themselves to a number of provinces and fell by the wayside, but the federal government was able, by exploiting its wartime emergency powers, to find the constitutional flexibility to meet the needs of the war and post-war emergencies. However, in 1949, the federal government took the initiative again. It secured an amendment to the B.N.A. Act which gave it powers of amendment in matters which were considered to concern it alone. In giving Parliament powers analagous to those of the provincial legislatures in section 92(1), the federal government asserted that it was acting within the agreement reached at the Constitutional Conference of 1936. In the following year it convened a constitutional conference with the provinces to finish the job.

At an initial meeting in January, a subcommittee of Attorneys-General was set up to work out proposals in detail. The subcommittee concluded that there were six different categories and subsequently proceeded to try to fit the provisions of the B.N.A. Act and other constitutional acts into these six pigeon-holes. When the full conference met in Quebec later in the year to see if agreement could be reached, it transpired that it could not decide what went into each pigeon-hole until accord could be reached on the amending formula for each. It was hoped that the conference would be able to reconvene to persevere in its efforts, but in fact it did not. While there are a number of reasons for the failure of the conference, one of the most important was the shadow cast over its deliberations by the earlier unilateral action of the federal authorities in putting through their own amending powers. While there was no barrier to the federal government taking this initiative, the fact that they had proceeded to deal with the category "matters which concern the federal government alone" without consultation was resented by some provinces who felt the whole area of amendment should be a matter of joint discussion.

So the issue rested for another decade. Then, in 1960, a new federal government and a changed atmosphere brought about a fresh attack on the problem. By 1960 the "status" argument had assumed a greater urgency so that "patriation" appeared to be more important than the details of the amending formula. Almost every year a new member achieved Commonwealth status, and for Canada to remain attached to the United Kingdom by the umbilical cord of its own constitution seemed to be nothing but a preposterous anomaly.

For this reason the federal government, in summoning the Constitutional Conference in 1960, hoped that attention would be focussed initially on the "patriation" problem, trusting that if agreement could be reached on this first, there would be less difficulty in coming to terms on the amending formula. This did not commend itself to the conference. The two questions are inseparable in the sense that there would be little use in re-enacting the constitution in Canada if there were no machinery for its amendment. And there remained two problems left over from the conference of 1950: the extent of entrenchment; and the need to devise a formula for the delegation of legislative authority from one level of government to the other. The earlier conference had agreed that the latter, which would provide some element of flexibility if the agreed constitution rigidly entrenched the distribution of legislative power, should be further explored.

The problem of defining the area of the entrenched clauses of the constitution has been the rock upon which most negotiations on the constitutional amending formula have broken. Because the courts have interpreted the phrase "property and civil rights" so that it includes practically the whole area of social legislation, they have interposed an effective barrier against uniform legislation in this field in Canada, except by such skilful evasions as the Family Allowances Act, or through constitutional amendment, as in the case of unemployment insurance and old-age pensions. This interpretation has enabled the province of Quebec to assert the right to develop its own unique approach to social welfare, and to regard this whole field as an entrenched area of provincial jurisdiction. This position is perhaps best expressed in the *Tremblay Report*:

> Quebec, in particular, could not easily consent to the amendment of section 92 by a simple majority of provinces without renouncing not only part of its political autonomy but also its cultural autonomy, that is to say, the power of organizing independently the social life of its population according to its own conception of Man and life in society. For Quebec is was not merely a matter of greater material security, but of the maintenance and progress of the French-Canadian group as such.[13]

This is a fact which must be faced. Some degree of uniformity in social or other legislation, even if it does not include Quebec, may have to be achieved by the delegation of authority from one level of government to the other. This possibility had been denied by the

13. *Report of the Royal Commission of Enquiry on Constitutional Problems.* (Quebec, 1956). p. 167.

Supreme Court in the *Nova Scotia Delegation* case, so that its benefits could not be achieved without an alteration in the constitution. It was perhaps for this reason that the 1950 conference agreed that delegation should be on the agenda of future discussions. For the price of agreement might be a formula which fell short of uniformity by allowing a province to "contract out" of arrangements which did not suit it, but were strongly desired by the others.

After the 1960 conference there were lengthy discussions among the various governments, at the end of which the Minister of Justice, Mr. Davie Fulton, submitted a draft on December 1, 1961 to the provinces for their approval. It was intended to proceed with this proposal in Parliament during the 1961-62 session. However, there were objections to the proposals from some provinces and the matter was not in fact dealt with before dissolution. The short and distracted life of the next Parliament was not conducive to progress with any business, no matter how uncontentious. A further election and a change of government in 1963 seemed bound to delay, if not destroy, the real progress which the Fulton formula embodied.

It had at last come to grips with the problem of rooting the British North America Act in Canadian legal soil. To accomplish this, a necessary first step must be to secure the repeal of section 7 of the Statute of Westminster, so that a final abrogation of British legislative power would have the effect of completing Canadian sovereignty.[14]

The Fulton proposals sought to embody in a single enactment the two connected proposals of patriation and amending procedure. Part I of the proposed act conferred on the Parliament of Canada the power to "make laws repealing, amending and re-enacting any provisions of the Constitution of Canada." Section 7 "signed off" the authority of the British Parliament in a single curt sentence: "No Act of the Parliament of the United Kingdom passed after the coming into force of this Act shall extend or be deemed to extend to Canada or to any province or territory thereof." The Statute of Westminster

14. While it is true in a strict legal sense that nothing the British Parliament can do will remove its supremacy over the Canadian constitution (for no Parliament can make a law which binds future Parliaments), this is of little practical importance. As Lord Sankey said, "The Imperial Parliament could, as a matter of abstract law, repeal or disregard section 4 of the Statute [of Westminster]. But that is theory and has no relation to realities." *British Coal Corporation v. the King* (1935) A.C. 500 at p. 520. For a full discussion of the technical legal difficulties involved in constitutional repatriation, or "autochthony"—the rooting of a constitution in one's own sovereign soil—see K.C. Wheare, *The Constitutional Structure of the Commonwealth*, (London, 1960). Chapter V.

was included in the enumeration of the enactments comprising "the Constitution of Canada."

A number of matters were entrenched so that they could not be altered without the unanimous consent of all the provincial legislatures: the draft act itself; section 51A of the B.N.A. Act (safeguarding provincial minimum representation in the House of Commons); the powers of the legislature of a province to make laws; the rights and privileges secured by the constitution to the legislature or government of a province; the assets or property of a province; and the use of the English or French languages.

Provisions of the constitution that referred to one or more, but not all of the provinces, required the concurrence of the legislatures of the provinces to which the amendment referred. This section took precedence over the provisions of the entrenching clauses.

Education was dealt with separately. Amendments affecting education required the consent of all of the provinces except Newfoundland. Amendments respecting education in Newfoundland required the concurrence of the Newfoundland legislature only.

Other matters, not covered by the entrenching clause, the education clause, or the clause dealing with matters which concern some, but not all provinces, required the concurrence of the legislatures of two-thirds of the provinces representing at least fifty percent of the population.

The second part of the Fulton formula dealt with the question of delegation. It proposed to add a new section 94A to the constitution, the effect of which would be to enable the Parliament of Canada to delegate any matter within its authority to the provincial legislatures, but the provinces could only delegate power to the federal Parliament under heads (6) prisons; (10) local works and undertakings; (13) property and civil rights; and (16) generally local matters, of section 92 of the B.N.A. Act. Delegation of provincial powers to Parliament required the consent of at least four provinces, unless it was declared that the matter was of concern to less than that number. The consent of a province to delegation could be revoked, whereupon the delegation of authority would cease to have effect in the revoking province.

The Fulton formula did not escape criticism. To the government of Saskatchewan it was too rigid to provide a workable amending formula. They regretted that the proposal so heavily entrenched provincial powers, and had made the delegation power so narrow as to be of doubtful use. They also found cause for regret that the proposed entrenched areas did not include a bill of rights.

Inevitably there were those who found the Fulton proposals unsatisfactory because they were not rigid enough. Not unnaturally, in this group was to be found the government of Quebec. A vital objection from their point of view was that nothing overt had been done to modify the 1949 amendment, which had conferred considerable and vague powers of amendment on the Parliament of Canada.

In 1964 the Pearson government revived the question, and it was the subject of a federal-provincial conference in Charlottetown in September of that year. Perhaps stimulated by the centennial of the Charlottetown Conference which had led to Confederation, the delegates agreed, at least in principle, "to conclude the repatriation of the B.N.A. Act without delay" and "to complete a procedure for amending the Constitution of Canada based on draft legislation proposed at the Constitutional Conference of 1961, which they accepted in principle."[15] No doubt many people, recalling the events of a century before, felt that it was time to complete the project for the Centennial of Confederation in 1967.

The Fulton-Favreau formula, as it became, dealt with the problem of the 1949 amending formula by revising it and incorporating it, together with a revised form of the provincial amending power in section 92(1), into the proposed amending procedure. The power of Parliament to amend the constitution was more specifically defined as applying to "the Constitution of Canada in relation to the executive Government of Canada, and the Senate and House of Commons." However, safeguards were inserted to protect the representation of the provinces in the Senate, and the proportionate representation of the provinces in the House of Commons. Other technical changes were made in the original draft, and a new part was added which would have the effect of making both the French and the English texts of the constitution official.

At last, it appeared, all of the governments concerned had finally reached agreement, and this in itself must rank as a monumental achievement. But the appearance of agreement was deceptive. For the Quebec government was to have second thoughts and to refuse, after a period of ambiguous silence, to seek the concurrence of the Quebec legislature in the formula. Two things seem to have contributed to this change of heart. In the first place, Mr. Lesage was then engaged in seeking to curtail the veto powers of the Legislative Council, the last remaining second chamber in a provincial legislature. Mr. Lesage hit upon the expedient of asking the federal

15. Favreau, *The Amendment of the Constitution of Canada.* p. 30.

government to seek an amendment to the B.N.A. Act to accomplish this purpose. This would have to be done before the adoption of the Fulton-Favreau formula, because the formula would have the effect (which no one seems to have foreseen) of virtually entrenching the position of the Legislative Council in Quebec, since its agreement to a curtailment of its powers would not be easy to achieve. This embarrassing necessity did not improve the atmosphere of the discussion of constitutional amendment in Quebec.[16]

A second reason was probably more compelling. The Fulton-Favreau formula provoked an unexpected storm of criticism in Quebec itself. It was argued that one effect of the formula would be to impose a new restraint on Quebec's constitutional development. This was because the new constitution, by requiring unanimous consent for the diminution of provincial powers, imposed the same obstacle to their increase, so that any one province could veto such change desired by all the others. While there was no consensus among the experts in this matter, this prospect was enough to be decisive in a period when Quebec was clearly moving in the direction of seeking special status and powers in the constitution. For that reason, concurrence in the Fulton-Favreau formula was too great a risk for a Quebec government to take. And so again, stalemate resulted.[17]

Nevertheless discussions continued. Mr. Trudeau, when Minister of Justice, had attempted to widen the area of discussion of constitutional reform to include a charter of human rights in the constitution. The focus of discussion at the same time narrowed. The question of delegation appeared to have lost some of its urgency, and there was a tendency to press on with amendment and leave questions of jurisdiction to be settled under what might be expected to be a more satisfactory amending formula. After considerable preliminary discussion, a new formula to break the constitutional deadlock emerged from the federal-provincial conference held at Victoria in February, 1971. The conference agreed in principle both on the matters of substance that would have to be part of the new constitution and on an amending procedure. On June 14, 1971, the

16. The request to the British Parliament to alter the powers of the Quebec Legislative Council was transmitted by the Government of Canada, but had not been proceeded with when Mr. Lesage suffered electoral defeat. His successor, fortified by a large majority in the upper chamber, succeeded in persuading the Legislative Council to agree to its own abolition in 1968.

17. The exchange of letters between Mr. Lesage and Mr. Pearson is reprinted in Canada. *House of Commons Debates.* January 28 and March 24, 1966.

Victoria Conference reconvened. After exhaustive examination of "best efforts" drafts of Attorneys-General and officials, a text emerged which all of the participants agreed to lay before their respective governments, which would then decide if the proposals could be submitted to their legislatures for ratification.

In summary, the Victoria Charter proposed to place in the constitution a statement of fundamental political rights; a form of protection for linguistic rights; constitutional provisions governing the Supreme Court of Canada; a declaration of principle that governments were committed to promote equality of opportunity and to reduce regional disparities throughout Canada; and a constitutional requirement for federal-provincial consultation and co-operation.[18]

An important part of the Charter was a new amending formula. The procedure enabled amendments to be made by proclamation of the Governor General when so authorized by resolutions of the Senate and House of Commons and a majority of the provinces that included (1) every province which at any time had had a population of at least twenty-five percent of the population of Canada (i.e. Ontario and Quebec); (2) at least two of the Atlantic provinces; (3) at least two of the Western provinces which, according to the latest census, had a combined population of at least fifty percent of the Western provinces. It was also provided that in these amendments, the Senate would have a power to delay a resolution passed by the Commons for ninety days rather than a veto. Amendments affecting one or more, but not all of the provinces, would require the consent of the Senate and House of Commons and of each of the provinces to which the amendment applies. This procedure applied not only to amendments affecting the jurisdiction of the two levels of government but also to a number of other matters: the office of the Queen, the Governor General and the Lieutenant-Governor; yearly sessions of Parliament and the provincial legislatures; the maximum duration of Parliament and the legislatures; the powers of the Senate; the number of members which a province is entitled to in the Senate and the residence qualification of Senators; the rights of a province to a number of members in the House of Commons not less than the number of Senators; the principle of proportionate representation of provinces in the House of Commons; and the use of the two languages.

It was known that the government of Quebec wished to restore

18. The text is reproduced in the Report of the Special Joint Committee of the Senate and of the House of Commons on the Constitution of Canada (1972) pp. 106-10.

provincial primacy in social policy before the new constitution came into force. To counter this position an interim solution was proposed in the form of a revision of section 94A (covering federal jurisdiction over old age pension and supplementary benefits) which would prohibit the federal government from introducing new legislation on these matters unless it had "at least ninety days before such introduction, advised the government of each province of the substance of the proposed legislation and requested its views thereon." It was hoped that this, together with the promise of further negotiation and close co-operation in social welfare administration would soften Quebec's resistance to the Charter.

This, in fact, did not turn out to be the case. Premier Bourassa, after consulting his Cabinet, found himself unable to recommend adoption of the Charter, and so the Victoria Conference ended like all the others, in failure. Consequently, the federal government let it be known that no further negotiations about constitutional matters would be initiated by them until such time as the situation had altered to make success likely. As if to underline this position, the federal government proceeded to disband the secretariat of the constitutional conference, an intergovernmental body of officials which had been assembled in Ottawa to co-ordinate the review of the continuing constitutional conference in 1968.

On the other hand, discussions continued between the two levels of government in the hope that the impasse, which was largely but not entirely between Quebec and Ottawa, could be ended. Both parties were agreed on the necessity of integrated welfare policy, and the federal position essentially was that—as long as their constitutional jurisdiction remained unimpaired—they were prepared to make administrative arrangements to accommodate the provinces. Thus, it was agreed that total welfare payments to needy families should be determined by provincial authorities in accordance with provincial priorities, and in consequence federal family allowance payments would be varied in accordance with provincial directives.

The discussion of constitutional reform did not end at Victoria. Indeed while the discussions leading up to Victoria were going on the matter was being canvassed in another arena. For a variety of reasons the federal government had shown little enthusiasm for a parliamentary enquiry in these matters, but with some reluctance had permitted a joint committee of both Houses to be set up to consider the problem. After a two-year study that body reported on March 16, 1972. Such a report, under the Canadian system of government, could not have more than persuasive force. Whatever fears the government might have had about the effect of the Committee's work, it is probable that the inquiry did a considerable amount of good. The Committee travelled indefatigably about the country, holding hearings in many places. This exercise undoubtedly had a useful effect in bringing the issues of constitutional reform much closer to the average elector, and it is probable that the Committee's report was more sensitive to the nature of the issues as understood by the electorate than as discussed by governments, which spend too much time talking to one another. While the recommendations were unlikely to appeal strongly to any government, they could not fail to be part of the context of further negotiations and therefore are worth noting.

In general, the Committee was in accord with the main lines of the Victoria Charter. In one respect it went further, by recommending that the federal power over economic matters be enlarged, and extended in time of crisis to such things as price and wage control. At the same time it was recommended that jurisdiction over social and cultural policy be decentralized in order to ensure the primacy of provincial authority.

In an attempt to deal with the question of the autodetermination of Quebec, the Committee spoke in vague terms of the right of a people to determine its own destiny, and recommended that, in case a clear majority of a provincial electorate decided in favour of independence, the federal government should resort to negotiation and abjure force. Nevertheless they rejected the possibility of including the right of secession in the constitution. Two members of the Committee from Quebec publicly dissented from this ambiguous declaration and urged that the right of autodetermination of a province be written into the constitution. Their purpose in urging this was not to support such a policy, but to make Quebec secession less likely because it had become legally possible.

As the seventies wore on the issue of Quebec separation, now manifested in the Parti Quebecois which had been elected to office in 1976, assumed the top place on the agenda of Canadian politics. But it was not the only issue, because the demand for a greater decentralization of the Canadian federal system seemed to be acquiring widespread support. This appeared to be particularly true in the Western provinces, and the phrase "western alienation" also entered the political vocabulary.

Wishing no doubt to appear to comprehend the dimensions of the problem the federal government resorted in 1977 to the appointment of a commission to study it, headed by Jean-Luc Pepin, who was a former minister then in political eclipse, and John Robarts, who as premier of Ontario had initiated in 1967 the televised conference on the future of Canadian federalism. Perhaps to emphasize the importance of the exercise, the Pepin-Robarts commission was described as the Task Force on Canadian Unity.

The recommendations of the Task Force, entitled *A Future Together*, was issued in January 1979. They identified the problem of Canadian unity around the twin themes of duality and regionalism. They argued that diversity was a source of strength in the Canadian union and in general favoured greater decentralization. The two orders of government were, in their view, equal under the constitution and they deplored what they perceived to be the attitude of some politicians and civil servants in Ottawa in regarding their provincial counterparts as inferiors. An assignment of powers sufficient to guarantee Quebec the capacity to nourish and defend its culture and social institutions should be available to all provinces, even though such powers might be claimed by Quebec alone. Special status in this form held no terrors for them. In general they appeared to dislike concurrent jurisdiction or ambiguous allocation of power between the two levels of government. A clearer definition of constitutional boundaries would reduce the level of conflict between the levels of government.

They sensed a fairly widespread desire for significant modification in some of the institutions of government as a way of ameliorating federal-provincial conflict. Nowhere is this more evident than in their proposals for the abolition of the Senate and its replacement by a Council of the Federation "composed of provincial delegations to whom provincial governments could issue instructions, each delegation being headed by a person of ministerial rank or on occasion by the premier."[19] This body would have sixty members, roughly in accordance with provincial populations, but weighted somewhat in favour of the smaller provinces. Federal government ministers would be able to present and defend federal policies in areas of provincial interest but not have the right to vote. The Council would have no powers over matters of exclusive federal jurisdiction, but would have a suspensive veto over areas of concurrent jurisdiction "where there is provincial paramountcy or in areas where central legislative authority combined with provincial administrative

19. *A Future Together.* (Ottawa, 1979). p. 97. They noted the similarity of their proposal, which seems to be based on the apparent role of the West German Bundesrat, to those of the government of British Columbia, the Ontario Advisory Committee on Confederation, and the constitutional committees of the Canadian Bar Association and the Canada West Foundation.

responsiblity is specified in the constitution."[20] Special approval of the Council would be required for ratification of treaties in matters of provincial jurisdiction, the exercise of the federal spending power in areas of provincial jurisdiction, and the ratification of the proclamation of a state of emergency. In addition appointments to the Supreme Court and certain federal regulatory agencies such as The Canadian Transport Commission and the National Energy Board would require ratification by the Council. The "sober second thought" role of the Senate would disappear but be replaced by an enlarged and strengthened House of Commons. Federal-provincial conferences of first ministers should be institutionalized and put on a regular annual basis, and standing committees of both the House of Commons and the provincial legislatures should be established to monitor federal-provincial conferences and agreements.

All of these proposals involved a more rigid separation of powers between the two levels of government, combined with a substantial intrusion of provincial governments into what had previously been the untrammelled sphere of operations of the central government. This is a mirror image of the constitution at Confederation, when the federal government, through the appointment of the Lieutenant-Governor and the use of his power of reservation and its own power of disallowance was able to penetrate provincial institutions and powers. The Task Force recommended the abolition of reservation and disallowance, and proposed that the Lietuenant-Governor be appointed on the advice of the provincial premier. These, and similar proposals, suggested a very much more decentralized federal system. Whatever appeal such recommendations might have to provincial governments and to the public, there can be no question that they were unlikely to appeal to the federal government, which meanwhile was unveiling its own proposals for constitutional reform. These took the form of a Constitutional Amendment Bill which was tabled in the House of Commons in June, 1978.

In an accompanying statement, entitled *A Time for Action*, the Prime Minister set forth the ambitious scope of Bill C-60, which was to put the constitution of Canada together in one place, and sought to remedy the deficiencies which the government perceived in present constitutional arrangements. A large part of the written constitution was based on old British statutes so that it "bears the imprint of a colonial period that has long since passed" and thus little understood by the public. The constitution also lacked a

20. *Ibid.* p. 98.

preamble or statement of principles, and much of it was written in obscure and anachronistic language. It contained no declaration of basic rights and freedoms, while the inadequacy of the protection of the French language had strengthened separatism in Quebec. The division of legislative powers was "neither as precise, as functional nor as explicit as might be wished." The Senate inadequately represented regional views and the Supreme Court was not enshrined in the constitution. Finally, the amendment process was inadequate and still needed to be complemented by the intervention of the British Parliament.

The Bill sought to alter those parts of the constitution which lay within the authority of Parliament, while other parts would only become effective when provincial agreement was secured. Years of fruitless negotiation by cautious officials and self-conscious ministers had demonstrated the truth of the old adage that it is nearly impossible for a committee to write a document in clear and inspiring prose. Unfortunately the federal draftsmen were no more successful. The statement of aims of the Canadian federation was a striking example of lumbering prose containing some sentences running up to one hundred words. One cannot imagine it engraved in the memories of later generations of school children.

The operative parts of the bill began with what was in effect a re-enactment of the 1960 Bill of Rights, to which were added new mobility rights governing the capacity of all Canadians to move to and reside in any province or territory, and enjoy equal protection of the laws therein and to hold property and pursue a livelihood there. To these were added the guarantee of political rights, including the maximum life of legislatures and parliaments, and their annual convocation. The principles of the Official Languages Act were written into the constitution, as well as the right to education in either language "where numbers warrant." The extension of these rights, which the bill entrenched as far as the federal government was concerned, would, of course, require implementation by the provinces.

A whole section of the bill sought to place in the constitution a number of statutory provisions relating to the institutions of the federal government. It also sought to put in statutory form such matters as the powers of the Governor General, many of which are now governed by conventions of the constitution, as well as the Cabinet, including the conventions of responsible government. The Queen's Privy Council for Canada was to be re-christened the Council of State for Canada. It is not easy to translate conventions of the constitution into statutory form and in general this particular exercise is best forgotten. It is not clear what position the Queen would occupy in the new constitution. It is debatable whether the Governor General has more powers or less, or whether he has the power either to appoint or dismiss the Prime Minister. The provisions regarding the dissolution of Parliament are less than clear, as are those governing under what conditions a government has lost the confidence of the House of Commons. What is perhaps worst about this part is that it would make these delicate arrangements subject to judicial interpretation, which would seriously imperil their flexibility.

The section which engendered the most controversy was that which would alter the name, composition, and powers of the Senate which would become a body called the House of the Federation with members indirectly elected—half by the House of Commons and half by the provincial legislatures. This new second chamber would have new powers over measures deemed to be of linguistic significance as well as the right to confirm senior judicial and executive appointments.

A later part of the bill sought to re-enact the provisions of the British North America Act governing the distribution of legislative powers between the two levels of government. While no new amending formula was designated, the bill provided methods by which its various provisions would be implemented.

While the Constitutional Amendment bill could not be said to have aroused general support either from provincial governments or from the public, its ultimate fate was settled when a joint committee of both Houses compelled the government to refer the part of the bill referring to Senate reform to the Supreme Court. The decision of that court that section 91(1) did not permit the Parliament of Canada to alter the composition or role of the Senate in a substantial way was the main reason why the bill was allowed to die on the order paper.

The defeat on May 20, 1980, of the Quebec referendum on Sovereignty Association, to which a contributing factor had been the promise of "constitutional renewal" made by proponents of the "No" vote, led to fresh efforts to reach agreement. A series of urgent preliminary negotiations took place between federal and provincial ministers over the summer to prepare for a summit of first ministers in September. The summit failed to reach agreement. However, buoyed by poll results and bound by their own promises in the Quebec referendum debate, the federal government decided to move ahead on constitutional reform without provincial agreement. In October, a set of resolutions was introduced in Parliament seeking authority to patriate the constitution, to place a charter of rights and freedoms in the constitution, and to provide an amending formula. The issues of decentralization and a re-allocation of powers between the two levels of government was largely ignored, no doubt in the expectation that the amending formula would provide a mechanism for them to be addressed by subsequent intergovernmental negotiation.[21]

If Bill C-60 had sought to deal with the problem of amendment by indirection, by inviting the provinces to adhere to its provisions before they came into force, the 1980 resolutions met the problem head on. They sought to impose the charter of rights on both federal and provincial authorities, and provided for an interim method of amendment which could be altered or replaced if there was unanimous agreement with the provinces within two years. The amending procedure provided was essentially the Victoria formula of a majority of the provinces in the four regions there specified. A further provision made it possible to substitute a referendum instead of legislative approval, thus making it possible to appeal directly to the people of a province over the head of its legislature. The Charter included not only the usual civil and political rights, but also the protection of the two official languages and the right to education in the minority language, and mobility rights. Also included in the constitutional provisions was a recognition of the principle of equalization, which bound Parliament to ensure that all provinces be financially able to provide essential public services "without imposing an undue burden of provincial taxation."

All of these proposals had been on the constitutional agenda for years, and appeared to enjoy wide public support. Some of them were objectionable to a number of provincial governments, but the element which aroused most opposition was the method of achieving them, which abruptly departed from the intergovernmental consensus which had been a central feature of constitutional change in the past. This appeared to violate what had been widely assumed to be a convention of the constitution. Indeed, what was at issue was not only a convention of the Canadian constitution, but also of the British constitution. The federal government, before embarking on its unilateral course, had been reassured by an opinion from counsel

21. Subsequently in 1982 the government published *The Charter of Rights and Freedoms: A guide for Canadians* in explanation of the significance of the Charter to the public.

that there was no legal impediment to the procedure which it envisaged. Since the objectionable part of the procedure was a matter of constitutional convention, rather than law, the issue might not lend itself to authoritative resolution in the courts.

In terms of the British constitution the issue hinged on the role of the British Parliament. Section 4 of the Statute of Westminster appeared to enshrine an existing convention that British acts of Parliament affecting the Dominions should be at their request and with their consent. Does there nevertheless remain a discretion in the British Parliament to refuse or modify such request, or is its role now purely that of a rubber stamp? In theory, no British Parliament is bound by the actions of its predecessors, so that the Statute of Westminster itself could be unilaterally repealed at Westminster. Is there now a limitation of the sovereignty of the British Parliament, or does the Statute of Westminster lay down a rule of construction for the guidance of the courts? On this matter the authorities differ.[22] Is the British Parliament bound to implement a request from Canada, or has it the right to demur if a province protests that it is being deprived of rights it hitherto possessed under the constitution? One thing is certain, British ministers have repeatedly asserted that the role is automatic and they have in fact regarded the provinces as not having the *locus standi* to be heard.[23] However, in the past, objection had come from only a single province, and the objection of eight out of ten might be a different matter.

In fact there was a great deal of provincial lobbying in London which led the Select Committee on Foreign Affairs of the British House of Commons to take provincial objection into account. While the Committee had no legislative power as such, its reports were likely to give an indication of the degree of difficulty an amending bill might encounter in Parliament. That, to a government with a very tight parliamentary timetable, might be a serious cause for concern.

In its First Report of January 21, 1981, the Foreign Affairs Committee had argued that the British government still had responsibility in these matters and should refuse to implement the proposed amendment if the procedure in Canada appeared to be defective. In a Second Report, dated April 15, they emphasized that they were not passing judgment on the substance of the request but only on

22. See K.C. Wheare, *The Statute of Westminster and Dominion Status.* Fifth Edition. (London, 1953) pp. 153 ff.

23. See Gerin-Lajoie. *Constitutional Amendment in Canada.* pp. 153 ff.

whether it had been made "in a proper manner." They concluded that "the UK Parliament need not automatically accede to the request unless the request is made *with an appropriate level and distribution of Provincial concurrence*" (their emphasis). Since the proposal had not followed the federal principle it was in their view tainted. Essentially this was a problem with the British political system and one for the United Kingdom to deal with.

The necessity of provincial consent in the circumstances was a matter of whether such a convention existed in the Canadian constitution. Was this a matter which could be resolved by the Canadian courts? Generally speaking the courts do not concern themselves with conventions of the constitution but only with matters of strict law. However, it is possible for a court to assimilate a constitutional convention into the law of the constitution if the rule appears to be clear and certain.[24] Alternatively, a court may recognize that a convention has been established but not go so far as to apply it as a judicial rule. Both possibilities were implicit in the references to three provincial courts of appeal. These references, which were heard early in 1981, in essence posed three questions: do the Trudeau proposals affect provincial powers; is there a convention that such amendments will not be proceeded without provincial consent; is provincial consent a legal requirement of the constitution? The answers of the three provincial courts were various. The Manitoba court upheld the position of the federal government in a 3-2 decision, the Quebec court reached the same conclusion by a majority of 4-1, while the Newfoundland court was unanimous in supporting the provincial position. In the Supreme Court the appeals from the three decisions were taken together, even though the questions were somewhat differently worded.

The Court, having heard argument on the appeals at the end of April, mulled over the questions during the summer and finally delivered judgment on September 28. They had no difficulty with the first question. In a unanimous opinion they found that the Trudeau proposals did in fact affect the rights and powers of the provinces. On the second question the Court was divided. The six justices in the majority found that there was indeed a constitutional convention which had been established that a substantial provincial consent must precede a resolution seeking amendments which affected provincial rights and powers, but unfortunately they failed

24. As Sir Kenneth Wheare put it, if a court recognizes a constitutional custom "as a rule it will apply it in the determination of a dispute before it, then that custom has ceased to be non-legal rule, and has joined the body of law strictly so called." *The Statute of Westminster*...p.2.

to "quantify" the degree or, if so, kind of consent required. The three dissenters, including the Chief Justice, found that no such convention existed. The answer to the third question was divided by the Court into two parts. The Majority felt that the proposed amendment package violated the norms of the constitution established by convention. Nevertheless, seven of the justices ruled that the federal government's action was legal.[24A]

The decision of the Supreme Court did not make the situation much clearer, and left a number of questions unanswered. The Court found a convention of the constitution which Canadians did not know existed (even though the principal actors had apparently conducted themselves in the past in conformity with it) in disposing of a case in which one of the principal issues was an amendment which would have established an amending formula in the constitution that required provincial participation, but they failed to specify what the convention is. What number of provinces constitute "substantial" compliance with the convention? Is provincial consent to be signified by provincial legislatures, or is it sufficient for governments alone to consent? They did not say. The two judges who supported both the existence of a convention and the consequence that the whole thing was illegal were at least consistent, as were the three who found no convention and no illegality. The four who recognized the existence of the convention and also made up the majority who found the package legal were responsible for the resulting confusion as to what in fact the Court had decided. What was perhaps more serious was that no one had asked them what may, in the long run, have been the crucial question: was the position of Quebec in the federal system sufficiently unique that any conventional formula implicitly recognized a Quebec veto on constitutional change?

Nevertheless, the decision of the Court acted as a catalyst in bringing about a conclusion to the dispute. A flurry of informal discussions took place between the federal and provincial governments in search of a compromise, culminating in a First Minister's Conference at the beginning of November. There ground was given on both the Charter and the amending formula by both the federal and most provincial governments. Most of the dissident provinces had particularly disliked the referendum provisions in the federal proposal. The eight dissidents had agreed on an alternative called the Vancouver compromise, which was in essence the proposal advanced by the government of Alberta. This provided that an

24A. *Reference Re: Amendment of the Constitution of Canada* 125 D.L.R. 3d 1 (1981).

amendment required the support of the federal government and two-thirds of the provinces with at least fifty percent of the population, and that a province which did not agree could opt out of the amendment and receive fiscal compensation for benefits lost in the amendment. This, in the end, was partially acceptable to the federal government if the compensation was limited to powers relating to "education or other cultural matters." The federal government also agreed that there should be a "notwithstanding" clause which would enable Parliament, or a provincial legislature, to enact laws, for a five-year renewable period, nothwithstanding the provisions of section 2 and sections 7 to 15 of the Charter. These concessions were sufficient to secure the adherence of seven of the eight dissenting provinces to the whole package. Thereafter the resolutions went through their appointed stages in Parliament on an agreed time limit, were transmitted to the Queen and thence to the British government. The latter was able to press the amending legislation through without serious difficulty, since agreement by nine provinces could hardly be perceived as evidence of substantial dissent. The new Constitution and Charter were proclaimed by the Queen in Ottawa on April 17, 1982. The long road to patriation was at last at an end.

The price was the isolation of Quebec and the apparent destruction of what it had assumed to be its special place in the constitution. The government of Quebec had itself contributed to this outcome. The historical position of Quebec, from which no previous government had departed, was to oppose any constitutional arrangement which undermined what had in fact become an effective veto on constitutional change. And yet the Quebec government had agreed in the April compromise with its dissident provincial partners on the Vancouver formula. Why? The most likely explanation for this was that it was based on the calculation that the Trudeau proposals would fail in the face of such substantial provincial opposition. Even so, it was surely a dangerous step to give up a historic position for a temporary tactical advantage. The present amending formula is the result of a hasty compromise and may well be revised in the future. The achievement of one that is more sensitive to the peculiar position of Quebec is likely to remain on the public agenda for some time.

In any event, amendments to the constitution are not everyday events. They require both a sense of urgency and a considerable effort of will. Accordingly they are not the usual solution to the many facets of ongoing federal-provincial relations.

FEDERAL-PROVINCIAL DIPLOMACY

In a modern federal state the reach of government is such that it is difficult to administer any policy area which does not touch both levels of government at sensitive points. As a result administrative co-operation had become the means by which it has been possible to carry out programs and policies on a national scale, even though they cut across the jurisdiction of both levels of governments.

In the period after the Second World War both levels of government perceived that seeking to settle conflicts of jurisdiction in the courts had all of the characteristics of a zero-sum game. Indirectly this tendency towards co-operation rather than constitutional conflict was made easier because the courts seem to have abandoned the "watertight compartment" view of the distribution of power in the federal system, and to have taken a more benevolent view of a kind of concurrent jurisdiction in which it was possible to achieve a unified system of control through administrative delegation or enforcement power from one sovereign legislature to the agents of the other.

The development of a large number of jointly financed and jointly administered programs in such fields as social security and public health were the result of federal initiatives in areas which were entirely, or partly, in provincial jurisdiction. This neatly skirted the apparent constitutional barrier, which in pre-war years had seemed insuperable, to the achievement of common programs with common standards which applied throughout the whole country. The result was achieved through piecemeal adjustments between the executive branches of the two levels of government. Co-ordination was achieved through *ad hoc* or standing committees composed of officials from the two levels of government.

The federal-provincial conference was the major innovation in the Canadian federal system during the post-war years. This informal and extra-constitutional device took many forms. At the summit of the process was the First Ministers' Conference. This body, presided over by the Prime Minister, includes all of the provincial premiers. The principal participants are usually accompanied by their ministers of intergovernmental affairs, other ministers if the subject warrants it, and the normal bevy of civil service advisers. There are also regular meetings of ministers covering particular subjects. Such meetings are usually supported by continuing meetings of officials to deal with the more technical topics and prepare the ground for further ministerial meetings. By 1964 there were one hundred such committees, and their number has not declined since.[25]

These meetings, which consume thousands of hours, involve the discussion of a vast range of matters of joint concern to the two levels of government. Discussion, bargaining, and often agreement cover matters ranging from constitutional amendments, tax-sharing, the joint funding of shared programs, to the reconciliation of legal norms. One of the most striking characteristics of this phenomenon is that a wide range of public policy issues is worked out through secret negotiation and then presented to Parliament and the provincial legislatures in agreed form for ratification, so the normal legislative process of debate and open compromise is replaced by agreements which are no longer discussable or negotiable by the time they become public.[26] This system of executive federalism, as it has been called, has had the effect of vastly strengthening the executive at the expense of the legislature, and the significance of this has not been lost on those who publicly mourn the decline in the influence and role of Parliament.

What are the perceived advantages in this procedure? It did make possible solutions to problems created by the need to fit modern demands on the state into a constitutional framework designed in the very different conditions of the nineteenth century. The essence of the problem was that only the federal government had the fiscal resources to support such programs, which were beyond the means of all but the richest provinces, and totally beyond the means of most provinces, even though the constitutional division of powers had placed these matters completely in provincial hands. A tolerable result could be achieved by intergovernmental co-operation without the trauma and frustration of seeking a constitutional amendment, or the high risks associated with resort to the courts.

One of the most striking of these developments had been a change in the balance of sophistication between the two levels of government. At the end of the war the federal government had a large, experienced, and expert bureaucracy to support policy inno-

25. See Edgar Gallant. "The Machinery of Federal-Provincial Relations." *Canadian Public Administration.* VIII:4 (December, 1965) pp. 516–26.

26. The best full-length treatment of the phenomenon is Richard Simeon. *Federal-Provincial Diplomacy.* (Toronto, 1972). The closest student of the problem over the years has been Professor Donald Smiley. See, for his most recent discussion, Chapter IV of his *Canada in Question: Federalism in the Eighties.* (Toronto, 1980).

vation and implementation by ministers. All provinces without exception came out of the war with small, old-fashioned bureaucratic structures unable to match their federal counterparts in knowledge, and in this case knowledge led to power. It was not uncommon in the early first ministers' conferences after the war for a provincial premier to be accompanied only by his Attorney-General. It was not long before this imbalance began to be corrected.

It was necessary for the provinces to develop accounting and control procedures sufficient to manage programs up to federal standards and this in itself led to improvements in the administrative capacities of the provinces. It was only the next step for provincial governments to realize that they were committing the bulk of their resources to joint programs funded by matched grants from the federal government at the expense of programs outside the interest of the federal planners. One illustration of this was that federal policies led to large joint expenditures for improving health care, leaving the provinces with limited funds to deal with education, which at the time was not—for political reasons—a federal priority.

As the provinces built up their own staffs of experts they became more and more capable of bargaining with their federal counterparts on equal intellectual terms. By the time the negotiations took place on the Canada Pension Plan in 1963–64 the provincial experts were clearly better prepared than their federal counterparts and succeeded in radically altering the original federal proposal. This growth in provincial bureaucratic capability should not be underestimated as a major factor in the decentralization of the Canadian federal system which took place in the sixties and seventies.

The system of federal adjustment by negotiation became so pervasive that it appeared to be displacing the courts as the principal mechanism of adjustment in the system. Intergovernmental bargaining as an alternative to resort to the courts as a way of managing conflict was successful in a number of situations where inappropriate jurisdictional boundaries prevented the implementation of generally agreed upon programs, even when there were complex jurisdictional problems, as was the case in pensions.

However by making the provinces the effective administrative agencies of programs for which the federal government had a major and increasing financial responsibility created grave problems for the federal government itself. The real growth of the economy was at a dead stop, while costs due to inflation were exerting strong upward pressure on the federal deficit because so much federal expenditure was committed to statutory obligations of which the major components were debt charges and established fiscal transfer programs. Since transfer programs are negotiated normally for five-year periods, federal efforts to retrench imposed heavier burdens on the provinces.

A further difficulty about the system of executive federalism is that it worked in the past because the goals and interests of the two levels of government were complementary. Until the sixties they shared the same objectives and could agree on the best policy and administrative outcome. The system's chances of working become slight when the objectives of the parties are not congruent, which appears to be the case in such matters as a common policy on energy and resource management. The fact that the two sides are resorting more and more to the courts for conflict resolution shows that the limits of federal-provincial negotiation are narrower than was thought in the heyday of executive federalism.

A UNION DISUNITED

Canada is not simply a federal system of the American type, garnished by a limited number of special safeguards such as the protection of the French language in the federal courts and in Parliament. It would be more accurate to describe it as two federal systems, of very different types, compelled to co-exist within the same constitutional structure. On the one hand, juridicially speaking, it is a federation of provinces each of which retains, within its own boundaries, a limited degree of self-government. Constitutionally, each of these provinces is the same as any other province, with only minor differences in the constitution. Any agreed change in the constitution could lead to an increase, or decrease, in the powers of the federal government. Such a system could, as some of the Fathers of Confederation expected, develop in time into a unitary state as the geographical barriers to efficient large-scale administration were overcome, and the "nationalizing" effects of education, the communications media and the increasing mobility of the population eroded regional sentiments.

There is, however, a sense in which the union is not a federation of provinces at all, but a union of the two "founding peoples" whose primary purpose is to preserve and foster the separate identity of each. It is possible that, over and above the federal distribution of power between the federal and provincial authorities, the constitution should recognize this so that special guarantees and institutions at both levels of government nourish and protect the language and culture of the French and English, particularly that of the weaker group. Such was the view of the matter which was to be found both in the recommendations of the Royal Commission on Bilingualism and Biculturalism as well as in Prime Minister Trudeau's proposed Charter of Human Rights of 1968 and in certain provisions of the Constitutional Amendment Bill of 1978. To a considerable degree they are now a part of the Charter in the 1982 Constitution Act.

A simpler view of the matter, widely accepted by French-Canadians in Quebec, is that Canada is a bi-national state in which the federal government epitomizes the "national state" for English-speaking Canadians, but that the only acceptable "national state" for French-Canadians is the province of Quebec. To some, the logic of this position leads them to assert that Quebec must separate from Confederation if the national rights and aspirations of French-Canadians are to be fulfilled.[27] At the other extreme there are those who would be content if Quebec, which is not "a province like the others," had a sufficiently "special" status within the union to give it a decisive, and in most cases exclusive, voice in all matters important to it. The other provinces, if they wish, can leave these important powers to Ottawa, but not Quebec. For those in Quebec who do not think that special status is a politically realistic objective, it seems a better strategy to capitalize on the desire for greater decentralization emanating from the other provinces, and aim at the same objective through a much greater decentralization of the system.[28]

While there is much in both the nature and the expectations of French-Canadian nationalism that is new, the fact is indisputable that French-Canadians have survived as a socially and culturally distinct group for over two centuries in a country in which the English-speaking majority controlled the levers of power. In part they survived through a combination of magnanimity and realism which, from time to time, recognized or reinforced the instruments of survival. The Royal Proclamation of 1760, and more particularly the

27. In the referendum of 1980 the Parti Quebecois put forward a proposal for Sovereignty-Association, involving political separation but continued economic union with certain common economic institutions. See *Quebec-Canada: A New Deal.* (Quebec, 1979).

28. This was the view of the Quebec Liberal Party in its Beige Paper. The Constitutional Committee of the Quebec Liberal Party. *A New Canadian Federation.* (Montreal, 1980).

Quebec Act, freed them in the use of their religion and their language from the effects of the English legal and constitutional system which would have eroded both. The Constitutional Act of 1791, by setting them apart in a separate province where they were in an overwhelming majority, provided a political setting in which they were able to learn to operate unfamiliar but useful political institutions. So effectively did they do so that the union of 1840 failed in its object of submerging them. The emergence of a federal system in which the province of Quebec retained the basic social and legal system under its jurisdiction was a consequence of the unacknowledged but functioning "federalism" of the united province of Canada.

The predominant position of the clergy among the traditional French-Canadian elites no doubt dictated the strategy of survival in the nineteenth century. This was essentially to preserve the French-Canadian society as a largely rural and static one, insulated as far as possible from contaminating contact with the bustling industrialization of the cities, and animated by a marked distrust of the state as an instrument of national development. By a policy of withdrawing into the fortress-province of Quebec it was possible to put up a dogged resistance to the aggressive expansion of the English-speaking majority. The costs of such a strategy were high, in terms of both the economic welfare of the French-Canadian *habitant*, and in the necessity to write-off as lost those who emigrated either to the United States or to the rest of Canada. And an attempt to arrest this emigration by the colonization of infertile areas of the province was, by and large, a failure which brought heavy social costs to the colonists.

What was the attitude of English-speaking Canadians to the "French fact" during most of the first century after Confederation? It must be said that even the most liberal of them regarded French Canada as little more than a transitory source of trouble and discomfort which, in the long run, would somehow be solved by the ultimate penetration of the forces of "progress" into Quebec. Meanwhile it was best to let sleeping dogs lie. And so the two groups coexisted in the mutual incomprehension of their two solitudes. On the English-speaking side there was an element of deep-seated Protestant suspicion of the Roman Catholic Church, a feeling that the French language was an anomaly in an English-speaking continent, and a feeling that French-Canadians were both backward and reactionary and thus an obstacle to the forces of progress in Canada. There was a touch of the North American radical belief that a good state could be built in the New World only by destroying the cultural roots of "foreigners," who must be assimilated in order to build a new Canada.[29]

Against this persistent pressure the French-Canadian reaction was to husband their political strength, to limit as far as possible the impact of twentieth-century industrialization on the *habitant* whose backwardness and ignorance, so it was thought, would be a solid barrier against the secular and integrating forces of urban and industrial society. It suited the purposes of Premier Maurice Duplessis to maintain this situation, though he found the encouragement of the exploitation of Quebec's natural resources by big business a useful source of both tax revenue and party funds. But the policy of immobilism died with him, and after his death came the deluge.

Even resource-development industries create an urban proletariate, and Quebec could not be isolated from the enormous social effects of wartime and post-war Canadian industrialization. The death of Duplessis opened a Pandora's box of new social forces, from which his own party was not totally immune. A new elite pattern quickly emerged in French-Canada. In the past, leadership had been the exclusive preserve of the ancient professions: the church, law, and medicine. In rural and small-town Quebec the professional classes had preserved their power unimpaired, and were able to act as brokers between the mass of French-Canadians and the larger structures of corporate and political power which were transcontinental and alien in character.

There has emerged a new and more broadly based pattern of power within the French-Canadian community, in which the engineers and managers of industrial society are more important than the traditional classes. It was possible for the intellectuals of an earlier generation to accept the myth of the mystical virtue of subsistence agriculture as the ultimate sources of political and moral strength of French Canada. But this dream of bucolic *survivance* has little attraction now.

Where the old nationalism was defensive, the new nationalism aims at creating something new. "Its aim," says Professor Charles Taylor, "is not to defend the traditional way of life, but to build a modern French society on this continent. In its pure form, practi-

29. For a perceptive discussion of these attitudes held by as eminent a member of the liberal establishment as John W. Dafoe, see Ramsay Cook, *The Politics of John W. Dafoe and the Free Press.* (Toronto, 1963) pp. 292–3.

cally the only value it has in common with the old is the French language itself."[30] It thus has the quality not only of a rejection of the dominant Anglo-Saxon values of North America, but of a revulsion against nearly all of the traditional values of French Canada. The carriers of this new nationalism are what Professor Taylor calls the new intelligentsia, who include intellectuals, journalists, teachers, economists and others of the new breed of civil servants who began to play a major role in Quebec after 1960.

Spurred onward by nationalists in a hurry in the communications industries, and by civil servants exhilarated by the feeling that they are making a revolution of modernization, political leaders have been borne along on a tide of rising expectations from government. For it is above all to the power of the state that the leaders of this new Quebec look for the satisfaction of new wants and the generation of economic development which will enlarge the opportunities for all. For them, these things must be done by their own state of Quebec, and not by Ottawa. For this there are two reasons: the new elites wish to share in the management of the new society, and Quebec has much ground to cover to catch up with the rest of Canada. For this reason, incidentally, the social priorities during the Quiet Revolution of the sixties were somewhat different from those articulated in Ottawa. Given the scarcity of both financial and human resources available at any one time, their priorities for collectivised welfare for the ill, the aged and the disadvantaged were low compared with the need to put resources into education and economic growth.

It needs to be remembered that the B.N.A. Act has never been a very effective protector of the rights deemed necessary by French-speaking Canadians for their survival as a distinct group. Their education rights in the Manitoba school controversy, as well as their efforts to preserve French as a language in the Ontario schools, were first taken away by an unsympathetic majority, and then confined to limbo by the insistence of the courts that minority education rights in the constitution were a matter of religion and not of language. The absence of constitutional protection for linguistic and cultural rights inevitably made the provincial rights of Quebec the only refuge in the constitution for the aspirations of French-Canadian nationalism.

Just as the British North America Act found no room for the aspirations of an older kind of national objective, it was equally

30. Charles Taylor, "Nationalism and the Political Intelligentsia: A Case Study." *Queen's Quarterly*. LXXII:1 (Spring, 1965).

unable, without substantial change, to accommodate the new ones. There is a certain irony in the fact that many of the adjustments now taken for granted, and indeed regarded as unduly modest, by important sections of French-Canadian opinion, are set out in the Report of the Royal Commission on Constitutional Problems which was set up by the Duplessis regime and which reported in 1956. Their proposals had little appeal at the time to Mr. Duplessis, but they are now part of the common stock of discussion in Quebec. They include not only the provision of a massive provincial program of welfare and education with the tax revenues to support it, but changes in important federal institutions such as the Senate, whose composition should be altered to represent the provinces directly (or better still, the "founding races," but of course appointed by the province). Furthermore the Supreme Court should no longer be the final court of appeal in civil law cases, and should be replaced by a more "representative" constitutional court.

Generally speaking, the aspirations of many French Canadians aim at constitutional modifications of several kinds. The imperfect separation of judicial power in the constitution, which places in the hands of an agency appointed by the federal authority, the Supreme Court of Canada, both the interpretation of the constitution and the final disposition of questions peculiar to Quebec civil law, must, in this view, be altered. Daniel Johnson lent his authority to the proposal "to create a genuine constitutional tribunal whose composition would reflect the federal character of our institutions and the Canadian cultural duality."[31] This reflects a noticeable distrust in Quebec of the Supreme Court of Canada as a body capable of giving credible and acceptable decisions affecting the powers and rights of the province. Thus for example neither the Liberal government of Jean Lesage nor the Union Nationale of Daniel Johnson would have been content to leave to the Court a final decision on either offshore mineral rights or the Quebec-Labrador boundary, preferring instead to have these matters settled by intergovernmental negotiation. Only the Parti Quebecois is able to profit by the renewed tendency to substitute litigation for negotiation and to have it both ways. If they win, they have strengthened provincial jurisdiction; if they lose they have found yet another demonstration of the failure of the federal system to protect Quebec interests.

In the field of executive power there appear to be two important

31. *The government of Quebec and the Constitution.* (Quebec, n.d.) p. 45. This is a reproduction of Mr. Johnson's statement to the fourth meeting of the Tax Structure Committee at Ottawa, September 14-15, 1966.

issues. One is partly a matter of the domestic constitution of Quebec, since it raises the question of the form as well as the character of the executive in the province. The other relates to the competence of the province to have a "treaty power" and an international presence to go with its exclusive jurisdiction in the field of education defined very broadly.

The first question involves both the "dignified" parts of the constitution and the symbolism associated with them. Some of this has practical significance in provinces other than Quebec. The Lieutenant-Governor, with his shadowy and now irrelevant powers of reservation, is a federal appointee. If he is a purely ceremonial figure in the constitution, then it can be argued quite reasonably that a province, which has now in any event to pay for a good deal of whatever pomp he can muster, might as well have his appointment governed by its own constitution. From this view there would probably be little dissent in Canada generally, though it is likely that the federal government prefers to treat a change in the Lieutenant-Governor's status as a minor bargaining counter in negotiations of constitutional reform.

In Quebec, however, there would be little resistance to going a good deal further than this. The monarchy has now become rather remote from life. To most French Canadians it probably symbolizes not the virtues of constitutional government, but an inexplicable refusal of English-speaking Canadians to cut the umbilical cord of colonial rule. The next step beyond this righteous republicanism is an apparent yearning for a "presidential" system in Quebec. Quebec cabinets, perhaps even more than most provincial cabinets, have always tended to be one-man bands. The strain which this imposes, within a parliamentary system, on the leader of a government is almost unbearable, as the death in office of three Quebec premiers in ten years testifies. It is easy to understand why some form of relief is sought. A presidential system would relieve the "chief executive" of the strain of parliamentary duties, and also personalize and strengthen the leadership. A system of separation of powers which this implies might also free the legislature from executive dominance, and lead to some strengthening of democratic institutions.

The second manifestation of desire to alter the executive arm of the constitution centres on the still unresolved question of the treaty power. The courts have made it plain that the implementation of treaties which concern matters of exclusive provincial jurisdiction lies with provincial legislatures. But the provinces of Canada are not states in international law, and therefore they cannot negotiate treaties or deal directly with foreign states or international agencies as if they were. It is a well-known fact that this situation is not accepted without question in Quebec. To the Quebec government, the logic of the situation is that if the province has the exclusive jurisdiction, it "should have, within the limits of Canadian foreign policy, a recognized capacity to negotiate and sign her own agreements with foreign governments on matters subject to her internal jurisdiction."[32]

When it comes to the legislative aspects of government there are also problems. On the one hand there is a devotion to the "watertight compartment" theory of exclusive jurisdiction, which creates a disposition to oppose in principle the joint federal-provincial programs that characterize co-operative federalism. On the other hand there is an awareness that a number of areas of federal jurisdiction, such as monetary policy and trade policy, impinge so directly on the integrated planning of provincial policies that some form of direct representation in federal agencies, such as the Bank of Canada, is essential if provincial policy-making is to be effective. For the same reason, the Quebec Liberal Party's Beige Paper of 1980 argued strongly for direct provincial representation in the federal Parliament through a revised second chamber in place of the Senate.

These pressures come, it needs to be understood, from those who wish to preserve in some form or other, a federal system. What kind of federal system it will be is going to require long and difficult negotiation. This generalized pressure for what William Riker has called a new "federal bargain"[33] has to be balanced against other pressures in the system. There is probably a growing disenchantment with the desirability of a strong central government. But while the centrifigal forces in Quebec are shaped in the pattern of "national self-determination," those of the rest of Canada represent a frustrated regionalism. Provincial governments, particularly those situated in provinces with great natural wealth, find it easy to persuade themselves that they could produce better policies for their own people than those which emerge from the compromises of Ottawa.

Alienation from, and frustration with, the compromises of pan-Canadian "nation-building" have become the most visible signs of

32. *Ibid.* p. 72.

33. William H. Riker. *Federalism: Origin, Operation, Significance.* (Boston & Toronto, 1964).

system stress which appear to threaten the survival of the Canadian system. It is worth pointing out that these stresses take two forms and may not be susceptible to the same kind of institutional accommodation. One kind of alienation comes from a group with its own language and cultural institutions which is able to defend its distinctiveness because its strongest power base is a large province in which it is the over-whelming majority. The largest part of the group, which is located in Quebec, is thus able to control the strategy and centre its political objectives on maintaining the power of that province.

The other minorities generally lack the distinctiveness and specificity of French-Canadians. They are regional minorities in parts of the country which have lacked the electoral numbers to dominate national economic policy decisions. These regions have a long history of grievance against what they have perceived as oppressive policy imposed on them by the more powerful regions of Canada. Western resentment against the impact of the "National Policy" has a long history which culminated in the inter-war years when the western agricultural economy was in a state of collapse.

The Maritime provinces, which prospered briefly in the boom which was caused by the American Civil War, have tended to attribute the subsequent decline of their economies to the tariff and transportation policies of the federal government, which seemed intent on bringing the benefits of western expansion to the central provinces of Ontario and Quebec. The "Maritime Rights" movement was thus essentially a demand for compensation for the adverse effects of national policies. However, since the Maritime provinces have become more and more dependent on federal redistributive measures, they are likely to be reconciled to a strongly centralized federation.

On the other hand the Western provinces, as a result of the growing diversification and strength of their resource-based economies, have turned increasingly to the decentralization of the Canadian federal system. In spite of their growing economic strength they see themselves as disproportionately weak in a political and constitutional system which concentrates political power in a central government dominated by the more populous Ontario and Quebec. This has caused them to demand substantial transfers of constitutional authority to the provinces. The fissiparous tendencies in the system tend to conceal the competition for legitimacy between federal and provincial politicians in each province.

The centrifugal tendencies in the system are reinforced by the political and governmental systems which have been created by two levels of government operated under the rules of the Westminster system. Governments develop interests in their own right, as distinct from the people they represent. "Federalism, at least in the Canadian case," as Alan Cairns has argued, "is a function not of societies but of the constitution and more importantly of the governments that must work the constitution."[34] In other words, constitutional change is not merely a predictable response to wider societal changes, but a product of the interaction of governments and bureaucracies that are strategically placed to shape the process of change. These governmental bodies command large programs and resources of funds. They constitute in their own right a substantial part of the population, and they are able to carry out the struggle to defend and enlarge their "territory" without apparent significant support or interest from the public at large.

The basic division of state functions in a federal system has also led to political parties and interest groups conforming to the federal pattern as they play out their own roles within the system. Cairns adds

> Contrary to all predictions, post World War II Canadian politics has not displayed an irreversible trend to centralization, nor the manifestations of capitalist contradiction in polarized class politics, creative or otherwise. Instead, the provinces, aided by the secular trends which have enhanced the practical significance of their constitutionally-based authority, and by the deliberate improvement of their own bureaucratic power and capacity, have given a new salience to the politics of federalism and the territorially based diversities it emcompasses, reflects and fosters.[35]

This has imposed almost intolerable strain on the mechanism of conflict resolution in the system. When the provincial governments, and for its own reasons the federal government, found that conflict resolution by the courts was a high-risk enterprise, they put their faith increasingly in federal-provincial conferences. But the conditions for conflict resolution by this means are frequently absent.

Conflicts over jurisdiction reflect real differences in policy objectives which may be extremely difficult to reconcile. Furthermore the format of the federal-provincial conference of First Ministers

34. Alan C. Cairns, "The Governments and Societies of Canadian Federalism." *Canadian Journal of Political Science.* X:4 pp. 698–9.

35. *Ibid.* p. 720.

tends to enhance disagreement rather than promote compromise. Whereas in the early years these conferences were closed meetings they are now vast conclaves, jammed into the once magnificent concourse of the Ottawa railway station, constantly distracted by the steady flow of memoranda in which every line is carefully analyzed for hidden meaning. Meanwhile, at the opening and closing sessions, the principals are pinned under the television lights as they read discourses intended to be consumed by their own electors, who are presumed to need reassurance that their champions are posturing for their benefit and protection. Even the press interviews of each head of government are carefully monitored by the others so that a response can be mounted at once. The atmosphere is that of a summit of great powers, rather than of a closed diplomatic conference seeking diplomatic solutions. When the participants have finally withdrawn from public view, their attitudes and positions have hardened to the point where negotiation is difficult.

On most issues the conflict is not in fact a simple confrontation between the federal government and a unified phalanx of provinces. If there are "separatists" in the West, it is not likely that they will be appeased by a near-partition of Canada into two separate cultural units. Indeed, it is possible that some of the disenchantment with the present federal system in many parts of English-speaking Canada is not at bottom regionalism at all, but a backlash against the burdens of accommodation with French-speaking Canadians.

Given the mounting pressures on the federal system as it now exists, it is clear that something will have to change. The price of failure to adapt may well lead to the collapse of the system. This is easy to see, but what to do? Are some options more plausible than others? Decisions which may be both irreversible and disastrous are daunting to comtemplate. Meanwhile suggested solutions abound. Since the Pearson years the agenda for constitutional reform has contained three major items. The first, now largely accomplished, is the achievement of an entrenched Charter of Rights including linguistic rights. The second involves institutional modifications to improve the responsiveness of the system to regional strains. The third, which Liberal governments have continued to place as the last stage of the process, is the partition of powers between the two levels of government.

The second stage, currently under discussion, involves a number of institutional modifications in the central government. One of these consists in the advocacy of a variety of modifications of the electoral system to diminish the adverse effects of an electoral system which consistently over-represents "mainstream" majorities at the expense of minority and frequently regional interests. The effects of this are exacerbated by the fact that the main political parties have grave difficulty in gaining seats in the House of Commons on a country-wide basis. It is further argued that the tight party discipline associated with the Westminster system unduly limits the capacity of Members of Parliament to represent regional interests and contributes to the weakness of Parliament as an institution. For these difficulties many answers have been proposed but none has mustered enough support to overcome the inertia of governments.

In the beginning the federal Cabinet was one of the most sensitive of intrastate federal institutions. For more than the first half-century after Confederation provincial representation in the Cabinet was one of the major sources for the accommodation of provincial and regional interests. This is no longer the case, and would not be so even if every province could be strongly represented in the Cabinet and the government caucus. Not only has the Cabinet tripled in size to a point where it is no longer an effective body for such a purpose, but also the nature of government business has changed so that ministers are no longer area representatives but the spokesmen for functional departments. It is no longer possible for the Cabinet to play the meliorative role it did when its principal function was the equitable distribution of patronage.

Strong provincial governments are now demanding changes in the direction of intrastate federalism which would involve direct penetration by provincial governments into the structure of the federal government. This has involved not only the demand for provincially-appointed representatives on regulatory and policy-making boards, but also direct representation of provincial governments in a new second chamber which would replace the Senate.

How far the implementation of all or any of these proposals would reduce regional alienation is unclear. What is a little more certain is that they would weaken the coherence and authority of central government institutions to the point where its capacity to deal with urgent and common policies might become questionable.

Can the federal system itself adapt to these new strains? The possible solutions were set out a number of years ago by Mr. A.W. Johnson.[36] Since at that time he held a position in the federal civil service which involved him directly in these matters, it was neces-

36. "The Dynamics of Federalism in Canada." *Canadian Journal of Political Science*. I:1 (March, 1963) pp. 18–39.

sary for him to deploy his arguments with some delicacy in exploring the themes of unity and diversity which have made Canada a federal state. He found four main choices, some of which were to be advocated by others in more or less extreme form in the continuing debate over the next decade. The first possibility was greater centralization, a natural concomitant of the growing interdependence of all countries and the consequent erosion of many of the characteristics of the nation state. However true this might be in the long run, events in Canada have tended to move in the opposite direction. Certainly Quebec, in his view, would rather separate than be submerged, and there is little evidence that the other provincial governments would be much more submissive to a process which would defeat the very purpose of federalism.

At the other extreme, there might be a progressive decentralization of government powers which, by eliminating a large part of the role of the federal government, would diminish conflict within the system. But the cost of this would be high, for the fiscal and economic policies of the federal government would fade before the growth of provincial power. The federal government would have to lean more heavily on monetary and trade policies, and these would only be effective if decisions over them came to be shared with the provinces.

A third possibility, already to some extent a reality, would be to increase the asymetricality of the system by giving special status to Quebec so that it would have some powers not possessed by other provinces. At the same time some of these powers could be exercised by the federal government over the rest of Canada, which would become much more highly centralized. Quebec might gradually become an associate state, accepting only limited common institutions operating at the federal level. One of the results of such an arrangement would be that the effects of federal tax measures, whether aimed at stability or growth, would be felt only outside Quebec, while the economic benefits would be shared by the whole country. To a considerable extent the effectiveness of these policies could depend on the willingness of the Quebec authorities voluntarily to adjust their taxation and expenditure policies in a manner consonant with federal objectives. It is faily clear that in these matters, as well as in foreign trade policy and regional development policy, there would have to be consultation between Quebec and the federal authorities to reach agreement on effective measures. But would this not mean that the Quebec authorities would achieve a veto over effective economic policy for the country as a whole?

Such a shift in the balance of power would naturally lead other provinces and regions to seek the satisfaction of a similar degree of autonomy, and thus the end result would be an unstable drift to general decentralization and possibly ultimate disintegration.

Such a decentralization of economic policy into the hands of the government of Quebec further raises the question of what should be the role of ministers and members of Parliament from Quebec. Should they be permitted to vote on (and perhaps effectively decide) questions affecting the rest of Canada, but exclusively controlled by the government and legislature of Quebec in the part of Canada which they represent in the federal Parliament?

A fourth possibility is to recognize as unavoidable the growing interdependence of the two levels of government as the reach of the public sector extends. The solution lies not in a major shift of power from one level of government to the other but adherence to the concept of a strong federal government and strong regional governments. Consistent with this would be adjustments of a major or minor sort to tidy up the constitution and bring it up to date through constitutional amendment. At the same time it is assumed that the federal government's role in shared-cost programs as a means of influencing provincial decisions will diminish. Even if the federal government continues to initiate new shared-cost programs in new policy areas as a means of developing a necessary degree of uniformity, Johnson argued that it should divest itself of these programs once they become fully established, and transfer to the provinces full fiscal resources to continue them. At the time when the federal government is slowing down its initiatives in fields of provincial jurisdiction, it should take a harder line in defending its own jurisdiction against provincial encroachment. The new areas of federal initiative should be in generating programs to meet specific regional needs, which would mean giving up the principle that all federal programs should be capable of equal and similar application in all parts of Canada. Consistent with this conception of the federal government as primarily concerned with equalizing areas of the country which are disadvantaged is a much more aggressive federal role in promoting a bilingual-bicultural policy throughout the country.

While the fourth possibility holds out the greatest prospect for continuing health in the federal system, it is perhaps less easy to share its confident assumptions at a time when the efficacy of all governments is seriously questioned. Nevertheless, Johnson's prescription is based on the assumption that there is a commn need, which can be identified and asserted, for the federal government to do a number of things which will contribute to the common good. Some of these things lie in the realm of economic policy. Both stability and growth as objectives of economic policy require intelligent action by large units of government. But units of government whose principal objectives are economic have difficulty in mobilizing support to carry out their policies. The reason for this is that the pay-off from economic measures is often in the future, and the short-run effects, by imposing apparent sacrifices and frustrating present economic needs of particular groups, encounter resistance. It is extremely difficult to carry on government on nothing but bread-and-butter issues, because economic choices between jam today and jam tomorrow do not have much appeal in themselves. To make and enforce imaginative and long-run economic decisions requires a degree of government support which must be bolstered by other means. Governments, in other words, have to appeal successfully to people's sense of pride and achievement in a community with which they can identify.

There are not many signs at the moment that the idea of Canada as a useful reality is very close to the surface in the minds of many Canadians. There have been times in the past when this sentiment was largely the result of a shared sense of history. To the extent that Canadian history concerns itself with French-English relations, it is perceived as a story of conflict, lacking the ingredients of a "usable past." And yet it is difficult to believe that there is not something unique and valuable in the Canadian experience, from which the world has something to learn and which ought to be cherished. It has been no mean feat to have developed a political system in which two distinct cultural groups have survived, though in somewhat chilly amity. But it has been a political system in which the temperature has been fairly low, and the level of civility correspondingly high. The rapid social transformation which has shaken up its power structure has destroyed most of the old political alliances of the past. It may be that they will not be replaced and no underlying sentiment for unity will be recreated. However, if a strong central government is to emerge, it will do so because there exists visible support for unity.

A strong federal government, in other words, must generate and maintain a solid political base. While a majority government is not an end in itself, it is a step in the direction of strong government, for periods of a minority government are simply reflections of weakening of the bonds of the system. The "forces of unity" must be strengthened in order to achieve some balance with the "forces of diversity." Mr Trudeau, before his conversion to active politics, wrote:

> Caught between centripetal and centrifugal forces, Canada's future, like its past, may continue to oscillate between times of federal and times of provincial predominance, depending upon the immediate needs of the people and the temper of their various politicians. (For it must not be forgotten that these latter have a vested interest in strengthening *that* level of government at which *they* operate.) Or—more likely—the political future of Canada will lie in the direction of greater centralization in some areas and greater decentralization in others. But at all times, co-operation and interchange between the two levels of government will be, as they have been, an absolute necessity. In that sense, I doubt whether federalism in the classical sense has ever existed, that is to say a federalism which would have divided the totality of its sovereign powers between regional and central governments with such sharpness and adequacy that these governments would have been able to carry on their affairs in complete independence of one another.[37]

In recent years there has been a rich flowering of proposals to solve Canadian problems by rethinking the basic assumptions of the system and modifying the machinery of the constitution to adapt it to present conditions. However, neither thinking the unthinkable, nor tinkering with the machinery of the union will cure the ailments of the body politic. As the Joint Parliamentary Committee on the Constitution, in a rare burst of eloquence, put it, "A community that is unable to justify its existence to itself will eventually find that it cannot survive by structure alone."[38]

37. Pierre Elliot Trudeau, *Federalism and the French Canadians.* (Toronto, 1968) p. 134. The quotation is from the essay "The Practice and Theory of Federalism", which was first published in 1961. While the phrase "co-operation and interchange between the two levels of government will be, as they have been, an absolute necessity" reflects the conventional wisdom of Canadian federalism, it must not be forgotten that executive federalism cannot bear the strain of the system if other institutions fail to adapt to changing needs. Donald Smiley's *Canada in Question: Federalism in the Eighties.* (Toronto, 1980) somberly considers these issues.

38. *Final Report.* p. 6.

INDEX